Advice from a Pro

Seven Money Mantras for a Richer Life (p. 10)
Choosing a Financial Planner (p. 25)
Competencies of Successful People (p. 37)
Career Advancement Tips (p. 45)
Crisis Steps to Take If Budget Deficits Occur Repeatedly (p. 88)
A Sideline Business Can Reduce Your Income Taxes (p. 107)
Buy a Home to Reduce Taxes (p. 123)
Endorse Your Checks Properly (p. 140)
Protect Yourself from Bad Check Fees (p. 140)
Guard Your Privacy (p. 162)
Control and Reduce Your Credit Card Debt (p. 192)
Avoid the Minimum Payment Trap (p. 194)
Tips for Buying Online (p. 214)
How to Buy a Used Vehicle (p. 223)
Cancel Private Mortgage Insurance as Soon as Possible (p. 241)
Applying the Large-Loss Principle to Property and Liability Insurance (p. 292)
Be Smart When Shopping for an Individual Plan (p. 305)
Maintain Your Medical Care Plan Between Jobs (p. 310)
Don't Be Fooled by Vanishing-Premium or Return-of-Premium Policies (p. 333)
Buy Term and Invest the Rest (p. 342)
Buy Shares of Stock Directly Using a Dividend-Reinvestment Plan (p. 371)
When to Sell an Investment (p. 376)
Check Your Stockbroker's Background (p. 410)
Zero-Coupon Bonds Pay Phantom Interest (p. 422)
Invest Only "Fun Money" Aggressively (p. 442)
How to Calculate Breakeven Prices for Option Contracts (p. 479)
How to Collect Retirement Benefits and Social Security from a Divorced Spouse (p. 493)
Buy Your Retirement on the Layaway Plan (p. 497)
Ten Things Every Spouse Must Know (p. 534)

Decision-Making Worksheets

Compare Salary and Living Costs in Different Cities (p. 41)
What Is Your Work-Style Personality? (p. 40)
Assessing the Benefits of a Second Income (p. 44)
Keeping Track of Your Job Search Progress (p. 47)
Choosing Between Low-Interest-Rate Dealer Financing and a Rebate (p. 212)
Comparing Automobile Financing and Leasing (p. 218)
Should You Buy or Rent? (p. 236)
Should You Refinance Your Mortgage? (p. 257)
Buying Automobile Insurance (p. 288)
Determining Disability Income Insurance Needs (p. 313)
The Needs-Based Approach to Life Insurance (p. 326)
Estimating Your Retirement Savings Goal in Today's Dollars (p. 495)

ninth edition

personal finance

with personal financial planner worksheets

E. Thomas Garman
Virginia Tech University,
Professor Emeritus

Raymond E. Forgue
University of Kentucky

Houghton Mifflin Company
Boston New York

Executive Publisher: George Hoffman
Executive Editor: Lise Johnson
Sponsoring Editor: Mike Schenk
Senior Marketing Manager: Nicole Moore
Senior Project Editor: Margaret Park Bridges
Senior Photo Editor: Jennifer Meyer Dare
Senior Composition Buyer: Chuck Dutton
New Title Project Manager: James Lonergan
Editorial Assistant: Katilyn Crowley

Publisher: George Hoffman
Sponsoring Editor: Mike Schenk
Marketing Manager: Nicole Moore
Editorial Assistant: James Hamilton
Editorial Assistant: Jill Clark
New Title Project Manager: Susan Peltier

Custom Publishing Editor: Dan Luciano
Custom Publishing Production Manager: Christina Battista
Project Coordinator: Katherine Roz

Cover Image: stock.xchng

Printed in the United States of America.

ISBN-13: 978-0-547-08433-6
ISBN-10: 0-547-08433-1
1043388

1 2 3 4 5 6 7 8 9 – CM – 09 08 07

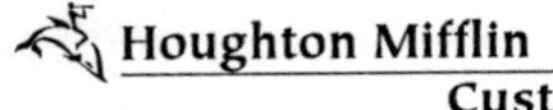

222 Berkeley Street • Boston, MA 02116

Address all correspondence and order information to the above address.

Brief Contents

PART 1 Financial Planning 1

1 Understanding Personal Finance 2
2 Career Planning 30
3 Financial Statements, Tools, and Budgets 58

PART 2 Money Management 95

4 Managing Income Taxes 96
5 Managing Checking and Savings Accounts 130
6 Building and Maintaining Good Credit 158
7 Credit Cards and Consumer Loans 182
8 Vehicle and Other Major Purchases 206
9 Buying Your Home 230

PART 3 Income and Asset Protection 265

10 Managing Property and Liability Risk 266
11 Managing Health Expenses 298
12 Life Insurance Planning 320

PART 4 Investments 351

13 Investment Fundamentals 352
14 Investing in Stocks and Bonds 384
15 Investing Through Mutual Funds 432
16 Real Estate and High-Risk Investments 460

PART 5 Retirement and Estate Planning 485

17 Retirement Planning 486
18 Estate Planning 520

Contents

PART 1

Financial Planning 1

1 Understanding Personal Finance 2

The Building Blocks to Achieving Personal Financial Success 4
Spend Less to Save and Invest 5
Financial Success and Happiness 5
Using the Building Blocks 5

The Economy Affects Your Personal Financial Success 6
Where Are We in the Business Cycle? 6
What Is the Future Direction of the Economy? 8
What Is the Future Direction of Inflation, Prices, and Interest Rates? 8

Think Like an Economist When Making Financial Decisions 11
Opportunity Costs in Decision Making 11
Marginal Utility and Costs in Decision Making 12
Marginal Income Tax Rate in Decision Making 12

The Time Value of Money: Setting Dollar Values on Financial Goals 14
Calculating Future Values 15
Calculating Present Values 17

Make Smart Money Decisions at Work 19
Flexible Benefit Plans Offer Tax-Free Money 19
Making Decisions About Employer-Sponsored Health Care Plans 19
Making Decisions About Employer's Flexible Spending Accounts 20
Making Decisions About Participating in Employer Life, Disability, and Long-Term Care Insurance Plans 21
Making Decisions About Participating in Your Employer's Retirement Plan 21

Where to Seek Expert Financial Advice 24
How Financial Planners Are Compensated 25

Big Picture Summary of Learning Objectives 27

Let's Talk About It 27

Do the Numbers 27

Financial Planning Cases 28

On the 'Net 29

GOOD MONEY HABITS IN PERSONAL FINANCE 4

DID YOU KNOW?...
The Top 3 Financial Missteps in Personal Finance 6
How to Be Financially Literate 7
State Lotteries Use Time Value of Money Calculations 15
Examples of Good Financial Behaviors 21
Examples of Poor Financial Behaviors 24

ADVICE FROM A PRO...
Seven Money Mantras for a Richer Life 10
Choosing a Financial Planner 25

2 Career Planning 30

Key Steps in Successful Career Planning 32
Create Your Career Goal and Plan 33
Clarify Your Interests 34
Review Your Abilities, Experiences, and Education 34
Identify Your Values 35
Consider Costs, Benefits, and Lifestyle Trade-offs 35
Align Yourself with Tomorrow's Employment Trends 36
Take Advantage of Networking 37
Target Preferred Employers 38
Be Willing to Change Career Goals and Plans 39

Know Your Preferred Work-Style Personality 39

Financial and Legal Aspects of Employment 41
Compare Salary and Living Costs in Different Cities 41
Place Values on Employee Benefits 42
Know Your Legal Employment Rights 43

Effective Employment Search Strategies 46
Assemble a Résumé 46
Identify Job Opportunities 46
Write an Effective Cover Letter 49
Obtain Strong Reference Letters 50
Apply 51
Interview for Success 51
Negotiate and Accept the Job 53

Big Picture Summary of Learning Objectives 55

Let's Talk About It 55

Do the Numbers 55

Financial Planning Cases 55

On the 'Net 56

GOOD MONEY HABITS IN UNDERSTANDING CAREER PLANNING 33

DID YOU KNOW?...
The Top 3 Financial Missteps in Career Planning 34
How to Work at Home Online 41
Value of Additional Education 42
What You Give Up When Cashing Out Your 401(k) Account 45
Résumé Buzzwords for Skills, Traits, and Technical Expertise 46
Prospective Employers Can Check Your Credit Report 49
How to Interview over a Meal 53
How to Deal with Rejection 54
How to Get a Raise 54

ADVICE FROM FROM A PRO…
Competencies of Successful People 37
Career Advancement Tips 45

DECISION-MAKING WORKSHEET
What Is Your Work-Style Personality? 40
Assessing the Benefits of a Second Income 44
Keeping Track of Your Job Search Progress 47

3 Financial Statements, Tools, and Budgets 58

Financial Values, Goals, and Strategies 60
Values Define Your Financial Success 60
Financial Goals Follow from Your Values 61
Financial Strategies Guide Your Financial Success 63

Financial Statements Measure Your Financial Health and Progress 64
The Balance Sheet Is a Snapshot of Your Financial Status Right Now 65
Strategies to Increase Your Net Worth 67
The Cash-Flow Statement Tracks Where Your Money Came From and Went 67

Financial Ratios Assess Your Financial Strength and Progress 72
Basic Liquidity Ratio: Can I Pay for Emergencies? 74
Asset-to-Debt Ratio: Do I Have Enough Assets Compared with Liabilities? 74
Debt Service-to-Income Ratio: Can I Meet My Total Debt Obligations? 75
Debt Payments-to-Disposable Income Ratio: Can I Pay My Debts? 75
Investment Assets-to-Total Assets Ratio: Do I Need to Invest More? 75
Other Ways to Assess Financial Progress 76

Financial Record Keeping Saves Time and Makes You Money 76

Reaching Your Goals Through Budgeting: Your Spending/Savings Action Plan 78
Action Before: Set Financial Goals 78
Action Before: Make and Reconcile Budget Estimates 80
Action Before: Plan Cash Flows 81
Action During Budgeting Period: Control Spending 85
Action After: Evaluate Budgeting Progress 86
Financial Software and Planning Tools Make Managing Your Money a Snap 87

Big Picture Summary of Learning Objectives 90

Let's Talk About It 91

Do the Numbers 91

Financial Planning Cases 92

On the 'Net 94

GOOD MONEY HABITS IN FINANCIAL STATEMENTS, TOOLS, AND BUDGETS 61

DID YOU KNOW?…
The Financial Planning Process 60
Life Planning Issues When You Find the Right Partner 64
Wealth-Building Principles 79
The Top 3 Financial Missteps in Budget Planning 85

ADVICE FROM A PRO
Crisis Steps to Take If Budget Deficits Occur Repeatedly 88

PART 2

Money Management 95

4 Managing Income Taxes 96

Progressive Income Taxes and the Marginal Tax Rate 98
The Progressive Nature of the Federal Income Tax 98
The Marginal Tax Rate Is Applied to the Last Dollar Earned 98
The Marginal Tax Rate Affects Your Financial Decisions 99
Your Effective Marginal Tax Rate Is Probably 43 Percent 100
Your Average Tax Rate Is Lower 100

Eight Steps in Calculating Your Income Taxes 100
1. Determine Your Total Income 101
2. Determine and Report Your Gross Income After Subtracting Exclusions 104
3. Subtract Adjustments to Income 105
4. Subtract Either the IRS's Standard Deduction for Your Tax Status or Your Itemized Deductions 106
5. Subtract the Value of Your Personal Exemptions 110
6. Determine Your Preliminary Tax Liability 110
7. Subtract Tax Credits for Which You Qualify 111
8. Calculate the Balance Due the IRS or the Amount of Your Refund 113

Avoid Taxes Through Proper Planning 116
Practice Legal Tax Avoidance, Not Tax Evasion 116
A Dollar Saved from Taxes Is Really Two Dollars—or More 116
Strategy: Reduce Taxable Income via Your Employer 116
Strategy: Make Tax-Sheltered Investments 118
Strategy: Postpone Income 123
Strategy: Bunch Deductions 124
Strategy: Take All of Your Legal Tax Deductions 124
Strategy: Buy and Manage a Real Estate Investment 125

Big Picture Summary of Learning Objectives 126

Let's Talk About It 126

Do the Numbers 127

Financial Planning Cases 127

On the 'Net 128

GOOD MONEY HABITS IN MANAGING INCOME TAXES 98

DID YOU KNOW?…
How to Determine Your Marginal Tax Rate 100
Determine Whether You Should File an Income Tax Return 101
Ways to Pay Income Taxes 102
Keep Your Tax Records a Long Time 109

Income Tax Preparation Guidance 110
Cafeteria Plans Offer Tax-Free Employee Benefits 117
Consider the Tax Consequences of Managing Income Taxes 120
How to Compare Taxable and After-Tax Yields 122
Overwithholding 124
Top 3 Financial Missteps in Managing Income Taxes 126

ADVICE FROM A PRO
A Sideline Business Can Reduce Your Income Taxes 107
Buy a Home to Reduce Taxes 123

5 Managing Checking and Savings Accounts 130

What Is Monetary Asset Management? 132
The Three Tools of Monetary Asset Management 132
Who Provides Monetary Asset Management Services? 133

Tool #1—Interest-Earning Checking Accounts 135
Types of Checking Accounts 136
Checking Account Minimum-Balance Requirements 136

Tool #2—Savings Accounts 138
Statement Savings Accounts 138
Certificates of Deposit 139
How to Save 142
Savings Account Interest 143

Tool #3—Money Market Accounts 145
Super NOW Accounts 145
Money Market Deposit Accounts 145
Money Market Mutual Funds 146
Asset Management Accounts 147

Electronic Money Management 147
Electronic Money Management Can Be Easy But Is Not Always Free 148
Consumer Protection Regulations 149

The Psychology of Money Management 150
Managing Money and Making Financial Decisions Are Different 151
People Ascribe Strong Emotions to Money 151
How to Talk About Financial Matters 151
Complications Brought by Remarriage 153

Big Picture Summary of Learning Objectives 154

Let's Talk About It 155

Do the Numbers 155

Financial Planning Cases 155

On the 'Net 157

GOOD MONEY HABITS IN MANAGING CHECKING AND SAVINGS ACCOUNTS 132

DID YOU KNOW?...
Top 3 Financial Missteps in Managing Checking and Savings Accounts 134
What Happens When You Write a Check 137
Payment Instruments for Special Needs 137
How to Ladder Your CDs 141
How to Reconcile Your Bank Accounts 142
The Tax Consequences of Saving for Children's College 144
How Ownership of Accounts (and Other Assets) Is Established 146
Using Plastic in Monetary Asset Management 148
How to Protect Your Privacy When Banking Online 149
How to Develop Money Sense in Children 152

ADVICE FROM A PRO
Endorse Your Checks Properly 140
Protect Yourself from Bad Check Fees 140

6 Building and Maintaining Good Credit 158

Reasons For and Against Using Credit 160
Good Uses of Credit 160
The Downside of Credit 161

You Should Set Your Own Debt Limit 163
Debt Payments-to-Disposable Income Method 163
Ratio of Debt-to-Equity Method 165
Continuous-Debt Method 165
Dual-Earner Households Should Consider a Lower Debt Limit 165

Obtaining Credit and Building a Good Credit Reputation 167
The Credit Approval Process 167
Your Credit Reputation 169

Sources of Consumer Loans 172
Depository Institutions Loan Money to Their Banking Customers 172
Sales Finance Companies Loan Money to Buy Consumer Products 172
Consumer Finance Companies Make Small Cash Loans 173
Stockbrokers Loan Money to Their Clients 173
Insurance Companies Loan Money to Their Policyholders 173

Dealing with Overindebtedness 175
Ten Signs of Overindebtedness 175
Federal Law Regulates Debt Collection Practices 176
Steps to Take to Get Out from Under Excessive Debt 176
Bankruptcy as a Last Resort 177

Big Picture Summary of Learning Objectives 179

Let's Talk About It 180

Financial Planning Cases 180

On the 'Net 181

GOOD MONEY HABITS IN BUILDING AND MAINTAINING GOOD CREDIT 160

DID YOU KNOW?...
How to Manage Student Loan Debt 166
The Top 3 Financial Missteps with Credit 167

Sources of Protection from Direct Medical Care Costs 301
Health Maintenance Organizations 302
Traditional Health Insurance 303
Consumer-Driven Health Care 303
What Types of Care Are Covered? 305

Making Sense of Your Medical Plan Benefits 305
What Types of Care Are Covered? 305
Who Is Covered? 306
When Does Coverage Begin and End? 307
How Much Must You Pay Out of Your Own Pocket? 308

Planning for Long-Term Care 310

Protecting Your Income During Disability 312
Level of Need 313
Important Disability Income Insurance Policy Provisions 314

Big Picture Summary of Learning Objectives 316

Let's Talk About It 316

Do the Numbers 317

Financial Planning Cases 317

On the 'Net 318

GOOD MONEY HABITS IN MANAGING HEALTH EXPENSES 301

DID YOU KNOW?...
Top 3 Financial Missteps in Managing Health Expenses 301
How Medicare Differs from Medicaid 304
It Is a Bad Idea to Be Young and Uninsured 306
How to Avoid Duplication of Employee Health Care Benefits 307
About Supplemental Health Plans 307
The Tax Consequences of Managing Health Expenses 310
Workers' Comp Pays If You Are Hurt on the Job 311
How to Affordably Manage Health-Related Risk 315

ADVICE FROM A PRO...
Be Smart When Shopping for an Individual Plan 305
Maintain Your Medical Care Plan Between Jobs 310

DECISION-MAKING WORKSHEET
Determining Disability Income Insurance Needs 313

12 Life Insurance Planning 320

How Much Life Insurance Do You Need? 322
What Needs Must Be Met? 322
What Dollar Amount Do You Need? 324

There Are But Two Basic Types of Life Insurance 328
Term Life Insurance 328
Some Forms of Cash-Value Life Insurance Pay a Fixed Return 330
Some Forms of Cash-Value Life Insurance Pay a Variable Return 332

Understandig Your Life Insurance Policy 334
Policy Terms and Provisions Unique to Life Insurance 335
Settlement Options Allow the Beneficiary to Decide How to Receive the Death Benefit 337
Policy Features Unique to Cash-Value Life Insurance 337

Step-by-Step Strategies for Buying Life Insurance 340
First Ask Whether or Not, and For How Much, Your Life Should Be Insured 340
Then Properly Integrate Your Life Insurance into Your Overall Financial Planning 340
Where and How to Buy Your Life Insurance 343

Big Picture Summary of Learning Objectives 347

Let's Talk About It 348

Do the Numbers 348

Financial Planning Cases 348

On the 'Net 350

GOOD MONEY HABITS IN LIFE INSURANCE PLANNING 322

DID YOU KNOW?...
Top 3 Financial Missteps When Protecting Loved Ones Through Life Insurance 325
How Insurance Policies Are Organized 335
About Life Insurance After Divorce 340
The Tax Consequences of Protecting Loved Ones Through Life Insurance 341
How to Layer Your Term Insurance Policies for $60 per Month 344
About Life Insurance Sales Commissions 345

ADVICE FROM A PRO...
Don't Be Fooled by Vanishing-Premium or Return-of-Premium Policies 333
Buy Term and Invest the Rest 342

DECISION-MAKING WORKSHEET
The Needs-Based Approach to Life Insurance 326

PART 4 Investments 351

13 Investment Fundamentals 352

Starting Your Investment Program 354
Investing Is More Than Saving 354
Are You Ready to Invest? 354
Decide Why You Want to Invest 355
Where Can You Get the Money to Invest? 355
What Investment Returns Are Possible? 356

Discover Your Investment Philosophy 357
How to Handle Investment Risk 357
Ultraconservative Investors Are Really Just Savers 358
What Is Your Investment Philosophy? 358
Should You Take an Active or Passive Investing Approach? 360

Identify the Kinds of Investments You Want to Make 361
Do You Want to Lend or Own? 362
Making Short-, Intermediate-, and Long-Term

Investments 362
Choose Investments for Their Components of Total Return 362

Risks and Other Factors Affect the Investor's Return 363
Random and Market Risk 363
Other Types of Investment Risks 364
Transaction Costs Reduce Returns 365
Leverage May Increase Returns 365

Establishing Your Long-Term Investment Strategy 367
Long-Term Investors Understand Market Timing 368
Strategy 1: Buy and Hold Anticipates Long-Term Economic Growth 369
Strategy 2: Dollar-Cost Averaging Buys at "Below-Average" Costs 370
Strategy 3: Portfolio Diversification Reduces Portfolio Volatility 372
Strategy 4: Asset Allocation Keeps You in the Right Investment Categories at the Right Time 372
Strategy 5: Modern Portfolio Theory Evolves from Asset Allocation 375

Creating Your Own Investment Plan 376

Big Picture Summary of Learning Objectives 380

Let's Talk About It 380

Do the Numbers 381

Financial Planning Cases 381

On the 'Net 382

GOOD MONEY HABITS IN INVESTING FUNDAMENTALS 355

DID YOU KNOW?...
Americans Are Lousy at Investing Their Money 359
The Tax Consequences in Investment Fundamentals 366
Calculate the Real Rate of Return (After Taxes and Inflation) on Investments 368
Employers Offer Automatic Portfolio Rebalancing 373
Top 3 Financial Missteps in Investing 375

ADVICE FROM A PRO...
Buy Shares of Stock Directly Using a Dividend-Reinvestment Plan 371
When to Sell an Investment 376

14 Investing in Stocks and Bonds 384

The Role of Stocks and Bonds in Investments 386
Common Stock 386
Preferred Stock 387
Bonds 387
An Illustration of Stocks and Bonds: Running Paws Cat Food Company 388

The Major Characteristics of Common Stocks 390
Match Your Investment Choices Using P/E Ratio and Beta 390
Income Stocks 391
Growth Stocks 391
Value Stocks 392
Speculative Stocks 392
Tech Stocks 392
Blue-Chip Stocks 392
Large-Cap, Small-Cap, and Midcap Stocks 393

How to Evaluate Stock Values 394
Use Fundamental Analysis to Evaluate Stocks 394
Corporate Earnings Are Most Important 395
Numerical Measures to Evaluate Stock Prices 395

Calculating a Stock's Potential Rate of Return 397
Use Beta to Estimate the Risk of the Investment 397
Estimate the Market Risk 398
Calculate Your Required Rate of Return 398
Calculate the Stock's Potential Rate of Return 398
Compare the Required Rate of Return with the Potential Rate of Return on the Investment 400

How to Use the Internet to Evaluate and Select Stocks 400
Begin by Setting Criteria for Your Stock Investments 400
Basic Investment Information 401
Stock Screening 401
Security Analysts' Research Reports 402
Corporate News 402
Stock Research Firms 404
Economic Data 404
Stock Market Data 404
Securities Exchanges (Stock Markets) 405
Looking Up a Stock Price 406
Using Portfolio Tracking to Monitor Your Investments 407

Buying and Selling Stocks 407
Discount, Online, and Full-Service Brokers 407
Broker Commissions and Fees 410
How to Order Stock Transactions 410
Margin Buying and Selling Short Are Risky Trading Techniques 413

Investing in Bonds 417
Corporate, U.S. Government, and Municipal Bonds 417
Unique Characteristics of Bond Investing 420
Evaluating Bond Prices and Returns 422

Big Picture Summary of Learning Objectives 427

Let's Talk About It 428

Do the Numbers 428

Financial Planning Cases 429

On the 'Net 431

GOOD MONEY HABITS IN INVESTING IN STOCKS AND BONDS 386

DID YOU KNOW?...
How Stock Dividends and Stock Splits Work 389
Most Stocks Are Cyclical and Some Are Countercyclical 393
About Employee Stock Options 396
How to Use Online Stock Calculators 401
How Over-the-Counter Securities Transactions Are Executed 408
Initial Public Offerings of Securities 408
Regulations Protect Against Investment Fraud 409

The Tax Consequences of Investing in Stocks and Bonds 413
How to Determine a Margin Call Stock Price 415
Top 3 Financial Missteps of Investing in Stocks and Bonds 416
How Far Bond Prices Will Move When Interest Rates Change 424
How to Estimate the Selling Price of a Bond After Interest Rates Have Changed 425

ADVICE FROM A PRO...
Check Your Stockbroker's Background 410
Zero-Coupon Bonds Pay Phantom Interest 422

15 Investing Through Mutual Funds 432

Why Invest in Mutual Funds? 434
Net Asset Value 434
Dividend Income and Capital Gains 435
Advantages of Investing Through Mutual Funds 436
Unique Mutual Fund Services 437

Fund Objectives, Types, and Characteristics 440
Income Objective 440
Growth Objective 441
Growth and Income Objective 443

Fees and Charges of Mutual Fund Investing 444
Load and No-Load Funds 444
Disclosure of Fees in Standardized Expense Table 446
What's Best: Load or No Load? Low Fee or High Fee? 446

Selecting Funds in Which to Invest 448
Review Your Investment Philosophy and Investment Goals 448
Eliminate Funds Inappropriate for Your Investment Goals 451
Load or No-Load Funds? 452
Investment Advice Needed? 452
Screen and Compare Funds That Meet Your Investment Criteria 453
Monitor Your Mutual Fund Portfolio 455

Big Picture Summary of Learning Objectives 456

Let's Talk About It 457

Do the Numbers 457

Financial Planning Cases 457

On the 'Net 459

GOOD MONEY HABITS IN MUTUAL FUNDS 435

DID YOU KNOW?...
Mutual Fund Disadvantages 437
Other Investment Companies 439
Stable-Value Funds Available in Employer-Sponsored Retirement Plans 441
Quant Funds 443
Top 3 Financial Missteps in Mutual Fund Investing 444
The Total Long-Term Returns for Stock Mutual Funds Are Roughly the Same 448
How to Learn About Mutual Funds 451
About Mutual Fund Volatility 453
The Tax Consequences of Mutual Fund Investing 454

ADVICE FROM A PRO...
Invest Only "Fun Money" Aggressively 442

16 Real Estate and High-Risk Investments 460

Making Money Investing in Real Estate 462
Current Income and Capital Gains 462
Current Income Results from Positive Cash Flow 463
Price Appreciation Leads to Capital Gains 463
Leverage Can Increase an Investor's Return 464
Beneficial Tax Treatments 465

Pricing and Financing Real Estate Investments 467
Pay the Right Price 467
Financing a Real Estate Investment 469

Disadvantages of Real Estate Investing 469

Investing in Collectibles, Precious Metals, and Gems 471
Collectibles 471
Gold and Other Metals 474
Precious Stones and Gems 476

Investing in Options and Futures Contracts 476
Options Allow You to Buy or Sell an Asset at a Predetermined Price 476
Commodities Futures Contracts 480

Big Picture Summary of Learning Objectives 482

Let's Talk About It 482

Do the Numbers 483

Financial Planning Cases 483

On the 'Net 484

GOOD MONEY HABITS IN REAL ESTATE AND HIGH-RISK INVESTMENTS 462

DID YOU KNOW?...
What to Do Before Investing in Real Estate 464
Top 3 Financial Missteps in Real Estate and High-Risk Investment Investing 465
About Real Estate Seminars 467
Timesharing Is Not an Investment 470
The Tax Consequences of an Income-Producing Real Estate Investment 472
Scams Abound in Collectibles, Precious Metals, and Gems 475
How to Make Sense of Option Contracts 477
About Hedge Funds 480
Sure Ways to Lose Money in Investing 481

ADVICE FROM A PRO...
How to Calculate Breakeven Prices for Option Contracts 479

PART 5

Retirement and Estate Planning 485

17 Retirement Planning 486

Retirement Planning Is Your Responsibility 488

Understanding Your Social Security Retirement Income Benefits 489
- Your Contributions to Social Security and Medicare 490
- How You Become Qualified for Social Security Benefits 490
- How to Estimate Your Social Security Retirement Benefits 491
- Check the Accuracy of Your Social Security Statement 493

How to Calculate Your Estimated Retirement Needs in Today's Dollars 494
- Projecting Your Annual Retirement Expenses and Income 494
- An Illustration of Retirement Needs 494
- Suggestions to Fund Erik's Retirement Goal 497

Why Invest in Tax-Sheltered Retirement Accounts? 498
- Your Contributions May Be Tax Deductible 498
- Your Earnings Are Tax Deferred 498
- You Can Accumulate More Money 498
- You Have Ownership and Portability 499
- Your Withdrawals Might Be Tax Free 499

Employer-Sponsored Retirement Plans 500
- Defined-Contribution Retirement Plan—Today's Standard 500
- Defined-Benefit Retirement Plan—Yesterday's Standard 502
- Cash-Balance Plan—The Newest Retirement Deal 504
- Additional Employer-Sponsored Plans 505

You Can Also Contribute to Personal Retirement Accounts 506
- Individual Retirement Accounts 506
- Keoghs and SEP-IRAs 509

Use Financial Advice and Monte Carlo Simulations 509
- Investment Advice for Retirement Assets 509
- Monte Carlo Simulations to Help Guide Retirement Investment Decisions 510

Living in Retirement Without Running Out of Money 513
- Figure Out How Many Years Your Money Will Last in Retirement and Make Monthly Withdrawals Accordingly 513
- Buy an Annuity and Receive Monthly Checks 514
- Consider Working Part Time 515

Big Picture Summary of Learning Objectives 516

Let's Talk About It 517

Do the Numbers 517

Financial Planning Cases 518

On the 'Net 519

GOOD MONEY HABITS IN RETIREMENT PLANNING 488

DID YOU KNOW?...
- *About Women and Retirement Planning* 490
- *How to Avoid Rollover Penalties When Changing Employers or Retiring* 503
- *Retirement Plan Insurance* 505
- *Tax-Sheltered Retirement Accounts Offer Flexibility* 507
- *Negative Impacts of Withdrawing Money Early from a Tax-Sheltered Retirement Account* 508
- *Retirement Withdrawals That May Avoid the 10% IRS Penalty* 508
- *Top 3 Financial Missteps in Retirement Planning* 510
- *If You Choose "Low-Cost" Over "High-Cost" Funds* 510
- *How to Invest 401(k) or IRA Money* 511
- *Tax Consequences in Retirement Planning* 514

ADVICE FROM A PRO...
- *How to Collect Retirement Benefits and Social Security from a Divorced Spouse* 493
- *Buy Your Retirement on the Layaway Plan* 497

DECISION-MAKING WORKSHEET
- *Estimating Your Retirement Savings Goal in Today's Dollars* 495

18 Estate Planning 520

How Your Estate is Transferred 522
- Probate 522
- Probate and Nonprobate Property 522
- Transfer Your Estate by Contracts 523
- Transfer the Rest of Your Estate by Will 524

Use of Trust to Transfer Assets and Reduce Estate Taxes 527
- Living Trusts 528
- Testamentary Trusts 529

Prepare Advance Directive Documents in Case You Become Incapacitated 530
- Powers of Attorney 530
- Advance Medical Directives 530

Checklist to Settle and Transfer Your Estate 532

Estate and Inheritance Taxes 533

Big Picture Summary of Learning Objectives 535

Let's Talk About It 535

Do the Numbers 536

Financial Planning Cases 536

On the 'Net 537

GOOD MONEY HABITS IN ESTATE PLANNING 522

DID YOU KNOW?...
- *How to Transfer Retirement Assets* 524
- *Last Will and Testament of Harry Johnson* 525
- *Spouses Have Legal Rights to Each Other's Estates* 528

Use of a Charitable Remainder Trust to Boost Current Income 529
Top 3 Financial Missteps in Estate Planning 533

ADVICE FROM A PRO…
Ten Things Every Spouse Must Know 534

Appendixes A-1

Appendix A: Present and Future Value Tables A-2
Appendix B: Estimating Social Security Benefits A-12
Appendix C: Glossary A-15

Preface

A Note to the Student

Within ten years of graduation, the typical college graduate will purchase three vehicles for more than $25,000 each; spend several thousand dollars on furniture and other household items; shell out a few thousand dollars in interest on credit cards; pay thousands of dollars to the Internal Revenue Service in income and Social Security taxes; buy a life insurance policy; contribute $2000 to $4000 annually to an employer-sponsored tax-sheltered retirement plan; and make a $15,000 to $30,000 down payment to purchase a home valued at more than $200,000. Though this book will give you the skills you need to balance your checkbook and balance your personal budget so that you can perform each of these financial tasks, it is also our hope that it will assist you in making sound financial decisions that will positively affect the balance of your life. Our goal as authors is to give you the knowledge, tools, attitudes, and skills you need to be financially sound and strike your own personal balance. Along with the text, we have developed a full, rich student website that you can use to learn as much as possible from your efforts and, perhaps more importantly, develop your own financial plans.

To the Instructor

This ninth edition of *Personal Finance* appropriately balances *all* the pieces of financial planning. It provides your students with the tools and knowledge they need for their short- and long-term financial success. In addition to updating and enhancing the quality of the content, this edition truly stimulates student interest in a half dozen new ways.

What is the greatest challenge in teaching personal finance? Instructors tell us "to connect all the pieces in a comprehensive manner," "to cover all the material in one course," "to accommodate different learning styles," "to show students the relevancy of the topics," "to visualize real-life examples," "to get students to do a reality check on their own finances," "to make topics interesting that are important later in life," "to teach the time value of money with lots of Excel spreadsheet exercises," "to deliver an effective e-package (including self-tests and decision-making worksheets)," and "to stimulate student interest such that the instructor receives verbal and nonverbal feedback in class." We have listened and responded. The ninth edition addresses those needs precisely. We have made many changes . . . for the better.

Topical Coverage of the Ninth Edition

We have carefully constructed the ninth edition to address instructors' concerns about getting through all the necessary material for this course. The new, streamlined table of contents consists of 18 chapters total broken into 5 Parts: Financial Planning, Money Management, Income and Asset Protection, Investments, and Retirement and Estate Planning. A **new** chapter on Career Planning provides students with the steps they need for successful career planning.

Features

We have carefully designed pedagogical features to strengthen learning opportunities for students. Each feature is designed to communicate vital information meaningfully and to maintain student interest. The following features support student understanding and retention.

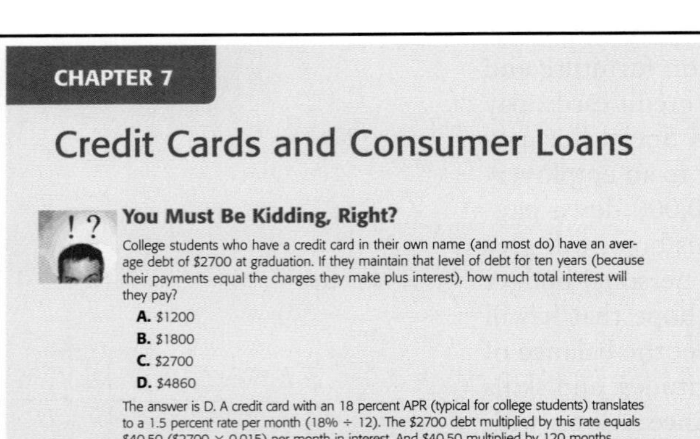
CHAPTER 7

Credit Cards and Consumer Loans

You Must Be Kidding, Right?

College students who have a credit card in their own name (and most do) have an average debt of $2700 at graduation. If they maintain that level of debt for ten years (because their payments equal the charges they make plus interest), how much total interest will they pay?

A. $1200
B. $1800
C. $2700
D. $4860

The answer is D. A credit card with an 18 percent APR (typical for college students) translates to a 1.5 percent rate per month (18% ÷ 12). The $2700 debt multiplied by this rate equals $40.50 ($2700 × 0.015) per month in interest. And $40.50 multiplied by 120 months equals $4860. You must pay more than the amount you charge plus any interest owed for each month in order to reduce your credit card debt and avoid paying many thousands of dollars in interest over the years. Otherwise, you will be in debt forever!

New to this edition, "You Must Be Kidding, Right?" Instructor alert! If you typically skip the opening case, now is the time to change your ways. This feature opens every chapter with a short narrative about a financial topic and a question with four possible answers. The often surprising answers provide an excellent opportunity to engage students in the chapter concepts.

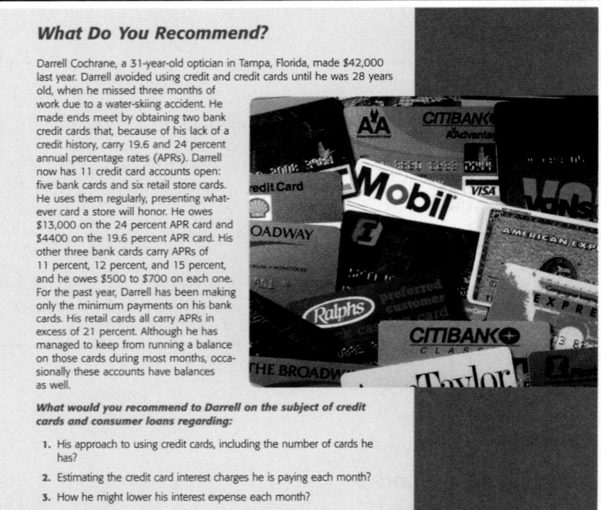
What Do You Recommend?

Darrell Cochrane, a 31-year-old optician in Tampa, Florida, made $42,000 last year. Darrell avoided using credit and credit cards until he was 28 years old, when he missed three months of work due to a water-skiing accident. He made ends meet by obtaining two bank credit cards that, because of his lack of a credit history, carry 19.6 and 24 percent annual percentage rates (APRs). Darrell now has 11 credit card accounts open: five bank cards and six retail store cards. He uses them regularly, presenting whatever card a store will honor. He owes $13,000 on the 24 percent APR card and $4400 on the 19.6 percent APR card. His other three bank cards carry APRs of 11 percent, 12 percent, and 15 percent, and he owes $500 to $700 on each one. For the past year, Darrell has been making only the minimum payments on his bank cards. His retail cards all carry APRs in excess of 21 percent. Although he has managed to keep from running a balance on those cards during most months, occasionally these accounts have balances as well.

What would you recommend to Darrell on the subject of credit cards and consumer loans regarding:

1. His approach to using credit cards, including the number of cards he has?
2. Estimating the credit card interest charges he is paying each month?
3. How he might lower his interest expense each month?
4. Consolidating his credit card debts into one installment loan?

Pretest/Posttest Chapter Opening Case: "What Do You Recommend?" These concise, realistic cases are presented at the beginning of each chapter and are followed by leading questions tying the most important fundamental concepts in the chapter. The case acts as a pretest because students will be able to offer only simplistic, experience-based opinions and suggestions to respond to the questions. This will communicate to students how much they have to learn from reading the chapter. "What Would You Recommend Now?" appears as part of the end-of-chapter pedagogy. At that point, student responses should be informed, practical, and action oriented.

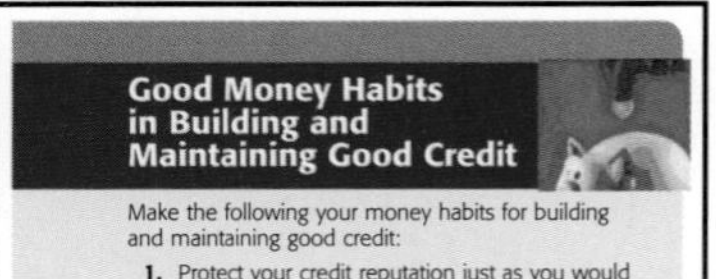
Good Money Habits in Building and Maintaining Good Credit

Make the following your money habits for building and maintaining good credit:

1. Protect your credit reputation just as you would guard your personal reputation.
2. Calculate your own debt limits before taking on any credit.
3. Obtain copies of your credit bureau reports regularly, and challenge all errors or omissions on them.
4. Never cosign a loan for anyone, including relatives.
5. Always repay your debts in a timely manner.

New to this edition, "Good Money Habits in Personal Finance" boxes concisely list the "right kind of advice" for readers desiring success in their personal finances throughout their lives.

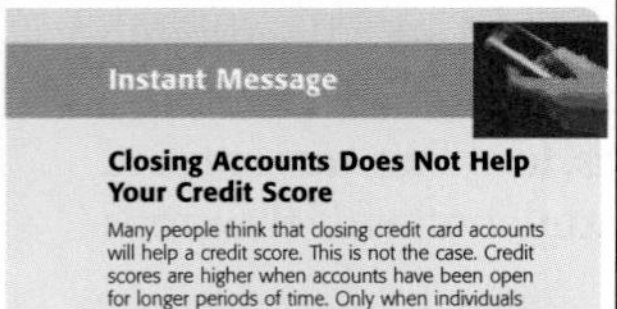
Instant Message

Closing Accounts Does Not Help Your Credit Score

Many people think that closing credit card accounts will help a credit score. This is not the case. Credit scores are higher when accounts have been open for longer periods of time. Only when individuals have ten or more cards should they consider closing some accounts and, even then, they should close their newest accounts, not the oldest.

New to this edition, "Instant Messages" provide quick, practical information on a variety of financial issues and opportunities.

"Decision-Making Worksheets" guide students to their best personal finance decisions following a step-by-step process.

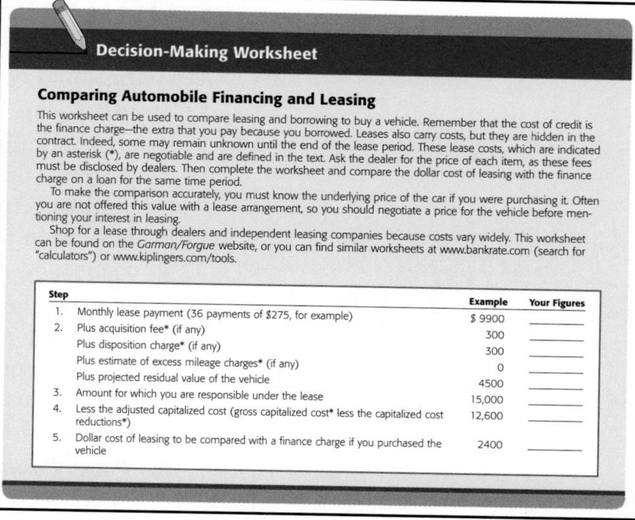

Decision-Making Worksheet

Comparing Automobile Financing and Leasing

This worksheet can be used to compare leasing and borrowing to buy a vehicle. Remember that the cost of credit is the finance charge—the extra that you pay because you borrowed. Leases also carry costs, but they are hidden in the contract. Indeed, some may remain unknown until the end of the lease period. These lease costs, which are indicated by an asterisk (*), are negotiable and are defined in the text. Ask the dealer for the price of each item, as these fees must be disclosed by dealers. Then complete the worksheet and compare the dollar cost of leasing with the finance charge on a loan for the same time period.

To make the comparison accurately, you must know the underlying price of the car if you were purchasing it. Often you are not offered this value with a lease arrangement, so you should negotiate a price for the vehicle before mentioning your interest in leasing.

Shop for a lease through dealers and independent leasing companies because costs vary widely. This worksheet can be found on the *Garman/Forgue* website, or you can find similar worksheets at www.bankrate.com (search for "calculators") or www.kiplingers.com/tools.

Step		Example	Your Figures
1.	Monthly lease payment (36 payments of $275, for example)	$ 9900	______
2.	Plus acquisition fee* (if any)	300	______
	Plus disposition charge* (if any)	300	______
	Plus estimate of excess mileage charges* (if any)	0	______
	Plus projected residual value of the vehicle	4500	______
3.	Amount for which you are responsible under the lease	15,000	______
4.	Less the adjusted capitalized cost (gross capitalized cost* less the capitalized cost reductions*)	12,600	______
5.	Dollar cost of leasing to be compared with a finance charge if you purchased the vehicle	2400	______

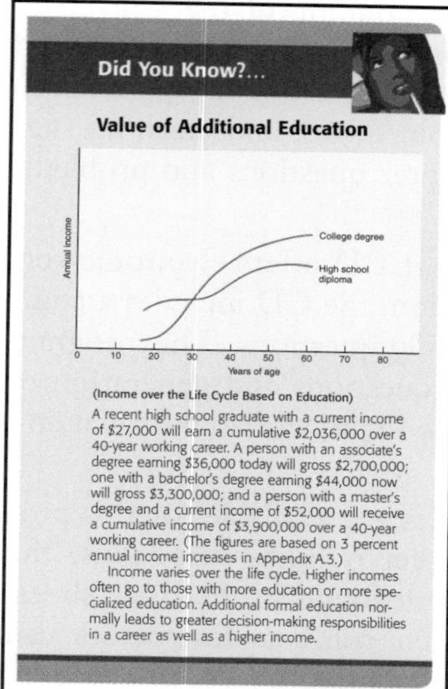

Did You Know?...

Value of Additional Education

(Income over the Life Cycle Based on Education)

A recent high school graduate with a current income of $27,000 will earn a cumulative $2,036,000 over a 40-year working career. A person with an associate's degree earning $36,000 today will gross $2,700,000; one with a bachelor's degree earning $44,000 now will gross $3,300,000; and a person with a master's degree and a current income of $52,000 will receive a cumulative income of $3,900,000 over a 40-year working career. (The figures are based on 3 percent annual income increases in Appendix A.3.)

Income varies over the life cycle. Higher incomes often go to those with more education or more specialized education. Additional formal education normally leads to greater decision-making responsibilities in a career as well as a higher income.

"Did You Know? . . ." boxes have interesting, catchy titles that encourage students to actually read the information, and research demonstrates this technique works.

"Advice from a Pro" boxes, written by some of the nation's very best personal finance experts, offer expert, real-world advice on getting out of credit card debt, making purchases online, buying a used car, and paying for retirement on the layaway plan plus many other topics.

End-of-Chapter Pedagogy. The end-of-chapter pedagogy carefully directs student learning of the concepts and principles key to success in personal finance.

What Do You Recommend Now? The same leading questions pertaining to the case at the beginning of the chapter are repeated in this section. At this point, however, instructors can anticipate higher-quality responses and a deeper level of understanding because students have read the chapter. Suggested answers appear in the *Instructor's Resource Manual.*

What Do You Recommend Now?

Now that you have read the chapter on buying housing, what do you recommend to Libby Clark regarding:

1. Buying or renting housing in the Denver area?
2. Steps she should take prior to actively looking at homes?
3. Finding a home and negotiating the purchase?
4. The closing process in home buying?
5. Selecting the type of mortgage to fit her needs?
6. Things to consider regarding the sale of her home should she ultimately be promoted to a position in another of the four regions?

Big Picture Summary of Learning Objectives. Three to four sentences review the chapter content following each of the chapter learning objectives.

Let's Talk About It. Students are given an opportunity to converse about their personal experiences related to the chapter by addressing these questions.

Do the Numbers. These questions apply the relevant quantitative mathematical calculations utilized in personal finance decision making. The student website includes calculators for these exercises.

Financial Planning Cases. Students must apply key concepts when analyzing typical personal financial problems, dilemmas, and challenges that face individuals and couples. Because the cases are designed to be both continuous *and* independent of the other chapters' cases, each case can be analyzed by itself. The series of case questions requires data analysis and critical thinking, and this effort reinforces mastery of chapter concepts.

On the 'Net. This end-of-chapter feature offers two or three Internet-based exercises, activities, and focused questions that expand the student's learning in a guided manner, allowing the student to research and apply chapter concepts while finding the answers.

New to this edition, Glossary. A comprehensive end-of-text glossary that includes detailed definitions of all key terms and concepts.

Complete Instructor Support

- ***Instructor's Resource Manual.*** Written by Karin Bonding of the University of Virginia, this ancillary includes a variety of useful components: suggested course outlines to emphasize a general, insurance, or investments approach to personal finance; a summary overview; learning objectives; and teaching suggestions. Answers and solutions to all end-of-chapter questions and problems have been provided by Raymond Forgue.

- ***HMTesting Instructor CD.*** This instructor support CD offers electronic versions of the IRM and PowerPoint slides. In addition, the CD includes a computerized *Test Bank*, which contains more than 2500 questions. This program is very user friendly and permits editing of test questions and generation of class exams. The test bank is offered in a Printable Diploma-based format and includes 100 to 200 questions per chapter.

Are You Ready to Invest?

- You balance your budget.
- You are able to save regularly.
- You use credit wisely.
- You carry adequate insurance.

- ***PowerPoint slides.*** Two sets of downloadable slides are available for this program. The Basic PowerPoint slides contain chapter outlines that follow the text. The Premium slides include all of the content found in the Basic slides, along with supplemental art questions and video content. Instructors can select which set best suits their in-classroom presentation needs. In addition, Classroom Response System ("Clicker") slides with question-and-answer PPT slides for in-class drill and knowledge testing are a new option available to instructors with the ninth edition of the text.
- ***Instructor website.*** The instructor website that accompanies *Personal Finance* provides a wealth of supplemental materials to enhance learning and aid in course management. Features of the site include Basic and Premium PowerPoint slides, downloadable *Instructor Resource Manual* files, an Updated Content section that highlights changes in personal finance, personal finance online calculators and Web links, and much more.

- ***EduSpace powered by Blackboard/WebCT.*** EduSpace allows flexible, efficient, and creative ways to present learning materials and opportunities. In addition to course management benefits, instructors may make use of an electronic grade book, receive papers from students enrolled in the course via the Internet, and track student use of communication and collaboration functions.

Kiplinger

- **New to this edition,** ***Instructor DVD—featuring personal finance tips from The Kiplinger Co.*** This Instructor DVD features video discussions with numerous personal finance professionals from The Kiplinger Co. These discussions contain personal finance tips illustrating and explaining pertinent topics such as job searching, income taxes, student loans, mortgage shopping, and more. The video clips from the DVD will also be available as streaming content in EduSpace.

Complete Student Support

- *My Personal Financial Planner* is a handbook for students to use in planning and organizing their personal finances. This booklet contains worksheets, schedules, and planners for financial planning. Some of the worksheets mimic the calculations and planning exercises covered in the book, others are for your use in developing your own financial plans and activities.
- **Student website** with *Your Guide to an A.* The student website accompanying *Personal Finance* contains many useful study aids and resources:

  The free open-access student website includes an *ACE Practice* Test for each chapter, online versions of several in-text features, a full glossary, a list of updated content, and more. A selection of the worksheets from the *My Personal Financial Planner* workbook are also available online. These can be copied and printed for students to turn in, as assigned, to their instructor.

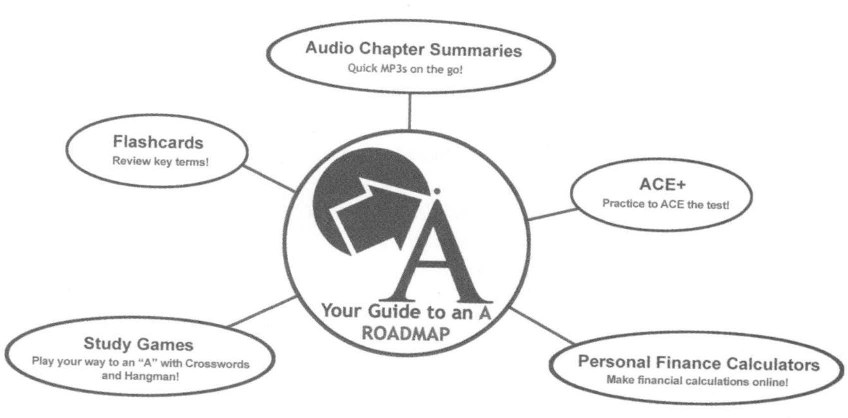

  The password-protected *Your Guide to an A* student website includes additional premium content. This site includes all the open-access resources **plus** *ACE Plus Tests* (two 25-question tests per chapter); audio chapter reviews; hangman, crossword, and drill flashcard games for each chapter; and a new set of Excel spreadsheet calculators to assist students in decision making and problem solving.
- **New to this edition, Excel spreadsheet calculators.** Over 50 Excel calculators prepared by the authors are on the student website. Most of the "Decision-Making Worksheets" from the book have been included, as well as all the major formulas from the text. You can use these materials to complete class assignments and end-of-chapter *Do the Numbers* and *Financial Planning Cases* AND to create key parts of your own personal financial plan.

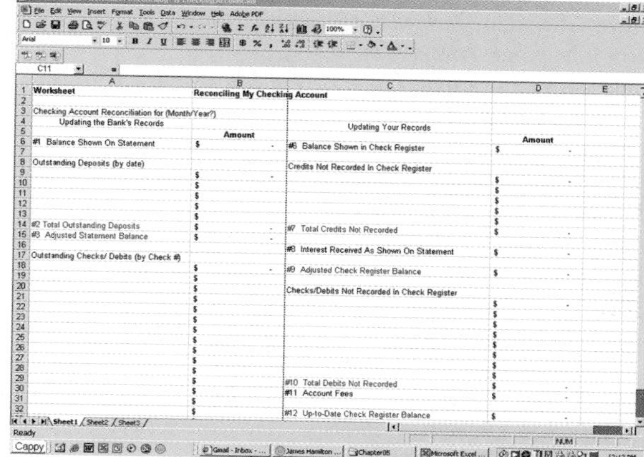

Acknowledgments

We would like to thank our reviewers and other experts, who offered helpful suggestions and criticisms to this and previous editions. This book is their book, too. We especially appreciate the assistance of the following individuals:

Tim Alzheimer, *Montana State University*
Gary Amundson, *Montana State University–Billings*
Dori Anderson, *Mendocino College*
Robert E. Arnold, Jr., *Henry Ford Community College*
Bala Arshanapalli, *Indiana University Northwest*
Hal Babson, *Columbus State Community College*
Anne Bailey, *Miami University*
Rosella Bannister, *Bannister Financial Education Services*
Richard Bartlett, *Muskingum Area Technical College*
Anne Baumgartner, *Navy Family Service Center–Norfolk*
John J. Beasley, *Georgia Southern University*
Kim Belden, *Daytona Beach Community College*
Pamela J. Bennett, *University of Central Arkansas*
Daniel A. Bequette, *Hartwell College*
Peggy S. Berger, *Colorado State University*
David Bible, *Louisiana State University–Shreveport*
George Biggs, *Southern Nazarene University*
Robert Blatchford, *Tulsa Junior College*
Susan Blizzard, *San Antonio College*
Karin B. Bonding, *University of Virginia*
Dean Brassington, *Financial Educator Services*
Anne Bunton, *Cottey College*
Paul L. Camp, *Galecki Financial Management*
Chris Canellos, *Stanford University*
Andrew Cao, *American University*
Diana D. Carroll, *Carson–Newman College*
Gerri Chaplin, *Joliet Junior College*
Steve Christian, *Jackson Community College*
Ron Christner, *Loyola University*
Charlotte Churaman, *University of Maryland*
Carol N. Cissel, *Roanoke College*
Thomas S. Coe, *Xavier University of Louisiana*
Edward R. Cook, *University of Massachusetts–Boston*
Patricia Cowley, *Omni Travel*
Kathy Crall, *Des Moines Area Community College*
Sheran Cramer, *University of Nebraska–Lincoln*
Ellen Daniel, *Harding University*
Joel J. Dauten, *Arizona State University*
Carl R. Denson, *University of Delaware*
Dale R. Detlefs, *William M. Mercer, Inc.*
A. Terrence Dickens, *California State University*
Charles E. Downing, *Massasoit Community College*
Alberto Duarte, *InCharge Education Foundation*
Sidney W. Eckert, *Appalachian State University*
Jacolin P. Eichelberger, *Hillsborough Community College*
Gregory J. Eidleman, *Alvernia College*
Richard English, *Augustana College*
Evan Enowitz, *Grossmont College*
Don Etnier, *University of Maryland–European Division*
Judy Farris, *South Dakota State University*
Vicki Fitzsimmons, *University of Illinois*
Fred Floss, *Buffalo State College*
Paula G. Freston, *Colby Community College*
H. Swint Friday, *University of South Alabama*
Caroline Fulmer, *University of Alabama*
Wafica Ghoul, *Davenport University*
Joel Gold, *University of South Maine*
Elizabeth Goldsmith, *Florida State University*
Joseph D. Greene, *Augusta State University*
Paul Gregg, *University of Central Forida*
Jeri W. Griego, *Laramie County Community College*
Michael P. Griffin, *University of Massachusetts–Dartmouth*
Richard C. Grimm, *Grove City College*
David R. Guarino, *Standard & Poor's*
Hilda Hall, *Surry Community College*
Patty Hatfield, *Bradley University*
Andrew Hawkins, *Lake Area Technical Institute*
Janice Heckroth, *Indiana University of Pennsylvania*
Diane Henke, *University of Wisconsin–Sheboygan*
Roger P. Hill, *University of North Carolina–Wilmington*
Jeanne Hilton, *University of Nevada*
Laura Horvath, *University of Detroit Mercy*
David Houghton, *Northwest Nazarene College*
George Hruby, *University of Akron*
Samira Hussein, *Johnson County Community College*
Roger Ignatius, *University of Maine-Augusta*
James R. Isherwood, *Community College of Rhode Island*
Naheel Jeries, *Iowa State University*
Karen Jones, *SWBC Mortgage Corporation*
Marilyn S. Jones, *Friends University*
Ellen Joyner, *Liberty National Bank–Lexington*
Virginia W. Junk, *University of Idaho*
Peggy D. Keck, *Western Kentucky University*
Dennis Keefe, *Michigan State University*
Jim Keys, *Florida International University*
Haejeong Kim, *Central Michigan University*
Jinhee Kim, *University of Marylan–College Park*
Karen Eilers Lahey, *University of Akron*
Eloise J. Law, *State University of New York–Plattsburgh*
Andrew H. Lawrence, *Delgado Community College*
David W. Leapard, *Eastern Michigan State University*
Charles J. Lipinski, *Marywood University*
Janet K. Lukens, *Mississippi State University*
Ruth H. Lytton, *Virginia Tech University*
Kenneth Marin, *Aquinas College*
Kenneth Mark, *Kansas Community College*
Julia Marlowe, *University of Georgia*
Lee McClain, *Western Washington University*
Billy Moore, *Delta State University*
John R. Moore, *Navy Family Services Center–Norfolk*
Diane R. Morrison, *University of Wisconsin–La Crosse*
Steven J. Muck, *El Camino College*
Randolph J. Mullis, *WEATrust*
James Nelson, *East Carolina State University*
Donald Neuhart, *Central Missouri State University*
Oris L. Odom II, *University of Texas–Tyler*
William S. Phillips, *Memphis State University*
John Piccione, *Rochester Institute of Technology*

Carl H. Pollock, Jr., *Portland State University*
Angela J. Rabatin, *Prince George's Community College*
Gwen M. Reichbach, *Dealers' Financial Services*
Mary Ellen Rider, *University of Nebraska*
Eloise Lorch Rippie, *Iowa State University*
Edmund L. Robert, *Front Range Community College*
Clarence C. Rose, *Radford University*
David E. Rubin, *Glendale Community College*
Michael Rupured, *University of Georgia*
Peggy Schomaker, *University of Maine*
Barry B. Schweig, *Creighton University*
Elaine D. Scott, *Bluefield State University*
James Scott, *Southwest Missouri State University*
Wilmer E. Seago, *Virginia Tech University*
Kim Simons, *Madisonville Community College*
Marilyn K. Skinner, *Macon Technical Institute*
Rosalyn Smith, *Morningside College*
Horacio Soberon-Ferrer, *University of Florida*
Edward Stendard, *St. John Fisher College*
Mary Stephenson, *University of Maryland-College Park*
Eugene Swinnerton, *University of Detroit Mercy*
Lisa Tatlock, *The Master's College*
Francis C. Thomas, *Port Republic, New Jersey*
Stephen Trimby, *Worcester State College*
John W. Tway, *Amber University*
Shafi Ullah, *Broward Community College*
Dick Verrone, *University of North Carolina–Wilmington*
Jerry A. Viscione, *Boston College*
Stephen E. Wagner, *Attorney at Law, Blacksburg, Virginia*
Rosemary Walker, *Michigan State University*
Grant J. Wells, *Michigan State University*
Jon D. Wentworth, *Southern Adventist University*
Dorothy West, *Michigan State University*
Gloria Worthy, *State Technical Institute-Memphis*
Rui Yau, *South Dakota State University*
Alex R. Yguado, *L.A. Mission College*
Robert P. Yuyuenyongwatana, *Cameron University*
Martha Zenns, *Jamestown Community College*
Larry Zigler, *Highland College*
Virginia S. Zuiker, *University of Minnesota*

This ninth edition also has benefited from the contributions of some of the United States' best personal finance experts, who have shared some specialized expertise by contributing to a series of boxes titled "Advice from a Pro":

Dennis R. Ackley, *Ackley & Associates*
M. J. Alhabeeb, *University of Massachusetts–Amherst*
Jan D. Andersen, *California State University–Sacramento*
Anthony J. Campolo, *Columbus State Community College*
Martin Carrigan, *The University of Findlay, Ohio*
Brenda J. Cude, *University of Georgia*
Lorraine R. Decker, *Decker & Associates Inc.*
Elizabeth Dolan, *University of New Hampshire*
Jonathan Fox, *The Ohio State University*
Carol S. Fulmer, *The University of Alabama*
Jordan E. Goodman, *MoneyAnswers.com*
Linda Gorham, *Berklee College of Music*
Sue Alexander Greninger, *University of Texas at Austin*
Reynolds Griffith, *Stephen F. Austin State University*
Holly Hunts, *Montana State University*
Alena C. Johnson, *Utah State University*
Hyungsoo Kim, *University of Kentucky*
Joan Koonce, *University of Georgia*
Constance Y. Kratzer, *New Mexico State University*
Frances C. Lawrence, *Louisiana State University*
Allen Martin, *California State University-Northridge*
Cora Newcomb, *Technical College of the Lowcountry, South Carolina*
Eve Pentecost, *University of Alabama*
Aimee D. Prawitz, *Northern Illinois University*
Kathleen Prochaska-Cue, *University of Nebraska-Lincoln*
Michelle Singletary, *The Washington Post*
Robert O. Weagley, *University of Missouri–Columbia*
Dana Wolff, *Southeast Technical Institute*

We definitely wish to thank the many students who had the opportunity to read, critique, and provide input for various components of the *Personal Finance* project. Please keep sending us your e-mails. Jing-Jang Xiao (University of Rhode Island) prepared the financial calculator appendix found on the website.

This edition of *Personal Finance* benefited enormously from the editorial efforts of Joanne Butler. In addition to being a fine manager and editor, she brought much insight, creativity, intelligence, and wisdom to the project. Helen Medley's accuracy check efforts were incomparable. Carol O'Connell did a superlative job supervising the production of this edition with its challenging format. We would also like to thank Karin Bonding for her contributions to the *Instructor's Resource Manual* and Amy Forgue for efforts on the PowerPoint slides.

A project of this dimension could never have been completed without the patience, support, understanding, and sacrifices of our friends and families during the book's development, revision, and production. Tom Garman, professor emeritus and fellow at Virginia Tech University, lives in Summerfield, Florida, and stays in contact with his children and their spouses and significant others: Dana, Julia, Scott, David, Alieu, Isatou, Kumba, Alimatou, and Ousman. Thanks are owed to all. Tom also credits the mentors in his life—Ron West, Bill Boast, Bill McDivitt, and John Binnion—for guiding him along the way, particularly through their noble examples of compassion, commitment, and excellence. Tom now serves as president of the nonprofit Personal Finance Employee Education Foundation (www.PersonalFinanceFoundation.org). Ray Forgue, recently retired from the University of Kentucky, lives near Greenville, South Carolina, where he proudly watches over son Matthew and daughter Amy as they commence their working careers. Ray wishes to thank his mother, Mary, and brothers Bob, Gary, Joe, and Dave for their patience over the years as he spent time during vacation and holiday visits working on this book. Special thanks to Snooky, whose assistance on the first edition of *Personal Finance* continues to shine through to this current edition.

Finally, we wish to say "thank you" to the hundreds of personal finance instructors around the country who have generously shared their views, in person and by letter and e-mail, on what should be included in a high-quality textbook and ancillary materials. You demand the best for your students, and we've listened. *Personal Finance* is your book! The two of us and the superlative team of people at Houghton Mifflin have tried very hard to meet your needs in every possible way. We hope we have exceeded your expectations. Why? Because we share the belief that students need to study personal finance concepts thoroughly and learn them well so that they will be truly successful in their personal finances.

E. Thomas Garman
ethomasgarman@yahoo.com

Raymond E. Forgue
perfinypm@yahoo.com

P.S. Dear students: If you are going to save any of your college textbooks, be certain to keep this one because the basic principles of personal finance are everlasting. Also, you might want to present the book as a gift to a significant other, spouse, or parent.

PART 1

CHAPTER 1 Understanding Personal Finance

CHAPTER 2 Career Planning

CHAPTER 3 Financial Statements, Tools, and Budgets

CHAPTER 1

Understanding Personal Finance

You Must Be Kidding, Right?

Se Ri Pak invests $250 a month, or $3000 a year, in her 401(k) retirement account, which earns an 8 percent annual return. After 35 years, how much money will she have in the account over and above the amounts she will contribute through the years?

A. $105,000

B. $210,000

C. $471,000

D. $576,000

The answer is D, $471,000 ($576,000 − $105,000). Se Ri will contribute $105,000 ($3000 × 35). Se Ri makes the big money ($471,000) off "the compounding money," not on the amount of money ($105,000) she put into her retirement plan. It's all about the magic of compound interest!

LEARNING OBJECTIVES

After reading this chapter, you should be able to:

1. **Use** the building blocks to achieving financial success.
2. **Understand** how the economy affects your personal financial success.
3. **Apply** economic principles when making financial decisions.
4. **Perform** time value of money calculations in personal financial decision making.
5. **Make** smart decisions about your employee benefits.
6. **Identify** the professional qualifications of providers of financial advice.

What Do You Recommend?

Lauren Crawford, age 23, recently graduated with her bachelor's degree in library and information sciences. She is about to take her first professional position as an archivist with a civil engineering firm in a rapidly expanding area in the U.S. Southwest. While in school, Lauren worked part time, earning about $8000 per year. For the past two years, she has managed to put $1000 each year into an individual retirement account (IRA). Lauren owes $15,000 in student loans on which she is obliged now to begin making payments. Her new job will pay $45,000. Lauren may begin participating in her employer's 401(k) retirement plan immediately, and she can contribute up to 6 percent of her salary to the plan.

What do you recommend to Lauren on the importance of personal finance regarding:

1. Participating in her employer's 401(k) retirement plan?
2. Understanding the effects of income taxes on her decision to participate in her employer's 401(k) plan?
3. Factoring the current state of the economy into her personal financial planning?
4. Using time value of money considerations to project what her IRA might be worth at age 63?
5. Using time value of money considerations to project what her 401(k) plan might be worth when she is age 63 if she were to participate fully?

FOR HELP with studying this chapter, visit the Online Student Center:

www.college.hmco.com/pic/garman9e

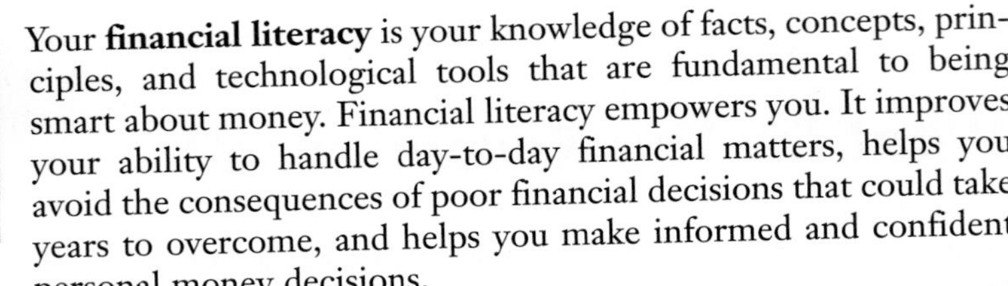

Good Money Habits in Personal Finance

Make the following your money habits in understanding personal finance:

1. Spend significantly less than you make and save using a pay-yourself-first approach.
2. Stay up-to-date with current economic conditions and the knowledge to manage your personal finances.
3. When making financial decisions, use marginal and opportunity costs and time value of money calculations.
4. Establish financial goals and take actions to achieve them.
5. Take advantage of tax sheltering through your employer's benefits program.
6. Believe in compounding by allowing your money to work for you over time by earning interest on top of the principal and other accrued interest.
7. Keep debt under control.
8. Take responsibility for managing your own financial success.

Your **financial literacy** is your knowledge of facts, concepts, principles, and technological tools that are fundamental to being smart about money. Financial literacy empowers you. It improves your ability to handle day-to-day financial matters, helps you avoid the consequences of poor financial decisions that could take years to overcome, and helps you make informed and confident personal money decisions.

Personal finance is the study of personal and family resources considered important in achieving financial success; it involves how people spend, save, protect, and invest their financial resources. Topics in personal finance include financial and career planning, budgeting, tax management, cash management, credit cards, borrowing, major expenditures, risk management, investments, retirement planning, and estate planning. A solid understanding of personal finance topics offers you a better chance of success in facing the financial challenges, responsibilities, and opportunities of life. Such successes might include paying minimal credit costs, not paying too much in income taxes, purchasing automobiles at low prices, financing housing on excellent terms, buying appropriate and fairly priced insurance, selecting successful investments that match your needs, planning for a comfortable retirement, and passing on your estate with minimal transfer costs.

Financial responsibility means that you are accountable for your future financial well-being and that you strive to make good decisions in personal finance. Studying personal finance will help you avoid financial mistakes and show you how to take advantage of financial opportunities. At the beginning of each chapter, we provide a short case vignette titled "What Do You Recommend?" Each case focuses on the financial challenges that can be experienced by someone who has not learned about the material in that chapter. You will be asked to think about what advice you might give the person as you study the chapter. Then at the end of each chapter, you will again be asked to provide more informed advice based on what you have learned. You will be smarter then!

The goal of this book is to provide you access to up-to-date information and rational suggestions to empower you to be able to make informed decisions about spending, managing money, maintaining creditworthiness, purchasing insurance, and saving and investing. Good decision making means you will control your personal financial destiny.

financial literacy Knowledge of facts, concepts, principles, and technological tools that are fundamental to being smart about money.

personal finance The study of personal and family resources considered important in achieving financial success; it involves how people spend, save, protect, and invest their financial resources.

financial responsibility Means that you are accountable for your future financial well-being and that you strive to make wise personal financial decisions.

The Building Blocks to Achieving Personal Financial Success

1 LEARNING OBJECTIVE
Use the building blocks to achieving financial success.

Today's marketplace provides a constant barrage of messages suggesting that you can spend and borrow your way to financial success, security, and wealth. These messages are very enticing for those starting out in their financial lives. In truth, overspending and overuse of consumer credit actually *impede* financial success!

Many people think that being wealthy is a function of how much you earn or inherit. In reality, it is much more closely related to your ability to understand the trade-offs and decisions that generate wealth for you. A **trade-off** is giving up one thing for another. For example, it is wise to give up some current spending in order to enjoy a financially comfortable retirement.

trade-off Giving up one thing for another.

You have to do only a *few* things right in personal finance during your lifetime, as long as you don't do too many things wrong. Personal finance is not rocket science. You can succeed very well in your personal finances by making appropriate plans and taking actions to implement those plans.

Spend Less to Save and Invest

First, recognize that financial objectives are rarely achieved without forgoing or sacrificing current *consumption* (spending on goods and services). This restraint is accomplished by putting money into **savings** (income not spent on current consumption) for use in achieving future goals. Some savings are actually **investments** (assets purchased with the goal of providing additional income from the asset itself). By saving and investing, people are much more likely to have funds available for future consumption.

savings Income not spent on current consumption.

investments Assets purchased with the goal of providing additional income from the asset itself.

Effective financial management often separates the haves from the have-nots. The haves, observes Virginia Tech professor Celia Hayhoe, are those people who learn to live on less than they earn and are the savers and investors of society. The have-nots are the spenders who live paycheck to paycheck, usually with high consumer debt. In short, follow the adage to "Spend some and save some."

Saving for future consumption represents a good illustration of the human desire to achieve a certain **standard of living.** This standard is what an individual or group earnestly desires and seeks to attain, to maintain if attained, to preserve if threatened, and to regain if lost. At any particular time, individuals actually experience their **standard of living.** In essence, your **level of living** is where you would like to be, and your level of living is where you actually are.

standard of living Material well-being and peace of mind that individuals or groups earnestly desire and seek to attain, to maintain if attained, to preserve if threatened, and to regain if lost.

Financial Success and Happiness

Financial success is the achievement of financial aspirations that are desired, planned, or attempted. Success is defined by the person that seeks it. Some define financial success as being able to actually live according to one's standard of living. Many seek financial security, which provides the comfortable feeling that your financial resources will be adequate to fulfill any needs you have as well as most of your wants. Others want to be wealthy and have an abundance of money, property, investments, and other resources. A fundamental truth of personal finance is that you cannot build financial security or wealth unless you spend less than you earn. As a result, you cannot reach your standard of living without somewhat restricting your level of living as you save and invest. That's the trade-off.

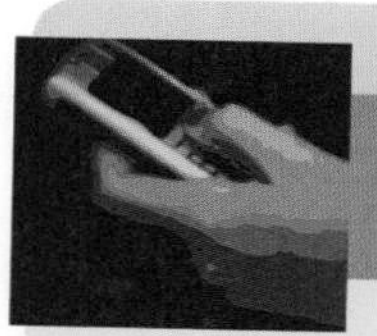

Instant Message

Buy Happiness With Money

Twenty-five percent of Americans believe that you can buy happiness with money.

Financial happiness encompasses a lot more than just making money. It is the satisfaction you feel about money matters. People who are happy about their finances are likely to be in control of their money, and this happiness spills over in a positive way to feelings about their overall enjoyment of life. Financial happiness is in part a result of practicing *good financial behaviors*—the subject of this book. Examples of such behaviors include paying bills on time, spending less than you earn, knowing where your money goes, and investing some money for the future. The more good financial behaviors you practice, the greater your financial happiness. In fact, just making progress toward achieving financial goals contributes to financial happiness.

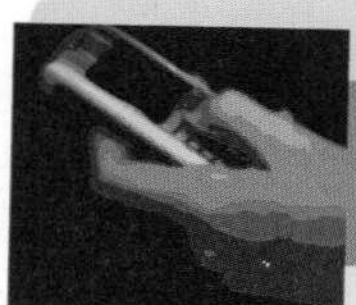

Instant Message

Frequently Heard Advice

The most frequently heard advice from financial advisers is to reduce your debts so you can save more.

Using the Building Blocks

Bridging the gap between one's level of living and one's desired standard of living involves learning about how to achieve financial success. Figure 1.1 shows how the building blocks of a financially

Figure 1.1
The Building Blocks of Your Financial Success

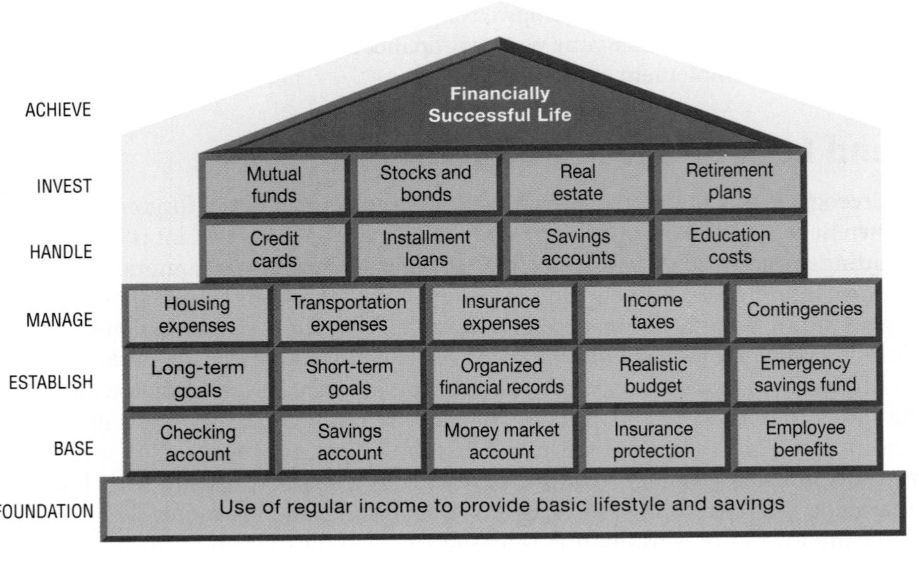

successful life fit together. Financial success and happiness come from using the building blocks of personal finance, such as having a foundation of regular income to provide basic lifestyle and savings, and establishing a financial base using employee benefits and checking and savings accounts. Other building blocks include setting financial goals, controlling expenditures, managing income taxes, handling credit cards, and investing in mutual funds and retirement plans. All of these factors are examined in the remaining chapters of the text.

Did You Know?...

The Top 3 Financial Missteps in Personal Finance

People slip up in personal finance when they do the following:

1. Only think about money matters when they have a financial problem
2. Spend more than they earn
3. Get financial advice from amateurs

CONCEPT CHECK 1.1

1. Describe financial success.
2. What is financial happiness?
3. What are the building blocks to achieving financial success?

The Economy Affects Your Personal Financial Success

2 LEARNING OBJECTIVE
Understand how the economy affects your personal financial success.

Your success in personal finance depends in part on how well you understand the economic environment; the current stage of the business cycle; and the future direction of the economy, inflation, and interest rates.

Where Are We in the Business Cycle?

economic growth A condition of increasing production (business spending) and consumption (consumer spending) in the economy and hence increasing national income.

An **economy** is a system of managing the productive and employment resources of a country, state, or community. The U.S. federal government attempts to regulate the country's overall economy to maintain stable prices (low inflation) and stable levels of employment (low unemployment). In this way, the government seeks to achieve sustained **economic growth,** which is a condition of increasing production (business spending) and consumption (consumer spending) in the economy—and hence increasing national income. Government policies also affect the economy. For example, tax cuts put money into consumers' pockets, which they are then likely to spend. Tax increases, in contrast, depress consumer demand.

Growth in the U.S. economy varies over time. The **business cycle** (also called the **economic cycle**) is a process by which the economy grows and contracts over time, and it can be depicted as a wavelike pattern of rising and falling economic activity in which the same pattern occurs again and again over time. As illustrated in Figure 1.2, the phases of the business cycle are *expansion* (when the economy is increasing), *peak* (the end of an expansion and the beginning of a contraction), *contraction* (when the economy is falling), and *trough* (the end of a contraction and beginning of an expansion).

The preferred stage of the economic cycle is the expansion phase, where production is at high capacity, unemployment is low, retail sales are high, and prices and interest rates are low or falling. Under these conditions, consumers find it easier to buy homes, cars, and expensive goods on credit, and businesses are encouraged to borrow to expand production to meet the increased consumer demand. The stock market also rises because investors expect higher profits.

As the demand for credit increases, short-term interest rates rise because more borrowers want money. Consumers and businesses purchase more goods, exerting upward pressure on prices. Eventually, prices and interest rates climb high enough to stifle consumer and business borrowing, send stock prices down, and choke off the expansion. The result is a period of negligible economic growth or even a decline in economic activity.

In such situations, the economy often contracts and moves toward a **recession.** The federal government's Business Cycle Dating Committee officially defines a recession as "a recurring period of decline in total output, income, employment and trade, usually lasting from six months to a year and marked by widespread contractions in many sectors of the economy." During recessions, consumers become pessimistic about their future buying plans. The typical U.S. recession is marked by an average economic decline of 2 percent that lasts for ten months with an average unemployment rate exceeding 6 percent. There have been three recessions in the past 25 years.

Did You Know?...

How to Be Financially Literate

The financially illiterate easily incur excessive levels of consumer debt, pay too much interest on debt, spend money unconsciously or frivolously, delay saving for retirement, fall prey to investment scams, buy the wrong kind of life insurance, and ultimately are unable to reach their financial objectives. They may not even have any financial goals. It is not fun going through life mired in financial problems and "learning from bad experiences."

Financial literacy is not widespread. Obstacles to financial literacy include a lack of knowledge about personal finance, the complexity of financial decisions, and the lack of time to learn about personal finance. People today face the challenge of saving, investing, and managing their own retirement funds, so it is no wonder that many feel less than competent, a bit confused, and a little anxious about financial matters.

But we are not talking about you! You are taking a course in personal finance, so you are already ahead in your money matters. So keep reading and studying. You will be financially literate!

business cycle/economic cycle Business cycles can be depicted as a wavelike pattern of rising and falling economic activity; the phases of the business cycle include expansion, peak, contraction (which may turn into recession), and trough.

recession A recurring period of decline in total output, income, employment and trade, usually lasting from six months to a year and marked by widespread contractions in many sectors of the economy.

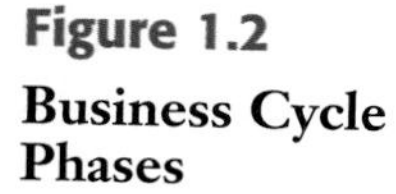

Figure 1.2
Business Cycle Phases

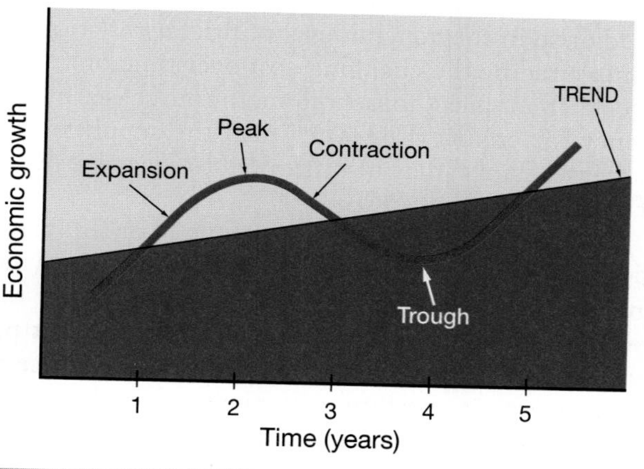

Eventually the economic contraction ends, and consumers and businesses become more optimistic. The economy then moves beyond the trough toward expansion, where levels of production, employment, and retail sales begin to improve (usually rapidly), allowing the overall economy to experience some growth from its previously weakened state. The entire business cycle may take four to five years.

What Is the Future Direction of the Economy?

To make sound financial decisions, you need to know both the current state of the business cycle and the direction in which it may be headed in the next few years. For example, when the economy begins to show clear signs of a slowdown, it may be a good time to invest in fixed-interest securities because interest rates are sure to fall as the government lowers its own interest rates to boost the economy. A point at which the economy is in the trough of a recession may be an excellent time to invest in stocks because the economy will soon expand and stock prices will rise. Using your knowledge of where we are in the business cycle and tracking a few economic statistics will guide you to make modest adjustment in your long-term financial strategy.

gross domestic product (GDP) The nation's broadest measure of economic health, it reports how much economic activity (all goods and services) has occurred within the U.S. borders during a given period.

Track the Gross Domestic Product The **gross domestic product (GDP)** is the broadest measure of the economic health of the nation because it reports how much economic activity (all goods and services) has occurred within the U.S. borders. The government regularly announces the rate at which the GDP has grown during the previous three months (www.bea.gov/newsreleases/rels.htm). An annual rate of less than 2 percent is considered low growth; 4 percent or more is considered vigorous growth.

Track the Employment Report The federal government's *Employment Report* tracks the number of jobs created every month (www.bls.gov/ces). More new jobs means more consumer spending.

index of leading economic indicators (LEI) A composite index reported monthly by the Conference Board that collects relevant economic data for business, governments, and individuals' use.

Track the Index of Leading Economic Indicators The **index of leading economic indicators (LEI)** is a composite index, reported monthly by the Conference Board, that suggests the future direction of the U.S. economy (www.conference-board.org). The LEI averages 21 components of growth from different segments of the economy, such as building permits, factory orders, and new private housing starts.

Track the Consumer Confidence Index The *consumer confidence index* gives a sense of consumers' willingness to spend, which spurs the economy (www.conference-board.org). Growing confidence suggests increased consumer spending.

What Is the Future Direction of Inflation, Prices, and Interest Rates?

inflation A steady and sustained rise in general price levels across economic sectors; measured by the changing cost over time of a "market basket" of goods and services that a typical household might purchase.

Inflation and interest rates typically move in the same direction. **Inflation** is a steady rise in the general level of prices; deflation involves falling prices. Inflation is measured by the changing cost over time of a "market basket" of goods and services that a typical household might purchase. Inflation occurs when the supply of money (or credit) rises faster than the supply of goods and services available for purchases. It also may be attributed to excessive demand or sharply increasing costs of production.

Inflation can be self-perpetuating. Workers may ask for higher wages, thereby adding to the cost of production. In response to the increases in the costs of labor and raw materials, manufacturers will charge more for their products. Lenders, in turn, will require higher interest rates to offset the lost purchasing power of the loaned funds. Consumers will lessen their resistance to price increases because they fear even higher prices in the future. In times of moderate to high inflation, buying power declines rapidly, and people on fixed incomes suffer the most.

How Inflation Affects Income and Consumption When prices are rising, an individual's income must rise at the same rate to maintain its **purchasing power,** which is a measure of the goods and services that one's income will buy. From an income point of view, inflation has significant effects. Consider the case of Scott Marshall of Chicago, a single man who took a job in retail management three years ago at a salary of \$32,000 per year. Since that time, Scott has received annual raises of \$800, \$900, and \$1000, but he still cannot make ends meet because of inflation. Although Scott received raises, his current income of \$34,700 (\$32,000 + \$800 + \$900 + \$1000) did not keep pace with the annual inflation rate of 4.0 percent (\$32,000 × 1.04 = \$33,280; \$33,280 × 1.04 = \$34,611; \$34,611 × 1.04 = \$35,996). If Scott's cost of living rose at the same rate as the general price level, in the third year he would be \$1296 (\$35,996 − \$34,700) short of keeping up with inflation. He would need \$1296 more in the third year to maintain the same purchasing power that he enjoyed in the first year.

purchasing power Measure of the goods and services that one's income will buy.

Personal incomes rarely keep up in times of high inflation. Your **real income** (income measured in constant prices relative to some base time period) is the more important number. It reflects the actual buying power of the **nominal income** (also called **money income**) that you have to spend as measured in current dollars. Rising nominal income during times of inflation creates the illusion that you are making more money, when in actuality that may not be true.

real income Income measured in constant prices relative to some base time period. It reflects the actual buying power of the money you have as measured in constant dollars.

nominal income Also called money income, it is income that has not been adjusted for inflation and decreasing purchasing power.

To compare your annual wage increase with the rate of inflation for the same time period, you first convert your dollar raise into a percentage, as follows:

$$\text{Percentage change} = \frac{\text{nominal income after raise} - \text{nominal income last year}}{\text{nominal income last year}} \times 100 \qquad (1.1)$$

For example, imagine that John Bedoin, a single parent and assistant manager of a convenience store in Columbia, Missouri, received a \$1600 raise to push his \$37,000 annual salary to \$38,600. Using Equation (1.1), John calculated his percentage change in personal income as follows:

$$\frac{(\$38{,}600 - \$37{,}000)}{\$37{,}000} = 0.043 \times 100 = 4.3\%^*$$

After a year during which inflation was 4.0 percent, he did better than the inflation rate because his raise amounted to 4.3 percent. Measured in real terms, John's raise was 0.3 percent (4.3 − 4.0). In dollars, his real income after the raise can be calculated by dividing his new nominal income by 1.0 plus the previous year's inflation rate (expressed as a decimal):

$$\text{Real income} = \frac{\text{nominal income after raise}}{1.0 + \text{previous inflation rate}} \qquad (1.2)$$

$$\frac{\$38{,}600}{1 + 0.040} = \$37{,}115$$

Clearly, a large part of the \$1600 raise John received was eaten up by inflation. To John, only \$115 (\$37,115 − \$37,000) represents real economic progress, while \$1485 (\$1600 − \$115) was used to pay the inflated prices on goods and services. The \$115 real raise is equivalent to 0.31 percent (\$115 ÷ \$37,000) of his previous income, reflecting the difference between John's percentage raise in nominal dollars and the inflation rate.

How Inflation Is Measured The U.S. Bureau of Labor Statistics measures inflation on a monthly basis using the **consumer price index (CPI).** The CPI is a broad measure of changes in the prices of all goods and services purchased for

consumer price index (CPI) A broad measure of changes in the prices of all goods and services purchased for consumption by urban households.

*This equation shows how the percentage change is calculated for any difference between two measurements. Divide the difference between measurement 1 and measurement 2 by the value of measurement 1. For example, a stock selling for \$65 per share on January 1 and for \$76 on December 31 of the same year would have risen 16.92 percent during the year: (\$76 − \$65) ÷ \$65 = 0.1692 or 16.92%.

Advice from a Pro...

Seven Money Mantras for a Richer Life

1. It's not an asset if you are wearing it!
2. Is this a need or is it a want?
3. Sweat the small stuff.
4. Cash is better than credit.
5. Keep it simple.
6. Priorities lead to prosperity.
7. Enough is enough!

Michelle Singletary
Nationally syndicated Washington Post *columnist ("The Color of Money") and author of* 7 Money Mantras for a Richer Life: How to Live Well with the Money You Have

consumption by urban households. The prices of more than 400 goods and services (a "market basket") sold across the country are tracked, recorded, weighted for importance in a hypothetical budget, and totaled. In essence, the CPI is a cost of living index. The index has a base time period—or starting reference point—from which to make comparisons. The 1982–1984 time period represents the base period of 100. For example, if the CPI were 220 on January 1, 2010, the cost of living would have risen 120.0 percent since the base period [(220 − 100) ÷ 100 = 1.2 or 120%]. Similarly, if the index rises from 220 to 228 on January 1, 2011, then the cost of living will have increased by 3.6 percent over the year [(228 − 220) ÷ 220 = 0.036 or 3.6%].

When prices rise, the purchasing power of the dollar declines, but not by the same percentage. Instead, it falls by the *reciprocal amount* of the price increase (the counterpart ratio quantity needed to produce unity). In the preceding illustration where prices increase between 2010 and 2011, prices rose 3.6 percent, whereas the purchasing power of the dollar declined 3.5 percent over the same period. [The previous year base of 220 divided by the index of 228 equals 0.965; the reciprocal is 0.035 (1 − 0.965), or 3.5%]

Inflation pushes up the costs of the products and services we consume. If automobile prices rose 20 percent over the past five years, for example, then it will take $28,800 now to buy a car that once sold for $24,000. Conversely, the purchasing power of the car-buying dollar has fallen to 83.3 percent of its original power ($24,000 ÷ $28,800) five years ago. If your market basket of goods and services differs from that used to calculate the CPI, you might have a very different *personal inflation* rate (the rate of increase in prices of items purchased by a particular person). Inflation pushes up the cost of borrowing, so monthly car payments and home mortgage rates increase when inflation rises.

federal funds rate The rate that banks charge one another for overnight loans; set by the Federal Reserve Board.

Track the Federal Funds Rate to Forecast Inflation You can forecast interest rates by paying attention to changes in the **federal funds rate,** which is the rate that banks charge one another on overnight loans. Because it is set by the **Federal Reserve Board** (an agency of the federal government commonly referred to as the **Fed**) and regularly reported by the news media, the federal funds rate provides an early indication of Fed policy and trends for longer-term interest rates. When the Fed believes the economy is growing too fast, it raises the rate and in turn lenders raise their rates for short-term loans, thereby making it more costly to borrow and spend. As a result, spending in the economy slows.

interest The price of borrowing money.

How Inflation Affects Borrowing, Saving, and Investing **Interest** is the price of money. During times of high inflation, interest rates on new loans for cars, homes, and credit cards rise. Even though nominal interest rates for savers rise as well, the increases do not provide "real" gains if the inflation rate is higher than the interest rate on savings accounts or certificates of deposit.

Smart investors recognize that the degree of inflation risk is higher for long-term lending (5 or 20 years, for example) than for short-term lending (such as a year) because the likelihood of error when estimating inflation increases when lots of time is involved. Therefore, long-term interest rates are generally higher than short-term interest rates. Similarly, stock market investors are negatively affected when inflation causes businesses to pay more when they borrow, thereby reducing their profits, and depressing stock prices. Throughout your financial life, you will want to factor the impact of inflation into your financial decisions so as to avoid its negative effects.

The Fed meets regularly to discuss the economy and review federal interest rates.

CONCEPT CHECK 1.2

1. Summarize the phases of the business cycle.
2. Describe two statistics that help predict the future direction of the economy.
3. Give an example of how inflation affects income and consumption.
4. Explain how the federal government measures inflation.

Think Like an Economist When Making Financial Decisions

3 LEARNING OBJECTIVE
Apply economic principles when making financial decisions.

Understanding and applying basic economic principles will affect your financial success. The most important of these are opportunity costs, marginal utility and costs, and marginal income tax rate.

Opportunity Costs in Decision Making

opportunity cost The opportunity cost of any decision is the value of the next best alternative that must be forgone.

The **opportunity cost** of a decision is the value of the next best alternative that must be forgone. Examples of personal opportunity costs are time, effort, and health, and examples of financial opportunity costs are interest, safety, and liquidity. Using the concept of opportunity costs allows you to address the personal consequences of choices because every decision inevitably involves trade-offs. For example, suppose that instead of reading this book you could have gone to a movie or watched television, but mainly you wanted to sleep. The lost benefit of that sleep—the next best alternative—is the opportunity cost when you choose to read. Knowing the opportunity cost of alternatives aids decision making because it indicates whether the decision made is truly the best option.

In personal finance, opportunity cost reflects the best alternative of what one could have done instead of choosing to spend, save, or invest money. For example, by deciding to put $2000 into a stock mutual fund for retirement rather than keeping the funds readily available in a savings account, you are giving up the option of using the money for a down payment on a new automobile. Keeping the money in a savings account has the opportunity cost of the higher return on investment that the stock mutual fund might pay. This opportunity to earn a higher rate of return is a primary consideration when making low-risk investment decisions.

Other challenging opportunity cost decisions are renting versus buying housing, buying a new or used car, buying or leasing a vehicle, working or borrowing to pay for college, purchasing life insurance or not, and starting early or late to save and invest for retirement. Another opportunity cost decision often is returning to college for a graduate degree.

If these costs are underestimated, then decisions will be based on faulty information, and judgments may prove wrong. Properly valuing the costs and benefits of alternatives represents a key step in rational decision making. The opportunity cost mathematics of the rent versus buy decision is illustrated later in Chapter 9.

Instant Message

Save $4.66 for Every $1 Not Saved Earlier

If you want to retire at age 63, you will have to save about $4.66 beginning at age 40 to make up for every dollar you did not save at age 20.

Marginal Utility and Costs in Decision Making

Utility is the ability of a good or service to satisfy a human want. A key task in personal finance is to determine how much utility you will gain from a particular decision. For example, if you decide to spend $70 on a ticket to a concert, you might begin by thinking about what you might gain from the expenditure. Perhaps you'll enjoy a nice evening, good music, and so on. **Marginal utility** is the extra satisfaction derived from having one more incremental unit of a product or service. **Marginal cost** is the additional (marginal) cost of one more incremental unit of some item. When known, this cost can be compared with the marginal utility received. Thinking about marginal utility and marginal cost can help in decision making because it reminds us to compare only the most important variables. It requires that we examine what we will really gain if we also experience a certain extra cost.

marginal utility The extra satisfaction derived from gaining one more incremental unit of a product or service.

marginal cost The additional (marginal) cost of one more incremental unit of some item.

To illustrate this idea, assume that you consider spending $150 instead of $90 (an additional $60) for a front-row seat at the concert. What marginal utility will you gain from that decision? Perhaps an ability to see and hear more or the satisfaction of having one of the best seats in the facility. You would then ask yourself whether those extra benefits are worth 60 extra dollars. In practice, people are inclined to seek additional utility as long as the marginal utility exceeds the marginal cost.

In another example, imagine that two new automobiles are available on a dealership lot in Ferndale, Michigan, where retired engineer Charlene Hicks is trying to make a purchase decision. Both vehicles are similar models, but one is a Mercury and the other is a Ford. The Mercury, with a sticker price of $29,100, has a moderate number of options; the Ford, with a sticker price of $30,800, has numerous options. Marginal analysis suggests that Charlene does not need to consider all of the options when comparing the vehicles. Instead, the concept of marginal cost says to compare the benefits of the additional options with the additional costs—$1700 in this instance ($30,800 − $29,100). Charlene need decide only whether the additional options are worth $1700.

Marginal Income Tax Rate in Decision Making

When making financial decisions, consider the economic effects of paying income taxes. Of particular importance is the **marginal tax rate,** which is the tax rate at which your last dollar earned is taxed. As income rises, taxpayers pay progressively higher marginal income tax rates. Financially successful people often pay U.S. federal income taxes at the 25 percent, or higher, marginal tax rate. For example, if Juanita Martinez, an unmarried office manager working in Atlanta, Georgia, has a taxable income of

marginal tax rate The tax rate at which your last dollar earned is taxed.

$66,000 and receives a $1000 bonus from her employer, she has to pay an extra $250 in taxes on the bonus income ($1000 × 0.25 = $250). Juanita also has to pay state income taxes of 6 percent, or $60 ($1000 × 0.06 = $60), and Social Security taxes of 7.65 percent, or $76.50 ($1000 × 0.0765 = $76.50). Therefore, Juanita pays an **effective marginal tax rate** of nearly 40 percent (25% + 6% + 7.65% = 38.65%), or $386.50, on the extra $1000 of earned income.

People who pay high marginal tax rates can do better by making tax-exempt investments, such as buying bonds issued by various agencies of states and municipalities. For example, Serena Miller, a married chiropractor with two children from Cleveland, Ohio, currently has $5000 in utility stocks earning 5 percent, or $250 ($5000 × 0.05), annually. She pays $62.50 in federal income tax on that income at her 25 percent marginal tax rate ($250 × 0.25), leaving her with $187.50 after taxes. Alternatively, a tax-exempt $5000 state bond paying 4 percent will provide Serena with a better after-tax return, $200.00 instead of $187.50. That is, she would receive $200.00 tax free from the state bond ($5000 × 0.04) compared with $187.50 ($250 − $62.50) after taxes on the income from the stocks.

The Very Best Kind of Income Is Tax-Exempt Income The very best kind of income, as this discussion implies, is **tax-exempt income,** which is income that is totally and permanently free of taxes. By legally avoiding paying one dollar in income taxes, you gain by not paying that dollar in taxes and, therefore, you receive the alternative use for that dollar. You also benefit by not having to earn another dollar to replace the one that might have been paid in taxes.

tax-exempt income Income that is totally and permanently free of taxes.

The Second Best Kind of Income Is Tax-Sheltered Income The second-best kind of income for individuals is **tax-sheltered** (or **tax-deferred) income**—that is, income that is exempt from income taxes in the current year but that will be subject to taxation in a later tax year. Figure 1.3 shows that tax-sheltered returns on savings and investments provide much greater returns than returns on which income taxes have to be paid because more money remains available to be invested. In addition, tax-sheltered funds grow more rapidly because compounding (the subject of the next section in this chapter) is enhanced when larger dollar amounts

tax-sheltered income Income exempt from income taxes in the current year but that will be subject to taxation in a later tax year.

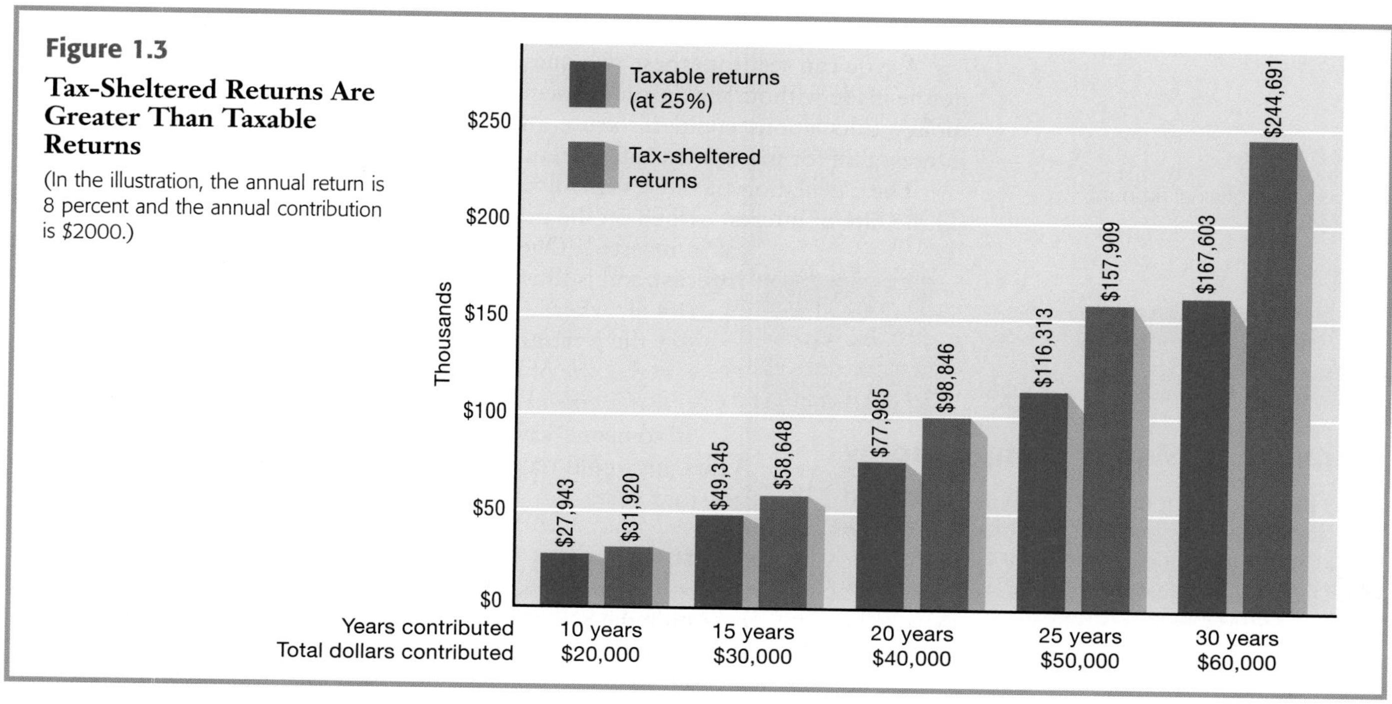

Figure 1.3
Tax-Sheltered Returns Are Greater Than Taxable Returns
(In the illustration, the annual return is 8 percent and the annual contribution is $2000.)

grow during the last years of an investment. Realize that eventually one must pay income taxes on the income deferred.

CONCEPT CHECK 1.3

1. Define *opportunity cost* and give an example of how opportunity costs might affect your financial decision making.
2. Explain and give an example of how marginal analysis makes some financial decisions easier.
3. Describe and give an example of how income taxes can affect financial decision making.

The Time Value of Money: Setting Dollar Values on Financial Goals

4 LEARNING OBJECTIVE
Perform time value of money calculations in personal financial decision making.

A dollar in your pocket today is worth more than a dollar received five years from now. Why? Time is money.

The **time value of money** is perhaps the single most important concept in personal finance. It adjusts for the fact that dollars to be received or paid out in the future are not equivalent to those received or paid out today. It is easy to understand that a dollar received today is worth more than a dollar received five years from now because today's dollar can be saved or invested and in five years you expect it to be worth more than a dollar. The time value of money involves two components: future value and present value.

time value of money (TVM) A method by which one can compare cash flows across time, either as what a future cash flow is worth today (present value) or what an investment made today will be worth in the future (future value).

Two Common Questions in Personal Finance To illustrate the time value of money, two questions in personal finance are commonly asked:

1. What will an investment (or a series of investments) be worth after a period of time? This question asks for a future value.
2. How much has to be put away today (or as a series of investments) to provide some dollar amount in the future? This question asks for a present value.

As you can see from these two questions, comparisons between time periods cannot be made without making adjustments to money values. Accordingly, time value of money calculations compare future and present values by taking into account the interest rate (or investment rate of return) and the time period involved.

The calculation of interest involves (1) the dollar amount, called the **principal,** (2) the rate of interest earned on the principal, and (3) the amount of time the principal is invested. One way of calculating interest is called **simple interest** and is illustrated by the **simple interest formula** where

principal The original amount invested.

$$i = prt \text{ where} \quad (1.3)$$
p = the *principal* set aside
r = the *rate* of interest
t = the *time* in years that the funds are left on deposit

If someone saved or invested $1000 at 8 percent for four years, he would receive $320 in interest ($1000 × 0.08 × 4) over the four years.

Instant Message

Reinvesting Means Compounding

If you earn 6 percent on a $1000 bond and spend your $60 annual interest every year for 20 years, you will have received $1200. But if you can reinvest your interest at 6 percent, you would net $2,262. Aha, the power of compounding.

Compounding But something is missing here. The simple interest formula assumes that the interest is withdrawn each year and only the $1000 stays on deposit for the entire four years. Most people do *not* invest this way. Instead, they leave the interest earned in the account so that it will earn additional interest. This earning of interest on interest is referred to as compound interest. And compound interest is always assumed in time value of money calculations.

compounding When interest on an investment itself earns interest.

Earning compound interest (or **compounding**) is the best way to build investment values over time. Because of compound interest, money grows much faster when the income from an investment is left in the account. In fact, the deposit of $1000 in our example would grow to $4,661 after 20 years (the calculation is described in the following paragraph). Many of the techniques for building wealth that we describe in this book are based on compounding. The way to build wealth is to make money on your money, not simply to put money away. Yes, you need to put money away first. But compounding over time is what really builds wealth.

Compounding serves as the basis of all time value of money considerations. To see how this works, let us look again at our example in which $1000 is invested at 8 percent for four years. Here is how the amount invested (or principal) would grow using compounding:

At the end of year 1, the $1000 would have grown to $1080 [$1000 + ($1000 × 0.08)].
At the end of year 2, the $1080 would have grown to $1166.40 [$1080 + ($1080 × 0.08)].
At the end of year 3, the $1166.40 would have grown to $1259.71 [$1166.40 + ($1166.40 × 0.08)].
At the end of year 4, the $1259.71 would have grown to $1360.49 [$1259.71 + ($1259.71 × 0.08)].

Due to the effects of compounding, this investor would have earned an additional $40.49 ($360.49 − $320). While this amount might not seem like much, realize that a $1000 investment for a longer period—say, 40 years—earning 8 percent interest would grow to $21,724.52, providing $20,724.52 in interest over that time period. Simple interest would have resulted in only $3200 in interest ($1000 × 0.08 × 40). The benefit of compounding over that time period is an additional $17,524.52 in interest ($20,724.52 − $3200).

The results are even more dramatic if $1000 is invested at the end of each year for 40 years. The total at the end of 40 years would be $259,056, with $219,056 representing the interest on the invested funds. This illustration suggests one of the cardinal rules of personal financial planning: Getting rich is not a function of investing a lot of money. It is the result of investing regularly for long periods of time.

Did You Know?...

State Lotteries Use Time Value of Money Calculations

How often have you heard or seen reports of lottery jackpots reaching extremely high amounts? Does the lottery actually pay out these amounts? Not really. Let's assume a lucky ticket holder wins a jackpot of $100 million. The announced jackpot is based on the assumption that the winner will receive the amount in a series of 20 annual payments of $5 million each, adding up to the $100 million advertised total. In fact, the lottery will invest a lump sum right away to fund the annual payments made over the 20 years. It needs to invest only $57,349,500 at 6 percent to fund the stream of $5 million payments ($5 million × 11.4699 from the 6 percent column and 20-year row of Appendix Table A.4). Alternatively, lottery winners may be permitted to take a "cash option" instead of the annual payments. In this case, a winner of a $100 million jackpot who chooses the cash option would receive only $57,349,500. The winner would also have to pay federal taxes, and perhaps state and city income taxes on this amount, resulting in an after-tax jackpot of closer to $35 million.

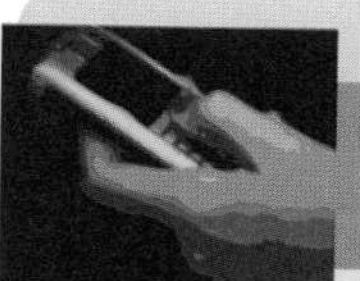

Instant Message

Compound Your Way to Wealth

One of the greatest investment strategies is compounding. Only through compounding will you attain the serious growth of your wealth over time.

Two Types of Time Value of Money Calculations

Essentially there are two types of time value of money calculations: (1) converting present values to future values (as illustrated in the preceding example) and (2) converting future values to present values. Within each type, the calculations differ slightly depending on whether a lump sum is involved or whether a series of payments (an annuity) is involved.

Calculating Future Values

Future value *(FV)* is the valuation of an asset projected to the end of a particular time period in the future. You can calculate the future value of a lump sum or the future value of a series of deposits.

future value The valuation of an asset projected to the end of a particular time period in the future.

Table 1.1 Future Value of $1 After a Given Number of Periods

Periods	1%	2%	3%	4%	5%	6%	7%	8%	9%	10%
1	1.0100	1.0200	1.0300	1.0400	1.0500	1.0600	1.0700	1.0800	1.0900	1.1000
2	1.0201	1.0404	1.0609	1.0816	1.1025	1.1236	1.1449	1.1664	1.1881	1.2100
3	1.0303	1.0612	1.0927	1.1249	1.1576	1.1910	1.2250	1.2597	1.2950	1.3310
4	1.0406	1.0824	1.1255	1.1699	1.2155	1.2625	1.3108	1.3605	1.4116	1.4641
5	1.0510	1.1041	1.1593	1.2167	1.2763	1.3382	1.4026	1.4693	1.5386	1.6105
6	1.0615	1.1262	1.1941	1.2653	1.3401	1.4185	1.5007	1.5869	1.6771	1.7716
7	1.0721	1.1487	1.2299	1.3159	1.4071	1.5036	1.6058	1.7138	1.8280	1.9487
8	1.0829	1.1717	1.2668	1.3686	1.4775	1.5938	1.7182	1.8509	1.9926	2.1436
9	1.0937	1.1951	1.3048	1.4233	1.5513	1.6895	1.8385	1.9990	2.1719	2.3579
10	1.1046	1.2190	1.3439	1.4802	1.6289	1.7908	1.9672	2.1589	2.3674	2.5937

Future Value of a Lump Sum Equation (1.4) can be used to calculate the future value of a lump sum:

$$FV = (\text{Present value of sum of money})\ (i + 1.0)^n \qquad (1.4)$$

where i represents the interest rate and n represents the number of time periods. Applying this formula to our earlier example of investing $1000 at 8 percent for four years, we obtain

$$\$1360.49 = (\$1000)\ (1 + 0.08)^4$$

or

$$\$1360.49 = (\$1000)(1.08)(1.08)(1.08)(1.08)$$

While mathematically correct, these calculations can be cumbersome when using long time periods. Table 1.1 provides a quick and easy way to determine the future dollar value of an investment. For the preceding example, use the table in the following manner: Go across the top row to the 8 percent column. Read down the 8 percent column to the row for four years to locate the factor 1.3605 (at the intersection of the green column and row). Multiply that factor by the present value of the cash asset ($1000) to arrive at the future value ($1360.50).

Appendix Table A.1 provides an even more complete table for calculating the future value of lump-sum amounts. Figure 1.4 demonstrates the effects of various com-

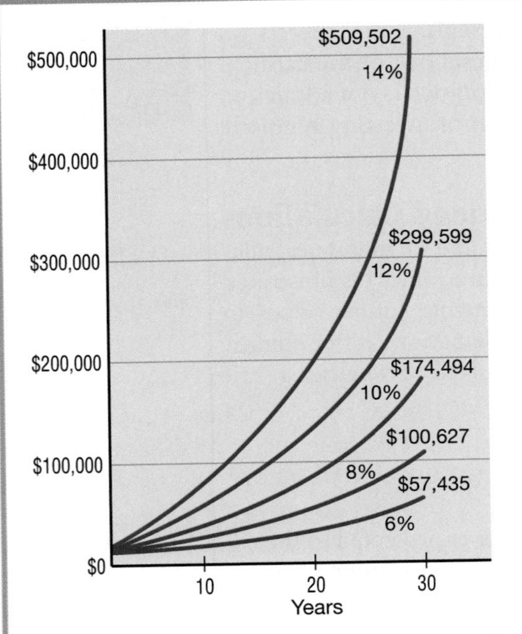

Figure 1.4
Future Value of $10,000 with Interest Compounded Annually After a Given Number of Periods

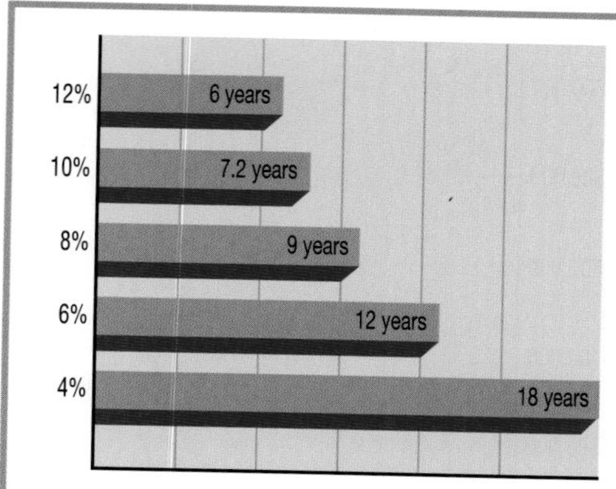

Figure 1.5

The Rule of 72 Illustrated

(Dividing the interest rate earned into 72 reveals how many years it takes for the principal to double.)

pounded returns on a $10,000 investment. The $10,000 will grow to $57,435 in 30 years with an interest rate of 6 percent. Compounding $10,000 at 10 percent yields $174,494 over the same time period; at 14 percent, it yields a whopping $509,502! For practice you might want to confirm these results using Appendix Table A.1.

Rule of 72 Reveals Number of Years for Principal to Double The **rule of 72** is a handy formula for figuring the number of years it takes to double the principal using compound interest. You simply divide the interest rate that the money will earn *into* the number 72. For example, if interest is compounded at a rate of 7 percent per year, your principal will double in 10.3 years (72 ÷ 7); if the rate is 6 percent, it will take 12 years (72 ÷ 6). The rule of 72 (see Figure 1.5) also works for determining how long it would take for the price of something to double given a rate of increase in the price. For example, if college tuition costs were rising 8 percent per year, the cost of a college education would double in just over nine years. In addition, the rule of 72 can be used to calculate the number of years before prices will double given a certain inflation rate. Just divide the inflation rate into 72.

rule of 72 A formula for figuring the number of years it takes to double the principal using compound interest; simply divide the interest rate that the money will earn *into* the number 72.

Future Value of an Annuity People often save for long-term goals by putting away a series of payments. Appendix Table A.3 provides a complete table for calculating the future value of a stream of deposited amounts, referred to as an annuity. Figure 1.6 graphically demonstrates the effects of various compounded returns on a $2000 annual investment made at the end of each year. The $2000 will grow to $91,524 in 20 years (read across the interest rate row in Appendix Table A.3 to 8 percent and then down the column to 20 years to obtain the factor of 45.762 to multiply by $2000) and to $226,566 in 30 years at an 8 percent rate. Compounding $2000 at 10 percent yields $114,550 in 20 years and $328,988 over 30 years; at 14 percent, it becomes $713,574 after 30 years! For practice you might want to confirm these results using Appendix Table A.3.

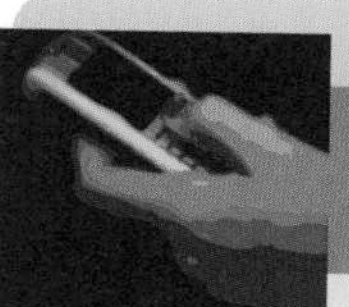

Instant Message

Assume Your Investments Earn 5% to 6%

When planning for long-term financial goals, assume your investments will earn 3 percent after inflation or at least 5 percent to 6 percent a year. Your investment returns could be higher. (See Chapter 13.)

Calculating Present Values

Present value (or **discounted value**) is the current value of an asset (or stream of assets) that will be received in the future. You can calculate the present value of a lump sum to be received in the future or the present value of a series of payments to be received in the future.

present value The current value of an asset (or stream of assets) that will be received in the future; also known as discounted value.

Present Value of a Lump Sum The present value of a lump sum is the current worth of an asset to be received in the future. Alternatively, it can be thought of as the amount you would need to set aside today at a given rate of inter-

Figure 1.6
Future Value of $2000 Annual Investments

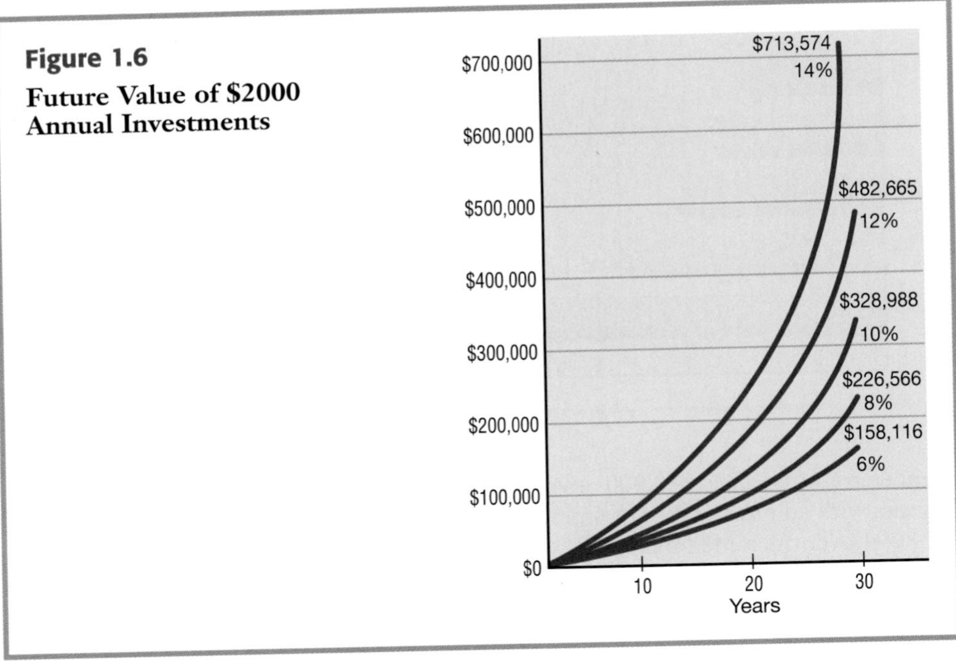

est for a given time period so as to have some desired amount in the future. Suppose you want to have $20,000 for the down payment on a new home in ten years. What would you need to set aside today to reach this goal if you could invest your money and receive a 7 percent return? Using Appendix Table A.2 you could look across the interest rate rows to 7 percent and then down to ten years to obtain the factor of 0.5083. Multiplying $20,000 by this factor reveals that $10,166 set aside today would allow you to reach your goal. (Note the connection here to the rule of 72: 7 percent divided into 72 is approximately 10.28, meaning that the investment would double in about 10.28 years. Indeed, $10,166 would approximately double to $20,000 in ten years.)

Instant Message

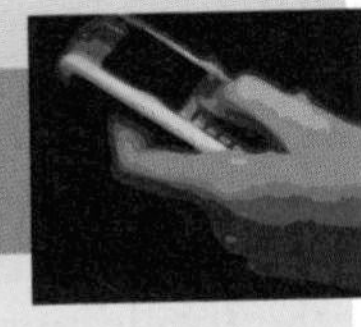

Web Calculators

Present and future value calculations can be readily performed on the Internet. Among the best calculators are those found at the following websites:

- **USA Today** (www.usatoday.com/money/perfi/calculators/calculator.htm)
- **Financial Calculators** (www.fincalc.com/)
- **KJE** (www.dinkytown.net/)
- **Bankrate.com** (www.bankrate.com)
- **CNNMoney** (cgi.money.cnn.com/tools/)
- **Fool.com** (www.fool.com/calcs/calculators.htm?source=LN)
- **Fidelity** (www.moneychimp.com/calculator/compound_interest_calculator.htm)

Present Value of an Annuity The present value of an **annuity** is the current worth of a stream of payments to be received in the future. Alternatively, it can be thought of as the amount you would need to set aside today at a given rate of interest for a given time period so as to receive that stream of payments. Suppose you want to have $30,000 per year for 20 years during your retirement. What amount would you need to have invested at retirement to reach this goal if you could invest your money and receive a 7 percent return? Using Appendix Table A.4 you could look across the interest rate rows to 7 percent and then down to 20 years to obtain the factor of 10.5940. Multiplying $30,000 by this factor reveals that $317,820 (10.5940 × $30,000) set aside at retirement would fund this stream of payments. Note the beauty of compound interest in this result. It takes only $317,820—not $600,000—to fund a $30,000 per year retirement for 20 years if you can earn 7 percent on your financial nest egg.*

annuity A stream of payments to be received in the future.

*If you are using a financial calculator for time value of money calculations, see "How to Use a Financial Calculator" on the *Garman/Forgue* website, or you can use the present and future value calculators found on the *Garman/Forgue* website, college.hmco.com/business.students.

CONCEPT CHECK 1.4

1. Explain the difference between simple interest and compound interest, and describe why that difference is critical.
2. What are the two components used when figuring the time value of money?
3. Use Table 1.1 to calculate the future value of [a] $2000 at 5 percent for four years, [b] $4500 at 9 percent for eight years, and [c] $10,000 at 6 percent for ten years.

Make Smart Money Decisions at Work

5 LEARNING OBJECTIVE
Make smart decisions about your employee benefits.

Smart decisions about your employee benefits can increase your actual income by thousands of dollars each year. To do so wisely, select among employer-sponsored plans for health care, out-of-pocket spending for health and dependent care, life insurance, disability, long-term care, and retirement. These decisions often require you to calculate the tax-sheltered aspects of the employee benefits. Your benefits package might also include dental and vision care, child care, elder care, subsidized food services, and an educational assistance program.

An **employee benefit** is compensation for employment that does not take the form of wages, salaries, commissions, or other cash payments. Examples include paid holidays, health insurance, and a retirement plan. The value of employee benefits often amounts to 30 percent or more of one's salary. Some employee benefits are tax sheltered, such as flexible spending accounts and retirement plans. Tax sheltered in this situation means that the employee avoids paying current income taxes on the value of the benefits received from the employer. The taxes may be postponed, or deferred, until a later date (usually a good idea)—perhaps until retirement, when the individual's income tax rate might be lower.

employee benefit Compensation for employment that does not take the form of wages, salaries, commissions, or other cash payments.

Flexible Benefit Plans Offer Tax-Free Money

A **flexible benefit plan,** also known as a **cafeteria plan,** is an employer-sponsored plan that gives the employee a choice of selecting either cash or one or more qualifying nontaxable benefits. For example, an employer might offer $2500 annually to each employee to spend on one or more benefits, and you pay no income taxes on the value of the benefits. A flexible benefits plan might offer dependent care, adoption assistance, medical expense reimbursements, insurance, or transportation benefits. Employees select the benefits they want. Employees working for employers that offer a cafeteria plan avoid having to pay out-of-pocket money for certain expenses.

flexible benefit plan An employer-sponsored plan that gives the employee a choice of selecting either cash or one or more qualifying nontaxable benefits; also known as a cafeteria plan.

Making Decisions About Employer-Sponsored Health Care Plans

Many employers offer: employees a choice of **health care plans.** Employees usually can make a decision to change health plans once a year as well as when one's family situation changes, such as marriage. The premium for an unmarried employee could be $5000 or more annually depending upon the amount of coverage provided. Fortunately, the premiums for employees are either paid for entirely or subsidized by the employer. Some employers pay perhaps the first $3000 of annual premiums for employee health care coverage and require that employees pay the remainder.

health care plan An employee benefit designed to pay all or part of the employee's medical expenses.

Partly because of soaring costs of health care coverage, employers often offer multiple policies. These can range from an expensive plan, perhaps with a $6600 premium, that offers comprehensive coverage requiring little out-of-pocket spending by the employee to an inexpensive **high-deductible health care plan,** perhaps with a $3100 premium, requiring larger out-of-pocket health care spending by the employee. The **deductible** is the amount paid to cover expenses before benefits begin. Employees, especially healthy ones, hope to save money on premiums by choosing these policies.

high-deductible health care plan A plan that requires individuals pay a higher deductible to cover medical expenses before insurance plan payments begin; chosen to save money on premiums.

Younger employers, particularly those who are typically healthy, often select high-deductible plans to save on the cost of premiums. For example, if an employer pays only the first $3000 in health care premiums for employees, an employee selecting the high-cost plan described previously has to pay $3600 ($6600 − $3000) annually, or $300 a month in premiums. This contrasts with a $100 annual premium for employees who select the high-deductible plan ($3100 − $3000). If the person experiences lots of health care expenses, he/she will have to pay additional costs.

Some employers also offer **health savings accounts (HSAs).** This special savings account is intended for people who have a high-deductible health care plan (with annual deductibles of at least $1000 for individuals and $2000 for families). Employees make tax-deductible contributions to a savings account to be used for eligible expenses. Employers may also contribute. The employee invests HSA funds and the money in the account grows tax free. Withdrawals are made to pay for medical expenses. The limits on contributions to an HSA savings account are $2900 per year for individuals and $5800 for families. The money in the account does not vanish if you don't spend it within a certain time period.

health savings accounts (HSAs) Special savings account intended for people who have a high-deductible health care plan (with annual deductibles of at least $1000 for individuals and $2000 for families).

The tax-advantaged aspect of making a health care plan choice adds another dimension to making the best personal financial decision. Because many workers have an effective marginal tax rate (discussed earlier in the chapter) of nearly 40 percent, that same percentage can be *saved* or not spent by giving it to the government in taxes. The worker who contributes $3000, for example, to a health savings account saves approximately $1200 ($3000 × 0.40), further reducing his or her health care expenses.

Instant Message

Don't Pay Extra Taxes

Contributing $1000 to a tax-advantaged employee benefit plan saves a worker as much as $400 that does not have to be paid to the government in taxes.

Making Decisions About Employer's Flexible Spending Accounts

A **flexible spending account (FSA)** is an employer-sponsored account that allows employee-paid expenses for medical or dependent care to be paid with an employee's pretax dollars rather than after-tax income. Under a typical FSA, the employee agrees to have a certain amount deducted from each paycheck, and that amount is then deposited in a separate account called a flexible spending account. As eligible expenses are incurred, the employee requests and receives reimbursements from the account.

flexible spending account (FSA) An employer-sponsored account that allows employee-paid expenses for medical or dependent care to be paid with an employee's pretax dollars rather than after-tax income.

Funds in a **dependent care FSA account** may be used to pay for the care of a dependent younger than age 13 or the care of another dependent who is physically or mentally incapable of caring for himself or herself and who resides in the taxpayer's home. Funds in a **health care FSA account** may be used to pay for qualified, unreimbursed out-of-pocket expenses for health care.

The tax advantage of an FSA occurs because the amounts deducted from the employee's salary avoid federal income tax, Social Security taxes, and, in most states, state income taxes, thereby allowing selected personal expenses to be paid with pretax (rather than after-tax) income. Paying the expenses with **pretax dollars** (money income that has not been taxed by the government) lowers taxable income, decreases take-home pay, and increases effective take-home pay because of the reimbursements. The maximum annual contribution limits are usually $5000 for dependent care FSA and $2000 to $3000 for medical care FSA.

pretax dollars Money income that has not been taxed by the government.

Younger workers who anticipate few medical costs usually do not sign up for a medical FSA, although FSAs do pay for eyeglasses, contacts, copayments, and some over-the-counter medications. Workers with children or others to take care of financially, such as elderly or disabled parents, often sign up for dependent care FSA. Only 20 percent of eligible employees participate in flexible spending accounts even though doing so saves money.

Before enrolling in an FSA, you need to estimate your expenses carefully so that the amount in the FSA does not exceed anticipated expenses. According to Internal Revenue Service (IRS) regulations, unused amounts are forfeited and are not returned to the employee—a condition called the "use it or lose it" rule. However, employers may offer a 2½-month grace period during which time you can continue to spend the previous year's FSA money. Many employers offer debit cards that withdraw money directly from an employee's FSA.

Did You Know?...

Examples of Good Financial Behaviors

Good financial behaviors to follow include these:

1. Develop a plan for financial future.
2. Start or increase savings.
3. Follow a budget or spending plan.
4. Reduce personal debts.
5. Pay credit card bills in full each month.
6. Control or reduce living expenses.
7. Comparison shop for purchases.
8. Use a credit/budget counselor if debt becomes unmanageable.
9. Use a financial planner when faced with complicated financial issues.
10. Set aside an emergency fund sufficient to live on for three months.
11. Contribute to a flexible spending account at work.
12. Calculate how much money you will need for retirement.
13. Sign up to participate in your employer's retirement plan.
14. Save and invest amounts sufficient to fund a financially successful retirement.

Making Decisions About Participating in Employer Life, Disability, and Long-Term Care Insurance Plans

Life, disability, and long-term care insurance coverage is often available through employers. While the premiums charged for the group of employees for life insurance are not as low as those available in the general marketplace, some employers pay for part or all of employees' premiums. Coverage is typically one or two times the employee's salary. So sign up for free or subsidized life insurance at work. The premiums for disability and long-term care insurance are often less expensive when purchased through one's employer. See Chapters 10, 11, and 12 to begin to purchase any needed insurance coverage.

Making Decisions About Participating in Your Employer's Retirement Plan

More than half of all workers are covered by an employer-sponsored, defined-contribution **retirement plan,** also called a **tax-sheltered retirement plan.** These include 401(k) plans and similar 403(b) and 457 plans. Employer-sponsored retirement plans provide four distinct advantages.

tax-sheltered retirement plan Employer-sponsored, defined-contribution retirement plans including 401(k) plans and similar 403(b) and 457 plans.

First Advantage: Tax-Deductible Contributions Tax-sheltered retirement plans provide tremendous tax benefits compared with ordinary savings and investment plans. Because pretax contributions to qualified plans reduce income, the current year's tax liability is lowered. The money saved in taxes can then be used to partially fund a larger contribution, which creates even greater returns. The 401(k) plan lets the IRS help employees finance their retirement plans because of the income taxes saved.

As Table 1.2 illustrates, you can save substantial sums for retirement with minimal effects on your monthly take-home pay. For example, a single person with a monthly taxable income of $4000 in the 25 percent marginal tax bracket who forgoes consumption and instead places $500 into a tax-sheltered retirement plan every month reduces monthly take-home pay from $3175 to $2800, or $375—that is certainly not an enormous amount. The net effect is that it costs that person only $375 to put away that $500 per month into a retirement plan. The

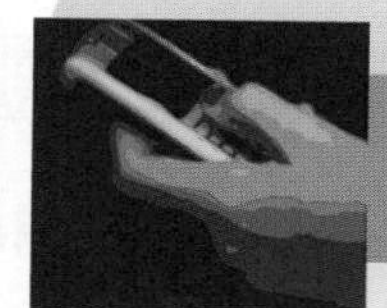

Instant Message

Living More Years Than Working

You will likely work full time for 45 years, from ages 22 to 67, so saving for retirement during those years is critical since you are likely to live 20 more years during retirement.

Table 1.2 It Costs Only $375 a Month to Save $6000 a Year for Retirement

Monthly salary	$4000	Monthly salary	$4000
Pretax retirement plan contribution	0	Pretax retirement plan contribution	500
Taxable income	4000	Taxable income	3500
Federal taxes*	825	Federal taxes*	700
Monthly take-home pay	3175	Monthly take-home pay	2800
You put away for retirement	0	Cost to put away $500 per month ($3175 – $2800)	375
		You put away for retirement	6000

*From Chapter 4; 25 percent income tax rate, single.

immediate "return on investment" equals a fantastic 25 percent ($125 ÷ $500). In essence, the taxpayer puts $375 into his or her retirement plan and the government contributes $125. (Without the plan, the taxpayer would pay the $125 directly to the government.) A taxpayer paying a higher marginal tax rate realizes even greater gains. Because a substantial part of your contributions to a tax-sheltered retirement plan comes from money that you would have paid in income taxes, it costs you less to save more.

Second Advantage: Employer's Matching Contributions To encourage saving for retirement, many employers "match" all or part of their employees' contributions, perhaps up to 6 percent of salary. An employee who saves $375 might receive an additional $375 a month from his/her employer. That's a 100 percent return on the employee's $375!

Third Advantage: Tax-Deferred Growth Because interest, dividends, and capital gains from qualified plans are taxed only after funds are withdrawn from the plan, investments in tax-sheltered retirement plans grow tax free. The benefits of tax deferral can be substantial.

For example, if a person in the 25 percent tax bracket invests $2000 at the beginning of every year for 30 years and the investment earns an 8 percent taxable return compounded annually, the fund will grow to $167,603 at the end of the 30-year period. If the same $2000 invested annually was instead compounded at 8 percent within a tax-sheltered program, it would grow to $244,691! The higher amount results from compounding at the full 8 percent and not paying any income taxes. (Figure 1.3 on page 13 illustrates these differences in returns.) Indeed, when the funds are finally taxed upon their withdrawal some years later, the taxpayer may be in a lower marginal tax bracket.

Instant Message

Income Does Not Create Wealth

People do not get wealthy by earning an income. Real wealth comes from increases in the value of assets over time, such as their home or the growth of their investments within a 401(k) retirement program.

Fourth Advantage: Starting Early Really Pays Off Big Recall the rule of 72, which can be used to calculate the number of years it would take for a lump-sum investment to double. A 9 percent rate of return doubles an investment every eight years. Waiting eight years to begin saving results in the loss of one doubling. Unfortunately, it is the *last* doubling that is lost, as illustrated in Table 1.3. In that example, $48,000 ($96,000 – $48,000) is lost due to a hesitancy to invest $3000. This is a tremendous opportunity cost for waiting eight years to start.

The gains are awesome when the one starts early and makes regular, continuing investments instead of delaying. For example, a worker who starts saving $25 per week in a qualified retirement plan at age 23 will have about $616,390 by age 65, assuming

Careful planning can result in a much more comfortable lifestyle when you retire.

Table 1.3 Starting to Save Early Versus Starting Late

Starting Earlier		Starting Later	
Age	**$ Value**	**Age**	**$ Value**
23	$ 3,000	23	$ 0
31	6,000	31	3,000
39	12,000	39	6,000
47	24,000	47	12,000
55	48,000	55	24,000
63	$96,000	63	$48,000

Starting to save $3000 eight years earlier (age 23 instead of 31) earns the investor an extra $48,000 ($96,000 – $48,000) assuming a compound growth rate of 9 percent.

an annual rate of return of 9 percent. Waiting until age 33 to start saving, instead of beginning at age 23, results in a retirement fund of *only* about $242,230. The benefit of starting to invest early is about $374,000 ($616,390 – $242,230). And the total extra dollars invested over the ten years was a mere $13,000. Putting in $13,000 early results in an extra $374,000. This effect occurs because most of the power of compounding appears in the last years of growth.

CONCEPT CHECK 1.5

1. Summarize the benefits of participating in a high-deductible health care plan at work.
2. Show a math example of why many employees participate in a tax-sheltered employee benefit plan, such as an HSA or 401(k) plan.
3. List two ways you can maximize the benefits from a tax-sheltered retirement program.

Did You Know?...

Examples of Poor Financial Behaviors

Poor financial behaviors to avoid include the following:

1. Purchasing something expensive that was wanted but not needed
2. Reaching the maximum limit on credit card
3. Spending more money than available
4. Making credit purchase after running out of money
5. Obtaining cash advance on a credit card after running out of money
6. Using cash advance on a credit card to pay another
7. Receiving an overdue notice from a creditor
8. Paying credit card bill late
9. Paying service charge for paying a utility bill late
10. Making vehicle loan/lease payment late
11. Paying rent/mortgage late
12. Borrowing money from a coworker
13. Obtaining cash advance from employer
14. Borrowing from 401(k) retirement plan at work
15. Taking old employer's 401(k) money in cash when changing jobs
16. Writing a check with insufficient funds ("bounce" a check)

Where to Seek Expert Financial Advice

6 LEARNING OBJECTIVE
Identify the professional qualifications of providers of financial advice.

At various points in their lives, many people rely on the advice of a professional to make financial plans and decisions. Often this consultation is focused on a narrow area of their finances. Professional financial advisers, such as a family lawyer, tax preparer, insurance agent, credit counselor, or stockbroker, can be helpful. Too often these people are not impartial because they are salespeople for specific financial services. They typically want to sell you something rather than have your best interests at heart. People often find it helpful to obtain the services of more broadly qualified financial experts.

financial planner An investment professional who evaluates the personal finances of an individual or family and recommends strategies to set and achieve long-term financial goals.

A **financial planner** is an investment professional who evaluates the personal finances of an individual or family and recommends strategies to set and achieve long-term financial goals. A good financial planner should be able to analyze a family's total needs in such areas as investments, taxes, insurance, education goals, and retirement and pull all of the information together into a cohesive plan. The planner may help a client select and prioritize goals and then rearrange assets and liabilities to fit the client's lifestyle, stage in the life cycle, and financial goals. When appropriate, planners should make referrals to outside advisers, such as attorneys, accountants, trust officers, real estate brokers, stockbrokers, and insurance agents. Effective financial advice helps you make better day-to-day financial decisions so you have more to spend, save, invest, and donate.

You can check the background of the planner you are considering. Self-regulatory organizations and government agencies are available to help.

- The Certified Financial Planner Board of Standards [(888) 237-6275; www.cfp.net] assists those searching for a CFP as well as accepts complaints.
- The National Association of Insurance Commissioners [(816) 842-3600; www.naic.org] directs inquiries to the appropriate state agency where you can check on planners who also sell insurance products.
- Financial Industry Regulatory Authority (FINRA) [(800) 289-9999; www.finra.org] oversees securities brokers.

Advice from a Pro...

Choosing a Financial Planner

When interviewing financial planners, ask them these questions:

1. Am I permitted a no-cost, initial consultation, and how much time is allowed?
2. What education, formal training, and credentials do you have to practice financial planning, is this your primary activity, and how long have you been in financial planning?
3. Are you licensed as an investment or life insurance broker?
4. How long have you resided in the community, and who can vouch for your professional reputation?
5. Will you provide references that I can contact from three or more clients you have counseled for at least two years?
6. Will you or an associate be involved in evaluating and updating the plan you suggest, and how often are formal reviews held with the client?
7. What process do you follow to identify a client's financial goals?
8. How do you evaluate investment performance, and how often?
9. May I see representative examples of financial plans, monitoring reports, and portfolios or actual case studies of your clients?
10. How are you personally compensated, and if you earn commissions, how are they earned and from whom?
11. May I have a copy of the contract you use with clients?
12. To whom do I take a complaint, if I had one?

Joan Koonce
University of Georgia

- The Securities and Exchange Commission [(800) 732-0330; www.sec.gov] regulates investment advisers and all securities dealers.

How Financial Planners Are Compensated

Financial planners earn their income in one of four ways:

1. **Commission-only financial planners/brokers** live solely on the commissions they receive on the financial products (such as investments or insurance) they sell to their clients. In this case, the plan will be "free," but a commission will be paid to the adviser by the source of the financial product, such as an insurance company or mutual fund. Advantage: Save money if you make only a few transactions.
2. **Fee-based financial planner/brokers** charge an up-front fee for providing services and charge a commission on any securities trades or insurance purchases that they conduct on your behalf. Advantage: Unlimited consultations with broker.
3. **Fee-offset financial planners/brokers** charge an annual or hourly fee. That fee will be reduced by any commissions earned off the purchase of financial products sold to the client. Advantage: Fee will be reduced as you trade investments.
4. **Fee-only financial planners** earn no commissions and work solely on a fee-for-service basis—that is, they charge a specified fee (typically \$50 to \$200 per hour or 1 percent of the client's assets annually) for the services provided. They usually need five or more one-hour appointments to analyze a client's financial situation and to present a thorough plan. Fee-only planners do not sell financial products, such as

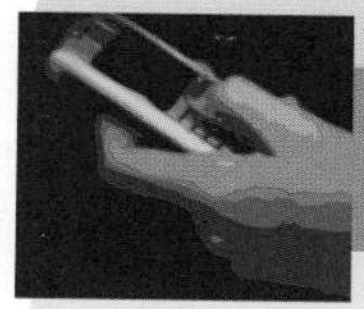

Instant Message

Paying for Financial Advice

One way or another, you will pay to get financial advice—commissions, fees, both, your mistakes—so assess the total costs up front as well as the opportunity costs.

Table 1.4 Financial Planner Professional Certifications

Many financial planners have voluntarily undergone training and satisfied various qualifications for particular professional certifications, as shown in Table 1.4. Certification examinations often require three years of work experience prior to sitting for the examination.

Certification	Description	Contact Information
Certified Financial Planner (CFP®)	Comprehensive financial planning; best-known certification	(800) 322-4237 www.cfp.net
Chartered Financial Consultant (ChFC)	Comprehensive financial planning in insurance industry	(888) 263-7265 www.theamericancollege.edu
Chartered Life Underwriter (CLU)	Life inurance	(888) 263-7265 www.theamericancollege.edu
Certified Public Accountant (CPA)	Income tax and estate planning	(888) 777-7077 www.aicpa.org
Personal Financial Specialist (PFS)	Personal finance credential for CPAs	(888) 777-7077 www.aicpa.org
Certified Trust and Financial Advisor (CTFA)	Trust, taxes, and personal finance credential for bankers	(202) 663-5092 http://www.aba.com
Accredited Financial Counselor (AFC)	Financial counseling and money management	(614) 485-9650 www.afcpe.org
Mutual Fund Chartered Counselor (MFCC)	Mutual funds	(800) 237-9990 www.cffp.edu
Registered Investment Adviser (RIA)	Investment adviser	(202) 551-6999 www.sec.gov

stocks or insurance. As a result and unlike other financial planners/brokers, they are not inclined to recommend products that earn them the highest commission. Finding a true fee-only financial planner is challenging. Advantage: Receive unbiased advice.

Remember, it's your money and your financial future. So when you use the services of a financial planner, don't be intimidated. Ask the hardest questions and don't leave the planner's office until you understand the answers.

CONCEPT CHECK 1.6

1. What are the four ways financial planners may be compensated?
2. Describe two professional certification programs for financial planners.

What Do You Recommend Now?

Now that you have read the chapter on the importance of personal finance, what do you recommend to Lauren in the case at the beginning of the chapter regarding:

1. Participating in her employer's 401(k) retirement plan?
2. Understanding the effects of income taxes on her decision to participate in her employer's 401(k) plan?

3. Factoring the current state of the economy into her personal financial planning?
4. Using time value of money considerations to project what her IRA might be worth at age 63?
5. Using time value of money considerations to project what her 401(k) plan might be worth at age 63 if she were to participate fully?

Big Picture Summary of Learning Objectives

1 Use the building blocks to achieving financial success.

Financial success and happiness comes from using the building blocks of personal finance, such as having a foundation of regular income to provide basic lifestyle and savings, and establishing a financial base using employee benefits and checking and savings accounts. Other building blocks include setting financial goals, controlling expenditures, managing income taxes, handling credit cards, and investing in mutual funds and retirement plans.

2 Understand how the economy affects your personal financial success.

Using your knowledge of where we are in the business cycle and tracking a few economic statistics will guide you to make modest adjustment in your long-term financial strategy.

3 Apply economic principles when making financial decisions.

Understanding and applying the basic economic principles of opportunity cost, marginal utility and cost, and marginal income tax rate will affect your financial success. The opportunity cost of a decision is the value of the next best alternative that must be forgone. Marginal cost is the additional (marginal) cost of one more incremental unit of some item. When known, this cost can be compared with the marginal utility received. One's marginal tax rate is the tax rate at which your last dollar is taxed.

4 Perform time value of money calculations in personal financial decision making.

Dollars to be received or paid out in the future are not equivalent to those received or paid out today. A dollar received today is worth more than a dollar received a year from now because today's dollar can be saved or invested; by next year, you expect it to be worth more than a dollar. The time value of money involves two components: future value and present value. The four basic time value of money calculations involve finding the future value of a lump sum, the future value of an annuity, the present value of a lump sum, and the present value of an annuity.

5 Make smart decisions about your employee benefits.

Smart decisions can increase your actual income by thousands of dollars each year. You need to wisely select among your employer-sponsored plans for health care, out-of-pocket spending for health and dependent care, life insurance, disability, and retirement. These decisions often require you to calculate the tax-sheltered aspects of the employee benefits.

6 Identify the professional qualifications of providers of financial advice.

When choosing a financial planner, know that many professional designations are meaningful in this field, such as CFP® and ChFC. Costs may be charged on a fee-only, commission-only, fee-based, or fee-offset basis.

Let's Talk About It

1. Where is the United States in the economic cycle now, and where does it seem to be heading? List some indicators that suggest in which direction it may move.
2. What are some common mistakes that people make in personal finance? Which three are the worst, and why?
3. People regularly make decisions in personal finance that have opportunity costs. List five financial decisions you have made recently and identify the opportunity cost for each.

Do the Numbers

1. As a graduating senior, Gwen Kumora of Manhattan, Kansas, is eager to enter the job market at an anticipated annual salary of $34,000. Assuming an average inflation rate of 5 percent and an equal cost-of-living raise, what will Gwen's salary be in 10 years? In 20 years? (Hint: Use Appendix Table A.1 or calculations on the *Garman/Forgue* website.) To make real economic progress, how much of a raise (in dollars) does Gwen need to receive next year?

2. Rachael Berry, a freshman horticulture major at the University of Minnesota, has some financial questions for the next three years of school and beyond. Answers to these questions can be obtained by using Appendix Table A or the *Garman/Forgue* website.
   (a) If Rachael's tuition, fees, and expenditures for books this year total $12,000, what will they be during her senior year (three years from now), assuming costs rise 6 percent annually? (Hint: Use Appendix Table A.1 or the *Garman/Forgue* website.)
   (b) Rachael is applying for a scholarship currently valued at $5000. If she is awarded it at the end of next year, how much is the scholarship worth in today's dollars, assuming inflation of 5 percent? (Hint: Use Appendix Table A.2 or the *Garman/Forgue* website.)
   (c) Rachael is already looking ahead to graduation and a job, and she wants to buy a new car not long after her graduation. If after graduation she begins a savings program of $2400 per year in an investment yielding 6 percent, what will be the value of the fund after three years? (Hint: Use Appendix Table A.3 or the *Garman/Forgue* website.)
   (d) Rachael's Aunt Karroll told her that she would give Kathryn $1000 at the end of each year for the next three years to help with her college expenses. Assuming an annual interest rate of 6 percent, what is the present value of that stream of payments? (Hint: Use Appendix Table A.4 or the *Garman/Forgue* website.)
3. Using the present and future value tables in Appendix A, the appropriate calculations on the *Garman/Forgue* website, or a financial calculator, calculate the following:
   (a) The future value of $400 in two years that earns 5 percent.
   (b) The future value of $1200 saved each year for ten years that earns 7 percent.
   (c) The amount a person would need to deposit today with a 5 percent interest rate to have $2000 in three years.
   (d) The amount a person would need to deposit today to be able to withdraw $6000 each year for ten years from an account earning 6 percent.
   (e) A person is offered a gift of $5000 now or $8000 five years from now. If such funds could be expected to earn 8 percent over the next five years, which is the better choice?
   (f) A person wants to have $3000 available to spend on an overseas trip four years from now. If such funds could be expected to earn 7 percent, how much should be invested in a lump sum to realize the $3000 when needed?
   (g) A person who invests $1200 each year finds one choice that is expected to pay 9 percent per year and another choice that may pay 10 percent. What is the difference in return if the investment is made for 15 years?
   (h) A person invests $50,000 in an investment that earns 6 percent. If $6000 is withdrawn each year, how many years will it take for the fund to run out?
4. You win a contest. The prize is cash, and you are offered several alternative payment plans. Which plan should you choose? Assume you can earn 5 percent on your money and ignore inflation.
   (a) $30,000 today
   (b) $40,000 in five years
   (c) $10,000 one year from today and $25,000 two years later
   (d) $4000 per year starting today for the next ten years
5. Using the rule of 72, calculate how quickly $1000 will double to $2000 at interest rates of 2 percent, 4 percent, 6 percent, 8 percent, and 10 percent.

Financial Planning Cases

Case 1
Reasons to Study Personal Finance

Lindsey Beliveau Bailey of Redding, California, is a senior in college, majoring in sociology. She anticipates getting married a year or so after graduation. Lindsey has only one elective course remaining and is going to choose between another advanced class in sociology and one in personal finance. As Lindsey's friend, you want to persuade her to take personal finance. Give some examples of how Lindsey might benefit from the study of personal finance.

Case 2
A Closer Look at Lifetime Financial Objectives

You have been asked to give a brief speech on how to achieve financial success. Define financial success and financial happiness, and summarize the building blocks to achieving financial success.

On the 'Net

Go to the Web pages indicated to complete these exercises. You can also go to the *Garman/Forgue* website at college .hmco.com/business/students for an expanded list of exercises. Under General Business, select the title of this text. Click on the Internet Exercises link for this chapter.

1. Visit the Bureau of Labor Statistics Consumer Price Index homepage at http://www.bls.gov/cpi/ and link to information for various areas of the country and metropolitan areas of various sizes. Describe how prices have been changing for your area and city size during the past year.
2. Visit the Conference Board website, http://www .conference-board.org/economics/consumer Confidence.cfm/, for the latest information on the consumer confidence index and the index of leading economic indicators. What do the indexes say about the direction of the economy over the next six months to one year?
3. Visit the website of the Financial Planning Association at http://www.fpanet.org/member/about/principles/ ethics.cfm. Read through the code of ethics for members of the organization. What does the code tell you about the members?

Visit the Garman/Forgue website ...

@college.hmco.com/business/students

Under General Business, select *Personal Finance 9e*. There, among other valuable resources, you will find a complete glossary, ACE questions, links to help you complete the chapter exercises, and links to other personal finance sites.

CHAPTER 2

Career Planning

You Must Be Kidding, Right?

Jessica Springsteen is contemplating going to graduate school at night for a master's degree so she can advance her career and earn more than her current $44,000 salary income. She is a sales account manager for a health care organization, and she has a small online business selling gourmet foods. How much more income can Jessica expect over an anticipated 40-year career if she obtains the advanced degree?

A. $100,000

B. $300,000

C. $600,000

D. $900,000

The answer is C, $600,000. Over a 40-year working career, a person with a postgraduate degree can expect to earn more than $3 million, and this is about $600,000 more than a person with a bachelor's degree will earn. Getting an advanced degree is no guarantee of a bigger income, but the likelihood of such a reality is high!

LEARNING OBJECTIVES

After reading this chapter, you should be able to:

1 **Identify** the key steps in successful career planning.

2 **Clarify** your work-style personality.

3 **Analyze** the financial and legal aspects of employment.

4 **Practice** effective employment search strategies.

What Do You Recommend?

Arthur Linkletter, age 21, expects to graduate next spring with a bachelor's degree in business administration. Arthur's grades are mostly Cs and Bs, and he has worked part time throughout his college career. Arthur is vice president of the Student Marketing Association on his campus. He would like to work in management or marketing for a medium- to large-size employer. Because he loves the outdoors, Arthur thinks he would prefer a job in the Northwest, perhaps in northern California, Oregon, or Washington.

What would you recommend to Arthur on the importance of career planning regarding:

1. Clarifying his values and lifestyle trade-offs?
2. Enhancing his career-related experiences before graduation?
3. Creating career plans and goals?
4. Understanding his work-style personality?
5. Identifying job opportunities?

FOR HELP with studying this chapter, visit the Online Student Center:

www.college.hmco.com/pic/garman9e

Career planning in the twenty-first century is an absolute necessity. Going from job to job may be okay for American teenagers and college students. And working for $12, $15, or $20 an hour and changing jobs for a $2-per-hour raise might be okay for a couple of years. But for many working adults, that's not an agreeable job advancement pattern. A **career** is the lifework chosen by a person to use personal talent, education, and training, and the general progression of one's career may include a number of related jobs.

career The lifework chosen by a person to use personal talent, education, and training.

You *can* control much of your financial future with effective career planning. Moving through the years in a career of your choice not only translates into jobs that are personally satisfying but also improves your level of living. A career translates into a base of income, employee benefits, additional educational experiences, advancement opportunities, and confidence in a secure financial future. Treat your career as a high priority, do-it-yourself project, and take control of where you are going and how you are going to get there.

Key Steps in Successful Career Planning

1 **LEARNING OBJECTIVE**
Identify the key steps in successful career planning.

Career planning can help you identify an employment pathway that aligns your interests and abilities with the tasks expected and one that supports your preferred lifestyle. You might take a job primarily to earn income. When you start looking for employment positions in your career path, you consider income, of course, but you also keep in mind opportunities for continued training, personal growth, and advancement. A career that suits you will give you opportunities to display your abilities in jobs you find satisfying while providing balance between work and your personal life.

Career planning and financial planning go hand in hand. You can't advance very far in planning your financial life without also planning a career that will pay you adequately. We include a chapter on career planning quite early in this book so that the principles and other information in the remaining chapters are relevant to you personally and to the way you want to make your living.

career planning Finding employment that will use your interests and abilities and that will support you financially.

Career planning doesn't stop when you take your first career job. Rather, career planning is a vibrant process that lasts throughout your life. Every time your life circumstances change, you will likely reconsider your career. But first you have to start. As you plan your career, you need to perform several steps, and you should take care to carry each step out to the best of your ability. Why? Because your actions and the impression you make upon prospective employers will affect the probability of getting a good job in your field that satisfies your interests and provides an income to meet your financial needs. The time and effort you put into your career planning effort will affect how much income you earn and how far you advance in your career. First, let's take a look at the key steps to successful career planning.

Figure 2.1
Steps in Career Planning

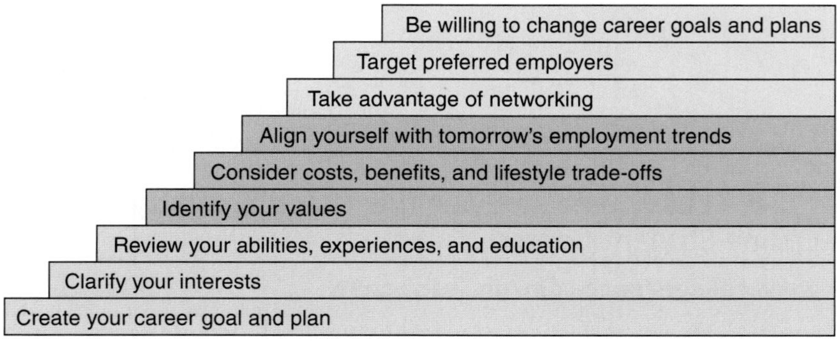

Create Your Career Goal and Plan

The workplace has changed dramatically. People used to take a single job and remain at the same company until they retired. Now, people change jobs five to ten times during their working years. You are not likely to remain with one employer a lifetime let alone ten years. You probably will completely change careers two or three times.

Thinking about a career goal helps you focus on what you want to do for a living. A **career goal** can be a specific job (e.g., cost accountant, teacher, human resources manager) or a particular field of work (e.g., health care, communications, construction). It helps guide you to do the kind of work you want in life rather than drift from job to job. Formulating a career goal requires thinking about your interests, skills, and experiences and learning about different careers and employment trends. The process of establishing a career goal motivates you to consider career possibilities that you may not have thought of otherwise.

To create a career goal, explore the jobs, careers, and trends in the employment marketplace that fit your interests and skills. Ask people about careers. Search websites such as those for the *Occupational Outlook Handbook* (www.bls.gov/oco/) and the *Occupational Outlook Quarterly* (www.bls.gov/opub/ooq/ooqhome.htm). Research the education requirements.

A *career plan* identifies employment that interests you; fits your abilities, skills, work style, and lifestyle; and provides strategic guidance to help you reach your career goal. It includes short-, medium-, longer-, and long-term goals as well as future education and work-related experiences that will serve to advance your career interests. Figure 2.2 provides an illustrative career plan.

Good Money Habits in Understanding Career Planning

Make the following your money habits in career planning:

1. Take the time to plan and make the effort required to obtain employment in your career.
2. Identify your career planning values and live them in your selection of jobs and in your performance at work.
3. Do not miss an opportunity to continually enhance your education and professional training.
4. Understand your preferred work-style personality.
5. Practice effective employment search strategies, especially interviewing skills.

career goal Identifying what you want to do for a living, whether a specific job or field of employment

Figure 2.2

Career Goals and Plans for Harry Johnson

Harry Johnson began his working career following graduation from college by obtaining employment with a small commercial interior design firm. He has an undergraduate degree from a university accredited by the American Society of Interior Designers. He is happy that his first professional job is in his major field of interest.

Initial career goal: To become an interior designer. To design, plan, and supervise commercial/contract design projects.

Long-term career goal (20-plus years): Own or become a partner in a medium- to large-size commercial/contract interior design firm.

Short-term plans and goals in career establishment stage (3 to 6 years): Gain work experience in current job; receive employer compliments on quality of work; obtain continuing education credits for professional growth and development; secure higher-level design responsibilities, such as lead professional design team; volunteer for committee responsibilities in local and state professional associations; obtain substantial increases in income; receive promotions; learn operational aspects and marketing of the company.

Medium-term plans and goals in professional growth stage (7 to 12 years): Be promoted to the level of senior designer; consider going to work for another employer as a senior designer and, if necessary, move to another community; volunteer for higher-level service in professional associations; obtain a master of fine arts degree in interior design; become assistant to the firm's general manager.

Longer-term plans and goals in advancement stage (13 to 20 years): Become general manager of commercial design firm; seek out potential partners and sufficient financing to either buy out or start up a medium-size design firm.

Did You Know?...

The Top 3 Financial Missteps in Career Planning

People slip up in career planning when they do the following:

1. Don't learn as much as possible about a company before going for an interview
2. Change jobs and cash out all the money in their employer-sponsored retirement savings plan instead of leaving it there, transferring it to their new employer's 401(k) plan, or moving it to a rollover IRA account
3. Fail to use the COBRA law (Consolidated Omnibus Budget Reconciliation Act) to elect to continue participating in their old employer's medical health plan benefits for up to 18 months

Clarify Your Interests

Your **interests** are topics and activities about which you have feelings of curiosity or concern. Interests engage or arouse your attention. They reflect what you like to do. Interests, including occupational interests, are likely to vary over time.

You might consider making a list of your top ten interests. On that list will probably be some things you enjoy but have not done recently. Because of conflicting interests and alternative claims on your time, you cannot pursue all your interests. It is important in career planning to evaluate your interests; if you plan your career with your interests in mind, you will increase the likelihood of career satisfaction.

Interest inventories are measures that assist people in assessing and profiling the interests and activities that give them satisfaction. They compare how your interests are similar or dissimilar to the interests of people successfully employed in various occupations; the theory behind these interest inventories is that individuals with similar interests are often attracted to the same kind of work. These inventories can help you identify possible career goals that match your strongest personal interests.

The Strong Interest Inventory assessment is considered by many to be the gold standard of career exploration tools. The opportunity to take one or more interest inventory assessments, usually for free or at a nominal cost, is available at most colleges and state-supported career counseling facilities. These assessments can also be completed online for a fee. (See, for example, www.discoveryourpersonality.com/Strong.html and www.careercc.com/career_assessment.shtml.)

interests Long-standing topics and activities that engage your attention.

interest inventories Scaled surveys that assess career interests and activities.

Review Your Abilities, Experiences, and Education

Reviewing your abilities, aptitudes, experiences, and education is a key step in career planning. The purpose is to see how well they match up with your career-related interests.

professional abilities Job-related activities that you can perform physically, mentally, artistically, mechanically, and financially.

Abilities Your professional **abilities** are the qualities that allow you to perform physically, mentally, artistically, mechanically, or financially job-related tasks. Most of us think of *ability* as a word describing how well we do something, a proficiency, dexterity, or technique, particularly one requiring use of the mind, hands, or body. Other examples of abilities include being skilled in working with people, being able to easily meet the public, and being good at persuading people. Employer surveys indicate that the single most important ability needed for career success in the twenty-first century is computer skills. Also very highly ranked are communication skills and honesty/integrity. Consider making a list of your top ten abilities.

aptitudes The natural abilities and talents that individuals possess.

Aptitudes are the natural abilities and talents that people possess. Aptitudes suggest that you have a tendency or inclination to learn and develop certain skills or abilities. Are you good with numbers? Do you find public speaking easy to do? Do you enjoy solving problems? What are your natural talents? Consider making a list of your top ten aptitudes.

Experiences College graduates have much more going for them than a degree and a string of part-time job experiences. Reviewing your experiences is a step in career planning. Evaluate what you have been doing in your life, including jobs and internships; participation in student organizations and community and church groups; leadership on school projects; and volunteer activities.

Those still in college can enhance their résumés by learning as much as possible in school, participating in clubs and other student organizations (including volunteering for committees and campus projects), getting involved in a faculty research project, and attending off-campus professional meetings in their major. Academic advisers can provide suggestions. Employers want workers with good writing and public speaking talents, strong computer skills, fluency in a second language, and an understanding of global commerce and industry. Experiences that use and develop these traits are a big plus for job seekers.

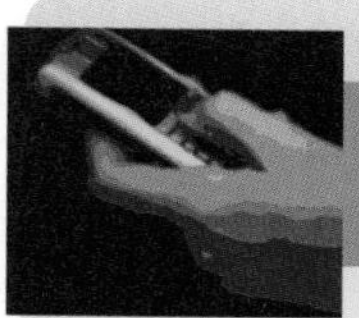

Instant Message

Education and Earnings

Adults with a bachelor's degree earn an average of $55,000 compared with $33,000 for high school graduates and $81,000 for those with advanced degrees, reports the U.S. Census Bureau.

Education and Professional Training Going to college is excellent preparation for your career and your life. But college may not have provided you with all the skills and abilities to be successfully employed. A review of your abilities, experiences, and education may suggest you need to seek additional education and professional training.

Identify Your Values

Thinking about and discovering what you want out of life gives you guidance for what to do to lead a satisfying life. Understanding yourself enables you to select a career path that best suits you. This is a key step in career planning.

Values are the principles, standards, or qualities considered worthwhile or desirable. Values provide a basis for decisions about how to live, serving as guides we can use to direct our actions. For something to be a value, it must be prized, publicly affirmed, chosen from alternatives, and acted upon repeatedly and consistently. Values are not right or wrong, or true or false; they are personal preferences.

values The principles, standards, or qualities that you consider desirable.

People may place value on family, friends, helping others, religious commitment, security, honesty, pleasure, good health, material possessions, financial achievement, and a satisfying career. Examples of conflicting values are family versus friends, stability versus adventure, religious beliefs versus actions, and work versus leisure. When you make important decisions, you might be wise to think carefully to clarify your values before taking action. Consider making a list of your ten most important values.

Consider Costs, Benefits, and Lifestyle Trade-offs

Selecting a career involves making decisions about costs and benefits and **lifestyle trade-offs.**

lifestyle trade-offs Weighing the demands of particular jobs with your social and cultural preferences.

Costs and Benefits When making career choices, you must weigh the benefits against the costs. The benefits could include a big salary, likelihood of personal growth and job advancements, and high job satisfaction. For some, the pluses might include the psychic benefit of a prestigious job with a high income. The costs might include living in a less desirable geographic area and climate, being too far from friends and family, sitting at a desk all day, working long hours, and doing too much travel.

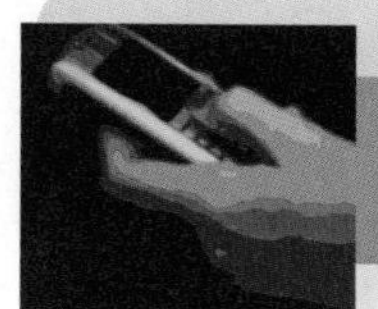

Instant Message

Take a Temporary Job When Looking for Permanent Employment

Accepting a temporary job eases the pressure of taking the first decent real job opportunity offered. It also gives you a chance to network, develop new skills, and perhaps convert the temporary job into a full-time position. The downside is that you have to conduct your full-time job search activities after working hours.

Lifestyle Trade-offs When considering any career, think about what lifestyle or social and cultural factors are important to you. For example, if access to big-name live entertainment, museums, and artistic activities is important, then working and living in a rural area may not be appropriate. If you like to visit new places, you may choose a career that involves frequent travel.

Consider the following lifestyle options in your decision making:

- Urban/rural setting
- Close/far from work
- Own/rent housing

Career planning should take lifestyle preferences into consideration.

- City/suburban life
- Warm/cold climate
- Near/far from relatives
- Constant/variable climate

In addition, employers in certain careers provide more support for working parents. Employer-subsidized child care as well as flexible work hours might be available at a "family-friendly" workplace.

These are all quality-of-life issues, your quality of life. The challenges are greater for dual-career couples because they must communicate effectively when considering the impact of one person's career decisions on the other. (Chapter 5 offers some tips on communication skills.) Remember, you always have the freedom to change your life and career objectives as you learn more about yourself and the world of work.

Instant Message

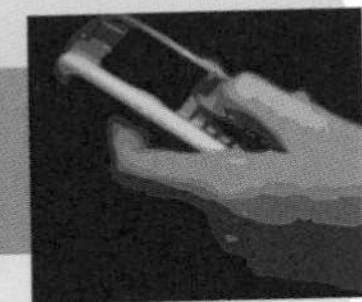

More Women Than Men Are Attending College

More women than men are going to college. Statistics show that nearly six in ten college students are women, and that proportion is expected to continue to increase.

Align Yourself with Tomorrow's Employment Trends

Right now, you may be focused on school—graduating and getting a good job. But you also need to find out where the jobs will be in the future. The job market today is rapidly changing—a result of economic downturns, corporate restructuring, downsizing, and globalization—and the career path you are considering now may not continue to be a good choice in the years ahead.

What, then, are the trends in employment? The aging U.S. population will create jobs in the service industries of finance, insurance, health care, recreation, and travel. Jobs are gravitating to existing population centers, particularly in warmer climates that have superior transportation systems. Jobs in manufacturing are largely going overseas to Mexico, Asia, Europe, and other countries, with the U.S. job market primarily demanding highly skilled workers in the service industries. Strong job growth is projected for the twenty-first century in computer technology, busi-

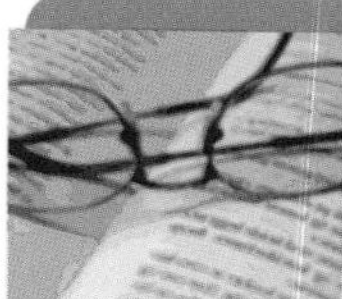

Advice from a Pro

Competencies of Successful People

People who are successful in their chosen careers, with their finances, and/or in life in general often possess and exhibit certain competencies.

1. Set goals in the various aspects of life and track progress toward attaining goals.
2. Use organizational tools such as lists as well as time management techniques.
3. Exhibit integrity.
4. Understand their motives and behave ethically.
5. Make a quality effort every time.
6. Accept accountability for their decisions and actions.
7. Exhibit good written and oral communication skills.
8. Demonstrate strong computer skills.
9. Open to new ideas.
10. Adapt easily to change.
11. Share knowledge to assist and mentor others.
12. Acquire advanced education and technical training and are life-long learners.
13. Take on new assignments and capitalize on the new skills learned.
14. Anticipate problems and work proactively to implement solutions.
15. Work well in teams and know when to lead and when to follow.
16. Project an image consistent with organizational values.
17. Understand operations, structure and culture of organization.
18. Loyal to and supportive of company and boss.

Caroline S. Fulmer
The University of Alabama
Certified Leadership Trainer for the Achieve Global Corporation

ness services, social services, child care, wholesale and retail sales, food services, hospitality, retirement facilities, travel, and human resources. All require good communication skills. High-demand occupations tend to pay high salaries and offer career advancement opportunities. They often require good computer skills. Table 2.1 shows the projected job growth in high-wage, high-growth occupations in the United States.

Take Advantage of Networking

Professional networking is the process of making and using contacts, such as individuals, groups, or institutions, to obtain and exchange information in career planning. Every person you know or meet is a possible useful contact. Networking requires that you make a conscious effort to use people you know and meet to maximize your job search process. Networking involves utilizing your social contacts, taking advantage of casual meetings, and asking for personal referrals. Most of your contacts will not be able to hire you, but they could refer you to the person who can, or they may be able to give you useful information about a potential employer.

professional networking Making and using contacts with individuals, groups, and other firms to exchange career information.

Maintain a continually growing list of people who are family, neighbors, friends, college associates, coworkers, previous supervisors, teachers, professors, alumni, business contacts, and others you know through civic and community organizations such as churches and business and social groups. Take note of where your contacts work and what types of jobs they have. Ask these people for 10 to 20 minutes of their time so you can seek information and suggestions from them. Perhaps meet at their workplaces (where you might meet other potential networking contacts), and afterward send them thank-you notes.

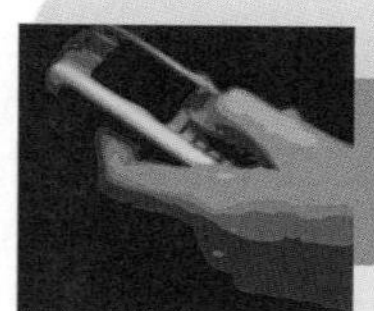

Instant Message

Network Your Way into a Company

The best way to find work at a company is to try to network your way in. Find someone you know who knows someone else in the company and can arrange an introduction.

Table 2.1 Projected High-Wage, High-Growth Occupations*

Job Title	Employment in 2014	Median Annual Income
General and operations managers	2,100,000	$115,000
Property association managers	454,000	60,000
Business operations specialists	396,000	79,000
Computer system analysts	640,000	100,000
Sales managers	403,000	122,000
Medical/health service managers	305,000	102,000
Training and development specialists	261,000	74,000
Marketing managers	228,000	153,000
Industrial engineers	205,000	98,000
Compensation benefits managers	70,000	100,000
Technical writers	62,000	81,000
Human resource managers	72,000	122,000
Media and communications	46,000	61,000
Air traffic controllers	28,000	153,000
Accountants/auditors	1,440,000	76,000
Child and social workers	324,000	51,000
Public relations specialists	231,000	66,000
Market research analysts	227,000	81,000
Advertising promotions managers	77,000	95,000

*Source: Bureau of Labor Statistics, Table I5, High-wage, high-growth occupations, by educational attainment cluster and earnings; authors' income projections to 2014.

As many as three-quarters of all job openings may never be listed in want ads, so the people in your network become a vital source of information about employment opportunities. For this reason, expanding the number of people in your network is advantageous; some of the people you know will also likely share their networking contacts. Networking is the number one way people are successful in their job search.

Target Preferred Employers

preferred employer Identifying employers that would suit you best.

Answering classified job advertisements probably is not the best way to start a career, unless you are lucky and the job listed is actually in your field of interest. A key step in the career search process is to think about both the industries in which you would prefer employment and which employers might be best for you.

If, for example, you want to work in the health care industry, you must research it. Get on the Internet. Go to the library. Visit the websites of health trade associations. Learn as much as you can about the health care industry. How broad is the industry? What types of companies are at the retail level? At the wholesale level? What kinds of firms provide services to the industry? Which companies are the largest? Which have the fastest growth rates? Which employers have employment facilities in geographic areas that are of interest to you? What are the leading companies? Which are the "employers of choice" that are family friendly or offer especially good benefits? What are the employee benefits at different companies? Knowing the industry and specific employers of interest to you tells you whom to target for employment in your career path.

Be Willing to Change Career Goals and Plans

Your career plan should be realistic and flexible. Your career interests and goals will change over time, especially as you continue your education, gain work experience, and see how your friends fare with their jobs and avocations. Teaching music education might be your first career, but you may eventually realize that the accompanying small income could keep you on a tight financial budget forever. This issue might encourage you to consider a total career change—perhaps to sales in the music industry or a related field, where incomes are higher.

Some people go the other way. For example, after some years in the field of accounting, you might change career goals and go to work in your longtime interest area of horticulture, which pays less. Your interests might evolve over time as well. For example, a person with a full-time job in retail store management might decide to turn a hobby of gun collecting into selling guns as an online business. Staying in a career path but changing jobs occurs, too. For example, some hospital nurses decide after a few years that they have made a wrong career choice. While the job pays well, it involves shift work and very long days. Those who want to remain in the nursing profession may decide to leave the hospital setting and go to work for a nursing home or college health facility.

Assessing yourself and your career plans every few years is important to achieving success in your working life. What do you find satisfying and not so satisfying? Honest answers will help you, particularly as your interests evolve. Your work experiences should hone your abilities and skills. Learning new skills on the job is common, and if that is not happening in a job, move on and change employers and perhaps careers.

CONCEPT CHECK 2.1

1. Distinguish between a job and a career.
2. How do your values affect your trade-offs in career planning?
3. What can be done to enhance your abilities and experiences without working in a job situation?
4. What are the components of career plans and goals?

Know Your Preferred Work-Style Personality

2 LEARNING OBJECTIVE
Clarify your work-style personality.

Every job requires the worker to function in relation to data, people, and things in differing work environments and corporate cultures. Your **work-style personality** is a unique set of ways of working with and responding to your job requirements, surroundings, and associates. When making a career selection, you must balance your work-style personality against the demands of the work environment.

work-style personality Your own ways of working with and responding to job requirements surroundings, and associates.

You can begin by rating each work value as shown in the "Decision-Making Worksheet: What Is Your Work-Style Personality." Next, go back to the list and circle the activities that you prefer to do "most often." Armed with this information, you can now more clearly decide on careers that are most suitable for you.

CONCEPT CHECK 2.2

1. Summarize the three major parts of your work-style personality.

Decision-Making Worksheet

What Is Your Work-Style Personality?

It would be useful for you to consider a number of work values critical to the process of career selection, particularly in the areas of work conditions, work purposes, and work relationships. Rate how you value the following work values as either very important in my choice of career (VI), somewhat important in my choice of career (SI), or unimportant in my choice of career (UI).

Work-Style Factor	Your Rating of Importance		
	VI	SI	UI
1. Work Conditions			
Independence and autonomy			
Time flexibility			
Change and variety			
Change and risk			
Stability and security			
Physical challenge			
Physical demands			
Mental challenge			
Pressure and time deadlines			
Precise work			
Decision making			
2. Work Purposes			
Truth and knowledge			
Expertise and authority			
Esthetic appreciation			
Social conditions			
Material gain			
Achievement and recognition			
Ethical and moral			
Spiritual and transpersonal			
3. Work Relationships			
Working alone			
Public contact			
Close friendships			
Group membership			
Helping others			
Influencing others			
Supervising others			
Controlling others			

For additional values clarification, go back to the list and *circle the activities* that you want to do more often. The goal is to match your highest work-style values to career choices with similar work-style requirements.

Source: Adapted from D. C. Borchard, J. J. Kelly, and N. P. K. Weaver, *Your Career: Choices, Chances, Changes* (Dubuque, IA: Kendall/Hunt, 1990), Chapter 11.

Financial and Legal Aspects of Employment

This section examines financial and legal aspects of employment to consider when analyzing your career plans, and it includes the Decision Making Worksheet: Assessing the Value of a Second Income.

3 LEARNING OBJECTIVE
Analyze the financial and legal aspects of employment.

Compare Salary and Living Costs in Different Cities

Incomes range by geographic region, community, and size of employer. Median household income is lowest in the South, a little higher in the Midwest, higher still in the West, and highest in the Northeast. These regional differences reflect the industrial base, unemployment rates, general economic conditions, costs of living (especially for housing and transportation), and the supply and demand for skilled workers. Incomes in rural areas are usually much lower than in urban areas. The highest incomes are paid in metropolitan areas exceeding 1 million in population. Higher salaries are paid in the largest communities for the reasons just mentioned but also because employers compete for the most skilled workers since so many people often live in these communities. Employers with fewer than 100 employees typically pay lower salaries for comparable positions than do larger employers.

Did You Know?...

How to Work at Home Online

Technology has made it possible for many people to work at home online, as 1 in 15 workers has such an alternative work arrangement. Some people work off site for an employer, telecommuting (or teleworking) and perhaps spending one day every two weeks at the company office. Other people are self-employed entrepreneurs who run microbusinesses. A good computer and software make it possible.

Lots of scams exist in the work-at-home industry, especially selling overpriced products and services that people don't need or want. See scam information at the National Fraud Information Center (www.fraud.org/tips/internet/workathome.htm).

Many excellent legitimate job opportunities exist. Examples of online employment are Web hosting, desktop publishing, information processing, database administration, researcher, public relations, employee assistance counseling, telemarketing, personal care services, data entry, accounting, consulting, technical writing, editing, debt counseling, and project management. For ideas on working at home, see the Small Business Administration (www.sba.gov), National Association for the Self-Employed (www.nase.org), and Service Corps of Retired Executives (www.score.org).

Compare Using City Indexes Comparing salary offers from employers located in different cities can be tricky without sufficient information on the approximate cost of living in each community. Sometimes those costs vary drastically. Information from the Internet reveals, for example, that life in a high-cost city such as Seattle is more expensive than life in a lower-cost city such as Portland, Oregon. The data are reported in index form, with the "average cost" community being given a rating of 100.

The following example demonstrates how to compare salary offers in two cities. Assume the Seattle (city 1) index is 138, and Portland's (city 2) is 114. You want to compare the buying power of a salary offer of $52,000 in Portland with a $65,000 offer in Seattle. The costs can be compared using Equations (2.1) and (2.2).

$$\text{Salary in city 1} \times \frac{\text{index city 2}}{\text{index city 1}} = \text{equivalent salary in city 2} \qquad 2.1$$

$$\text{Seattle salary of \$65,000} \times \frac{114}{138} = \text{\$53,696 in buying power in Portland}$$

Thus, the $65,000 Seattle salary offer would buy $53,695 of goods and services in Portland, an amount more than the Portland offer of $52,000. All things being equal (and they are both nice cities), the Seattle offer is slightly better ($53,696 − $52,000 = $1,695).

city indexes Comparing wages and cost of living for various employment locations.

To compare the buying power of salaries in the other direction, reverse the formula:

$$\text{Salary in city 2} \times \frac{\text{index city 1}}{\text{index city 2}} = \text{equivalent salary in city 1} \qquad 2.2$$

$$\text{Portland salary of \$52,000} \times \frac{138}{114} = \text{\$62,947 in buying power in Seattle}$$

Thus, the $52,000 Portland offer can buy only $62,947 of goods and services in Seattle—an amount less than the $65,000 Seattle salary offer. All things being equal, the Seattle offer is still better. For fairer comparisons, add the value of employee benefits and redo the calculations.

Compare Salaries and Living Costs on the 'Net You may compare salary figures and the cost of living in different communities at the following websites:

- CityRating.com (http://www.cityrating.com/costofliving.asp)
- CNNMoney.com (http://cgi.money.cnn.com/tools/costofliving/costofliving.html)
- Moving.com (http://www.moving.com/find_a_place/relosmart/rs.asp)
- Salary.com (http://swz.salary.com/costoflivingwizard/layoutscripts/coll_start.asp)

Did You Know?...

Value of Additional Education

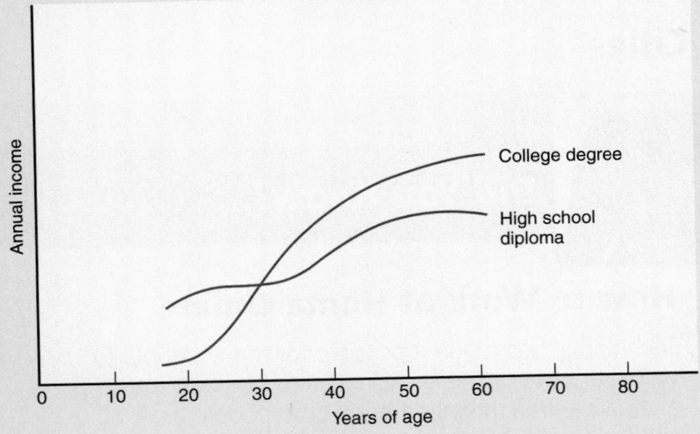

(Income over the Life Cycle Based on Education)

A recent high school graduate with a current income of $27,000 will earn a cumulative $2,036,000 over a 40-year working career. A person with an associate's degree earning $36,000 today will gross $2,700,000; one with a bachelor's degree earning $44,000 now will gross $3,300,000; and a person with a master's degree and a current income of $52,000 will receive a cumulative income of $3,900,000 over a 40-year working career. (The figures are based on 3 percent annual income increases in Appendix A.3.)

Income varies over the life cycle. Higher incomes often go to those with more education or more specialized education. Additional formal education normally leads to greater decision-making responsibilities in a career as well as a higher income.

Place Values on Employee Benefits

Employee benefits are tremendously important to employees, especially when comparing the benefits provided by one employer with another. **Nonsalary benefits** (or **employee benefits**) are forms of remuneration provided by employers to employees that result in the employee not having to pay out-of-pocket money for certain expenses. Examples include paid vacations, health care, paid sick leave, child care, tuition reimbursement, and financial planning services.

The topic of "making smart money decisions at work" was examined in Chapter 1, which provided details on selecting among employer benefits such as health care plans (including health savings accounts), flexible spending plans (such as dependent and health care FSA accounts), insurance (such as life, disability, and long-term care), and employer retirement plans.

You can place a monetary value on each employee benefit that is available. Some nonsalary benefits might not be applicable, such as child care if you are single. Others are supervaluable, such as a health plan, since a policy purchased in the private market for a single person might have a premium of $5000 a year. To put monetary values on employee benefits, you may (1) place a market value on the benefit or (2) calculate the future value of the benefit. See www.salary.com to calculate the value of your employee benefits.

nonsalary benefits Forms of remuneration provided by employers to employees that result in the employee not having to pay out-of-pocket money for certain expenses; also known as employee benefits.

Place a Market Value on the Benefit If instead of enjoying a certain employee benefit, you had to pay out-of-pocket dollars for it, you can easily determine its market value. Private child care might cost $300 a week in your community; thus, when provided free from your employer, that is a whopping $15,000 ($300 × 50 weeks) saved annually. Actually, it is more because you would likely have to earn perhaps $22,000 to have $15,000 left over after paying $7000 in income and Social Security taxes. An employer-provided paid-for life insurance policy with a face value of $50,000 might cost $600 if you had to buy it yourself.

Calculate the Future Value of the Benefit The best income is income that is never taxed, called tax-exempt income. Chapter 1 examined this topic. Many employee benefits are of this type and that's great from your personal finance per-

Seattle has a lot to offer, but it comes at a price.

spective. Future value calculations come into play when you are trying to place a value on an employee benefit that is tax sheltered. Such income is exempt from income taxes in the current year but is subject to taxation in a later tax year. An employer that provides a 401(k) retirement plan offers a valuable benefit. If an employer provides a match of $1200 a year to the regular contributions of the employee, for example, those $1200 contributions will eventually be the worker's money. And it will grow free of income taxes until the funds are withdrawn. Over 20 years, the annual employer contributions of $1200 grow to more than $44,000 (using Appendix A.3) at 6 percent annual return. That's a good employee benefit!

Know Your Legal Employment Rights

You have legal rights both during the hiring process and after you are hired. When selecting employees, employers may not discriminate based on gender, race, color, national origin, age, marital status, pregnancy, or mental or physical disabilities (if the person can perform the essential job tasks). Laws in many states and cities also prohibit discrimination against gays and lesbians in the hiring process.

Once hired, you have many rights. Employers must do the following:

- Pay the minimum wage established by federal, state, or local laws
- Provide unemployment insurance
- Provide workers' compensation benefits to any employee who is injured or becomes ill on the job
- Pay Social Security taxes to the government, which are then credited to the employee's lifetime earnings account maintained by the Social Security Administration

Once hired, the law requires that hourly employees be paid overtime for extra work hours put in beyond the standard 40-hour workweek. (Salaried employees are not paid overtime, and the vast majority of college graduates have salaried jobs.) In addition, a woman cannot be forced to go on maternity leave before she wants to do so if she does choose to take leave. You have the rights not to be unfairly discriminated against or harassed and to be employed in a safe workplace.

Decision-Making Worksheet

Assessing the Benefits of a Second Income

A second income might add surprisingly little to your total earnings because of all the costs associated with earning it. In this example, a nonworking spouse is considering a job that pays $30,000 annually. The accurate net amount of the extra $30,000 income is a mere $9,205, thus adding only $767 a month to total earnings.

1. Second Income	
Annual earnings	$30,000
Value of benefits (life insurance)	300
Total 1	$30,300
2. Expenses	
Federal income taxes (25% rate × $30,000)	$ 7,500
State/local income taxes (6% rate × $30,000)	1,800
Social Security taxes (7.65% × $30,000)	2,295
Transportation and commuting (50 weeks @$40)	2,000
Child care (8 months after-school only)	3,200
Lunches out (50 weeks, twice a week at $10)	1,000
Work wardrobe (including dry cleaning)	1,200
Other work-related expenses (magazines, dues, gifts)	300
Take-out food for supper (too tired to cook; $100 month)	1,200
Guilt complex purchases (to make up for time lost with others)	600
Total 2	$21,095
3. Net Value of Second Income	
Total of 1 from above	$30,300
Subtract total of 2 from above	21,095
Accurate net amount of second income	$ 9,205

You have the right to take leave for personal or family medical problems, pregnancy, or adoption. You also have the right to privacy in such personal matters. When you leave an employer, you have the right to continue your health insurance coverage, perhaps for as long as 18 months, by paying the premiums yourself. If you believe you have been wronged, you can assert your legal rights.

CONCEPT CHECK 2.3

1. Summarize how education level and age affect income.
2. Explain how to compare salary and living costs in different cities.
3. What two techniques can be used to place monetary values on employee benefits?
4. Choose three career advancement tips and explain how each one might apply in someone's personal situation.

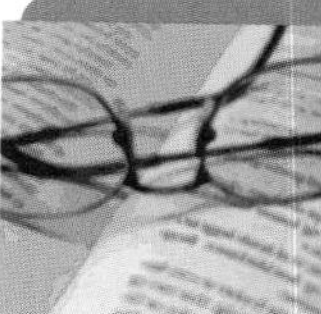

Advice from a Pro

Career Advancement Tips

The essence of career advancement is to build your job-related knowledge and skills for the future by learning. You do not want to fall behind your coworkers and those who work for other employers, as they may be your future job market competitors. To advance in your career, consider the following:

1. Ask one or two people to serve as your mentors, people with whom you can regularly discuss your career progress. A **mentor** is an experienced person, often a senior coworker, who offers friendly career-related advice, guidance, and coaching to a less experienced person.
2. Volunteer for new assignments.
3. Sign up for employer-sponsored seminars and training opportunities.
4. Attend meetings and conferences in your field.
5. Complete certification programs offered by professional associations.
6. Take advanced college courses and complete a graduate degree.
7. Stay alert to what is happening in your career field by reading professional and trade publications.
8. Be up-to-date on current events and business and economic news by reviewing websites and reading newspapers, news magazines, and business periodicals.
9. Be actively involved in something besides work, such as coaching children's athletics, playing softball, singing in a choral group, or teaching reading to illiterate adults.
10. Change jobs when appropriate to obtain a different or better position that advances your career, or when deemed necessary to entirely alter your career.

Dana Wolff
Southeast Technical Institute

Did You Know?...

What You Give Up When Cashing Out Your 401(k) Account

When changing jobs, nearly half of workers unwisely cash out all the money in their employer-sponsored retirement plan instead of leaving it with the old employer, transferring it to a new employer's 401(k) plan, or moving it to an IRA rollover account. If an individual has $50,000 in a 401(k) account and cashes it out, that person gives up $233,000 in future dollars over the following 20 years.

	If you cash out $50,000:	If you roll over $50,000:
20% federal income tax withholding	−$10,000	
5% additional tax (in 25% tax bracket)	−2,500	
10% early-withdrawal penalty	−5,000	
5% state/local income tax	−2,500	
Total withdrawn	−$20,000	+$50,000
Money spent on new car, TV, home repair, vacation, etc.	−$30,000	Money invested in another tax-deferred retirement account that earns 8 percent annually
Total	−$50,000	+$50,000
Additional investment actions taken	None	None
Investment balance after 20 years	$0	$233,050

Effective Employment Search Strategies

4 LEARNING OBJECTIVE
Practice effective employment search strategies.

Once you have undertaken some career planning, you will want to get a job in your preferred career field. This is a process that takes much effort. A successful job search might require 25 to 30 hours per week of your time. Effective search strategies follow.

Assemble a Résumé

résumé Summary record of your education, training, experience, and other qualifications.

chronological format Résumé that provides your information in reverse order, with most recent first.

skills format Résumé that emphasizes your aptitudes and qualities.

functional format Résumé that emphasizes career-related experiences.

The Internet is a valuable resource for you in all aspects of career planning, including preparing a résumé. A **résumé** is a summary record of your education, training, experience, and other qualifications. It is often submitted with a job application. Your résumé, usually one or two pages in length, should be carefully written and contain zero errors or inconsistencies in message, content, and appearance.

Its primary function is to provide a basis for screening people out of contention for jobs. When you supply a résumé, you are providing documentation for some kind of subjective evaluation against unknown criteria. Large employers, recruiters, and local and national websites screen résumés, and computer software is frequently used to scan them instead of humans. Use key buzzwords from the job description such as "Microsoft Office" so the scanning process picks them up.

When it is necessary to technically fulfill a requirement in the employment process, tailor a special edition of your résumé to fit that special set of circumstances. Résumés are usually presented in a **chronological format** (information in reverse order with most recent first), **skills format** (aptitudes and qualities), or **functional format** (career-related experiences). See Figures 2.3, 2.4, and 2.5 for sample résumés. Colleges have career centers with sample résumés and professional staff who can offer personal advice. You can also find examples of résumés on the Internet.

Monster.com has 500,000 online résumés and ResumeMailman .com forwards résumés to recruiters. Simply posting your résumé on an Internet site or sending out résumés is not conducting a significant job search. Realize, of course, that your current employer can view your résumé if it is posted on the Internet.

Did You Know?...

Résumé Buzzwords for Skills, Traits, and Technical Expertise

When preparing your résumé, it is important to include buzzwords for skills, traits, and technical expertise that a potential employer will identify as desirable. This is especially important when computer software is used to scan résumés. Following are examples of good buzzwords:

- Attributes: honesty, integrity
- Skills: oral, written, editing, mediating
- Interests: fun, avocations, volunteer efforts
- Teamwork: coordinated, designed, developed, led, researched
- Computer literacy and expertise: list programs and applications
- Job responsibilities: initiated, managed, monitored, planned, trained, supervised
- Job accomplishments: achieved, administered, built, created, designed, implemented, organized, produced

Identify Job Opportunities

The next step is to identify job opportunities that fit your skill set and provide opportunities for advancement in your career. Use the following resources, and keep track of your job search progress using the Decision-Making Worksheet.

Career Fairs **Career fairs** are university-, community-, and employer-sponsored opportunities for job seekers to meet with perhaps hundreds or even thousands of potential employers over one or more days. Here you can schedule brief screening interviews with a dozen or more employers in a single day. Career fairs are advertised in local newspapers, on television, and on the Internet. Searech "career fairs" on the Internet as well as at CareerBuilder.com and NationalCareerFairs.com.

Classified Advertisements Advertisements in newspapers and professional and trade publications—as well as their Internet equivalents—are an excellent starting place in the job search process. Larger newspapers, such as the *Atlanta Constitution* and *Chicago Daily News* advertise jobs in large geographic areas. Others such as the

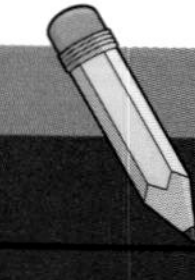

Decision-Making Worksheet

Keeping Track of Your Job Search Progress

The job search process involves a tremendous number of details. Below is a list of task areas in worksheet format that you can use to help keep track of your job search progress. Create lots of columns to the right so you can input important information, such as dates.

1. Identify your values. _____ _____ _____

2. Decide on economic, psychic, and lifestyle trade-offs. _____ _____ _____

3. Clarify career-related interests. _____ _____ _____

4. Review abilities, experiences, and education. _____ _____ _____

5. Identify employment trends. _____ _____ _____

6. Create career goals and plans. _____ _____ _____

7. Target preferred employers. _____ _____ _____

8. Analyze your work-style personality. _____ _____ _____

9. Compare salary and living costs in different cities. _____ _____ _____

10. Place values on employee benefits. _____ _____ _____

11. Create an expanding list of networking contacts. _____ _____ _____

12. Obtain excellent letters of reference. _____ _____ _____

13. Compile revealing personal stories. _____ _____ _____

14. Assemble a résumé. _____ _____ _____

15. Assemble a cover letter. _____ _____ _____

16. Identify job opportunities: _____ _____ _____

- **a.** Career fairs. _____ _____ _____
- **b.** Classified advertisements. _____ _____ _____
- **c.** Employment agencies. _____ _____ _____
- **d.** Internet. _____ _____ _____

17. Interviewing _____ _____ _____

Research the company. _____ _____ _____

Create responses for anticipated interview questions. _____ _____ _____

Create positive responses to list of negative questions. _____ _____ _____

Evaluate your interview performance. _____ _____ _____

18. Send a thank-you note. _____ _____ _____

19. Accept the job. _____ _____ _____

ous sales experience or who seemed to possess terrific potential.

(a) If Jimmy actually was well suited for sales, which work values and work-style factors do you think he would rate as "very important"?

(b) What would you recommend to Jimmy regarding how to find out about the depth of his interest in a sales career?

(c) Assuming Jimmy has appropriate personal qualities and academic strengths to be successful in a sales career, what additional strategies should he consider to better market himself?

Case 2
Career Promotion Opportunity

Nina and Ting Guo of Des Plaines, Illinois, have been together for eight years, having married just after completing college. Nina has been working as an insurance salesperson ever since. Ting began working as a family counselor for the state of Illinois last year after completing his master's degree in counseling. Recently Nina's boss commented confidentially that he was going to recommend Nina to be the next person to be promoted, given a raise of about $15,000, and relocated to the home office in St. Louis, Missouri. Nina thinks that if offered the opportunity she would like to take it, even if it means that Ting will have to resign his new job.

(a) What suggestions can you offer Nina when she gets home from work and wants to discuss with her husband her likely career promotion?

(b) What lifestyle factors and costs and benefits issues should Nina and Ting probably discuss?

Case 3
Victor and Maria Hernandez

Throughout this book, we will present a continuing narrative about Victor and Maria Hernandez. Following is a brief description of the lives of this couple.

Victor and Maria, both in their late 30s, have two children: John, age 13, and Joseph, age 15. Victor has had a long sales career with a retail appliance store. Maria works part time as a dental hygienist. Victor is somewhat satisfied with his career but has always wondered about a career as a teacher in a public school. He would have to take a year off work to go to college to obtain his teaching certificate, and that would mean giving up his $43,000 salary. Victor expects that he could earn about the same income as an inner-city teacher.

(a) What is the future value of $43,000 over 20 years at six percent? (Hint: Use Appendix A.1.)

(b) What if Victor could earn $4000 each year teaching in the summers? What is the future value of earning those annual amounts over 20 years at six percent? (Hint: Use Appendix A.3.)

Case 4
Harry and Belinda Johnson

Throughout this book, we will present a continuing narrative about Harry and Belinda Johnson. Following is a brief description of the lives of this couple.

Harry graduated with a bachelor's degree in interior design last spring from a large Midwestern university near his hometown. Belinda has a degree in business finance from a university on the West Coast. Harry and Belinda both worked on their school's student newspapers and met at a conference during their junior year in college. They were married last June and live in an apartment in Kansas City.

(a) Harry receives $3000 in interest income annually from a trust fund set up by his deceased father's estate. The amount will never change. What will be the buying power of $3000 in ten years if inflation rises at 3 percent a year? (Hint: Use Appendix A.2.)

(b) Belinda and Harry have discussed starting a family but decided to wait for perhaps five years in order to get their careers off to a good start and organize their personal finances. They also know that having children is expensive. They figure that the extra expense of a child would be about $5000 annually until high school graduation. How much money will they likely cumulatively spend on a child over 18 years? (Hint: Use Appendix A.3.)

On the 'Net

Go to the Web pages indicated to complete these exercises. You can also go to the *Garman/Forgue* website at college.hmco.com/business/students for an expanded list of exercises. Under General Business, select the title of this text. Click on the Internet Exercises link for this chapter.

1. Go to the website for the *Occupational Outlook Handbook* at http://www.bls.gov/oco/home.htm. Select two occupational areas that are of interest to you and for each determine the likely starting salary, career path, future salary expectations, and demand for people with the skills appropriate for the occupation.
2. Go to the website for the Bureau of Labor Statistics' assessment of the labor outlook in the United States

at http://www.bls.gov/bls/employment.htm. Browse through the information provided to determine the current national unemployment rate for the nation as a whole and for a city/area of interest to you. Compare current statistics with those of one year ago and with projections for five and ten years in the future.

Visit the Garman/Forgue website...

@college.hmco.com/business/students

Under General Business, select *Personal Finance 9e*. There, among other valuable resources, you will find a complete glossary, ACE questions, links to help you complete the chapter exercises, and links to other personal finance sites.

CHAPTER 3

Financial Statements, Tools, and Budgets

You Must Be Kidding, Right?

The median net worth of American families is $93,000, and the mean amount is $448,000. (Those with high net worth pull the mean above the median.) What are the median and mean figures for families headed by a person less than 35 years of age?

A. $17,000 and $88,000

B. $30,000 and $128,000

C. $47,000 and $178,000

D. $60,000 and $198,000

The answer is A, $17,000 median and $88,000 mean. Median net worth goes up with age. It is $83,000 for families ages 35 to 44, $174,000 for ages 45 to 54, and $298,000 for ages 55 to 64. It all about saving money and building wealth over time!

LEARNING OBJECTIVES

After reading this chapter, you should be able to:

1. **Identify** your financial values, goals, and strategies.
2. **Use** balance sheets and cash-flow statements to measure your financial health and progress, just as businesses do.
3. **Evaluate** your financial strength and progress using financial ratios.
4. **Maintain** the financial records necessary for managing your personal finances.
5. **Outline** and work toward achieving your financial goals through budgeting.

What Do You Recommend?

Robert and Nicole Patterson, both age 26, have been married for four years and have no children. Robert is a licensed electrician earning $46,000 per year, and Nicole earns $41,000 annually as a middle-school teacher. Robert would like to go to half time on his job and return to school on a part-time basis; he is one year short of finishing his bachelor's degree in engineering. His education expenses would be about $10,000 per year, which could be partially covered by student loans. He has not yet discussed his plans with Nicole.

Robert and Nicole have recently started saving for retirement through their employment and have set aside some savings for emergencies. They have substantial credit card debt and are still paying off their student loans. The couple rents a two-bedroom apartment. Robert always thought it smart to save all of their receipts, bank statements, and other financial documents. His system for organizing their records is very simple; each month he puts everything in a manila envelope and then puts the 12 envelopes into a box at the end of the year.

Robert knows that his educational plans will have financial implications for the couple. He wants to factor these financial issues into his discussion with Nicole about his plans. To this point, they have never developed financial statements or explicit financial goals.

What do you recommend to Robert for his talk with Nicole on the subject of financial planning regarding:

1. Determining what they own and owe?
2. Better understanding their patterns of family income and expenditure?
3. Using the information in Robert's newly prepared financial statements to summarize the family's financial situation?
4. Evaluating their financial progress?
5. Setting up a record-keeping system to better serve their needs?
6. Starting a budgeting process to guide saving and spending?

FOR HELP with studying this chapter, visit the Online Student Center:

www.college.hmco.com/pic/garman9e

It is becoming harder to afford "the basics" in America. Housing, gasoline, food, entertainment, and health care costs continue to rise. To maintain the lifestyle people want, many spend every dollar they earn. They live paycheck to paycheck. Some turn to debt. Three in 10 people rate themselves as fair or poor in managing money and say they are living beyond their means. They do not set financial goals. They do not save to build up a rainy-day fund to pay the unexpected bill. This chapter provides the nitty-gritty details on how to go about becoming financially successful. You can attain your financial goals by setting goals and strategies that are consistent with your values. Along the way, you follow your spending plan, take appropriate actions to achieve results, and regularly measure your financial strength and progress.

Financial Values, Goals, and Strategies

1 LEARNING OBJECTIVE
Identify your financial values, goals, and strategies.

financial planning The process of developing and implementing a coordinated series of financial plans to help achieve financial success.

Identifying your financial values and goals sets the stage for financial success. Values and goals keep a balance between spending and saving and help you stay committed to your financial plans. Once goals are set, you can develop the strategies necessary for their achievement. **Financial planning**, the process of developing and implementing a coordinated series of financial plans, can help you achieve financial success. By planning your finances, you seek to manage your income and wealth so that you reach your financial goals.

Figure 3.1 provides an overview of effective personal financial planning, and Table 3.1 illustrates one couple's overall financial plan. Your managerial efforts push you toward achieving financial success. The couple has made plans in 15 specific areas spread across three broad categories: *spending*, *risk management*, and *capital accumulation*. Many people ignore certain areas (retirement planning is a common example) and act with only partial knowledge in other areas (relying on their employers' often inadequate disability income insurance, for example). Yet achieving success in financial matters requires effective financial planning in all 15 specific areas. The chapters in this book will provide enough detail so that you will feel confident and competent as you implement your financial plans that address all 15 areas.

Did You Know?...

The Financial Planning Process

The financial planning process includes the following steps:

1. Setting realistic financial and personal goals
2. Evaluating where you are now financially
3. Developing a plan to reach your goals
4. Putting your plan into action
5. Monitoring your plan to stay on track with changing goals and circumstances

Source: The Financial Planning Association, www.FPAnet.org, reprinted with permission from the Financial Planning Association.

Values Define Your Financial Success

Your values provide the underlying support and rationale for your financial and lifestyle goals. Your **values** are your fundamental beliefs about what is important, desirable, and worthwhile. They serve as the basis for your goals. All of us differ in the ways we value education, spiritual life, health, employment, credit use, family life, and many other factors. Personal financial goals grow out of these values because we inevitably consider some things more important or desirable than others. We express our values, in part, by the ways we spend, save, invest, and donate our money.

One major benefit of financial planning is using money wisely. People who are smart about personal finance typically value saving some of their income. They adhere to the personal finance philosophy of "Pay myself first." If you earn money, shouldn't you be "paid" first? Successful money managers do this instead of spending it all, or even worse by spending more than they earn by using lots of credit. They establish a current spending level based on the necessities of life. They set aside money for future spending, such as for a vehicle purchase, home, child's education, vacation home, and living expenses during the years of retirement.

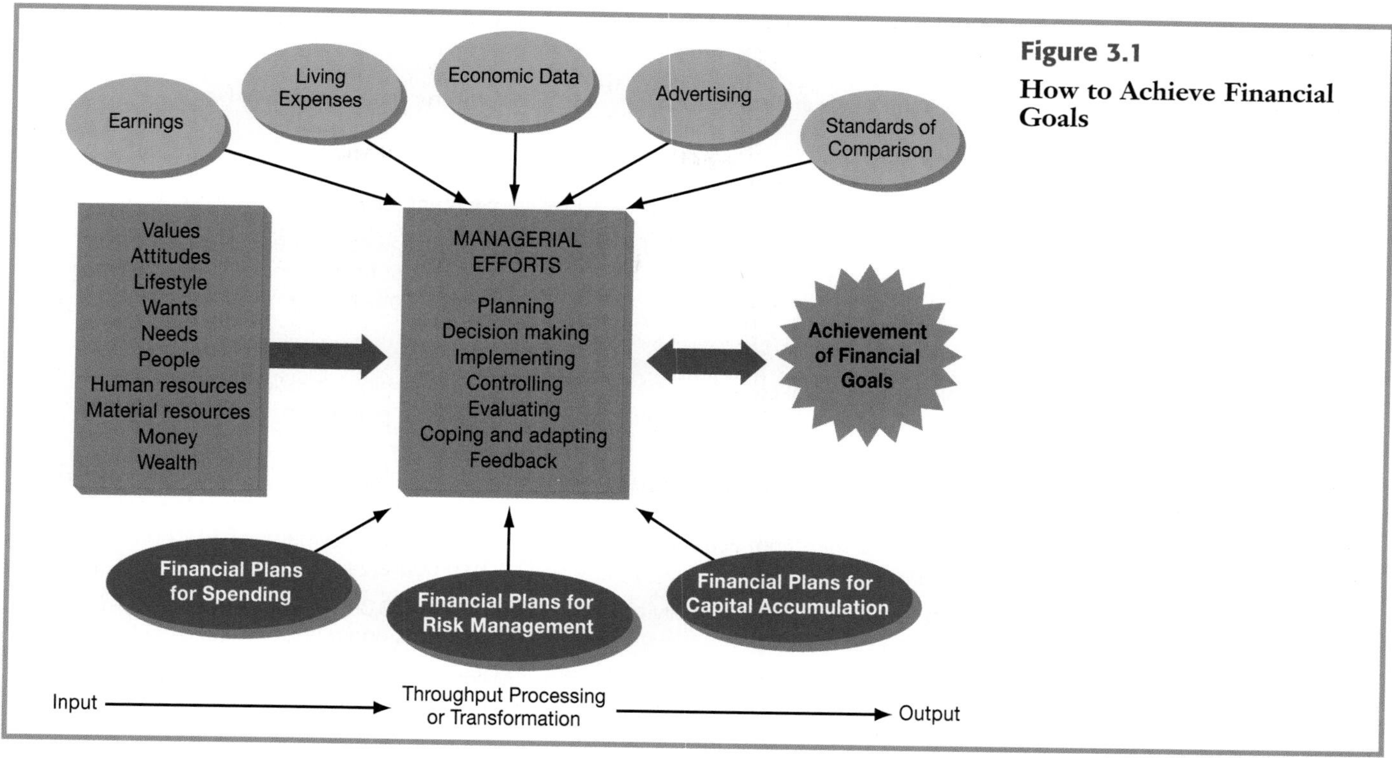

Figure 3.1
How to Achieve Financial Goals

Financial Goals Follow from Your Values

Successful financial planning evolves from your financial goals. **Financial goals** are the specific long-, intermediate-, and short-term objectives to be attained through financial planning and management efforts. Financial and lifestyle goals should be consistent with your values. To serve as a rational basis for financial actions, they must be stated explicitly in terms of purpose, dollar amounts, and the projected dates by which they are to be achieved.

Setting goals helps you visualize the gap between your current financial status and where you want to be in the future. Examples of general financial goals include finishing a college education, paying off debts (including education loans), meeting financial emergencies, taking a vacation, owning a home, accumulating funds to send children through college, owning your own business, creating a better peace of mind, ensuring family harmony, and having financial independence at retirement. None of these goals, however, is specific enough to guide financial behavior. Specific goals should be measurable, attainable, relevant, and time related. Saving for retirement should begin with a calculation of how much money you will need in retirement (see Chapter 17), and saving for retirement should start soon after you begin a full-time job. Saving for a child's education should begin when your first child is born, if not earlier.

Consider the example of Heather Vogel, a dance instructor from Cincinnati, Ohio. Heather has just made the last $347 payment on her four-year car loan. She does not like being in debt, so she does not want to take out such a large loan again. Heather

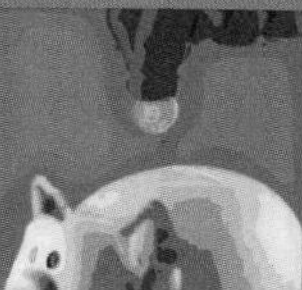

Good Money Habits in Financial Statements, Tools, and Budgets

Make the following your money habits in financial planning statements, tools, and budgets:

1. Identify your financial values, goals, and strategies so you can always keep a balance between spending and saving and stay committed to your financial plans.
2. Develop your own balance sheet and update it annually.
3. Develop your own cash-flow statements monthly or quarterly and compile them into an annual statement each year.
4. Calculate your financial ratios annually to assess your financial progress.
5. Develop a list of your financial goals. Start with the shorter-term goals and then expand your list to longer-range goals. Update and revise your goals annually.
6. Start an uncomplicated personal financial record-keeping system that meets your needs.

Table 3.1 Financial Plans, Goals, and Objectives for Harry (Age 23) and Belinda (Age 22) Johnson, Prepared in February 2008

Financial Plan Areas	Long-Term Goals and Objectives	Short-Term Goals and Objectives
FOR SPENDING		
Evaluate and plan major purchases	Purchase a new car in two years.	Begin saving $200 a month for a down payment for a new car.
Manage debt	Keep installment debt under 10 percent of take-home pay.	Pay off charge cards at end of each month and do not finance any purchases of appliances or other similar products.
FOR RISK MANAGEMENT		
Medical costs	Avoid large medical costs.	Maintain employer-subsidized medical insurance policy by paying $135 monthly premium.
Property and casualty losses	Always have renter's or homeowner's insurance. Always have maximum automobile insurance coverage.	Make semiannual premium payment of $220 on renter's insurance policy. Make premium payments of $440 on automobile insurance policy.
Liability losses	Eventually buy $1 million liability insurance.	Rely on $100,000 policy purchased from same source as automobile insurance policy.
Premature death	Have adequate life insurance coverage for both as well as lots of financial investments so the survivor would not have any financial worries.	Maintain employer-subsidized life insurance on Belinda. Buy some life insurance for Harry. Start some investments.
Income loss from disability	Buy sufficient disability insurance.	Rely on sick days and seek disability insurance through private insurers.
FOR CAPITAL ACCUMULATION		
Tax fund	Have enough money for taxes (but not too much) withheld from monthly salaries by both employers to cover eventual tax liabilities.	Confirm that employer withholding of taxes is sufficient. Have extra money withheld to cover additional tax liability because of income on trust from Harry's deceased father.
Revolving savings fund	Always have sufficient cash in local accounts to meet monthly and annual anticipated budget expense needs.	Develop cash-flow calendar to ascertain needs. Put money into revolving savings fund to build it up quickly to the proper balance. Keep all funds in interest-earning accounts.
Emergency fund	Build up monetary assets equivalent to three months' take-home pay.	Put $150 per month into an emergency fund until it totals one month's take-home pay.
Education	Maintain educational skills and credentials to remain competitive. Have employer assist in paying for Belinda to earn a master of business administration (MBA). Have Harry complete a master of fine arts (MFA), possibly a PhD in interior design.	Both take one graduate class per term.
Savings	Always have a nice-size savings balance. Regularly save to achieve goals. Save a portion of any extra income or gifts. Save $26,000 for a down payment on a home to be bought within five years.	Save enough to pay cash for a good-quality DVD player. Pay off Visa credit card balance of $390 soon. Begin saving $400 per month for a down payment on a new home.
Investments	Own substantial shares of a conservative mutual fund that will pay dividends equivalent to about 10 percent of family income at age 45. Own some real estate and common stocks.	Start investing in a mutual fund before next year.

Table 3.1 Financial Plans, Goals, and Objectives for Harry (Age 23) and Belinda (Age 22) Johnson Prepared in February 2008—cont'd

Financial Plan Areas	Long-Term Goals and Objectives	Short-Term Goals and Objectives
Retirement	Retire at age 60 or earlier on income that is the same as the take-home pay earned just before retirement.	Establish individual retirement accounts (IRAs) for Harry and Belinda before next year. Contribute the maximum possible amount to employer-sponsored retirement accounts.
Estate planning	Provide for surviving spouse.	Each spouse makes a will.

would like to put at least part of the money she has been paying monthly for the loan into a savings account, which would allow her to replace her current vehicle in five years. Heather figures that it would take about $22,500 to buy a similar inexpensive high-mileage vehicle in five years. She assumes she could earn a 3 percent return on her savings and, using Appendix Table A.3, has determined that she would need to save $4238 per year ($22,500 ÷ 5.3091 for five years at 3 percent interest from Appendix Table A.3), or roughly $353 per month.

Heather's thinking offers a good example of how financial goal setting works. She recognized the value she put on staying out of debt and proceeded to the general goal of paying cash for her next car. After determining an overall dollar amount needed, she broke that amount down into first annual and then monthly amounts. For only $6 more per month than she has been paying on her loan ($353 − $347), Heather will be able to pay cash for her next car. This is the small sacrifice she is willing to make to avoid using credit to buy a vehicle in the future.

Financial Strategies Guide Your Financial Success

financial strategies Preestablished action plans implemented in specific situations.

Financial strategies are preestablished plans of action to be implemented in specific situations. Heather Vogel implemented a very effective strategy in the preceding example. That is, when a loan has been repaid, start a savings program with the same monthly payment amount. Saving may be easier for Heather if she arranges for the amount she'd like to save to be automatically deposited from her paycheck into her savings account. Another effective savings strategy is to arrange for one-half of every raise to go into savings before you become accustomed to the additional income.

Heather's actions have nothing to do with her earning more money. Many people think that being wealthy is a function of how much you earn or inherit. Accumulating wealth is much more related to your ability to understand trade-offs among current and future wants and make the sacrifices that will save money and generate wealth for you. In Heather's case, all that remains for her to do is to put the strategy into action. She can then review her strategy annually and adjust it as necessary to keep pace with her shifting circumstances.

To sum up, successful financial planning includes the following elements that guide behavior: (1) specified values that underlie the plans, (2) explicitly stated financial goals, and (3) logical and consistent financial strategies. Smart financial strategies will be presented throughout this book, as they help you keep a balance between spending and saving. Only after this values-based process is complete do you take actions to achieve the goals. In other words, your financial planning comes before you take action.

CONCEPT CHECK 3.1

1. Summarize the financial planning process.
2. Explain the relationships among financial values, goals, and strategies.

Did You Know?...

Life Planning Issues When You Find the Right Partner

Personal finances are complex enough for just one person, but when two people join their financial lives together, things can get very complicated. When you find the right partner, it is smart to do the following:

- ***Change beneficiaries.*** Life insurance policies, retirement accounts, and mutual fund accounts all have beneficiaries (the people who will receive the funds at your death) named when you set them up. (See Chapters 12, 15, 17, and 18.)
- ***Coordinate employee benefits.*** Couples often have two incomes today, so each has a menu of employee benefits from which to choose. As a result, one spouse may drop a benefit that is being received via the other's plan. For example, if one partner receives family coverage for health care for free or at a low monthly cost, perhaps the other can drop that aspect of his or her own plan. One spouse might then be able to add another benefit at no cost, such as paid education expenses. Your employee benefits officer can help you decide which options to select.
- ***Update life insurance coverage.*** Focus on term life insurance for the bulk of your needs. (See Chapter 12.)
- ***Review auto and homeowner's insurance coverages.*** Also inventory your personal property. (See Chapter 10.)
- ***Get out of debt.*** One or both of you may bring debts into the new family. Because a couple can live together a little more cheaply than two individuals who live apart, funds can be freed up to pay off credit card, student, and other loans. This debt reduction has an added benefit: It sets the stage for getting a mortgage to buy your first home. (See Chapters 6, 7, and 9.)
- ***Update names with government agencies.*** If one or both partners' names are changed as a result of your new status, you need to notify the Social Security Administration and driver's licensing office of that change. You will need to show your marriage certificate as proof of the change.
- ***Save for retirement separately.*** Day-to-day living expenses will go down somewhat when you team up as a couple. Use some of that money to allocate additional amounts to your individual retirement plans. (See Chapter 17.)
- ***Update estate transfer plans.*** With a new number one in your life, you should change (or set up) your will, durable power of attorney, living will, and health care surrogate designations. (See Chapter 18 for more information on these documents.)
- ***Close redundant bank and credit accounts.*** Reducing the number of accounts that each partner brings into the marriage can save money on account fees. Decide which accounts are yours, mine, or ours. Having excess credit cards can reduce your credit scores and exposes you to the potential for overuse. (See Chapters 5 and 6 for more on managing accounts.)
- ***Manage money together.*** All of the topics in this chapter on financial planning should be undertaken as a team. (See Chapter 5 for how to effectively discuss money matters.)

financial statements Compilations that show financial conditions, including balance sheets and cash-flow statements.

2 LEARNING OBJECTIVE
Use balance sheets and cash-flow statements to measure your financial health and progress.

balance sheet (or net worth statement) Snapshot of assets, liabilities, and net worth on a particular date.

Financial Statements Measure Your Financial Health and Progress

Financial statements are compilations of personal financial data designed to communicate information on money matters. They are used—often along with other financial data—to indicate the financial condition and behavior of an individual or family. The two most useful statements are the balance sheet and the cash-flow statement.

A **balance sheet** (or **net worth statement**) describes an individual's or family's financial condition on a specified date (often January 1) by showing assets, liabilities, and net worth. It provides a current status report and includes information on what you own, what you owe, and what the net result would be if you paid off all of your debts. It answers the question "Where are you financially right now?"

A **cash-flow statement** (or **income-and-expense statement**) lists and summarizes income and expense transactions that have taken place over a specific period of time, such as a month or a year. It tells you where your money came from and where it went. It answers the question "Where did your money go?"

cash-flow statement (or income and expense statement) Summary of all income and expense transactions over a specific time period.

The Balance Sheet Is a Snapshot of Your Financial Status Right Now

To benchmark where you are on the wealth-building scale, determine your net worth. If you are indeed serious about your financial success, then you will sit down soon with pencil and paper or at your computer to see exactly where you stand. You do so by preparing your balance sheet, which summarizes the value of what you own minus what you owe. Your balance sheet should be updated at least once each year so that you can assess your progress. Net worth grows slowly. If you are successful in your career and follow the basic principles outlined in this book, there is no reason why you cannot have a net worth of $1 million, or $2 million or more, later in your life. Net worth typically peaks for people in their 60s and declines thereafter as they live off their financial nest egg in retirement.

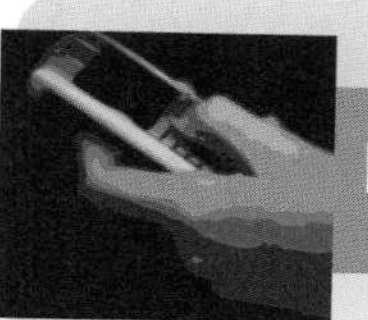

Instant Message

Turn Your Goals into Reality

The path toward turning a wish into reality begins with writing it down. If buying a condo is your goal, tape a photograph of a beautiful one on your refrigerator. Then tell others about your financial goal. Your mind will figure ways to make it into a reality.

Components of the Balance Sheet

A balance sheet consists of three parts: assets, liabilities, and net worth. Your **assets** include everything you own that has monetary value. Your **liabilities** are your debts—amounts you owe to others. Your **net worth** is the dollar amount left when what is owed is subtracted from the dollar value of what is owned—that is, if all the assets were sold at the listed values and all debts were paid in full. Your net worth is the true measure of your financial wealth.

assets Everything you own that has monetary value.

liabilities What you owe.

net worth What's left when you subtract liabilities from assets.

What Is Owned—Assets

The assets section of the balance sheet lists items valued at their **fair market value**—what a willing buyer would pay a willing seller, not the amount originally paid or what it might be worth a year from now. It is useful to classify assets as monetary, tangible, or investment assets.

Monetary assets (also known as **liquid assets** or **cash equivalents**) include cash and low-risk near-cash items that can be readily converted to cash with little or no loss in value such as checking and savings accounts. They are primarily used for maintenance of living expenses, emergencies, savings, and payment of bills.

monetary assets/liquid assets/cash equivalents Assets that can be used as cash.

Tangible (or **use**) **assets** are personal property whose primary purpose is to provide maintenance of one's everyday lifestyle. Tangible assets, such as furniture and vehicles, generally depreciate in value over time.

tangible (use) assets Personal property used to maintain your everyday lifestyle.

Investment assets (also known as **capital assets**) include tangible and intangible items that have a relatively long life and high cost and that are acquired for the monetary benefits they provide, such as generating additional income and appreciation (or increasing in value). Examples include stocks and bonds. Investment assets generally appreciate and are dedicated to the maintenance of one's future level of living.

investment (capital) assets Tangible and intangible items acquired for their monetary benefits.

Following are some examples of each kind of asset.

Monetary Assets

- Cash (including cash on hand, checking accounts, savings accounts, savings bonds, certificates of deposit, and money market accounts)
- Tax refunds due
- Money owed to you by others

Tangible Assets

- Automobiles, motorcycles, boats, bicycles
- House, condominium, mobile home
- Household furnishings and appliances

- Personal property (jewelry, furs, tools, clothing)
- Other "big ticket" items

Investment Assets

- Stocks, bonds, mutual funds, gold, partnerships, art, IRAs
- Life insurance and annuities (cash values only)
- Real property (and anything fixed to it)
- Personal and employer-provided retirement accounts

short-term (current) liability Obligation paid off within one year.

long-term liability Debt that comes due in more than one year.

What Is Owed—Liabilities The liabilities section of the balance sheet summarizes debts owed, including both personal and business-related debts. The debt could be either a **short-term** (or **current**) **liability**, an obligation to be paid off within one year, or a **long-term liability**, debts that do not have to be paid in full until more than a year from now. To be accurate, record debt obligations at their current payoff amounts (excluding future interest payments). Following are some examples of items to include in the liabilities section of a balance sheet, with some suggested subheadings.

Short-Term (or Current) Liabilities

- Personal loans owed to other people
- Credit card and charge account balances
- Other open-end credit obligations
- Professional services unpaid (doctors, dentists, chiropractors, lawyers)
- Taxes unpaid
- Past-due rent, utility bills, and insurance premiums

Long-Term Liabilities

- Automobile loans
- Real estate mortgages
- Home equity (second mortgage) loan
- Consumer installment loans and leases (although a lease is technically not a debt)
- Education loans
- Margin loans on securities

Net Worth—What Is Left Net worth is determined by subtracting liabilities from assets, as indicated in Equation (3.1), the *net worth formula:*

$$\text{Assets} - \text{liabilities} = \text{net worth} \tag{3.1}$$

or

$$\text{What is owned} - \text{what is owed} = \text{net worth}$$

This formula assumes that if you converted all assets to cash and paid off all liabilities, the remaining cash would be your net worth. For example, if your items of value had a fair market value of $8000 and the amount you owe to others is $4500, your net worth, or wealth, is $3500 ($8000 − $4500). Figure 3.2 shows household net worth figure by age group. Calculating your net worth will give you a reading on where you stand and point out any trouble spots on your balance sheet.

Sample Balance Sheets The total assets on a balance sheet must equal the total liabilities plus the net worth. Both sides must balance, which is the source of the name "balance sheet." You decide how much detail to include to show your financial condition accurately on a given date.

The balance sheets shown in Table 3.2 (page 68) and Table 3.3 (page 69) reflect the degree of detail that might be included for a traditional college student and a couple with two children, respectively. Notice that Table 3.2 includes very few items. This pattern is typical of single people who have not acquired many objects of value. Observe also the excess of liabilities over assets. This situation is not unusual for college students, for whom debts often seem to grow much faster than assets do. In this case, the person is technically **insolvent** because he or she has a negative net worth.

insolvent Carrying a negative net worth.

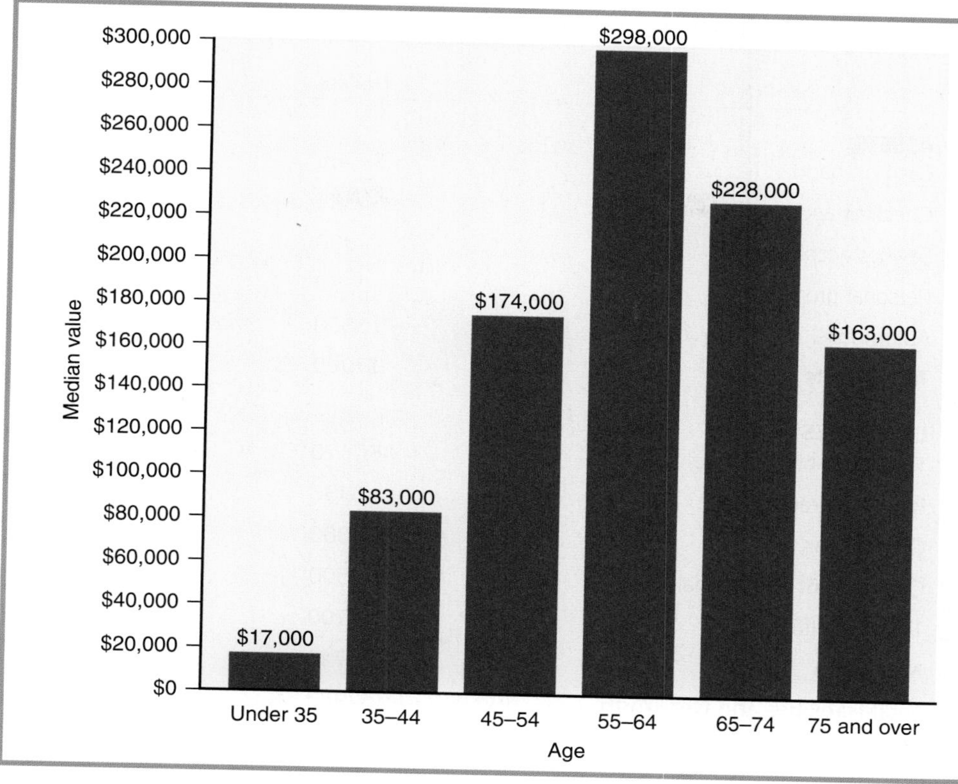

Figure 3.2
Net Worth by Age
Source: Base data from Survey of Consumer Finances. Authors' estimates for 2009.

When students graduate and take on full-time jobs, typically their balance sheets change dramatically after a few years. The balance sheet in Table 3.3 shows greater detail and more items, reflecting the increasing financial complexity that typically occurs at later stages in a person's life.

Strategies to Increase Your Net Worth

You can increase your net worth by increasing assets, decreasing liabilities, or doing both. One way to increase assets and net worth is to cut back on spending. Perhaps consider forgoing the cup of coffee or soda you buy each day as you head to class, as any decrease in spending leaves money in the bank as an asset. Reducing expenses on high-cost items such as housing and transportation will have an even greater effect on assets. A second way to increase net worth is to increase income to build assets or pay down debts. For example, as you earn more money, perhaps consider saving most of the difference between your new income and your old income rather than using the added money for more spending. Paying off debt, especially high-interest credit card balances, increases net worth.

The Cash-Flow Statement Tracks Where Your Money Came From and Went

The cash-flow (or income and expense) statement summarizes the total amounts that have been received and spent over a period of time, usually one month or one year. It shows whether you were able to live within your income during that time period. It reflects the flow of funds in and out.

A cash-flow statement includes three sections: **income** (total income received); **expenses** (total expenditures made); and **surplus** (or **net gain** or **net income**), when total income exceeds total expenses, or **deficit** (or **net loss**), when expenses exceed

expenses Total expenditures made in a specified time.

Table 3.2 Balance Sheet for a College Student—William Soshnik, January 1, 2008

	Dollars	Percent
ASSETS		
Cash on hand	$ 85	1.07
Checking account	335	4.21
Savings account	800	10.05
Personal property*	3140	39.45
Automobile	3600	45.23
Total Assets	**$7960**	100.00
LIABILITIES		
Telephone bill past due	$ 70	0.88
Bank loan—automobile	3130	39.32
College loan	1000	12.56
Government educational loan	4500	56.53
Total Liabilities	**$8700**	109.30
Net Worth	($ 740)	−9.30
Total Liabilities and Net Worth	**$7960**	100.00

*At fair market value, list includes clothing, $400; dresser, $50; television, $150; chair, $30; table, $40; desk, $120; cooking/dining items, $50; and computer equipment, $2300.

cash basis Only transactions involving actual money received or money spent are recorded.

income. Such statements are usually prepared on a **cash basis**, meaning the only transactions recorded are those involving actual money received or money that was spent.

Income/Cash Coming In You may think of income as simply what is earned from salaries or wages, but there are other types of income that you should include on a cash-flow statement, such as the following:

- Bonuses and commissions
- Child support and alimony
- Public assistance
- Social Security benefits
- Pension and profit-sharing income
- Scholarships and grants
- Interest and dividends received (from savings accounts, investments, bonds, or loans to others)
- Income from the sale of assets
- Other income (gifts, tax refunds, rent, royalties, capital gains)

Expenses/Cash Going Out All expenditures made during the period covered by the cash-flow statement should be included in the expenses section. The number and type of expenses shown will vary for each individual and family. Many people categorize expenses according to whether they are fixed or variable.

fixed expenses Expenses that recur at fixed intervals.

variable expenses Expenses over which you have substantial control.

Fixed expenses are usually paid in the same amount during each time period; they are often contractual. Examples of such expenses include rent payments and automobile installment loans. It is usually takes quite an effort to reduce a fixed expense.

Variable expenses are expenditures over which an individual has considerable control. Food, entertainment, and clothing are variable expenses, for example. Some categories, such as savings, can be listed twice, as both fixed and variable expenses. The following are examples of fixed and variable expenses that you might include in a cash-flow statement:

Fixed Expenses

- Savings and investments
- Retirement contributions (employer's plan, IRA)

Table 3.3 Balance Sheet for a Couple with Two Children—Victor and Maria Hernandez, January 1, 2008

	Dollars	Percent
ASSETS		
Monetary Assets		
Cash on hand	$ 260	0.08
Savings account	1,500	0.48
Victor's checking account	600	0.19
Maria's checking account	700	0.23
Tax refund due	700	0.23
Rent receivable	660	0.21
Total monetary assets	**$4,420**	1.43
Tangible Assets		
Home	$176,000	56.79
Personal property	9,000	2.90
Automobiles	11,500	3.71
Total tangible assets	**$196,500**	63.40
Investment Assets		
Fidelity mutual funds	$ 4,500	1.45
Scudder mutual fund	5,000	1.61
General Motors stock	2,800	0.90
New York 2016 bonds	1,000	0.32
Life insurance cash value	5,400	1.74
IRA	6,300	2.03
Real estate investment	84,000	27.10
Total investment assets	**$109,000**	35.17
Total Assets	**$309,920**	100.00
LIABILITIES		
Short-Term Liabilities		
Dentist bill	$ 120	0.04
Credit card debt	1,545	0.50
Total short-term liabilities	**$1,665**	0.54
Long-Term Liabilities		
Sales finance company: automobile	$ 7,700	2.48
Savings and loan: real estate	92,000	29.69
Total long-term liabilities	**$ 99,700**	32.17
Total Liabilities	**$101,365**	32.71
Net Worth	$208,555	67.29
Total Liabilities and Net Worth	**$309,920**	100.00

- Housing (rent, mortgage, loan payment)
- Automobile (installment payment, lease)
- Insurance (life, health, liability, disability, renter's, homeowner's, automobile)
- Installment loan payments (appliances, furniture)
- Taxes (federal income, state income, local income, real estate, Social Security, personal property)

Variable Expenses

- Meals (at home and away)
- Utilities (electricity, water, gas, telephone)
- Transportation (gasoline and maintenance, licenses, registration, public transportation, tolls)
- Medical expenses
- Child care (nursery, baby-sitting)
- Clothing and accessories (jewelry, shoes, handbags, briefcases)
- Snacks (candy, soft drinks, other beverages)
- Education (tuition, fees, books, supplies)
- Household furnishings (furniture, appliances, curtains)
- Cable television (beyond basic services)
- Personal care (beauty shop, barbershop, cosmetics, dry cleaner)
- Entertainment and recreation (hobbies, socializing, health club, tapes/CDs, videotape/DVD rentals, movies)
- Charitable contributions (gifts, church, school, charity)
- Magazine subscriptions
- Vacations and long weekends
- Credit card payments
- Savings and investments
- Miscellaneous (postage, books, magazines, newspapers, personal allowances, domestic help, membership fees)

There is no rigid list of categories to be used in the expenses section, but you do need to classify all of your expenditures in some way. Rather than just use fixed and

Lattes are a variable expense that can add up quickly.

variable expenses categories, you might also separate expenditures into savings/investments, debts, insurance, taxes, and household expenses. The more specific your categories, the deeper your understanding of your outlays.

Cash Surplus (or Cash Deficit) The surplus (deficit) section shows the amount of cash remaining after you have itemized income and subtracted expenditures from income, as illustrated by the following calculations using Equation (3.2), *the surplus/deficit formula*. (A business would call this amount its net profit or net loss.)

$$\text{Surplus (deficit)} = \text{total income} - \text{total expenses} \quad (3.2)$$

or $$\$1100 \text{ surplus} = \$12{,}500 - \$11{,}400$$

$$(\$800 \text{ deficit}) = \$14{,}900 - \$15{,}700$$

A surplus demonstrates that you are managing your financial resources successfully and do not have to use savings or borrow money to make financial ends meet. When the calculation shows a surplus, that amount is then available (in your checking and savings accounts) to spend, save, invest, or donate. A surplus is not really cash lying around on the kitchen table; it is the cash value reflected in the accounts on your balance sheet. Figure 3.3 shows the typical personal financial situation over the life cycle in present value dollars, from the wealth accumulation years through retirement.

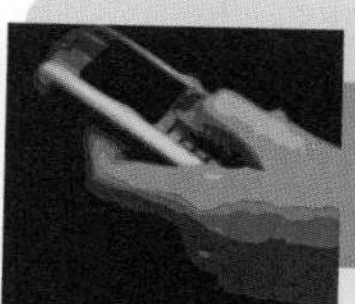

Instant Message

Take the Wheel of Your Personal Finances

Financial expert Angie Hollerich says that it is easy to be a passenger, but it takes courage to take the wheel and control of your own personal finances.

Sample Cash-Flow Statements Table 3.4 and Table 3.5 show the cash-flow statements for a college student and a couple with two children, respectively. Table 3.5 vividly highlights the additional income needed to rear children and shows the increased variety of expenditures that characterize a family's

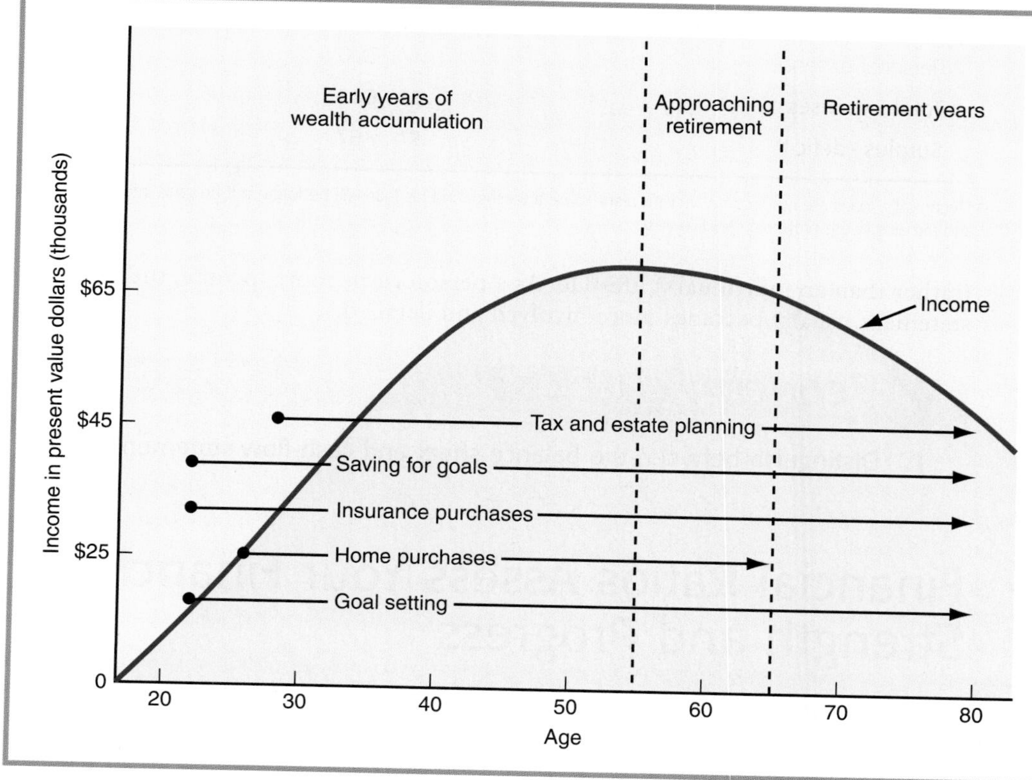

Figure 3.3

Personal Finance over the Life Cycle

Table 3.4 Cash-Flow Statement for a College Student—William Soshnik, January 1–December 31, 2008

	Dollars	Percent
INCOME		
Wages (after withholding)	$ 4,650	39.71
Scholarship	1,750	14.94
Government grant	2,500	21.35
Government loan*	2,600	22.20
Tax refund	210	1.79
Total Income	**$11,710**	**100.00**
EXPENSES		
Room rent (includes utilities)	$ 1,500	12.81
Laundry	216	1.84
Food	1,346	11.49
Automobile loan payments	1,292	11.03
Automobile insurance	778	6.64
Books and supplies	932	7.96
Tuition	3,160	26.99
Telephone	282	2.41
Clothing	475	4.06
Gifts	300	2.56
Automobile expenses	600	5.12
Health insurance	102	0.87
Recreation and entertainment	360	3.07
Personal expenses	300	2.56
Total Expenses	**$11,643**	99.43
Surplus (deficit)	**$ 67**	0.57

*Technically, loans are not income. William plans to be a teacher, and his loan will be forgiven if he goes into teaching and remains in the profession for five years.

(rather than an individual's) lifestyle. As a person earns more income, the cash-flow statement usually becomes more involved and detailed.

CONCEPT CHECK 3.2

1. Distinguish between the balance sheet and cash-flow statement.

Financial Ratios Assess Your Financial Strength and Progress

3 LEARNING OBJECTIVE
Evaluate your financial strength and progress using financial ratios.

Financial ratios are numerical calculations designed to simplify the process of evaluating your financial strength and the progress of your financial condition. Ratios serve as tools or yardsticks to develop saving, spending, and credit-use pat-

Table 3.5 Cash-Flow Statement for a Couple with Two Children—Victor and Maria Hernandez, January 1, 2008–December 31, 2008

	Dollars	Percent
INCOME		
Victor's gross salary	$43,180	65.42
Maria's salary (part time)	12,500	18.94
Interest and dividends	1,800	2.73
Bonus	600	0.91
Tax refunds	200	0.30
Net rental income	7,720	11.70
Total Income	**$66,000**	100.00
EXPENSES		
Fixed Expenses		
Mortgage loan payments	$12,000	18.18
Real estate taxes	2,400	3.64
Homeowner's insurance	760	1.15
Automobile loan payment	4,400	6.67
Automobile insurance and registration	1,191	1.80
Life insurance premiums	1,200	1.82
Medical insurance (employee portion)	2,980	4.52
Savings at credit union	1,260	1.91
Federal income taxes	6,800	10.30
State income taxes	3,100	4.70
City income taxes	720	1.09
Social Security taxes	4,260	6.45
Personal property taxes	950	1.44
Retirement IRAs	4,000	6.06
Total Fixed Expenses	**$46,021**	69.73
Variable Expenses		
Food	$ 4,900	7.42
Utilities	2,100	3.18
Gasoline, oil, maintenance	3,100	4.70
Medical expenses	1,245	1.89
Medicines	750	1.14
Clothing and upkeep	1,950	2.95
Church	1,200	1.82
Gifts	900	1.36
Personal allowances	1,160	1.76
Children's allowances	960	1.45
Miscellaneous	500	0.76
Total variable expenses	**$18,765**	28.43
Total Expenses	**$64,786**	98.16
Surplus (deficit)	**1,214**	1.84

terns consistent with your goals. Calculators for these ratios can be found on the *Garman/Forgue* website.

Basic Liquidity Ratio: Can I Pay for Emergencies?

liquidity Speed and ease with which an asset can be converted to cash.

basic liquidity ratio Number of months you could meet expenses using only monetary assets if all income ceases.

Liquidity is the speed and ease with which an asset can be converted to cash. You can use the **basic liquidity ratio** to determine the number of months that you could continue to meet your expenses using only your monetary assets if all income ceases. A high ratio is desirable. For example, compare the monetary assets on the balance sheet for Victor and Maria Hernandez in Table 3.3 ($4420) with their monthly expenses in Table 3.5 ($64,786 ÷ 12 = $5399) using Equation (3.3):

$$\text{Basic liquidity ratio} = \frac{\text{monetary (liquid) assets}}{\text{monthly expenses}} \tag{3.3}$$

$$= \frac{\$4420}{\$5398}$$

$$= 0.82$$

This financial ratio suggests that the Hernandezes may have insufficient monetary assets, unable to support them for even one month (0.82) if they faced with a loss of income. According to researchers at the University of Texas, experts recommend that people have monetary assets equal to three months' expenses in emergency cash reserves. Surveys reveal that more than half of American families do not have that much savings. The exact amount of monetary assets necessary depends on your family situation and your job. A smaller amount may be sufficient for your needs if you have adequate income protection through an employee benefit program, are employed in a job that is definitely not subject to layoffs, or have a partner who works for money income. Households dependent on the income from a self-employed person with fluctuating income need a larger emergency cash reserve.

Asset-to-Debt Ratio: Do I Have Enough Assets Compared with Liabilities?

asset-to-debt ratio Compares total assets with total liabilities.

The **asset-to-debt ratio** compares total assets with total liabilities. It provides you with a broad measure of your financial liquidity. This ratio measures solvency and ability to pay debts, as shown in Equation (3.4). A high ratio is desirable. Calculations based on the figures in the Hernandezes' balance sheet (Table 3.3) show that the couple has ample assets compared with their debts because they own items worth more than three times what they owe. (Reversing the mathematics shows that they owe less than one-third of what they own.)

$$\text{Asset-to-debt ratio} = \frac{\text{total assets}}{\text{total debt}} \tag{3.4}$$

$$= \frac{\$309{,}920}{\$101{,}365}$$

$$= 3.057$$

If you owe more than you own, then you are technically insolvent. While your current income may be sufficient to pay your current bills, you still do not have enough assets to cover all of your debts. Many people in such situations seek credit counseling, and some eventually declare bankruptcy. (These topics are discussed in Chapter 6, "Building and Maintaining Good Credit.") Many college students are temporarily insolvent, and that's okay because their earning capacity suggests that in only a few years their net worth will change for the better.

Instant Message

Emergency Savings Breaks the Cycle of Debt

With some money in emergency savings, perhaps $500 or $2000, to pay for vehicle repairs and unexpected travel, you never will have to pay with plastic for things that are not in your budget.

Debt Service-to-Income Ratio: Can I Meet My Total Debt Obligations?

The **debt service-to-income ratio** provides a view of your total debt burden by comparing the dollars spent on gross annual debt repayments (including rent or mortgage payments) with gross annual income. A ratio of 0.36 or less is desirable. Using data in Table 3.5, Equation (3.5) shows that the Hernandezes' $16,400 in annual loan repayments ($12,000 for the mortgage loan and $4400 for the automobile loan) amount to 24.85 percent of their $66,000 annual income. A ratio of 0.36 or less indicates that gross income is adequate to make debt repayments, including housing costs, and implies that you usually have some flexibility in budgeting for other expenses. This ratio should decrease as you grow older.

debt service-to-income ratio Compares dollars spent on gross annual debt with gross annual income.

$$\text{Debt service-to-income ratio} = \frac{\text{annual debt repayments}}{\text{gross income}} = \frac{\$16{,}400}{\$66{,}000} = 24.85\% \quad (3.5)$$

Debt Payments-to-Disposable Income Ratio: Can I Pay My Debts?

The **debt payments-to-disposable income ratio** divides monthly disposable personal income (not gross income) into monthly debt repayments (excluding mortgage debt). (**Disposable personal income** is the amount of your income remaining after taxes and withholdings for such purposes as insurance and union dues.) It estimates funds available for debt repayment. A ratio of 15 percent or less is desirable. A debt payments-to-disposable income ratio of 16 percent or more is considered problematic because the person is making high debt payments and quickly would be in serious financial trouble if a disruption in income occurred.

debt payments-to-disposable income ratio Divides monthly disposable personal income into monthly debt repayments.

disposable personal income Amount of income remaining after taxes and withholding.

In the Hernandezes' case, their disposable monthly income from Table 3.5 is $3932.50 [($66,000 − $2980 − $6800 − $3100 − $720 − $4260 − $950) ÷ 12]. Their monthly debt repayments from Table 3.5 are $366.67 ($4400 ÷ 12). The result using Equation (3.6) is a debt payments-to-disposable income ratio of 9.32 percent.

$$\text{Debt payments-to-disposable income ratio} = \frac{\text{monthly nonmortgage debt repayments}}{\text{disposable income}} = \frac{\$366.67}{\$3932.50} = 9.32\% \quad (3.6)$$

Investment Assets-to-Total Assets Ratio: Do I Need to Invest More?

The **investment assets-to-total assets ratio** compares the value of your investment assets with your net worth. This ratio reveals how well an individual or family is advancing toward their financial goals for capital accumulation, especially as related to retirement. A ratio of 50 percent or higher is desirable. A ratio of 10 percent might be appropriate for people in their 20s, 11 to 30 percent for those in their 30s, and above 30 percent for people in their 40s. Inserting the data from their balance sheet in Table 3.3 into Equation (3.7) shows that the Hernandezes have a ratio of 0.352 or 35.2 percent. As you can see, a little more than one-third of their total assets is made up of investment assets, a typical proportion for this stage in their lives.

investment assets-to-total assets ratio Compares investment asset value with net worth.

$$\text{Investment assets-to-total assets ratio} = \frac{\text{investment assets}}{\text{total assets}} = \frac{\$109{,}000}{\$309{,}920} = 0.352 \qquad (3.7)$$

Other Ways to Assess Financial Progress

You can use other data from your balance sheet and cash-flow statement to help analyze your finances. Consider the assets listed on the balance sheet for Victor and Maria Hernandez in Table 3.3. Do they have too few monetary assets compared with tangible and investment assets? Experts recommend that 15 to 20 percent of your assets be in monetary form and that this proportion increase as you near retirement. Do you have too much invested in one asset, or have you diversified, like the Hernandezes? Have your balance sheet figures changed in a favorable direction since last year? Is a growing proportion of your income coming from your investments? Are you making progress toward your financial goals? If not, ask: "Am I spending money where I really want to?" "In which categories can I reduce expenses?" "Could I increase income?"

CONCEPT CHECK 3.2

1. Distinguish between the basic liquidity ratio and debt-service-to-income ratio.

Financial Record Keeping Saves Time and Makes You Money

4 LEARNING OBJECTIVE
Maintain the financial records necessary for managing your personal finances.

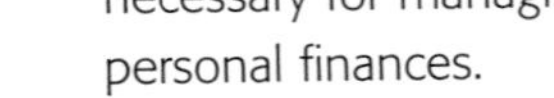

financial records Documents that evidence financial transactions.

Financial records are documents that evidence financial transactions, such as bills, receipts, credit card receipts and statements, bank records, tax returns, brokerage statements, and paycheck stubs. Your financial records will help determine where you are, where you have been, and where you are going financially. They also help you save money as well as make money. Good records enable you to review the results of financial transactions as well as permit other family members to find them in an emergency. Organized records help you take advantage of all available tax deductions when filing income taxes and provide you with more dollars to spend, save, invest, or donate. Table 3.6 shows categories of financial records and the contents that might be included in each.

Some records may be safely stored at home in a fire-resistant file cabinet or a safe. Other records should be kept in a **safe-deposit box.** Safe-deposit boxes are secured lock boxes available for rent ($50 to $250 per year) in banks. Two keys are used to open such a box. The customer keeps one key, and the bank holds the other. Many people keep duplicates of important records at their workplace or with relatives because the likelihood of records at both locations being stolen or destroyed simultaneously is very small. You can purge or shred some of your records when you no longer need them, such as non-tax-related checks and credit card receipts more than a year old, expired insurance policies, and financial reports when supplanted with updated summary information.

CONCEPT CHECK 3.2

1. List some advantages of keeping good financial records.
2. Name three financial records that might best be kept in a safe-deposit box.

Table 3.6 Financial Records: What to Keep and Where

Category	Contents: In Home Files and Fireproof Home Safe	Contents: In Safe-Deposit Box
Financial plans/ budgeting	Financial plans Balance sheets and cash-flow statements Current budget List of safe-deposit box contents Names and contact information for financial advisers	Names and contact information for financial advisers Copy of written financial plans, goals, and budgets
Career and employment	Current résumé College transcripts Letters of recommendation Employee benefits descriptions Written career plans	
Banking and financial services	Checkbook, unused checks, and canceled checks List of locations and account numbers for all bank accounts Checking and savings account statements Locations and access numbers for safe-deposit boxes Account transaction receipts	List of financial institutions and account numbers for all financial services accounts Certificates of deposit
Taxes	Copies of all income tax returns, both state and federal, for the past three years, including all supporting documentation Receipts for all donations of cash or property Log of volunteer expenses Receipts for property taxes paid	Copies of all income tax filings, both state and federal, for the past three years Records of securities purchased and sold
Credit	Utility and telephone bills Monthly credit card statements Receipts of credit payments List of credit accounts and telephone numbers to report lost/stolen cards Unused credit cards Credit reports and scores	List of credit accounts and telephone numbers to report lost/stolen cards
Housing, vehicles, and consumer purchases	Copies of legal documents (leases, mortgage, deeds, titles) Property appraisals and inspection reports Home repair/home improvement receipts Warranties Owners manuals for purchases Auto registration records Vehicle service and repair receipts Receipts for important purchases	Original legal documents (leases, mortgage, deeds, titles) Copies of property appraisals Vehicle purchase contracts (until vehicle is sold) Photographs or videos of valuable possessions
Insurance	Original insurance policies List of insurance policies with premium amounts and due dates Premium payment receipts Calculation of life insurance needs Insurance claims forms and reports Medical records for family, including immunization records and list of prescription drugs	List of all insurance policies with company and agent names and addresses and policy numbers Listing with photographs or videotape of personal property
Investments	Records of stock, bond, and mutual fund transactions and certificate numbers Mutual fund statements Statements from brokers Reports from financial planner Company annual reports Retirement plan quarterly and annual reports Documents on business interests Written investment philosophy Written investment strategies	Contact information for all investment needs Stock and bond certificates Rare coins, stamps, and other collectibles

Continued

Table 3.6 Financial Records: What to Keep and Where—cont'd

Category	Contents: In Home Files and Fireproof Home Safe	Contents: In Safe-Deposit Box
Retirement	Pension and retirement plan information Retirement statements Copies of all retirement plan transactions Copy of Social Security card Trust agreements Information on Social Security	Extra copy of all retirement plan transactions and statements
Estate planning	Copy of will Copies of advance directives (wills, living wills, medical powers of attorney, durable powers of attorney with originals with attorney) Copies of trust documents (originals with trustees/attorney)	Copy of will (original of all estate planning documents should be placed in attorney's office)
Personal information	Copy of birth certificate and marriage license Religious documents Copy of divorce decree, property settlement, and custody agreement Receipts for alimony and child support payments Custodial information for your children, relatives, and/or elderly parent	Passports while not being used Military and adoption papers Originals of birth, marriage, death certificates Originals of Social Security cards Originals of divorce decrees, property settlements, and custody agreements Master list of all important documents and their location Memory stick or CD containing soft copies of many financial records

Reaching Your Goals Through Budgeting: Your Spending/Savings Action Plan

5 LEARNING OBJECTIVE
Achieve your financial goals through budgeting.

Your financial success is largely a matter of choice, not a matter of chance. Your budget is where you make and implement those choices. Your budget is your plan for spending and saving. Budgeting forces you to consider what is important in your life, what things you want to own, how you want to live, what it will take to do that, and, more generally, what you want to achieve in life. The budgeting process gives you control over your finances, and it empowers you to achieve your financial goals while simultaneously (and successfully) confronting any unforeseen events. In short, budgeting answers the question, "What is my spending/savings action plan?"

Some people do all their budgeting mentally—and do so successfully. Good for them! Many of us, however, need to see the actual numbers on paper or on a computer screen. A **budget** is a paper or electronic document used to record both planned and actual income and expenditures over a period of time. Your budget represents the major mechanism through which your financial plans are carried out and goals are achieved.

budget Paper or electronic document used to record both planned and actual income and expenditures over a period of time.

Figure 3.4 illustrates how to think about financial statements and budgeting. The cash-flow statement focuses on *where you have been* financially, the balance sheet shows *where you are* financially at the current time, and the budget indicates *where you want to go* in the future.

Action Before: Set Financial Goals

Creating and following a spending plan has three stages: before, during, and after. Before establishing your budget, take action to set financial goals. **Long-term goals** are financial targets or ends that an individual or family wants to achieve perhaps more than five years in the future. Such goals provide direction for overall financial plan-

long-term goals Financial targets to achieve more than five years in the future.

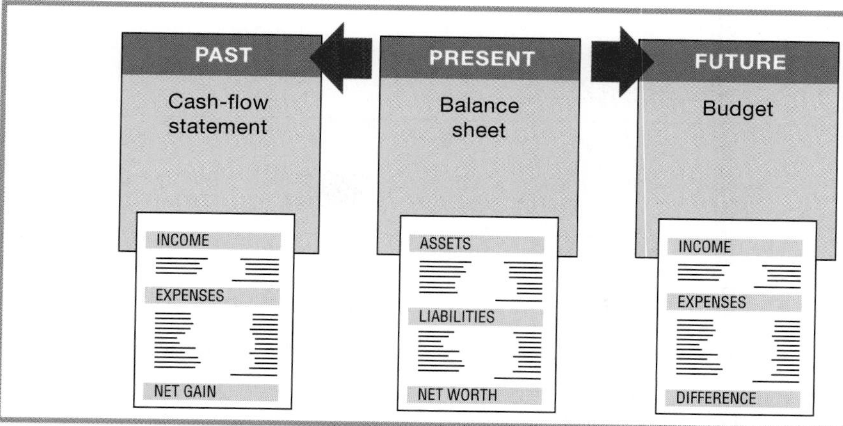

Figure 3.4
About Financial Statements and Budgets

ning as well as shorter-term budgeting. An example of a long-term goal is to create a $1 million retirement fund by age 60. Goals must be specific. They should contain dollar-amount targets and target dates for achievement.

If you have a small income or large debts, it may be unrealistic to think of long-term goals until any current financial difficulties are resolved. You may be unable to do much more than take care of immediate necessities, such as housing expenses, food, and utility bills. In such instances, you need to focus on short-term efforts to improve your financial situation. You may need to focus on paying down debt, not adding to it.

Intermediate-term goals are financial targets that can be achieved between one year and perhaps three to five years. Examples of intermediate-term goals are creating an emergency fund amounting to three months of income within four years, saving $22,500 within three years for a down payment on a home, taking a $4000 vacation to China in two years, paying off $8000 in credit card debt in one and a half years, and paying off a college loan in five years. **Short-term goals** are financial targets or ends that can be achieved in less than a year, such as finishing college, paying off an auto loan, increasing savings, purchasing assets (i.e., vehicle, furniture, television, stereo, clothes), reducing high-interest debt, taking an annual vacation, attending a wedding, buying life insurance, and making plans for retirement.

You need to be as clear as possible about what your financial goals are. The goals worksheet in Figure 3.5 (page 80) provides examples of how much to save to reach long-, intermediate-, and short-term goals. People can view such savings as a fixed expenditure (such as withholding from a paycheck to contribute to an employer's retirement plan or to transfer to a savings account). Other savings may be a variable such as saving what is left over after all expenditures are made.

Prioritizing your goals makes sense. But what are your most important goals? One certain priority should be to pay off high-interest credit cards as soon as possible. Another is to contribute as much as you can afford to a retirement plan. Many college graduates buy a new car soon after getting their first job to celebrate having "made it." Before you're lured into following suit, give careful consideration to your priorities and remember that every action carries not only the dollar cost of the action taken but also the opportunity cost of the alternatives forgone. To achieve your long-term goals, you may have to sacrifice by deferring some of your short-term desires.

Did You Know?...

Wealth-Building Principles

1. Set financial goals and objectives.
2. Find money to save and pay off high-cost debt.
3. Start early.
4. Save automatically.
5. Take advantage of free dollars at work.
6. Use government tax breaks.
7. Buy a home and pay it off.
8. Don't spend accumulated wealth without good reason.
9. Make wealth accumulation, not consumption, your main financial priority.
10. Be patient and optimistic.

Source: National City Corporation, NationalCity.com. Used with permission.

intermediate-term goals Financial targets that can be achieved within one to five years.

Figure 3.5
Goals Worksheet for Harry and Belinda Johnson

Date worksheet prepared Feb. 20, 2008

1 LONG-TERM GOALS	2 AMOUNT NEEDED	3 MONTH & YEAR NEEDED*	4 MONTHS TO SAVE	5 DATE START SAVING	6 MONTHLY AMOUNT TO SAVE (2 ÷ 4)
European vacation	$3,000	Aug. 2010	30	Feb. '08	$100
Down payment on new auto	5,000	Oct. 2011	45	Jan. '08	111

Date worksheet prepared Feb. 20, 2008

1 INTERMEDIATE-TERM GOALS	2 AMOUNT NEEDED	3 MONTH & YEAR NEEDED*	4 MONTHS TO SAVE	5 DATE START SAVING	6 MONTHLY AMOUNT TO SAVE (2 ÷ 4)
Down payment on home	$26,078	Dec. 2013	60	Jan. '08	$435

Date worksheet prepared Feb. 20, 2008

1 SHORT-TERM GOALS	2 AMOUNT NEEDED	3 MONTH & YEAR NEEDED*	4 MONTHS TO SAVE	5 DATE START SAVING	6 MONTHLY AMOUNT TO SAVE (2 ÷ 4)
Partial down payment on new auto	$1,332	Dec. '08	12	Jan. '08	$111
House fund	4,815	Dec. '08	12	Jan. '08	401
Christmas vacation	700	Dec. '08	12	Jan. '08	58
Summer vacation	600	Aug. '08	6	Mar. '08	100
Anniversary party	250	June '08	5	Feb. '08	50

*Goals requiring five years or more to achieve require consideration of investment return and after-tax yield, which will be presented in Chapter 4.

Action Before: Make and Reconcile Budget Estimates

Before the month begins, you make and reconcile budget estimates of income and expenditures. Here you resolve conflicting needs and wants by revising estimates as necessary. You can't have everything in life—especially this month—even though you might want it.

budget estimates Projected dollar amounts to receive or spend in a budgeting period.

take-home pay/disposable income Pay received after employer withholdings for taxes, insurance, and union dues.

discretionary income Money left over after necessities such as housing and food are paid for.

Make Budget Estimates **Budget estimates** are the projected dollar amounts in a budget that one plans to receive or spend during the period covered by the budget. Begin by estimating total gross income from all sources, and review take-home pay and then discretionary income. For example, Jonny Deppe's annual gross income is $60,000 and after employer withholdings for taxes, insurance, and union dues, his **take-home pay** (also called **disposable income**) is $48,000. This is the money available for spending, saving, investing, and donating. Focus also on your **discretionary income.** This is the money left over once the necessities of living are covered, such as paying for housing, food, and other necessities. It is usually the money that is really "controllable" and often makes up the bulk of your variable expenses. After Jonny pays his rent, food, utilities, and car payment, his discretionary income is $18,000.

Table 3.7 presents budget estimates for a college student, a single working person, a young married couple, a married couple with two young children, and a married couple with two college-age children. The college student's budget requires monthly withdrawals of previously deposited savings to make ends meet. The single working person's budget allows for an automobile loan, but not much else. The young married couple's budget permits one automobile loan, an investment program, contributions to individual retirement accounts, and significant spending on food and entertainment. The budget of the married couple with two young children allows for only an inexpensive automobile loan payment even though one spouse has a part-time job to help with the finances. The budget of the married couple with two college-age children permits a home mortgage payment, ownership of two paid-for automobiles, savings and investment programs, and a substantial contribution for college expenses.

It is essential to make reasonable budget estimates. If you have seven Christmas gifts to buy and expect to spend $50 for each, it's easy to make an estimate of $350. If you want to go out to dinner once each week at $50 per meal, estimate an expense of $200 per month. Avoid using unrealistically low figures by simply being fair and honest in your estimates. Then add up your totals.

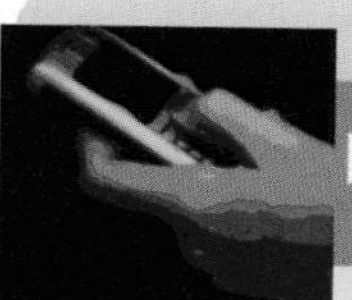

Instant Message

Set Reachable Goals at First

Establishing unrealistic short-term goals sets up a high likelihood of failure. Instead, set financial targets that are almost too easy to meet. For example, you may want to save $350 per month to use as a down payment on a home in five years. That may seem like a lot. Start perhaps painlessly by saving $100 per month for a few months. Then put away $150 for two months, $200 for two months, then $250, then $300, and finally $350.

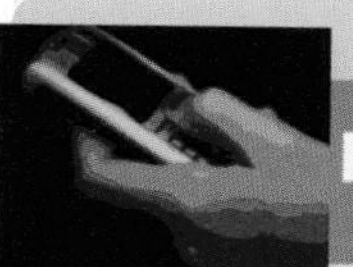

Instant Message

List the Benefits of Reaching Your Financial Goals

List the benefits to yourself that will occur when you reach a particular financial goal. You are likely to achieve a financial goal when you are convinced that it is "your goal," when you make an emotional commitment to the goal, when your short-term goals lead to your long-term goals, and when you can visualize receiving the benefits of your goals.

Revise Budget Estimates Sometimes the math is alarming! When initial expense estimates exceed income estimates, three choices are available: (1) earn more income, (2) cut back on expenses, or (3) try a combination of more income and fewer expenses. The process of reconciling needs and wants is a healthy exercise. It helps identify your priorities by telling you what is important in your life at the current time, and it identifies areas of sacrifice that you might make. Revising your short-term financial goals may also be required.

You have no choice: You must reconcile conflicting wants to revise your budget until total expenses do not exceed income. Perhaps you can change some "must have" items to "maybe next year" purchases. Perhaps you can keep some quality items but reduce their quantity. For example, instead of $200 for four meals at restaurants each month, consider dining out twice each month at $60 per meal. You'll save $40 and still have two really nice meals. Your actions on money matters override your words, so act accordingly.

Table 3.8 presents the annual budget for Harry and Belinda Johnson and reflects their efforts to reconcile their budget estimates until the total planned expenses fall below the total planned income. Harry and Belinda are "paying themselves first," in the amount of $400 per month, to save to buy their own home. The Johnsons have a little way to go to fully reconcile their annual budget estimates.

Action Before: Plan Cash Flows

Before the month begins, you plan your cash flows. Income usually remains somewhat constant month after month, but expenses do rise and fall sharply. As a result, people occasionally complain that they are "broke, out of money, and sick of budgeting." This challenge can be anticipated by using a cash-flow calendar and eliminated with a revolving savings fund.

The budget estimates for monthly income and expenses in Table 3.8 have been recast in summary form in Table 3.9, providing a **cash-flow calendar** for the Johnsons. This is a very useful budgeting tool. Annual estimated income and expenses are recorded in this calendar for each budgeting time period in an effort to identify surplus or deficit situations. In the Johnsons' case, planned annual income exceeds

cash-flow calendar Budget estimates for monthly income and expenses.

Table 3.7 Sample Monthly Budgets for Various Family Units

Classifications	College Student	Single Working Person	Young Married Couple	Married Couple with Two Young Children	Married Couple with Two College-Age Children
INCOME					
Salary	$ 300	$2800	$2200	$3500	$4400
Salary	0	0	2100	860	1600
Interest and dividends	5	15	15	15	80
Loans/scholarships	300	0	0	0	0
Savings withdrawals	570	0	0	0	500
Total Income	$1175	$2815	$4315	$4375	$6580
EXPENSES					
Fixed Expenses					
Retirement contributions	$ 0	$ 20	$ 360	$ 180	$ 340
IRA	0	20	160	180	200
Savings (withheld)	0	20	20	10	100
Housing	350	750	900	1100	1300
Health insurance	0	0	60	150	140
Life and disability insurance	0	0	20	60	40
Homeowner's or renter's insurance	0	0	40	60	80
Automobile insurance	0	80	90	60	140
Automobile payments	0	280	345	220	0
Loan 1 (TV and stereo)	0	80	80	40	0
Loan 2 (other)	0	40	40	0	50
Federal and state taxes	30	455	715	600	710
Social Security taxes	23	210	330	305	385
Real estate taxes	0	0	0	0	40
Investments	0	0	60	100	300
Total Fixed Expenses	$ 403	$1955	$3220	$3065	$3825
Variable Expenses					
Other savings	$ 0	$ 60	$ 150	$ 0	$ 0
Food	180	230	270	340	350
Utilities	40	80	90	140	145
Automobile gas, oil, maintenance	0	90	110	90	100
Medical	10	30	40	70	50
Child care	0	0	0	260	0
Clothing	20	50	60	50	40
Gifts and contributions	10	20	40	60	80
Allowances	20	75	60	100	180
Education	400	0	0	0	1500
Furnishing and appliances	10	10	30	20	20
Personal care	10	45	25	30	30
Entertainment	40	120	100	60	120
Vacations	17	30	40	30	60
Miscellaneous	15	20	80	60	80
Total variable expenses	$ 772	$ 860	$1095	$1310	$2755
Total Expenses	$1175	$2815	$4315	$4375	$6580

Table 3.8 Annual Budget Estimates for 2009 for Harry and Belinda Johnson

	Jan.	Feb.	Mar.	Apr.	May	June	July	Aug.	Sept.	Oct.	Nov.	Dec.	Yearly Total	Monthly Average
INCOME														
Harry's salary	$2,500	$2,500	$2,500	$2,500	$2,500	$2,500	$2,575	$2,575	$2,575	$2,575	$2,575	$2,575	$30,450	$2,537.50
Belinda's salary	3,000	3,000	3,300	3,300	3,300	3,300	3,300	3,300	3,300	3,300	3,300	3,300	39,000	3,250.00
Interest	24	24	24	25	26	27	27	28	30	31	33	33	332	27.67
Trust	0	0	0	0	0	0	0	0	3,000	0	0	0	3,000	250.00
Total Income	**$5,524**	**$5,524**	**$5,824**	**$5,825**	**$5,826**	**$5,827**	**$5,902**	**$5,903**	**$8,905**	**$5,906**	**$5,908**	**$5,908**	**$72,782**	**$6,065.17**
EXPENSES														
Fixed Expenses														
Rent	$ 900	$ 900	$ 900	$ 900	$ 900	$ 900	$ 950	$ 950	$ 950	$ 950	$ 950	$ 950	$11,100	$ 925.00
Health insurance	135	135	135	135	135	135	135	135	135	135	135	135	1,620	135.00
Life insurance	9	9	9	9	9	9	9	9	9	9	9	9	108	9.00
Home purchase fund	400	400	400	400	400	400	400	400	400	400	400	400	4,800	400.00
Renter's insurance	0	0	0	0	0	220	0	0	0	0	0	0	220	18.33
Automobile insurance	0	0	0	0	0	440	0	0	0	0	0	440	880	73.33
Auto loan payment	285	285	285	285	285	285	285	285	285	285	285	285	3,420	285.00
Student loan	145	145	145	145	145	145	145	145	145	145	145	145	1,740	145.00
Savings/emergencies	24	24	70	150	85	150	150	28	150	150	150	150	1,281	106.75
Harry's retirement plan	150	150	150	150	150	150	154	154	154	154	154	154	1,824	152.00
Belinda's retirement	120	120	132	132	132	132	132	132	132	132	132	132	1,560	130.00
Health club	50	50	50	50	50	50	50	50	50	50	50	50	600	50.00
Cable television	35	35	35	35	35	35	35	35	35	35	35	35	420	35.00
Federal income taxes	767	767	848	848	848	848	854	854	854	854	854	854	10,050	837.50
State income taxes	266	266	284	284	284	284	289	289	289	289	289	289	3,402	283.50
Social Security	421	421	444	444	444	444	450	450	450	450	450	450	5,318	443.17
Total fixed expenses	$3,707	$3,707	$3,887	$3,967	$3,902	$4,627	$4,038	$3,916	$4,038	$4,038	$4,038	$4,478	$48,343	$4,028.58
Variable Expenses														
Savings/investments	$ 0	$ 0	$ 0	$ 0	$ 0	$ 0	$ 0	$ 0	$3,000	$ 0	$ 0	$ 0	$3,000	$ 250.00
Revolving savings fund	140	140	140	140	140	0	250	0	215	190	0	0	1,355	112.92
Food	350	350	350	350	350	350	350	350	350	350	350	350	4,200	350.00
Utilities	150	150	150	150	100	100	100	100	100	125	125	150	1,500	125.00
Telephone	70	70	70	70	70	70	70	70	70	70	70	90	860	71.67
Auto expenses	115	115	115	115	115	115	115	115	115	115	115	115	1,380	115.00
Medical	100	100	100	100	100	100	100	100	100	100	100	100	1,200	100.00
Clothing	180	180	180	180	180	180	180	180	180	180	180	180	2,160	180.00
Church and charity	100	100	100	100	175	100	100	100	100	100	100	100	1,275	106.25
Gifts	80	80	160	75	120	20	20	60	60	60	60	20	815	67.92
Christmas gifts	0	0	0	0	0	0	0	0	0	0	400	300	700	58.33
Public transportation	60	60	60	60	60	60	60	60	60	60	60	60	720	60.00
Personal allowances	200	200	200	200	200	200	200	200	200	200	200	200	2,400	200.00
Entertainment/meals	240	240	240	240	240	240	240	240	240	240	240	240	2,880	240.00
Automobile license	0	0	0	0	0	40	0	0	0	0	0	0	40	3.33
Vacation (Christmas)	0	0	0	0	0	0	0	0	0	0	0	700	700	58.33
Vacation (summer)	0	0	0	0	0	0	0	600	0	0	0	0	600	50.00
Anniversary party	0	0	0	0	0	250	0	0	0	0	0	0	250	20.83
Miscellaneous	32	32	72	78	74	75	79	62	77	78	75	75	809	67.42
Total variable expenses	$1,817	$1,817	$1,937	$1,858	$1,924	$1,900	$1,864	$2,237	$4,867	$1,868	$2,075	$2,680	$26,844	$2,237
Total Expenses	**$5,524**	**$5,524**	**$5,824**	**$5,825**	**$5,826**	**$6,527**	**$5,902**	**$6,153**	**$8,905**	**$5,906**	**$6,113**	**$7,158**	**$75,187**	**$6,265.58**
Difference (available for spending, saving, and investing)	$0	$0	$0	$0	$0	−$700	$0	−$250	$0	$0	−$205	−$1,250	−$2,405	
Revolving savings withdrawals						700		250			205	200	1355	
Uncovered shortfall	$0	$0	$0	$0	$0	$0	$0	$0	$0	$0	$0	−$1,050	−$1,050	

Table 3.9 Cash-Flow Calendar for Harry and Belinda Johnson

Month	1 Estimated Income	2 Estimated Expenses	3 Surplus/Deficit (1 − 2)	4 Cumulative Surplus/Deficit
January	$ 5,524	$ 5,524	$ 0	$ 0
February	5,524	5,524	0	0
March	5,824	5,824	0	0
April	5,825	5,825	0	0
May	5,826	5,826	0	0
June	5,827	6,527	−700	−700
July	5,902	5,902	0	−700
August	5,903	6,153	−250	−950
September	8,905	8,905	0	−950
October	5,906	5,906	0	−950
November	5,908	6,113	−205	−1,155
December	5,908	7,158	−1,250	−2,405
Total	**$72,782**	**$75,187**	**−2,405**	

revolving savings fund Variable budgeting tool that places funds in savings to cover large irregular or higher-than-usual expenses.

Instant Message

Rules for Successful Budgeting

1. Keep it simple.
2. Make it personal.
3. Keep it flexible.
4. Be positive.

Instant Message

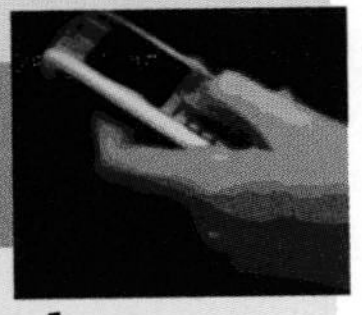

Cut the Dollars Not the Pennies

Harvard law professor and bankruptcy expert Elizabeth Warren says that you should not cut out the caffe lattes to manage your money better. Instead of making penny cuts, enjoy the coffee and then make real dollar cuts elsewhere in your spending such as in housing, cars, preschool, child care, and health care. And cut back on the credit card charges.

expenses. The couple starts out the year with many expenses, resulting in deficits for the next six months. Later in the year, income usually exceeds expenses, but they are still faced with a deficit at year's end.

Effective management of cash flow can involve curtailing expenses during months with financial deficits, increasing income, using savings, or borrowing. If you borrow money and pay finance charges, the credit costs will further increase your monthly expenses.

For this reason alone, it is smart to "borrow from yourself" by using a **revolving savings fund.** This is a variable expense classification budgeting tool into which funds are allocated in an effort to create savings that can be used to balance the budget later so as to avoid running out of money. Establishing such a fund involves planning ahead—much like a college student does when saving money all summer (creating a revolving savings fund) to draw on during the school months. You establish a revolving savings fund for two purposes: (1) to accumulate funds for large irregular expenses, such as automobile insurance premiums, medical costs, Christmas gifts, and vacations, and (2) to meet occasional deficits due to income fluctuations.

Table 3.10 shows the Johnsons' revolving savings fund. When preparing their budget, the Johnsons realized that in June, August, November, and December they were going to have significant deficits. They decided to begin setting aside $140 per month to cover the June deficit. To do so, they decided to wait to start building their emergency fund. By June they had $700 in their revolving savings fund to cover the June deficit. Continued use of the revolving savings fund helped them meet the August and November deficits as well.

The Johnsons will still be $1050 short in December. Lacking that much money, the couple has three alternatives: (1) use some of Harry's trust fund money to cover the deficit, (2) dip into their

Table 3.10 Revolving Savings Fund for Harry and Belinda Johnson

Month	Large Expenses	Amount Needed	Deposit into Fund	Withdrawal from Fund	Fund Balance
January		$ 0	$ 140	$ 0	$ 140
February		0	140	0	280
March		0	140	0	420
April		0	140	0	560
May		0	140	0	700
June	Party and insurance	700	0	700	0
July		0	250	0	250
August	Vacation	250	0	250	0
September		0	215	0	215
October		0	190	0	405
November	Holiday gifts	205	0	205	200
December	Holiday gifts and vacation	1250	0	200	0
Total		**$2405**	**$1355**	**$1355**	**–$1050**

emergency savings in December, or (3) cut back on their expenses enough throughout the year to create sufficient surpluses. Ideally, the Johnsons want to have sufficient emergency funds by the end of the year to establish their revolving savings fund for the following year. Cutting back on expenses may be their best option.

Did You Know?...

The Top 3 Financial Missteps in Budget Planning

People slip up in budget planning when they do the following:

1. Fail to plan for occasional, nonmonthly expenditures
2. Underestimate how much they spend each month
3. Use credit cards to "balance" their budget

Action During Budgeting Period: Control Spending

Budget controls are techniques to maintain control over personal spending so that planned amounts are not exceeded. They give feedback on whether spending is on target and provide information on overspending, errors, emergencies, and exceptions or omissions. Following are examples of budget controls:

Monitor Unexpended Balances to Control Overspending The number one method to control overspending is to monitor unexpended balances in each of your budget classifications. You can accomplish this task by using a budget design that keeps a declining balance, as illustrated by parts (a) and (b) of Figure 3.6 (page 89). Other budget designs, such as those shown in parts (c) and (d) of Figure 3.6, need to be monitored differently. As illustrated in parts (c) and (d) of the figure, simply calculate subtotals every week or so, as needed, during a monthly budgeting period.

Budget for Shopping Trips Set a budget for every shopping trip, and don't spend a penny more.

Use a Subordinate Budget A **subordinate budget** is a detailed listing of planned expenses within a single budgeting classification. For example, an estimate of $1200 for a vacation could be supported by a subordinate budget as follows: motel, $700; restaurants, $300; and entertainment, $200.

subordinate budget Detailed listing of planned expenses within a single budgeting classification.

Pay by Check to Record the Purpose of Expenditures Each check contains a space to record the purpose. The check stub or register also provides a place to record explanations of expenditures. If you use automatic teller machines (ATMs) to withdraw cash or use debit cards to pay for day-to-day expenditures, record these withdrawals in the check register *immediately*. Retain the paperwork and write the purpose of each expense on the back of each. Deposit all checks received to your checking account without receiving a portion in cash; if you need cash, write a check or make an ATM withdrawal.

Keep Track of Credit Transactions Some people do not record their credit transactions until they receive a statement. It is easy to continue buying on credit without recognizing the amount of indebtedness until the statement arrives. Record each credit transaction when it occurs; if you misplace a receipt, you still have a record available for verification.

budget exceptions When budget estimates differ from actual expenditures.

Justify Exceptions to Avoid Lying to Yourself **Budget exceptions** occur when budget estimates in various classifications differ from actual expenditures. Exceptions usually take the form of overexpenditures, but can also occur in the over- or underreceipt of earnings. Simply spending extra income instead of recording it is not being honest with yourself. Recording the truth—by writing a few words to explain the exception—gives you the information to control your finances. If the exception is an expenditure, then immediately determine how to make up for the overexpenditure by reducing other expenses in your spending plan.

envelope system Placing exact amounts into envelopes for each budgetary purpose.

For the Strongest Control, Use the Envelope System The **envelope system** of budgeting entails placing exact amounts of money into envelopes for purposes of strict budgetary control. Here you place money equal to the budget estimate for the various expenditure classifications in envelopes at the start of a budgeting period and write the classification name and the budget amount on the outside of each envelope. As expenditures are made, record them on the appropriate envelope and remove the proper amounts of cash. When an envelope is empty, funds are exhausted for that classification.

Action After: Evaluate Budgeting Progress

budget variance Difference between amount budgeted and actual amount spent or received.

Evaluation occurs at the end of each budgeting cycle. The purpose is to determine whether the earlier steps in your budgeting efforts have worked, and it gives you feedback to use for the next budget cycle. You review by comparing actual amounts with budgeted amounts, evaluating whether your objectives were met, and assessing the success of the overall process as well as your progress toward your short- and long-term goals.

In some budget expenditure classifications, the budget estimates rarely agree with the actual expenditures—particularly in variable expenses. A **budget variance** is the difference between the amount budgeted and the actual amount spent or received. The remarks column, as illustrated in parts (c) and (d) of Figure 3.6 (page 89), can help clarify why variances occurred. Overages on a few expenditures may cause little concern. If excessive variances have prevented you from achieving your objectives or making the budget balance, then take some action. Serious budget controls might have to be instituted or current controls tightened.

Whatever your goals, it feels good when you make progress toward them, and it is thrilling to achieve them. If you did not achieve some of your objectives, you can determine why and then adjust your budget and objectives accordingly. It is "okay" to revise your plans. Suppose the Johnsons find that they are unable to set aside the

Instant Message

Get Started on a Wealth-Building Goal

Set a wealth-building goal and strategy that will allow you to achieve the goal, such as building a retirement fund by contributing to a 401(k) retirement plan or saving for the down payment on a home. Find the money to save by reducing expenses or earning extra income.

Keep to a budget when shopping, and use checks to keep track of purchases.

planned $400 for their new home. By evaluating their budget, they find that unexpected medical expenses and an out-of-state trip to visit a sick relative led them to dip into their savings. Because they understand why the objective was not achieved, they can set their sights on reaching the goal during the next budgeting time period.

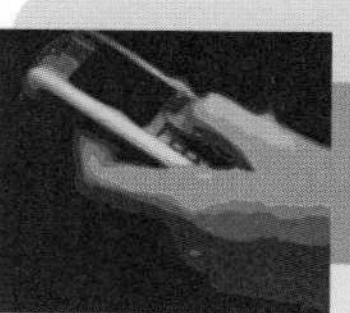

Instant Message

Manage Your Finances Using Web Portals

Some comprehensive Web portals on personal finances are Yahoo! Finance (finance.yahoo.com), MSN Money Central (moneycentral.com), and Quicken.com (quicken.com). You will find all kinds of easy-to-use financial tools, including bill paying, banking, vehicle loan rate comparisons, mortgage shopping, online tax preparation, stock screening, stock quotes, online brokers, retirement calculators, and breaking news stories.

Financial Software and Planning Tools Make Managing Your Money a Snap

Financial software and planning tools, including many on the Internet, make managing your money—including record keeping—a snap. Financial software offers many benefits. Laborious calculations are sharply reduced, banking transactions can be performed with automatic updating of financial records, the balance sheet and cash-flow statements are automatically updated when transactions occur, and your financial plans can be developed.

Quicken and Microsoft Money are the two most popular user-friendly brands of personal finance software. Both provide complete financial planning systems. Several other programs focus primarily on income tax preparation, including TurboTax, which works with your day-to-day financial software to help you do your taxes. Many companies have financial planning tools and calculators on their websites, including CNNmoney.com, Fool.com, Kiplinger.com, USAToday.com, and Yahoo.com.

Record Keeping In the process of budgeting, **record keeping** is the process of recording the sources and amounts of dollars earned and spent. Recording the estimated and actual amounts for both income and expenditures helps you monitor your money flow. Keeping track of income and expenses is the only way to collect sufficient information to evaluate how close you are to achieving your financial objectives. For those who keep records on paper, Figure 3.6 shows four samples of self-prepared record-keeping formats that vary in complexity. Most people record earnings and expenditures when they occur. When writing in the "activity" and "remarks" columns in your record, be descriptive because you may need the information later.

record keeping Recording sources and amounts of dollars earned and spent.

Advice from a Pro

Crisis Steps to Take If Budget Deficits Occur Repeatedly

If you always run out of money before the month is over, you may need to take some drastic steps to get your finances under control. Consider the following:

1. Stop using credit cards.
2. Spend only cash or money that you have, and leave debit and credit cards at home.
3. Stop making ATM withdrawals and getting cash back from purchases to use for pocket money.
4. Reduce or stop spending on luxuries such as eating out, clothing, movies, entertainment, memberships, hobbies, clothing, CDs, DVDs, and expanded cable channels.
5. Drop landline telephone service and use only a cell phone.
6. Use a list when shopping, and stick to it.
7. Avoid shopping malls and discount stores.
8. Sell an asset, especially one that requires additional expenses, such as a second car.
9. Move to lower-cost housing.
10. Increase income by working overtime or finding a second job.

Alena C. Johnson
Utah State University

Adding Up Actual Income and Expenditures After the budgeting period has ended—usually at the beginning of a new month—you need to add up the actual income received and expenditures made during that period. You can perform this calculation on a form for each budget classification, as shown in parts (a) and (b) of Figure 3.6 or on a form with all income and expenditure classifications, as in parts (c) and (d) of Figure 3.6. Such calculations indicate where you may have overspent within your budget categories. If you are new at budgeting, do not be too concerned about overspending; it occurs in some classifications almost always, only to be balanced by underspending in other categories. Use such information to refine your budget estimates in the future. In three or four months, you will be able to estimate your expenses much more accurately. The *Garman/Forgue* website provides budgeting software as well as numerous other templates, calculators, and worksheets that you can use in your own personal financial planning.

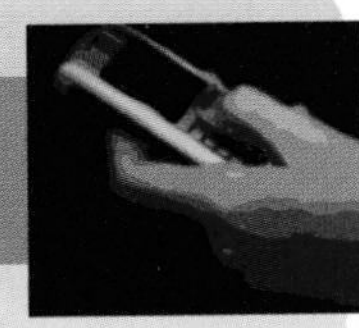

Instant Message

Instant Budget Analyses on the Internet

To compare your spending with that of people like you, describe your situation on the CNNMoney website at cgi.money.cnn.com/tools/instantbudget/instantbudget_101.jsp.

What to Do with Budgeted Money Left Over at the End of the Month At the end of the budgeting time period, some budget classifications may still have a positive balance. For example, perhaps you estimated the electric bill at $100, but it was only $80. You may then ask, "What do I do with the $20 surplus?" You also may ask, "What happens to budget classifications that were overspent?"

People handle the **net surplus** (the amount remaining after all budget classification deficits are subtracted from those with surpluses) in any of the following ways:

net surplus Amount remaining after all budget classification deficits are subtracted from those with surpluses.

- Carry the surpluses forward
- Put into a revolving savings fund
- Build a cash reserve by depositing in a savings account
- Pay down credit card debt
- Put toward a mortgage or other loan
- Invest in a retirement account
- Spend like "mad money"

Figure 3.6
Record-Keeping Formats

(a)

Food Budget: $90

DATE	ACTIVITY	AMOUNT	BALANCE
2-6	Groceries	$ 20	$ 70
2-9	Dinner out	18	52
2-14	Groceries	11	

(b)

DATE	ACTIVITY	AMOUNT BUDGETED	EXPENDITURES	BALANCE
2-1	Budget estimate	$ 90		$ 90
2-6	Groceries		$ 20	70
2-9	Dinner out		18	52
2-14	Groceries		11	41
2-20	Groceries		25	16
2-28	February Totals	$ 90	$ 74	$16

(c)

DATE	ACTIVITY	EXPENDITURES Food Budget: $90	Clothing Budget: $30	Auto Budget: $60	Rent Budget: $275	Savings Budget: $60	Utilities Budget: $40	TOTAL Budget: $680	REMARKS
2-1	Gasoline			10				10	
2-6	Groceries	20						20	Had friends over
2-8	Gasoline			17				17	Good price
2-9	Dinner out	18						18	
2-14	Groceries	11						11	Pepsi on sale
2-15	Subtotals	/49		/27				/76	

(d)

			INCOME			EXPENDITURES								REMARKS
			Salary	Other	TOTAL	Food	Clothing	Auto	Rent	Savings	Utilities		TOTAL	
	Estimates		700	40	740	90	30	60	275	60	40		680	
	Balance forwarded from January		—	—	—	6	—	14	—	—	2		28	
	Sum		700	40	740	96	30	74	275	60	42		708	
DATE	ACTIVITY	CASH IN												
2-1	Paycheck	700	700											
2-1	Texaco-gasoline							10					10	
2-6	Safeway-groceries					20							20	Had friends over
2-8	7/11-gasoline							17					17	Good price
2-9	Dinner out-pizza					18							18	
2-14	Giant-groceries					11							11	Pepsi on sale
2-15	Subtotals	/700				/ 49		/27					/76	
2-16	Cell phone										41		41	
2-28	Totals	700		40	740	83	28	27	275	60	41		660	Good month

The budgeting form in part (d) of Figure 3.6 allows for carrying balances forward to the next period. Some people carry forward deficits, with the hope that having less available in a budgeted classification the following month will motivate them to keep expenditures low. Because variable expense estimates are usually averages, it is best not to change the estimate based on a variation that occurs over just one or two months. If estimates are too high or low for a longer period, you will want to make adjustments.

Using financial software for budgeting takes the drudgery out of making and using a spending plan. And it gets to be easy after a few months. Budgeting can help you succeed financially.

CONCEPT CHECK 3.5

1. List two actions that should be performed before establishing a budget.
2. What are budget estimates and offer some suggestions on how to go about making budget estimates for various types of expenses.
3. Distinguish between a cash flow calendar and a revolving savings fund, and tell why each is important.
4. Offer three suggestions for effective budget controls.

What Do You Recommend Now?

Now that you have read the chapter on financial planning, what do you recommend to Robert for his talk with Nicole on the subject of financial planning regarding:

1. Determining what they own and owe?
2. Better understanding their patterns of family income and expenditure?
3. Using the information in Robert's newly prepared financial statements to summarize the family's financial situation?
4. Evaluating their financial progress?
5. Setting up a record-keeping system to better serve their needs?
6. Starting a budgeting process to guide saving and spending?

Big Picture Summary of Learning Objectives

1 Identify your financial values, goals, and strategies.

By identifying your financial values, goals, and strategies, you can always keep a balance between spending and saving and stay committed to your financial success. You may create financial plans in three broad areas: plans for spending, plans for risk management, and plans for capital accumulation.

2 Use balance sheets and cash-flow statements to measure your financial health and progress.

Financial statements are compilations of personal financial data designed to furnish information on money matters. The balance sheet provides information on what you own, what you owe, and what the net result would be if you paid off all your debts. The cash-flow statement lists income and expenditures over a specific period of time, such as the previous month or year.

3 Evaluate your financial strength and progress using financial ratios.

Financial ratios are numerical calculations designed to simplify the process of evaluating your financial strength and the progress of your financial condition. Ratios serve as tools or yardsticks to develop saving, spending, and credit-use patterns consistent with your goals.

4 Maintain the financial records necessary for managing your personal finances.

Your financial records will help determine where you are, where you have been, and where you are going financially. They also help you make money.

5 Achieve your financial goals through budgeting.

Budgeting is all about logical thinking about your finances. Budgeting forces you to consider what is important in your life, what things you want to own, how you want to live, what it will take to do that, and, more generally, what you want to achieve in life. A budget is a process used to record both projected and actual income and expenditures over a period of time, and it represents the major mechanism through which your financial plans are carried out and goals are achieved.

Let's Talk About It

1. What are your three most important personal values? Give an example of how each of those values might influence your financial plans.
2. College students often have little income and many expenses. Does this reduce or increase the importance of completing a cash-flow statement on a monthly basis? Why?
3. Of the financial ratios described in this chapter, which two might be most revealing for the typical college student? Which two are the most revealing for a retiree?
4. Do you have a budget? Why or why not? What do you think are the major reasons why people do not make formal budgets?
5. What is the biggest budget-related mistake that you have made? What would you do differently?

Do the Numbers

1. Review the financial statements of Victor and Maria Hernandez (Table 3.3 and Table 3.5) and respond to the following questions:
   (a) Using the data in the Hernandezes' balance sheet, calculate an investment assets-to-net worth ratio. How would you interpret the ratio? The Hernandez family appears to have too few monetary assets compared with tangible and investment assets. How would you suggest that they remedy that situation over the next few years?
   (b) Comment on the couple's diversification of their investment assets.
   (c) Calculate the asset-to-debt ratio for Victor and Maria. How does this information help you understand their financial situation? How do their total assets compare with their total liabilities?
   (d) The Hernandezes seem to receive most of their income from labor rather than investments. What actions would you recommend for them to remedy that imbalance over the next few years?
   (e) The Hernandezes want to take a two-week vacation next summer, and they have only eight months to save the necessary $2400. What reasonable changes in expenses and income might they consider to increase net income and make the needed $200 per month?
2. John Green has been a retail salesclerk for six years. At age 35, he is divorced with one child, Amanda, age 7. John's salary is $36,000 per year. He regularly receives $250 per month for child support from Amanda's mother. John invests $100 each month ($50 in his mutual fund and $50 in U.S. savings bonds). Using the following information, construct a balance sheet and a cash-flow statement for John.

ASSETS	**Amount**
Vested retirement benefits (no employee contribution)	$3000
Money market account (includes $150 of interest earned last year)	5000
Mutual fund (includes $200 of reinvested dividend income from last year)	4000
Checking account	1000
Personal property	5000
Automobile	3000
U.S. savings bonds	3000

LIABILITIES	**Outstanding Balance**
Dental bill (pays $25 per month and is included in uninsured medical/dental)	$ 450
Visa (pays $100 per month)	1500
Student loan (pays $100 per month)	7500

ANNUAL EXPENSES	**Amount**
Auto insurance	$ 780
Rent	9100
Utilities	1200
Phone	680
Cable	360
Food	3000
Uninsured medical/dental	1000
Dry cleaning	480
Personal care	420
Gas, maintenance, license	2120
Clothes	500
Entertainment	1700
Vacations/visitation travel	1300
Child care	3820
Gifts	400
Miscellaneous	300
Taxes	6400
Health insurance	2440

3. Sharon and Dick DeVaney of West Lafayette, Indiana, have decided to start a family next year, so they are looking over their budget (illustrated in Table 3.7 as the "young married couple"). Sharon thinks that she can go on half-salary ($1050 instead of $2100 per month) in her job as a graduate assistant for about 18

months after the baby's birth; she will then return to full-time work.

(a) Looking at the DeVaneys' current monthly budget, identify categories and amounts in their $4315 budget where they realistically might cut back $1050. (Hint: Federal and state taxes should drop about $290 as their income drops.)

(b) Assume that Sharon and Dick could be persuaded not to begin a family for another two to three years until Sharon finishes graduate school. What specific budgeting recommendations would you give them for handling (i) their fixed expenses and (ii) their variable expenses to prepare financially for an anticipated $1050 loss of income for 18 months as well as the expenses for the new baby?

(c) If the DeVaneys' gross income of $4315 rises 6 percent per year in the future, what will their income be after five years? (Hint: See Appendix Table A.1 or the *Garman/Forgue* website.)

Financial Planning Cases

Case 1
Manipulation of a Cash-Flow Statement

Using the cash-flow statement developed by William Soshnik (see Table 3.4), enter the data from the *Garman/Forgue* website. The program will calculate the totals.

(a) Print the cash-flow statement, and compare the results with the text for accuracy.

(b) What original source records might William use to develop his cash-flow statement?

(c) Use the data in the cash-flow statements for William (Table 3.4) and for Victor and Maria Hernandez (Table 3.5) to advise William on how his financial life will change as he becomes older.

Case 2
Budget Control for a Recent Graduate

Joseph Jackson, a political scientist from Tucson, Arizona, graduated from college eight months ago and is having a terrible time with his budget. Joseph has a regular monthly income from his job and no really large bills, but he likes to spend. He exceeds his budget every month, and his credit card balances are increasing. Choose three budget control methods that you could recommend to Joseph, and explain how each one could help him gain control of his finances.

Case 3
A Couple Creates an Educational Savings Plan

Stanley Marsh and Wendy Testaburger of Gary, Indiana, have two young children and have been living on a tight budget. Their monthly budget is illustrated in Table 3.7 on page 81 as the "married couple with two young children." Wendy and Stanley are nervous about not having started an educational savings plan for their children. Wendy has just begun working on a part-time basis at a local accounting firm and earns about $860 per month; this income is reflected in the Marsh-Testaburgers' budget. They have decided that they want to save $200 per month for the children's education, but Wendy does not want to work more hours away from home.

(a) Review the family's budget and make suggestions about how to modify various budget estimates so that they could save $200 per month for the education fund.

(b) Briefly describe the effect of your recommended changes on the Marsh-Testaburgers' lifestyle.

Case 4
Victor and Maria Hernandez

Victor and Maria, both in their late 30s, have two children: John, age 13 and Joseph, age 15. Victor has had a long sales career with a major retail appliance store. Maria works part time as a dental hygienist. The Hernandezes own two vehicles and their home, on which they have a mortgage. They will face many financial challenges over the next 20 years, as their children drive, go to college, and leave home and go out in the world on their own. Victor and Maria also recognize the need to further prepare for their retirement and the challenges of aging.

Victor and Maria Hernandez Think About Their Financial Statements and Budgets

Victor and Maria Hernandez spent some time making up their first balance sheet, which is shown in Table 3.3.

(a) Victor and Maria are a bit confused about how various financial activities can affect their net worth. Assume that their home is now appraised at $192,000 and the value of their automobile has dropped to $9500. Calculate and characterize the effects of these changes on their net worth.

(b) If Victor and Maria take out a bank loan for $1545 and pay off their credit card debts totaling $1545, what effects would these changes have on their net worth?

(c) If Victor and Maria sell their New York 2016 bond and put the cash into their savings account, what effects would this move have on their net worth ratio?

(d) Use the sample budgets in Table 3.7 to explain to the couple how their budget might change when their children go to college.

Case 5

Harry and Belinda Johnson

Harry graduated with a bachelor's degree in interior design last spring from a large Midwestern university near his hometown. Belinda has a degree in business finance from a university on the West Coast. Harry and Belinda both worked on their school's student newspapers and met at a conference during their junior year in college. They were married last June and live in an apartment in Kansas City. They currently own one car and Belinda uses public transportation to commute to work. Harry and Belinda look forward to advancing in their careers, buying their own home, and having children.

The Johnsons' Financial Statements Suggest Budgeting Problems

Harry and Belinda both found jobs in the same city. Harry works at a small interior design firm and earns a gross salary of $2500 per month. He also receives $3000 in interest income per year from a trust fund set up by his deceased father's estate; the trust fund will continue to pay that amount until 2020. Belinda works as a salesperson for a regional stock brokerage firm. She earns $3000 per month, and when she finishes her training program in another two months, her gross salary will increase $300 per month. Belinda has many job-related benefits, including life insurance, health insurance, and a credit union. The Johnsons live in an apartment located approximately halfway between their places of employment. Harry drives about 10 minutes to his job, and Belinda travels about 15 minutes via public transportation to reach her downtown job. Harry and Belinda's apartment is very nice, but small, and it is furnished primarily with furniture given to them by their families. Soon after starting their first jobs, Harry and Belinda decided to begin their financial planning. Each had taken a college course in personal finance, so after initial discussion, they worked together for two evenings to develop the two financial statements presented below and on the next page.

(a) Briefly describe how Harry and Belinda probably determined the fair market prices for each of their tangible and investment assets.

(b) Using the data from the cash-flow statement developed by Harry and Belinda, calculate a basic liquidity ratio, asset-to-debt ratio, debt service-to-income ratio, debt payments-to-disposable income ratio, and investment assets-to-total assets ratio. What do these ratios tell you about the Johnsons' financial situation? Should Harry and Belinda incur more debt?

(c) The Johnsons enjoy a high income because both work at well-paying jobs. They have spent parts of three evenings over the past several days discussing their financial values and goals together. As shown in the upper portion of Figure 3.5, they have established three long-term goals: $3000 for a European vacation to be taken in 2½ years, $5000 needed in October 2011 for a down payment on a new automobile, and $26,078 for a down payment on a home to be purchased in December 2013. As shown in the lower portion of the figure, the Johnsons did some calculations to determine how much they had to save for each goal—over the near term—to stay on schedule to reach their long-term goals as well as pay for two vacations and an anniversary party. After developing their balance sheet and cash-flow statement, the Johnsons made a budget for the year (shown in Table 3.8). They then reconciled various conflicting needs and wants until they found that total annual income exceeded expenses. Next, they created a revolving savings fund (Table 3.10) in which they were careful to include enough money each month to meet all of their short-term goals. When developing their cash-flow calendar for the year (Table 3.9), they noticed a problem: substantial cash deficits during four months of the year. In fact, despite their projected high income, they anticipate a deficit for the year. To meet this problem, they do not anticipate increasing their income, using savings, or borrowing. Instead, they are considering modifying their needs and want to reduce their budget estimates to the point where they would have a positive balance for the year. Make specific recommendations to the Johnsons on how they could make reductions in their budget estimates. Do not offer suggestions that would alter their new lifestyle drastically, as the couple would reject these ideas.

Balance Sheet for Harry and Belinda Johnson—January 1, 2008

	Dollars	Percent
ASSETS		
Monetary Assets		
Cash on hand	$ 1,178	5.48
Savings (First Federal Bank)	890	4.14
Savings (Far West Savings and Loan)	560	2.60
Savings (Smith Brokerage Credit Union)	160	0.74
Checking account (First Federal Bank)	752	3.50
Total monetary assets	**$ 3,540**	16.45

Tangible Assets		
Automobile (3-year-old Toyota)	$ 11,000	51.13
Personal property	2,300	10.69
Furniture	1,700	7.90
Total tangible assets	**$15,000**	69.72
Investment Assets		
Harry's retirement account	$ 1,425	6.62
Belinda's retirement account	1,550	7.20
Total investment assets	**$ 2,975**	13.83
Total Assets	**$21,515**	100.00
LIABILITIES		
Short-Term Liabilities		
Visa credit card	$ 390	1.81
Sears card	45	0.21
Dental bill	400	1.86
Total short-term liabilities	**$ 835**	3.88
Long-Term Liabilities		
Student loan (Belinda)	$ 3,800	17.66
Automobile loan (First Federal Bank)	8,200	38.11
Total long-term liabilities	$ 12,000	55.78
Total Liabilities	$ 12,835	59.66
Net Worth	$ 8,680	40.34
Total Liabilities and Net Worth	$ 21,515	100.00

Cash-Flow Statement for Harry and Belinda Johnson July 1–December 31, 2007 (First Six Months of Marriage)

	Dollars	Percent
INCOME		
Harry's gross income ($2500 × 6)	$ 15,000	41.64
Belinda's gross income ($3000 × 6)	18,000	49.97
Interest on savings account	24	0.07
Harry's trust fund	3,000	8.33
Total Income	**$36,024**	100.00
EXPENSES		
Fixed Expenses		
Rent	$ 5,400	14.99
Renter's insurance	220	0.61
Automobile loan payment	1,710	4.75
Automobile insurance	420	1.17
Medical insurance (withheld from salary)	750	2.08
Student loan payments	870	2.42
Life insurance (withheld from salary)	54	0.15
Cable television	540	1.50
Health club	300	0.83
Savings (withheld from salary)	900	2.50
Harry's retirement plan (6% of salary)	900	2.50
Belinda's retirement plan (4% of salary)	720	2.00
Federal income taxes (withheld from salary)	4,600	12.77
State income taxes (withheld from salary)	1,600	4.44
Social Security (withheld from salary)	2,520	7.00
Automobile registration	90	0.25
Total fixed expenses	**$21,594**	59.94
Variable Expenses		
Food	$ 2,300	6.38
Utilities	750	2.08
Telephone	420	1.17
Gasoline, oil, maintenance	700	1.94
Doctor's and dentist's bills	710	1.97
Medicines	345	0.96
Clothing and upkeep	1,900	5.27
Church and charity	800	2.22
Gifts	720	2.00
Christmas gifts	350	0.97
Public transportation	720	2.00
Personal allowances	1,040	2.89
Entertainment	980	2.72
Vacation (holiday)	700	1.94
Vacation (summer)	600	1.67
Miscellaneous	545	1.51
Total variable expenses	**$13,580**	37.70
Total Expenses	**$35,174**	97.64
Surplus (deficit)	**$ 850**	2.36

On the 'Net

Go to the Web pages indicated to complete these exercises. You can also go to the *Garman/Forgue* website at college.hmco.com/business/students for an expanded list of exercises. Under General Business, select the title of this text. Click on the Internet Exercises link for this chapter.

1. Visit *Kiplinger's Personal Finance Magazine* website at http://www.kiplinger.com/tools/. There you will find a link to a long list of calculators that can be used in various present and future value calculations. Select four that you believe would be particularly useful in the aspects of personal financial planning that were discussed in this chapter.
2. Visit the website for SRI Consulting at http://www.sric-bi.com/VALS/presurvey.shtml where you will find the VALS questionnaire. This short questionnaire will help you identify your values in the context of the values of other members of American society.
3. Visit the website for the Economic Policy Institute at http://www.epi.org/content.cfm/datazone_fambud_budget where you can find an example of a family budget for many areas of the United States. Calculate the budget for an area of interest to you. How useful do you think such a calculator would be for a family interested in developing its own budget?

Visit the Garman/Forgue website...

@college.hmco.com/business/students

Under General Business, select *Personal Finance 9e.* There, among other valuable resources, you will find a complete glossary, ACE questions, links to help you complete the chapter exercises, and links to other personal finance sites.

PART 2

CHAPTER 4 Managing Income Taxes

CHAPTER 5 Managing Checking and Savings Accounts

CHAPTER 6 Building and Maintaining Good Credit

CHAPTER 7 Credit Cards and Consumer Loans

CHAPTER 8 Vehicle and Other Major Purchases

CHAPTER 9 Buying Your Home

CHAPTER 4

Managing Income Taxes

You Must Be Kidding, Right?

Bharat Persaud's employer gave him a $2000 bonus last year, and when Bharat was filling out his federal income tax form, he discovered that $1000 of it moved him from the 15 percent marginal tax rate to 25 percent. How much tax will Bharat pay on the $1000?

A. $150

B. $180

C. $250

D. $380

The answer is C. The federal marginal tax rate is applied to your last dollar of earnings. The first $1000 of Bharat's bonus is taxed at the marginal tax rate of 15 percent ($150), but the second $1000 is taxed at 25 percent ($250). Be aware of your marginal tax rate!

LEARNING OBJECTIVES

After reading this chapter, you should be able to:

1. **Explain** the nature of progressive income taxes and the marginal tax rate.
2. **Differentiate** among the eight steps involved in calculating your federal income taxes.
3. **Use appropriate strategies** to avoid overpayment of income taxes.

What Do You Recommend?

Jeffrey Hutchinson and Amber Martin plan to get married in two years. Jeffrey earns $44,000 per year managing a fast-food restaurant. He also earns about $10,000 per year selling jewelry that he designs at craft shows held monthly in various nearby cities. Right after they get married, Jeffrey plans to go back to college full time to finish the last year of his undergraduate degree. Amber earns $58,000 annually working as an institutional sales representative for an insurance company. Both Jeffrey and Amber each contribute $100 per month to their employer-sponsored 401(k) retirement accounts. Jeffrey has little additional savings, but Amber has accumulated $18,000 that she wants to use for a down payment on a home. Amber also owns 300 shares of stock in an oil company that she inherited four years ago when the price was $90 per share; now the stock is worth $130 per share. Jeffrey and Amber live in a state where the state income tax is 6 percent.

What would you recommend to Jeffrey and Amber on the subject of managing income taxes regarding:

1. Using tax credits to help pay for Jeffrey's college expenses?
2. Determining how much money Amber will realize if she sells the stocks, assuming she pays federal income taxes at the 25 percent rate?
3. Buying a home?
4. Increasing contributions to their employer-sponsored retirement plans?
5. Establishing a sideline business for Jeffrey's jewelry operation?

FOR HELP with studying this chapter, visit the Online Student Center:

www.college.hmco.com/pic/garman9e

Online Study Center

Avoid Taxes Through Proper Planning

3 LEARNING OBJECTIVE
Use appropriate strategies to avoid overpayment of income taxes.

While the U.S. tax laws are strict and punitive about compliance (although the IRS audits less than 0.5 percent of all returns), they remain neutral about whether the taxpayer should take advantage of every "break" and opportunity possible. Economist John Maynard Keynes said, "The avoidance of taxes is the only intellectual pursuit that carries any reward." The strategies described here will enable you to reduce your tax liability.

Practice Legal Tax Avoidance, Not Tax Evasion

Tax evasion involves deliberately and willfully hiding income, falsely claiming deductions, or otherwise cheating the government out of taxes owed. It is illegal. A waiter who does not report tips received and a baby-sitter who does not report income are both evading taxes, as is a person who deducts $150 in charitable contributions but who fails to actually make the donations.

tax avoidance Reducing tax liability through legal techniques.

Tax avoidance means reducing tax liability through legal techniques. It involves applying knowledge of the tax code and regulations to personal income tax planning. Tax evasion results in penalties, fines, interest charges, and a possible jail sentence. In contrast, tax avoidance boosts your income because you pay less in taxes; as a result, you will have more money available for spending, saving, investing, and donating.

A Dollar Saved from Taxes Is Really Two Dollars—or More

These three reasons ought to motivate you to find legal ways to reduce your tax liability.

opportunity cost Most valuable alternative that must be sacrificed to satisfy a want or need.

1. **The opportunity cost.** As noted in Chapter 1, the most valuable alternative that must be sacrificed to satisfy a want is called an opportunity cost. An opportunity cost is measured in terms of the value of this forgone option, and it is reflected by the cost of what one must do without or what one could have bought instead. By paying $1 in taxes, you lose the alternative use of that dollar.
2. **Earning another dollar to replace one given to the IRS.** If you pay a dollar too much in taxes, you may need to earn another dollar to replace it. A dollar saved in taxes, therefore, may be viewed as two dollars in your pocket.
3. **Earnings on a dollar not given to the IRS.** If the two dollars saved are invested, the earnings from that investment further expand your savings.

Strategy: Reduce Taxable Income via Your Employer

It may seem illogical to suggest that to lower your tax liability you should reduce your income. The objective is to reduce *taxable* income. Reducing your federal taxable income also will reduce the personal income taxes imposed by state and local governments. Three useful ways of reducing taxable income are premium-only plans, dependent care flexible spending accounts, and defined-contribution retirement plans. Employees often are already paying for these expenses out of their own pockets with after-tax dollars, thus these plans allow people to reduce taxes on money they are already spending.

Contributions to these employer-sponsored plans are entirely free of federal, state, and Social Security and Medicare taxes. The amount withheld to pay for the benefit is deducted from a worker's salary before taxes are calculated. In effect, the IRS subsidizes or helps pay for part of your planned expenses. If your effective marginal tax rate is 43 percent, that is how much savings you obtain by participating. So if you contribute $5000 in pretax income per year to one or more employer-sponsored plans, you immediately save $2150 because you do not have to pay that amount to the IRS.

Premium-Only Plan Many large employers offer a **premium-only plan (POP)** that allows employees to withhold a portion of their pretax salary to pay their premium contributions for employer-provided health benefits. Benefits could include health, dental, vision, and disability insurance. Amounts withheld are not reported to the IRS as taxable income. For example, if Nhon Ngo, a restaurant manager in Dallas, has $40 per month ($480 annually) withheld through his employer to pay for his share of the employer-sponsored health insurance premium, he saves $206 [$480 × 0.43 (effective marginal tax rate)] a year because he does not have to send that amount to the government in taxes.

Transportation Reimbursement Plan A transportation reimbursement plan is a similar pretax program. This employer plan allows you the opportunity to save money by using payroll deduction with pretax salary dollars to pay for work-related transportation expenses, such as transit passes, vanpool commuting, and qualified parking. If Nhon contributes $600 in pretax income to his employer's transportation plan, he saves $258 ($600 × 0.43).

Did You Know?...

Cafeteria Plans Offer Tax-Free Employee Benefits

Employers often offer some benefits via a **cafeteria plan.** This is a program in which the employer gives the employee a specified number of credits that the employee can "spend" on different employee benefit plans or contribute to a flexible spending account. A cafeteria plan might offer tax-free benefits such as accident and health insurance, group life insurance, long-term disability insurance, dependent care, adoption assistance, medical expense reimbursements, or transportation benefits. For example, an employer might offer $4000 annually to each employee to spend on these benefits. The employee is not taxed on the value of the benefits.

Typically, there are sufficient employer credits for employees to choose a low-cost medical plan and a small amount of life insurance coverage without having to contribute their own money. If employees choose more costly benefits, they will have to make contributions out of their own money. Some plans give the employee a choice of selecting either cash or the benefits. Employees working for employers that offer a cafeteria plan avoid having to pay out-of-pocket money for certain expenses.

Dependent Care Flexible Spending Account An attractive benefit for employees who pay for child care or provide care for a parent is a salary reduction plan known as a **flexible spending account (FSA).** This is also called an **expense reimbursement account.** An FSA allows an employee to fund qualified medical expenses on a pretax basis through salary reduction to pay for out-of-pocket unreimbursed expenses for health care (usually a maximum of $3000 annually) and dependent care (maximum $5000 annually) that are not covered by insurance. Examples are annual deductibles, office copayments, over-the-counter drugs, prescriptions, and orthodontia. The salary reductions are not included in the individual's taxable earnings reported on Form W-2, and reimbursements from an FSA account are tax free.

flexible spending account (FSA) or expense reimbursement account Allows employees to fund qualified medical or dependent expenses on pretax basis by reducing take-home salary.

Suppose Nhon in the preceding example has $1200 annually withheld through his employer to be used to pay out-of-pocket medical expenses (e.g., eyeglasses, chiropractors, physician copayments) plus another $3000 to pay out-of-pocket expenses for dependent care of his child. Nhon's $4200 ($1200 + $3000) in FSA withholdings reduces his costs by $1806 ($4200 × 0.43).

FSAs are subject to a **use-it-or-lose-it rule,** which means that any unspent dollars in the account at the end of the year are forfeited and not returned to the employee. The IRS allows a 2½-month additional "grace period" if your employer provides this extension. As a result, you should make conservative estimates of your expenses when you elect your choices. For example, if you had $1000 withheld for medical expenses but spent only $700 over the year, the balance of $300 goes back to your employer, not to you.

use-it-or-lose-it rule An IRS regulation requiring that unspent dollars in a flexible spending account at the end of a calendar year be forfeited, unless the employer allows a three-month grace period for spending the funds.

Defined-Contribution Retirement Plan Contributing money to a qualified employer-sponsored retirement plan reduces income taxes. A **defined-contribution retirement plan** (described in Chapters 1 and 17) is an IRS-approved retirement plan sponsored by an employer to which employees may make pretax contributions that lower their tax liability. The most popular plan is known as a **401(k) retirement plan,** although other variations exist as well.

defined-contribution retirement plan IRS-approved retirement plan sponsored by employers that allows employees to make pretax contributions that lower their tax liability.

The amount of money that an employee contributes to his or her individual account is not taxable income to the employee. For example, if you contribute $2000 to your employer's retirement plan, this immediately saves you $500 that you will not have to pay in taxes, assuming you pay taxes at the 25 percent marginalized tax rate.

An extra benefit of a defined-contribution retirement plan is that employers often offer full or partial **matching contributions** to employees' accounts up to a certain proportion and/or limit of the contributions made by the employee participant. For example, if you invest $2000 into your 401(k) plan and your employer matches half of what you contribute, that is an immediate return of 50 percent ($1000 ÷ $2000) on your investment! The employer's "match" is essentially free money.

matching contributions Employer programs that match employees' 401(k) contributions up to a particular percentage.

All of the dollars in a qualified retirement plan are likely to be invested in alternatives such as stocks and stock mutual funds, where they will grow free of income taxes. Income taxes must be paid when withdrawals are made, presumably during retirement.

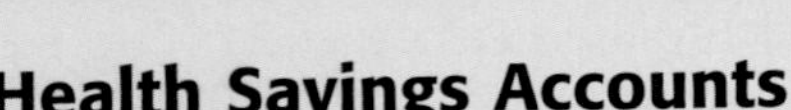

Instant Message

Health Savings Accounts

A health savings account (HSA) is funded by an employee working for an employer who offers a high-deductible health plan (HDHP) from which tax-free distributions can be taken to pay for qualified medical expenses that are not reimbursed by the HDHP. An employee can contribute about $2850 annually to an HSA (about $5650 for family coverage). Any unspent money in the account rolls over to the next year.

Strategy: Make Tax-Sheltered Investments

Investments are often made with **after-tax dollars,** which means that the individual earned the money and paid income taxes on it. They take their after-tax money and invest it. (Investment alternatives are examined in Chapters 13 through 16.) The returns earned from these investments usually result in taxable income.

after-tax dollars Money on which employee has already paid taxes.

Tax laws encourage certain types of investments or other taxpayer behaviors by giving them special tax advantages over other activities. As a result, numerous **tax-sheltered investments** exist. The tax laws allow certain income to be exempt from income taxes in the current year or permit an adjustment, reduction, deferral, or elimination of income tax liability. When making investment decisions, investors should consider tax-sheltered investments.

tax-sheltered investments Investments that yield returns that are tax advantaged.

Some of the best tax-sheltering opportunities are offered to people who wish to save and invest for their retirement. Retirement accounts are not investments themselves but rather the "housing" for tax-advantaged investments. Several additional tax-sheltered opportunities exist that can help reduce one's tax liability.

Investing with Pretax Income Making an investment contribution with **pretax income** means that you do not have to pay taxes this year on the income. For example, Britney Speigel made a $1000 contribution into an IRA that qualified as an adjustment to income. Britney's $1000 will not count as taxable income this year. This will save her $250 ($1000 × 0.25), assuming she pays income taxes at the 25 percent rate. Instead of paying the $250 in taxes on the $1000 in income, she can invest the $1000 in a stock mutual fund (discussed in Chapter 15) within her IRA account. Britney's $1000 includes $250 that otherwise would have gone to the government in taxes. This tax shelter is available with most retirement accounts. In effect, investing with pretax income is an interest-free deferral of taxes, $250 in this case, to fund one's investment.

pretax income Income before taxes are calculated.

Tax-Deferred Investment Growth When interest, dividends, or capital gains are **tax deferred,** the investor does not pay the current-year tax liability. For example, if Adam Reynolds received $2000 in interest from his investments, he would owe $500 in income taxes this year assuming he pays at the 25 percent marginal tax rate. If his investments were either in tax-deferred alternatives or made within tax-deferred accounts, the law allows the taxes to be paid sometime in the future (or perhaps never at all). This benefit is substantial. Investments can grow faster because the money that would have gone to the government in taxes every year can remain in the investment to accumulate. The tax-free growth of such investments is called **tax-deferred compounding.**

tax deferred Interest, dividends, or capital gains that are allowed to grow without taxes until distributions are taken.

tax-deferred compounding Tax-free growth of tax-deferred investments.

Assume that Kyle Broflosken, who pays combined federal and state income taxes at the 30 percent rate, opens two mutual fund accounts: a regular taxable investment account and a tax-sheltered IRA investment account. Kyle puts $1000 into each account. One year later, each account is worth $1090. The extra $90 in each case represents investment growth derived from interest, dividends, and capital gains. The $90 increase in the regular taxable account is considered taxable income. If Kyle took out $27 to pay the tax liability, that would leave a net amount of $1063 in the account. In contrast, the whole $90 increase in the tax-sheltered account can stay there and continue to grow at a pretax annual rate of return rather than an after-tax rate. This means that the extra $27 in the tax-sheltered account is an asset that Kyle can keep out of Uncle Sam's reach for years and years; it can be invested and reinvested again and again. By the time income taxes must finally be paid—probably during retirement—Kyle might be in a lower tax bracket. In effect, the government "loans" tax-free money to Kyle to help fund his retirement plan.

IRA The amount contributed (up to $5000 annually) to an **individual retirement account (IRA)** is considered an adjustment to income, which reduces your current-year income tax liability. Investments inside the IRA (such as stocks and stock mutual funds) accumulate tax free. Income taxes are owed on any eventual withdrawals, likely during retirement. This type of IRA is also known as a **traditional individual retirement account.**

(traditional) individual retirement account (IRA) Investment accounts that reduce current year income and that are allowed to accumulate tax free.

Roth IRA Contributions (up to $4000 annually) to a **Roth IRA** accumulate tax free and withdrawals are tax free. There is no tax break on contributions, as they are made with after-tax money. This is an excellent investment vehicle for people with a long-term investment horizon. IRAs are examined in Chapter 17.

Roth individual retirement accounts Investments made with after-tax money; the interest on such accounts is allowed to grow tax free, and withdrawals are also tax free.

Coverdell Education Savings Account Contributions of up to $2000 per year of after-tax money may be made to a **Coverdell education savings account** (also known as an **education savings account** and formerly known as an **education IRA**) to pay the future education costs for a child younger than age 18. Earnings accumulate tax free and withdrawals for qualified expenses are tax free. The money can be used to pay for public, private, or religious school expenses, from kindergarten through trade school or college, including tuition, fees, room and board, tutoring, uniforms, home computers, Internet access and related technology, transportation, and extended day care.

Qualified Tuition (Section 529) Programs There are two types of **qualified tuition (Section 529) programs**. Under the **prepaid educational service plan,** an individual purchases tuition credits today for use in the future. Also known as a **state-sponsored prepaid tuition plan,** this program allows parents, relatives, and friends to purchase a child's future college education at today's prices by guaranteeing that amounts prepaid will be used for the future tuition at an approved institution of higher education in a particular state. The funds may be used to pay for tuition only—not room, board, or supplies.

prepaid educational service plan Type of qualified tuition program that allows purchase of a child's future college education at today's prices, locking in tuition prices.

The second qualified (Section 529) tuition program, called a **college savings plan,** is set up for a designated beneficiary. You may contribute up to $12,000 per year per child of after-tax money to a 529 college savings plan. Withdrawals are tax free if made for qualified education expenses such as tuition, room, and board. If one child does not go to college, the funds may be transferred to another relative. One may contribute to both a Section 529 plan and an education IRA for the same beneficiary in the same year.

Government Savings Bonds **Series EE** and **Series I** government savings bonds are promissory notes issued by the federal government. The income is exempt from state and local taxes. You may defer the income tax until final maturity (30 years) or report the

Did You Know?...

Consider the Tax Consequences of Managing Income Taxes

This is an example of how one couple—model taxpayers—took numerous tax deductions to reduce their income taxes. Ron and Marilyn West of Longmont, Colorado, have a complex income return because they have both made it a habit to learn about tax-saving strategies and to take advantage of them whenever possible. The Wests have a son in elementary school and a daughter in college; Ron's disabled mother, who requires in-home nursing care, lives in their home as well. Because Marilyn went to work immediately after high school, she only recently started taking college classes at night. Last year, she spent $1000 on night-school tuition.

Part of the Wests' income comes from tax-exempt sources. The table shows their total income and demonstrates how they arrived at a very low final tax liability. The couple has taken advantage of applicable exclusions, adjustments, deductions, exemptions, and credits. Their deductions and tax credits, typical for a couple with three dependents, result in a tax liability of only $3044. The marginal tax rate for the West family is 15 percent. Their average tax rate for all income is 3.0 percent ($3044 ÷ $100,550). For a family with such a substantial income, they have been quite successful in lowering their tax liability.

Total Income		
Ron's salary (self-employed)	$ 54,200	
Marilyn's salary	35,570	
Marilyn's year-end bonus	1,000	
State income tax refund (itemized last year)	180	
Interest on savings account	350	
Interest on tax-exempt state bonds	2,000*	
Gift from Marilyn's mother	2,500*	
Carpool income (Ron's van pool)	250*	
Reimbursements from flexible spending accounts	4,500*	
Total all income		$100,550
Minus* Excludable Income		
($2,000 + $2500 + $250 + $4,500 from above)		– $ 9,250
Gross Income		$91,300
Adjustments to Income		
Contribution—Ron's retirement account	$ 4,000	
Contribution—Marilyn's IRA	2,500	
Flexible spending account for health care	500	
Flexible spending account for dependent care	4,000	
College tuition and fees (daughter)	3,000	
Minus Adjustments to Income		– 14,000
Adjusted Gross Income (AGI)		$77,300
Deductions		
Medical expenses (includes long-term care premiums)	$ 6,900	
Exclusion (7.5% of AGI)	– 5,798	
Total net medical expenses	$1,102	

Taxes		
Real property	$2,800	
Personal property (vehicles)	210	
Total deductible taxes	$3,010	
Interest Expenses		
Home mortgage interest	$10,800	
Home-equity loan interest	460	
Total deductible interest expenses	$11,260	
Contributions		
Church	$1,200	
Other qualified charities	240	
Charitable travel	90	
Total deductible contributions	$1,530	
Casualty or Theft		
Lost diamond ring (uninsured)	$8,100	
Insurance reimbursement	– 0	
Reduction	– 100	
Exclusion (10% of AGI)	– 7,730	
Total deductible casualty loss	$ 270	
Miscellaneous		
Union dues (Ron)	$480	
Safe-deposit box	30	
Unreimbursed job expenses	460	
Cost of Ron looking for a new job	900	
Investment publications	60	
Financial planning tax advice	150	
Tax publications	40	
Subtotal	2,120	
Less 2% of AGI	– 1,546	
Total net miscellaneous deductions	$574	
Total Itemized Deductions		– 17,746
Minus Exemptions (5 @$3400)		– 17,000
Taxable Income		$42,554
Tax Liability (from Table 4.3)	$5,604	
Tax Credits		
Hope Scholarship credit (Marilyn)	–1,000	
Dependent care credit (Ron's mother)	– 960	
Child tax credit (son)	– 600	
Minus total tax credits		–2,560
Final Tax Liability		$3,044

interest annually. Reporting the interest in a child's name is advisable when it can be offset totally by the child's standard deduction. You may exclude accumulated interest from bonds from income tax in the year you redeem the bonds to pay qualified educational expenses. (See Chapter 14 for more information on these and similar bonds.)

municipal bonds (munis) Long-term debt issued by state and local governments and their agencies to finance public improvement projects; usually tax-free interest to buyer.

Municipal Bonds **Municipal bonds** (also called **munis**) are long-term debts issued by local governments and their agencies used to finance public improvement projects. Interest is free from federal and state taxes if the bond is purchased in one's state of residence. Taxpayers in higher-income brackets (28 percent or more) often take advantage of these kinds of investments. (See Chapter 14.) Smart investors choose the bonds that pay the better return after payment of income taxes. The formula to decide whether a taxable investment or nontaxable investment is better for you appears in the box "Compare Taxable and After-Tax Yields."

Did You Know?...

How to Compare Taxable and After-Tax Yields

Investors may choose to put their money into vehicles that provide taxable income, such as stocks, corporate bonds, and stock mutual funds. Taxpayers also have the opportunity to lower their income tax liabilities by investing in tax-exempt municipal bonds, money market funds that invest in municipal bonds, and other tax-exempt ventures. (These investment alternatives are discussed in Chapter 14.)

Because of their tax-exempt status, these investments offer lower nominal returns than taxable alternatives. But after considering the effects of taxes, the actual return to an investor on a tax-exempt investment may be higher than the after-tax yield on a taxable corporate bond.

To find out whether a taxable investment pays a higher after-tax yield than a tax-exempt alternative, the investor must determine the after-tax yield of each alternative. The **after-tax yield** is the percentage yield on a taxable investment after subtracting the effect of federal income taxes that will need to be paid on the investment. The after-tax yield on a tax-exempt investment is the same as the nominal yield because you do not have to pay income taxes on income from this kind of investment. So the question is, "How does the investor calculate the after-tax yield on a taxable investment?"

When you know the taxable yield, use Equation (4.1) to determine the equivalent after-tax yield on a taxable investment. Only then can you decide which investment is better. For example, suppose Bobby Bigbucks pays income taxes at the 35 percent combined federal and state marginal tax rate and is considering buying either a municipal bond that pays a 3.5 percent yield or a taxable corporate bond that pays a 5.7 percent yield. Equation (4.1) calculates the equivalent after-tax yield on the corporate bond:*

$$\begin{aligned}\text{After-tax yield} &= \text{taxable yield} \times (1 - \text{federal marginal tax rate})\\ &= 5.7 \times (1.00 - 0.35)\\ &= 5.7 \times 0.65 \qquad (4.1)\\ &= 3.71\end{aligned}$$

The answer is 3.71 percent. Thus, a 5.7 percent taxable yield is equivalent to an after-tax yield of 3.71 percent. Eureka! Now Bobby knows that he should buy the corporate bond paying 5.7 percent because its after-tax yield of 3.71 percent is higher than the 3.5 percent paid by the municipal bond. These differences may look small, and they are, but over time they add up. For example, the extra 0.21 percent (3.71 − 3.50) yield on a $20,000 bond investment for 20 years amounts to $840 [$20,000 × 0.0021 × 20 (bond interest is not compounded)]. That's real money!†

The higher your federal tax rate, the more favorable tax-exempt municipal bonds become as an investment compared with taxable bonds. The tax-exempt status of municipal bonds does not apply to capital gains. When you sell an investment for more than what you paid for it, you will owe federal income taxes on the capital gain.

*This and similar equations can be found and used on the *Garman/Forgue* website.
†The formula can be reversed to solve for the equivalent taxable yield when one knows the tax-exempt yield. To continue the example, the return for Bobby on a 3.71 percent tax-exempt bond is equivalent to a taxable yield of 5.7 percent [3.71 ÷ (1.00 − 0.35)]. If Bobby finds a tax-exempt bond paying more than 3.71 percent, he should consider buying it.

Advice from a Pro

Buy a Home to Reduce Taxes

Hanna Pallagrosi of Rome, New York, took a sales position at a retail chain store two years ago, where she earned a gross income of $46,736. Hanna wisely made a $1000 contribution to her IRA. Her itemized deductions came to only $3800, so she took the standard deduction and personal exemption amounts. The result was a tax liability of $6046. Hanna was not happy about paying what she thought was a large tax bill that year.

Gross income	$46,736
Less adjustment to income	– 1,000
Adjusted gross income	45,736
Less value of one exemption (old figure)	– 3,200
Subtotal	42,536
Less standard deduction (old figure)	– 5,000
Taxable income	37,536
Tax liability (from old tax table not shown)	$ 6,046

Last year Hanna did not receive a raise. Nonetheless, Hanna continued to contribute $1000 into her IRA. To reduce her federal income taxes, she also became a homeowner after using some inheritance money to make the down payment on a condominium. During the year, she paid out $9126 in mortgage interest expenses and $1995 in real estate taxes. After studying various tax publications, Hanna determined that she had $3814 in other itemized deductions that, when combined with the interest and real estate taxes, totaled $14,935. These deductions reduced Hanna's tax liability dramatically.

Gross income	$46,736
Less adjustment to income	– 1,000
Adjusted gross income	45,736
Less itemized deductions	–14,935
Subtotal	30,801
Less value of one exemption	– 3,400
Taxable income	27,401
Tax liability (from Table 4.3)	$ 3,723

Hanna correctly concluded that the IRS "paid" $2323 ($6046 – $3723) toward the purchase of her condominium and her living costs because she did not have to forward those dollars to the government. An additional benefit for Hanna is that she now owns a home whose value could appreciate in the future. The best advice is to buy a home to reduce income taxes.

Frances C. Lawrence
Louisiana State University

Here is an example to illustrate the benefits of municipal bonds. Assume that Lauren Rider, a retiree living in Lincoln, Nebraska, currently has $100,000 in a certificate of deposit earning 4.5 percent, or $4500 annually ($100,000 × 0.045). She pays $1125 in tax on this income at her 25 percent federal marginal tax rate ($4500 × 0.25), leaving her a net after-tax return of $3375. Investing in a tax-exempt $100,000 municipal bond paying 3.9 percent would provide Lauren with a better after-tax return. She would receive $3900 ($100,000 × 0.039) tax free from a municipal bond, compared with $3375 ($4500 – $1125) after taxes on the certificate of deposit. The increase in her after-tax income would be $525 ($3900 – $3375).

Capital Gains on Housing A big tax shelter is available to homeowners when they sell their homes. Those with appreciated principal residences are allowed to avoid taxes on capital gains of up to $500,000 if married and filing jointly and on gains up to $250,000 if single. The home must have been owned and used as the taxpayer's private residence for two out of the past five years prior to the date of the sale.

Strategy: Postpone Income

Another way to reduce income tax liability is to postpone income. This goal is achieved by purposefully making arrangements to receive some of this year's income in the next year, when your marginal tax rate might be lower, perhaps only 25 percent rather than

28 percent. A 3 percent tax savings (paying at the 25 percent rate rather than 28 percent) on $2000 of income is $60 ($2000 × 0.03), enough to pay for a meal in a quality restaurant. For example, if you expect a year-end commission check of $2000, the extra income this year might be enough to push you into a higher marginal tax bracket. If your employer is willing to give the commission check a January date, the income need not be reported until the following year.

You might expect to be in a lower tax bracket in the following year because you anticipate less sales commissions or know that you will not work full time (for example, if you return to school, have a child, or decide to travel). Retired people may be able to postpone withdrawals of income from retirement plans, and entrepreneurs may delay billing customers for work.

Strategy: Bunch Deductions

Many people find that they do not have enough itemized deductions to exceed the standard deduction amount. By shifting the payment dates of some deductible items, you can increase your deductions. For example, if a single person has about $5000 of deductible expenses this year, she could prepay some items in December to push the total over the $5350 threshold and benefit by taking the excess deductions now. The next year she can take the standard deduction amount instead of itemizing.

bunching deductions For taxpayers who do not meet floor for itemizing deductions every year, strategy of prepaying expenses in one year so that itemizing works every other year.

This process is known as **bunching deductions.** Items that may be prepaid include medical expenses, dental bills, real estate taxes, state and local income taxes, the January payment of estimated state income taxes, personal property taxes that have been billed (e.g., on autos and boats), dues in professional associations, and charitable contributions. You may mail the payments or charge them on credit cards by December 31.

Strategy: Take All of Your Legal Tax Deductions

Although you should not spend money just to create a tax deduction, you are encouraged to take all of the deductions to which you are entitled. One way to increase itemized deductions, for example, is to purchase a home with a mortgage loan. The large amounts of money homeowners expend for both interest and real estate taxes are deductible.

Here are some other approaches to increase your deductions and keep more tax dollars in your pocket. Assume you are in the 15 percent marginal tax bracket and itemize deductions. Cash contributions made to people collecting door to door or at a shopping center during holidays are deductible, even though receipts are not given. Fifty dollars in contributions deducted can save you $7.50 in taxes. Instead of throwing out an old television set, donate it. An $80 charitable contribution for a TV will save you $12 in taxes. These amounts may sound like "small change," but lots of little tax deductions can quickly add up to more than $100, and that's real money!

Expenses for business-related trips can be a fruitful area for tax deductions. If you are in the 15 percent tax bracket and take one business trip per year, perhaps incurring $400 in deductible expenses, you will save another $60 in taxes, assuming your miscellaneous deductions already exceed 2 percent of your AGI. The IRS also permits tax deductions for the costs expended on occasional job-hunting trips. In other words, depending on your tax bracket, the U.S. government pays the bill for 15 or 25 percent of such expenditures.

Did You Know?...

Overwithholding

Overwithholding occurs when employees have their employers withhold more in estimated taxes than the tax liability ultimately due the government. Approximately four-fifths of all taxpayers practice overwithholding, which is a form of forced savings. These taxpayers receive their refunds (which averaged more than $2300 last year) approximately six weeks after filing their income tax returns. The IRS does not pay interest on such refunded monies, so overwithholding has an opportunity cost—the interest you could be earning on such amounts. If you anticipate that your tax liability will be lower than the amount in the federal government's withholding schedule, you can file a new W-4 form with your employer to decrease the amount withheld, which will in turn increase the amount of your take-home income.

Strategy: Buy and Manage a Real Estate Investment

Tax losses are paper losses in the sense that they may not represent actual out-of-pocket dollar losses. They are created when deductions generated from an investment (such as depreciation and net investment losses) exceed the income from an investment.

Taxpayers are allowed to deduct certain real estate losses against ordinary taxable income, such as salary, interest, dividends, and self-employment earnings. Deductions are allowed for real estate investors who (1) have an adjusted gross income of $150,000 or less and (2) actively participate in the management of the property. Here the investor may deduct up to $25,000 of net losses from a "passive investment," such as real estate, against income from "active" sources, such as salary. For example, a residential real estate investment property might generate an annual cash income $1000 greater than the out-of-pocket operating costs associated with it. After depreciation expenses on the building are taken as a tax deduction, the resulting $1500 tax loss may then be used to offset other income. This tax break begins to phase out for those with an AGI of $100,000.

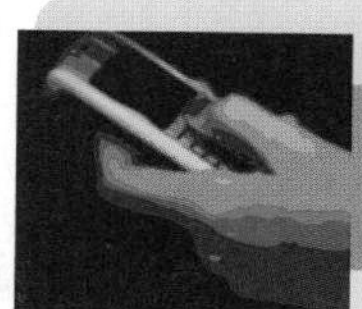

Instant Message

Kiddie Tax for Children Under Age 18

If a child is under age 18 and has net investment income exceeding $1700, the excess is taxed as though it were the income of the parent. This is called the **kiddie tax.** The parent's marginal tax rate is probably higher than that of the child, which is usually 10 percent.

tax losses Paper losses that may not represent actual losses created when deductions generated from an investment exceed income from the investment.

CONCEPT CHECK 4.3

1. Distinguish between two types of tax-sheltered investment returns.
2. Explain how to reduce income taxes via your employer, and name three employer-sponsored plans to do so.
3. Summarize the differences between an individual retirement account (IRA) and a Roth IRA.
4. Identify three strategies to avoid overpayment of income taxes (different from above), and summarize the essence of each.

Certain real estate losses are tax deductible.

Did You Know?...

Top 3 Financial Missteps in Managing Income Taxes

People slip up in managing income taxes when they do the following:

1. Turn all your income tax planning over to someone else
2. Overwithhold too much income to receive a refund next year
3. Ignore the impact of income taxes in your personal financial planning

What Do You Recommend Now?

Now that you have read the chapter on managing income taxes, what advice can you offer Jeffrey Hutchinson and Amber Martin in the case at the beginning of the chapter regarding:

1. Using tax credits to help pay for Jeffrey's college expenses?
2. Determining how much money Amber will realize if she sells the stocks, assuming she pays federal income taxes at the 25 percent rate?
3. Buying a home?
4. Increasing contributions to their employer-sponsored retirement plans?
5. Establishing a sideline business for Jeffrey's jewelry operation?

Big Picture Summary of Learning Objectives

1 Explain the nature of progressive income taxes and the marginal tax rate.

The federal personal income tax is a progressive tax because the tax rate increases as a taxpayer's taxable income increases. The marginal tax rate is applied to your last dollar of earnings. Your effective marginal tax rate is probably 43 percent.

2 Differentiate among the eight steps involved in calculating your federal income taxes.

There are eight steps in calculating your income taxes. Certain types of income may be excluded. Regulations permit you to subtract adjustments to income, exemptions, deductions, and tax credits before determining your final tax liability.

3 Use appropriate strategies to avoid overpayment of income taxes.

You can reduce your tax liability by following certain tax avoidance strategies, such as putting your money in tax-sheltered investments, reducing taxable income via your employer, and investing pretax money for tax-deferred compounding. Other strategies are to postpone income, bunch deductions, take all your legal deductions, and buy and manage a real estate investment.

Let's Talk About It

1. Many college students choose not to file a federal income tax return, assuming that the income taxes withheld by employers "probably" will cover their tax liability. Is such an assumption correct? What are the negatives of this practice if the employers withheld too much in income taxes? What are the negatives if the employers did not withhold enough in income taxes?
2. Long-term capital gains are taxed at a rate of 15 or 5 percent. What is your opinion on the fairness of these lower capital gains tax rates as compared with the marginal rates applied to income earned from employment that range as high as 35 percent?
3. Some college students earn money that is paid to them in cash and then do not include this as income when they file their tax returns. What are the pros and cons of this practice?

4. Identify two possible sideline businesses that you might engage in to reduce your income tax liability.
5. Name three tax credits that a college student might take advantage of while still in college or during the first few years after graduation.
6. Identify five strategies to reduce income tax liability that you will likely take advantage of in the future.

Do the Numbers

1. What would be the tax liability for a single taxpayer who has a gross income of $33,975? (Hint: Use Table 4.3, and don't forget to first subtract the value of a standard deduction and one exemption.)
2. What would be the marginal tax rate for a single person who has a taxable income of (a) $20,210, (b) $27,800, (c) $26,055, and (d) $90,230? (Hint: Use Table 4.3.)
3. Find the tax liabilities based on the taxable income of the following people: (a) married couple, $74,125; (b) married couple, $53,077; (c) single person, $27,880; (d) single person, $53,000. (Hint: Use Table 4.3.)
4. Joseph Addai determined the following tax information: gross salary, $59,400; interest earned, $90; IRA contribution, $1000; personal exemption, $3400; and itemized deductions, $3950. Calculate Joseph's taxable income and tax liability. (Hint: Use Table 4.3.)
5. Brandon and Rachael Timmerman determined the following tax information: gross salaries, $234,000 and $222,000, respectively; interest earned, $11,000; qualified retirement plan contributions, $60,000; personal exemptions, $6800; and itemized deductions, $26,000. Calculate the Timmermans' taxable income and tax liability. (Hint: Use Table 4.2.)
6. Anthony Clark determined the following tax information: salary, $144,000; interest earned, $2000; personal exemption, $3400; itemized deductions, $9000; qualified retirement plan contribution, $7000. Calculate Anthony's taxable income and tax liability. (Hint: Use Table 4.2.)

Financial Planning Cases

Case 1

A New Family Calculates Income and Tax Liability

Stephanie Nichols and her two children, Austin and Alexandra, moved into the home of her new husband, Glenn Sandler, in Ames, Iowa. Stephanie is employed as a union organizer, and her husband manages a vegetarian food store. The Nichols-Sandler family income consists of the following: $40,000 from Stephanie's salary; $42,000 from Glenn's salary; $10,000 in life insurance proceeds from a deceased aunt; $140 in interest savings; $4380 in alimony from Stephanie's ex-husband; $14,200 in child support from her ex-husband; $500 cash as a Christmas gift from Glenn's parents; $90 from a friend who rides to work in Stephanie's vehicle; $60 in lottery winnings gained from playing the lottery at $5 every week; $170 worth of dental services traded for a quilt Stephanie gave to the dentist; and a $1600 tuition-and-books scholarship Stephanie received to go to college part time last year.

(a) What is the total of the Nichols-Sandler reportable gross income?

(b) After putting $2800 into qualified retirement plan accounts last year, what is their adjusted gross income?

(c) How many exemptions can the family claim, and how much is the total value allowed the household?

(d) How much is the allowable standard deduction for the household?

(e) Their itemized deductions are $12,200, so should they itemize or take the standard deduction?

(f) What is their taxable income for a joint return, and what is their marginal tax rate?

(g) What is their final federal income tax liability? (Hint: Use Table 4.3.)

(h) If Stephanie's and Glenn's employers withheld $6000 for income taxes, does the couple owe money to the government or do they get a refund? How much?

Case 2

Taxable Versus Tax-Exempt Bonds

Art Williams, radio station manager in Franklin County, New Jersey, is in the 25 percent federal marginal tax bracket and pays an additional 5 percent in taxes to the state of New Jersey. Art currently has more than $20,000 invested in corporate bonds bought at various times that are earning differing amounts of taxable interest: $10,000 in ABC earning 5.9 percent; $5000 in DEF earning 5.5 percent; $3000 in GHI earning 5.8 percent; and $2000 in JKL earning 5.4 percent. What is the after-tax return of each investment? To calculate your answers, use the after-tax yield formula (or the reversed formula) on page 122, or the *Garman/Forgue* website.

Case 3
Taxable Versus Nontaxable Income

Identify each of the following items as either part of taxable income or an exclusion from taxable income for LaDainian Tomison and Megan Smithfield, a married couple from San Diego:

(a) LaDainian earns $45,000 per year.
(b) LaDainian receives a $1000 bonus from his employer.
(c) Megan receives $40,000 in commissions from her work.
(d) Megan receives $300 in monthly child support.
(e) LaDainian pays $200 each month in alimony.
(f) LaDainian contributes $2000 to his retirement account.
(g) Megan inherits a car from her aunt that has a fair market value of $3000.
(h) LaDainian receives a $5000 gift from his mother.

Case 4
Victor and Maria Reduce Their Income Tax Liability

The year before last, Victor earned $51,000 from his retail management position and Maria earned $45,000 as a dental hygienist. After they took the standard deduction and claimed four exemptions (themselves plus their two children), their federal income tax liability was about $12,500. After hearing from friends that they were paying too much in taxes, the couple vowed to try to never again pay that much. Therefore, the Hernandezes embarked on a yearlong effort to reduce their income tax liability. This year they tracked all of their possible itemized deductions, and both made contributions to qualified retirement plans at their places of employment.

(a) Calculate the Hernandezes' income tax liability for this year as a joint return (using Table 4.3) given the following information: gross salary income (Victor, $55,000; Maria $49,000); state income tax refund ($400); interest on checking and savings accounts ($250); carpool income from Maria's coworkers ($240); contributions to qualified retirement accounts ($6000); itemized deductions (real estate taxes, $4000; mortgage interest, $6000; charitable contributions, $2700); and exemptions ($3400 each) for themselves and their two children.
(b) List five additional strategies that Victor and Maria might consider for next year's tax planning to reduce their tax liability.

Case 5
The Johnsons Calculate Their Income Taxes

Several years have gone by since Harry and Belinda graduated from college and started their working careers. They both earn good salaries. They believe that they are paying too much in federal income taxes. The Johnsons' total income last year included Harry's salary of $60,000, Belinda's salary of $90,000, $400 interest on savings and checking, and $3000 interest income from the trust that is taxed in the same way as interest income from checking and savings accounts.

(a) What is the Johnsons' reportable gross income on their joint tax return?
(b) What is the total value of their exemptions?
(c) How much is the standard deduction for the Johnsons?
(d) The Johnsons are buying a home that has monthly mortgage payments of $3000, or $36,000 a year. Of this amount, about $32,000 goes for interest and real estate property taxes, both of which are tax deductible. The couple has an additional $6400 in itemized deductions, thus they have a total of $38,400 ($32,000 + $6400). Using these numbers and Table 4.2, calculate their taxable income and tax liability.
(e) Assuming they had a combined $24,000 in federal income taxes withheld, how much of a refund will the Johnsons receive?
(f) What is their marginal tax rate?
(g) Based on gross income, what is their average tax rate?
(h) List three additional ways that the Johnsons might reduce their tax liability next year.

On the 'Net

Go to the Web pages indicated to complete these exercises. You can also go to the *Garman/Forgue* website at college.hmco.com/business/students for an expanded list of exercises. Under General Business, select the title of this text. Click on the Internet Exercises link for this chapter.

1. Visit the website for the Internal Revenue Service. Use the search function to find "Publication 501." Use this publication to determine (a) whether you must file a return, (b) who can claim you as an exemption, and (c) how much your standard deduction is.

2. Visit the website for the Internal Revenue Service's primary tax information document for taxpayers—Publication 17, *Your Federal Income Tax*—at http://www.irs.gov/publications/p17/index.html. Scroll down the menu to "Education Credits." There you will find information on the Hope Scholarship credit and the lifetime learning credit. How might these two credits help you lower your or your parents' overall federal income tax bill?
3. Visit the website for the Federation of Tax Administrators at http://www.taxadmin.org/fta/rate/. Click on "tax rates." There you will find a table with tax rates for all states that levy an income tax. Based on what you found, what is your combined federal and state marginal tax rate?

Visit the Garman/Forgue website...

@college.hmco.com/business/students

Under General Business, select *Personal Finance 9e.* There, among other valuable resources, you will find a complete glossary, ACE questions, links to help you complete the chapter exercises, and links to other personal finance sites.

CHAPTER 5

Managing Checking and Savings Accounts

You Must Be Kidding, Right?

Patti Patterson realized about two weeks ago that she had misplaced her ATM card. At first she was not worried because she reasoned that it had to be somewhere in the house. Last week she received her savings account statement. She looked at her statement today and found that $200 had been illegally withdrawn from her account on five different occasions ($1000 total). She immediately called her bank to report the fraudulent withdrawals. How much of this money will Patti lose because of the unauthorized withdrawals?

A. $0 **B.** $50 **C.** $500 **D.** $1000

The answer is C, $500. Because Patti waited more than two days after realizing the card was lost to report it to her financial institution, federal law states that she is liable for the first $500 in unauthorized uses. If she had notified the bank within two days, her loss would have been only $50. If Patti failed to notify her bank of the loss within 60 days, the law states that she would lose all of the money taken fraudulently. It's smart to immediately report a lost debit card!

LEARNING OBJECTIVES

After reading this chapter, you should be able to:

1 **List** and define the tools of monetary asset management and identify the types of financial services firms that provide those tools.

2 **Earn** interest and pay no or low fees on your checking accounts.

3 **Make** the best use of the benefits of savings accounts.

4 **Explain** the importance of placing excess funds in a money market account.

5 **Describe** electronic money management, including your legal protections.

6 **Discuss** your personal finances and money management more effectively with loved ones.

What Do You Recommend?

Mark Rosenberg and Trina Adams are to be married in two months. Both are employed full time and currently have their own apartments. Once married, they will move into Trina's apartment because it is larger. They plan to use Mark's rent money to begin saving for a down payment on a home to be purchased in four or five years. Mark has a checking account at a branch of a large regional commercial bank near his workplace where he deposits his paychecks. He also has three savings accounts—one at his bank and two small accounts at a savings and loan association near where he went to college. Mark pays about $30 per month in fees on his various accounts. In addition, he has a $10,000 certificate of deposit (CD) from an inheritance; this CD will mature in five months. Trina has her paycheck directly deposited into her share draft account at the credit union where she works. She has a savings account at the credit union as well as a money market account at a stock brokerage firm that was set up years ago when her father gave her 300 shares of stock. She also has $4300 in an individual retirement account invested through a mutual fund.

What would you recommend to Trina and Mark on the subject of managing checking and savings accounts regarding:

1. Where they can obtain the monetary asset management services that they need?
2. Their best use of checking accounts and savings accounts as they begin saving for a home?
3. The use of a money market account for their monetary asset management?
4. Their use of electronic banking in the future?
5. How they can best discuss the management of their money and finances?

FOR HELP with studying this chapter, visit the Online Student Center:

www.college.hmco.com/pic/garman9e

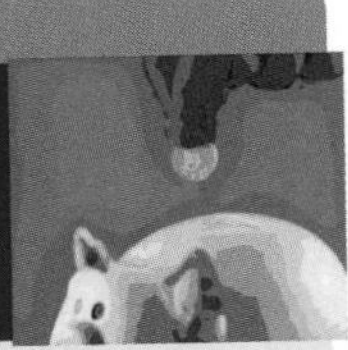

Good Money Habits in Managing Checking and Savings Accounts

Make the following your money habits when managing checking and savings accounts:

1. Use a free, interest-earning checking account for your day-to-day spending needs.
2. Use high-interest savings accounts for funds you will not need for six months to about five years in the future.
3. Use investments for needs that will not occur until five or more years in the future.
4. Maintain an emergency fund sufficient to cover three months of expenses.
5. Buy certificates of deposit when saved funds will not be needed until a specific future date.
6. Reconcile your account statements monthly.

Your financial success will depend heavily on how well you save money. Savings allows you to accumulate excess funds, or **monetary assets.** These assets were defined in Chapter 3 as cash and low-risk, near-cash items that can be readily converted to cash with little or no loss in value. If you are a typical college student, your monetary assets are the largest component of your net worth and are the major focus of the activities you consider "personal finance."

People use monetary assets in one of three ways. First, they spend them. They buy food, clothing, entertainment, and a long list of products and services. Spending often requires cash or the use of a check or a debit card to access funds in a checking account. (Using credit is covered in Chapters 6 and 7.) Checking accounts are appropriate places to keep money that you will spend within the next three to six months or so. The second way that people use monetary assets is to set aside funds to meet needs that will occur six months to five years in the future. You could keep these funds in a checking account, but savings accounts pay more interest. With savings accounts, the focus is on holding money safely until needed in the future. The third way that people use monetary assets is to make investments. Here the goal is to earn an even better return and actually earn money on your money. Investments are the best places to put money you will not need for 5, 10, or even 20 years in the future. The beauty of investments is that over long periods of time it is quite possible to earn three or four times more than the original amount deposited. Investments are examined in Chapters 13 through 16.

monetary assets Cash and low-risk, near-cash items that can quickly be converted into cash.

1 LEARNING OBJECTIVE
List and define the tools of monetary asset management and identify the types of financial services firms that provide those tools.

monetary asset (cash) management How you handle your monetary assets.

liquidity Ease with which an asset can be converted to cash.

What Is Monetary Asset Management?

Monetary asset (cash) management encompasses how you handle all of your monetary assets, including cash on hand, checking accounts, savings accounts and certificates of deposit, and money market accounts. The goal is to maximize interest earnings and to minimize fees while keeping funds safe and readily available for living expenses, emergencies, and saving and investment opportunities. Successful monetary asset management allows you to earn interest on your money while maintaining reasonable liquidity and safety. **Liquidity** refers to the speed and ease with which an asset can be converted to cash. Your funds are safe when they are free from financial risk.

The Three Tools of Monetary Asset Management

As illustrated in Figure 5.1, monetary asset management relies on three major tools:

1. Low-cost, interest-earning checking accounts from which to pay ongoing, current living expenses.
2. Interest-earning savings accounts in local financial institutions in which you deposit funds for upcoming expenditures or to accumulate funds for future investments.
3. Money market accounts in local financial institutions or other financial services

Checking account	Savings account	Money market account
• NOW checking (pays interest)	• Statement savings (+1/4%) • Certificate of deposit (+1% to +3%)	• Money market deposit account (+1/2%) • Super NOW (+3/4%) • Money market mutual fund (+1% to +5%) • Asset management account (+1% to +5%)

Figure 5.1
The Three Tools of Asset Management
(Percents are the amounts above NOW accounts.)

providers. These accounts pay higher interest rates than checking and savings accounts. They have limited check-writing privileges and, thus, are a cross between a checking and a savings account.

Who Provides Monetary Asset Management Services?

The **financial services industry** comprises companies that provide monetary asset management and other services. The firms in this industry provide checking, savings, and money market accounts. Quite often they also provide credit, insurance, investment, and financial planning services. These firms include depository institutions such as banks and credit unions, stock brokerage firms, mutual funds, financial services companies, and insurance companies. Table 5.1 matches these various types of firms with the financial products and services that they sell. As you can see, there is considerable overlap among the services they sell. For example, State Farm, which most people recognize as an insurance company, also owns a mutual fund and a bank.

financial services industry Companies that provide monetary asset management and other services.

Table 5.1 Today's Providers of Monetary Asset Management Services

Providers	What They Sell	Examples of Well-Known Company Names
Depository institutions (banks, mutual savings banks, savings and loan associations, and credit unions)	Checking, savings, lending, credit cards, investments, and trust advice	Bank One, Chase, Wells Fargo, Wachovia, Everbank (online)
Mutual funds	Money market mutual funds, tax-exempt funds, bond funds, and stock funds	Fidelity, T. Rowe Price, Vanguard
Stock brokerage firms	Securities investments (stocks and bonds), mutual funds, and real estate investment trusts	Merrill Lynch, Goldman/Sachs
Financial services companies	Checking, savings, lending, credit cards, securities investments, real estate, investments, insurance, accounting and legal advice, and financial planning	American Express, A. G. Edwards, Raymond James
Insurance companies	Property and liability, health and life insurance, credit services, financial planning services	Allstate, Aetna, State Farm

depository institutions Organizations licensed to take deposits and make loans.

Depository Institutions **Depository institutions** are organizations licensed to take deposits and make loans. They all can offer some form of government account insurance on their customers' deposits and are government regulated. They offer a wide range of financial services. Examples of depository institutions are commercial banks, savings banks, and credit unions. Although each is a distinct type of institution, people often call them all simply *banks*.

Commercial banks are corporations chartered under federal and state regulations. They offer numerous consumer services, such as checking, savings, loans, safe-deposit boxes, investment services, financial counseling, and automatic payment of bills. Accounts in federally chartered banks are insured against loss by the **Bank Insurance Fund (BIF) of the Federal Deposit Insurance Corporation (FDIC),** which is an agency of the federal government.

Savings banks (or **savings and loan associations–S&Ls**) focus primarily on accepting savings and providing mortgage and consumer loans. They offer checking services through interest-earning NOW accounts (discussed later in this chapter). Savings banks generally pay depositors an interest rate about 0.10 to 0.20 percentage points higher than the rate found at commercial banks. The FDIC insures accounts in all federally chartered savings banks through the FDIC's **Savings Association Insurance Fund (SAIF).**

A **mutual savings bank (MSB)** is similar to a savings bank in that it also accepts deposits and makes housing and consumer loans. These banks are legally permitted in only 17 states, primarily those in the eastern United States. They are called "mutual" because the depositors own the institution and share in the earnings. Generally, MSBs have the FDIC's BIF coverage. Like savings banks, they offer interest-earning checking accounts to checking customers.

A **credit union (CU)** also accepts deposits and makes loans. Credit unions operate on a not-for-profit basis and are owned by their members. The members/owners of the credit union all share some common bond, such as the same employer, church, trade union, or fraternal association. People in the family of a member are also eligible to join. Federally chartered credit unions have their accounts insured through the **National Credit Union Share Insurance Fund (NCUSIF),** which is administered by the National Credit Union Administration (NCUA). State-chartered credit unions are often insured by NCUSIF, and most others participate in private insurance programs. Credit unions usually pay higher interest rates and charge lower fees than commercial banks, savings banks, or MSBs.

Did You Know?...

Top 3 Financial Missteps in Managing Checking and Savings Accounts

People slip up in managing checking and savings accounts when they do the following:

1. Pay high fees unnecessarily
2. Keep most of your excess funds in your checking account where it earns you very little interest
3. Fail to reconcile your accounts on a regular basis

credit union (CU) Member-owned, not-for-profit federally insured financial institutions that provide checking, savings, and loan services to members.

Deposit Insurance Is a Real Plus Deposits in depository institutions are insured against loss of both the amount on deposit and the accrued interest by various insurance funds. This **deposit insurance** for your deposits at any one institution works as follows:

deposit insurance Insures deposits, both principal amounts and accrued interest, up to $100,000 per account for most accounts ($200,000 for retirement accounts).

1. The maximum insurance on all of your single-ownership (individual) accounts (held in your name only) is $100,000.
2. The maximum insurance on all of your joint accounts (accounts held with other individuals) is $100,000.
3. The maximum insurance on all of your retirement accounts is $200,000.
4. A maximum of $100,000 in insurance per beneficiary is available for **"payable on death accounts"** (accounts set up so that the funds go to a spouse, child, parent, or sibling upon the death of the account holder).

Thus, individuals might have several increments of insurance for their accounts at any one institution. Funds on deposit at other institutions will also have these same limits. So if you had $80,000 in individual accounts at each of two different institutions, you would have a total of $160,000 of deposit insurance.

Other Financial Services Providers Other providers offer monetary asset management services. Most purchase private insurance to cover potential losses in their monetary asset accounts. No insurance is available for stocks, bonds, and other investment accounts.

Mutual funds are investment companies that raise money by selling shares to the public and then invest that money in a diversified portfolio of investments. Most have created mutual fund accounts that can be used for monetary asset management purposes. For example, cash management accounts in mutual funds provide a convenient and safe place to keep money while awaiting alternative investment opportunities. Note that money deposited in a mutual fund is not insured by the federal government, although some mutual fund companies purchase insurance privately for the noninvestment portions of customers' accounts. Mutual funds are the subject of Chapter 15.

mutual funds Investment companies that raise money by selling shares to the public and then invest that money in a diversified investment portfolio.

Stock brokerage firms are licensed financial institutions that specialize in selling and buying stocks, bonds, and other investments. Such firms provide advice and assistance to investors and earn commissions based on the buy and sell orders that they process for their clients. Stock brokerage firms typically offer money market mutual fund accounts (operated by mutual funds) into which clients may place money while waiting to make investments. The noninvestment portion of an account (for example, cash held in the account prior to making an investment) is insured by the Securities Investor Insurance Corporation, a nongovernment entity.

Insurance companies provide property, liability, health, life, and other insurance products. Many offer monetary asset services, such as money market accounts. Some also offer vehicle loans and credit cards.

CONCEPT CHECK 5.1

1. Identify the primary goals of monetary asset management.
2. Explain the circumstances when it would be appropriate to have funds in a checking account, a savings account, or in investments.
3. Describe the primary differences between depository institutions and other financial services providers.
4. Describe your insurance protections when you have funds on deposit in a depository institution.

Tool #1—Interest-Earning Checking Accounts

2 LEARNING OBJECTIVE

Earn interest and pay no or low fees on your checking accounts.

A **checking account** at a depository institution allows you to write checks against amounts you have on deposit. Checks transfer your deposited funds to other people and organizations. Checking accounts also can be accessed by using a **debit** (or **check**) **card** in an automated teller machine (ATM) or a point-of-sale (POS) terminal at a retail store. When you use a debit card, funds are instantaneously removed from your account. They are given to you as cash or sent electronically to an account owned by any other person or organization you designate to receive the funds. You can also access your checking account via telephone or home computer. When you use a checking account, record the date, check number, amount of the check, and to whom it was written into the **check register** you received when you obtained your blank

checking accounts At depository institutions, allow depositors to write checks against their deposited funds, which transfer funds to other people and organizations.

Checks transfer your deposited funds.

checks. Also subtract the amount of the check from your previous balance in the account. Deposits into the account are added as they occur, as well. This section examines the types of checking accounts available and checking account charges, fees, and penalties.

interest-earning checking account Any account on which you can write checks that pays interest.

tiered interest Common type of NOW account that pays lower interest on smaller deposits and higher interest on larger balances.

stop-payment order Notifying your bank not to honor a check when it's presented for payment.

Types of Checking Accounts

Checking accounts may or may not pay interest. If you have an account that does not pay interest, you may pay no fees or lower fees than an account that does pay interest. However, interest-paying accounts with no or very low fees are available since all depository institutions can offer some form of **interest-earning checking account** [also called a **negotiable order of withdrawal (NOW) account**]. A **share draft account** is the credit-union version of a NOW account. Its name arises because members of the credit union actually own the organization and their deposits are called shares. Costs for a share draft account are often lower than those for a checking account at a bank or savings bank. NOW accounts and share draft accounts may pay higher interest rates on larger balances (such as amounts above $1000). The combination of a base rate and a higher rate is called **tiered interest.** For example, an account might pay 2.1 percent on the first $2000 and 3.0 percent on any additional funds in the account.

A **lifeline banking account** offers access to certain minimal financial services that every consumer needs—regardless of income—to function in our society. An applicant's income and net worth determine acceptance into a lifeline program. The cost of lifeline banking accounts is extremely low, often about $5 per month; however, they do not pay interest.

Instant Message

Free Checking Is Not Totally Free

More and more banks are offering "free" checking accounts. What this means is that there is no minimum-balance requirement or monthly maintenance fee on the account and no activity fee for writing too many checks. However, there will be fees for writing bad checks, using another bank's ATM, inactivity on the account, and many others.

Checking Account Minimum-Balance Requirements

Most interest-earning checking accounts have a minimum-balance requirement that, if not met, will result in the assessment of a

Did You Know?...

What Happens When You Write a Check

Years ago checks were sent from institution to institution and ultimately were returned to account holders as **canceled checks.** That rarely happens anymore, as checks are now processed electronically. Instead, you are simply sent a listing of the checks you have written that have been paid, or **cleared,** by the depository institution. Some banks also send customers monthly **image statements** that show miniature computer pictures of their checks.

When you write a check, you either simultaneously make a copy that serves as your record that the check was written or record the transaction in your check register. The check itself is treated in one of two ways. First, in the traditional method, the check is sent to your bank so that the funds can be paid to whomever you had written the check. Second, in the method now being frequently used, the check is scanned by the receiving bank (or even the business to which you gave it) and an electronic **substitute check** is created and transmitted immediately to your bank. As a result the check can clear your bank in a matter of minutes or hours. Your checking account statement will indicate which checks cleared via a substitute check. Substitute checks are an acceptable version of the original check written by you. Under the Check Clearing for the 21st Century Act, your bank must quickly correct any errors in the processing of your check if the substitute check and the original check are both paid by your bank. Check your statement each month to ensure that this type of error has not occurred.

A **stop-payment order** tells your bank not to honor a check when it's presented for payment. To issue such an order, you can telephone your bank and stop payment on the check. In any event, a stop-payment order works only if the check has not yet cleared. And with electronic processing, check clearing can occur in a matter of minutes as can debit card transactions. Be aware that if the verbal stop-payment order is not followed up with a written instruction to the bank, the person or merchant to whom the check was written can still cash the check after 14 days. Even with a written request, the check can be cashed after six months unless the order has been renewed.

Did You Know?...

Payment Instruments for Special Needs

There are four types of payment instruments that you might find useful from time to time.

Traveler's Checks

Traveler's checks are issued by large financial institutions (such as American Express, Visa, and Carte Blanche) and sold through various outlets. They are accepted almost everywhere. Purchasers typically pay a fee of 1 percent of the amount of the traveler's checks, or $1 per $100. Traveler's checks come in specific U.S. denominations ($10, $20, $50, and $100) and in many foreign currencies. All traveler's check companies guarantee replacement of lost checks if their serial numbers are identified.

Money Orders

Many financial institutions, retailers such as Wal-Mart, and the U.S. Postal Service sell money orders. A **money order** is a checking instrument bought for a particular amount. Money orders are written for relatively small amounts, and the fee charged—usually from $0.50 to $8.00—is based on the amount of the order.

Certified Checks

A **certified check** is a personal check drawn on your account on which your financial institution imprints the word **certified,** signifying that the account has sufficient funds to cover its payment. The financial institution simultaneously places a hold on that amount in the account and then waits for the check to come back through the banking system before actually subtracting the funds. Checks certified by an officer of the financial institution generally cost $5 to $15.

Cashier's Checks

To be even more certain that a check is good, some payees insist on receiving payment in the form of a **cashier's check.** Such a check is made out to a specific party and drawn on the account of the financial institution itself; thus, it is backed by the institution's finances. To obtain such a check, you would pay the financial institution the amount of the cashier's check and have an officer prepare and sign it. Generally, a fee of $5 to $15 is charged.

Instant Message

Using Checking Accounts in Budgeting

Copies of your written checks, your check register, and your debit card receipts are very useful in budgeting as they provide a record of money spent. Keep track of all checks written and retain all debit card receipts until you can verify their accuracy in your account statement.

monthly fee. In addition, interest is usually not paid for a month when the account falls below the minimum. An account with no minimum-balance requirement is preferable but not always available. Checking account users must consider the amount of interest that will be lost and the fees that will be imposed.

Decision making becomes more difficult when the institution offers an interest-earning account in combination with either a minimum- or average-balance requirement. With a **minimum-balance account,** the customer must keep a certain amount (perhaps $500 or $700) in the account throughout a specified time period (usually a month or a quarter) to avoid a flat service charge (usually $5 to $15). A fee is assessed whenever the triggering event occurs—that is, when the balance drops below the specified minimum. With an **average-balance account,** a service fee is assessed only if the average daily balance of funds in the account drops below a certain level (perhaps $800 or $1000) during the specified time period (usually a month or a quarter).

In addition to monthly fees, institutions may assess lots of other fees. People interested in getting their money's worth in banking would be wise to avoid as many of the charges shown in Table 5.2 as possible.

traveler's checks Financial instruments issued by extremely large institutions that are accepted virtually anywhere in the world upon countersignature.

certified check Personal check on which your financial institution imprints the word *certified,* signifying that the account has sufficient funds to cover its payment.

minimum-balance account Checking account that requires customers to keep a certain minimum amount for a specified time period to avoid fees.

average-balance account Checking account for which service fees are assessed if the account's average daily balance drops below a certain level during specified time.

✓ CONCEPT CHECK 5.2

1. Distinguish between an interest-paying checking account and a lifeline account.
2. What is meant by *free checking?*
3. List three checking account fees or penalties that you could easily avoid by using your account appropriately.

Tool #2—Savings Accounts

3 LEARNING OBJECTIVE
Make the best use of the benefits of savings accounts.

savings account Account that provides an accessible source of emergency cash and a temporary holding place for extra funds that will earn some interest.

time deposits Savings accounts that financial institutions expect to remain on deposit for an extended period.

The second tool of monetary asset management is a **savings account.** A savings account provides you with a readily accessible source of emergency cash and a temporary holding place for funds in excess of those needed for daily living expenses. Interest rates on savings accounts are typically 0.20 to 0.50 percentage points higher than those paid on interest-paying checking accounts.

Funds on deposit in a savings account are considered time deposits rather than **demand deposits** (another term for checking accounts). **Time deposits** are savings that are expected to remain on deposit in a financial institution for an extended period. Institutions have a rule requiring that savings account holders give 30 to 60 days' notice for withdrawals, although this restriction is seldom enforced. Some time deposits are **fixed-time deposits,** which specify a period that the savings *must* be left on deposit, such as six months or three years; certificates of deposit (CDs) fit this description.

Statement Savings Accounts

The typical savings account offered by financial institutions is the **statement savings account** (also called a **passbook savings account**). Statement savings accounts permit frequent deposits or withdrawals of funds. No fees are assessed as long as a low minimum

Table 5.2 Costs and Penalties on Checking and Savings Accounts

Account Activity	Reasons for Assessing Costs or Penalties	Assessed on Checking or Savings
Automated teller machine (ATM) transactions	A customer's account is assessed a fee (often $1) for each transaction on an ATM; an additional fee may be charged for using an ATM not owned by the financial institution.	Checking, savings
Telephone, computer, or teller information	Fees are assessed for access or requests for account information by telephone, by computer, or in person (often $2 per transaction) after a number of free requests (perhaps three) have been made.	Checking, savings
Maintenance fees on a minimum-balance account (often waived if paychecks are directly deposited electronically)	The account balance falls below a set minimum amount, such as $300. A set fee of $5 to $15 per month is often charged.	Checking
Maintenance fees on an average-balance account (often waived if paychecks are directly deposited electronically)	The average daily account balance for the month falls below a set amount, such as $500. The cost is usually based on a set fee, a scaled amount (the more the account falls below the average, the greater the cost), or a percentage of the amount the account falls below the average.	Checking
Stop-payment order	A customer asks the financial institution to not honor a particular check; the fee is $15 to $30 per check.	Checking
Bad check "bounced" for insufficient funds	Costs of $20 to $40 or more are assessed for each check written or deposited to your account marked "insufficient funds."	Checking
Early account closing	Charges are assessed if a customer closes an account within a month or quarter of opening it. Charges range from $5 to $10.	Checking, savings
Delayed use of funds	Amounts deposited by check cannot be withdrawn until rules allow it.	Checking, savings
Inactive accounts	A monthly penalty may be assessed for inactive accounts (ones with no activity for six months to a year).	Checking, savings
Excessive withdrawals	Some savings institutions assess a penalty ($1 to $3) when withdrawals exceed a certain number per month.	Savings
Early withdrawal	Amounts withdrawn before the end of a quarter earn no interest for that quarter.	Savings
Deposit penalty	Deposits made during the current quarter earn no interest until the beginning of the next quarter.	Savings

balance ($25 to $100) is maintained. Statement savings account holders are provided with printed receipts to document their account transactions, and transactions usually can be accessed through ATMs. The process for opening a savings account is similar to that for a checking account.

All depository institutions offer time deposits. In the following subsections, we examine ways to save, savings account interest, the implications of the Truth in Savings Act, and grace periods.

Certificates of Deposit

A **certificate of deposit (CD)** is an interest-earning savings instrument purchased for a fixed period of time. The required deposit amounts range from $100 to $100,000, while the time periods range from seven days to eight years. The interest rate in force when the CD is purchased typically remains fixed for the entire term of the deposit. Depositors collect their principal and interest when the CD expires. Certificates of deposit are insured through the FDIC or the NCUSIF if purchased through an insured depository institution.

certificate of deposit (CD) An interest-earning savings instrument purchased for a fixed period of time.

Advice from a Pro

Endorse Your Checks Properly

Endorsement is the process of writing on the back of a check to legally transfer its ownership, usually in return for the cash amount indicated on the face of the check. Choosing the proper type of endorsement can protect you from having the check cashed by someone else against your wishes.

A check with a **blank endorsement** contains only the payee's signature on the back. Such a check immediately becomes a bearer instrument, meaning that anyone who attempts to cash it very likely will be allowed to do so, even if the check has been lost or stolen. You would be wise to never make a blank endorsement prior to depositing or cashing a check.

A **special endorsement** can be used to limit who can cash a check; to make this kind of endorsement, you write the phrase *Pay to the order of [name]* on the back along with your signature. A special endorsement can easily be put on a check that you want to sign over to another person. Such a "two-party check" is hard to cash other than by depositing it in an account at a financial institution.

A **restrictive endorsement** uses the phrase *For deposit only* written on the back along with the signature. It authorizes the financial institution to accept the check only as a deposit to an account. No one else can cash such a check. Checks deposited by mail should always be endorsed this way. In addition, you can include the name of the financial institution and the account number as part of the endorsement to make it even more restrictive.

Kathleen Prochaska-Cue
University of Nebraska–Lincoln

Advice from a Pro

Protect Yourself from Bad Check Fees

A **bad check** is one for which there are insufficient funds in the account. If funds to cover the check are not available, the bank will charge you a fee of perhaps $25 or even $40, and the merchant to whom the check was written will charge you a similar fee. The fees could total $80 for one bad check!

Almost all banks in the United States subscribe to Chex Systems, a company that lists several million people who have either written bad checks in the past or committed checking account fraud. It does not matter to Chex Systems whether the overdraft was later repaid—the person's name stays on the list anyway. Most banks and credit unions will not open a new account for five years for anyone on the list. (You can get a copy of your Chex Systems report at www.chexhelp.com.) Writing too many bad checks will also reflect poorly on a person's credit rating. (This topic is examined in Chapter 6.)

Your bank offers three ways to avoid bad check fees:

1. **Automatic funds transfer agreement.** The amount necessary to cover a bad check will be transmitted from your savings account to your checking account, as long as you keep sufficient funds in your savings account. An automatic funds transfer agreement is usually the least expensive of these three alternatives.
2. **Automatic overdraft loan agreement.** The needed funds will be automatically loaned to you by your bank or charged to your Visa or MasterCard account as a cash advance. Note that the loan may be advanced in fixed increments of $100. If you need only $10, for example, you will consequently be responsible for paying interest on amounts not needed. A cash advance fee of $10 or more may also be assessed.
3. **Bounce protection agreement.** The bank will honor checks written against insufficient funds up to a certain limit, such as $1000. In return, the customer must pay a $20 to $30 fee for each overdraft check and has one week to repay the funds. Bounce protection protects only against the fees that might be charged by a merchant to whom the check was written. Be aware that your bank might automatically sign you up for bounce protection unless you specifically decline it.

Cora Newcomb
Technical College of the Lowcountry, South Carolina

Did You Know?...

How to Ladder Your CDs

Most people who place money in CDs like them because the funds are insured and, thus, have no risk. But that is not exactly true. You see, when you put money in a CD, you have locked in an interest rate. What if rates in general go up while your money is in the CD? You are stuck at the lower rate. Or if rates come down, you will have to renew at the lower rate when the CD matures. Laddering is a technique that smoothes out the fluctuations in interest rates.

Here's how laddering works. Let's say you have $10,000 you would like to put into a CD. To start, simply go to bankrate.com and find the best rate you can get at the time. Then you purchase five CDs: CD #1 for $2000 for a one-year term, CD #2 for $2000 for a two-year term, CD #3 for $2000 for a three-year term, CD #4 for $2000 for a four-year term, and CD #5 for $2000 for a five-year term. If you want to have fewer rungs on the ladder, simply divide your initial funds by three or four rather than five.

As the CDs mature, you renew each of them for five years. After five years, you continue to have one CD mature each year, and you renew at the highest current market rate you can find (you do not have to stay with the same financial institution). As interest rates fluctuate over time, you always have some CDs at lower rates and some at higher rates. As a result, you are always earning an average rate overall, thus avoiding the possibility of having all of your money accruing very low rates. And you always will be able to access at least some of your money within a relatively short time frame.

Interest rates on longer-term CDs are usually higher than the comparable rates on shorter-term instruments. This difference is meant to reward savers for accepting higher risk: The longer they own a CD, the more their money is subject to inflation risk. The purchasing power of their funds on deposit and the interest received goes down because of inflation. This is why longer-term savers demand higher returns than shorter-term savers.

Variable-rate certificates of deposit (or **adjustable-rate CDs**) are also available. These instruments pay an interest rate that is adjusted (up ordown) periodically. Typically, savers are allowed to "lock in," or fix, the rate at any point before their CDs mature. This variability detracts from the main virtue of the fixed-rate CD—predictability. The best variable-rate CDs have a guaranteed minimum interest rate. **Bump-up CDs** allow savers to bump up the interest rate once to a higher market rate, if available, and to add up to 100 percent of the initial deposit whenever desired.

Money withdrawn from a CD before the end of the specified time period is subject to interest penalties. For certificates held less than one year, the depositor may lose a minimum of one month's interest; on certificates held more than a year, the depositor may lose a minimum of three months' interest. If the penalty exceeds the interest amount, you will get back less than you deposited. Consequently, before putting money into a CD, make sure that it is appropriate to tie up your funds in this way.

Because you do not make deposits and withdrawals after initially investing in a CD, you have no reason to restrict yourself to a nearby institution when searching for the highest yields. Lists of institutions paying the highest yields on CDs are updated weekly at www.bankrate.com. You might also check with a stockbroker for high CD yields because brokerage firms often buy CDs in volume to resell to individuals as **brokered certificates of deposit.** All types of CDs are excellent tools for managing monetary assets, and as banking deposits, they enjoy the added protection of federal deposit insurance.

automatic funds transfer agreement Agreement whereby the amount necessary to cover a bad check will be transmitted from your savings account to your checking account.

automatic overdraft loan agreement Arrangement whereby the needed funds will be automatically loaned to you by your bank or charged to your Visa or MasterCard account as a cash advance.

brokered certificates of deposit CDs purchased through a stock brokerage firm.

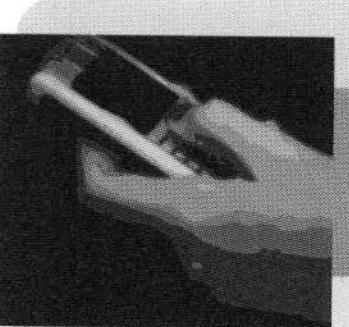

Instant Message

Uninsured CDs

Beware that some so-called CDs are actually "investment certificates." They are not insured and can be recalled by the financial institution and reissued at a lower interest rate prior to their maturity. Always ask "Is this a CD or an investment certificate?"

Did You Know?...

How to Reconcile Your Bank Accounts

It is a very good idea to maintain records of the activities occurring in your various banking accounts. You should record all checks written, debit card transactions, and deposits in your check register as they take place. It is also a good idea to go online every few days to confirm deposit and withdrawal (or checking) transactions.

You also should conduct an **account reconciliation** in which you compare your records with your bank's records, checking the accuracy of both sets of records and identifying any errors. The best time to do so is when you receive your monthly account statement from your bank. Account reconciliation is a three-step process:

1. Bring your own records up-to-date.
2. Bring the bank's records up-to-date.
3. Reconcile the results from Steps 1 and 2.

If the revised balance in your records and the revised balance from the bank statement differ, you will need to find where the error occurred. First, check the additions and subtractions in your records. Next, make sure that all previous entries in your records are properly reported on the account statement.

Looking for errors when Steps 1 and 2 yield differing results is a necessary but tedious task. Fortunately, it is less likely to be necessary today because of electronic banking. Many people go online frequently to check their balances and review their account activity for accuracy. In this way, they can catch errors early and are always very confident that their balances are exactly as shown in their own records. Here is a table you can use to guide your reconciling efforts.

	Amount	Comment
STEP 1: Bring Your Own Records Up-to-Date		
1. Enter balance from your check register.	$	
2. Add deposits not yet recorded.	$	
3. Subtract checks and other withdrawals not yet recorded.	$	
4. Subtract bank fees and charges included in the monthly statement and not yet recorded.	$	
5. Add interest earned.	$	
ADJUSTED CHECKBOOK REGISTER BALANCE	$	
STEP 2: Bring the Account Statement Up-to-Date		
1. Enter ending balance from bank statement.	$	
2. Add deposits made since bank statement closing date.	$	
3. Add outstanding checks written since bank statement closing date.	$	
ADJUSTED BANK STATEMENT BALANCE	$	

STEP 3: Compare adjusted checkbook register balance and adjusted bank statement balance. If the two balances do not match, identify where the error occurred.

account reconciliation Comparing your records with your bank's records, checking the accuracy of both sets of records, and identifying any errors.

How to Save

Americans have the lowest savings rates among the major countries of the world. When asked, they typically complain that there simply is no money left over at the end of the month. In a sense, they are correct, but they are thinking about savings in the wrong way. Wise financial planners take a different approach. They follow the adage "pay yourself first," which means to treat savings as the first expenditure after—or even before—getting paid. Build savings into your budget right from the beginning. In this way, you can effectively build funds to provide for large, irregular expenditures or unforeseen expenses; meet short-term goals; or save for retirement, a down payment on a home, or children's college education. Saving is not glamorous; slow and steady wins the race.

Your first savings goal is to accumulate enough money to cover living expenses (perhaps 70 percent of gross income) for three to six months. This money will serve as an **emergency fund** in case of job layoff, long illness, or other serious financial calamity. For a person with a $30,000 gross annual income, a three-month emergency fund would be $5250 ($30,000 ÷ 12 = $2500; $2500 × 0.70 = $1750 for each month). People who should consider keeping more funds available—perhaps income to cover six months to a year of living expenses—include those who depend heavily on commissions or bonuses or who own their own businesses.

Most people do not have a sufficient emergency fund. Instead, they rely on credit cards when an emergency or unforeseen need arises. This is an unwise way to manage finances. Other savings goals can be broken down into short-term goals and then monthly savings amounts calculated using the methods discussed in Chapter 3. If you have more than one or two goals, you can set up savings, or investment, accounts for each goal. In this way, you can keep track of your progress and keep money separately identified.

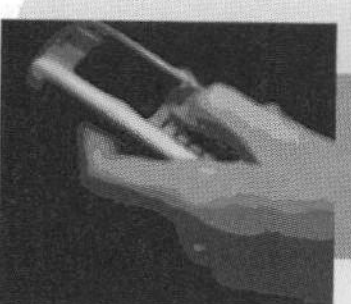

Instant Message

Be a Regular Saver

Start saving regularly when you are young. Break long-term goals into short-term benchmarks. Then when sufficient amounts are accumulated, move the funds from savings into higher-yielding investments.

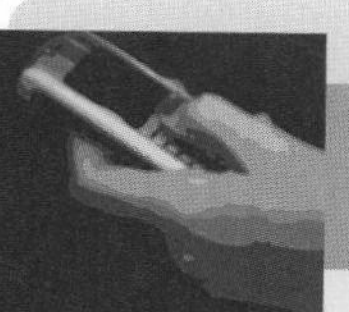

Instant Message

Use a Savings Calculator

A very easy-to-use savings calculator can be found at http://partners.financenter.com/kiplinger/calculate/us-eng/savings03.fcs. You can determine how much to save to reach your goal or find out what your savings will be worth at a future date.

Savings Account Interest

The calculation of interest to be paid on deposits in financial institutions is primarily based on four variables:

1. Amount of money on deposit
2. Method of determining the balance
3. Interest rate applied
4. Frequency of compounding (such as annually, semiannually, quarterly, monthly, or daily)

The Truth in Savings Act requires depository institutions to disclose a uniform, standardized rate of interest so that depositors can easily compare various savings options. This rate, called the **annual percentage yield (APY),** is a percentage based on the total interest that would be received on a $100 deposit for a 365-day period given the institution's annual rate of simple interest and frequency of compounding. The more frequent the compounding, the greater the effective return for the saver. The institution must use the APY as its interest rate in advertising and in other disclosures to savers.

annual percentage yield (APY) Return on total interest received on $100 deposit for 365-day period, given institution's simple annual interest rate and compounding frequency.

Wise money managers select the savings option that pays the highest APY and avoid institutions that assess excessive costs and penalties. Given the same APY, savers should choose an institution that compounds interest daily. Comparison shopping could easily earn you an extra $10 to $20 each year on a $1500 savings account balance. Smart savers also consider the fees and penalties outlined in Table 5.2 when deciding where to open a savings account.

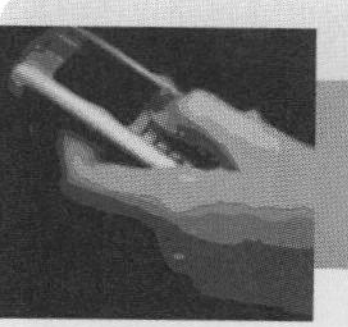

Instant Message

Focus on the APY

The best checking or savings account is the one with the highest APY. Once you have selected the account, make sure you manage it so that you avoid fees.

An account with a grace period provides the depositor with a small financial benefit. A **grace period** is the period (in days) during which deposits or withdrawals can be made and still earn the same interest as other savings from a given day of the interest period. For example, if deposits are made by the tenth day of the month, interest might be earned from the first day of the month. For withdrawals, the grace period

grace period Period (in days) for which deposits or withdrawals can be made without any penalty.

Did You Know?...

The Tax Consequences of Saving for Children's College

A long-term goal of many families is saving for their children's college education. The best ways follow:

Put Money in a Section 529 College Savings Plan. Named after the related section of the Internal Revenue Service Code, many states have established a **Section 529 college savings plan.** Deposits into a 529 plan are not deductible, but withdrawals for qualified educational expenses are tax free. Section 529 plans offer two options: prepaid tuition or an investment plan. A state-sponsored prepaid tuition plan allows parents, relatives, and friends to purchase a child's future college education at today's prices by guaranteeing that today's payment will be used for the future tuition payments at an approved institution of higher education in a particular state. In a 529 investment plan, the state offers an investment program from which to draw when the child is in college.

Put Money in a Coverdell Education Savings Account (ESA). Nondeductible contributions up to a maximum of $2000 per year may be made to a Coverdell education savings account (formerly known as an education IRA) to pay the future education costs for a child younger than age 18. The money and earnings on the account can be withdrawn later tax free to pay for public, private, or religious school expenses, K–12 (expires in 2011), trade school, or college, including tuition, fees, tutoring, uniforms, home computers, educational computer software, and room and board.

Put Money for College in a Custodial Account. A **custodial account** is one opened in the name of a child younger than age 14 under the provisions of the Uniform Gifts to Minors Act (or Uniform Transfers to Minors Act). These funds can be used for college expenses. Beginning in 2008, taxpayers in the 10 percent and 15 percent tax brackets will be able to sell assets, such as stocks or mutual funds, without paying any capital gains taxes. However, a so-called **kiddie tax rule** applies to unearned income (such as interest and dividends) of a minor child. This rule limits the ability of children to have their unearned income taxed at the child's low tax rate (presumably lower than the parent's tax rate). For children younger than age 18, the first $850 of unearned income (the income earned from an investment) earned on custodial account assets is tax free to the child. The next $850 is taxed at the child's tax rate. Unearned income in excess of $1700 is taxed at the parent's (likely higher) rate. When children reach age 18, they will pay tax solely based on their own income tax bracket. Assets held in a custodial account for a long time should not be sold until the individual reaches age 18. At that point, the kiddie tax rules will no longer apply and, assuming the child falls into one of the two lowest tax brackets, he or she will qualify for the 10 or 5 percent tax rate on capital gains, making the profit largely free of federal taxes.

Discount bonds (also called **zeroes** or **zero bonds**) are municipal, corporate, and government bonds that pay no annual interest. Discount bonds are sold to investors at sharp discounts from their face value and may be redeemed at full value upon maturity. For example, a $100 **Series EE savings bond** sold by the federal government can be purchased for $50, one-half its face amount. The interest, which is usually compounded semiannually, accumulates within the bond itself, and the return to the investor comes from redeeming the bond at its stated face value at the maturity date. Parents can invest in discount bonds through a custodial account to help pay for a child's college education. The phantom income "paid" to the child is generally so small that little, if any, income taxes are due each year as the interest accrues. An advantage of Series EE savings bonds is that taxes on the interest that accrues each year are deferred until redemption. The interest is tax free at redemption if the proceeds are used to fund the child's college education.

Put Money in a Roth IRA. Contributions to a Roth IRA account and the earnings within it accumulate tax free, and withdrawals are entirely free of tax after age 59½. Withdrawals before age 59½ are subject to the IRS's early distribution 10 percent withdrawal penalty. Before age 59½, the contributions to a Roth IRA account, but not the *earnings,* can be used for college expenses (or any purpose) without incurring the penalty. Withdrawals of deposits in a traditional IRA for college expenses also avoid the 10 percent penalty, but income taxes are due on the amounts withdrawn.

Section 529 Plan Provides a tax-free way to save for college.

generally ranges from three to five days. Thus, if a saver withdrew money from an account within three to five days of the end of the interest period, the savings might still earn interest as if the money remained in the account for the entire period.

CONCEPT CHECK 5.3

1. Describe reasons to keep money in a savings account rather than a checking account.
2. Distinguish between statement savings accounts and CDs.
3. Explain the benefits of a pay-yourself-first approach to saving.
4. Describe how can you use information about APY to your advantage.

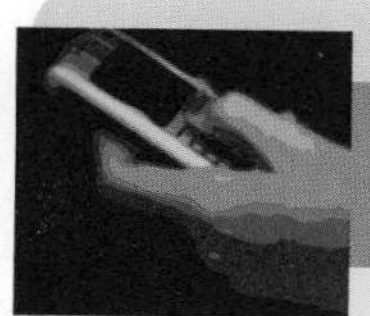

Instant Message

Interest Is Taxable

Any interest earned on your checking and savings accounts must be reported as income on your federal and state income tax returns. Your financial institutions should send you a Form 1099 statement that reports your interest income for the previous year; that information also is sent to the IRS.

Tool #3—Money Market Accounts

4 LEARNING OBJECTIVE

Explain the importance of placing excess funds in a money market account.

Most people use checking and savings accounts as the cornerstones of their monetary asset management efforts. When income begins to exceed expenses on a regular basis, perhaps by $200 or $300 each month, a substantial amount of excess funds can quickly build up. Although this situation is a comfortable one, it is wise from a monetary asset management point of view to move some of the excess funds into an account that pays more interest.

A **money market account** is any of a variety of interest-earning accounts that pays relatively high interest rates (compared with regular savings accounts) and offers some limited check-writing privileges. A money market account provides both checking and savings tools at a higher interest rate. Such accounts are offered by banks, savings banks, credit unions, stock brokerage firms, financial services companies, and mutual funds. The types of money market accounts are super NOW accounts, money market deposit accounts, money market mutual funds, and asset management accounts.

money market account Interest-earning accounts that pay relatively high interest rates and offer limited check-writing privileges.

Super NOW Accounts

A **super NOW account** is a government-insured money market account offered through depository institutions. It takes the form of a high-interest NOW account with limited checking privileges (usually a maximum of six checks per month). The initial minimum deposit typically ranges from $1000 to $2500. If the average balance falls below a specified amount (such as $1000), the account reverts to earning interest at the lower rate offered on a regular NOW checking account. Depositors can withdraw their funds (using checks or a debit card or electronically) at any time without penalty.

Money Market Deposit Accounts

A **money market deposit account (MMDA)** is also a government-insured money market account offered through a depository institution. It has minimum-balance requirements and tiered interest rates that vary with the size of the account balance. Institutions are allowed to establish fees for transactions and account maintenance, and account holders typically are limited to three to six transactions each month. Often the customer must deposit $1000 to open an account. If the average monthly

money market deposit account (MMDA) Government-insured money market account with minimum-balance requirements and tiered interest rates.

Did You Know?...

How Ownership of Accounts (and Other Assets) Is Established

When you open a new account, you will be asked to sign a **signature card** that can be used to verify the signatures of the owners of the account. Accounts can be owned either individually or jointly.

An **individual account** has one owner who is solely responsible for the account and its activity. At the death of the individual owner, the account becomes part of his or her estate and will go to heirs in accordance with the owner's will. If desired, individual accounts can be set up with a **payable at death designation,** whereby a person is named in the account to receive the funds upon the death of the individual owner. This allows that person to gain quick access to the funds after the owner's death but does not give the person any rights to the account while the owner is still alive.

A **joint account** has two or more owners, each of whom has legal rights to the funds in the account. The forms of joint ownership discussed here apply to all types of property, including automobiles and homes, as well as checking and savings accounts. Three types of joint ownership exist:

1. **Joint tenancy with right of survivorship** (also called simply **joint tenancy**) is the most common form of joint ownership, especially for husbands and wives. In this case, each person owns the whole of the asset and can dispose of it without the approval of the other(s). With accounts at financial institutions, the financial institution will honor checks or withdrawal slips possessing any of the owners' signatures. An advantage of a joint account is that in case of death of one of the owners, the property continues to be owned by the surviving account holder(s).
2. **Tenancy in common** is a form of joint ownership in which two or more parties own the asset, but each retains control over a separate piece of the property rights. In most states, the ownership shares are presumed to be equal unless otherwise specified. When one owner dies, however, his or her share in the asset is distributed to his or her heirs according to the terms of a will (or if no will exists, according to state law) instead of automatically going to the other co-owners.
3. **Tenancy by the entirety,** which exists in about 30 states, is restricted to property held between a husband and a wife. Under this arrangement, no one co-owner can sell or dispose of his or her portion of an asset without the permission of the other. This restriction prevents transfers by one owner without the knowledge of the other.

Generally, dual-earner couples prefer to own some property together and some property separately. If you own a business and default on a loan, for example, your creditors usually cannot attach your home if it is in your spouse's name. Nonworking spouses, however, should get their name on all deeds and investments; in the event of divorce, courts typically award property to the people who legally own it. In **community property** states—in which most of the money and property acquired during a marriage are legally considered the joint property of both spouses—the rights of both husbands and wives are equally protected. (These jurisdictions include Arizona, California, Idaho, Louisiana, Nebraska, Nevada, New Mexico, Puerto Rico, Texas, Washington, and Wisconsin.)

---

individual account Has one owner who is solely responsible for the account and its activity.

joint tenancy with right of survivorship (also simply called joint tenancy) Arrangement whereby each person owns the whole of the asset and can dispose of it without the approval of the other(s).

community property Arrangement in which most of the money and property acquired during a marriage are legally considered the joint property of both spouses.

money market mutual fund (MMMF) Money market account in a mutual fund rather than at a depository institution.

balance falls below a certain amount, such as $2500, the entire account earns interest at the lower rate of a regular NOW account. MMDAs generally pay higher interest rates than super NOW accounts.

Money Market Mutual Funds

A **money market mutual fund (MMMF)** is a money market account in a mutual fund investment company (rather than at a depository institution). It pools the cash of thousands of investors and earns a relatively safe and high return by buying debts with very short-term maturities (always less than one year). Interest is calculated daily, and an investor can withdraw funds at any time. Money market mutual funds typically pay the highest rate of return that can be earned on a daily basis by small investors.

MMMFs, which require a minimum deposit ranging from $500 to $1000, can prove convenient in cases of special financial needs because checks can be drawn on the account. On the other hand, the minimum check limit is often $200, which serves to discourage use of the MMMF as an everyday checking account. At least three dozen mutual funds offer unlimited check writing with no minimums on check amounts, however. Electronic transfers are permitted, but ATMs cannot be used because MMMFs are not depository institutions. Although MMMFs are not insured by any federal agency, they are considered extremely safe. Some funds buy only debts of the U.S. government and therefore are virtually risk free. To open an MMMF account, you can contact a mutual fund company; more details are provided in Chapter 15.

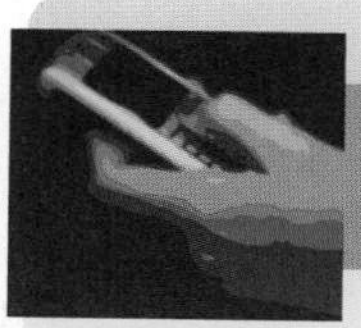

Instant Message

It Is Easy to Find a Money Market Mutual Fund

You can find money market mutual funds easily online. Some of these MMMFs are managed by American Century (americancentury.com), Dreyfus (dreyfus.com), Fidelity (fidelity.com), Scudder (scudder.com), and T. Rowe Price (troweprice.com).

Asset Management Accounts

An **asset management account** (**AMA;** also known as an **all-in-one account**) is a multiple-purpose, coordinated package that gathers most of the customer's monetary asset management vehicles into a unified account and reports them on a single monthly statement. Included in this package might be transactions in a money market mutual fund and in checking, credit card, debit card, loan, and stock brokerage accounts. Also known as **central asset accounts,** AMAs are offered through depository institutions, stock brokerage firms, financial services companies, and mutual funds. Such an account enables you to conduct all of your financial business with one institution. Typically, $10,000, spread across all subaccounts, is required to open an AMA. Some AMAs assess an annual fee, usually $100. Notice that this would be a 1 percent fee on a $10,000 deposit ($100 ÷ $10,000) and reduce your return by 1 percentage point.

asset management account (AMA, central asset accounts, or all-in-one account) Multiple-purpose, coordinated package that gathers most monetary asset management vehicles into a unified account and reports activity on a single monthly statement to the client.

Institutions that offer AMAs use computer programs to manage the funds in these accounts. Daily or weekly, the program checks the various subaccounts and **sweeps** funds in and out of the MMMF to ensure that the highest interest rates apply to the funds. AMAs usually have other features that attract investors as well—for example, free credit and debit cards, a rebate of 1 percent on credit card purchases, free traveler's checks, inexpensive term life insurance, and a free investment advisory newsletter.

CONCEPT CHECK 5.4

1. Explain the benefits of opening a money market account.
2. Distinguish between a super NOW account and a money market account.
3. Identify the feature of depository institution accounts not available with money market mutual funds.
4. List some benefits of an asset management account.

Electronic Money Management

5 LEARNING OBJECTIVE
Describe electronic money management, including your legal protections.

Monetary asset management can be summed up today with the phrase "paper, plastic, or neither." "Paper" comprises the traditional cash- and check-based systems. "Plastic" is the use of a debit or other type of card to access your funds via an ATM or point-of-sale (POS) terminals at a store. "Neither" is the use of your computer to access and use your accounts.

Did You Know?...

Using Plastic in Monetary Asset Management

There are many types of plastic devices used to access your money.

1. **ATM cards** allow you to withdraw money from or transfer money among your checking and savings accounts at an automatic teller machine. You must use a personal identification number (PIN) to use the card.
2. **Debit cards** do ATM cards one better—you can use them to make purchases via a point-of-sale (POS) terminal at retail outlets. Using a debit card to make a purchase immediately transfers money from your account. You typically use a PIN or provide your signature when using a debit card.
3. **Stored-value cards** contain a magnetic strip or bar code that encrypts the amount of money stored via the card. They are much like a mini-checking account you can use wherever the card is accepted. A gift card is an example of a stored-value card. So are cards given for refunds and rebates. Some stored-value cards can be "reloaded" with additional funds such as Wal-Mart's reloadable VISA debit card.
4. **Electronic benefits transfer (EBT) cards** are used by the government to pay military personnel and provide Social Security and other government benefits. They are much like a stored-value card, but the holder does not "load" the card—the payer does so.
5. **Credit cards** allow you make purchases or obtain cash with credit from the bank or retailer that issued the cards. These are debts that must be paid back, often with interest.

Most major banks now provide access to their banking services via websites. "Internet banks" operate entirely online. **Electronic money management** occurs whenever transactions are conducted without using paper documents. Most of these activities involve **electronic funds transfers (EFTs),** in which funds are shifted electronically (rather than by check or cash) among your various accounts and to and from other people and businesses.

electronic funds transfers (EFTs) Electronic fund transfers among various accounts or to and from other people and businesses.

Electronic Money Management Can Be Easy But Is Not Always Free

There are costs assessed for the use of some electronic banking.

ATM transaction fee Payments levied each time an ATM is used.

An **ATM transaction fee** may be assessed for using an ATM. Fees may be levied by your financial institution as well as by the institution that provides the ATM if you are using an ATM linked to a national network. For example, you might pay your institution $1 to $3 and another $1 to $3 (or more) to the machine provider. Making frequent, small withdrawals can be expensive: a $2 ATM fee is 10 percent of a $20 withdrawal but just 1 percent of a $200 withdrawal.

Transaction fees of $1 to $3 also may be assessed whenever you make a purchase via a point-of-sale terminal at a retail store. This is most likely to happen when you use a PIN number. Such a usage is called an "online" transaction and occurs when you hit the "debit" button on the terminal. You can usually avoid the fee if you hit "credit" instead and the transaction becomes an "off-line" transaction. Rather than use your PIN, you sign for the purchase. The transaction is still a debit transaction but is processed in a way that costs less for your bank. You also have additional legal protections for "off-line" transactions as discussed later.

Instant Message

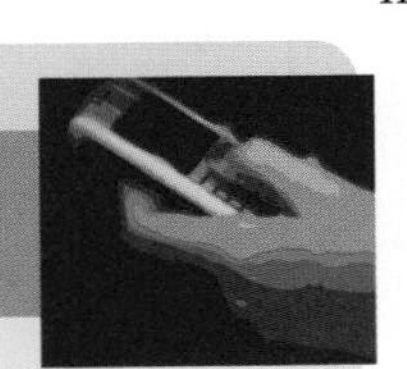

Reduce and Avoid ATM Fees

Minimize your ATM fees by making fewer large withdrawals rather than more frequent small withdrawals. Avoid fees altogether by using your own bank's ATMs.

Fees can be assessed for other uses of electronic money management. Some banks charge for online banking services such as bill paying and verification of your account balances. Often these fees for these services are a fixed monthly rate for all usage that may be cheaper than writing checks and mailing payments. These paper-based services are often free.

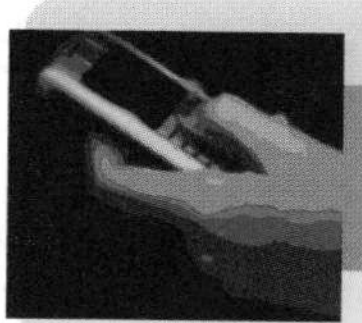

Instant Message

Use Direct Deposit to Save Money—and Time

Many financial institutions offer no-fee checking accounts to customers who have their paychecks electronically sent from their employer via **direct deposit.** In addition, the institution may charge a lower interest rate on loans and credit card accounts for customers who use direct deposit.

Consumer Protection Regulations

Federal and state regulations have been adopted to provide protections for the use of debit cards and other electronic banking. The Electronic Funds Transfer Act is the governing law, and the Federal Reserve Board's Regulation E provides specific guidelines on ATM and debit card liability. Cards can be issued only if the card cannot be used until validated and the user is informed of his or her liability for unauthorized use as well as other terms and conditions. When you sign up for electronic banking services, the depository institution must inform you of your rights and responsibilities in a written **disclosure statement.**

Users must be provided with written receipts when using an ATM or POS terminal. These receipts show the amount of the transaction, the date on which it took place, and other pertinent information. General protection of a customer's account takes the form of a **periodic statement** sent by the financial institution that shows all electronic transfers to and from the account, fees charged, and opening and closing balances. Smart users of electronic banking services and electronic funds transfers regularly compare the information on this periodic statement with their written receipts.

periodic statements Consumer-protecting recaps that show all electronic transfers to and from accounts, fees charged, and opening and closing balances.

Fixing Errors If you find an error in your periodic statement, notify the issuing organization in writing as soon as possible. Use the notification procedures found in the disclosure statement accompanying your monthly statement. If the institution needs more than ten business days to investigate and correct a problem, generally it must return the amount in question to your account while it conducts the

Did You Know?...

How to Protect Your Privacy When Banking Online

Your privacy is a big concern whenever you conduct banking transactions online. Here are some tips for reducing the risk:

- Never check your bank account online via wireless systems away from home. These are easily hacked. Even home wireless systems are at risk, however.
- Avoid using someone else's computer to manage your account. If you do, shut down the computer completely when finished.
- Do not provide any account information if you get an unsolicited e-mail. It's likely from a scam artist.
- When finished, always hit the log off button at the top of the page instead of just closing the browser window.
- Regularly change your password and keep it to yourself.
- Study your statements. Ask about anything that looks unusual or the least bit in error.
- Make and save paper copies of all your online transactions until you can verify their accuracy on your next account statement.

Did You Know?...

How to Develop Money Sense in Children

A major theme of this chapter is that checking, savings, and investments are an integral part of reaching your financial goals. By progressively building savings funds, you can achieve financial success. Parents can help children develop money sense by providing them with opportunities to manage their own money while still young and guiding this behavior toward appropriate patterns. Parents can do the following to increase their children's ease in handling money:

1. **Give an allowance.** Even children as young as five years old should have some money of their own. An allowance should be the source of these funds in the preteen years. The amounts of allowance should fit the family income level. Allowances are a means for teaching money management.
2. **Encourage work.** Once children reach their preteen years, there are many opportunities to earn their own money. When children see what it takes to make money, it is easier for them to know the real cost of spending.
3. **Set reasonable limits.** Children should be given age-appropriate limits for spending in various categories and should be required to save a portion, perhaps 50 percent, of their money. But parents should not stop children from "wasting their money" or bail them out of every mistake. We learn best from experience, not from what someone else tells us is best.
4. **Teach them to make good choices through increasingly complex activities.** The dollar amounts and the areas of discretionary spending can increase as the child becomes older. A seven-year-old might be allowed to spend his or her own money on toys, snacks, and gifts to charity at church or school. A 14-year-old might be allowed to buy meals and clothing as well. More responsibility and autonomy should be given only as the child exhibits the ability to handle previous, less complicated tasks.
5. **Help them learn to wait.** Children should have autonomy over at least some of their own money. But the remainder, perhaps 50 percent, should be saved. Then when children desire some high-cost item, they can see that saving for a while can help them reach their goal.
6. **Talk about family finances with children.** In many families, money matters are a taboo subject. Children need to see that parents must work at managing the family finances. They should know what it costs to raise a family and to make ends meet. Otherwise, kids will grow up with unrealistic expectations and behaviors that will be passed on to their children.
7. **Be a role model.** Children learn more from what they see than what they are told. Avoid borrowing money from a child. They will learn that credit is easy. And, certainly, pay them back on time if you do borrow. Otherwise, they will think they can borrow without paying back. Save money yourself, and tell your children that saving means that you can't have something you, or they, want right way.

Instant Message

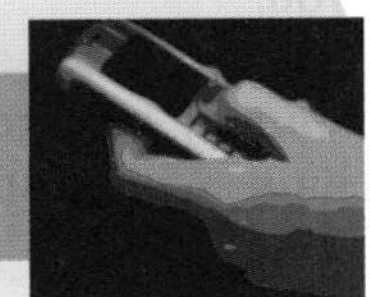

Lifeline Banking May Save You Money

College students who are independent of their parents may qualify for a very low-cost lifeline banking account.

Use Positive "I" Statements Messages focusing on "I" describe the behavior in question, the feelings you experienced because of the behavior, and any tangible effect on you. For example, a spouse might say, "I feel upset when we use credit cards because I do not know where we will find the money to pay the bills at the end of the month." "I" messages say three things: what (the behavior), I feel (feelings), because (reason). Using "I" messages helps build stronger relationships because they tell the other person "I trust you to decide what change in behavior is necessary." Beware of "I" statements that begin with "I need you to ...." "You" statements are blaming statements, such as "You always ...," "You never ...," and "If you don't, I will ...." These statements have a high probability of being condescending to

Each member of the family should be aware of and involved with important financial decisions.

other people, of making them feel guilty, and of implying that their needs and wants are not as important as yours.

Be Honest and Talk Regularly Achieving consensus requires that each person be honest when talking about money matters. It further demands that couples regularly talk about finances. Be prepared to compromise. When you make decisions together, act on them. Focus attention on both current financial activities and issues as well as long-term financial planning. Use these discussions to forge overall long-term strategies for dealing with your family finances. Once the proper base has been established, short-term issues are more likely to fall into place.

Complications Brought by Remarriage

Remarriage merges financial histories, values, and habits as well as households. Some remarried couples—and those choosing to live together following a previous relationship—have substantial combined incomes bolstered by child-support payments from a former spouse. In many cases, at least one person may be paying (instead of receiving) alimony and child support. When "his," "her," and "our" children are included in the household, living expenses can be quite steep. Special concerns for blended families include determining who assumes financial responsibility for biological offspring and stepchildren; handling resentment over alimony and child-support payments; and managing unequal assets, incomes, responsibilities, and debts. Even gift giving can become a quandary.

Many remarried people use "his" and "hers" funds and require the legally responsible parent owing financial support to a previous spouse or to children to make such payments out of his or her own money. Professor Jean Lown of Utah State University suggests that, "What is best is what the couple can agree on."

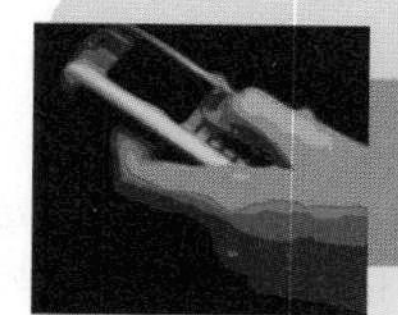

Instant Message

Press "Credit" When Using Your Debit Card

Debit card fees are now much more common when you make purchases with the card. Press the "credit" key instead and sign your name on the receipt and no fee is charged.

CONCEPT CHECK 5.6

1. Explain why it is difficult for many people in relationships to talk about money matters.
2. Identify four ways you could more effectively communicate about money matters.
3. List four things that parents can do to help their children be better money managers.

What Do You Recommend Now?

Now that you have read the chapter on managing checking and savings accounts, what would you recommend to Mark Rosenberg and Trina Adams in the case at the beginning of the chapter regarding:

1. Where they can obtain the monetary asset management services that they need?
2. Their best use of checking accounts and savings accounts as they begin saving for a home?
3. The use of a money market account for their monetary asset management?
4. Their use of electronic banking in the future?
5. How they can best discuss the management of their money and finances?

Big Picture Summary of Learning Objectives

1 List and define the tools of monetary asset management and identify the types of financial services firms that provide those tools.

Maximizing interest earnings and minimizing fees on savings and checking accounts is the goal of monetary asset management. The five primary providers of monetary asset management services include depository institutions (such as banks and credit unions), stock brokerage firms, mutual funds, financial services companies, and insurance companies.

2 Earn interest and pay no or low fees on your checking accounts.

The first tool of monetary asset management is an interest-earning checking account that is used to pay monthly living expenses. When setting set up an account, consider charges, fees, and penalties.

3 Make the best use of the benefits of savings accounts.

Your second tool of monetary asset management is a savings account in which you can place funds not needed for six months to five years into the future. Some longer-term savings instruments such as certificates of deposit allow you to safely earn even higher returns if you are willing to forgo liquidity.

4 Explain the importance of placing excess funds in a money market account.

Your third tool of monetary asset management is a money market account. When your income begins to exceed expenses on a regular basis, it is wise to move excess funds into such an account, which typically pays a higher interest rate. The funds can be left in the account while you consider other investment options. Money market accounts include super NOW accounts, money market deposit accounts, money market mutual funds, and asset management accounts.

5 Describe electronic money management, including your legal protections.

Electronic money management occurs whenever banking transactions are conducted via computers without the customer using paper documents. Electronic banking includes the use of automatic teller machines (ATMs), point-of-sale (POS) terminals, debit cards, and stored-value cards. The Electronic Funds Transfer Act protects consumers who use electronic money management.

6 Discuss your personal finances and money management more effectively with loved ones.

Recognize the psychological and emotional aspects of money and identify your own approaches to money. Communicate openly and frequently about money matters by using "I" statements.

Let's Talk About It

1. Describe some examples of checking and savings account transactions that result in assessment of costs or penalties.
2. You know someone who recently wrote several bad checks. Explain to him the relative benefits of having an automatic funds transfer agreement versus an automatic overdraft loan agreement.
3. When would you recommend using an individual account, a joint tenancy with right of survivorship account, and a tenancy by the entirety account for money management needs?
4. When might it be appropriate for you to open a money market account?
5. What should you do if your ATM or debit card is lost or stolen? Why?
6. Have you ever had a disagreement with a friend or family member over a money issue? How might you communicate differently now than you did previously?

Do the Numbers

1. Twins Barbara and Mary are both age 22. Beginning at age 22, Barbara invests $2000 per year for eight years and then never sets aside another penny. Mary waits ten years and then invests $2000 per year for the next 30 years. Assuming they both earn 8 percent, how much will each twin have at age 65? (Hint: Use Appendix Tables A.1 and A.3 or visit the *Garman/Forgue* website.)
2. You need to amass $20,000 in the next ten years to help with a relative's college expenses. You have $10,000 available to save. What annual percentage rate must be earned to realize the $20,000? (Hint: Use Appendix Table A.1 or visit the *Garman/Forgue* website.)
3. You want to create a college fund for a child who is now three years old. The fund should grow to $30,000 in 15 years. If a current investment yields 7 percent, how much must you invest in a lump sum now to realize the $30,000 when needed? (Hint: Use Appendix Table A.2 or visit the *Garman/Forgue* website.)
4. How many years of investing $2000 annually at 8 percent will it take to reach a goal of $20,000? (Hint: Use Appendix Table A.3 or visit the *Garman/Forgue* website.)
5. You plan to retire in 22 years. To provide for your retirement, you initiate a savings program of $6000 per year yielding 7 percent. What will be the value of the retirement fund at the beginning of the 23rd year? (Hint: Use Appendix Table A.3 or visit the *Garman/Forgue* website.)

Financial Planning Cases

Case 1
A Lobbyist Considers Her Checking Account Options

Shudan Lee, a lobbyist for the textile industry living in Springfield, Virginia, has maintained a checking account at a commercial bank for three years. The bank requires a minimum balance of $100 to avoid an account charge, and Shudan has always maintained this balance. Recently, she heard that a nearby savings and loan association is offering NOW accounts paying 3 percent interest on the average daily balance of the account. This institution requires a minimum balance of only $300, but a forfeiture of monthly interest occurs if the account falls below this minimum. Given her past habits at the commercial bank, Shudan feels that the $300 minimum would not be too difficult to maintain. She is seriously thinking about moving her money to the NOW account.

(a) What is the main reason Shudan should move her checking account?

(b) What should Shudan know about the differences among NOW accounts offered at various financial institutions?

(c) If Shudan maintained an average balance of $350 in a NOW checking account earning 3 percent interest, how much interest would she have earned on her money after one year? (Hint: Use Appendix Table A.1 or visit the *Garman/Forgue* website. Do not forget to subtract Shudan's initial lump-sum deposit from the derived answer.)

(d) How much more would Shudan have earned in one year if she decided to invest in a money market mutual fund paying 4 percent interest instead of the NOW account? (Hint: Use Appendix Table A.1 or visit the *Garman/Forgue* website.)

Case 2
Deciding Among the Tools of Monetary Asset Management

Kwaku Addo earns $4200 per month take-home pay and has the funds directly deposited in his checking account. He spends only about $3500 per month, and the excess funds have been building up in his account for about one year.

(a) What other types of accounts are available to Kwaku?

(b) How might he manage his accounts to earn as much interest as possible and keep his money safe?

(c) How might he use electronic money management to accomplish these tasks?

Case 3
Use of a Computer Banking Service

Trent Searle, a service station owner from Roy, Utah, pays a $10 monthly fee for a computerized home banking service. His friend Scott Simpson feels that Trent is wasting his money on the service. Trent has a net income of $3000 per month, plus other earnings from some investments. In addition, he is part owner of an apartment complex, which gives him approximately $1000 per month in income. He always tries to put his excess earnings into solid investments so that they might bring future income and security.

(a) What specific computer banking services would help a person such as Trent?

(b) Justify Trent's paying the $10 monthly fee for computer banking.

Case 4
Victor and Maria Hernandez Need to Save Money Fast

The Hernandez family is experiencing some financial pressures, even though the couple has a combined income of $66,000. Also, their eldest son, Joseph, will start college in only three years. Maria is contemplating going to work full time to add about $15,000 to the family's annual income.

(a) If Maria begins working full time, how much federal income and Social Security tax will the couple pay on this amount if their marginal tax rate is 25 percent and the Social Security and Medicare tax rate is 7.65 percent?

(b) How much should they save annually for the next three years if they want to build up Joseph's college fund to $20,000, assuming a 7 percent rate of return and ignoring taxes on the interest? (Hint: Use Appendix Table A.1 or visit the *Garman/Forgue* website.)

(c) Given their 25 percent marginal tax rate, what is the Hernandezes' after-tax return and how would that affect the amount they would need to save each year?

(d) What savings options are open to the Hernandezes that could reduce or eliminate the effects of taxes on their savings program?

Case 5
How Should the Johnsons Manage Their Cash?

In January, Harry and Belinda Johnson had $3540 in monetary assets (see page 93): $1178 in cash on hand; $890 in a statement savings account at First Federal Bank earning 1.5 percent interest compounded daily; $560 in a statement savings account at the Far West Savings and Loan earning 1.5 percent interest compounded semiannually; $160 in a share account at the Smith Brokerage Credit Union earning a dividend of 1.6 percent compounded quarterly; and $752 in their non–interest-earning regular checking account at First Interstate.

(a) What specific recommendations would you give the Johnsons for selecting a checking account and savings account that will enable them to effectively use the first and second tools of monetary asset management?

(b) Their annual budget, cash-flow calendar, and revolving savings fund (see Tables 3.8, 3.9, and 3.10 on pages 83–85) indicate that the Johnsons will have additional amounts to deposit in the coming year. What are your recommendations for the Johnsons regarding use of a money market account? Why?

(c) What savings instrument would you recommend for their savings, given their objective of saving enough to purchase a new home? Support your answer.

(d) If the Johnsons could put most of their cash on hand ($1000) into a money market account earning 4 percent, how much would they have in the account after one year?

On the 'Net

Go to the Web pages indicated to complete these exercises. You can also go to the *Garman/Forgue* website at college.hmco.com/business/students for an expanded list of exercises. Under General Business, select the title of this text. Click on the Internet Exercises link for this chapter.

1. Visit the website for *Economic Review*, published by the Federal Reserve Bank of Kansas City, where you will find an article (scroll down) on electronic payment mechanisms in retail trade. What is the major reasoning behind the contention in the article that such forms of payment are more evolutionary than revolutionary?
2. Visit the website for Bankrate.com at http://www.bankrate.com/brm/rate/chk_sav_home.asp for information about checking accounts. Use the search box to find articles on "Check 21," which governs check clearing and processing. How might the rules of Check 21 affect your use of your checking account?
3. Visit the Bankrate.com website at http://www.bankrate.com/brm/rate/deposits_home.asp where you will find information about rates of return on certificates of deposit. What is the best rate for a one-year CD and a five-year CD in a large city near your home (look in the state, then the city)? How do these rates compare with the average rates nationally and the highest rates nationally?
4. Visit the website for Federal Reserve Bank of Chicago at http://www.chicagofed.org/. Use the search box to find articles on "internet bank." Read the article titled "What You Should Know About Internet Banking." After reading the information, make a list of important positive and negative aspects of Internet banking. Is Internet banking right for you?

Visit the Garman/Forgue website ...

@college.hmco.com/business/students

Under General Business, select *Personal Finance 9e.* There, among other valuable resources, you will find a complete glossary, ACE questions, links to help you complete the chapter exercises, and links to other personal finance sites.

CHAPTER 6

Building and Maintaining Good Credit

You Must Be Kidding, Right?

People with no prior credit history or one that shows poor repayment patterns in the past often wonder if they will ever be able to get credit. Simply put, why would any lender want to trust them? Which of the following is true today about the availability of credit for people in such situations?

A. No one will ever grant them credit.

B. If they wait a few years, their situation could change.

C. If they keep searching, they will find a lender that will treat them like everyone else.

D. Credit is relatively easy to obtain.

The answer is D. There are plenty of lenders that accept people with no or poor credit histories. The reason is the interest rate they will charge. Charging a high rate makes them willing to grant credit to high-risk applicants. Building and maintaining your good credit history will get you low interest rates!

LEARNING OBJECTIVES

After reading this chapter, you should be able to:

1. **Explain** reasons for and against using credit.
2. **Establish** your own debt limit.
3. **Achieve** a good credit reputation.
4. **Describe** common sources of consumer credit.
5. **Identify** signs of overindebtedness and describe options available for debt relief.

What Do You Recommend?

Carrie Savarin, age 25, is a nurse practitioner with the local health department. She earns $50,000 per year, with about $4000 of her income coming from overtime pay. Her employer provides a qualified tax-sheltered retirement plan to which Carrie contributes 4 percent of her salary and for which she receives an additional 4 percent matching contribution from her employer. (She could contribute up to 6 percent with an equal employer match.) Carrie has $19,000 in outstanding student loans on which she will pay $354 per month over the next five years, and her total credit card debt is $3000. Otherwise, she is debt free. Carrie would like to purchase a new or late-model used car to replace the car she has been driving since her senior year in high school. She has $2000 to use as a down payment.

What would you recommend to Carrie on the subject of building and maintaining good credit regarding.

1. Factors she should consider regarding her ability to take on additional debt?
2. The impact of her current debt on her ability to obtain a loan to buy a vehicle?
3. Where she might obtain financing for a vehicle loan?
4. The effect of taking on a loan on her overall financial planning?

FOR HELP with studying this chapter, visit the Online Student Center:

www.college.hmco.com/pic/garman9e

Online Study Center

Did You Know?...

How to Manage Student Loan Debt

You should minimize your student loan debt because large debts make it more challenging to meet other financial goals such as buying a home and saving for retirement. Here are some tips for managing student loan debt:

1. **Choose the most advantageous repayment pattern allowed.** The standard repayment plan for student loan debt calls for equal monthly installments paid over ten years, but to pay the debt off faster, you can establish a graduated repayment plan whereby the payments are lower in the early years but then increase in later years.
2. **Pay electronically.** Make arrangements to have the monthly payment transferred electronically out of a checking account and you can receive a reduction in the interest rate.
3. **Make your repayments on time, every time.** In some programs, if you make the first 48 payments on time, the interest rate will be reduced by 2 percentage points. Failing to repay in a timely manner can have dire consequences, including forfeiture of federal and state income tax refunds, as well as Social Security and veterans' benefits.
4. **Consolidate your student loans.** Consolidating your education loans means that all your existing loans are paid off and one new loan is created. This strategy may allow for a much more convenient repayment schedule. The interest rate may be lower, the monthly payment is usually lower, and the amount of time for repayment may be longer under the new loan. Loans can be consolidated through a private bank or through one of three government programs: Collegiate Funding Services (www.cfsloans.com), Sallie Mae (www.salliemae.com), or Federal Direct Consolidation Loans (www.loanconsolidation.ed.gov).

Double incomes should not mean double debt.

CONCEPT CHECK 6.2

1. Distinguish among the debt payments-to-disposable income, ratio of debt-to-equity, and continuous-debt methods for setting your debt limit.
2. What are the threshold levels for both the debt payments-to-disposable income and ratio of debt-to-equity methods that would indicate that a person is carrying too much debt?
3. Discuss how dual-earner households should consider their ability to carry additional debt.

Obtaining Credit and Building a Good Credit Reputation

3 LEARNING OBJECTIVE
Achieve a good credit reputation.

Credit is widely and readily available to many of us today. It is not unusual for a customer to walk into a retail store such as Target or Home Depot and be offered a credit card account that can be used immediately. However, if the applicant has not used credit previously (no credit) or if he or she has failed to honor credit agreements in the past (bad credit), an offer of credit is typically not extended. Your success in obtaining credit hinges on an understanding the credit approval process and having a good credit reputation.

The Credit Approval Process

To obtain credit, you must first complete a credit application. Based on the information in this application, the lender will investigate your credit history. The information is then evaluated (sometimes instantly via computer), and the lender decides whether to extend credit. When an application is approved, the rules of the account are contained in the credit agreement.

Did You Know?...

The Top 3 Financial Missteps with Credit

People slip up in building and maintaining good credit when they do the following:

1. Make late payments on credit cards
2. Pay more than 15 percent of disposable income toward nonmortgage debt payments
3. Fail to regularly check the accuracy of credit bureau files

You Apply for Credit A **credit application** is a form or interview that requests information that sheds light on your ability and willingness to repay debts. This information helps lenders make informed decisions about whether they will be repaid by borrowers. Answering questions completely and honestly both on an application form and during an interview (if any) is important. If inconsistencies arise during the lender's subsequent investigation of the applicant's credit history, the lender could refuse the request for credit or charge a higher interest rate. At the time of application, always ask for a copy of the rules governing the account, including the APR and various repayment terms. However, these terms are not final and can change when the actual decision to lend is made. That is why you should read all credit contracts before signing.

Approximately 12 percent of all people who apply for credit are denied. Half of the unsuccessful applicants have no established **credit history** (a continuing record of a person's credit usage and repayment of debts) or their credit history contains negative information. A bad credit history is like having high blood pressure—you may not know you have a problem until something bad happens, such as when your loan application is rejected.

credit application Form or interview that provides information about your ability and willingness to repay debts.

credit history Continuing record of a person's credit usage and repayment of debts.

The Lender Conducts a Credit Investigation Upon receiving your completed credit application, the lender conducts a **credit investigation** and compares the findings with the information on your application. The goal of the investigation is to assign a **credit rating** to the applicant; this rating is the lender's evaluation of the applicant's creditworthiness. In assigning a credit rating, lenders will look at the applicant's prior credit usage; repayment patterns; and other important characteristics, such as income, length of employment, home ownership status, and credit history.

To conduct its investigation, the lender obtains a **credit report** from a **credit bureau** that keeps records of many borrowers' credit histories. Lenders pay a fee for each credit report requested. Credit bureaus compile information from merchants, utility companies, banks, court records, and creditors. Most of the more than 2000 local credit bureaus in the United States belong to national groups that collectively have access to the credit histories of more than 160 million adults.

Lenders use a **credit scoring** system (also known as **risk scoring**) in which a statistical measure is used to rate applicants on the basis of various factors deemed relevant to creditworthiness and the likelihood of repayment. All three of the major credit-reporting bureaus calculate and report credit scores to lenders. You also have the right to know your scores, although you usually must pay a fee to do so. The most well-known score is the FICO score developed by Fair, Isaac and Company.

credit report Information compiled by a credit bureau from merchants, utility companies, banks, court records, and creditors about your payment history.

credit bureau Firm that collects and keeps records of many borrowers' credit histories.

credit scoring (risk scoring) system Statistical measure used to rate applicants based on various factors deemed relevant to creditworthiness and the likelihood of repayment.

The Lender Decides Whether to Accept the Application and Under What Terms The approval or rejection of credit is based on the lender's judgment of the willingness and ability of the applicant to repay the debt. If the application is accepted, a contract is created that outlines the rules governing the account. For credit cards, this contract is called a **credit agreement.** For loans, the contract is called a **promissory note** (or simply, the **note**).

The actual lender always makes the decision about whether to grant credit. Credit scoring simply allows lenders to categorize credit users according to the perceived level of risk. Under the concept of **tiered pricing,** lenders may offer lower interest rates to applicants with the highest credit scores while charging steeper rates to more risky applicants. Even people with low credit scores usually can find some lender that will say yes, however. The interest rates will be higher for those borrowers. Of course,

credit agreement Contract that stipulates repayment terms for credit cards.

promissory note (note) Contract that stipulates repayment terms for a loan.

unfair discrimination Making distinctions among individuals based on unfair criteria when granting credit.

Did You Know?...

Unfair Credit Discrimination Is Unlawful

The Equal Credit Opportunity Act (ECOA) prohibits certain types of **unfair discrimination** (making distinctions among individuals based on unfair criteria) when granting credit. Under this law, a lender must notify an applicant within 30 days about the lender's acceptance or rejection of a credit application. The ECOA also requires the creditor to provide the applicant with a written statement, if requested, detailing the reasons for refusing credit. Rejecting a credit application due to poor credit history is legal. Conversely, it is illegal to reject applicants on the basis of gender, race, age, national origin, religion, or receipt of Social Security income or public assistance. Credit applications cannot ask for information that could be used in a biased manner, such as marital status and childbearing plans. (Applicants may offer such information voluntarily, however.) If discrimination is proved in court, the lender may be fined as much as $10,000.

A creditor cannot require an applicant to disclose income from alimony, separate maintenance payments, or child support payments. If the borrower wants this income to be counted during the lender's evaluation of the application, the creditor can consider whether that income stream is received consistently. Information about a spouse or former spouse may not be requested unless the spouse will use the account, it is a joint account, or repayment of debts will rely on the spouse's income or other financial support. The law requires that credit granted in both spouses' names be used to build a credit history for the parties as a couple as well as for each individual spouse.

Review your credit report annually to make sure it is accurate.

for approved purposes. (One in five complaints to the Federal Trade Commission involves credit bureaus.) FCRA is partially enforced by consumers.

If you find an error or omission, you should immediately take steps to correct the information. Here's how:

1. Notify the credit bureau that you wish to exercise your right to a reinvestigation under FCRA. Specifically, you should ask the bureau to "reaffirm" the item. If the credit bureau responds by stating that the information is accurate, you have the right to challenge the item with the lender involved.
2. The bureau must reinvestigate the information within 30 days. If it cannot complete its investigation within 30 days, it must drop the information from your credit file.
3. If the information was erroneous, it must be corrected. If a report containing the error was sent to a creditor investigating your application within the past six months, a corrected report must be sent to that creditor.
4. If the credit bureau refuses to make a correction (perhaps because the information was "technically correct"), you may wish to provide your version of the disputed information (in 100 words or less) by adding a **consumer statement** to your credit bureau file. This statement will be included with any credit reports by that bureau.
5. Negative information in your file is generally not reportable after a period of seven years except for bankruptcy data, for which the time limit is ten years.

consumer statement Your version of a credit issue that shows up on your credit report when the credit bureau refuses to drop a disputed claim.

CONCEPT CHECK 6.3

1. Summarize the basic steps that occur when someone applies for credit.
2. What is a credit history, and what role do credit bureaus play in the development of your credit history?
3. What is a credit score, and what five major factors go into its calculation?
4. Identify five actions you can take to build a good credit reputation.
5. Summarize the protections provided under the Fair Credit Reporting Act.

Did You Know?...

The Effects of Divorce on Your Credit

The breakup of a marriage affects the creditworthiness of both partners. The Federal Trade Commission makes the following suggestions for individuals seeking a divorce.

Pay careful attention to credit accounts held jointly, including mortgages, second mortgages, and credit cards. The behavior of one divorcing spouse will continue to affect the other individual as long as the accounts are held in both names. One party could make credit card charges, for example, and refuse to pay the debt, leaving the financial burden on the other party. When possible, ask creditors to close joint accounts and reopen them as individual accounts. Never accept a creditor's verbal assurance, either over the telephone or in person, that an account has been closed. Always insist on written confirmation, including the effective date of the account closure.

When debts were accumulated in both names, a divorce decree has no legal effect on who technically owes which debts. Creditors can legally collect from *either* of the divorcing parties. If the person absolved of responsibility for the debt under the divorce decree is forced by a creditor to pay off the account, he must then go to court to seek enforcement of the divorce decree and collect reimbursement from the former spouse.

Both before and after a divorce, get a copy of your credit report. Check it for accuracy and challenge any problem areas, such as accounts that continue to be shown in both names.

4 LEARNING OBJECTIVE
Describe common sources of consumer credit.

Sources of Consumer Loans

Today's consumers have many sources of consumer loans from which to choose. Most consumer lending occurs through depository institutions and sales finance companies. Other sources include consumer finance companies, stockbrokers, and insurance companies. Table 6.3 shows the interest rates charged and example payment amounts and finance charges from these various sources of consumer loans.

Depository Institutions Loan Money to Their Banking Customers

Depository institutions include commercial banks, mutual savings banks, savings banks, and credit unions (see Chapter 5 for more detailed descriptions of these institutions). They tend to make loans to their own customers and to noncustomers with good credit histories. For most loans, depository institutions offer highly competitive rates, partly because the funds loaned are obtained primarily from their depositors. The interest rate commonly ranges from 9 to 16 percent. Research indicates that many people who go elsewhere for loans actually meet the qualifications for depository institution lending and end up paying a higher interest rate than necessary.

Sales Finance Companies Loan Money to Buy Consumer Products

sales finance company Seller-related lender whose primary business is financing sales for its parent company.

A **sales finance company** is a seller-related lender (such as GMAC Financial Services for General Motors Corporation and Ford Motor Credit) whose primary business is financing the sales of its parent company. Such firms specialize in making purchase loans, often with the item being bought serving as the collateral for the loan. Because the seller often works in close association with the sales finance company, credit can be approved on the spot.

Sales finance companies require collateral and deal only with customers who are considered medium to good risks. Thus, their interest rates are often competitive with

Table 6.3 What It Costs to Borrow Money

Lender	Annual Percentage Rate	Two-Year Loan		Five-Year Loan	
		Monthly Payment	Finance Charge	Monthly Payment	Finance Charge
Life insurance company	6	$44.32	$ 63.68	$19.33	$159.80
Sales finance company	8	45.23	85.52	20.28	216.80
Credit union	10	46.14	107.36	21.25	275.00
Commercial bank	12	47.07	129.68	22.24	334.40
Mutual savings bank	12	47.07	129.68	22.24	334.40
Savings and loan association	12	47.07	129.68	22.24	334.40
Bank credit card	18	49.92	198.08	25.39	523.40
Consumer finance company	24	52.87	268.88	28.77	726.20

Credit costs money. Just how much can be seen by considering the cost of borrowing $1000 for two years and for five years from various sources at various interest rates.

those offered by depository institutions. Their interest rates may be even lower than those offered by other sources if the seller subsidizes the rate to encourage sales—as with the special low-APR financing often offered on new cars, for example. Most new-car loans today are made by sales finance companies.

Consumer Finance Companies Make Small Cash Loans

A **consumer finance company** specializes in making relatively small loans and is, therefore, also known as a **small-loan company.** These lenders range from the well-recognized Household Finance Corporation (HFC) and Beneficial Finance Corporation (BFC) to many local neighborhood lenders. Such companies make both secured and unsecured loans and require repayment on a monthly installment basis. The interest rates they charge are higher than those available from depository lenders because consumer finance companies focus on borrowers with low credit scores.

consumer finance company/small loan company Firm that specializes in making relatively small secured or unsecured loans that require monthly installment payments.

Approximately one-fifth of all loans granted by consumer finance companies are for the purpose of debt consolidation (described later). Other common uses of such loans are for travel, vacations, education, automobiles, and home furnishings. Some small-loan companies specialize in making loans by mail. They advertise in newspapers and magazines and on the Internet to attract borrowers, who complete a credit application and receive approval via mail.

Stockbrokers Loan Money to Their Clients

Many people build significant assets in investment accounts that may be earmarked for their children's college education, their own retirement, or other specific needs. If you have a margin account (see Chapter 14), you can borrow from your stockbroker using your investments as collateral. Although many people prefer not to tap into these funds directly, it may be possible to borrow from or against these accounts. For example, it may be possible to borrow from certain employer-sponsored, tax-sheltered retirement accounts (see Chapter 17), depending on the rules of the plan. Care must be taken to ensure that the loan plus interest is repaid so that the savings goal can still be met. Tax consequences may arise if retirement account loans are not repaid.

Insurance Companies Loan Money to Their Policyholders

Insurance companies, such as State Farm or Allstate, offer car loans and credit cards to their policyholders. They may make these loans out of their own funds or have bank subsidiary companies set up to handle such loans. Insurance companies loan only

Did You Know?...

About Alternative Lenders

A number of avenues through which to obtain credit are available that may not look like credit. Credit can come from unusual sources, including payday lenders, rent-to-own stores, and pawnshops.

Payday lenders (which are banned in some states) are businesses that grant credit when they honor a personal check but agree not to deposit the check for a week or longer. The fees for check cashing are sometimes 20 percent or more of the amount of the check, pushing the APR (if the check is held for later deposit) to several hundred percent or higher.

A **rent-to-own program** provides a mechanism for buying an item with little or no down payment by renting it for a period of time, after which it is owned. Furniture, appliances, and electronic entertainment items are commonly sold via the rent-to-own approach. This form of credit is often used by people who believe they cannot qualify for credit purchases. These programs have two big drawbacks for consumers. First, the renter does not own the item until the final payment is made. Paying late or stopping payments will cause the products to be seized with no allowance being made for the previous "rental" payments. Second, the actual cost for renting items is often exorbitantly high. For example, a TV worth $300 might be rented for $15 per week for one year, producing a finance charge of $480 (52 × $15 − $300).

A **pawnshop** is a lender that offers single-payment loans, often ranging from $100 to $500, for short time periods (typically one or two months), after the borrower turns over an item of personal property to the pawnshop. The dollar amount loaned is typically equal to one-third or less of the value of the item pawned. In most states, a borrower need merely turn over the item, present identification, and sign on the dotted line. The pawnshop owner can legally sell the item if the borrower fails to redeem the property by paying the amount due, plus interest, within the time period specified. The pawnshop typically charges an interest rate of about 5 percent per month plus a 2 percent monthly storage fee; thus, the annual combined "interest" amounts to 84 percent [(5 + 2) × 12]. Clearly, pawnshops represent the lender of last resort for borrowers.

payday lenders Businesses that grant credit by honoring a personal check but agree not to deposit the check for a week or longer (until payday).

rent-to-own programs Provide a mechanism for buying an item with little or no down payment by renting it to the borrower for a period of time after which the borrower owns the merchandise.

to their customers with high credit scores. As a consequence, they can be a low-cost source from which to borrow money.

Policyholders who have cash-value life insurance policies can obtain loans based on the cash values built up in their policies. (This topic is examined in Chapter 12.) An advantage to borrowing on a cash-value life insurance policy is that the interest rates are low, ranging from 4 to 6 percent even though the policyholders actually borrow their own money. Many people fail to pay back such loans because no fixed schedule of repayment is established and insurance companies do not pressure borrowers to repay the debt. If the insured person dies before repaying the loan, the life insurance company will deduct the amount of the loan from the amount that would otherwise be paid on the policy.

CONCEPT CHECK 6.4

1. List the four types of depository institutions that are sources of credit for consumers.
2. Distinguish between a sales finance company and a consumer finance company.
3. Summarize how stockbrokers and insurance companies serve as sources of consumer credit.
4. Explain where you would go to obtain credit at the lowest cost.

Dealing with Overindebtedness

5 LEARNING OBJECTIVE
Identify signs of overindebtedness and describe options that are available for debt relief.

People become **overindebted** when their excessive personal debts make repayment difficult and cause financial distress. There are ways to get out from under this burden.

overindebted When one's excessive personal debts make repayment difficult and cause financial distress.

Ten Signs of Overindebtedness

1. **Exceeding debt limits and credit limits.** Are you spending more than 20 percent of your take-home pay on credit repayments? Do you sometimes reach the maximum approved credit limits on your credit cards?
2. **Not knowing how much you owe.** Have you lost track of how much you owe? Do you avoid reality by not adding up the total? Are you afraid to add up how much debt you have?
3. **Running out of money.** Are you using credit cards on occasions when you previously used cash? Are you borrowing to pay insurance premiums, taxes, or other large, predictable bills? Are you borrowing to pay for regular expenses such as food or gasoline? Do you try to borrow from friends and relatives to carry you through the month?
4. **Paying only the minimum amount due.** Do you pay the minimum payment—or just a little more than the minimum—on your credit cards instead of making large payments to more quickly reduce the balance owed?
5. **Requesting new credit cards and increases in credit limits.** Have you applied for additional credit cards to increase your borrowing capacity? Have you asked for increases in credit limits on your current credit cards? Have you obtained a cash advance on one credit card to make the payment on another card?
6. **Paying late or skipping credit payments.** Are you late more than once a year in paying your mortgage, rent, car loan, or utility bills? Do you frequently pay late charges? Are you juggling bills to pay the utilities, rent, or mortgage? Are creditors sending overdue notices?
7. **Using debt-consolidation loans.** Are you borrowing, perhaps from a new source, to pay off old debts? Such action may temporarily reduce pressure on your budget, but it also indicates that you are overly indebted.
8. **Taking add-on loans.** Taking **add-on loans,** also called **flipping,** occurs when you refinance or rewrite a loan for an even larger amount before it has been completely repaid. Suppose that a loan of $1000 has been repaid down to $400. You decide to refinance the debt balance of $400 by borrowing $2000 and using the additional $1600 ($2000 − $400) for other purposes.
9. **Experiencing garnishment. Garnishment** is a court-sanctioned procedure by which a portion of the debtor's wages are set aside by the debtor's employer to pay debts. Wages and salary income, including that of military personnel, can be garnished. The Truth in Lending Act prohibits more than two garnishments of one person's paycheck. The total amount garnished cannot represent more than 25 percent of a person's disposable income for the pay period or more than the amount by which the weekly disposable income exceeds 30 times the federal minimum wage (whichever is less). In addition, the law prohibits garnishment from being used as grounds for employment discharge.
10. **Experiencing repossession or foreclosure. Repossession** is a legal proceeding by which the lender seizes an asset (called **foreclosure,** if the property is a home) for nonpayment of a loan. When a lender repossesses property, the borrower may still owe on the debt because of a deficiency balance. A **deficiency balance** occurs when the sum of money raised by the sale of the repossessed collateral fails to cover the amount owed on the debt plus any repossession expenses (collection, attorney, and court costs) paid by the creditor.

garnishment Court-sanctioned procedure by which a portion of debtors' wages are set aside by their employers to pay debts.

repossession/foreclosure Legal proceeding by which the lender seizes an asset.

deficiency balance Occurs when money raised by sale of repossessed collateral doesn't cover the amount owed on the debt plus any repossession expenses.

Did You Know?...

The Effect of Using Voluntary Repossession to Get Out of Debt

Consider the tale of Betty Peterson, a corporal in the army from San Diego, California, whose husband lost his job. In an attempt to reduce expenditures, Betty voluntarily turned her Chevrolet HHR back to the finance company while still owing $11,000 on the debt. A month later, she was notified that the vehicle had been sold at auction for $7800; the proceeds were reduced to only $7100, however, due to collection and selling costs of $500 and attorney fees of $200. Betty was billed for a deficiency balance of $3900 ($11,000 − $7100). She would have been much better off had she sold the vehicle herself, as vehicles at auction usually sell for much less than their book values.

Federal Law Regulates Debt Collection Practices

The federal **Fair Debt Collection Practices Act (FDCPA)** prohibits third-party debt collection agencies from using abusive, deceptive, and unfair practices in the legitimate effort to collect past-due debts. **Debt (or credit) collection agencies** are firms that specialize in making collections that could not be obtained by the original lender. In some cases, they assist the original lender (for a fee); in other cases, they take over (purchase) the debt and become the creditor. When a debtor offers to make payment for several debts, the FDCPA requires that the amount paid must be applied to whichever debts the debtor desires. Banks, dentists, lawyers, and others who conduct their own collections (second-party collectors) are exempt from the provisions of the FDCPA. Nevertheless, many states have enacted similar laws that govern these second-party collectors.

Collection agencies are prohibited from telephoning the debtor at unusual hours, making numerous repeated telephone calls during the day, not applying payments to amounts under dispute, using deceptive practices (such as falsely claiming that their representatives are attorneys or government officials), making threats, or using abusive language. They also cannot telephone a debtor's employer. Even with these limitations, collection agencies can be irritatingly persistent when collecting past-due accounts. If the collection effort is not successful, as a last resort the creditor may take the debtor to court to seek a legal judgment against the debtor; this judgment may be collected by repossessing some of the debtor's property or garnishing wages.

Fair Debt Collection Practices Act (FDCPA) Prohibits third-party debt collection agencies from using abusive, deceptive, or unfair practices to collect past-due debts.

debit collection agency Firm that specializes in collecting debts that the original lender could not collect.

Steps to Take to Get Out from Under Excessive Debt

Even the most well-meaning credit user can become overextended as a result of illness, unemployment, or divorce. What should you do if you realize that you are overly indebted?

1. **Determine your account balances and the payments required.** Find out exactly what it would take to pay off your balances today. This amount is not the same as the total of your remaining payments and probably includes penalties and late charges if you have been unable to keep up with your payments. Also ask your lenders to give you a monthly payment dollar amount needed to pay off the debts by the date previously agreed.
2. **Focus your budget on debt reduction.** Calculate the percentage of your budget necessary to make the payments on your debts, and then add 5 percent. Use this extra money to help pay your creditors by applying the extra money to the debt with the highest APR. The sacrifices required will pay off in the long run. Remember, paying off debts provides a better "rate of return" than putting money into savings and investments, so invest your money in debt repayment first.
3. **Contact your creditors.** Try to work out a new payment plan with your creditors. Many lenders, including those that finance automobiles, may let you skip a payment. They want to see you solve your financial problems so you can avoid

Instant Message

Student Loans Can Cause High Debt-to-Equity Ratios

Recent college graduates who have large education loans have high debt-to-equity ratios. If the ratio does not improve within three years after graduating, a serious debt problem may exist.

bankruptcy. Creditors are more likely to work with borrowers who come to them first rather than after collection efforts begin.

4. **Take on no new credit.** Return your credit cards to the issuer or lock them up so that you cannot use them. Disciplined action to reduce debt should show results in only a few months. If progress does not occur, seek professional help.
5. **Refinance.** Determine whether some loans can be refinanced to obtain a lower interest rate, especially mortgage loans. (See Chapter 9 for details.) Even if you refinance, keep making the same payment so you will pay the new loan off more quickly. Obtaining a debt-consolidation loan might be appropriate for someone who has acquired too much debt, but you should avoid the temptation to use this strategy simply to lower your total monthly payments. However, it is smart to use debt consolidation to lower APRs.
6. **Find good help.** You may be able to obtain free budget and credit advice from your employer, credit union, or labor union. Also, many banks and consumer finance companies offer advice to help financially distressed debtors, as do nonprofit **credit counseling agencies (CCAs).** Such an agency can make arrangements with unsecured creditors to collect payments from overly indebted consumers to repay debts, and it can provide individuals with credit counseling, assistance with financial problems, educational materials on credit and budgeting, and a **debt management plan (DMP).** A DMP is an arrangement whereby the consumer provides one monthly payment (usually somewhat smaller than the total of previous credit payments) that is distributed to all creditors. Creditor concessions, such as reduced interest rates, may also allow debtors to repay what they owe more quickly than would otherwise be possible. Credit counseling services are provided at a nominal cost on a face-to-face basis, online, or via the telephone. Seek an agency that is a not-for-profit agency that has 501(c)3 status from the IRS and that will do a full budget review for you. You can obtain consumer information and a referral by contacting the Association of Independent Consumer Credit Counseling Agencies [(800) 450-1794; www.aiccca.org] or the National Foundation for Credit Counseling [(800) 388-2227; www.nfcc.org].
7. **Avoid bad help.** Many companies claim that they want to help people in debt. A **credit repair company** (also known as a **credit clinic**) is a firm that offers to help improve or fix a person's credit history for a fee. Some are not so reputable, however. Avoid firms that charge a hefty advance payment ($250 to $2000).

In reality, no company can remove or "fix" accurate but negative information in anyone's credit history. You can improve your future credit history by making on-time repayments. And you can correct errors in your credit bureau files on your own for free with little effort.

credit counseling agency (CCA) Agency that can arrange payment schedules with unsecured creditors for overly indebted consumers and can provide individuals with credit counseling.

debt management plan (DMP) Arrangement whereby consumer provides one monthly payment (usually somewhat smaller than the total of previous credit payments) that is distributed to all creditors.

credit repair company (credit clinic) Firm that offers to help improve or fix a person's credit history for a (usually hefty) fee.

bankruptcy Constitutionally guaranteed right that permits people (and businesses) to ask a court to find them officially unable to meet their debts.

discharged debts Debts (or portions thereof) that are excused as a result of a bankruptcy.

Bankruptcy as a Last Resort

When debts are so overbearing that life seems really bleak—a situation that may be aggravated by recent unemployment, illness, disability, death in the family, divorce, or small-business failure—many people consider filing a petition in federal court to declare bankruptcy. **Bankruptcy** is a constitutionally guaranteed right that permits people (and businesses) to ask a court to find them officially unable to meet their debts. Federal laws allow bankruptcy for consumers in two forms: Chapter 13 and Chapter 7. Some debts are never excused **(discharged)** through either Chapter 13 or 7 bankruptcies. Such debts include education loans that have come due within the previous seven years, fines, alimony, child support, income taxes for the most recent three years, and debts for causing injury while driving under the influence of alcohol or drugs.

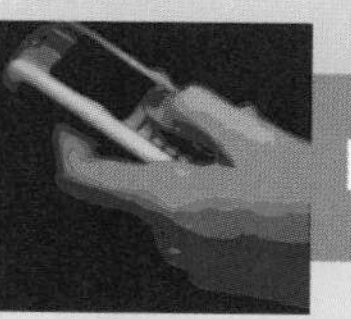

Instant Message

Debt Management Plans and Your Credit Score

Entering into a debt management plan will not lower your credit score. However, the credit score is not the only factor that lenders use when judging creditworthiness. Some lenders will look on a debt management plan unfavorably and deny credit or charge higher APRs for people who have been on a plan, compelling those people to search more extensively for good credit terms.

Before you can file for bankruptcy under either Chapter 7 or Chapter 13, you must complete credit counseling with an agency approved by the United States Bankruptcy Trustee's office.* The purpose of this counseling is to give you an idea of whether you really need to file for bankruptcy or whether an informal repayment plan would get you back on your economic feet. Once your bankruptcy case is over, you'll have to attend another counseling session, this time to learn personal financial management. Only after you submit proof to the court that you have fulfilled this requirement can you get a bankruptcy discharge wiping out your debts.

Chapter 13 of the Bankruptcy Act (wage earner or regular income plan) Designed for individuals with regular incomes who might be able to pay off some or all of their debts given certain court protections.

Chapter 13—Regular Income Plan

Chapter 13 of the Bankruptcy Act (also known as the **wage earner** or the **regular income plan**) is designed for individuals with regular incomes who might be able to pay off some or all of their debts given certain protections of the court. Under this plan, the debtor submits a debt repayment plan to the court that is designed to repay as much of the debt as possible, typically in three to five years. After the debtor files a petition for bankruptcy, the court issues an automatic **stay**—a court order that temporarily prevents all creditors from recovering claims arising from before the start of the bankruptcy proceeding. This action protects the debtor from collection efforts by creditors, including garnishments. Typically, no assets may be sold by the debtor or repossessed by the lender after a stay is granted.

After the court notifies all creditors of the petition for bankruptcy, a hearing is scheduled. With the help of a **bankruptcy trustee** (an agent of the bankruptcy court), who verifies the accuracy of a bankruptcy petition at a hearing and who distributes the assets according to a court-approved plan, the proposed repayment plan is reviewed (and modified, if necessary) and finally approved by the court. The debtor must then follow a strict budget while repaying the obligations. During this time, the bankrupt person cannot obtain any new credit without the permission of the trustee. If the debtor makes all scheduled payments, he or she is discharged of any remaining amounts due that could not be repaid within the repayment period.

Instant Message

"Chase"ing College Students on Facebook

As an indicator of how important the college market is to credit card companies, Chase Bank is Facebook's exclusive credit card sponsor, and ads for Chase credit cards have begun to appear on the popular social-networking website.

Chapter 7 of the Bankruptcy Act—Immediate Liquidation Plan (straight bankruptcy) Provides for the liquidation of assets with proceeds applied to paying off excusable debts to the degree possible.

Chapter 7—Immediate Liquidation Plan

Chapter 7 of the Bankruptcy Act, also called **straight bankruptcy,** provides for an immediate liquidation of assets. This option is permitted when it would be highly unlikely that substantial repayment could ever be made. Petitioners who have higher incomes may be required to repay some of their debt under Chapter 13.

When Chapter 7 is allowed, most of the bankrupt person's assets are given over to the bankruptcy trustee. Any assets that serve as collateral for loans are turned over to the appropriate secured creditors. Most of the remaining assets are sold, and the proceeds of the sales are distributed to the unsecured creditors of the bankrupt person. Any leftover debt is usually discharged by the court when the debtor emerges from bankruptcy. State and federal laws govern what assets the debtor can keep. In general, bankrupt people are allowed to keep a small amount of equity in their homes, an inexpensive automobile, and limited personal property.

Bankruptcy should be used as a last resort rather than as a quick fix or cure-all for overuse of credit. Bankruptcy remains on one's credit record for ten years. Because employers, landlords, and creditors check credit reports, people who have declared bankruptcy typically face years of trouble when renting housing,

Instant Message

Debt Reduces Your Ability to Save and Invest

Saving and investing over long periods of time is the key to building wealth. Taking on excessive debts early in life may compromise your goal of being financially successful.

*To find an approved agency, go to www.usdoj.gov/ust and click "Credit Counseling and Debtor Education."

obtaining home loans, and getting credit cards. A discharged debtor usually emerges with little, if any, debt and a much improved net worth but cannot use Chapter 7 again for at least eight years. Therefore, some creditors will lend to bankrupt individuals, albeit at much higher interest rates than usual.

CONCEPT CHECK 6.5

1. Identify four signs of overindebtedness.
2. List the major provisions of the Fair Debt Collection Practices Act.
3. What services are provided by a credit counseling agency and how might a debt management plan work to provide relief for someone who is having debt problems?
4. Distinguish between Chapter 7 and Chapter 13 bankruptcy and explain who might be forced to use Chapter 13 rather than Chapter 7.

What Do You Recommend Now?

Now that you have read this chapter on building and maintaining good credit, what would you recommend to Carrie Savarin regarding:

1. Factors she should consider regarding her ability to take on additional debt?
2. The impact of her current debt on her ability to obtain a loan to buy a vehicle?
3. Where she might obtain financing for a vehicle loan?
4. The effect of taking on a loan on her overall financial planning?

Big Picture Summary of Learning Objectives

1 Explain reasons for and against using credit.

People borrow for a variety of reasons—for example, to deal with financial emergencies, to have goods immediately, and to obtain discounts in the future. Perhaps the greatest disadvantage of using credit is the ensuing loss of financial flexibility in personal money management. The annual percentage rate (APR) provides the best approximation of the true cost of credit.

2 Establish your own debt limits.

It is important to establish your own debt limit. Three methods can be used: the debt payments-to-disposable income method, the ratio of debt-to-equity method, and the continuous-debt method.

3 Achieve a good credit reputation.

In the process of opening a credit account, the lender investigates your credit history, obtains a credit score (such as a FICO score) from a credit bureau, and then determines whether to grant credit and under what conditions.

4 Describe the common sources of consumer credit.

Major sources of consumer loans include depository institutions (commercial banks, savings and loan associations, and credit unions), sales finance companies, and consumer finance companies. Loans are also available through insurance companies and stockbrokers. Depository institutions typically offer the best interest rates, although sales finance companies sometimes offer low rates to increase sales of the products being financed. In any case, only those people with high credit scores qualify for the best rates from any source.

5 Identify signs of overindebtedness and describe the options that are available for debt relief.

Among the signals of being overly indebted are exceeding credit-limit guidelines and running out of money too often. People experiencing serious financial difficulties can obtain professional assistance through nonprofit credit counseling agencies or by contacting an attorney about bankruptcy.

Let's Talk About It

1. If there is such a thing as good debt, what types of debt do you consider to be "good"? What types do you consider to be "bad"?
2. What aspects of your financial life make you creditworthy? What aspects would make it difficult for you to obtain credit?
3. How might students judge whether they are taking on too high a level of student loan debt?
4. If you wanted to borrow money to buy a new or used car, where would you turn? Why?
5. Are you concerned that the major national credit bureaus may have files containing information about you? What do you think about the process required to correct errors in those files?
6. Is it too easy for college students to get credit cards, and do you know anyone who has gotten into financial difficulty because of overuse of credit cards?
7. How do you feel about bankruptcy? When might bankruptcy be justified in your opinion? When might it not be justified?

Financial Planning Cases

Case 1
Reducing Expenses to Buy a New Car

Courtney Bennett graduated from college and accepted a position in Manhattan, Kansas, as a librarian in the public library. Courtney has no debts, and her budget is shown in the first column of Table 6.2 on page 164. She now faces the question of whether to trade in her old car for a new one requiring a monthly payment of $330. Taking the role of a good friend of Courtney, suggest how Courtney might cut back on her expenses so that she can afford the vehicle.

(a) What areas might be cut back?

(b) How much in each area might be cut back?

(c) After finishing your analysis, what advice (and possibly alternatives) would you offer Courtney about buying the new car?

Case 2
Preparation of a Credit-Related Speech

Jacob Marchese of Auburn, Alabama, is the credit manager for a regional chain of department stores. He has been asked to join a panel of community members and make a ten-minute speech to graduating high-school seniors on the topic "Using Credit Wisely." In the following outline that Jacob has prepared, provide him with some suggested comments.

(a) What is consumer credit?

(b) Why might graduates use credit?

(c) How can graduates use credit wisely?

Case 3
Debt Consolidation as a Debt Reduction Strategy

Justin Granovsky, an assistant manager at a small retail shop in Las Vegas, Nevada, had an unusual amount of debt. He owed $5400 to one bank, $1800 to a clothing store, $2700 to his credit union, and several hundred dollars to other stores and individuals. Justin was paying more than $460 per month on the three major obligations to pay them off when due in two years. He realized that his take-home pay of slightly more than $2100 per month did not leave him with much excess cash. Justin discussed an alternative way of handling his major payments with his bank's loan officer. The officer suggested that he pool all of his debts and take out an $11,000 debt-consolidation loan for seven years at 14 percent. As a result, he would pay only $206 per month for all his debts. Justin seemed ecstatic over the idea.

(a) Is Justin's enthusiasm over the idea of a debt-consolidation loan justified? Why or why not?

(b) Why can the bank offer such a "good deal" to Justin?

(c) What compromise would Justin make to remit payments of only $206 as compared with $460?

(d) If you assume that the debt-consolidation loan will cost more in total interest, what would be a justification for this added cost?

Case 4
Victor and Maria Advise Their Niece

Victor and Maria have always enjoyed a close relationship with Maria's niece Teresa, who graduated from college with a pharmacy degree. Teresa recently asked Maria for some assistance with her finances now that her education debts are coming due. She owes $19,000 in student loans and earns $44,000 per year in disposable income. Teresa would like to take on additional debt to furnish her apartment and buy a better car.

(a) What advice might Maria give Teresa about managing her student loan debt?

(b) If next year Teresa were to consolidate her loans into one loan at 8 percent interest, what advice might Maria give regarding Teresa's overall debt limit using both the debt payments-to-disposable income method and the continuous-debt method? (Hint: Use Table 7.1 on page 199 or visit the *Garman/Forgue* website to calculate monthly payments for various time periods.)

Case 5
The Johnsons Attempt to Resolve Their Credit and Cash-Flow Problems

Harry and Belinda have a substantial annual joint income—more than $70,000, in fact. Nevertheless, they expect to experience some cash-flow deficits during several months of the upcoming year (see Tables 3.8 and 3.9 on pages 83 and 84).

To resolve this difficulty, the couple is considering two options. One option is to open a credit card account and use it exclusively for those expenditures that will cause the deficits they face. Or they could talk to their bank about opening a line of credit that would allow them to borrow money by simply calling the bank and having money placed in their checking account.

(a) What are the advantages and disadvantages of the Johnsons opening these accounts?

(b) What financial calculations should Harry and Belinda undertake to see whether they could afford to borrow more money at this time?

(c) What might Harry and Belinda do before applying for credit to ensure that they will pay the lowest interest rate possible?

On the 'Net

Go to the Web pages indicated to complete these exercises. You can also go to the *Garman/Forgue* website at college.hmco.com/business/students for an expanded list of exercises. Under General Business, select the title of this text. Click on the Internet Exercises link for this chapter.

1. Visit the website for obtaining a free credit report at http://www.annualcreditreport.com to order a copy of your credit report. Check the accuracy of the report and follow the directions provided to correct any errors. If no report is available on you, it should be because you have never used credit. If you have used credit and there is no report, you should notify the credit bureaus of this error.
2. Visit the website for the Federal Reserve Board at www.federalreserve.gov/consumers.htm. Locate its online copy of the *Consumer Handbook on Credit Protection Laws*. Identify one additional protection not discussed in this book that is provided by each of the following laws: the Fair Credit Billing Act, the Equal Credit Opportunity Act, and the Fair Credit Reporting Act.
3. Visit the website for Fair, Isaacs and Company at www.myfico.com/CreditEducation. Read up on how credit scoring works. Identify three actions you could take to improve your credit score.

Visit the Garman/Forgue website ...

@college.hmco.com/business/students

Under General Business, select *Personal Finance 9e*. There, among other valuable resources, you will find a complete glossary, ACE questions, links to help you complete the chapter exercises, and links to other personal finance sites.

CHAPTER 7

Credit Cards and Consumer Loans

You Must Be Kidding, Right?

College students who have a credit card in their own name (and most do) have an average debt of $2700 at graduation. If they maintain that level of debt for ten years (because their payments equal the charges they make plus interest), how much total interest will they pay?

A. $1200

B. $1800

C. $2700

D. $4860

The answer is D. A credit card with an 18 percent APR (typical for college students) translates to a 1.5 percent rate per month (18% ÷ 12). The $2700 debt multiplied by this rate equals $40.50 ($2700 × 0.015) per month in interest. And $40.50 multiplied by 120 months equals $4860. You must pay more than the amount you charge plus any interest owed for each month in order to reduce your credit card debt and avoid paying many thousands of dollars in interest over the years. Otherwise, you will be in debt forever!

LEARNING OBJECTIVES

After reading this chapter, you should be able to:

1. **Compare** the common types of consumer credit, including credit cards and installment loans.
2. **Describe** the types and features of credit card accounts.
3. **Manage** your credit card accounts to avoid fees and finance charges.
4. **Describe** the important features of consumer installment loans.
5. **Calculate** the interest and annual percentage rate on consumer loans.

What Do You Recommend?

Darrell Cochrane, a 31-year-old optician in Tampa, Florida, made $42,000 last year. Darrell avoided using credit and credit cards until he was 28 years old, when he missed three months of work due to a water-skiing accident. He made ends meet by obtaining two bank credit cards that, because of his lack of a credit history, carry 19.6 and 24 percent annual percentage rates (APRs). Darrell now has 11 credit card accounts open: five bank cards and six retail store cards. He uses them regularly, presenting whatever card a store will honor. He owes $13,000 on the 24 percent APR card and $4400 on the 19.6 percent APR card. His other three bank cards carry APRs of 11 percent, 12 percent, and 15 percent, and he owes $500 to $700 on each one. For the past year, Darrell has been making only the minimum payments on his bank cards. His retail cards all carry APRs in excess of 21 percent. Although he has managed to keep from running a balance on those cards during most months, occasionally these accounts have balances as well.

What would you recommend to Darrell on the subject of credit cards and consumer loans regarding:

1. His approach to using credit cards, including the number of cards he has?
2. Estimating the credit card interest charges he is paying each month?
3. How he might lower his interest expense each month?
4. Consolidating his credit card debts into one installment loan?

FOR HELP with studying this chapter, visit the Online Student Center:

college.hmco.com/pic/garman9e

Good Money Habits in Credit Cards and Consumer Loans

Make the following your money habits in credit cards and installment loans:

1. Move credit card balances to lower-cost accounts, if necessary.
2. Never make convenience purchases on bank credit cards on which you carry a balance.
3. Pay your credit card balances in full each month, or no longer than two or three months later.
4. Check your monthly billing statements against your receipts for accuracy, and challenge discrepancies.
5. Use student loans for direct education expenses only rather than to maintain a better lifestyle.
6. Select installment loans that have a low annual percentage rate.

Instant Message

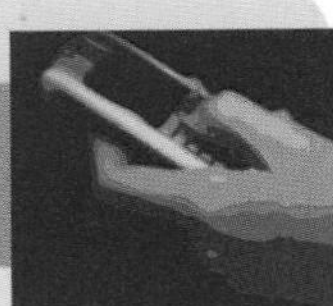

Pay Close Attention to the APR

Always inquire about the APR if it is not readily apparent, and use it to compare rates from other lenders to obtain the best deal.

You cannot borrow your way to financial success. Using any kind of credit requires deliberate thinking and planning. You need to first consider whether the reason you are borrowing is sound, and then decide in advance how you will repay the debt. This is especially true for credit cards. Credit card usage can be managed so that you pay no interest at all but only if you pay your balance in full every month. Planning for installment loans is also important because you commit to making a series of monthly payments for one to seven or more years. Smart borrowers understand the mathematics behind the calculation of the finance charges on these installment loans. Smart borrowers always focus on the **annual percentage rate (APR)** when comparing among various sources of credit. The APR is the cost of credit on a yearly basis as a percentage rate.

annual percentage rate (APR) The cost of credit on a yearly basis as a percentage rate.

Types of Consumer Credit

1 LEARNING OBJECTIVE

Compare the common types of consumer credit, including credit cards and installment loans.

Consumer credit is nonbusiness debt used by consumers for expenditures other than home mortgages. (Borrowing for housing has investment aspects that result in a separate classification; see Chapter 9.)

There are two types of consumer credit: installment credit and noninstallment credit.

- With **installment credit** (also called **closed-end credit**), the borrower must repay the amount owed plus interest in a specific number of equal payments, usually monthly. For example, an $18,000 automobile loan might require monthly payments of $380 for 60 months.
- **Noninstallment credit** includes single-payment, open-ended credit, and service credit. **Single-payment loans** are the easiest of the three to understand. As an example, a borrower might take out a loan of $2000 at 12 percent interest for one year. If so, a single payment of $2240 ($2000 + $240 interest; $2000 × 0.12) would be due at the end of one year.

With **open-ended credit** (also called **revolving credit**), credit is extended in advance of any transaction so that the borrower does not need to reapply each time credit is desired. Credit cards are an example of open-ended credit. Any amounts owed will be repaid in full in a single payment or via a series of equal or unequal payments, usually made monthly. The borrower can use the account as long as the total owed does not exceed his or her **credit limit.** This credit limit is set by the lender and is the maximum outstanding debt allowed on the credit account. Credit limits vary with the perceived creditworthiness of the borrower.

installment credit (closed-end credit) Credit arrangement in which the borrower must repay the amount owed plus interest in a specific number of equal payments.

noninstallment credit Single-payment, open-ended credit and service credit arrangements.

Open-ended credit can be used to make purchases and, in some cases, to obtain cash advances. It is the most convenient type of credit, and it is also the most abused. Many open-ended accounts—but not all—use a credit card. A **credit** (or **charge**) **card** is a plastic card identifying the holder as a participant in the charge account plan of a lender, such as a retailer or financial institution.

Cash advances may be obtained at any financial institution that issues the type of card (Visa, MasterCard, and so on) being used. A cash advance is a cash loan from a credit card account. In most cases, the borrower receives cash, such as from an ATM. Alternatively, the funds may be transferred electronically into the cardholder's checking account.

A **personal line of credit** is a form of open-ended credit that allows the borrower access to a prearranged revolving line of credit provided by the lender (usually a commercial bank, savings bank, credit union, or brokerage firm). The essence of a line of credit is that borrowers can obtain a cash advance when needed and not reapply for a loan each time they need money. Like credit card accounts, a personal line of credit includes a credit limit and a flexible repayment schedule. Some people also use the equity in their home as collateral for a line of credit. This arrangement is referred to as a **home-equity line of credit.**

Service credit is granted to consumers by public utilities, physicians, dentists, and other service providers that do not require full payment when services are rendered. For example, your electric company allows you to use electricity all month and then sends you a bill that may not be due for 10 to 15 days. Service credit usually carries no interest, although penalty charges and interest may apply if payments are made late. Service may eventually be cut off for continued slow payment or nonpayment of the debt.

open-ended (revolving) credit Arrangement in which credit is extended in advance of any transaction so that borrowers do not need to reapply each time they need to use credit.

credit limit Maximum outstanding debt that a lender will allow on an open-ended credit account.

CONCEPT CHECK 7.1

1. Distinguish between installment credit and open-ended credit.
2. Explain the basic features of revolving credit.
3. Describe how someone might use a personal line of credit.

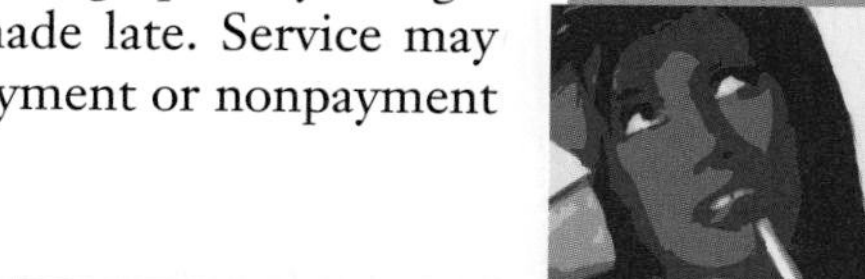

Did You Know?...

Top 3 Financial Missteps with Credit Cards and Consumer Loans

People slip up in credit cards and consumer loans when they do the following:

1. Fail to shop for the lowest APR on their credit cards and consumer loans
2. Regularly carry month-to-month balances on credit card accounts
3. Use a credit card rather than lower-cost installment loans to make expensive purchases

Credit Card Accounts

Credit card accounts allow the borrower to pay the balance in full at any time or carry over a balance owed from month to month (travel and entertainment cards are an exception). If a balance is carried over, a **minimum payment** must be made each month to cover interest and a small payment on the amount owed (the **principal**). If at least the minimum payment amount is not received by the due date, the cardholder may be declared in **default** (the borrower has failed to make a payment of principal or interest when due or meet any other requirement of a credit agreement). Most cardholders maintain balances and can do so for years even as other charges are added to the same account. As long as the total debt remains below the credit limit, the user may continue to make charges against the account.

cash advance The use of a credit card to obtain cash rather than to make a purchase.

personal line of credit Form of open-ended credit in which the lender allows the borrower access to a prearranged revolving line of credit.

2 LEARNING OBJECTIVE
Describe the types and features of credit card accounts.

Types of Credit Card Accounts

Credit card accounts include bank credit cards, retail credit cards, and travel and entertainment accounts (such as American Express's familiar "green card").

Bank Credit Cards A **bank credit card account** is an open-ended account at a financial institution (commercial bank, savings and loan association, or credit union) that allows the holder to make purchases almost anywhere. Visa, MasterCard, Discover, and Optima are the most commonly recognized bank card names. However, the actual lender is the financial institution. Visa, MasterCard, and the like are simply service providers that maintain the electronic network through which transactions are communicated. Participating merchants and financial institutions pay transaction fees to these service providers based on the dollar amounts charged. Virtually all financial institutions offer bank credit cards, as do a number of consumer products companies, such as AT&T, General Motors, Allstate

minimum payment Payment that must be made to a credit account each month to cover interest and a portion of the amount owed.

principal Total amount owed on a credit account not including interest.

bank credit card account Open-ended credit account with a financial institution that allows the holder to make purchases almost anywhere.

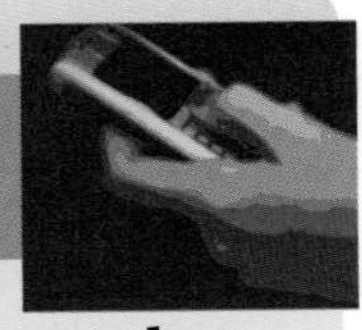

Instant Message

Cash Advances Are Very Expensive

Obtaining money via a credit card cash advance seems so easy. But it is expensive. First, there is a transaction fee. It is usually a percentage of the amount taken (2 percent is common), but there is often a minimum amount that makes the percentage much higher on small advances. Then there is the interest that begins to accrue immediately even if you are not carrying a balance on the card. Plus, the interest rate on cash advances is higher than for purchases.

Insurance, and Verizon. These companies contract with Visa, MasterCard, and a bank to offer **co-branded credit cards.**

Many bank credit card issuers periodically send **cash advance** (or **convenience**) **checks** to their cardholders. Of course, these instruments are not genuine checks but simply a check-equivalent way to take a cash advance. Customers can use these "checks" to make payments to others or themselves. If such a payment is used to make a payment on another credit card, it represents a **balance transfer.** If you receive convenience checks but do not want to use them, either put them in a safe place or destroy them immediately because they easily could be used fraudulently by someone else. As indicated in Figure 7.1 on page 188, a transaction fee is often charged for receiving cash advances, using convenience checks, or making balance transfers.

Some bank credit cards are a form of **prestige card,** often with a precious metal in the brand name such as "gold," "silver," or "platinum." These accounts require that the user possess higher credit qualifications and offer enhancements such as free traveler's checks and higher credit limits. Prestige cards may carry higher annual fees. Most holders of regular bank credit cards do not realize that they could obtain a higher credit limit on their standard card just by requesting one from the issuer.

cash advance (or convenience) checks A check-equivalent way to take a cash advance on a credit card.

balance transfer Full or partial payment on the balance of one credit card using a cash advance from another.

Some Visa and MasterCard credit cards are identified as **affinity cards**—that is, standard bank cards with the logo of a sponsoring organization imprinted on the face of the card. The issuing financial institution often donates a portion of the annual fee and a small percentage of the amounts charged (perhaps 0.25, 0.5, or 1 percent) to the sponsoring organization. Sponsors may include charitable, political, sports, or other organized groups, such as the Sierra Club or Mothers Against Drunk Driving. Supporters of the sponsoring organization may be motivated to use an affinity card because the organization receives money from each transaction. Creditors rightly calculate that fewer delinquencies will occur among the particular group of people, so they can afford to transfer some dollars to the named organization.

retail credit cards Allow customers to make purchases on credit at any of the outlets of a particular retailer.

Retail Credit Card Accounts A **retail credit card** allows a customer to make purchases on credit at any of the outlets of a particular retailer or retail chain. Examples of credit card accounts at retail stores include those offered by JCPenney, Best Buy, and Shell Oil. Many retailers have alliances with a financial institution to offer a bank credit card that carries the retailer's logo and can also be used anywhere the bank credit card can be used.

Some smaller retail establishments offer open-ended accounts that do not use a credit card as the vehicle for using the account. With these retail charge accounts, customers simply ask to have the purchase put on their account for repayment at a later date.

travel and entertainment (T&E) cards Bank credit cards that allow holders to make purchases at numerous businesses but that require the holder to repay the entire balance charged within 30 days.

Travel and Entertainment Cards **Travel and entertainment (T&E) cards** are similar to bank credit cards in that they allow holders to make purchases at numerous businesses. The entire balance charged must be repaid within 30 days, however. The best-known T&E cards are those issued by American Express, Diners Club, and Carte Blanche. Such cards are often used by businesspeople for food and lodging expenses while traveling. They are somewhat more difficult to obtain than bank cards because applicants must have higher-than-average incomes to qualify for an account; in addition, applicants must pay an annual membership fee of $35 or more. T&E cards are not accepted at as many outlets as are bank credit cards.

Did You Know?...

How to Close a Credit Card Account

Credit card accounts are open-ended credit and, therefore, can remain open for decades even if you never use the card or stop using it at some point. Accounts are not closed if you cut up the cards. Instead, the lender must be formally notified of your request before the account will be officially closed. Here's what to do:

1. Obtain the customer-service telephone number for the lender from your most recent monthly statement. If you do not have a recent bill, obtain a copy of your credit report, which will list the contact information for the lender.
2. Contact the lender to request the address to which you should send your cancellation request. It will not be same address to which you send your monthly payment.
3. Send a written request to close the account and request that the creditor send a confirmation that the account is, indeed, closed.
4. After 90 days, obtain a copy of your credit report (pay if necessary) from one of the three national credit bureaus. If the account shows as closed, obtain free copies from the other two bureaus as confirmation at the next free opportunity. If the account shows as still open at the first bureau, ask for a reinvestigation and also obtain copies from the other two bureaus to ensure the account shows closed appropriately.

Note that you cannot "close" an account on which you currently owe a balance. You can, however, ask the lender to no longer honor the card.

Common (But Not Always Beneficial) Aspects of Credit Card Accounts

Federal law requires credit card lenders to disclose all the rules governing the account to borrowers before they sign up for any card. Some of that information must be displayed in a uniform manner, as illustrated in the sample credit card disclosure box in Figure 7.1. The remainder of the information appears in the credit agreement (contract). Credit card issuers are free to change the rules on an account at any time as long as they notify the account holder of the change. This notification is usually included as an insert in the monthly bill for the account and often appears in very small print. You can avoid any penalties imposed by the new rules by paying off the account or by closing it. If you cannot pay the bill in full, you will be obligated to adhere to the new rules until you close the account. This section outlines some of the more important aspects of credit card accounts.

Teaser Rates Some cards carry a temporarily low introductory rate **(teaser rate)** to entice borrowers to apply for an account. Teaser APRs of 0 to 3.9 percent are common. In Figure 7.1, the teaser rate is 4.99 percent for purchases and 0.0 percent for balance transfers during the first six months the account is open. The APR typically reverts to a much higher fixed or variable interest rate after the introductory period ends. Some credit card borrowers take advantage of teaser rates by opening new accounts regularly and transferring the balances from other accounts to the new account to take advantage of the low introductory rate despite the high balance transfer fee that might exist. Customers with a good credit history can use this technique several times in succession. Lenders catch on to people who frequently take advantage of this technique, however, and become reluctant to offer teaser rates to them.

teaser rate A temporarily low introductory rate to entice borrowers to apply for a credit card.

CREDIT CARD DISCLOSURE INFORMATION

Figure 7.1

The Fair Credit and Charge Card Disclosure Act (FCCCDA) requires that key pieces of information be disclosed in direct-mail advertising and on applications for credit cards. An example of this required disclosure is provided here. To search for the best offers on credit cards, you can visit www.bankrate.com or www.cardtrack.com.

DETAILS OF RATE, FEE, AND OTHER COST INFORMATION	
As required by law, rates, fees, and other costs of this credit card offer are disclosed here. All account terms are governed by the Credit Card Agreement sent with the card. Account terms are not guaranteed for any period of time; all terms, including the APRs and fees, may change in accordance with the Agreement and applicable law.	
Annual Percentage Rate for purchases	The **introductory rate** (see notes below) is **4.99%** until the first billing after the sixth-month anniversary of the opening of the account. After that **9.99%** (variable rate).
Other APRs (all other APRs are variable)	**Balance Transfers:** The introductory rate is 0% until the first billing after the sixth-month anniversary of the opening of the account. After that **9.99%**. Cash Advances: **19.99%**. Default Rate: **27.99%** (see notes below).
Variable rate information	**Your APRs may vary** during each billing period. The rate for purchases and balance transfers is determined by adding 5.99% to the prime rate (see notes below). The rate for cash advances is determined by adding 15.99% to the prime rate but such rate will never be below 19.99%. The default is determined by adding no more than 23.99% to the prime rate.
Grace period for repayment of purchases	**Not less than 20 days** if you pay your total new balance in full each billing period by the due date. Payment must be received by 9 a.m. on the due date. There is **no grace period for balance transfers and cash advances.**
Method of computing the balance	**Average Daily Balance** (including new purchases).
Annual fee	**$25**
Minimum Finance Charge	**$1.00**
Miscellaneous fees	**Transaction fee for Cash Advances:** 3% of the amount of the transaction but not less than $20. **Transaction fee for Balance Transfers:** 3% of the amount of the transfer but not less than $50. There is no balance transfer fee during the six-month introductory period. **Late fee:** $15 on balances up to $500. $35 on balances over $500. **Over-the-limit fee:** $35. **Bounced check fee:** $35.
Notes	**Introductory rates:** Eligibility for introductory rate is subject to your maintaining good credit. Rates indicated in this offer are subject to change to reflect changes in the prime rate (see below) at the time of your application. **Default rate:** All of your APRs may increase if you default under any Card Agreement that you have with us because you fail to make a payment to us **or any other creditor** when due, you exceed your credit limit, or you make a payment to us that is not honored. Factors considered when determining your default rate may include the length of time your account with us has been open; the existence, seriousness, and timing of defaults under any Card Agreement you have with us; or other indications of account usage and performance on this or any other account you have with us **or any other creditor**. **Prime rate:** The prime rate (currently 4%) used to determine your APRs for each billing period is the U.S. prime rate published in the *Wall Street Journal* two business days prior to the billing date for that billing period.

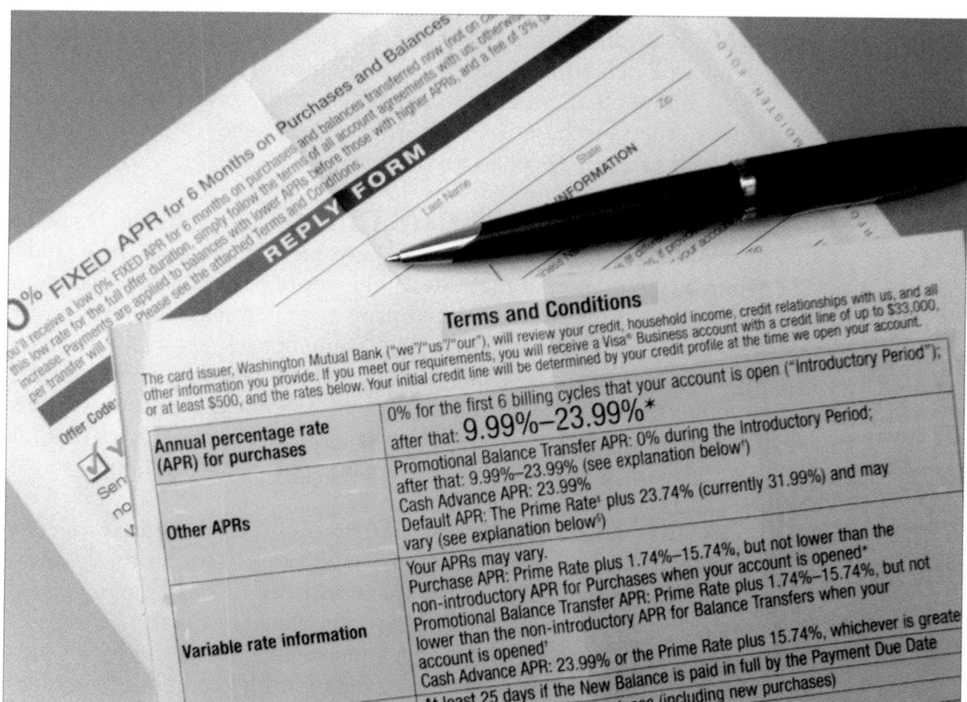

Extremely low rates are usually temporary. Read the fine print carefully.

Default Rates Usually the teaser rate will be rescinded and the regular rate on the account will be applied if the borrower makes a late payment even once during the introductory period. A more serious downside to most credit card accounts is the assessment of a **default rate.** A default rate is a high APR that is assessed whenever a borrower fails to uphold certain rules of the account, such as making on-time payments or staying within the specified credit limit. The disclosure notice in Figure 7.1 indicates that if you are late making a payment even once during the introductory period, you will not only lose the teaser rate but also see a default rate of perhaps 27.99 percent APR [23.99 percent plus 4 percent (the current prime rate)].

default rate A high APR that is assessed whenever a borrower fails to uphold certain rules of the account, such as making on-time payments or staying within the specified credit limit.

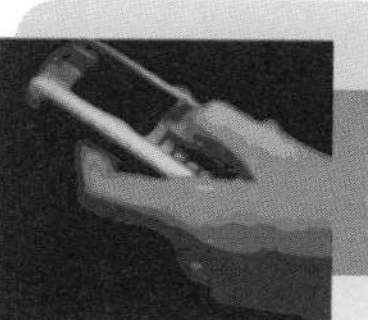

Instant Message

About 1 in 20 Credit Card Accounts Are in Default

Due to their ease of use, credit cards are now the primary source of consumer debt other than home mortgages. For the same reason, about 4.5 percent of all credit card accounts recently were more than 30 days past due.

It is understandable that a credit card company might want to raise the interest rate when a customer is having trouble paying on the account. In fact, many credit card companies now recheck their customers' credit reports on a regular basis after an account is opened to see whether a customer has taken on significantly higher levels of debt or is in any financial trouble. If it finds that the customer's credit report has changed significantly, the credit card company can decide whether the borrower is in **universal default** and, if so, apply the default rate. Under universal default, you can be charged a default rate on an account that you are handling well simply because you are having trouble with other accounts. In fact, being late just once or twice on one account can trigger universal default on other accounts. (Note the words "or any other creditor" in bold in Figure 7.1—they indicate that this company utilizes the concept of universal default.)

universal default Situation in which credit companies assign much higher rates to accounts because credit report rechecks indicate repayment problems in one or more other accounts with any lender.

Variable Interest Rates Credit card accounts (and installment loans) carry either fixed or variable interest rates. **Variable interest rates** go up and down, usually monthly or annually, according to changes in interest rates in the economy as a whole. The example in Figure 7.1 has a variable interest rate with the prime rate used as a base rate. The **prime rate** is a key measure of interest rates in the economy and its fluctuations drive the changes in rates for all types of variable-rate credit. Since the

variable interest rate cards Have rates that change monthly or annually according to general changes in the economy as a whole.

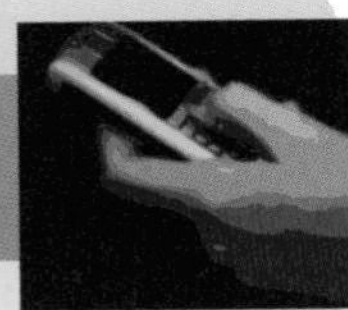

Instant Message

There Is Really No Such Thing as a Fixed-Rate Credit Card

Many bank credit cards are variable-rate cards. But even for those that are not, the card issuer can change the rate with as little as 30 days' notice.

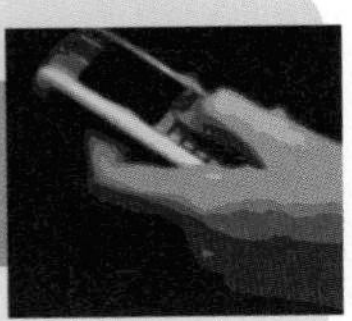

Instant Message

When in Doubt—"Opt Out"

Federal law states that consumers have the right to opt out of receiving unsolicited credit card offers, which are based on your credit report. To put a stop to the mailings, dial (888) 5-OPT-OUT or visit https://www.optoutprescreen.com.

year 2000, the prime rate has been as high as 9.4 percent and as low as 4 percent. As indicated in Figure 7.1, the card company lists the percentage rate that is added to the prime rate to determine the purchase (+5.99%), cash advance (+15.99%), and default rates (+23.99%) on the card.

Preapproved Credit Card Offers Companies interested in expanding their base of credit customers sometimes pay credit bureaus to prescreen their files and identify people who pass certain tests of creditworthiness. A company may then send applications for credit to the prescreened people. Some consumers will have been preapproved as part of this process, so they merely need to sign the notice to open the account. Note that being preapproved means only that you will be granted credit. Both the credit card debt limit and APR will be determined after you apply for an account.

Annual and Transaction Fees Some bank credit card lenders assess **annual fees** ranging from $25 to $50 (or more). In addition, lenders may charge a **transaction fee** (a small charge levied each time a card is used). The card illustrated in Figure 7.1 assesses transaction fees for cash advances and balance transfers. Some lenders even charge a fee for printing the monthly credit bill. Most fees are not required to be included in the APR calculation because they cannot be known in advance. Thus, an apparently low-rate card may turn into a high-cost card when all fees are considered.

Liability for Lost or Stolen Cards The Truth in Lending Act limits a cardholder's **credit card liability** for lost or stolen credit cards. Under the law, if you notify the card issuer within two days of a loss or theft, you are not legally responsible for any fraudulent usage of the card. After two days, your maximum liability for fraudulent usage of the card (including telephone calling cards) prior to your notification is $50. You are not responsible for any fraudulent usage after you notify the issuer of the loss. Although your financial liability is low, some companies nevertheless specialize in selling credit card insurance (for an annual premium ranging from $15 to $49) that will pay creditors for the first $50 of unauthorized use of an insured person's lost or stolen credit cards. Such insurance is profitable for insurance companies—but an unnecessary expense for you. If you are insistent, most credit card companies will waive the $50 fee for unauthorized use as a gesture of goodwill to keep you as a good customer.

annual fees Charges levied against cardholders for the privilege of having an open account but that are not included in the advertised APR.

transaction fees Charges levied against cardholders per use of the card but that are not included in the APR advertised.

Did You Know?...

About Secured Credit Cards

A **secured credit card** (also called a **collateralized credit card**) is backed by collateral in the form of a savings account opened at the financial institution that issues the card. Banks offering secured credit cards typically charge an application fee and require the applicant to make a deposit of $500 to $1000 into a savings account. The person then receives a credit limit in the same amount on a bank credit card. The savings balance cannot be withdrawn as long as the card is available for use. The deposit is refunded (with a small amount of interest) when the credit card balance is paid off and the account closed. Most people do not need a secured credit card, but those who have no alternative should consider obtaining one from a reputable institution, as scams abound in this market.

Late-Payment, Bounced Check, and Over-the-Limit Fees Late-payment fees of $30 or more are often applied when the borrower fails to make a payment by the due date. Most card issuers assess a similar charge if you write a bad check when making your monthly payment. Many credit card issuers charge a significant ($20 to $50) over-the-limit fee when the cardholder exceeds his or her credit limit. Each of these fees is much higher than necessary in terms of the actual cost to the lender for these rule violations. Indeed, they represent a significant source of profits for credit card issuers. The account illustrated in Figure 7.1 assesses a $35 fee for each of these offenses.

Credit Card Insurance Many lenders encourage borrowers to sign up for **credit life insurance** that pays the unpaid balance of a loan—to the lender—in the event of the borrower's death. Credit life insurance is grossly overpriced and is a cost that can be avoided. The same can be said for **credit disability insurance,** which repays the outstanding loan balance if the borrower becomes disabled (with "disability" usually being very narrowly defined), and credit unemployment insurance. The only exception might be credit life insurance for an account holder who cannot obtain life insurance through more traditional means.

CONCEPT CHECK 7.2

1. Distinguish among bank credit cards, retail credit cards, and travel and entertainment cards.
2. What are the differences and similarities between a cash advance and a balance transfer using a bank credit card?
3. Describe the positive and negative aspects of having a variable interest rate on a credit card.
4. What is a default rate, and how might a cardholder come to have to pay this interest rate?
5. Describe five common fees assessed on credit card accounts and how they can be avoided.

Managing Credit Cards Wisely

3 LEARNING OBJECTIVE
Manage your credit card accounts to avoid fees and finance charges.

Credit cards can be a positive tool in personal financial management—when used appropriately. It is important to manage their use wisely. To do so, you must understand and monitor your credit statements, correct errors when appropriate, and also recognize how finance charges are computed. Your goal should be to use the credit card in a manner that avoids all fees, including finance charges. This means paying your balance in full every month.

Credit Statements

Active charge account holders receive a monthly **credit statement** (also called a **periodic statement**) that summarizes the charges, payments, finance charges, and other activity on the account. The significant features of credit statements are the billing date, due date, transaction and posting dates, grace period, payment minimum, and credit for merchandise returns and billing errors obtained. You also need to know how to correct errors in your credit statements. Figure 7.2 shows a monthly statement for a credit card.

credit statement The monthly bill on a credit card account showing the charges and payments made, minimum payment required and due date among other information; also called a periodic statement.

Billing Date The **billing date** (sometimes called the **statement date** or **closing date**) is the last day of the month for which any transactions are reported on the statement. In Figure 7.2, this date is 5/22/08. Any transactions or payments made after this date will be recorded on the following month's credit statement. The statement is mailed to the card-

billing/closing/statement date The last day for which any transactions are reported on the credit statement.

Advice from a Pro...

Control and Reduce Your Credit Card Debt

If your credit card debt rises to a hard-to-manage level, consider the following suggestions:

1. Immediately stop using your credit cards, and do not open new credit accounts or accept any new credit offers.
2. Evaluate all of your budgeted expenditures and plan to devote the largest possible amounts toward paying off your credit card balances.
3. Work overtime or take another job. Devote any extra income, such as a tax refund, toward paying these debts.
4. Gather your most recent credit card statements, sit down with pencil and paper, and write down the balance of each debt and the interest rate. Then set a payoff date and calculate the monthly payment you will need to pay off the debt by that date using a calculator like the ones found at bankrate.com or money.cnn.com.
5. Consider transferring existing balances on high-interest rate accounts to an account with a lower interest rate. Use caution, however, because brief introductory periods, transaction fees, and penalties may eliminate any potential savings.
6. Pay the minimum amount due on your cards with low interest rates, and pay as much as possible on the cards with the highest interest rates. Continue to do so until all of your debts are paid off.
7. If after three to six months you are not making good progress toward paying off your credit card balances, consider seeking assistance from a nonprofit credit counseling agency. It can negotiate with your creditors to lower your payments and interest rates and to reduce or eliminate late fees and over-the-limit charges.

M. J. Alhabeeb
University of Massachusetts–Amherst

holder a day or so after the billing date. The billing date is generally the same day of each month, and the time period between billing dates is referred to as the **billing cycle.**

Due Date The due date is the specific day by which the credit card company should receive payment from you. In Figure 7.2, this date is 6/17/08. The period between the billing date and the due date—usually 20 to 25 days (with 20 days becoming more common)—represents the time allowed for statements and payments to be mailed and for the borrower to make arrangements to pay. Federal law states that bills must be mailed to cardholders at least 14 days before payments are due. The account illustrated in Figure 7.2 has a 25-day billing period. If payment is received later than the due date, a credit bureau may be notified of slow payment. If no payment is received, the company will begin collection efforts, often by mailing a "first notice" that a payment is overdue.

Transaction and Posting Dates The date on which a credit cardholder makes a purchase (or receives a credit, as described later in this chapter) is known as the **transaction date.** In the past, several days would pass before the credit card company was informed of the transaction and the charge was posted to the account (on the **posting date**). With the increased use of magnetic strip readers at retailers, however, these dates may be concurrent, with both matching the date on which the clerk or the customer "swipes" the card through the reader. Interest is charged from the posting date unless a grace period is offered; some lenders charge interest from the transaction date.

grace period Time period between the posting date of a transaction and the payment due date during which no interest accrues.

Grace Period A **grace period** is the time period between the posting date of a transaction and the due date, within which any new credit card purchases made during the billing cycle will avoid finance charges (also see Figure 7.1). Most cards provide a grace period only if the previous month's total balance was paid in full and on time.

Figure 7.2

Sample Statement for a Revolving Charge Account

Source: Courtesy of Pikeville National Bank, Pikeville, KY.

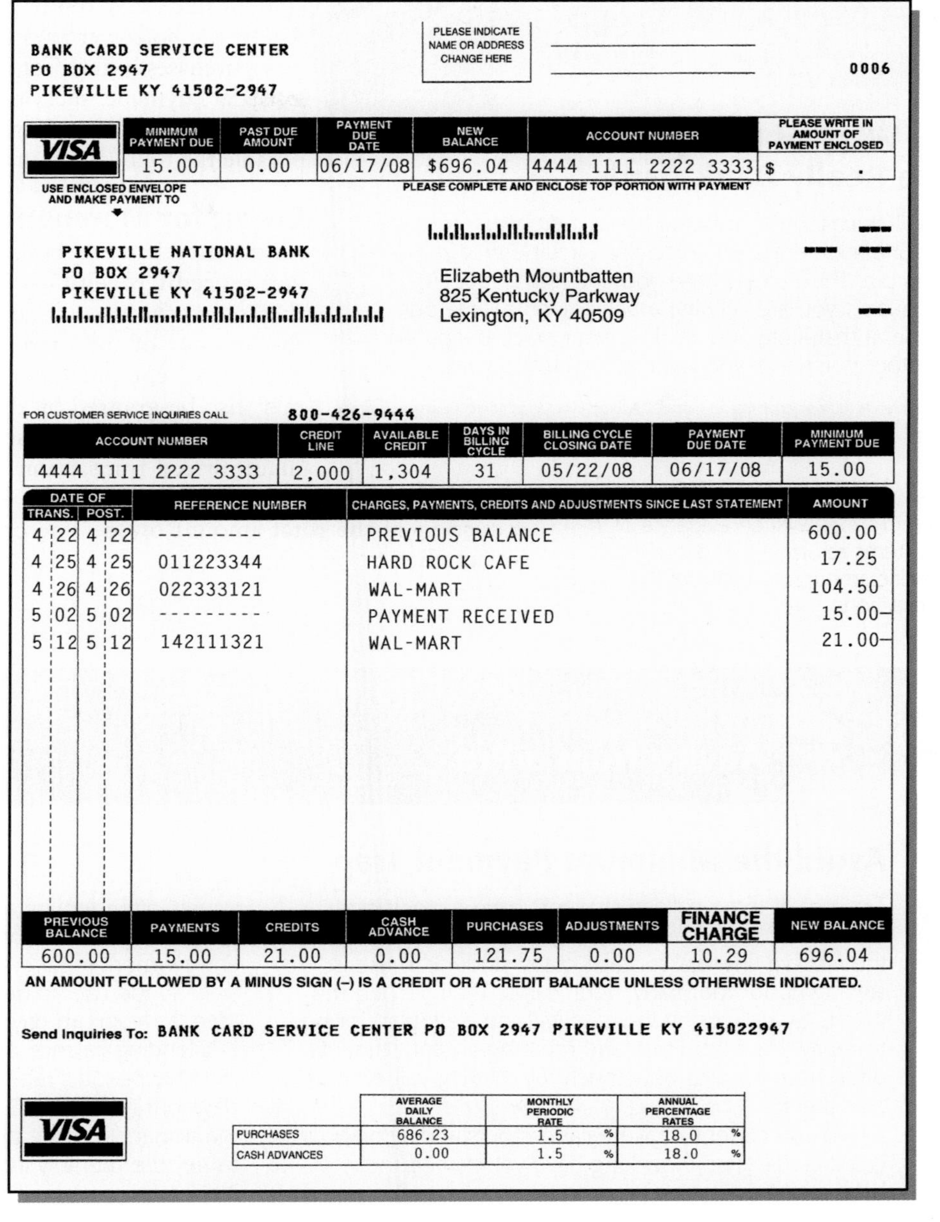

BANK CARD SERVICE CENTER
PO BOX 2947
PIKEVILLE KY 41502-2947

PLEASE INDICATE NAME OR ADDRESS CHANGE HERE

0006

VISA

MINIMUM PAYMENT DUE	PAST DUE AMOUNT	PAYMENT DUE DATE	NEW BALANCE	ACCOUNT NUMBER	PLEASE WRITE IN AMOUNT OF PAYMENT ENCLOSED
15.00	0.00	06/17/08	$696.04	4444 1111 2222 3333	$.

USE ENCLOSED ENVELOPE AND MAKE PAYMENT TO

PLEASE COMPLETE AND ENCLOSE TOP PORTION WITH PAYMENT

PIKEVILLE NATIONAL BANK
PO BOX 2947
PIKEVILLE KY 41502-2947

Elizabeth Mountbatten
825 Kentucky Parkway
Lexington, KY 40509

FOR CUSTOMER SERVICE INQUIRIES CALL 800-426-9444

ACCOUNT NUMBER	CREDIT LINE	AVAILABLE CREDIT	DAYS IN BILLING CYCLE	BILLING CYCLE CLOSING DATE	PAYMENT DUE DATE	MINIMUM PAYMENT DUE
4444 1111 2222 3333	2,000	1,304	31	05/22/08	06/17/08	15.00

DATE OF TRANS.	DATE OF POST.	REFERENCE NUMBER	CHARGES, PAYMENTS, CREDITS AND ADJUSTMENTS SINCE LAST STATEMENT	AMOUNT
4 22	4 22	---------	PREVIOUS BALANCE	600.00
4 25	4 25	011223344	HARD ROCK CAFE	17.25
4 26	4 26	022333121	WAL-MART	104.50
5 02	5 02	---------	PAYMENT RECEIVED	15.00-
5 12	5 12	142111321	WAL-MART	21.00-

PREVIOUS BALANCE	PAYMENTS	CREDITS	CASH ADVANCE	PURCHASES	ADJUSTMENTS	FINANCE CHARGE	NEW BALANCE
600.00	15.00	21.00	0.00	121.75	0.00	10.29	696.04

AN AMOUNT FOLLOWED BY A MINUS SIGN (–) IS A CREDIT OR A CREDIT BALANCE UNLESS OTHERWISE INDICATED.

Send Inquiries To: BANK CARD SERVICE CENTER PO BOX 2947 PIKEVILLE KY 415022947

VISA

	AVERAGE DAILY BALANCE	MONTHLY PERIODIC RATE	ANNUAL PERCENTAGE RATES
PURCHASES	686.23	1.5 %	18.0 %
CASH ADVANCES	0.00	1.5 %	18.0 %

About one-third of cardholders pay their bills in full by the due date and receive, in effect, an interest-free loan on their new purchases during the next billing cycle. It is a smart move to use one credit card for convenience items that are paid in full each month and another credit card for items for which paying off the balance each month is not possible. Use a no-annual-fee card for the convenience purchases and a low-APR card for purchases for which you carry a balance. Avoid cards that do not offer a grace period. In Figure 7.2, the cardholder has a previous unpaid balance, $600, and was charged interest on the unpaid balance as well as on the new charges made within the billing cycle, starting from the date they were posted to the account. Thus, this example lacks a grace period because of the unpaid balance on the card.

Minimum Payment Amount To meet their obligations, borrowers must make a **minimum payment** monthly that is no smaller than the amount required by the

minimum payment amount Lowest allowable monthly payment required by the lender.

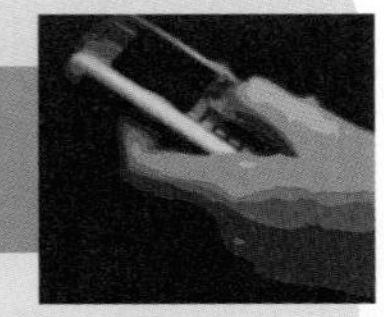

Instant Message

Be Wary of Using Store Cards That Are Really Bank Cards

Retail chains often co-brand their credit cards with a major bank credit card company. Circuit City is an example. This can increase your interest charges because if you are carrying a balance on a large purchase at that store you will lose your grace period on all other purchases you will make with that card.

creditor. In Figure 7.2, the cardholder has two options: pay the total amount due ($696.04) or make at least the minimum payment of $15. If the borrower pays the full amount due, finance charges on new purchases in the next billing cycle generally can be avoided. If a partial payment, such as the "total minimum payment due" of $15, is made, additional finance charges will be assessed and will be payable the following month.

Credit for Merchandise Returns and Errors If you return merchandise bought on credit, the merchant will issue you a **credit receipt**—written evidence of the items returned that notes the specific amount of the transaction. In essence, the amount of the merchandise credit is charged back to the credit card company and eventually to the merchant. A credit may also be granted by the credit card company when a billing error has been made (discussed in the next section) or when an unauthorized transaction appears. Credits obtained in the current month should appear on the next monthly statement as a reduction of the total amount owed. The credit statement in Figure 7.2 shows a $21 credit.

credit receipt Written evidence of any items returned that notes the specific amount and date of the transaction.

Advice from a Pro…

Avoid the Minimum Payment Trap

Two out of three college students have a credit card, with the average level of debt exceeding $2500. In fact, the first big financial mistake many students make is signing up for too many credit cards. Their second mistake is typically using the card with no clear plan for how to repay the debt. Third, and most significant, students often have no idea how much the interest will eventually cost them.

Do you currently have balances outstanding on your credit cards? If so, how long have you carried those balances? If you open an account in college and already have an unpaid balance of $2500 upon your graduation at age 22, you may find that the balance will not drop below $2500 for many years. This situation occurs when you continue to make purchases with the card but continue to send in only the required minimum payment amount. If $2500 is still owed on the account years later (perhaps when you reach age 37), then you have "permanent debt." In essence, you have never repaid the college charges. With an 18 percent APR, the finance charges on a principal of $2500 for 15 years will total $6750 (0.18 × $2500 × 15), almost three times as much as the debt itself!

The outlook is similarly bleak if you discontinue using the card for new purchases but still remit only the required minimum repayment amount. Credit card issuers often require a minimum monthly payment as low as 3 or 3 1/2 percent of the outstanding balance. This tiny payment requirement is mathematically guaranteed to keep the user in debt for many, many years. To illustrate, a minimum payment of $75 (3 percent) on an outstanding balance of $2500 with a 1.5 percent monthly periodic rate results in only one-half of the payment ($37.50 = $2500 × 0.015) going to reduce the actual debt (the principal). The other $37.50 is used to pay the monthly interest. At this rate of repayment, it will take more than six years to repay the $2500.

A ploy that card issuers frequently use is to allow cardholders to "skip a payment"—in essence, to make "a zero-dollar minimum payment." Interest will continue to accrue for the month during which no payment is made. This practice increases the total amount owed because the unpaid interest simply adds to the unpaid balance.

Such offers for a "low" or "zero-dollar" minimum payment perfectly illustrate the minimum payment trap. To avoid paying credit card charges for six to ten years, or even longer, you must make much larger monthly payments that go toward retiring your credit card balances. Better still, ask yourself—no, ask yourself twice—"Do I really need to charge it?"

Donald Stuhlman
Wilmington College, Delaware

Computation of Finance Charges

Companies that issue credit cards must tell consumers the APR applied as well as the method used to compute the finance charges. In addition, they must disclose the **periodic rate,** which is the APR for a charge account divided by the number of billing cycles per year (usually 12). For example, a periodic rate of 1.5 percent per month would result from an APR of approximately 18 percent (actually a bit higher because of compounding); both figures must be disclosed. Typically, the finance charge is calculated by first computing the **average daily balance**—the sum of the outstanding balances owed each day during the billing period divided by the number of days in the period. The periodic rate is then applied against that balance.

periodic rate The APR for a charge account divided by the number of billing cycles per year (usually 12).

average daily balance Sum of the outstanding balances owed each day during the billing period divided by the number of days in the period.

Correcting Errors on Your Credit Card Statement

The **Fair Credit Billing Act (FCBA)** helps people who wish to dispute billing errors on revolving credit accounts. In effect, the FCBA permits a **chargeback**—that is, the amount of the transaction is charged back to the business where the transaction

Fair Credit Billing Act (FCBA) Helps people who wish to dispute billing errors on revolving credit accounts.

chargeback The amount of the transaction is charged back to the business where the transaction originated in the case of a dispute or challenge by the cardholder.

Did You Know?...

How Credit Card Balances Are Calculated

Four methods are commonly used to calculate the average daily balance on a credit card billing statement:

1. **Average daily balance excluding new purchases.** The cardholder pays interest only on any balance left over from the previous month.
2. **Average daily balance including new purchases with a grace period.** The balance calculation includes the balance from the previous month and any new charges made during the billing cycle. The grace period allows for the exclusion of new charges made during the billing cycle only if the balance from the previous billing cycle was zero.
3. **Average daily balance including new purchases with no grace period.** The balance from the previous month and any new charges made during the billing cycle are included in the balance calculation, even if the previous month's balance was paid in full.
4. **Two-cycle average daily balance including new purchases.** This method is the least favorable for consumers, especially as they pay down the credit card balance. It eliminates the grace period on new purchases made during the current billing cycle, and it retroactively eliminates the grace period for the previous month each time the account carries a balance. The two-cycle method effectively doubles the finance charges and is a device for advertising one interest rate and charging another. Unlike with the one-cycle systems, in which each billing cycle stands alone, you must pay off your balance for at least two months to avoid finance charges.

The following chart illustrates how cardholders can sometimes be horribly (and legally) overcharged. It demonstrates how finance charges vary for a hypothetical situation in which a borrower charges $1000 per month and pays only the minimum payment, except for every third month when the balance is paid in full. Executing this scheme four times over the course of a year would result in the finance charges shown in the chart under the three most common ways of computing the average daily balance and for low-, average-, and high-interest cards.

	Annual Percentage Rate		
	12.0%	**17.3%**	**19.8%**
Average daily balance (excluding new purchases)	$ 40.00	$ 57.60	$ 66.00
Average daily balance (including new purchases)*	$ 80.00	$115.20	$132.00
Two-cycle average daily balance (including new purchases)	$120.00	$172.80	$198.00

*This is the most common method used by credit card issuers.

Shoppers frequently rely on purchase loans when buying "big ticket" items such as furniture and TVs.

Instant Message

Billing Errors Are Common

Data from the University of Michigan's Survey of Consumers shows that nearly one in six households reported a credit card problem during a recent year.

originated. Withholding payment to a credit card company is permitted when the cardholder alleges that a mathematical error has been made in a billing statement, when fraudulent use of the card appears to have occurred, or when (within certain reasonable limitations) a **goods and services dispute** asserts that the charges were for faulty, damaged, shoddy, defective, or poor-quality goods and services and you made a good-faith effort to try to correct the problem with the merchant. For goods and services disputes, the FCBA applies only to charges of more than $50 made in your home state or within 100 miles of your current mailing address. Most lenders apply the spirit of the FCBA to any goods and services disputes, regardless of the geographic distances involved.

You must make your billing error complaint within 60 days after the date on which the first bill containing the error was mailed to you. The lender then has 30 days to acknowledge your notification and, within 90 days, must either correct the error permanently, return any overpayment (if requested), or provide evidence of why it believes the bill to be correct (such as a copy of a charge slip you supposedly signed).

dunning letters Notices that make insistent demands for repayment.

While the dispute is being investigated, creditors cannot assess interest on or apply penalties for nonpayment of the disputed amount, send **dunning letters** (notices that make insistent demands for repayment), or send negative information about your account to a credit bureau without stating that "some items are in dispute." A lender that does not follow the procedures correctly cannot collect the first $50 of the questioned amount, even if the bill was correct. Back interest and penalties may be charged if the disputed item is proved to be legitimately owed.

Take several actions when disputing an item on a billing statement:

1. Send a written notice of the error to the credit card issuer. The notice must be in writing to qualify for the protections provided under the FCBA. Instead of sending the notice to the same address where repayments are normally remitted, examine the billing statement thoroughly, looking for an address under the heading "Send Inquiries to" or something similar.
2. Provide photocopies (not originals) of any necessary documentation. Keep the originals to challenge any finding by the company that no error occurred.
3. Withhold payment for disputed items. If possible, pay the remaining amount owed in full to isolate a disputed item. Under the provisions of the FCBA, the company must immediately credit your account for the amount in dispute.

4. After the dispute has been settled, review your credit bureau file to ensure that it does not include information regarding your refusal to repay the disputed amount.

CONCEPT CHECK 7.3

1. Describe how the finance charge is calculated on a credit card account.
2. What is the major benefit of having a credit card with a grace period?
3. Explain the steps you should take if you find an error on your credit card account billing statement.

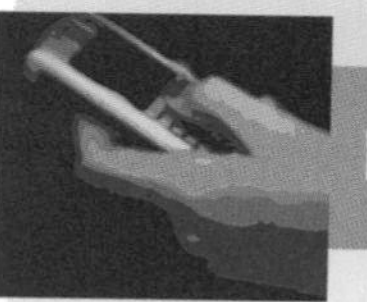

Instant Message

Homeowner's Insurance May Cover Lost Cards

Most homeowner's and renter's insurance policies pay for the $50 fee you might have to pay for unauthorized use of a lost or stolen credit card. (See Chapter 10 for details.)

Understanding Consumer Installment Loans

4 LEARNING OBJECTIVE
Describe the important features of consumer installment loans.

Consumers obtain installment credit in two ways. With a **cash loan,** the borrower receives cash and then uses it to make purchases, pay off other loans, or make investments. With a **purchase loan** (also called **sales credit**), the consumer makes a purchase on credit with no cash transferring from the lender to the borrower. Instead, the funds go directly from the lender to the seller. For example, a car buyer might obtain a purchase loan from the General Motors Acceptance Corporation (GMAC) to buy a new Pontiac Grand Am. With some purchase loans, the lender *is* the seller. For all consumer loans, the borrower will sign a formal **promissory note** (a written installment loan contract) that spells out the terms of the loan.

promissory note Written installment loan contract that spells out the terms of the loan.

Installment Loans Can Be Unsecured or Secured

Credit can either be unsecured or secured. An **unsecured loan** is granted solely based on the good credit character of the borrower. Sometimes unsecured loans are called **signature loans** because they are backed up by only the borrower's signature. Because unsecured loans carry higher risk than secured debts, the interest rate charged on them is substantially higher.

unsecured loan/signature loan Loan granted based solely on borrower's good creditworthiness.

A **secured loan** requires a cosigner or collateral. A **cosigner** agrees to pay the debt if the original borrower fails to do so. Being a cosigner is a major responsibility because a cosigner has the same legal obligations for repayment as the original borrower does. In case of default, a lender will go after the party—either the borrower or the cosigner—from whom it is more likely to collect the funds.

secured loan Loan that is backed by collateral or a cosigner.

A loan secured with **collateral** means that the lender has a security interest in the property that is pledged as collateral. For example, the vehicle itself is the collateral on an automobile loan. The item of collateral does not necessarily need to be the property purchased with the loan. Typically, the lender records a lien in the county courthouse to make the security interest known to the public. A **lien** is a legal right to seize and dispose of (usually sell) property to obtain payment of a claim. When the loan is repaid, the lien will be removed. (The borrower should make sure this removal occurs.)

lien A legal right to seize and dispose of (usually sell) property to obtain payment of a claim. Once loan is paid, the lien is removed.

In the event that the borrower fails to repay the loan, the creditor can exercise the lien and seize the collateral through repossession, sometimes without notice. Almost all credit contracts contain an **acceleration clause** stating that after a specific number of payments are unpaid (often just one), the loan is considered in default and all remaining installments are due and payable upon demand of the creditor. These

acceleration clause Part of a credit contract stating that after a specific number of payments are unpaid (often just one), the loan is considered in default and all remaining installments are due and payable upon demand of the creditor.

clauses protect the lender's interest but can prove very difficult for borrowers. Don't be fooled if you miss a payment and the lender does not exercise the acceleration clause immediately: It can do so at any time after default occurs. Do not ignore a warning letter from a creditor!

Purchase Loan Installment Contracts

Two kinds of contracts are used when purchasing goods with an installment loan:

- **Installment purchase agreements** (also called **collateral installment loans** or **chattel mortgage loans**), in which the title of the property passes to the buyer when the contract is signed
- **Conditional sales contracts** (also known as **financing leases**), in which the title does not pass to the buyer until the last installment payment has been paid

An installment purchase agreement provides a measure of protection for the borrower, as the creditor must follow all legal procedures required by state law when repossessing the property. Some state laws permit the lender to take secured property back as soon as the buyer falls behind in payments, possibly by seizing a car right from a person's driveway.

CONCEPT CHECK 7.4

1. Describe how a cash loan and a purchase loan differ.
2. Distinguish between a secured and an unsecured loan.
3. When might a lender enforce an acceleration clause on a loan and explain the impact of such an action by the lender.
4. Differentiate between an installment purchase agreement and a conditional sales contract.

5 LEARNING OBJECTIVE
Calculate the interest and annual percentage rate on consumer loans.

Truth in Lending Act (TIL) Requires lenders to disclose to credit applicants both the interest rate expressed as an annual percentage rate (APR) and the finance charge.

variable-rate (adjustable-rate) loans Loans for which the interest rate varies with the monthly payment going up or down, allowing the loan to be paid off by the original end date.

Calculating Interest on Consumer Loans

The federal **Truth in Lending Act (TIL)** requires lenders to disclose to credit applicants both the interest rate expressed as an annual percentage rate (APR) and the finance charge. As explained in Chapter 6, the APR is the relative cost of credit on a yearly basis expressed as a percentage rate. Any interest rate quoted by a lender must be the APR. The finance charge is the cost of credit expressed in dollars.

Calculating an Installment Loan Payment

Installment credit typically comes with a **fixed interest rate,** meaning that the rate will not change over the life of the loan. Lenders often offer **variable-rate loans** (also called **adjustable-rate loans**) to borrowers. When the loan rate varies, the monthly payment will go up or down, allowing the loan to be paid off by the same date as originally established in the contract.

To help you figure out the required monthly payment for different loan amounts, Table 7.1 shows various monthly installment payments used to repay a $1000 loan at commonly seen APR interest rates and time periods. For loans of other dollar amounts, divide the borrowed amount by 1000 and multiply the result by the appropriate figure from the table. For example, an automobile loan for $12,000, financed at 10 percent interest, might be repaid in 36 equal monthly payments of $387.24 ($32.27 × 12). A loan for $3550 at 16 percent for 24 months will require monthly payments of $173.81 ($48.96 × 3.550).

Table 7.1 Monthly Installment Payment (Principal and Interest) Required to Repay $1000*

	Number of Monthly Payments						
APR†	12	24	36	48	60	72	84
5	$85.61	$43.87	$29.97	$23.03	$18.87	$16.10	$14.13
6	86.07	44.32	30.42	23.49	19.33	16.57	14.61
7	86.53	44.77	30.88	23.95	19.80	17.05	15.09
8	86.99	45.23	31.34	24.41	20.28	17.53	15.59
9	87.45	45.68	31.80	24.88	20.76	18.03	16.09
10	87.92	46.14	32.27	25.36	21.25	18.53	16.60
11	88.38	46.61	32.74	25.85	21.74	19.03	17.12
12	88.85	47.07	33.21	26.33	22.24	19.55	17.65
13	89.32	47.54	33.69	26.83	22.75	20.07	18.19
14	89.79	48.01	34.18	27.33	23.27	20.61	18.74
15	90.26	48.49	34.67	27.83	23.79	21.14	19.27
16	90.73	48.96	35.16	28.34	24.32	21.69	19.86
17	91.20	49.44	35.65	28.85	24.85	22.25	20.44
18	91.68	49.92	36.15	29.37	25.39	22.81	21.02
19	92.16	50.41	36.66	29.90	25.94	23.38	21.61
20	92.63	50.90	37.16	30.43	26.49	23.95	22.21

*To illustrate, assume an automobile loan of $14,000 at 8 percent for five years. To repay $1000, the monthly payment is $20.28; therefore, multiply $20.28 (8% row and 60-month column) by 14 to give a monthly payment of $283.92. For amounts other than exact $1000 increments, simply use decimals. For example, for a loan of $14,500, the multiplier would be 14.5.

†For fractional interest rates of 5.5, 6.5, 7.5, and so on, simply take a monthly payment halfway between the whole-number APR payments. For example, the payment for 48 months at 9.5 percent is $25.12 ($25.36 − $24.88 = $0.48; $0.48 ÷ 2 = $0.24; $0.24 + $24.88 = $25.12).

The finance charge must include all mandatory charges to be paid by the borrower. In addition to interest, lenders may charge fees for a credit investigation; a loan application; or credit life, credit disability, or credit unemployment insurance. When fees are required, the lender must include them in the finance charge in dollars as part of the APR calculations. When the borrower elects these options voluntarily, the fees are not included in the finance charge and APR calculations, even though they raise the actual cost of borrowing. It is easy to calculate the finance charge on a consumer loan. First, multiply the monthly payment by the number of months and subtract the original amount borrowed. In the 36-month automobile loan example given earlier, the finance charge would be $1,940.64 [($387.24 × 36) − $12,000]. Second, add any other mandatory charges.

Finance Charge and APR Calculations for Installment Loans

Interest accounts for the greatest portion of the finance charge. Three methods are used to calculate interest on installment and noninstallment credit: the declining-balance (sometimes called the simple-interest) method, the add-on interest method, and the discount method. The add-on method predominates at banks, savings and loan associations, and consumer finance companies for installment loans for automobiles, furniture, and other credit requiring collateral. The declining-balance method is widely used by credit unions to calculate interest on loans. The declining-balance method is always used for credit cards and for most home mortgages.

The following discussion illustrates the calculation of the annual percentage rate for installment loans using each of the three methods.

declining-balance method Interest calculation method in which interest is assessed during each billing period (usually each month) based on the outstanding balance of the installment loan that billing period.

amortization Loan repayment method in which part of the payment goes to pay interest and part goes to repay principal. Extra payments toward principal shorten the life of the loan and decrease total amount of interest paid.

add-on interest method Interest is calculated by applying an interest rate to the amount borrowed times the number of years to arrive at the total interest to be charged.

The Declining-Balance Method With the **declining-balance method,** the interest assessed during each payment period (usually each month) is based on the outstanding balance of the installment loan. The lender initially calculates a schedule (such as that given in Table 7.2) to have the balance repaid in full after a certain number of months. The borrower may vary the rate of repayment by making payments larger than those scheduled or may repay the loan in full at any time.

Here is an illustration of the declining-balance method for an installment loan. As shown in Table 7.2, at the end of the first month, a periodic interest rate (the monthly rate applied to the outstanding balance of a loan) of 1.5 percent (18 percent annually divided by 12 months) is applied to the beginning balance of $1000, giving an interest charge of $15. Of the first monthly installment of $91.68, $15 goes toward the payment of interest and $76.68 ($91.68 – $15.00) goes toward payment of the principal.

For the second month, the outstanding balance is reduced to $923.32 ($1000 – $76.68). Since the balance is $78.68 lower, the interest portion of the payment drops to $13.85 (0.015 × $923.32). Because the declining-balance method of calculating interest on installment loans applies the periodic interest rate to the outstanding loan balance, the APR and the simple interest rate will differ only if fees (such as an application fee) boost the finance charge. (This method of paying off a loan, called **amortization,** is discussed in Chapter 9 when we examine home mortgage loans.) Note that declining-balance loans carry no prepayment penalties.

The Add-On Method The add-on method is a widely used technique for computing interest on installment loans. With this method, the interest is calculated and added to the amount borrowed to determine the total amount to be repaid. Equation (7.1) is used to calculate the dollar amount of interest. Note that the interest rate used in this equation for the add-on method is an add-on rate and should not be confused with the APR.

With the **add-on interest method,** interest is calculated by applying an interest rate to the amount borrowed times the number of years. The add-on interest formula given in Equation (7.1) is used as follows:

$$I = PRT \qquad (7.1)^*$$

where

I = Interest or finance charges
P = Principal amount borrowed
R = Rate of interest (simple, add-on, or discount rate)
T = Time of loan in years

*Calculations involving Equation (7.1) can be performed on the *Garman/Forgue* website.

Table 7.2 Sample Repayment Schedule for $1000 Principal Plus Interest Using the Declining Balance Method (1.5% per Month)

Month	Outstanding Balance	Payment	Interest	Principal	Ending Balance
1	$1000.00	$91.68	$15.00	$76.68	$923.32
2	923.32	91.68	13.85	77.83	845.49
3	845.49	91.68	12.68	79.00	766.49
4	766.49	91.68	11.50	80.18	686.31
5	686.31	91.68	10.29	81.39	604.92
6	604.92	91.68	9.07	82.61	522.31
7	522.31	91.68	7.83	83.85	438.46
8	438.46	91.68	6.58	85.10	353.36
9	353.36	91.68	5.30	86.38	266.98
10	266.98	91.68	4.00	87.68	179.30
11	179.30	91.68	2.69	88.99	90.31
12	90.31	91.66	1.35	90.31	0

For example, assume that Megan Broman of New York City borrows $2000 for two years at 9 percent add-on interest to be repaid in monthly installments. Using Equation (7.1), her finance charge in dollars is $360 ($2000 × 0.09 × 2). Adding the finance charge ($360) to the amount borrowed ($2000) gives a total amount of $2360 to be repaid. When this amount is divided by the total number of scheduled payments (24), we find that Megan must make 24 monthly payments of $98.33.

Calculating the APR When the Add-On Method Is Used Add-on rates and APRs are not equivalent. This is because the add-on calculation assumes the original debt is owed for the entire period of the loan. But of course the debt does go down as the debt is repaid. In the example just given, Megan does not have use of the total amount borrowed for the full two years. Equation (7.2) shows the **n-ratio method** of estimating the APR on her add-on loan.

$$\begin{aligned} \text{APR} &= \frac{Y(95P+9)F}{12P(P+1)(4D+F)} \qquad (7.2)^* \\ &= \frac{(12)(95 \times 24+9)(360)}{12(24)(24+1)[(4 \times 2000)+360]} \\ &= \frac{12(2289)(360)}{(288)(25)(8360)} \\ &= \frac{9{,}888{,}480}{60{,}192{,}000} \\ &= 16.4\% \end{aligned}$$

where

APR = Annual percentage rate
Y = Number of payments in one year
F = Finance charge in dollars (dollar cost of credit)
D = Debt (amount borrowed or proceeds)
P = Total number of scheduled payments

Using Equation (7.2), the APR is 16.4 percent. Note that the APR is approximately double the add-on rate because, on average, Megan has use of only half of the borrowed money during the entire loan period.

Applying the Rule of 78s to Determine Prepayment Penalties Most installment loan contracts that use the add-on method include a **prepayment penalty**—a special charge assessed to the borrower for paying off a loan early. Prepayment penalties take into consideration the reality that borrowers should pay more in interest early in the loan period when they have the use of more money and increasingly less interest as the debt shrinks over time. With an add-on method loan, however, the interest is spread evenly across all payments rather than declining as the loan balance falls. If an add-on method loan is paid off early, the lender will use some penalty method to compensate for the lower interest component applied in the early months.

prepayment penalty Special charge assessed to the borrower for paying off a loan early.

The **rule of 78s method** (also called the **sum of the digits method**) is the most widely used method of calculating a prepayment penalty. Its name derives from the fact that, for a one-year loan, the numbers between 1 and 12 for each month add up to 78 (12 + 11 + 10 + 9 + 8 + 7 + 6 + 5 + 4 + 3 + 2 + 1). For a two-year loan, the numbers between 1 and 24 would be added, and so on for loans with longer time periods.

rule of 78s method/sum of the digits method for calculating prepayment penalties A common method of calculating the prepayment penalty on a loan.

To illustrate the use of the rule of 78s method, consider the case of Devin Grigsby from Berea, Kentucky. He borrowed $500 for 12 months plus an additional $80 finance charge, and is scheduled to pay equal monthly installments of $48.33 ($580 ÷ 12). Assume Devin wants to pay the loan off after only six months. He might assume—

*Calculations involving Equation (7.2) can be performed on the *Garman/Forgue* website.

incorrectly—that he would owe only $250 more because after six months he had paid $250 (one-half) of the $500 borrowed and $40 (one-half) of the finance charge, for a total of $290 in payments ($48.33 × 6). Actually, Devin still owes $268.46, including a prepayment penalty of $18.46. To calculate this amount using the rule of 78s method, the lender adds together all of the numbers between 12 and 7 (12 for the first month, 11 for the second, and so on for six months): 12 + 11 + 10 + 9 + 8 + 7 = 57. The lender assumes that during the first six months $58.46 [(57 ÷ 78) × $80]—not $40—of the finance charges was received from the $290 in payments Devin had made on the loan.* Consequently, only $231.54 ($290.00 − $58.46) was paid on the $500 borrowed, leaving $268.46 ($500.00 − $231.54) still owed, for a prepayment penalty of $18.46 ($268.46 − $250.00).

discount method of calculating interest Interest is calculated based on discount rate multiplied by the amount borrowed and by number of years to repay. Interest is then subtracted from the amount of the loan and the difference is given to the borrower. In this method, interest is paid up-front before any part of the payment is applied toward the principal.

The Discount Method Occasionally, the discount method may be used to compute the interest on an installment loan. With the **discount method,** the interest is calculated based on a discount rate that is multiplied times the amount borrowed and multiplied by the number of years to repay. The interest is then subtracted from the amount of the loan and the difference is given to the borrower. Thus, the interest is paid up-front. When this method is applied to our earlier example involving Megan Broman, she would receive only $1640 [$2000 − ($2000 × 2 × 9%)] at the beginning of the loan period. Her monthly payment would be $83.33 ($2000 ÷ 24). Using Equation (7.2), the APR would be 19.8 percent (the APR rises because only $1640 is obtained while $2000 is repaid).

CONCEPT CHECK 7.5

1. Explain how the interest is calculated on a consumer loan that uses the declining-balance method.
2. Summarize how interest is calculated on a consumer loan that uses the add-on method.
3. What is the effect of the rule of 78s when a borrower repays an add-on method loan early?
4. Explain how the interest is calculated on a consumer loan that uses the discount method.

What Do You Recommend Now?

Now that you have read this chapter on credit cards and consumer loans, what would you recommend to Darrell Cochrane regarding:

1. His approach to using credit cards, including the number of cards he has?
2. Estimating the credit card interest charges he is paying each month?
3. How he might lower his interest expense each month?
4. Consolidating his credit card debts into one installment loan?

*If the loan was paid off after one month, the amount of interest paid is assumed to be 12⁄78 of the $80 finance charge, or $12.31. For a loan paid in full after two months, the amount of interest paid is assumed to be 23⁄78 of the total (12⁄78 for month 1 plus 11⁄78 for month 2), or $23.59.

Big Picture Summary of Learning Objectives

1 Compare the common types of consumer credit, including credit cards and installment loans.

Borrowers can use both installment and noninstallment credit. Open-ended credit is an example of noninstallment credit. It permits the customer to gain repeated access to credit without having to fill out a new application each time money is borrowed. The consumer may choose either to repay the debt in a single payment or to make a series of payments of varying amounts. Bank credit cards and travel and entertainment credit cards are the most commonly used open-ended credit accounts.

2 Describe the types and features of credit card accounts.

Credit card borrowers must adhere to all the rules of the account or risk being charged a number of punitive fees such as late-payment and bounced check fees. Borrowers also need to be wary of default rates, which may raise the APR on the account for any violation of the account rules. Some lenders apply default rates if the borrower falls behind in payments on other accounts, even if the borrower is in good standing on the lender's own account.

3 Manage your credit card accounts to avoid fees and finance charges.

Credit card statements provide a monthly summary of credit transactions and the calculation of any finance charges. Credit card issuers compute finance charges by multiplying the average daily balance by the periodic interest rate.

4 Describe the important features of consumer loans.

Consumer loans, also called installment loans, have several features that distinguish them from credit card accounts. Loans usually have a fixed payment for a fixed number of months. Once the loan is paid off, the account is closed and a new account would need to be opened if the person wants to take out another loan.

5 Calculate the interest and annual percentage rate on consumer loans.

Both the declining-balance and add-on methods are used to calculate the interest on installment loans, although the annual percentage rate formula gives the correct rate in all cases. With declining-balance loans, the dollar amount of interest incorporated in each monthly payment declines as the loan balance declines.

Let's Talk About It

1. If you wanted to borrow money to study abroad for a semester and could pay it back within two years after returning, would you prefer a single-payment loan, an installment loan, or a cash advance on a credit card?
2. Some credit cards offer a 1 percent or higher rebate for all purchases made on the card. How would you feel about using such a card to get those rebates with the intention of paying the balance off in full each month?
3. Do you feel that the much higher default interest rates are justified if you are not repaying a credit card on time? Does your opinion differ if the default rate was applied because you were in trouble on another account and not on the account charging the default rate?
4. How do you feel about the fact that interest costs are higher in the early months of a declining-balance loan than they are in the later months?
5. Are prepayment penalties such as that applied with the rule of 78s justified? Why or why not?

Do the Numbers

1. Kimberly Jensen and Rebecca Parker of East Lansing, Michigan, are both single. The pair share an apartment on the limited resources provided through Kimberly's disability check from Social Security and Rebecca's part-time job at a grocery store. The two grew tired of their old furniture and went shopping. A local store offered credit at an annual interest rate of 16 percent, with a maximum term of four years. The furniture they wish to purchase costs $2800, with no down payment required. Using Table 7.1 or the *Garman/Forgue* website, make the following calculations:
   (a) What is the amount of their monthly payment if they borrow for four years?
   (b) What are the total finance charges over that four-year period?
   (c) How would the payment change if Kimberly and Rebecca reduced the loan term to three years?
   (d) What are the total finance charges over that three-year period?
   (e) How would the payment change if they could afford a down payment of $500 with four years of financing?
   (f) What are the total finance charges over that four-year period given the $500 down payment?
   (g) How would the payment change if they could afford a down payment of $500 with three years of financing?
   (h) What are the total finance charges over that three-year period given the $500 down payment?

2. Talika Sampson, an antiques dealer from Miami, Florida, received her monthly billing statement for April for her MasterCard account. The statement indicated that she had a beginning balance of $600, on day 5 she charged $150, on day 12 she charged $300, and on day 15 she made a $200 payment. Out of curiosity, Talika wanted to confirm that the finance charge for the billing cycle was correct.
   (a) What was Talika's average daily balance for April without new purchases?
   (b) What was her finance charge on the balance in part (a) if her APR is 19.2 percent?
   (c) What was her average daily balance for April with new purchases?
   (d) What was her finance charge on the balance in part (c) if her APR is 19.2 percent?
   (e) What was her finance charge using the two-cycle average daily balance if her average daily balance for March was $800? (Hint: Add the March average daily balance to the April average daily balance, and then divide by 2 to obtain the two-cycle average daily balance.)
3. Elizabeth Mountbatten, a biologist from Lexington, Kentucky, is curious about the accuracy of the average daily balance shown on her most recent credit card billing statement, which appears in Figure 7.2 on page 193. Use the posting dates for her account to calculate her average daily balance and compare the result with the amount shown on the statement.
4. Timothy Sprater of Bozeman, Montana, has been shopping for a loan to buy a new car. He wants to borrow $18,000 for four or five years. Timothy's credit union offers a declining-balance loan at 9.1 percent for 48 months, resulting in a monthly payment of $448.78. The credit union does not offer five-year auto loans for amounts less than $20,000, however. If Timothy borrowed $18,000, this payment would strain his budget. A local bank offered him a five-year loan at a 9.34 percent APR, with a monthly payment of $376.62. This credit would not be a declining-balance loan. Because Timothy is not a depositor in the bank, he would also be charged a $25 credit check fee and a $45 application fee. Timothy likes the lower payment but knows that the APR is the true cost of credit, so he decided to confirm the APRs for both loans before making his decision.
   (a) What is the APR for the credit union loan?
   (b) Use the n-ratio formula to confirm the APR on the bank loan.
   (c) What is the add-on interest rate for the bank loan?
   (d) By how much would Timothy lower the APR on the bank loan if he opened an account to avoid the credit check and application fees?
5. Aaron Carson of Bishop, California, obtained a two-year installment loan for $1500 to buy some furniture eight months ago. The loan had a 12.6 percent APR and a finance charge of $204.72. His monthly payment is $71.03. Aaron has made eight monthly payments and now wants to pay off the remainder of the loan. The lender will use the rule of 78s method to calculate a prepayment penalty.
   (a) How much will Aaron need to give the lender to pay off the loan?
   (b) What is the dollar amount of the prepayment penalty on this loan?

Financial Planning Cases

Case 1
A Delayed Report of a Stolen Credit Card

Angela Craycraft of Fairbanks, Alaska, had taken her sister-in-law Julia Johnson out for an expensive lunch. When it came time to pay the bill, Joan noticed that her Visa credit card was missing, so she paid the bill with her MasterCard. While driving home, Angela remembered that she had last used the Visa card about a week earlier. She became concerned that a sales clerk or someone else could have taken it and might be fraudulently charging purchases on her card.

(a) Summarize Angela's legal rights in this situation.
(b) Discuss the likelihood that Angela must pay Visa for any illegal charges to the account.

Case 2
Clauses in a Car Purchase Contract

Virginia Rowland is a dentist in Hattiesburg, Mississippi, who recently entered into a contract to buy a new automobile. After signing to finance $18,000, she hurriedly left the office of the sales finance company with her copy of the contract. Later that evening, Virginia read the contract and noticed several clauses—an acceleration clause, a repossession clause, and a rule of 78s clause. When she signed the contract, Virginia was told these standard clauses should not concern her.

(a) Should Virginia be concerned about these clauses? Why or why not?
(b) Considering the rule of 78s clause, what will happen if Virginia pays off the loan before the regular due date?
(c) If Virginia had financed the $18,000 for four years at 7 percent APR, what would her monthly pay-

ment be, using the information in Table 7.1 or on the *Garman/Forgue* website?

Case 3
Victor and Maria Have a Billing Dispute

Maria Hernandez was reviewing her recent bank credit card account statement when she found two charges that she and Victor could not have made. The charges were for rental of a hotel room and purchase of a meal on the same day in a distant city. These charges totaled $219.49 out of the couple's $367.89 balance for the month.

(a) What payment should Maria make on the account?

(b) How should she notify her credit card issuer about the unauthorized use?

(c) Once the matter is resolved, what should Maria do to ensure that her credit history is not negatively affected by this error?

Case 4
The Johnsons' Credit Questions

Harry and Belinda need some questions answered regarding credit. Their seven-year-old car has been experiencing mechanical problems lately. Instead of buying a new set of tires, as planned for in March, they are considering trading the car in for a newer used vehicle so that Harry can have dependable transportation for commuting to work. The couple still owes $3600 to the bank for their current car, or $285 per month for the remaining 18 months of the 48-month loan. The trade-in value of this car plus $1000 that Harry earned from a freelance interior design job should allow the couple to pay off the auto loan and leave $1250 for a down payment on the newer car. The Johnsons have agreed on a sales price for the newer car of $14,250. The money planned for tires will be spent for other incidental taxes and fees associated with the purchase.

(a) Make recommendations to Harry and Belinda regarding where to seek financing and what APR to expect.

(b) Using the *Garman/Forgue* website or the information in Table 7.1, calculate the monthly payment for a loan period of three, four, and five years at 8 percent APR. Describe the relationship between the loan period and the payment amount.

(c) Harry and Belinda have a cash-flow deficit projected for several months this year (see Tables 3.8 and 3.9 on pages 83 and 84). Suggest how, when, and where they might finance the shortages by borrowing.

On the 'Net

Go to the Web pages indicated to complete these exercises. You can also go to the *Garman/Forgue* website at college.hmco.com/business/students for an expanded list of exercises. Under General Business, select the title of this text. Click on the Internet Exercises link for this chapter.

1. Visit the website for Bankrate.com at http://www.bankrate.com/brm/rate/cc_home.asp, where you will find information on bank credit card interest rates around the United States. View the information for the lenders in a large city nearest your home. How does the information compare with the interest rates charged on your own credit card account(s)? How do the rates in the city you selected compare with those found elsewhere in the United States?
2. Visit the website for Interest.com at http://auto-loan.interest.com/index.asp. There you will find an auto loan calculator that determines the monthly payment for any declining-balance loan given a specified time period, interest rate, and loan amount. Assume you wish to borrow $12,000 to buy a car. Vary the time period and interest rate of the loan to see how these variations affect your monthly payment.
3. Do you owe money on one or more credit cards? Visit the Bankrate.com website at http://www.bankrate.com and click on "More calculators" to find a calculator that will tell you how long it will take to pay off your balances.

Visit the Garman/Forgue website ...

@college.hmco.com/business/students

Under General Business, select *Personal Finance 9e*. There, among other valuable resources, you will find a complete glossary, ACE questions, links to help you complete the chapter exercises, and links to other personal finance sites.

CHAPTER 8

Vehicle and Other Major Purchases

You Must Be Kidding, Right?

When Ryan Levelle graduated from college three years ago, he really wanted a fully equipped Pontiac G6. His monthly payment would be about $350 per month, about $70 more than he could afford. So that Ryan could meet his budget, the dealer suggested that he lease the vehicle and offered a 42-month lease option at $270 per month for 12,000 miles per year. The contract had a $0.30 per mile fee at the end of the lease for any excess mileage. Now, with six more months on his lease, Ryan is already 1500 miles over the 42,000 (3.5 × 12,000) total mileage limit in his contract. What is Ryan's best option at this point?

A. Turn back the vehicle now and pay the $450 (1500 × $0.30) for excess mileage.

B. Try to cut back on his driving to minimize his excess mileage fee, which could be more than $2500 if he keeps driving at the same rate as he has been.

C. Stop driving the car and pay $450 for excess mileage when he turns it back at the end of the lease.

D. Continue driving the vehicle and buy it at the end of the lease by paying the residual value agreed upon when he entered into the contract.

The answer is D. None of the other options is financially practical. Ryan learned a hard lesson. Leases require a lower monthly payment but have hidden costs that often are not known until the very end of the contract!

LEARNING OBJECTIVES

After reading this chapter, you should be able to:

1. **Explain** the three steps in the planned buying process that occur prior to interacting with sellers.
2. **Describe** the five aspects of major purchases that require comparison shopping.
3. **Negotiate** and decide effectively when making major purchases.
4. **Evaluate** your purchase decisions and, if necessary, effectively seek redress.

What Do You Recommend?

David and Lisa Cosgrove of Tacoma, Washington, are in their early 40s and have three children. They own three vehicles. Lisa drives an almost-new Toyota Camry; David uses a five-year-old Ford pickup; and Amber, the couple's 17-year-old daughter, drives a ten-year-old Dodge Neon. Recently, a fire in their garage destroyed both the Neon and the Camry. The Cosgroves received an insurance settlement of $21,900 on Lisa's car, although the loan payoff amount was $22,800. Amber's Neon was not insured for fire. The couple wants to obtain replacement cars that are similar to those destroyed.

What would you recommend to David and Lisa on automobiles and other major purchases regarding:

1. How to search for two vehicles to replace those destroyed?
2. Whether to replace Lisa's vehicle with a new or used vehicle?
3. Whether to lease or buy a vehicle?
4. How to decide between a rebate and a special low APR financing opportunity if they decide to purchase a new vehicle for Lisa?
5. How to negotiate with the sellers of the vehicles?

FOR HELP with studying this chapter, visit the Online Student Center:

www.college.hmco.com/pic/garman9e

planned buying Thinking through all the details of a purchase from the initial desire to buy to your satisfaction after the purchase.

Planned buying entails thinking through all the details of a purchase from the initial desire to buy to your satisfaction after the purchase. You can use planned buying principles any time, but they are especially handy when you are buying a car or making other "big ticket" purchases. The seven distinct steps that lead you through the planned buying process are illustrated in Figure 8.1. Steps 1, 2, and 3 occur before you interact with sellers: determining your needs and wants, performing preshopping research, and fitting a purchase into your budget. Comparison shopping and other interactions with sellers comprise the fourth step in the buying process. Steps 5 and 6—negotiating and making the decision—follow. The seventh and final step—evaluation of the decision—is taken after making the purchase. After reading this chapter, you will understand enough about the planned buying process to save money when buying expensive goods while still meeting your needs and many of your wants.

1 LEARNING OBJECTIVE

Explain the three steps in the planned buying process that occur prior to interacting with sellers.

Do Your Homework

Let's look now at the first three steps, all of which should occur before you actually interact with sellers. They are, in a sense, the homework you do when preparing to buy.

What Do You Really Want?

need Item thought to be necessary.

want Item not necessary but desired.

A **need** is something thought to be a necessity; a **want** is unnecessary but desired. In truth, very few needs exist, yet in everyday language people talk often of "needing" certain things. In the planned buying process, it is best to avoid such thinking because once something is called a need, it may no longer be open to careful consideration. Instead, you should consider all purchase options to be wants. Of course, some wants are very important. The most important can be determined by prioritizing your wants. This approach allows for careful consideration of the benefits and costs of the options available. Costs should include opportunity costs as measured by some other goal or want that will become less attainable if a given want is satisfied. For example, buying a car with a retractable sunroof might mean that you cannot afford to purchase one with a remote start feature.

impulse buying Buying without fully considering priorities and alternatives.

generic products Goods that carry store brands or are sold under a general commodity name such as "whole-kernel corn" rather than a brand name, such as Del Monte.

Setting priorities becomes more difficult when a decision is complex such as when buying a car or home. Consider the case of Sharon Wilson, a respiratory therapist from St. Paul, Minnesota. Sharon has been late to work several times in the past few months because her 12-year-old car has been having mechanical problems. Sharon wants to avoid being late. But how? Should she buy a new car, a used car, lease a new car, repair her current car, or take the bus to work? After considering these options, Sharon decided to buy a new car. Now she must determine which features are of high or low priority. To do

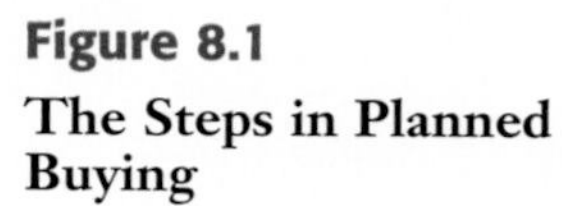

Figure 8.1
The Steps in Planned Buying

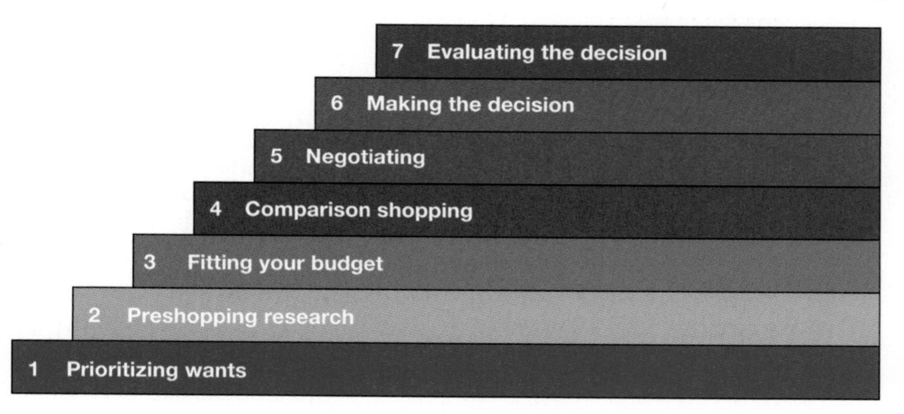

Did You Know?...

How to Buy Smart

The ways that people waste money could fill the pages of a very long book. Fortunately, buying wisely can save you 10 or more percent during the course of a year. Smart buyers should practice the following habits:

Do Not Buy on Impulse
Buying without fully considering priorities and alternatives is called **impulse buying.** For example, let's say you're looking for a laptop computer and you decide to buy one on sale at a discount store. While at the store, you pick up two video games that you had not planned to buy. The extra $150 spent on the unplanned purchase ruins most of the benefits of your careful shopping for the computer itself.

Pay Cash
Paying cash whenever possible can save money in two ways. First, it helps control impulse buying, which is a temptation when you're paying with a credit card. Second, using credit adds to the cost of items you buy.

Buy at the Right Time
You can save $5 or $10 a week on food simply by stocking up on advertised specials. New cars are least expensive at the end of the month and the model year. Many items, such as sporting goods and clothing, are marked down near certain holidays and at the end of each season. But be certain that what you buy on sale is something you will really use.

Do Not Pay Extra for a "Name"
Buying generic and store-brand products represents a good way to save money. **Generic products** are sold under a general commodity name such as "whole-kernel corn" rather than a brand name such as Del Monte. Store-brand products, such as those sold by Sears (Kenmore), Kroger, or Safeway, are actually made by the brand-name manufacturers. Gasoline, vitamins, medicines, laundry and other soaps, and many grocery items are all products with minor quality differences.

Recognize the High Price of Convenience
Buying a few items daily at a convenience store rather than using a shopping list during a weekly visit to a supermarket can raise food bills by perhaps 30 percent. Shopping for furniture and appliances in one's local community may be convenient, but better prices on the same items may be found in larger, more competitive shopping areas or online.

AUTOMOBILE FEATURE	PRIORITY LEVEL 1	2	3
Adjustable steering column			✔
Side-impact airbags		✔	
Air conditioning		✔	
AM-FM radio	✔		
Antilock brakes		✔	
Automatic transmission	✔		
Keyless locking system	✔		
CD player			✔
Cruise control		✔	
4-wheel (all-wheel) drive			✔
Power windows	✔		
Rear-window defroster	✔		
Sun roof / moon roof			✔
Theft-deterrent system			✔

Figure 8.2
Priority Worksheet (for Sharon Wilson)

Advice from a Pro...

Tips for Buying Online

People use the Internet to shop for appliances, vehicles, furniture, and other big-ticket items. Here's how you can become a better online shopper:

1. Use only secure sites. A secure site will feature a key or lock symbol on its screens or have a URL starting with "https" ("s" for secure). Sites displaying the VeriSign symbol must meet certain security standards.
2. Only do business with sellers for which you have complete contact information, including a "snail mail" (postal) address and telephone number.
3. Review shipping policies and costs as well as return policies before placing your order.
4. Never use a debit card for online purchasing. When the debit card transaction is executed, your cash is immediately transferred from your account to the seller's account. It may be difficult to persuade a seller to give you a refund when you pay by debit card. Purchases made via credit cards give you more protection because you may be able to ask that a purchase be charged back (see Chapter 6).
5. Print and keep copies of all purchase documents, warranties, credit card authorizations, and shipping notices.
6. Use only one particular credit card for online purchases. This practice will serve you well if your account number is stolen. In such a case, you can notify the one credit card issuer of the theft and block the card's future use without affecting your other accounts.
7. Check the site's privacy policy. Sites that display the TRUSTe symbol or Better Business Bureau Online seal have agreed to meet certain privacy standards.
8. Opt out of any list sharing that the seller might conduct with other merchants.
9. Do not use your regular e-mail address. Set up a free address at Yahoo!, Hotmail, or other provider and use it solely for online transactions. This will reduce the spam coming into your everyday e-mail account.

Brenda J. Cude
University of Georgia

$50 less in savings (she was saving to buy a vehicle). In addition, her transportation-related expenses would change as follows: gasoline, −$20; maintenance and repairs, −$50; and insurance costs, +$20. (Always get an insurance quote before buying a vehicle.) In all, these efforts would raise only $270, still $48 short of the amount she needs for the car. Sharon's alternatives are to make more cutbacks in her budget, work overtime, or get a part-time job. She could also reduce her payments to about $264 per month by taking out a longer, 60-month loan (13.05 × $20.28, from Table 7.1 on page 199). She should be wary about having to operate on such a tight budget for five years, however. Sharon will pay much more in interest with a longer-term loan and she might want to consider a less expensive new car or a used car.

CONCEPT CHECK 8.1

1. What is planned buying?
2. Distinguish between *needs* and *wants*, and explain why it may be better to act as if no needs exist.
3. Describe the types of information you need to be your own expert when making big-ticket purchases.
4. Summarize the process to determine whether you can afford a particular purchase.

Table 8.1 Fitting a Vehicle Payment into a Monthly Budget

	Prior Budget	Possible Cutbacks	New Budget
Food	$ 250	$ − 30	$ 220
Clothing/laundry	120	− 50	70
Vehicle maintenance and repairs	75	− 50	25
Auto insurance	60	20	80
Gasoline	90	− 20	70
Housing	450		450
Utilities	80		80
Telephone	50		50
Entertainment	150	− 50	100
Gifts	50	− 10	40
Church and charity	60		60
Personal care	60	− 10	50
Savings	200	− 50	150
Miscellaneous	70	− 20	50
TOTAL	**$1765**	**$ − 270**	**$1495**
Car payment			318
TOTAL WITH CAR PAYMENT	**$1765**	**$ − 270**	**$1813**

Use Comparison Shopping to Find the Best Buy

2 LEARNING OBJECTIVE
Describe the five aspects of major purchases that require comparison shopping.

After completing the first three steps in planned buying, it is time to begin interacting with sellers. These interactions begin with comparison shopping. **Comparison shopping** is the process of comparing products or services to find the best buy. A **best buy** is a product or service that, in the buyer's opinion, represents acceptable quality at a fair or low price for that level of quality. Purchasing the product with the lowest price does not necessarily ensure a best buy; quality and features count, too. You can begin your comparison shopping online, but most likely you will need to visit different stores and talk to sellers directly.

comparison shopping Process of comparing products or services to find the best buy.

best buy Product or service that, in the buyer's opinion, represents acceptable quality at a fair or low price for that quality level.

Comparison shopping takes time and effort, but the payoff in both satisfaction and savings can be considerable. During the early steps in the comparison shopping process, shoppers should narrow their choices to specific makes and models and desired options. Then they should visit the appropriate sellers again. This time, shoppers will be much closer to the decision to buy and will be ready to discuss details, although they should not buy at this point. When comparison shopping, tell the salesperson exactly what interests you and ask about price and any dealer incentives and rebates that apply. You should inquire about financing options, leasing, warranties, and service contracts. Finally, test-drive the vehicle. The goal is to narrow the choice even further prior to negotiating for the very best deal, which is the next step in the buying process.

Compare Prices

Prices on big-ticket items such as autos, furniture, appliances, and electronic equipment are rarely the same from seller to seller and vary from week to week. Hundreds or even thousands of dollars can be saved by searching for the best prices. Experts recommend use of the "rule of three," which says to compare at least three alterna-

Instant Message

Guard Your Privacy

Do not give out your Social Security number or allow the dealer to photocopy your driver's license before you go on a test drive. The dealer can then access your credit report and estimate how much you can afford to pay and your ability to obtain financing elsewhere.

tives before making any decision. When buying a car, compare the prices you find at dealers with the information from one of the websites devoted to vehicle prices listed on page 211.

Compare Financing Options

Sellers are not the only source of financing. Your bank or credit union loans money to make purchases. Also use websites such as bankrate.com or interest.com. Be on the lookout for "same as cash" offers on furniture, appliances, and electronics that allow you to delay interest or payment for, perhaps, 90 days to one year. If the product is paid off during this time period, you will not incur any finance charges. Be wary, however. Interest may be charged retroactively if a payment is late or if the purchase isn't fully paid off during the required time period.

Consider Leasing Instead of Buying

Leasing a new vehicle is an increasingly attractive option to people who are in the market for a car. About 20 percent of the new cars "sold" each year are actually leased. It is even possible to lease used cars. Is leasing a better deal than financing? You cannot answer this question until you understand some basics of leasing.

leasing Renting a product while ownership title remains with lease grantor.

When **leasing** a vehicle or any other product, you are, in effect, renting the product while the ownership title remains with the lease grantor. Regulation M issued by the Federal Reserve Board governs lease contracts. A requirement of this regulation is a mandatory disclosure of pertinent information about the lease that the consumer is considering. The disclosure form must summarize the offer of the lessor (leasing agency) to the lessee (consumer). The information in this form should be compared with the actual lease contract prior to signing to ensure that the lease signed is actually what was agreed upon verbally.

Did You Know?...

The Keys to a Safe Car

The following pointers may help you buy a safer vehicle:

- **Check government safety test results.** The federal government crash-tests motor vehicles to analyze their safety. For results on various makes and models, call the National Highway Traffic Safety Administration (NHTSA) "auto hotline" at (800) 424-9393 or visit www.safercar.gov.
- **Check on recalls.** When buying a used car, visit www.nhtsa.gov to see whether the vehicle has been recalled. If so, confirm that the repairs have been made to the car you're considering; if not, buy elsewhere. Dealers are required to fix for free vehicles recalled for safety reasons.
- **Consider a model with additional airbags.** All new cars have driver and passenger front-seat airbags. For added protection, consider new and used models that also provide side-impact airbags.
- **Look for antilock brakes.** Antilock brakes are believed to reduce the possibility of skidding during sudden stops. They are especially helpful in rain and inclement winter conditions.
- **Think about theft.** Some makes and models of vehicles are much more attractive to thieves than others. These vehicles also require higher auto insurance premiums. Visit www.nhtsa.gov and search "vehicle theft ratings."

Leasing Terminology Five terms are important in leasing:

1. The **gross capitalized cost (gross cap cost)** includes the price of the vehicle plus what the leasor paid to finance the purchase plus any other items the lessee agree to pay for over the life of the lease, including insurance or a maintenance agreement.
2. **Capitalized cost reductions (cap cost reductions)** are monies paid on the lease at its inception, including any down payment, trade-in value, or rebate.
3. The **adjusted capitalized cost (adjusted cap cost)** is determined by subtracting the capitalized cost reductions from the gross capitalized cost.
4. The **residual value** is the projected value of a leased asset at the end of the lease time period.
5. The **money factor** (or **lease rate** or **lease factor**) measures the rent charge portion of your payment. Although the money factor is sometimes described by dealers as a figure for comparing leases, lease forms must carry the following disclosure about the money factor: "This percentage may not measure the overall cost of financing this lease."

gross capitalized cost (gross cap cost) Includes vehicle price plus cost of any extra features such as insurance or maintenance agreements.

adjusted capitalized cost (adjusted cap cost) Subtracting the capitalized cost reductions from the gross capitalized cost.

residual value Projected value of leased asset at end of lease time period.

Always negotiate the purchase price before discussing a lease. Leasing requires an initial outlay of cash to pay for the first month's lease payment and a security deposit. Payments are based on the capitalized cost of the asset minus any capitalized cost reductions and the residual value. This difference represents the cost of using the asset during the lease period; when divided by the number of months in the contract, it serves to establish the base for the monthly lease payment. (Some new vehicles are offered with single-payment leases in which the entire difference between the capitalized cost and residual value is paid up-front.) With monthly payment leases, the payments are lower than monthly loan payments for equivalent time periods because you are paying for only the reduction in the asset's value—not its entire cost. To compare the costs of leasing versus buying, use the Decision-Making Worksheet, "Comparing Automobile Financing and Leasing."

Open- and Closed-End Leases A lease may be either open end or closed end. In an **open-end lease**, you must pay any difference between the projected residual value of the vehicle and its actual market value at the end of the lease period. When a vehicle depreciates more rapidly than expected, the holder of an open-end lease has to pay extra money when the lease expires. For example, a vehicle with an $11,000 residual value but a $10,250 market value would require an end-of-lease payment of $750 ($11,000 − $10,250). The Consumer Leasing Act limits this end-of-lease payment to a maximum of three times the average monthly payment.

Most vehicle leases are closed-end leases. In a **closed-end lease** (also called a **walkaway lease**), the holder pays no charge if the end-of-lease market value of the vehicle is lower than the originally projected residual value. However, closed-end leases may carry some type of end-of-lease charge if the vehicle has greater than normal wear or excess mileage. For example, a four-year closed-end lease might require a $0.30 per mile **excess mileage charge** in excess of 55,000 miles. If you actually drove the vehicle 60,000 miles during the four years, you would be charged an extra $1500 [$0.30 × 5000 (60,000 − 55,000)].

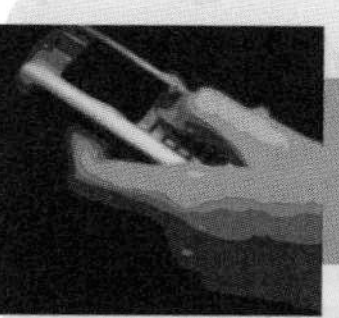

Instant Message

Buying Your Leased Vehicle

With either an open- or closed-end lease, you may purchase the vehicle at the end of the lease period. With an open-end lease, you would pay the actual cash value. With a closed-end lease, you would pay the residual value.

closed-end lease/walkaway lease Agreement in which the lessee pays no charge if the end-of-lease market value of the vehicle is lower than the originally projected residual value.

Additional Leasing Fees Other charges are possible with a lease. An **acquisition fee** is either paid in cash or included in the gross capitalization cost. It pays for a credit report, application fee, and other paperwork. A **disposition fee** is assessed when you turn in the vehicle at the end of the lease and the lessor must prepare it for resale. An **early termination charge** may also be levied if you decide to end the lease prematurely. Be wary of a lease with an early termination charge, even if you do not

early termination charge Charge if lessee turns car in before the end of lease period.

dealer holdback/dealer rebate Dealer incentive in which the manufacturer allows dealers to hold back a percentage of invoice price, thereby providing the dealer with additional profit on the vehicle.

billed from the manufacturer. But this may not be the price the dealer will have to pay when the vehicle is sold. Manufacturers often offer a **dealer holdback** (or **dealer rebate**) to dealers. A dealer holdback is a percentage of the invoice price that the dealer can hold back from (instead of paying to) the manufacturer, thereby providing the dealer with additional profit on the vehicle. Because of holdback incentives, dealers can sell a vehicle at or below invoice and still make a good profit. For example, a vehicle might have a sticker price of $27,890, an invoice price of $24,600, and a dealer holdback of 5 percent, or $1230. A negotiated price of $24,500 will still net the dealer a profit of $1130 [$1230 − ($24,600 − $24,500)]. Remember both the MSRP and invoice price are artificial numbers set by the manufacturer and dealer to allow room to negotiate a profitable price. For this reason, do not hesitate to negotiate for a price that is below the invoice price. Visit edmunds.com for a listing of recent dealer holdback offers on various makes and models of vehicles.

Instant Message

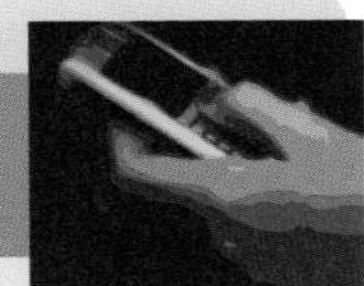

Negotiating a Vehicle Purchase

When buying a car, you should negotiate the deal in this order:

1. Get a firm price for the vehicle.
2. Negotiate the lowest possible APR through the dealer. Borrow elsewhere if the rate is lower.
3. Obtain a firm commitment on a trade-in allowance. Sell the vehicle yourself if the allowance is too low.

Negotiate Your Interest Rate Negotiating the interest rate, or APR, on a vehicle loan is not only possible but also essential to getting a good deal overall. Most vehicle borrowers accept that the dealer-arranged financing is the best the dealer can find. Buyers often do not know that the dealer benefits from having the borrower agree to a higher rate. Here is how the process works. The dealer asks the buyer to complete a loan application. The application is submitted to one or more lenders with whom the dealer has a preexisting affiliation. The lenders will assess the application and, if approved, suggest an APR. However, if the dealer suggests and gets an acceptance for a higher rate by the buyer (perhaps by saying that the buyer's credit score is low), the dealer (and salesperson) receives a higher fee for arranging the higher APR loan. In this way, the dealer can make money even if the profit off the sale of the vehicle itself is minimal. This is why it is so important to know your credit score and arrange the best financing you can on your own and accept the dealer financing only if it can beat your deal.

Negotiate Your Trade-in Getting a good deal on a vehicle purchase requires one more negotiation—your trade-in. You can pay a low price for the car you are buying, arrange a low-rate loan, and still not have a good deal if you do not receive what your trade-in is worth. Success here depends on knowing the value of your vehicle as a trade-in based on your preshopping research. The same online sources you used to get that information also have information on the average price at which similar vehicles are selling via private individuals. While it is true that trade-in values are usually lower than private sale values, you also have the costs of selling and the time involved if you decide not to accept the dealer's offer for your vehicle.

high-balling Sales tactic in which dealer offers a trade-in allowance that is much higher than the vehicle is worth.

Trade-ins are a way for a seller to make more money on the transaction. In one common sales technique, called **high-balling,** a dealer offers a trade-in allowance that is much higher than the vehicle is worth. This apparent generosity will look very good to a buyer. But beware, the dealer is likely making up for this elsewhere, possibly in a higher-than-necessary price for the purchased vehicle. You will not know whether you are being high-balled unless you know the value of your trade-in.

Negotiating a Car Deal: An Illustration

Thousands of dollars are at stake when you buy a vehicle. Consider the case of Gary Joseph, a production manager from Northville, Michigan. Gary was in the market for a newer car. He had done his homework and narrowed his choice of vehicles and options down to one model and two dealerships. He also had arranged his own financing at 6.6 percent APR. Finally, he also knew the trade-in value of his current vehicle.

Advice from a Pro...

How to Buy a Used Vehicle

Most consumer-buying experts recommend purchasing late-model used cars to get the most from your car-buying dollar. You need to be careful when buying a used vehicle, however. Following are some basic steps that can help you avoid getting a lemon:

1. **Decide how much you can afford to spend.** Decide in advance how much you can afford.
2. **Decide which features and options you want.** Decide on features such as power steering, air conditioning, or antilock brakes. Consider choosing an older model to obtain them without spending too much more.
3. **Search for reliable makes and models in your price range.** The Internet is an excellent source of used-car pricing information. In addition, you should consult the most recent April issue of *Consumer Reports* for its lists of recommended used vehicles in various price ranges.
4. **Start your search.** Start with online sources and also use classified advertisements in your local newspaper and used-vehicle advertising publications. All of the online information sources included in this chapter list local dealership offerings for specific makes and models.
5. **Select source.** New-car dealerships tend to offer the nicer, more reliable, and more expensive used vehicles. Used-car dealerships, on the other hand, tend to have the widest range of quality. Private individuals deserve your attention because they usually own the vehicle personally and know its history. Used cars sold by rental agencies such as Hertz and Avis can be good choices because the cars have been regularly maintained.
6. **Avoid credit rebuilders.** Dealers who use terms such as "credit rebuilders" or "buy here/pay here" give the impression that they are willing to lend to all buyers quickly and easily. While their standards are certainly lower, they also charge very high interest rates and offer contract terms that are very unforgiving of late or missed payments.
7. **Quickly rule out the unworthy.** Regardless of the source, immediately rule out any vehicle that seems to have a problem or raises a question in your mind. Do the same for sellers who do not seem cooperative. Too many vehicles are available to waste your time considering poor-quality vehicles or wrestling with uncooperative sellers.
8. **Check your selections carefully.** By now you should have narrowed your choice to two or three specific vehicles. Inspect them inside and out. Take along a friend who is knowledgeable about cars if you are not car savvy. Ask for maintenance records if the seller is an individual or a rental company. Ask the dealer for the name, address, and phone number of the previous owner and give that person a telephone call. Before you agree to buy any vehicle, ask your mechanic to examine it. Although the examination may cost $50 to $75, it could help you avoid purchasing a vehicle with problems and save hundreds of dollars in repairs later.
9. **Check your vehicle's history.** You want to know whether your vehicle has ever been wrecked or salvaged. You also want to know its ownership history. Carfax.com is good source of this information. Ask the seller to pay for this service. Vehicles coming off lease can be a good choice, and they are often still under original warranty.
10. **Negotiate and decide.** Never pay the asking price for a used vehicle. Get all verbal promises and guarantees in writing. If a seller will not put his or her words in writing, shop elsewhere. Finally, return to the quiet of your home to consider your alternatives and to make your final decision. If necessary, put down a small deposit to hold the vehicle for a day or two while you make your decision.

Aimee D. Prawitz
Northern Illinois University

Gary presented his list of desired options to the first dealer and was shown a suitable car on the lot. When Gary inquired about price, the salesperson asked what monthly payment would fit affordably in his budget. Gary countered by saying that his budget was not important and that he wanted to know the price for the vehicle. When the salesperson responded that it was the dealership's policy to get the affordable payment amount before answering any questions, Gary insisted on a price from the salesperson. The salesperson then asked Gary whether he would

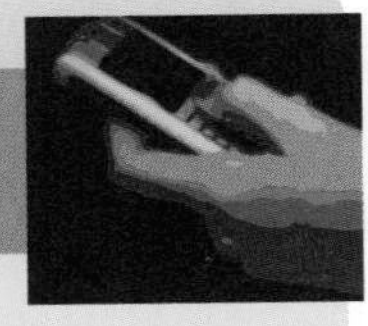

Instant Message

Play Good Cop–Bad Cop When Buying Vehicles

Many people are uncomfortable negotiating with sellers. Sellers understand this and are very good at putting people at ease with friendly talk and a supportive tone. But underneath, they are all business. How should you play the game? If you are a good negotiator, bring a friend along to be the friendly good cop while you focus on the deal and ask the hard questions. If you dislike negotiating, you can be the good cop, while your friend can ask the hard questions and focus on the business at hand.

be borrowing the money for the vehicle. Gary replied that he didn't know yet. The salesperson asked Gary if he had a trade-in vehicle. Gary replied, "Maybe, but let's get a price for the new car first." Finally, the salesperson gave him a price.

Gary said thank you and left the dealership, saying he would get back in touch with the salesperson. Later, he went to the other dealership and had a very similar discussion. He then went back and forth with the two dealers and obtained his best offer from the second dealer. Only then did Gary ask about the possibility of a loan. The salesperson arranged a loan with a 7.2 percent APR. Gary declined as he had a lower rate in hand. Then Gary asked about trading in his current car. The dealer offered him a trade-in allowance of $6200, $800 lower than what Gary knew the vehicle was worth ($7000) as a trade-in. Gary also knew he would likely be able to sell it himself for $7500. He countered the $7000 offer with that amount and ultimately accepted a $7200 trade-in allowance, thereby saving himself the time and money needed to sell the vehicle himself.

Gary did everything right. He focused first on price, playing one dealership off against the other. He arranged his own financing and took the lowest APR. He negotiated his trade-in separately. Notice that he never once talked about monthly payments with the dealer. He knew that the dealer could manipulate other aspects of the deal to fit Gary's monthly payment goal and still make plenty of money off the deal. Gary was not finished, however. As a smart shopper, he knew he should take the information he had and go home to make the final decision.

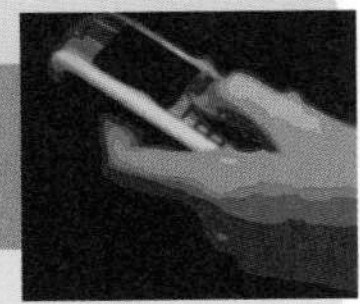

Instant Message

Buy Used Cars and Use Them Up

The best way to buy vehicles is to buy late-model used cars and drive them for ten or more years. New cars lose 25 percent of their value in the first year.

Make the Decision

It's unwise to make buying decisions for expensive purchases inside a retail store or showroom. By waiting until you get home to make the final decision, you are free of pressure from a salesperson and free of your own need to "get it over with." After taking some time to rationally consider all of the consequences of the purchase, you can return to the dealer's showroom and close the sale.

A decision-making grid allows you to visually and mathematically weigh the decision you are about to make. Table 8.2 depicts a grid for someone deciding among three different washing machines. The first task in developing such a grid is to determine the various criteria for making the decision. In Table 8.2, these factors include price, durability, and styling. Each criterion is assigned a weight that reflects the importance each has in the mind of the purchaser. Each brand and model under consideration is then given a score (from 1 to 10 in this case) that indicates how well it performs on that criterion. The score *(S)* is multiplied by the weight *(W)* to obtain a weighted score. The total of the weighted scores for each brand/model can then be compared with the totals for the other choices to determine which one "wins." In Table 8.2, Appliance C, which has a total score of 8.0, would be chosen. A grid of this type helps bring objectivity to your decision-making process and can be of benefit, especially when buying big-ticket items.

Finalizing a Car Deal

low-balling An attempt to raise an already negotiated price when it comes time to finalize the written contract.

After negotiating a good deal and making your final decision, it would be nice if you could simply return to the dealer and sign the necessary papers. But even then there is opportunity for the dealer to push for a little more profit. One technique that is used at this point is called **low-balling**. This involves an attempt to raise an already negotiated

Table 8.2 Decision-Making Grid (Illustrated for a Washing Machine)

Criteria	Decision Weight (*W*)	Appliance A		Appliance B		Appliance C	
		Score (*S*)*	*W* × *S*	Score (*S*)*	*W* × *S*	Score (*S*)*	*W* × *S*
Price	30%	9	2.7	7	2.1	5	1.5
Durability	25%	6	1.5	8	2.0	10	2.5
Features	20%	6	1.2	8	1.6	10	2.0
Warranty	15%	6	0.9	10	1.5	8	1.2
Styling	10%	10	1.0	6	0.6	8	0.8
TOTAL	**100%**		7.3		**7.8**		**8.0**

* Using a 10-point scale where 10 is the highest score.

price when it comes time to finalize the written contract. For example, after agreeing on the price of a vehicle with a buyer, the salesperson states that, as a formality, the approval of a manager is necessary. While the buyer is dreaming of driving home in the new car, the salesperson and the manager are talking about how much more they can get for the vehicle. When the salesperson returns, he or she indicates that there is a problem. Perhaps the trade-in value is too high, or the sticker price can't be discounted by quite as much as planned, or the price of a certain option has increased. In reality, of course, low-balling is simply a ruse to allow the dealer to get more money. Smart buyers stand firm and insist on the deal that had been negotiated.

Finally, it is time to sign the papers. Commonly at this point the salesperson turns the buyer over to another member of the sales team whose specific job it is to have all the papers signed to finalize the sale, the loan, and the transfer of the title and registration of the vehicle. Sign only a **buyer's order** that names a specific vehicle and all charges. And do so only after the salesperson and sales manager have signed *first*. Then verify that all aspects of the deal are as originally agreed, sign your name, and drive away in your new vehicle.

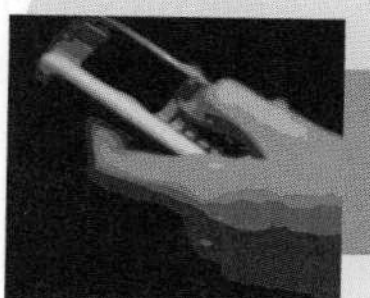

Instant Message

Use Leases to Save Money

Leases work best for people who wish to drive a new vehicle every two or three years. If you do choose a leasing option, your goal should be to lower your monthly cost rather than to buy more car. Otherwise, in just a few years, you will find that you have spent big bucks for a vehicle you must turn back in or pay extra to buy as a used vehicle.

buyer's orders Written offer that names a specific vehicle and all charges; only sign such offers after the salesperson and sales manager have signed *first*.

CONCEPT CHECK 8.3

1. List some of the complexities in vehicle buying, and offer your advice on how to get a best buy.
2. What three aspects of a vehicle purchase should be negotiated? In what order?
3. Why should you make major purchase decisions at home?
4. Summarize how to use a decision-making grid.

Evaluate Your Decision

4 LEARNING OBJECTIVE

Evaluate your purchase decisions and, if necessary, effectively seek redress.

The planned buying process comes full circle when you evaluate your decision. The purpose of this step is to determine where things went well and where they went less smoothly. The lessons learned will prove useful when you need to make a similar purchase in the future. Sometimes the process was so successful that you may want to compliment the seller.

Table 8.3 Complaint Procedure (Levels and Channels of Complaining)

Levels to Bring Your Complaint	Channels for Complaint
1. Local business	Salesperson → supervisor → manager/owner
2. Manufacturer	Consumer affairs department → president/chief executive officer
3. Self-regulatory organizations	Better Business Bureau → county medical societies → consumer action panels
4. Consumer action agencies	Private consumer action groups → media action lines → government agencies
5. Small-claims or civil court	Small-claims court → civil court

redress Process of righting a wrong.

alternative dispute resolution programs Industry- or government-sponsored programs that provide an avenue to resolve disputes outside the formal court system.

lemon laws State laws that provide guidelines for arbitrators to use to order a dealer's buyback of a "lemon" as defined under the law—commonly a car that has been in the shop four or more times to fix the same problem.

small-claims court State courts in which civil matters are often resolved without attorney assistance.

In other cases, you may want to complain about the product or service so as to obtain **redress**—that is, to right the wrong. This process should start with the actual seller, as indicated in Table 8.3. Seeking redress through the first three channels in the complaint procedures as shown in the table can rectify almost all consumer complaints.

Alternative dispute resolution programs are industry- or government-sponsored programs that provide an avenue to resolve disputes outside the formal court system. Vehicle manufacturers utilize these programs as part of their warranty procedures. **Mediation** is a procedure in which a neutral third party works with the parties involved in the dispute to arrive at a mutually agreeable solution. In **arbitration,** a neutral third party hears (or reads) the claims made and the positions taken by the parties to the dispute and then issues a ruling that is binding on one or both parties.

All states have enacted new-vehicle **lemon laws** that provide guidelines for arbitrators to use to order a dealer's buyback of a "lemon." A common definition of a lemon in these laws is a vehicle that was in the shop for repairs four times for the same problem in the first year after purchase. (For the specific definition in your state, visit www.carlemon.com.) To enforce a lemon law, the buyer must go through the warranty process specified in the owner's manual. Eventually, if the problem is not resolved, an arbitration hearing will be held through which the owner can request a buyback. Some states have also enacted used-vehicle lemon laws.

Sometimes your best efforts at redress may not prove successful. As a result, you might consider taking legal action in **small-claims court.** In this state court, civil matters are often resolved without the assistance of attorneys (in some states, attorneys are actually prohibited from representing clients in small-claims courts). Small-claims courts usually place restrictions on the maximum amount under dispute, typically ranging from $500 to $2500, for which a claim may be made in those courts. To file a small-claims court action, go to your local county courthouse and ask which court hears small claims.

CONCEPT CHECK 8.4

1 Outline the steps to go through to seek redress.
2. Distinguish between mediation and arbitration.
3. How do lemon laws work?

What Do You Recommend Now?

Now that you have read this chapter on vehicle and other major purchases, what do you recommend to David and Lisa Cosgrove regarding:

1. How to search for two vehicles to replace those destroyed?
2. Whether to replace Lisa's vehicle with a new or used vehicle?
3. Whether to lease or buy a vehicle?
4. How to decide between a rebate and a special low APR financing opportunity? Should they decide to purchase a new vehicle for Lisa?
5. How to negotiate with the sellers of the vehicles?

Big Picture Summary of Learning Objectives

1 Explain the three steps in the planned buying process that occur prior to interacting with sellers.

The planned buying process includes three steps that occur prior to interacting with sellers: prioritizing wants, obtaining information during preshopping research, and fitting the planned purchase into the budget. These steps represent the homework needed when preparing to buy.

2 Describe the five aspects of major purchases that require comparison shopping.

To interact effectively with sellers, you should comparison shop to find the best buy. When purchasing vehicles and other big-ticket items, this shopping process includes comparing prices, financing arrangements, leasing options, warranties, and extended warranties.

3 Negotiate and decide effectively when making major purchases.

Negotiating with sellers involves obtaining a fair price, low-cost financing, and a high trade-in allowance. After negotiating, the final decision should be made at home.

4 Evaluate your purchase decisions and, if necessary, effectively seek redress.

The planned buying process comes full circle when you evaluate your decision. The purpose of this step is to determine where things went well, where they went less smoothly, and how you can make better purchase decisions in the future. When things have not gone well, you can use mediation, arbitration, lemons laws, or small-claims court to resolve matters.

Let's Talk About It

1. Do you or a family member tend to buy name-brand versions of certain products? Which ones? Why or why not?
2. Are all of the steps in the planned buying process used when buying simple everyday products (such as a loaf of bread or a half-gallon of milk) or are they used only when buying big-ticket items?
3. What benefits do you see in leasing a vehicle? What negatives exist when leasing?
4. What is the worst purchase decision you have ever made? What step(s) in the planned buying process could you have done better in that situation?
5. When was the last time your were seriously dissatisfied with a purchase? Did you complain? Why or why not? If you complained, what was the outcome?

Do the Numbers

1. Amanda Forsythe of Tampa, Florida, must decide whether to buy or lease a car she has selected. She has negotiated a purchase price of $24,700 and could borrow the money to buy from her credit union by putting $3000 down and paying $515 per month for 48 months at 6.5 percent APR. Alternatively, she could lease the car for 48 months at $260 per month by paying a $3000 capital cost reduction and a $350 disposi-

tion fee on the car, which is projected to have a residual value of $8100 at the end of the lease. Use the Decision-Making Worksheet on page 218 to advise about Amanda whether she should buy or lease the car.

2. Kyle Parker of Fayetteville, Arkansas, has been shopping for a new car for several weeks. So far, he has negotiated a price of $27,000 on a model that carries a choice of a $2500 rebate or dealer financing at 2 percent APR. The dealer loan would require a $1000 down payment and a monthly payment of $564 for 48 months. Kyle has also arranged for a loan from his bank with a 7 percent APR. Use the Decision-Making Worksheet on page 212 to advise Kyle about whether he should use the dealer financing or take the rebate and use the financing from the bank.

Financial Planning Cases

Case 1
Purchase of a New Refrigerator

Tracy Sullivan, a financial consultant from Spokane, Washington, is remodeling her kitchen. Tracy, who lives alone, has decided to replace her refrigerator with a new model that offers more conveniences. She has narrowed her choices to two models. The first is a basic 20.2-cubic-foot model with a bottom freezer for $799. The second is a 25.4-cubic-foot model with side freezer for $999. Additional features for this model include icemaker, textured enamel surface, and ice and water dispenser. Tracy's credit union will loan her the necessary funds for one year at a 12 percent APR on the installment plan. Following is her budget, which includes $2140 in monthly take-home pay.

Food	$ 300
Entertainment	120
Clothing	60
Gifts	70
Charities	75
Car payment	330
Personal care	60
Automobile expenses	120
Savings	130
Housing	825
Miscellaneous	50
Total	**$2140**

(a) What preshopping research might Tracy do to select the best brand of refrigerator?

(b) Using the information in Table 7.1 on page 119 or the *Garman/Forgue* website, determine Tracy's monthly payment for the two models.

(c) Fit each of the two monthly payments into Tracy's budget.

(d) Advise Tracy to help her make her decision.

Case 2
A Dispute over New-Car Repairs

Christopher Hardison, a high school football coach from Oklahoma City, Oklahoma, purchased a new SUV for $28,000. He used the vehicle often; in fact, in less than nine months he had put 14,000 miles on it. A 24,000-mile, two-year warranty was still in effect for the power-train equipment, although Christopher had to pay the first $100 of each repair cost. After 16,500 miles and in month 11 of driving, the car experienced some severe problems with the transmission. Christopher took the vehicle to the dealer for repairs. A week later he picked the car up, but some transmission problems remained. When Christopher took the car back to the dealer, the dealer said that no further problems could be identified. Christopher was sure that the problem was still there, and he was amazed that the dealer would not correct it. The dealer told him he would take no other action.

(a) Was Christopher within his rights to take the car back for repairs? Explain why or why not.

(b) What logical steps might Christopher follow if he continues to be dissatisfied with the dealer's unwillingness or inability to repair the car?

(c) Should Christopher seek any help from the court system? If so, describe what he could do without spending money on attorney's fees.

Case 3
Victor and Maria Hernandez Buy a Third Car

The Hernandezes' older son, Hector, has reached the age at which it is time to consider purchasing a car for him. Victor and Maria have decided to give Maria's old car to Hector and buy a later-model used car for Maria.

(a) What sources can Victor and Maria use to access price and reliability information on various makes and models of used cars?

(b) What sources of used cars might be available to Victor and Maria, and what differences might exist among them?

(c) How might Victor and Maria check out the cars in which they are most interested?

(d) What strategies might Victor and Maria employ when they negotiate the price for the car they select?

Case 4
The Johnsons Decide to Buy a Car

The Johnsons have decided to move out of their apartment and into some form of owned housing. Although they have not decided what type of housing they will buy, they know that Belinda will no longer be able to ride the bus to work. Recognizing this fact, they are in the market for another car. They have decided not to buy a new car but think they have some room in their budget for a used car, given the raises each has received this year (see Table 3.8 on page 83). Harry and Belinda estimate that they could afford to spend about $3200 on an inexpensive used car by making a down payment of $600 and financing the remainder over 24 months at $120 per month.

(a) Make suggestions about how the $120 might be integrated into the Johnsons' budget (Table 3.8 on page 83) without changing the amount left over at the end of each month. Harry and Belinda want to retain that extra money to help defray some of the added expenses of home ownership.

(b) Which sources of used cars should they consider? Why?

(c) Assume that the Johnsons have narrowed their choices to two cars. Both have air conditioning, AM-FM radio, and automatic transmission. The first car is an eight-year-old Chevrolet Lumina with 102,000 miles; it is being sold for $3400 by a private individual. The hatchback-style car has a six-cylinder engine, and the seller has kept records of all repairs, tune-ups, and oil changes. The car will need new tires in about six months. The second car is a nine-year-old, two-door Ford Focus with 116,000 miles, being sold by a used-car dealership. It has a four-cylinder engine. Harry contacted the previous owner and found that the car was given in trade on a new car about three months ago. The previous owner cited no major mechanical problems but simply wanted a bigger car. The dealer is offering a written 30-day warranty on parts only. The asking price is $3200. Which car would you advise the Johnsons to buy? Why?

On the 'Net

Go to the Web pages indicated to complete these exercises. You can also go to the *Garman/Forgue* website at college.hmco.com/business/students for an expanded list of exercises. Under General Business, select the title of this text. Click on the Internet Exercises link for this chapter.

1. Visit the website for the Kelley Blue Book at http://www.kbb.com. For a used vehicle you currently own or one you would like to own, determine its "used car retail value," "trade-in value," and "private party value." Why do the three values differ?
2. Visit the website of *Consumer Reports* magazine at http://www.consumerreports.org and click on the "Cars" tab. You will be sent to a page containing tips on buying new and used cars. In what ways are the strategies similar and in what ways do they differ from the tips offered in this book for buying a used car?
3. Visit the website of the Federal Reserve Board at http://www.federalreserve.gov/consumers.htm where you will find a Web page titled "Keys to Vehicle Leasing" that expands upon the information in this book. Use this information to generate a list of pros and cons of leasing versus purchasing a vehicle. By clicking on "sample leasing form" on this Web page, you can view and print a copy of the required vehicle leasing disclosure form.

Visit the Garman/Forgue website ...

@college.hmco.com/business/students

Under General Business, select *Personal Finance 9e*. There, among other valuable resources, you will find a complete glossary, ACE questions, links to help you complete the chapter exercises, and links to other personal finance sites.

CHAPTER 9

Buying Your Home

You Must Be Kidding, Right?

Horst Brandt recently bought a new home and borrowed $140,000 at 6.75 percent interest for 30 years. His monthly payment for interest and principal will be $908. A friend suggested that Horst should have easily been able to find a loan at 6.5 percent with a monthly payment of $885. Horst dismissed his friend's comments, arguing that the difference in the monthly payments was no big deal. His friend replied, "Horst, it's not the monthly payment, it's the interest." How much more in interest will Horst pay over the life of the loan because he took a loan with the higher rate?

A. $350

B. $4200

C. $8460

D. $10,500

The answer is C. Horst will be making a higher payment for each and every month for 30 years. While the difference in the monthly payment seems small [$23 ($908 – $885) per month in this example], even a small difference in the interest rates on mortgage loans can add up to thousands of dollars in extra interest over the life of the loan. That is why searching for the lowest possible interest rate is so important when borrowing to buy a home!

LEARNING OBJECTIVES

After reading this chapter, you should be able to:

1 **Decide** whether renting or owning your home is better for you both financially and personally.

2 **Explain** the up-front and monthly costs of buying a home.

3 **Describe** the steps in the home-buying process.

4 **Distinguish among** the conventional and alternative ways of financing a home, and list the advantages and disadvantages of each.

5 **Identify** the important aspects of selling a home.

What Do You Recommend?

Libby Clark has worked for a major consumer electronics retailer since graduating from college. The company has operations across the country with regional headquarters in Atlanta, Denver, Minneapolis, and Boston. She has been based in the Atlanta area for the past three years and had begun thinking about buying a home there rather than renting her townhouse apartment. Then, last month, Libby was promoted to deputy regional director for the Denver region. The promotion represents a key step for becoming a regional director in four or five years. Regional directors may or may not be promoted from within their current region.

What do you recommend to Libby on the subject of buying a home regarding:

1. Buying or renting housing in the Denver area?
2. Steps she should take prior to actively looking at homes?
3. Finding a home and negotiating the purchase?
4. The closing process in home buying?
5. Selecting a type of mortgage to fit her needs?
6. Things to consider regarding the sale of her home should she ultimately be promoted to a position in another of the four regions?

FOR HELP with studying this chapter, visit the Online Student Center:

www.college.hmco.com/pic/garman9e

You may already be renting a place to live. But eventually you will have to decide between renting versus buying a home. At that point, you will have to estimate the financial benefits of renting versus buying and take a good hard look at what it really costs to buy a home. If you decide to buy, you will begin a complicated but rewarding process. This process will require that you obtain a **mortgage loan**—a loan to purchase real estate in which the property itself serves as collateral. The market has developed many types of mortgage loans, and borrowers need to understand the mathematics of mortgage loans—now more than ever before. Eventually you will want to sell your home, and understanding that process can help you get the most from your sale.

mortgage loan Loan to purchase real estate in which the property itself serves as collateral.

Should You Rent or Buy Your Home?

1 LEARNING OBJECTIVE
Decide whether renting or owning your home is better for you both financially and personally.

Most areas of the United States offer a wide variety of rented and owned housing. Whether to rent or buy depends on your preferences and what you can afford. In the short run, renting is usually less expensive than buying. In the long run, the opposite is true. Nearly 90 percent of all households headed by people younger than age 25 are rental households, compared with less than 20 percent of those headed by people aged 55 to 64.

Good Money Habits in Buying Your Home

Make the following your money habits when buying your home:

1. Read your leases and all other real estate contracts before signing.
2. Save the funds for a down payment in a tax-sheltered Roth IRA account.
3. Get your finances in order before shopping for a new home by reducing debt, budgeting better, and clearing up anything that keeps you from having a high credit score.
4. Buy a home as soon as it fits your budget and lifestyle so you can take advantage of special income tax deductions and the likelihood of substantial price appreciation over time.
5. Thoroughly explore mortgage loan sources and options to determine which one best fits your needs.
6. If you make a down payment of less than 20 percent on a home, cancel private mortgage insurance as soon as the equity in your home pushes the loan-to-value ratio to 80 percent.

Rented Housing

People may choose to rent their housing for several reasons. For some, the large down payment and high monthly loan payments are barriers to buying a home. Some people simply prefer the easy mobility of renting or want to avoid many of the responsibilities associated with buying. Prospective renters need to consider the monthly rental fees and related expenses, the lease agreement and restrictions, and tenant rights.

Rent, Deposit, and Related Expenses **Rent** is the cost charged for using an apartment or other housing space. It is usually due on a specific day each month, with a late penalty being assessed if the tenant is tardy in making the payment. Other fees could be assessed for features such as use of a clubhouse and pool, exercise facilities, cable television, and space for storage and for parking.

A **damage deposit** is an amount given in advance to a landlord to pay for repairing the unit beyond the damage expected from normal wear and tear. It is often charged before the tenant moves in and is often equal to one month's rent. You may also be required to pay a **security deposit** to ensure that you do not move without paying your rent. Again, this amount is often equal to the last month's rent payment. Thus, an apartment with a monthly rent of $800 might require payment of $800 for the first month's rent, an $800 security deposit, and an $800 damage deposit for a total of $2400.

rent Cost charged for using an apartment or other housing space.

lease In this context, a contract specifying both tenant and landlord legal responsibilities.

Lease Agreement and Restrictions A **lease** is a contract specifying the legal responsibilities of both the tenant and the landlord. It identifies the amount of rent and security deposit, the length of the lease (typically one year), payment responsibility for utilities and repairs, penalties for late payment of rent, eviction procedures for nonpayment of rent, and procedures to follow when the lease ends. Leases often state whether the security deposit accumulates interest, how soon the unit must be inspected for cleanliness after the tenant vacates the premises, and when the security deposit (or the balance) will be forwarded to the tenant. Local laws may also address these issues.

In the United States, two types of leases generally govern tenant-landlord relationships. The first provides for **periodic tenancy** (for example, week-to-week or month-to-month residency), where the agreement can be terminated by either of the parties if they give proper notice in advance (for example, one week or one month). Without such notice, the agreement stays in effect. This arrangement also typically applies in situations in which no written lease is established. The second type of lease provides for **tenancy for a specific time** (for example, one year). When this period expires, the agreement terminates unless notice is given by both parties that the agreement will be renewed.

Lease agreements may contain a variety of restrictions that are legally binding on tenants. For example, pets may or may not be permitted; when they are permitted, landlords often require a larger security deposit. Excessive noise from home entertainment systems or parties may be prohibited as well. To protect other renters from overcrowding, a clause may limit the number of overnight guests. An important restriction applies to **subleasing** (wherein an original tenant leases the property to another tenant). Here a tenant who moves before the lease expires may need to obtain the landlord's permission before someone else can take over the rental unit. The new tenant may even have to be approved, and the original tenant may retain some financial liability until the term of the original lease expires.

Tenant Rights Tenants have a number of legal rights under laws in most states and many local communities. Some important rights are as follows:

- Prohibitions against **harassment** (rent increases, eviction, or utility shutoff) for reporting building-code violations or otherwise exercising a tenant's legal rights.
- Assurances of some legally prescribed minimum standard of **habitability** for items such as running water, heat, and a working stove and the safety of access areas such as stairways.
- The right to make minor repairs and deduct the cost from the tenant's next rent payment. This right is subject to certain restrictions, such as giving sufficient prior written notification to the landlord.
- Prompt return of a security deposit, with limits placed on the kinds of deductions that can be made. Landlords must explain specific reasons for deductions. Some state laws require that interest be paid on security deposits.
- The right to file a lawsuit against a landlord for nonperformance. Such suits can be brought in a small-claims court.

Did You Know?...

How to Make Sure Your Security Deposit Is Returned

If you leave a rental unit clean and undamaged, you have a legal right to a refund of your security deposit when you move out. Several steps will help ensure that you receive a full refund:

- Make a list of all damages and defects when you first move into the unit. Have the landlord sign this list.
- Maintain the unit and keep it clean.
- Notify the landlord promptly (in writing, if necessary) of any maintenance problems and malfunctions.
- Give proper written notice of your intention to move out at least 30 days in advance of the lease expiration.
- Make a written list of all damages and defects after moving out but prior to turning over the keys. Have the landlord sign this second list.
- Use certified mail (with a return receipt) to request the return of your security deposit and to inform the landlord of your new address.
- Use small-claims court (see Chapter 8), if necessary, to obtain a court-ordered refund.

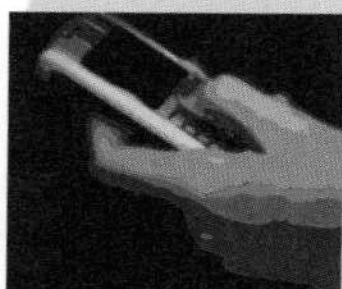

Instant Message

Always Obtain a Written Lease

Renting housing without a formal, written lease may seem like an easy and congenial way to do business, but it is fraught with potential for disagreements later. Always get your rental agreements in writing. Model leases can be found at nolo.com.

Owned Housing

Americans have historically favored single-family dwellings to satisfy their owned-housing desires. However, other alternatives such as condominiums, cooperatives, manufactured housing, and mobile homes have increased in popularity.

subleasing An arrangement in which the original tenant leases the property to another tenant.

Single-Family Dwellings A **single-family dwelling** is a housing unit that is detached from other units. Buyers have many choices available for both new and

single-family dwelling Housing unit that is detached from other units.

existing homes with varying floor plans and home features. Some people prefer the modern kitchens and other features found in newer homes; others prefer the larger rooms, higher ceilings, and completed landscaping of older homes.

Condominiums and Cooperatives The terms *condominium* and *cooperative* describe forms of ownership rather than types of buildings. These forms of ownership usually cost less than single-family dwellings, offer recreation facilities, and have reduced maintenance obligations.

condominium (condo) Form of ownership with the owners holding legal title to their own housing unit among many with common grounds and facilities owned by the developer or homeowner's association.

With a **condominium** (or **condo**), the owner holds legal title to a specific housing unit within a multi-unit building or project and owns a proportionate share in the common grounds and facilities. The entire complex is run by the owners through a **homeowner's association.** Besides making monthly mortgage payments, the condominium owner must pay a monthly **homeowner's fee** that is established by the homeowner's association. This fee covers expenses related to the management of the common grounds and facilities and insurance on the building. Some areas of concern for condominium owners include potential increases in homeowner's fees and limited resale appeal of the unit.

cooperative (co-op) Form of ownership in which owner holds a share of the corporation that owns and manages a group of housing units as well as common grounds and facilities; co-op owners pay a monthly management fee to an independent entity that carries out activities similar to those that homeowner associations do for condo owners.

With a **cooperative** (or **co-op**), the owner holds a share of the corporation that owns and manages a group of housing units. The value of this share is equivalent to the value of the owner's particular unit. The owner also holds a proportional interest in all common areas. A monthly fee for the cooperative covers the same types of items as does a condominium fee but also includes an amount to cover the professional management of the complex and payments on the cooperative's mortgage debt. (The pro-rata share for interest and property taxes is deductible on each shareholder's income tax return.)

Manufactured Housing and Mobile Homes **Manufactured housing** consists of fully or partially factory-built housing units designed to be transported (often in portions) to the home site. Final assembly and readying of the housing for occupancy occurs at the home site. **Mobile homes,** in contrast, are fully factory-assembled housing

It is important to factor homeowner's fees into the monthly income needed to purchase a condominium.

units that are designed to be towed on a frame with a trailer hitch. Mobile homes rarely appreciate in value like other forms of housing; in fact, they usually depreciate.

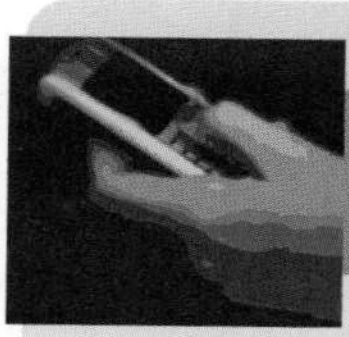

Instant Message

Understand Your Deed Restrictions

Most existing communities, new housing developments and cooperative and condominium associations have **deed restrictions** established by local zoning laws or by the developer. These rules govern such things as minimum lot size, the outside appearance and landscaping of the property, allowable secondary buildings, parking of vehicles, and other aspects of the use and appearance of the property. You should ask for and read the deed very carefully before buying.

deed restrictions Rules placed on the homeowner's use of a property by local government or a homeowner's association.

Who Pays More—Renters or Owners?

According to conventional wisdom, homeowners enjoy a financial advantage over renters when total housing costs are calculated over many years. Renters generally pay out less money in terms of annual cash flow. But owners receive annual income tax advantages, and they usually see increases in the value of their homes over time that greatly improve their financial situation.

Based on Cash Flow, Renters Appear to Win The Decision-Making Worksheet, "Should You Buy or Rent?" illustrates a comparison between a small condominium and an apartment with similar space and amenities. For the apartment, rent would total $1000 per month. Assume you could buy the condominium for $180,000 by using $36,000 in savings as a down payment and borrowing the remaining $144,000 for 30 years at 7 percent interest. As the worksheet shows, renting would have a cash-flow cost of $10,920 after a reduction for the interest that could be earned on your savings. Buying requires several expenses beyond the monthly mortgage payment, including an $1800 annual homeowner's fee. In this case, the cash-flow cost of buying is $17,621, or $6701 more than renting.

After Taxes and Appreciation, Owners Usually Win To make the comparison more accurate, you must consider the tax and appreciation aspects of the two options. If you rent, you would pay $360 ($1440 × 0.25) in income taxes on the interest on the amount in your savings account ($36,000) not used for a down payment. If you buy the condominium, $1464 of the $11,496 in annual mortgage loan payments during the first year will go toward the principal of the debt, and the remainder—$10,032 ($11,496 − $1464)—will go toward interest. Both mortgage interest and real estate property taxes qualify as income tax deductions. If you are in the 25 percent marginal tax bracket, your taxes would be reduced by $2508 ($10,032 × 0.25) as a result of deducting the mortgage interest and by $750 ($3000 × 0.25) as a result of deducting the real estate tax. In effect, every time you make a payment you will get some of it back from the government.

Condominiums also have a likelihood of appreciation, or increase, in the home's value. A conservative assumption would be that the condominium will increase in value by 2.5 percent per year. A home valued at $180,000 would, therefore, be worth $184,500 ($180,000 × 1.025) after one year, a gain of $4500. In this case, buying is financially better than renting by approximately $2881 ($11,280 − $8399).

CONCEPT CHECK 9.1

1. Explain the purpose and value of a lease for both the renter and the landlord.
2. Distinguish between periodic tenancy and tenancy for a specific time when renting housing.
3. Identify three ways that home buyers can save on their income taxes.
4. Illustrate how housing buyers pay less than renters when taxes and appreciation of housing values are considered.

Decision-Making Worksheet

Should You Buy or Rent?

This worksheet can be used to estimate whether you would be better off renting housing or buying. If you are renting an apartment and planning to buy a house, qualitative differences will enter into your decision. This worksheet will put the financial picture into focus. A similar worksheet can be found on the Ginnie Mae website at www.ginniemae.govYPTH/rent_vs_buy/rent_vs_buy_calc.asp?Section=YPTH.

	Example Amounts		Your Figures	
	Rent	**Buy**	**Rent**	**Buy**
Annual Cash-Flow Considerations				
Annual rent ($1000/month) or mortgage payments ($958.00/month)*	$12,000	$11,496	____	____
Property and liability insurance	360	725	____	____
Private mortgage insurance	N/A	0	N/A	____
Real estate taxes	0	3,000	____	____
Maintenance	0	600	____	____
Other housing fees	0	1,800	____	____
Less interest earned on funds not used for down payment (at 4%)	1,440	N/A	____	N/A
Cash-Flow Cost for the Year	**$10,920**	**$17,621**	____	____
Tax and appreciation considerations				
Less principal† repaid on the mortgage loan	N/A	1,464	N/A	____
Plus tax on interest earned on funds not used for down payment (25% marginal tax bracket)	360	N/A	____	N/A
Less tax savings due to deductibility of mortgage interest‡ (25% marginal tax bracket)	N/A	2,508	N/A	____
Less tax savings due to deductibility of real estate property taxes (25% marginal tax bracket)	N/A	750	N/A	____
Less appreciation on the dwelling (2.5% annual rate)	N/A	4,500	N/A	____
Net Cost for the Year	**$11,280**	**$ 8,399**	____	____

*Calculated from Table 9.4.
†Calculated according to the method illustrated in Table 9.2.
‡Mortgage interest tax savings equal total mortgage payments minus principal repaid multiplied by the marginal tax rate.

2 **LEARNING OBJECTIVE**

Explain the up-front and monthly costs of buying a home.

What Does It Cost to Buy a Home?

Buying housing represents the largest outlay of funds over most people's lifetime. Some of these costs occur up-front. The largest of these is usually the down payment. Others, such as the mortgage payment, occur monthly. A few items, such as real estate property taxes, require both an initial outlay and recurring monthly payments. Table 9.1 illustrates these outlays for the purchase of a $185,000 home with $25,000 down financed by a 30-year mortgage at 6.5 percent interest. This same example is used repeatedly

Did You Know?...

The Tax Consequences of Buying Your Home

Home ownership makes you eligible for three big tax breaks.

1. **Mortgage interest and real estate taxes are tax deductible on federal (and most state) income tax returns.** These amounts usually exceed the IRS's standard deduction (see Chapter 4). You can then take advantage of even more deduction opportunities that are available to taxpayers who itemize.
2. **The profits made by selling a home can be tax free.** If you sell a home for more than you originally paid, you have a *capital gain*. Gains are ordinarily taxable, but homeowners can avoid paying taxes on gains by buying a home that is more expensive, thus rolling the gain into the new home. In addition, capital gains of up to $500,000 if married and filing jointly, and up to $250,000 if single may be avoided. To qualify, the home must have been owned and used as the principal residence for two of the last five years prior to the date of the sale. In the first few years of home ownership, any appreciation likely will be offset by the anticipated sales commission. This explains the advice that you should not buy a home unless you know you will live in it for three years.
3. **You can save the funds to buy a home in a tax-sheltered account.** Individuals can use Roth IRAs (see Chapter 17) to save for retirement. Once the account is five years old, as much as $10,000 may be withdrawn tax free and penalty free, provided that a qualifying, first-time home buyer uses the funds for home-buying costs. This mechanism even allows parents or grandparents to make withdrawals from their Roth IRAs to help young family members buy their first home.

throughout this chapter to illustrate the costs of home buying (it is near the median price for first-time buyers).

Most Up-Front Costs Are Due at the Closing

First-time home buyers are often surprised by the high initial costs of buying a home. These costs include the down payment and closing costs. **Closing costs** include fees and charges other than the down payment and may vary from 2 to 10 percent of the mortgage loan amount. The down payment and closing costs must be paid at a meeting called the **closing** at which ownership of the property is transferred. All the parties to the purchase, sale, and the mortgage loan are represented at the closing. Up-front costs are indicated in green in Table 9.1.

closing costs Include fees and charges other than the down payment and may vary from 2 to 10 percent of the mortgage loan amount.

The Down Payment The **down payment** on a home is simply the portion of the purchase price that is not borrowed. The buyer actually writes a check to the seller for that amount. In this example, we assume that the prospective homeowner has $25,000 to use as a down payment on a $185,000 home and will, thus, need to borrow $160,000.

down payment Portion of the purchase price that is not borrowed.

Points A **point** (or **interest point**) is a fee equal to 1 percent of the total loan amount. Any charges for points must be paid in full when the home is bought, although sometimes they can be added to the amount borrowed. Lenders use points to increase their returns on loans. For example, a lender might advertise a loan as having an interest rate 0.25 percentage point below prevailing rates but then charge 1 point. Any points are, in effect, prepaid interest and compensate the lender for having a low interest rate. In our example, the lender charged 2 points on the $160,000 loan, resulting in a charge of $3200. By law, interest points must be included when calculating the APR for the loan. Interest points are deductible on federal income tax returns.

Point/or interest point Fee equal to 1 percent of the total mortgage loan amount.

Table 9.1 Illustrated Up-Front and Monthly Costs When Buying a Home (Purchase Price of a Home, $185,000 with $25,000 Down; Closing on July 1)

Home-Buying Costs	At Closing	Monthly
Payments Required Up-Front		
Down payment	$25,000	
Points (2)	3,200	
Attorney's fee	500	
Title search	200	
Title insurance (to protect lender)	320	
Title insurance (to protect buyer)	320	
Loan origination fee	800	
Credit reports	75	
Home inspection	400	
Recording fees	250	
Appraisal fee	250	
Termite and radon inspection fee	130	
Survey fee	100	
Notary fee	150	
Payments Required Monthly		
Principal and interest (from Table 9.3 for a $160,000 loan for 30 years at 6.5%)		$1,011.31
Mortgage insurance		53.33
Warranty insurance		30.00
Payments Required Up-Front and Then Monthly		
Property taxes ($2160 for the entire year, $1080 for first half-year, then $180 monthly)	1,080*	180.00
Homeowner's insurance ($1200 for the entire year; $600 for first half-year, then $100 monthly)	600†	100.00
Subtotal	**$33,375**	**$1,374.64**
Less amount owed by seller	−1,080*	—
Total	**$32,295**	**$1,374.64**

*Would be received from seller, who legally owes these taxes, and then deposited in escrow account to be available when the tax bill comes due at the end of the year.
†Would be paid to escrow account to be available when the premium for the next year is due.

Attorney Fees Home buyers should hire an attorney to review documents and advise and represent them prior to and during closing. Attorney fees commonly amount to 0.5 percent of the purchase price of the home, although some attorneys do this work for a flat fee ($500 in our example).

title Legal right of ownership interest to real property.

deed Written document used to convey real estate ownership.

Title Search and Insurance The **title** to real property is the legal right of ownership interest. In real estate transactions, the title is transferred to a new owner through a **deed,** which is a written document used to convey real estate ownership.

Four types of deeds are used:

1. A *warranty deed* is the safest, as it guarantees that the title is free of any previous mortgages.
2. A *special warranty deed* guarantees only that the current owner has not placed any mortgage encumbrances on the title.
3. A *quitclaim deed* transfers whatever title the current owner had in the property with no guarantee.

4. A *deed of bargain and sale* conveys title with or without a guarantee that the seller had an ownership interest.

A title search and the purchase of title insurance protect the buyer's title to the property. Your attorney or title company will conduct a **title search** by inspecting court records and prepare a detailed written history of property ownership called an **abstract.** The seller normally pays the fees for this process ($200 in our example). Lenders often require buyers to purchase **title insurance** because it protects the lender's interest if the title is later found faulty. Premiums for title policies vary among title companies. The one-time charge at closing may amount to 0.20 percent of the amount of the loan for each policy [$320 ($160,000 × 0.002) in our example]. Homeowners who wish to insure their own interest must purchase a separate title insurance policy (another $320 in our example).

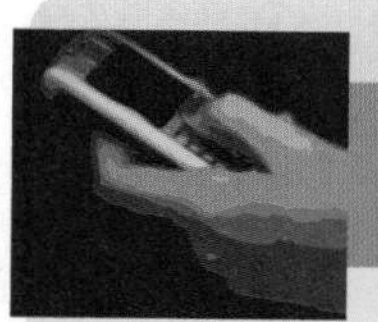

Instant Message

Joint Ownership Is Best When Couples Buy a Home

Both married and unmarried couples buying a home should generally put the ownership in both names using joint tenancy with right of survivorship. If one of the parties dies, the other will have clear title to the entire property.

Miscellaneous Fees When a prospective mortgage borrower applies for a loan, the lender may charge a **loan origination fee** at the closing to process the loan ($800 or half of a point in our example). In addition, credit reports ($75 in our example) are needed before a home buyer can obtain a loan—and the borrower pays the fee for this report as well. Another important up-front cost is the **home inspection** ($400 in our example) conducted to ensure that the home is physically sound and that all operating systems are in proper order. Title and deed recording fees ($250 in our example) are charged to transfer ownership documents in the county courthouse. An **appraisal fee** ($250 in our example) may be required to obtain a professionally prepared estimate of the fair market value of the property by an objective party. If you are charged an appraisal fee, you have the right to receive a copy of the appraisal. Occasionally, termite and radon inspections ($130 in our example) are required by local laws but are a good idea even when not required. A **survey** ($100 in our example) is sometimes required to certify the specific boundaries of the lot. Finally, separate **notary fees** ($150 in our example) may be charged for the services of those legally qualified to certify (or notarize) signatures.

title insurance Protects the lender's interest if the title search is later found faulty.

home inspection Conducted to ensure that the home is physically sound and that all operating systems are in proper order.

appraisal fee Fee charged for a professionally prepared estimate of the fair market value of the property by an objective party.

Monthly Costs Include Both Principal and Interest

Once a home is purchased, the monthly costs can consume as much as 30 or 40 percent of your disposable income. These costs include the portion of your monthly payment that goes to principal (the amount you owe) and interest. Other monthly costs include mortgage insurance, home warranty insurance, property taxes, and/or homeowner's insurance. Monthly costs are indicated in blue in Table 9.1.

Mortgage Principal and Interest A mortgage loan requires repayment of both *principal* ***(P)*** and *interest* ***(I)*****,** which are the first two letters of the acronym **PITI**, which real estate agents and lenders often use to indicate a mortgage payment that includes **p**rincipal, **i**nterest, real estate **t**axes, and homeowner's **i**nsurance. In the example in Table 9.1, the mortgage payment for principal and interest on a 30-year mortgage for $160,000 at 6.5 percent is $1011.31. (Later in this chapter, you will learn how the P and I components for any mortgage loan are calculated).

PITI Elements of a monthly real estate payment consisting of principal, interest, real estate taxes, and homeowner's insurance.

Mortgage Insurance Lenders expect an 80 percent **loan-to-value (LTV) ratio** when a home is purchased. The LTV ratio is simply the loan amount divided by the value of the home. An 80 percent LTV ratio translates into a 20 percent down payment, an amount that is difficult to come by for many first-time buyers. Fortunately, a number of special programs allow for down payments as low as 1 percent of the purchase price of the home. When a buyer makes a down payment that is less than 20 percent of the home's purchase price, the lender will require that the borrower obtain mortgage insurance.

loan-to-value (LTV) ratio Original or current outstanding loan balance divided by the home value.

Mortgage insurance Insures the difference between the amount of down payment required by an 80 percent LTV ratio and the actual, lower down payment.

Mortgage insurance insures the difference between the amount of down payment required by an 80 percent LTV ratio and the actual, lower down payment. In this way, the lender is assured of payment of the loan balance if the home were later repossessed for default and sold for less than the amount owed. Mortgage insurance may be obtained from several sources and can be canceled when the LTV ratio reaches 80 percent as the loan is paid down. You can obtain mortgage insurance from these sources.

private mortgage insurance (PMI) Mortgage insurance obtained from a private company rather than a government agency.

- **Private Mortgage Insurance. Private mortgage insurance (PMI)** is obtained from a private company rather than a government agency. The largest private mortgage insurer is the Mortgage Guaranty Insurance Corporation (MGIC, pronounced "magic"). The cost of PMI varies from 0.25 to 2.0 percent of the debt, depending on the degree to which the loan-to-value ratio exceeds 80 percent. In our example, the loan-to-value ratio is 86.5 percent ($160,000 ÷ $185,000). As a result, the annual private mortgage insurance premium is 0.4 percent of the mortgage loan (0.004 × $160,000) and is $640, or $53.33 per month ($640 ÷ 12).

  Instead of making monthly payments for PMI, it may be possible to obtain lender-paid mortgage insurance. In such a case, the lender pays the mortgage insurance premium and in return charges a higher interest rate on the loan of perhaps an additional ¼ to ¾ of a percentage point. In this way, the mortgage insurance premium is tax deductible because it represents part of the interest payments. But in this case, the insurance cannot be canceled when the LTV ratio hits 80 percent without completely refinancing the loan.

Federal Housing Administration (FHA) An arm of the U.S. Department of Housing and Urban Development (HUD) that insures loans that meet its standards to encourage home ownership.

- **FHA Mortgage Insurance.** To encourage lending, the **Federal Housing Administration (FHA)** of the U.S. Department of Housing and Urban Development (HUD) insures loans that meet its standards. To obtain such mortgage insurance, the borrower must be creditworthy and the home must meet the FHA's minimum-quality standards. (For information on HUD mortgage programs, visit www.hud.gov/buying/mortprog.cfm.) FHA mortgage insurance premiums may be paid as a single up-front, lump-sum payment or may be financed and paid in monthly amounts in the same way as private mortgage insurance.
- **VA Mortgage Insurance.** The federal **Department of Veterans Affairs (VA)** promotes home ownership among military veterans (active-duty, reserve, and National Guard veterans may qualify) by providing the lender with a guarantee against buyer default. In effect, the VA (www.homeloans.va.gov) guarantee operates much like FHA or private mortgage insurance—that is, the lender is guaranteed a portion of the loan's value in the event that the home must be repossessed and sold.

Home Warranty Insurance All homes for sale carry some type of implied warranty (see Chapter 8). In some states, home sellers must complete a form verifying the condition of home features and major mechanical equipment at the time of sale. A seller who knowingly hides serious defects might be liable, but the buyer will have to hire an attorney and sue to prove this point. Many new-home builders provide an express warranty good for one year on the new homes they sell.

Home warranty insurance, another option for the homeowner, operates much like a service contract (also discussed in Chapter 8). Insurance companies sell this type of insurance on existing homes through real estate agents and builders. The example in Table 9.1 has a $30-per-month home warranty insurance protection. Typically, the homeowner must pay the first $100 to $200 of any repair.

Some Fees Are Paid Both Up-Front and Then Monthly

escrow account Special reserve account at a financial institution in which funds are held until they are paid to a third party—in this case, for home insurance and for property taxes.

Some home-buying costs do not fit neatly into an up-front or monthly pattern. This is because they are billed annually. Property taxes and homeowner's insurance are examples. *Taxes (T)* and *insurance (I)* represent the last two letters of PITI. To ensure that these are paid when due, the lender usually requires that monthly installments be paid into an **escrow** account. An **escrow account** is a special reserve

Advice from a Pro...

Cancel Private Mortgage Insurance as Soon as Possible

Private mortgage insurance (PMI) is required for any mortgage loan for which the initial loan-to-value ratio is more than 80 percent, that is, the down payment is less than 20 percent of the house's purchase price. PMI premiums must be paid until the unpaid balance drops to 80 percent of the home's value. As the borrower makes mortgage payments over time, the amount of principal remaining to be paid will decline until eventually the 80 percent threshold is reached. At that point, the lender must notify the borrower of the opportunity to drop the PMI.

As illustrated in Figure 9.2, a borrower might start out owing \$160,000 or 86.5 percent of the value of the home. It takes about six years to reach the 80 percent threshold (\$148,000 = 0.80 × \$185,000) simply by making loan payments. The good news is that the value of the home may increase much faster than the loan principal declines. In the example in Figure 9.2, the 80 percent threshold will be reached in about three years because of the rising value of the home.

When that threshold is attained, the borrower can ask the lender to cancel the PMI. Lenders usually require an appraisal of the property before doing so, but the cost of the appraisal (perhaps \$300) represents money well spent. It is a smart move to make such a request, and it is even smarter to continue making the same monthly payment on the mortgage after the PMI is removed. The extra amount will be applied to the principal of the loan, thereby paying it off even sooner.

Ronald R. Jordan
Constance Y. Kratzer
New Mexico State University

account at a financial institution in which funds are held until they are paid to a third party. When the insurance and tax bills are due, the lender pays them out of the escrow account.

Real Estate Property Taxes Real estate property taxes must be paid to local governments and may range from 1 to 4 percent of the value of the home. The total property tax (\$2160 in our example) is due once each year when the government sends out its tax bill. However, if a buyer takes possession during the tax year, the buyer must pay the taxes accrued so far into the escrow account at the closing (\$1080, or 6 × \$180 here) to ensure that sufficient funds will be available when the bill comes due at the end of the year. Then the monthly amount (\$180 in our example) is paid thereafter into the escrow account. (Because it is the seller who really owed the taxes for the six months prior to the sale, the seller will pay the buyer \$1080 on the day of the closing.)

Homeowner's Insurance Lenders always require homeowners to insure the home itself in case of fire or other calamity. Both the home and its contents can be covered in a typical homeowner's insurance policy. (Chapter 10 covers this information in detail.) The annual premium for such insurance must be paid each year in advance (\$1200 in this example). Lenders require prepayment of the estimated insurance premium each month (\$100 here) into the escrow account. In our example illustrated in Table 9.1 on page 238, the purchaser must be prepared to pay one-half year's premium (\$600 here) on the closing day so that there will be sufficient funds in the account to pay the next year's full premium in six months when it is due.

Did You Know?...

About Real Estate Property Taxes

Real estate property taxes are based on the value of buildings and land. To calculate these taxes, local government officials first establish a **fair market value** for the owner's home and land. Next, the **assessed value** of the property is calculated. A home with a fair market value of \$160,000, for example, might have an assessed value of \$120,000. Although you can do little to influence the tax rate on real estate property, you can claim that assessed valuation of your home is too high. If your appeal is successful, your tax bill will be lowered accordingly. On a national basis, about one-half of all appeals succeed.

real estate property taxes Taxes assessed by local government agencies on the value of real estate to pay for schools and municipal services.

The Bottom Line?

The wise financial planner will carefully estimate all initial and monthly costs of housing. Focusing only on the down payment and the monthly payment for principal and interest does not tell the whole story. In our example, the borrower put only 13.5 percent of the purchase price ($25,000 ÷ $185,000) as a down payment but with points and other up-front costs actually had to come up with 17.46 percent ($32,295 ÷ $185,000) at the closing. Thus, the closing costs represented almost 4 percent (17.46% − 13.5%) of the purchase price. Similarly, the monthly payment for principal and interest was $1011.31, but the actual monthly outlay will be $1374.64, an increase of 36 percent [($1374.64 − $1011.31) ÷ $1011.31]. This is the real dollar amount that buyers must fit into their budget when trying to determine whether they can afford to buy a home.

CONCEPT CHECK 9.2

1. What is the standard down payment amount on a mortgage loan?
2. If you make a down payment that is lower than standard, identify the extra cost you will be required to pay.
3. Why do lenders use points in home loans, and who is responsible for paying points?
4. Explain why the down payment and mortgage principal and interest understate the actual up-front and monthly costs of home ownership.
5. When should you request that private mortgage insurance be canceled if such insurance was required at the time of purchase of a home?
6. Identify the components of PITI.

3 LEARNING OBJECTIVE
Describe the steps in the home-buying process.

The Steps of Home Buying

The steps in the home-buying process closely resemble the planned buying steps outlined in Chapter 8. It may take several weeks or months to find a home that represents a good value and another four to five months to actually move into the home. Special attention will need to be paid to the seven steps outlined in Figure 9.1.

Did You Know?...

The Top 3 Financial Missteps When Buying Housing

People slip up in buying their home when they do the following:

1. Fail to search for and negotiate for the lowest mortgage interest rate possible
2. Fail to request that private mortgage insurance be canceled when their loan-to-value ratio drops to 80 percent
3. Pay off a mortgage early when carrying credit card debt or not saving regularly through a qualified tax-sheltered retirement plan

Get Your Finances in Order

You need to be financially ready to buy a home. Three tasks ease the process considerably: doing a credit checkup, accurately estimating all monthly housing costs, and fitting projected housing costs into your budget.

Do a Credit Checkup Your credit history can make or break your chances of buying the home of your dreams. Obtain copies of your credit report and your credit scores from all three major credit reporting agencies (lenders use all three) about six months in advance of buying housing; you can then clear up any errors before the loan application process begins. See page 171 for the steps to take to correct errors in your credit report. Most people can improve their credit scores by correcting errors and rearranging credit accounts. See www.myfico.com for suggestions.

You should plan on it taking about 6 months to buy a home from the time you begin your efforts until you actually move in.

Timing	Step
6 months before moving in	**1. Get your finances in order.** • Ensure that your credit bureau file is accurate and request any updates or corrections as necessary. • Estimate all your expected monthly housing costs. • Adjust your budget to fit the costs expected.
3 to 5 months before moving in	**2. Prequalify for a mortgage.** • Shop for best rates. • Estimate affordability using front- and back-end ratios. • Consult several lenders and mortgage brokers.
2 to 4 months before moving in	**3. Search for a home online and in person.**
2 months before moving in	**4. Agree to terms with a seller.** • Negotiate a price with the seller and give the seller earnest money. • Have your lawyer go over the purchase contract with you. • Sign the purchase contract with the seller. • Have the home inspected by someone you hire.
1 to 2 months before moving in	**5. Obtain a mortgage loan.** • Formally apply for a mortgage from the desired lender. Consider locking-in an interest rate if rates are likely to go up before the closing. • Arrange for a lawyer to help you go over the contract and the good-faith estimate of closing costs.
2 to 4 weeks before moving in	**6. Prepare for the closing.** • Make moving arrangements. • Activate all utilities. • Initiate the change of address process.
The Big Day	**7. Attend the closing.** • Correct any errors in the contract or uniform settlement statement. • Sign your name. Write the big checks. • Celebrate!!!! Take family and friends out to dinner.

Figure 9.1

Steps in the Process of Buying a Home

Estimate Your Monthly Housing Costs Using Internet Resources

It is vital to have an accurate estimate of what you will have to pay on a monthly basis for your new home. It is not enough to just estimate the amount of the payment for principal and interest on your mortgage loan. Other costs can add up, too. Fortunately, resources available on the Internet make that task much easier.

1. Start by choosing the type of home you would like to own and the neighborhood in which you would like to live.
2. Go to the www.realtor.com website to search for housing that matches your interests. You will be able to estimate the selling price of similar housing and, by subtracting your available down payment amount, estimate the amount you will need to borrow.
3. Go to the www.bankrate.com website to estimate the current interest rates on mortgage loans in your market.
4. Use the calculator at www.bankrate.com to estimate the monthly payment for a loan of the amount you need at the prevailing interest rates.
5. Add an additional 30 to 40 percent (it was 36 percent in the Table 9.1 example) to the monthly payment on the loan for such things as homeowner's insurance, property taxes, maintenance, and upkeep.

Fit the Housing Costs into Your Budget Once you have an estimate of the monthly costs associated with buying a home, you will need to see how these costs fit into your budget. As discussed previously, you should include all likely components of the monthly payment into your budget: the principal and interest, property taxes, homeowner's insurance, mortgage insurance, and perhaps a home warranty fee. You should also consider any additional costs you might pay for utilities. Heating, air conditioning, electric, and water are all areas for which homeowners generally pay more than renters, and including a 50 percent increase for these into your budget is appropriate.

You can follow a similar process as outlined in Chapter 8 on pages 213-214 to fit your payment into your budget. If your budget cannot accommodate your estimate of monthly costs, you may need to revise your goals by downsizing the type of home you desire or choosing housing in another neighborhood. If so, readjust the estimate of your monthly housing costs and fit these revised numbers into your budget.

Prequalify for a Mortgage

At this stage, you can begin looking into whether you would qualify for a mortgage loan given the price range of homes that you like and your intended down payment.

Did You Know?...

The Income Needed to Qualify for a Mortgage

The table below gives you a quick idea of how much income you need to buy a home at a certain price using a front-end ratio of 28 percent. The illustration is for a 30-year loan with a 20 percent down payment. For each home price, the top figure in each row shows the monthly payment for principal, interest, real estate taxes, and homeowner's insurance for the interest rates; the bottom figure shows the required gross annual income to qualify for the loan. For example, a 7 percent loan on a $180,000 home requires a monthly payment of $1183 plus an income of $50,700 to qualify. Taxes and insurance are assumed to be 1.5 percent of the purchase price (divided by 12 months). Visit the *Garman/Forgue* website to perform these calculations for a variety of home prices and interest rates.

	Price of Home						
Interest Rate	**$120,000**	**$150,000**	**$180,000**	**$210,000**	**$240,000**	**$270,000**	**$300,000**
5.5	695	869	1,043	1,216	1,390	1,564	1,738
	29,800	37,200	44,700	52,100	59,600	67,000	74,500
6.0	725	907	1,088	1,269	1,451	1,634	1,814
	31,100	38,900	46,600	54,400	62,200	70,000	77,700
6.5	757	946	1,135	1,324	1,514	1,703	1,892
	32,400	40,600	48,700	56,800	64,900	73,000	81,100
7.0	789	986	1,183	1,380	1,577	1,775	1,971
	33,800	42,300	50,700	59,200	67,600	76,100	84,500
7.5	821	1,027	1,232	1,437	1642	1,848	2,053
	35,200	44,000	52,800	61,600	70,400	79,200	88,000
8.0	854	1,068	1,282	1,495	1,709	1,922	2,136
	36,600	45,800	54,900	64,100	73,200	82,400	91,500

You also need to make a preliminary decision about the time period of the loan and the choice between a fixed or variable interest rate (topics covered later in this chapter). One goal is to find the lowest APR for loans available to you. A good place to start is with the financial institutions in which you have your checking and savings accounts. In addition, you can search for low-rate loans at www.bankrate.com. Other helpful information can be found at the websites for the U.S. Department of Housing and Urban Development (www.hud.gov/buying/) and the Federal National Mortgage Association (www.homepath.com).

Once you have an idea of the interest rate you will pay, you can consult lenders to determine whether you would qualify for a mortgage in the amount you would like. Lenders use two rules of thumb to estimate the maximum affordability of housing expenses: the front-end ratio and the back-end ratio.

- The **front-end ratio** compares the total annual expenditures for housing (the principal and interest on the mortgage plus the real estate taxes and insurance) with the loan applicant's gross annual income. Generally, the total annual expenditures should not exceed 25 to 29 percent of gross annual income. Applying a 28 percent front-end ratio, a young couple with a combined gross annual income of $73,000 could qualify for a mortgage requiring total annual expenditures of less than $20,440 (0.28 × $73,000), or $1703 per month.
- The **back-end ratio** compares the total of all monthly debt payments (for the mortgage, real estate taxes, and insurance, plus auto loans and other debts) with gross monthly income. Generally, lenders require that monthly debt payments do not exceed 33 to 41 percent of gross monthly income. Applying a back-end ratio of 38 percent, the same couple could qualify for any loan that does not result in total monthly debt repayments exceeding $2311 [their monthly income of $6083 ($73,000 ÷ 12) × 0.38].

front-end ratio Compares the total annual PITI expenditures for housing with the loan applicant's gross annual income to assess the borrower's ability to pay the mortgage.

back-end ratio Compares the total of all monthly PITI expenditures plus auto loans and other debts with gross monthly income.

Many young couples base their ability to afford housing on their combined incomes. This locks them into a full-time, dual-income lifestyle once they have purchased a home. Family obligations may later disrupt their ability or willingness to continue that lifestyle. They might be better off gauging housing affordability on just one income or on part-time work for the second income.

About one-half of all mortgage loans today are arranged through a mortgage broker. A **mortgage broker** is an individual or company that acts as an intermediary between borrowers and lenders. In other words, a broker helps lenders find borrowers and borrowers find lenders. Either the lender or the borrower may pay the fee charged by the broker. If the lender pays this fee, the broker legally represents the lender. If the borrower pays it, the broker legally represents the borrower. Thus, if you want the broker to work to find you the lowest possible rate, you should be prepared to pay for the service.

mortgage broker Individual or company that acts as an intermediary between borrowers and lenders.

Moderate- and low-income families often find it difficult to save the 20 percent down payment required by lenders. FHA- and VA-insured loans (discussed earlier in this chapter) provide some opportunity for low down payments but are not available to all borrowers or on all homes. Other programs have been developed for low-income buyers and people buying homes for the first time. Lenders in your area can provide you with information about programs that target these special-needs groups. Through such programs, it may be possible to buy a home with a low (or no) down payment and at a low, government-subsidized interest rate.

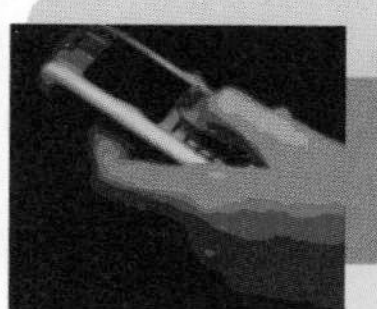

Instant Message

Keep Your Debts Low If You Want to Buy a Home

Student loan, car loan, and credit card payments can easily disqualify young home buyers based on the back-end ratio. If you plan on buying a house some day, you need to be very careful about how much debt you take on while in school and after graduation.

Search for a Home Online and in Person

Searching for a home requires a commitment of time. You do not want to be impulsive when you will be committing yourself to hundreds of thousands of dollars of expense. You can find housing in any number of ways, but the Internet has revolutionized the

Did You Know?...

How to Search for a Home

You can be a more effective home shopper if you do the following:

- Make a list in advance of special features or "must have" items that you are looking for in your new home.
- Drive around the neighborhood before you visit a property. Get out of the car and listen. Are there industrial noises or excessive highway noises? Any pet noises from the neighbors? Then ask the real estate agent and/or seller about any aspects that are of interest to you such as types of neighbors and availability of parks and schools.
- Look at only two or three properties in one day at most. Looking at too many homes at one time can be confusing and exhausting
- Bring a notepad and tape measure with you. Make sketches of the floor plans that you like. Bring along a camera or video equipment.
- Obtain written information describing details about the home. Ask about special home features, utility costs (you can confirm these with the utility company), and any recent improvements and repairs.
- Roll a small rubber ball along floors, countertops, and door frames to check for slopes and sags.
- Walk around the outside of the property to assess the external condition of the home and yard. Look for signs of water damage to the home or drainage issues in the yard.

home search process. You can narrow your choices to excellent prospects without ever leaving home. Simply go to realtor.com and search for homes in your community. You will be able to see floor plans, photos, descriptions of features and condition, and price-related information. Once you have found a home you would like to see, you can contact the seller or the real estate agent handling the property.

Agree to Terms with the Seller

Once you have your finances in order and have received assurances that you can qualify for a mortgage, you can start looking for a home in earnest. Sellers generally put a price on the property that is 5 to 15 percent higher than the amount that they actually expect to receive. Therefore, you may want to make an offer to buy that is somewhat lower than the asking price. Perhaps $10,000 to $30,000 is at stake here.

purchase offer/offer to purchase Written offer to purchase real estate.

Make an Offer to Buy The written offer to purchase real estate is called a **purchase offer** (or an **offer to purchase**). Of course, you will specify a price, but other aspects of the sale may be included in your offer as well. Examples of conditions include successful termite and radon inspections; a home inspection of the plumbing, heating, cooling, and electrical systems; and inclusion of the living room drapes and kitchen and other appliances. When you make an offer, you need to give the seller some **earnest money** as a deposit; 1 or 2 percent of the purchase price should be sufficient to show your good faith when making an offer to purchase the seller's property. This money is returned if the seller rejects the offer.

earnest money Funds given to seller as a deposit to hold the property until a purchase contract can be negotiated.

real estate broker (agent) Person licensed by a state to provide advice and assistance, for a fee, to buyers or sellers of real estate. Real estate brokers who are members of the National Association of Realtors often use the registered trademark of Realtor® to describe themselves.

Respond to a Counteroffer Most home sellers do not accept the first offer from a prospective buyer. Instead, they usually make a **counteroffer,** which is a legal offer to sell (or buy) a home at a different price and perhaps with different conditions from those outlined in the original offer. You can assume that a seller who is willing to make a counteroffer may also be willing to sell at a slightly lower price. Thus, if you make a counteroffer falling between the two prices, a sale will usually result. Of course, if you push the seller too far, you risk having the seller back out of the negotiations altogether. Plus, while

Did You Know?...

The Role of Real Estate Agents

A **real estate broker (agent)** is a person licensed by a state to provide advice and assistance, for a fee, to buyers or sellers of real estate. Real estate brokers who are members of the National Association of Realtors often use the registered trademark of **Realtor®** to describe themselves. Brokers typically earn a commission of 5 to 7 percent on the sale price of a home. The seller-not the buyer-usually pays this commission. **Flat-fee brokers,** who charge a flat fee for their services rather than a percentage-based commission, are also available in most real estate markets.

Almost any agent can show you housing that is **listed** (under contract with the seller and the broker) by the realty firm. In addition, many communities have a **multiple-listing** (or **open-listing**) **service,** which is an information and referral network among real estate brokers allowing properties listed with a particular broker to be shown by all other brokers.

Buyers should understand that a real estate agent can play three possible roles. The **listing agent** is the party with whom the seller signs the listing agreement. Listing agents advertise the property, show it to prospective buyers, and assist the seller in negotiations. They receive a commission when the home is sold and owe the seller undivided loyalty. A **selling agent** is any real estate agent that seeks out buyers for a home. Listing agents also play this role, but any real estate agent can search for buyers to whom to sell a property.

Most home buyers use a real estate agent in their search for a home. They should understand that the agent's legal obligation is to the party who will pay his or her fee or commission—generally the seller! Buyers should be wary of this potential conflict of interest and hire their own broker if they need such services. That is, home buyers who want an agent to represent their interests should obtain the services of a **buyer's agent.** This person serves as the buyer's representative in the real estate negotiations and transaction.

Why is the distinction among the three types of agents important? Consider the example of a buyer who has asked a selling agent to help him find a home. During negotiations, the potential buyer decides to offer $175,000 for a property with an asking price of $189,000 but tells the selling agent that he would be willing to go as high as $180,000. The selling agent would then be legally obligated to tell the seller about this $180,000 figure.

you are negotiating, the seller could be receiving offers from other prospective buyers. In some hot real estate markets, buyers compete with each other by offering sellers more than the asking price. In such a scenario, the highest bidder wins.

Negotiate and Sign a Purchase Contract A **purchase contract** (or **sales contract**) is the formal legal document that outlines the actual agreement that results from the real estate negotiations. It includes the final negotiated price and a list of conditions that the seller has agreed to accept. When the purchase contract is signed, the seller keeps the earnest money as a deposit.

You want to make sure that your earnest money is protected by including one or more **contingency clauses** in the purchase offer. These clauses specify that certain conditions must be satisfied before a contract is binding. One recommended clause would stipulate that the seller must refund the earnest money if the buyer cannot obtain satisfactory financing within a specified time period, usually 30 days. Other important contingency clauses should allow the buyer to opt out of the deal if the home fails to pass certain aspects of the home inspection (for example, the inspection uncovers a major structural defect). Of course, if at this point you simply change your mind about buying, you will forfeit your earnest money and may be sued for damages.

Apply for a Mortgage Loan

Only after you sign a purchase contract do you formally apply for a mortgage loan on the specific home you have selected. The potential lender usually approves or turns down this request within a few days.

multiple-listing (open-listing) service An information and referral network among real estate brokers allowing properties listed with a particular broker to be shown by all brokers.

listing agent The party with whom the seller signs the listing agreement; listing agent advertises the property, shows it to prospective buyers, and assists the seller in negotiations.

buyer's agent Serves as the buyer's representative in the real estate negotiations and transaction.

purchase contract/sales contract Formal legal document that outlines the actual agreement that results from the real estate negotiations.

contingency clauses Specify that certain conditions must be satisfied before a contract is binding.

good-faith estimate Lender's list of all the costs associated with the loan, including the annual percentage rate, application and processing fees, closing costs, and any other charges that must be paid when the deal is legally consummated.

When you apply for a mortgage, the lender must give you a **good-faith estimate** of all the costs associated with the loan, including the annual percentage rate, application and processing fees, and any other charges that must be paid when the deal is legally consummated. Table 9.1 on page 238 provides an example of the type of information in the good-faith estimate.

The exact interest rate on your mortgage may be the current rate at the time of application or the rate in force at the time of closing. If you expect rates to rise between the time you apply for the loan and the actual closing, you may wish to pay a small fee to obtain a **mortgage lock-in.** This agreement includes a lender's promise to hold a certain interest rate for a specified period of time, such as 60 days. It may be part of, but is not the same as, a **loan commitment** (or **loan preapproval**), which is a lender's promise to grant a loan.

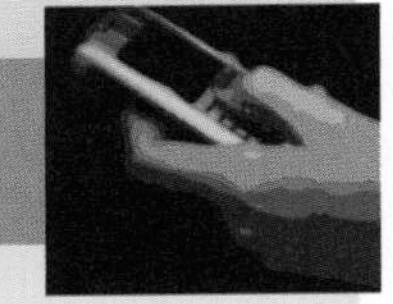

Instant Message

Buyers Have a Right to Full Disclosure

Federal law governs the information that must be disclosed to real estate purchasers. A list of these disclosures can be found by going to www.hud.gov and searching for the keyword "RESPA" to learn more about your rights under the Real Estate Settlement Procedures Act.

Prepare for the Closing

After you have obtained a mortgage, you are not yet finished. Of course, you will want to do all the usual tasks associated with moving; giving notification of your change of address, hiring a moving company (or not), getting your utilities shut off at your old residence and on at your new are examples. But there are two very important steps that can save you thousands of dollars and many headaches.

loan commitment/loan preapproval Lender's promise to grant a loan.

subprime market Market that serves higher-risk applicants at higher interest rates.

Hire Your Own Inspector Recall that you should always have a contingency clause included in your purchase contract so that you can back out of the deal if the house fails to pass the home inspection. The inspector should look for termite infestation, wood rot, and radon gas as well as examine the general condition of the home, including heating/cooling, plumbing, and electrical. You should pay the inspector yourself and should not choose one based on the recommendation of the seller's real estate agent. You want an independent person who is well qualified to look

Did You Know?...

Your Credit Score Affects the Mortgage Rate You Pay

Mortgage lenders charge interest rates based on your credit score. Here are illustrative credit scores and the corresponding mortgage loan interest rates.

Credit Score	APR
720–850	5.7%
700–719	5.9%
675–699	6.4%
620–674	7.6%
560–619	8.5%
500–559	9.3%

Loan applicants whose scores are lower than desired are turned down or, more commonly, referred to a lender in the **subprime market,** which serves higher-risk applicants. Many individuals who are placed in this market are happy to have obtained a loan. However, many borrowers fail to realize that they would have qualified for loans at standard rates if they had searched more extensively and taken steps to improve their credit scores.

out for your interests. If the inspector finds problems, you can negotiate with the seller for an adjustment in the purchase price of the home or, in severe cases, use the contingency clause to back out of the deal. Do not allow the seller to arrange the repair as the seller will likely settle for the cheapest and quickest solution, not necessarily the one that adequately repairs the problem.

Hire an Attorney The good-faith estimate that you receive is a legal document outlining your entire up-front and monthly home-buying costs. Hiring an attorney to go over the estimate and your purchase contract to ensure that everything is in order is money well spent. Many of the closing costs are negotiable, and your attorney can advise on how to keep these costs to a minimum.

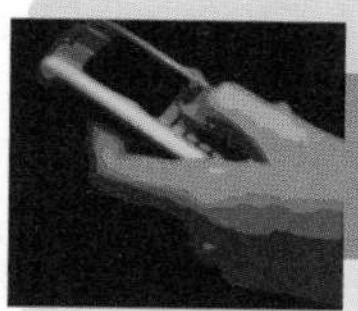

Instant Message

Maintain Your Credit Score While Waiting for Your Mortgage to Close

In the weeks leading up to the closing of your home, it is tempting to begin buying furniture, appliances, outdoor equipment, and other costly items. Think twice if doing so means racking up high balances on your credit cards. Your mortgage lender might want to raise your interest rate if you significantly change your credit score before the closing.

Sign Your Name on Closing Day

To complete the sale, the buyer, the seller, and their chosen representatives generally gather in the lender's office for the closing. At the closing, all required documents are signed and payments are made. A key document is the **uniform settlement statement,** which lists all of the costs and fees to be paid at the closing. You have the right to see this statement one business day before the closing so that you can avoid surprises and can compare the fees with the good-faith estimate provided earlier. Challenge all discrepancies.

uniform settlement statement Lists all of the costs and fees to be paid at the closing.

CONCEPT CHECK 9.3

1. Distinguish between the two rules of thumb that lenders use to assess housing affordability.
2. What services does a mortgage broker offer?
3. What services do real estate agents provide for buyers?
4. Why should a buyer be cautious about working with a seller's agent?
5. Explain the benefits of having contingency clauses in a home purchase agreement.

Financing a Home

4 LEARNING OBJECTIVE
Distinguish among conventional and alternative ways to finance a home, and list the advantages and disadvantages of each.

People often rent housing for five years or more while they save enough to make a down payment to purchase a home. Some couples postpone having children, while other people cut back on entertainment and vacations and put off making major purchases. Before buying, you must become knowledgeable about mortgage loans and learn how they are used to purchase a home.

The Mathematics of Mortgage Loans

Mortgage loans are available from depository institutions (described in Chapters 5 and 7) and mortgage finance companies. In exchange for the loan, the lender *(mortgagee)* has a **lien** on the real estate-that is, the legal right to take and hold property or to sell it in the event the borrower *(mortgagor)* defaults on the loan. **Foreclosure** is a process in which the lender sues the borrower to prove default and asks the court to order the sale of the property to pay the debt.

foreclosure Process in which the lender sues the borrower to prove default and asks the court to order the sale of the property to pay the debt.

The term *mortgage* receives its name from the concept of amortization, which is the process of gradually paying off a loan through a series of periodic payments to a lender. Each payment is allocated in two ways:

1. A portion goes to pay the simple interest on outstanding debt for that month multiplied by the periodic (monthly) interest rate.
2. The remainder goes to repay a portion of the **principal,** which is the debt remaining from the original amount borrowed.

As the principal is paid down, increasingly smaller portions of the payments will be required to pay interest while the portion of the payments devoted to the principal will grow larger. These changes in the allocation of each payment are illustrated in Figure 9.2.

Note the slow decline in the amount of each monthly payment going toward interest. A high proportion of each monthly payment during the early years of a mortgage loan is allocated to interest. This is because the outstanding debt remains very high. Table 9.2 shows the interest and principal payment amounts for the first three months of a $160,000, 30-year, 6.5 percent mortgage loan. For the first month, $866.67 goes for interest costs, and only $144.64 goes toward retirement of the principal of the loan. Table 9.3 provides a partial **amortization schedule** for the same loan. When you take out a mortgage loan, you will receive a full amortization schedule for each month of the loan listing all the monthly payments, the portions that will go toward interest and principal, and the debt remaining after each payment is made.

amortization schedule List that shows all the monthly payments, the portions that will go toward interest and principal, and the debt remaining after each payment is made throughout the life of the loan.

Typically, it takes many years of monthly payments to significantly reduce the outstanding balance of the loan. At any point, the amount that has been paid off (including the down payment) plus any appreciation in the value of the home represents the homeowner's **equity** (the dollar value of the home in excess of the amount owed on it). Figure 9.3 illustrates the buildup of equity in a home that results from reductions in the amount owed and the growth in the home's value. Note that the bulk of the increase in equity is a result of increases in the market value of the home. Additional payments can be directed toward the principal at any time to reduce the amount owed, increase equity, and reduce the eventual total amount of interest paid on the loan.

equity Dollar value of the home in excess of the amount owed on it.

Factors Affecting the Monthly Payment on a Mortgage

Three factors affect the monthly payment on a mortgage loan: the amount borrowed, the interest rate charged, and the length of maturity of the loan.

Figure 9.2

Change in Principal and Interest Components of the Monthly Payment on a $160,000 Mortgage Loan at 6.5 Percent Interest Rate for 30 Years

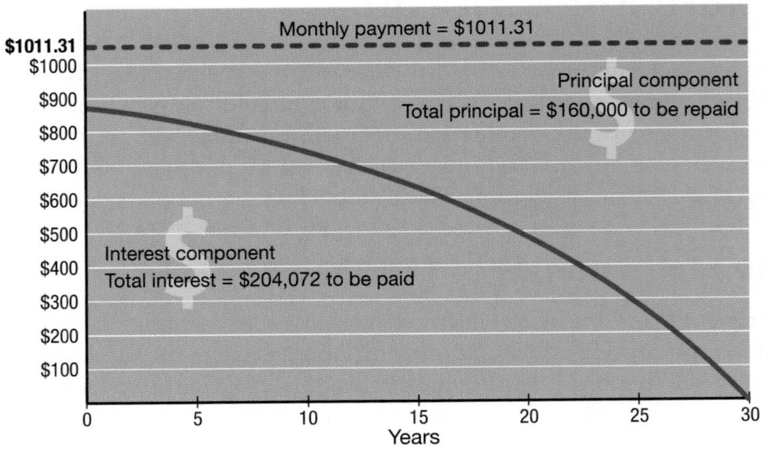

Table 9.2 Amortization Effects of Monthly Payment of $1011.31 on a $160,000, 30-Year Mortgage Loan at 6.5 percent

First Month			
	$160,000 × 6.5% × 1/12	=	$866.67 Interest payment
	$1011.31 − 866.67	=	$144.64 Principal repayment
	$160,000 − 144.64	=	$159,855.36 Balance due
Second Month			
	$159,855.36 × 6.5% × 1/12	=	$865.88 Interest payment
	$1011.31 − 865.88	=	$145.43 Principal repayment
	$159,855.36 − 145.43	=	$159,709.93 Balance due
Third Month			
	$159,709.93 × 6.5% × 1/12	=	$865.10 Interest payment
	$1011.31 − 865.10	=	$146.21 Principal repayment
	$159,709.93 − 146.21	=	$159,563.72 Balance due

Table 9.3 Partial Amortization Schedule for a $160,000, 30-year (360-Payment) Mortgage Loan at 6.5 Percent

Payment Number (Month)	Monthly Payment Amount	Portion Principal Repayment	Portion to Interest	Total of Payments to Date	Outstanding Loan Balance
1	$1011.31	$144.64	$866.67	$1011.31	$159,855.36
2	1011.31	145.43	865.88	2,022.62	159,709.93
3	1011.31	146.21	865.10	3,033.93	159,563.72
12	1011.31	154.33	856.98	12,135.72	158,057.31
24	1011.31	164.66	846.64	24,271.44	156,138.84
60	1011.31	200.01	811.30	60,678.60	149,577.55
120	1011.31	276.58	734.73	121,357.20	135,365.22
180	1011.31	382.46	628.85	182,035.80	115,712.16
240	1011.31	528.88	482.43	242,714.40	88,535.58
300	1011.31	731.34	279.97	303,393.00	50,955.32
360	1011.31	1005.86	5.45	364,071.60	0

The Amount Borrowed The payment schedule illustrated in Table 9.4 gives the monthly payment required for each $1000 of a mortgage loan at various interest rates. Using this table, you can calculate the monthly payment for mortgage loans of different amounts. For example, the $160,000 mortgage loan described earlier (6.5 percent for 30 years) costs $6.3207 per $1000 per month. Thus, 160 × $6.3207 equals $1011.31.

Making a down payment that is larger than required lowers the borrower's monthly payments. For example, a down payment of 30 percent, or $55,500, would lower the monthly payment on the loan to $818.53 [$6.3207 × ($185,000 − $55,500) ÷ 1000]. A smaller loan also carries lower total interest costs and may qualify for an interest rate that is perhaps 0.5 percentage points lower. In that case, the payment for the same loan would amount to only $776.42 [$5.9955 × ($185,000 − $55,500) ÷ 1000].

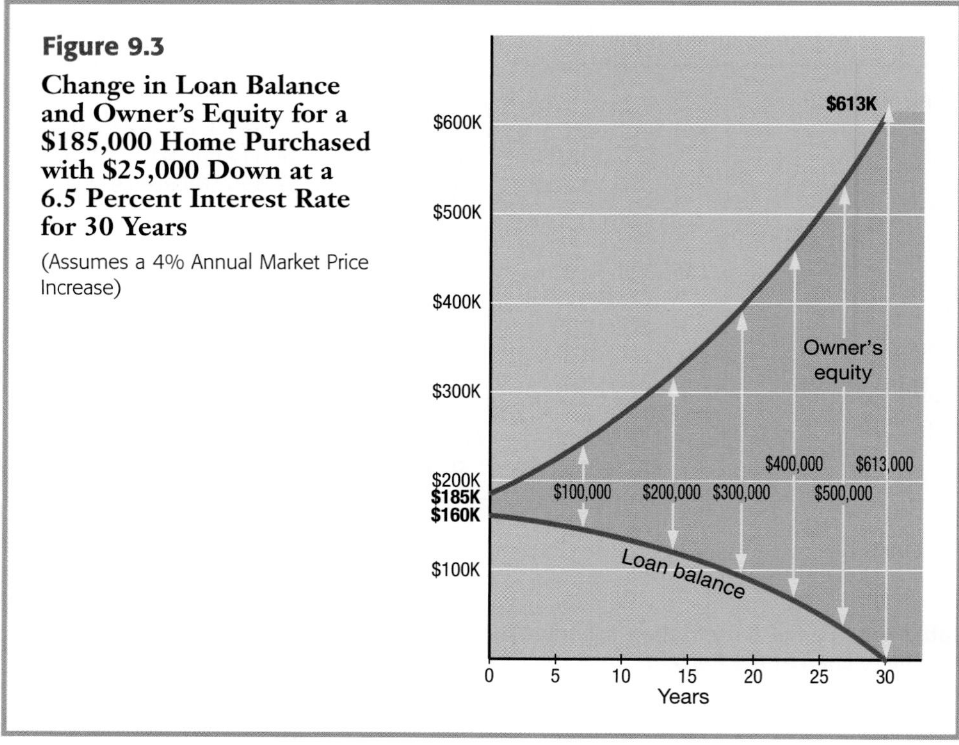

Figure 9.3
Change in Loan Balance and Owner's Equity for a $185,000 Home Purchased with $25,000 Down at a 6.5 Percent Interest Rate for 30 Years
(Assumes a 4% Annual Market Price Increase)

Table 9.4 Estimating Mortgage Loan Payments for Principal and Interest (Monthly Payment per $1000 Borrowed)

	Payment Period (Years)			
Interest Rate (%)	**15**	**20**	**25**	**30**
4.5	$ 7.6499	$6.3265	$5.5583	$5.0669
5.0	7.9079	6.5996	5.8459	5.3682
5.5	8.1708	6.8789	6.1409	5.6779
6.0	8.4386	7.1643	6.4430	5.9955
6.5	8.7111	7.4557	6.7521	6.3207
7.0	8.9883	7.7530	7.0678	6.6530
7.5	9.2701	8.0559	7.3899	6.9921
8.0	9.5565	8.3644	7.7182	7.3376
8.5	9.8474	8.6782	8.0523	7.6891
9.0	10.1427	8.9973	8.3920	8.0462
9.5	10.4422	9.3213	8.7370	8.4085
10.0	10.7461	9.6502	9.0870	8.7757

Note: To use this table to figure a monthly mortgage payment, divide the amount borrowed by 1000 and multiply by the appropriate figure in the table for the interest rate and time period of the loan. For example, a $160,000 loan for 30 years at 6.5 percent would require a payment of $1011.31 [($160,000 ÷ 1000) × 6.3207]; over 20 years, it would require a payment of $1192.91 [($160,000 ÷ 1000) × 7.4557]. For calculations for different interest rates, visit the *Garman/Forgue* website.

The Interest Rate The higher the interest rate, the higher the monthly payment on a mortgage loan (see Table 9.4). For example, a $1011.31 monthly payment is required for a $160,000 mortgage loan taken out for 30 years at 6.5 percent. If the interest rate were 7.5 percent, the monthly mortgage payment would be $1118.74 (160 × $6.9921), an increase of over $107. The effects are even greater when you consider the total of all the monthly payments and the total interest paid over the life of the loan. The 6.5 percent loan will have total payments of $364,072 (360 × $1011.31) with total interest of $204,072 ($364,072 − $160,000.00). For the 7.5 percent loan, total payments are $402,746 (360 × $1118.74) and total interest is $242,746 ($402,764 − $160,000.00). Thus, the added cost for the 30-year loan at 7.5 percent is $38,674 over the life of the loan.

Length of Maturity of the Loan Table 9.5 illustrates the relationships among maturity length, monthly payment, and interest cost for a $100,000 loan at various interest rates. A longer term of repayment results in a smaller payment (for loans with the same interest rate). More total interest is paid over the longer repayment time period despite the lower monthly payment. For example, the monthly payment on a 7 percent loan is $775 for 20 years but only $665 for 30 years. When the loan is paid back in 20 years, the total interest costs are much lower ($86,000 rather than $139,400, for a savings of $53,400).

Some borrowers opt for a mortgage loan with a comparatively short 15-year maturity. The advantages include a faster buildup of equity, lower total interest, and a quicker payoff of the loan. These advantages can also be gained with a 20- or 30-year mortgage by simply paying additional amounts toward the principal during the time period of the loan. It is wise to take a longer repayment period even if you plan to pay off the loan in 15 (or fewer) years. With that strategy, the faster payoff is optional rather than mandatory.

The Conventional Mortgage Loan

A **conventional mortgage** is a fixed-rate, fixed-term, fixed-payment mortgage loan. Borrowers like conventional mortgages because they are so predictable. For example, a $160,000 loan could be granted at a 6.5 percent annual interest rate over a period of 30 years with a fixed monthly payment of $1011.31. The payment is the same for month after month and year after year.

conventional mortgage A fixed-rate, fixed-term, fixed-payment mortgage loan.

Table 9.5 Monthly Payment and Total Interest to Repay a $100,000 Loan

	Interest Rate (%)				
Length of Loan	**6**	**6.5**	**7**	**7.5**	**8**
30 years	$600	$632	$665	$699	$734
	116,000	127,500	139,400	151,600	164,200
25 years	644	675	707	739	772
	93,200	102,500	112,100	121,700	131,600
20 years	716	745	775	806	836
	71,800	78,800	86,000	93,400	100,600
15 years	844	871	899	927	955
	51,900	56,800	61,800	66,900	71,900

Note: Figures are rounded. The top figure in each pair is the monthly payment, and the bottom figure is the total interest paid to the nearest $100.

You can use this table to calculate the monthly payment and total interest on any loan at these same interest rates. Simply divide the amount of the loan by $100,000 and multiply that figure by the amounts shown in the table. For example, the loan $160,000 at 6.5% for 30 years illustrated in this chapter has a monthly payment of $1011 (1.6 × $632) and total interest of $204,000 (1.6 × $127,500).

The Adjustable-Rate Mortgage Loan

adjustable-rate mortgage (ARM)/ variable-rate mortgage Mortgage in which the borrower's interest rate fluctuates according to some index of interest rates based on the rising or falling cost of credit in the economy—thus transferring interest rate risk to the borrower.

With an **adjustable-rate mortgage (ARM)**—sometimes called a **variable-rate mortgage**—the borrower's interest rate fluctuates according to some index of interest rates based on the rising or falling cost of credit in the economy. With an ARM, the risk of interest rate changes is assumed by the borrower, not the lender. As a consequence, the monthly payment could increase or decrease, usually on an annual basis, but sometimes monthly. Borrowers with ARMs should always determine the "worst case" scenario for interest rate increases under their loan contract and calculate the monthly payment that would result.

teaser rate Low interest rate that lenders sometimes use to lure buyers; these rates will be low for the first year or so and then will rise to more realistic rates.

ARM rates are usually 1 to 3 percentage points below conventional mortgage rates. Lenders sometimes offer an even lower **teaser rate** to entice people to borrow using an ARM. Such a loan will carry an interest rate for the first year or so that may be 1 to 2 percentage points below the regular ARM loan rates, a substantial savings over a conventional mortgage. Borrowers using an ARM with a teaser rate must be prepared for the higher monthly payments that will occur when interest rates rise in the future.

negative amortization Occurs when monthly payments are actually smaller than necessary to pay interest on the loan, which will result in a rising principal loan balance.

Most ARMs have **interest-rate caps** that limit the amount by which the interest rate can increase (perhaps no more than 2 percent per year and no more than 5 percent over the life of the loan). **Payment caps,** in contrast, limit the amount by which the payment can vary on an ARM. Having a loan with a payment cap but without an equivalent interest-rate cap is an invitation to **negative amortization,** which occurs when monthly payments are actually smaller than necessary to pay the interest. This practice will result in a principal loan balance that rises rather than falls. Variations of ARMs exist.

Instant Message

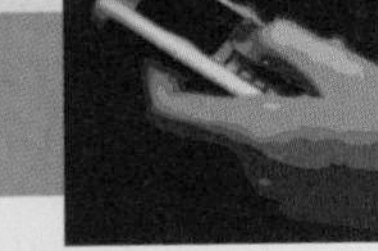

Be Wary of "Exotic" Mortgages

The high cost of housing has led many people to use "exotic" mortgages that are structured to have low monthly payments, especially in the early years. Loans with teaser rates and graduated-payment mortgages are a particular problem when people (such as those with low credit scores) use them to buy homes that are on the borderline of affordability. When the monthly payment goes up a few years into the loan, it may no longer be affordable. Such loans were a major reason for the foreclosure crisis of 2007.

Alternative Mortgage Loans

A number of new mortgage options have emerged in response to interest rate fluctuations and increasing costs for housing. Most alternative lending approaches aim to keep the monthly payment as low as possible, especially in the early years of the loan for first-time and lower-income buyers. The lower payments also permit borrowers to purchase larger, more expensive homes than they could afford with a traditional loan.

Interest-Only Mortgage With an **interest-only mortgage** loan, you pay only the interest on the mortgage in monthly payments for a fixed term. No monthly payment is made on the debt itself. After the end of that term, usually five to seven years, you can refinance, pay the balance in a lump sum, or start paying off the principal with a commensurate jump in the monthly payment. The obvious lure of an interest-only mortgage is its lower monthly payment.

interest-only mortgage Mortgage in which the borrower pays only the interest on the mortgage in monthly payments for a fixed term, then either refinances the principal, pays off the principal, or starts paying the higher monthly payment with the principal payments added in.

Graduated-Payment Mortgage With a **graduated-payment mortgage,** smaller-than-normal payments are required in the early years, but payments gradually increase to larger-than-normal payments in later years. The interest rate is fixed, but payments early in the life of the mortgage may be lower than necessary to pay even the interest, resulting in possible negative amortization. Graduated-payment mortgages are attractive to buyers who expect substantial increases in their income in the future.

Lender Buy-Down Mortgage With a **lender buy-down mortgage,** a base interest rate is set for the loan that is perhaps 0.5 percentage points higher than the interest rate for a conventional mortgage. For the first year, the borrower pays a rate 2 percentage points below the base rate. In the second year, the rate is 1 point below the base rate. In the third and future years, the base rate would be charged. These changes are known in advance and are contractual. First-time home buyers often use buy-down mortgages to take advantage of lower monthly payments in early years of the loan.

Rollover (Renegotiable-Rate) Mortgage A **rollover mortgage** consists of a series of short-term loans for two- to five-year time periods but with total amortization spread over the usual 25 to 30 years. The loan is renewed for each time period at the market interest rates that prevail at the time of the renewal.

Shared-Appreciation Mortgage With a **shared-appreciation mortgage,** the lender offers an interest rate about one-third less than the market rate. In exchange, the lender gains the right to receive perhaps one-third of any appreciation in the home's value when the home is sold or ten years after the time of the loan.

Growing-Equity Mortgage The **growing-equity mortgage (GEM)** is meant for people who design their loan in advance to reduce interest costs by paying off the mortgage loan early. One form of GEM is the **biweekly mortgage,** which calls for payments to be made every two weeks that represent half of the normal monthly payment. The borrower, therefore, makes 26 payments per year. For example, a $200,000, 7 percent, 30-year loan requires a $1330.60 monthly payment for a total of $15,967.20 (12 × $1330.60) paid in one year. On a biweekly basis with payments of $665.30 ($1330.60 ÷ 2), the total amount paid each year would be $17,297.80 ($665.30 × 26). The difference of $1330.60 ($17,297.80 − $15,967.20) is equivalent to one extra monthly payment per year and is applied to the principal of the loan. Under the biweekly repayment plan, a loan may be repaid in approximately 20 years, rather than the 30 years dictated by the monthly payment plan.

Setting up a loan as a GEM from the beginning forces you to make the agreed-upon additional payments. However, almost all mortgage lenders permit payment of additional amounts toward principal at any time as a way to get the loan paid off faster and reduce interest expenses. For example, even paying an additional $70 (or $1400.60) per month on the preceding loan would allow the loan to be paid off in just over 25 years and would save almost $50,000 in interest costs.

Assumable Mortgage With an **assumable mortgage,** the buyer pays the seller a down payment generally equal to the seller's equity in the home and takes responsibility for the mortgage loan payments for the remaining term of the seller's existing mortgage loan. The buyer's goal is to obtain the loan at the original interest rate, which should be below current market rates. This approach will work only if the original mortgage loan agreement does not include a **due-on-sale clause.** Such a clause requires that the mortgage loan be fully paid off if the home is sold. It can impose a burden on the seller because it prohibits a buyer from assuming the mortgage loan.

Seller Financing **Seller financing** occurs whenever the seller of a home agrees to accept all or a portion of the purchase price in installments rather than as a lump sum. Usually seller financing is a short-term arrangement, however, with payments based on amortization occurring over perhaps 20 years and a balloon payment due after perhaps five years. That is, all principal not paid after five years would be due at once.

In most seller financing, the buyer obtains the title to the property when the deal is closed and the contract is signed. In contrast, a **land contract** (or **contract for deed**) brings greater risk for the buyer because all terms in the contract (including payment of the debt) must be satisfied before transfer of title will occur. As a result, if you move before paying off the contract in full, you forfeit all

biweekly mortgage GEM that calls for payments of half of the normal payment to be made every two weeks; the borrower thus makes 26 payments a year and reduces the principal amount by one full payment each year; this reduces the mortgage term to about 20 years on a 30-year mortgage.

assumable mortgage Buyer pays the seller a down payment generally equal to the seller's equity in the home and takes responsibility for the mortgage loan payments for the remaining term of the seller's existing mortgage loan.

due-on-sale clause Requires that the mortgage loan be fully paid off if the home is sold. It can impose a burden on the seller because it prohibits a buyer from assuming the mortgage loan.

land contract/contract for deed Brings greater risk for the buyer because all terms in the contract (including payment of the debt) must be satisfied before transfer of title will occur.

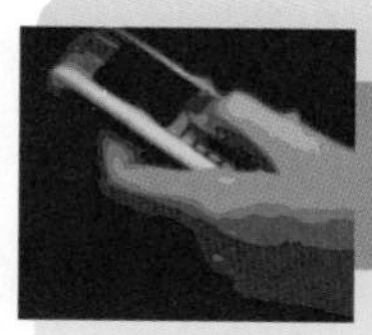

Instant Message

Be Cautious About Tapping Your Equity to Pay Other Debts

Homeowners sometimes take out a second mortgage or refinance a mortgage to pay off credit card debts and vehicle loans. As a result, they lower their overall interest rate and can deduct the interest when filing their taxes. But the downside is that they have traded short-term debt for long-term debt. They should pay this debt off as soon as possible.

Did You Know?...

About Second Mortgage Loans

Home values have increased significantly in recent years, allowing many people to see higher-than-expected increases in their home equity. You can use a second mortgage to borrow based on this home equity, with the property serving as collateral for both the first and second mortgage loans. A **second mortgage** is an additional loan on a residence besides the original mortgage. In case of default, the amount owed on the original mortgage must be paid first. Because of this additional risk, the interest rate on a second mortgage is often 2 to 5 percentage points higher than current market rates for first mortgages.

Historically, people have used second mortgages to pay for major remodeling projects, finance college costs for children, pay off medical bills, or start a business. Today, some people use these funds for everyday living expenses, an unwise practice dubbed "eating one's house."

Two types of second mortgages exist:

- The **home-equity installment loan,** where a specific amount of money is borrowed for a fixed time period with fixed monthly payments.
- The **home-equity line of credit,** where a maximum loan amount is established and the loan operates as open-ended credit, much like a credit card account. These line-of-credit loans often have variable interest rates and flexible repayment schedules.

The credit limit on a second mortgage loan is usually set at 80 percent (but can go as high as 125 percent)* of the home's appraised value minus the amount owed on the first mortgage. For example, a person with a home appraised at $200,000 with a balance owed of $100,000 on a first mortgage might be allowed to take out a $60,000 second mortgage [($200,000 × 0.80) − $100,000].

*Only the interest on borrowings up to 100 percent of the home's market value can be used as a deduction when filing state and federal income taxes.

second mortgage An additional loan on a residence besides the original mortgage, usually at a higher interest rate because in case of default, the first mortgage is paid first.

reverse mortgage/home-equity conversion loan Allows a homeowner older than age 61 to continue living in the home and to borrow against the equity in a home that is fully paid for and to receive the proceeds in a series of monthly payments, often over a period of 5 to 15 years or for life.

money paid in installments to the seller and any appreciation in the home's value. You build no equity until the contract is completed.

Reverse Mortgage. A **reverse mortgage,** also known as a **home-equity conversion loan,** allows a homeowner older than age 61 to borrow against the equity in a home that is fully paid for and to receive the proceeds in a series of monthly payments, often over a period of 5 to 15 years or for life. The contract allows the person to continue living in the home. Essentially, the borrower trades his or her equity in the home in return for either a fixed monthly income or a line of credit that can be drawn upon at the option of the homeowner. The most likely prospects for such loans are elderly people who have paid off their mortgages but are strapped for income. The mortgage does not have to be paid back until the last surviving owner sells the house, moves out permanently, or dies.

CONCEPT CHECK 9.4

1. Explain why the portions of a monthly mortgage payment that are allocated toward interest and toward principal will vary as the loan is repaid.
2. Distinguish between a conventional mortgage loan and an adjustable-rate loan.
3. Identify the two ways that home buyers build equity in their property.
4. Define negative amortization and describe one way that it might occur on a variable-rate loan.
5. Specify one advantage and one disadvantage of an interest-only mortgage loan.

Decision-Making Worksheet

Should You Refinance Your Mortgage?

It is sometimes advantageous to refinance an existing mortgage when interest rates decline. In **mortgage refinancing,** a new mortgage is obtained to pay off and replace an existing mortgage. Most often it is undertaken to lower the monthly payment on the home by taking out a loan with a lower interest rate.

The example here illustrates how to determine whether refinancing your mortgage is a wise choice. The original mortgage for $130,000 was obtained seven years ago at an 8 percent interest rate for 30 years. The monthly payment is $953.89. After seven years, the principal owed has declined to $120,200. If interest rates for new mortgages have declined to 6.5 percent, the owner could take out a new mortgage at the lower rate for a monthly payment of 840.28. Borrowing $120,200 for 23 years at 6.5 percent saves approximately $114 per month ($954 − $840). However, refinancing may have some up-front costs, including a possible prepayment penalty on the old mortgage and closing costs for the new mortgage. The question then becomes, will these costs exceed the monthly savings gained with a lower payment?

The following worksheet provides a means for estimating whether refinancing offers an advantage. It compares the future value of the reduced monthly payments (line 5) with the future value of the money used to pay the up-front costs (estimated here at 2%) of refinancing (line 8). The homeowner would need to estimate the number of months he or she expects to own the home after refinancing. Given an estimate of four years in this example, the net savings would be $1747 (subtracting line 8 from line 5), and refinancing would benefit the owner. A similar worksheet can be found at cgi.money.cnn.com/tools/cutmortgage/cutmortgage.html.

Decision Factor	Example	Your Figures
1. Current monthly payment	$ 954	_____
2. New monthly payment	840	_____
3. Monthly savings [(line 1 − line 2) × 12]	114	_____
4. Additional years you expect to live in the house	4	_____
5. Future value of an account balance after 4 years if the monthly savings were invested at 3% after taxes (using the calculator on the *Garman/Forgue* website)	5,806	_____
6. Prepayment penalty on current loan (1%)	1,202	_____
7. Points and fees for new loan (2%)	2,404	_____
8. Future value of an account balance after 4 years if the prepayment penalty and closing costs ($3606) had been invested instead at 3% after taxes (using the calculator on the *Garman/Forgue* website)	4,059	_____
9. Net saving after 48 months (line 5 − line 8)	$1,747	_____

It may also be possible to borrow more than the current balance on the existing loan, thereby utilizing some of the equity built up in the home. People do this sometimes to use some of the proceeds to pay off other debt or make a down payment on a vacation or investment property. Borrowers refinancing for more than the amount owed should understand that rebuilding the equity to its previous level may take many years.

mortgage refinancing New mortgage is obtained to pay off and replace an existing mortgage, usually at a lower interest rate.

Selling a Home

5 LEARNING OBJECTIVE
Identify the important aspects of selling a home.

While most of this chapter deals with buying a home, important considerations also arise when you are selling a home. It helps to do some minor painting, cleaning, and repairing before listing your home for sale. Sellers must disclose known defects in the home to the real estate agent as well as to potential buyers.

Should You List with a Broker or Sell a Home Yourself?

fizbo For sale by owner (FSBO).

Knowing that the sales commission to a broker on a $200,000 home could be $12,000 provides motivation for some homeowners to consider selling their homes themselves. The key to success in a **fizbo** (for **f**or **s**ale **b**y **o**wner) is to know what price to ask for your home. Asking too little could cost you much more than the commission paid to a broker. Setting the price too high keeps potential buyers away.

Many homeowners begin by contacting a few brokers to get their opinions on how much the home is worth. Brokers are often quite willing to give their opinions because the homeowner might list the home with them if it does not sell quickly. Placing a for-sale sign on your lawn and spending about $300 on advertising the property should keep your telephone ringing for a month or so with all types of inquiries.* If your home does not sell by then, you might consider listing it with a broker.

listing agreement Agreement that brokers require homeowners to sign that permits the broker to list the property exclusively or with a multiple-listing service.

Brokers require that homeowners sign a **listing agreement** permitting them to list the property exclusively or with a multiple-listing service. A multiple-listing service may work best because it allows every broker in the community to show and sell the home. Brokers "qualify" prospective buyers—distinguishing between serious buyers and people who are just looking or cannot afford the home. If your broker cannot find a buyer within 60 days, consider signing an agreement with another broker that might prove more aggressive in advertising and selling your property. If a sale occurs (or begins) during the time period of the listing agreement, you must pay a commission to the broker for any sale to a buyer not listed as an exception in the listing agreement.

*For more information on selling your own home, visit www.sellyourhomeyourself.com.

Fizbos can save a homeowner money but usually take longer to sell.

Selling Carries Its Own Costs

The largest selling cost is the **broker's commission.** These commissions often amount to 6 percent of the selling price of the home. Some sellers are unaware that brokers may negotiate their commission. Smart sellers also pay for a title search, a professional appraisal, and their own home inspection as well.

broker's commission Largest selling cost in selling a home; these commissions often amount to 6 percent of the selling price of the home.

Most mortgage loans are paid off before maturity because people move and sell their homes. Mortgage loan contracts often have a clause that specifies a **prepayment fee** or penalty, which can range from 1 to 3 percent of the original mortgage loan. On a $160,000 mortgage loan, for example, the charge might vary from $1600 to $4800. Usually, the penalty is only for an early payoff in the first few years of the loan.

Local communities may assess **real estate transfer taxes.** These taxes are paid by the seller and also possibly the buyer. The tax is based on the purchase price of the home or the equity the seller has in the home. These tax rates can be as high as 4 percent, that is, $8000 on a $200,000 home. When paid by the seller, they may affect the offer that the seller is willing to accept for the home.

real estate transfer taxes Community-assessed taxes paid by the seller and also sometimes by the buyer based on the purchase price of the home or the equity the seller has in the home.

Be Wary of Seller Financing

Some sellers who have experienced trouble when marketing their homes have successfully resorted to many variations of seller financing, although difficulties can arise with these options. Suppose you have a home worth $200,000 with a mortgage loan balance of $90,000 and equity of $110,000. The buyer assumes the existing mortgage loan, puts up $40,000 in cash, and takes out a second mortgage from *you* to repay the $70,000 over five years. At closing, the broker receives a commission of $12,000, and you come away with only $28,000 cash—a small sum to use in making a down payment on another home. Also, seller financing carries a risk that the buyer may not be able to make the second mortgage payments to you and could potentially default on the loan.

CONCEPT CHECK 9.5

1. List some disadvantages of trying to sell a home yourself.
2. List one advantage and one disadvantage of using a real estate broker to sell a home.
3. Describe two costs associated with selling a home.

What Do You Recommend Now?

Now that you have read the chapter on buying housing, what do you recommend to Libby Clark regarding:

1. Buying or renting housing in the Denver area?
2. Steps she should take prior to actively looking at homes?
3. Finding a home and negotiating the purchase?
4. The closing process in home buying?
5. Selecting the type of mortgage to fit her needs?
6. Things to consider regarding the sale of her home should she ultimately be promoted to a position in another of the four regions?

Big Picture Summary of Learning Objectives

1 Decide whether renting or owning your home is better for you both financially and personally.

When choosing housing, renters must consider the costs of rent, a security deposit, and related items. Home buyers can choose among single-family dwellings, condominiums, cooperative housing, manufactured housing, and mobile homes. Renters generally pay out less money in terms of cash flow in the short run, whereas owners enjoy tax advantages and generally see an increase in the market value of their homes, making them better off financially in the long run.

2 Explain the up-front and monthly costs of buying a home.

Home buyers understand that they will make a down payment and then make monthly principal and interest payments on their mortgage. What many don't understand is that closing costs for interest points and other aspects of the purchase can add an additional 5 percent or more to the amount needed up-front at the closing. Similarly, monthly charges for private mortgage insurance, homeowner's insurance, and real estate property taxes can add another 25 percent or more to their monthly payment for principal and interest.

3 Describe the steps in the home-buying process.

The home-buying process includes (a) getting your finances in order, (b) prequalifying for a mortgage, (c) searching for a home online and in person, (d) agreeing to terms with a seller, (e) obtaining a mortgage loan, (f) preparing for the closing, and (g) signing your name on closing day.

4 Distinguish among conventional and alternative ways to finance a home, and list advantages and disadvantages of each.

Mortgage loans for homes are amortized. Amortization is the process of gradually paying off a mortgage through a series of periodic payments to a lender, with a portion of each payment going toward the principal and another portion going toward the interest owed. Conventional mortgages and adjustable-rate mortgages are the most common types of housing loans. Numerous alternative types of mortgages are available that have reduced the importance of the long-term, fixed-rate mortgage loan and that provide new ways to keep the monthly payment as low as possible.

The mathematics of buying a home shows how loan payments are calculated and how the portion of each monthly payment that goes toward interest declines, resulting in the portion that goes toward the principal increasing with each subsequent payment.

5 Identify the important aspects of selling a home.

When selling a home, it is wise to consider the pros and cons of listing with a real estate broker versus selling the home yourself, the transaction costs of selling, and the pitfalls of seller financing.

Let's Talk About It

1. What do you see as the advantages and the disadvantages for you of renting or buying housing at the cur-

rent time? How might your feelings change in the future, such as within five years?

2. In the early years of the standard 30-year mortgage loan, as little as 10 percent of the monthly payment actually goes toward repaying the debt. As a result, it takes many, many years for the loan balance to come down to any significant extent. Explain how that affects your feelings about taking on such a long-term obligation.
3. What experts could you turn to for assistance during the home-buying and loan application processes? What conflicts of interest most concern you?
4. Would you prefer a fixed- or adjustable-rate mortgage to finance a home purchase? Why?
5. Some closing costs on a home purchase are negotiable. Would you feel comfortable entering into a discussion of these items? Why or why not?

Do the Numbers

1. Walter and Marcie Jensen of Atlanta, Georgia, both of whom are in their late 20s, currently are renting an unfurnished two-bedroom apartment for $880 per month, plus an additional $130 for utilities and $34 for insurance. They have found a condominium they can buy for $160,000 with a 15 percent down payment and a 30-year, 7 percent mortgage. Principal and interest payments are estimated at $905 per month, with property taxes amounting to $110 per month and a homeowner's insurance premium of $450 per year. Private mortgage insurance will cost the couple about $60 per month. Closing costs are estimated at $3200. The monthly homeowner's association fee is $275, and utility costs are estimated at $160 per month. The Jensens have a combined income of $57,000 per year, with take-home pay of $4100 per month. They are in the 25 percent tax bracket, pay $225 per month on an installment loan (ten payments left), and have $39,000 in savings and investments.
   (a) Can the Jensens afford to buy the condo? Use the results from the *Garman/Forgue* website or the information on pages 236-242 to support your answer. Also, consider the effect of the purchase on their savings and monthly budget.
   (b) Walter and Marcie think that their monthly housing costs would be lower the first year if they bought the condo. Do you agree? Support your answer.
   (c) If they buy, how much will Walter and Marcie have left in savings to pay for moving expenses?
   (d) Available financial information suggests that mortgage rates might drop over the next few months. If the Jensens wait until the rates drop to 6.0 percent, how much will they save on their monthly mortgage payment? Use the information in Table 9.4 or the *Garman/Forgue* website to calculate the payment.
2. Seth and Cassie Moore of Holyoke, Massachusetts, have an annual income of $120,000 and want to buy a home. Currently, mortgage rates are 7 percent. The Moores want to take out a mortgage for 30 years. Real estate taxes are estimated to be $4800 per year for homes similar to what they would like to buy, and homeowner's insurance would be about $720 per year.
   (a) Using a 28 percent front-end ratio, what are the total annual and monthly expenditures for which they would qualify?
   (b) Using a 36 percent back-end ratio, what monthly mortgage payment (including taxes and insurance) could they afford given that they have an automobile loan payment of $470, a student loan payment of $350, and credit card payments of $250? (Hint: Subtract these amounts from the total monthly affordable payments for their income to determine the amount left over to spend on a mortgage.)
   (c) If mortgage interest rates are around 7 percent and the Moores want a 30-year mortgage, use the information in the Did You Know box on page 244 to estimate how much they could borrow given your answer to part b.
3. Phillip Guadet of Monroe, Louisiana, has been renting a small, two-bedroom house for several years. He pays $950 per month in rent for the home and $300 per year in property and liability insurance. The owner of the house wants to sell it, and Phillip is considering making an offer. The owner wants $130,000 for the property, but Phillip thinks he could get the house for $120,000 and use his $25,000 in 5 percent certificates of deposit that are ready to mature for the down payment. Phillip has talked to his banker and could get a 7 percent mortgage loan for 25 years to finance the remainder of the purchase price. The banker advised Phillip that he would reduce his debt principal by $1850 during the first year of the loan. Property taxes on the house are $1800 per year. Phillip estimates that he would need to upgrade his property and liability insurance to $500 per year and would incur about $1000 in costs the first year for maintenance. Property values are increasing at about 3.5 percent per year in the neighborhood. Phillip is in the 25 percent marginal tax bracket.
   (a) Use Table 9.4 to calculate the monthly mortgage payment for the mortgage loan that Phillip would need.

(b) How much interest would Phillip pay during the first year of the loan?

(c) Use the Decision-Making Worksheet, "Should You Buy or Rent?" on page 236 to determine whether Phillip would be better off buying or renting based on his cash flow.

4. Kevin Tutumbo of Rochester Hills, Michigan, has owned his home for 15 years and expects to live in it for five more years. He originally borrowed $105,000 at 8 percent interest for 30 years to buy the home. He still owes $85,750 on the loan. Interest rates have since fallen to 6.5 percent, and Kevin is considering refinancing the loan for 15 years. He would have to pay 2 points on the new loan with no prepayment penalty on the current loan.

   (a) What is Kevin's current monthly payment?

   (b) Calculate the monthly payment on the new loan.

   (c) Advise Kevin on whether he should refinance his mortgage using the Decision-Making Worksheet, "Should You Refinance Your Mortgage?" on page 257.

Decision-Making Cases

Case 1

Michael and Jonathan Weigh the Benefits and Costs of Buying Versus Renting

Michael Higginbottom and Jonathan Van Ness of Binghamton, New York, are trying to decide whether to rent or purchase housing. Both men are single. Michael favors buying and Jonathan leans toward renting, and both seem able to justify their particular choice. Michael thinks that the tax advantages are a very good reason for buying. Jonathan, however, believes that cash flow is so much better when renting. See whether you can help them make their decision.

(a) Does the home buyer enjoy tax advantages? Explain.

(b) Discuss Jonathan's belief that cash flow is better with renting.

(c) Suggest some reasons why Michael might consider renting rather than purchasing housing.

(d) Suggest some reasons why Jonathan might consider buying rather than renting housing.

(e) Is there a clear-cut basis for deciding either to rent or to buy housing? Explain why or why not.

Case 2

Emma Chooses Among Alternative Mortgage Options

Emma Rafferty of San Mateo, California, has examined several options for new home financing. She has been favoring alternative mortgage plans because of the rising mortgage rates. Emma hopes that the market rate will drop in a couple of years.

(a) What broad concerns are present with alternative mortgages?

(b) What financing option would you suggest for Emma, assuming she is able to use any type of mortgage available? Why?

Case 3

Jeremy Decides to Sell His Home Himself

Jeremy Jorgensen of St. Paul, Minnesota, is concerned about the costs involved in selling his home, so he has decided to sell his home himself rather than pay a broker to do it.

(a) How would you advise Jeremy if he asked you whether he should sell the house himself or list with a broker? Explain your answer.

(b) Would Jeremy really save money by selling his home himself if he considers his time as part of his costs? Why or why not?

(c) Can you suggest any ways that Jeremy might reduce his selling costs without doing the selling himself? Explain.

Case 4

Victor and Maria Hernandez Learn About Real Estate Agents

Victor and Maria have been thinking about selling their home and buying a house with more yard space so that they can indulge their passion for gardening. Before they make such a decision, they want to explore the market to see what might be available and in what price ranges. They will then list their house with a real estate agent and begin searching in earnest for a new home.

(a) What services could a real estate agent provide for the couple, and what types of agents could represent them as they sell their current home?

(b) A friend has advised them that they really need a buyer's agent for the purchase of a new home. Explain to the Hernandezes the difference between buyer's and seller's agents.

Case 5
The Johnsons Decide to Buy a Condominium

Belinda Johnson's parents and maternal grandmother have combined their finances and presented Harry and Belinda with $25,000 with which to purchase a condominium. The Johnsons have shopped and found one that they like very much. They could either borrow from the condominium developer or obtain a loan from one of three other mortgage lenders. The financial details follow and are summarized in the table below.

(a) Which plan has the lowest total up-front costs? The highest?

(b) What would be the full monthly payment for PITI and PMI for each of the options?

(c) If the Johnsons had enough spare cash to make the 20 percent down payment, would you recommend lender 1 or lender 2? Why?

(d) Assuming that the Johnsons will need about $3000 for moving costs (in addition to closing costs), which financing option would you recommend? Why?

Financing Details on a Condominium Available to the Johnsons

Price: $140,000. Developer A will finance the purchase with a 10 percent down payment and a 30-year, 6.5 percent ARM loan with 2 interest points. The initial monthly payment for principal and interest is $796.41 ($126,000 loan after the down payment is made; 126 × $6.3207). After one year, the rate rises to 8 percent, with a principal plus interest payment of $921.91. At that point, the rate can go up or down as much as 2 percent per year, depending on the cost of an index of mortgage funds. There is an interest-rate cap of 5 percent over the life of the loan. Taxes are estimated to be about $1500, and the homeowner's insurance premium should be about $600 annually. A mortgage insurance premium of $78 per month must be paid monthly on the two 10 percent down options.

On the 'Net

To complete these exercises, go to the *Garman/Forgue* website at college.hmco.com/business/students. Under General Business, select the title of this text. Click on the Internet Exercises link for this chapter, and answer the questions that appear on the webpage.

Condo: Price, $140,000; Taxes, $1500; Insurance, $600

	Developer A	Lender 1	Lender 2	Lender 3
Loan term and type	30-year ARM*	30-year CON†	15-year CON	20-year REN‡
Interest rate	6.5%	7.5%	8%	7.5%
Down payment	$ 14,000	$ 28,000	$ 28,000	$ 14,000
Loan amount	126,000	112,000	112,000	126,000
Points	2,520	1,120	0	3,780
Principal and interest payment	796.41	783.12	1,070.33	1,015.04
PMI	78	0	0	78

*Adjustable-rate mortgage.
†Conventional.
‡Renegotiable every five years.

1. Visit the website for Bankrate.com (http://www.bankrate.com/brm/rate/mtg_home.asp), where you will find information on mortgage interest rates around the United States. View the information for the lenders in a large city near your home. How does the information compare with the interest rates on your own credit card account(s)? How do the rates in the city you selected compare with other rates found in the United States?
2. Visit the website for the United States Department of Housing and Urban Development, where you will find a calculator (http://www.hud.gov/buying/index.cfm#afford) that helps you determine the amount you can afford for the purchase of a home given your income and funds available for a down payment, closing costs, and other home-buying expenses. Enter the data requested for your current situation. What does the calculator tell you about your housing affordability? Change the entered data for some point in the future when you project a better financial situation for yourself. How do the results change?
3. Visit the website for the National Association of Realtors (realtor.com), where you can search for owned housing in various locales around the United States. Look for housing in your community of a type that would interest you and that is in your price range. Were you able to find housing that meets your criteria? Also search for similar housing in the San Diego, California (high-cost area), and Syracuse, New York (low-cost area), metropolitan areas. Compare these cost results with the housing found in your area.

Visit the Garman/Forgue website ...

@college.hmco.com/business/students

Under General Business, select *Personal Finance 9e*. There, among other valuable resources, you will find a complete glossary, ACE questions, links to help you complete the chapter exercises, and links to other personal finance sites.

PART 3

CHAPTER 10 Managing Property and Liability Risk

CHAPTER 11 Managing Health Expenses

CHAPTER 12 Life Insurance Planning

CHAPTER 10

Managing Property and Liability Risk

You Must Be Kidding, Right?

Tiffany Blake recently caused an automobile accident when she had a blowout on the freeway. Her car crossed the median and was struck by two other cars. The cost of repairs to Tiffany's car will be $13,200, which exceeds the car's $12,500 fair market value. The damage to the other two vehicles was $17,800 and $6400, respectively. Fortunately, no one was injured in the accident. On the advice of her insurance agent, Tiffany had purchased an auto insurance policy with a $500 collision deductible and liability limits of $25,000/$50,000/$15,000 when she purchased her car. What dollar amount of these losses will be covered by her policy?

A. $12,700 **B.** $27,000 **C.** $36,200 **D.** $37,400

The answer is B. Tiffany carried collision insurance, which covers her vehicle. The company will pay her $12,000, which is the fair market value of the vehicle less her $500 deductible. The company will take title to her vehicle, and she can use the $12,000 to find another car. The company will also pay $15,000 for the damage to the other vehicles. This is the limit for property damage liability under her policy. Tiffany will be personally responsible for the additional $9200 ($17,800 + $6,400 − $15,000) in damage to the other vehicles. Always buy high liability coverage limits!

LEARNING OBJECTIVES

After reading this chapter, you should be able to:

1 **Apply** the risk-management process to address the risks to your property and income.

2 **Explain** basic insurance terms and the relationship between risk and insurance.

3 **Design** a homeowner's or renter's insurance program to meet your needs.

4 **Design** an automobile insurance program to meet your needs.

5 **Describe** other types of property and liability insurance.

6 **Summarize** how to make an insurance claim.

What Do You Recommend?

George and Emily Cosgrove of Athens, Georgia, recently had a fire in their garage that destroyed two of their cars and did considerable damage to the garage and to the outside of their home. After receiving their reimbursements from their homeowner's and automobile insurance policies, the Cosgroves realized that they were severely underinsured. One vehicle was not insured for fire, and the insurance on their dwelling amounted to only 60 percent of its current replacement value.

What do you recommend to George and Emily about managing property and liability risk regarding:

1. The risk-management steps they should take to update their insurance coverages?
2. The relationship between severity and frequency of loss when deciding whether to buy insurance?
3. Adequately insuring their home?
4. The use of deductibles and policy limits to keep their automobile insurance premiums at a manageable level while still maintaining vital coverage?

FOR HELP with studying this chapter, visit the Online Student Center:

www.college.hmco.com/pic/garman9e

Up to this point, this book has focused on ways to manage your money and strategies for using financial resources to achieve your personal goals. But it is just as important to protect your resources and assets from the possibility of financial loss. Losses can result from accidents, acts of nature, illness or injury, and death. You can manage the risk of these losses through the effective use of insurance. Chapter 11 focuses on losses related to illness or injury, and Chapter 12 looks at losses related to death. This chapter focuses on losses that occur from accidents and acts of nature. Such losses stem from two possibilities. First, your property might be damaged. **Property insurance** protects you from financial losses resulting from the damage to or destruction of your property or possessions. Second, you might be held responsible, or liable, for losses suffered by others. **Liability insurance** protects you from financial losses suffered when you are held liable for the losses of others. The two major forms of property and liability insurance are insurance for your home and its contents and insurance for your ownership and use of vehicles.

property insurance Protection from financial losses resulting from the damage to or destruction of your property or possessions.

liability insurance Protection from financial losses suffered when you are held liable for others' losses.

risk Uncertainty about the outcome of a situation or event.

Risk and Risk Management

The Nature of Risk

1 LEARNING OBJECTIVE
Apply the risk-management process to address the risks to your property and income.

Risk is uncertainty about the outcome of a situation or event. It arises out of the possibility that the outcome will differ from what is expected. In the area of potential financial losses, risk consists of uncertainty about whether the financial loss will occur and how large it might be. There are two types of risk. **Speculative risk** exists in situations where there is potential for gain as well as for loss. Investments such as those made in the stock market involve speculative risk. **Pure risk** exists when there is no potential for gain, only the possibility of loss. Fires, automobile accidents, illness, and theft are examples of events involving pure risk. Insurance addresses pure risk.

Many people think of "odds" or games of chance when they hear the word **risk.** In fact, risk and chance are different concepts. The difference between the two is subtle but very important. An event with a 95 percent chance of occurring is highly likely to occur. Thus, both uncertainty and risk are low. An event with a 0.000001 percent chance of occurring is highly likely *not* to occur. Thus, both uncertainty and risk are low. When an event has a moderate chance of occurring—5 percent, for example—the uncertainty and risk are relatively high because it is difficult to predict the one person in 20 who will experience the event. In such cases, insurance often represents a wise choice for reducing risk.

Good Money Habits in Managing Property and Liability Risk

Make the following your money habits in managing property and liability insurance risk:

1. Always insure your home and vehicles.
2. Purchase insurance policies with very high liability limits to protect against the possibility of catastrophic losses.
3. Verify that your auto insurance policy covers rental car losses so you can wisely ignore sales pressure to purchase such overpriced coverage.
4. Always comparison shop for insurance locally as well as online.
5. Maintain a verifiable inventory of all your insured property so that you can collect what is coming to you in the event of a loss.
6. Once each year, reassess what types of and how much insurance coverage you need.

The Risk-Management Process

Risk management is the process of identifying and evaluating situations involving pure risk to determine and implement the appropriate means for its management. The goal is to minimize any risk or potential for risk through advance planning. Risk management entails making the most efficient arrangements before a loss occurs so as to minimize any after-loss effects on your financial status. It is an important part of overall personal financial management, as it preserves the benefits of your other financial planning efforts. Insurance is merely one of many possible ways of handling risk, and it is not always the best choice.

risk management Process of identifying and evaluating purely risky situations to determine and implement appropriate management.

Table 10.1 The Risk-Management Process

	Possessions	Activities	Accompanying Perils
Step 1 *Identify sources of risk.*	Vehicle House Jewelry	Driving Smoking Traveling	Accident Fire Theft
Step 2 *Estimate risk and potential losses.*	(a) Determine the likely frequency of losses associated with each exposure. (b) Determine the potential severity and magnitude of losses associated with each exposure.		
Step 3 *Choose how to handle risk.*	(a) Avoid risk. (b) Retain risk. (c) Control losses. (d) Transfer risk. (e) Reduce risk.		
Step 4 *Implement the risk-management plan.*	(a) Refrain from certain activities. (b) Take extra precautions. (c) Buy insurance.		
Step 5 *Evaluate and adjust the program.*			

The risk-management process involves five steps; Table 10.1 outlines these steps in the risk-management process.

Step 1: Identify Sources of Risk Sources of risk, called **exposures,** are the items you own and the activities in which you engage that expose you to potential financial loss. Owning and/or driving an automobile is a common exposure. In risk management, you take an inventory of what you own and what you do in order to identify your exposures to loss.

You face the possibility of loss in one of four ways:

1. First, you may suffer a loss to your property, such as can happen during a house fire.
2. Second, you could be held legally responsible for losses suffered by others such as if you cause an automobile accident.
3. Third, you may become ill or be injured and have costs associated with health care.
4. Fourth, you may suffer a loss of income as a result of illness, accident, or death.

You also need to identify the perils that you face. A **peril** is any event that can cause a financial loss. Fire, wind, theft, vehicle collision, illness, and death are all examples of perils.

peril Any event that can cause a financial loss.

Step 2: Estimate Risk and Potential Losses Once you identify your exposures to risk, you estimate both loss frequency and loss severity. **Loss frequency** refers to the likely number of times that a loss might occur over a period of time. **Loss severity** describes the potential magnitude of the loss(es).

Many people wonder whether they should buy insurance when loss frequency is low, for example if they are young and healthy or if they live in a safe neighborhood. This is not a good way to think about potential losses. If loss frequency is low, the insurance would simply cost less. Figure 10.1 illustrates the relationship between loss severity and loss frequency in risk management.

What is more important is loss severity. "How much might I lose?" is the question you should ask. When considering possible property losses, you simply make an esti-

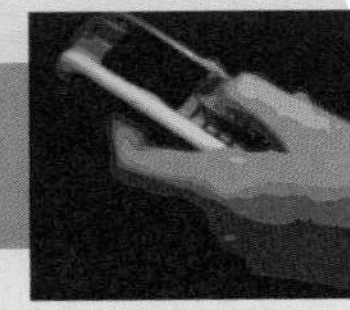

Instant Message

Driving Exposes You to Huge Potential Losses

The average driver will be involved in an accident approximately once every seven years, with the severity of these accidents ranging from a minor fender bender to catastrophic collisions bringing losses in the hundreds of thousands of dollars.

Did You Know?...

Top 3 Financial Missteps in Managing Property and Liability Risk

People slip up in managing property and liability risk when they do the following:

1. Buy only the legal minimum coverage on the liability insurance on their car
2. Fail to keep good records (e.g., lists, photos, receipts) that could serve to document insured property losses
3. Pay high premiums because they select low deductibles on property insurance for their home and car

mate of the value of the property. Liability losses are more complicated because the severity of the loss depends on the circumstances of the person you harm. For example, if you caused an accident that permanently disabled a young heart surgeon with three small children, you would be liable for the surgeon's care, lost earnings over the surgeon's lifetime, and future care and education of the children. A loss of several million dollars is not out of the question in such a situation.

Step 3: Choose How to Handle Risk The risk of loss may be handled in five ways: risk avoidance, risk retention, loss control, risk transfer, and risk reduction. Each strategy may be appropriate for certain circumstances, and the mix that you choose will depend on the source of the risk, the size of the potential loss, your personal feelings about risk, and the financial resources you have available to pay for losses.

- **Risk avoidance.** The simplest way to handle risk is to avoid it. With this approach, you would refrain from owning items or engaging in activities that expose you to possible financial loss. For example, choosing not to own an airplane or not to skydive limits your exposure. Avoiding risk is not always practical, however.
- **Risk retention.** A second way to handle risk is to retain or accept it. The risk that the shrubbery around your house might die during a dry spell is such a retained risk. Conscious risk retention plays an important role in risk management. Risk retention due to ignorance or inaction is not effective risk management. For example, many people unwisely put off the purchase of life insurance because they consider it to be a morbid, unpleasant task.
- **Loss control.** Loss control, the third method of handling risk, is designed to reduce loss frequency and loss severity. For example, installing heavy-duty locks and doors will reduce the *frequency* of theft losses. Installing fire alarms and smoke detectors cannot prevent fires but will reduce the *severity* of losses from them. Insurance companies often require loss-control efforts or give discounts to policyholders who implement them.
- **Risk transfer.** A fourth way to handle risk is to transfer it. In a risk transfer, an insurance company agrees to reimburse you for a financial loss. For example, a professional football team's star run

Figure 10.1

The Relationship Between Severity and Frequency of Loss

	HIGH SEVERITY	LOW SEVERITY
LOW FREQUENCY	Purchase insurance to cover the potentially large losses. Their infrequency will make premiums affordable.	Consider retaining risk because the frequency and severity of loss are both low.
HIGH FREQUENCY	Purchase insurance. Loss control efforts can be useful in reducing the necessarily high premiums.	Retain risk but also budget for losses that are likely to be frequent.

ning back might take out an insurance policy on his legs. In this case, the uncertainty is simply transferred from the running back or his team to an insurance company. Insurance represents one method of transferring risk, although not all risk transfers can be classified as insurance because insurance goes beyond merely transferring risk to the actual reduction of risk.

- **Risk reduction.** The fifth way to handle risk is to reduce it to acceptable levels. Insurance is used by policyholders when they arrange for all or a portion of their risk to be covered by an insurance company, thereby reducing their personal level of risk.

risk reduction Includes mechanisms, such as insurance, that reduce the overall uncertainty about the magnitude of loss.

Step 4: Implement the Risk-Management Program The fourth step in risk management is to implement the risk-handling methods you have chosen. For most households, this means buying insurance to transfer and reduce risk. This involves selecting types of policies and coverage, dollar amounts of coverage, and sources of insurance protection.

large-loss principle A basic rule of risk management that encourages us to insure the losses that we cannot afford and assume the losses that we can reasonably afford.

People often wonder what types of insurance to buy and how many dollars of coverage to choose. You should use the maximum possible loss as a guide for the dollar amount of coverage to buy. This way of thinking makes use of the **large-loss principle:** Insure the losses that you cannot afford and assume the losses that you can reasonably afford. In other words, pay for small losses out of your own pocket and purchase as much insurance as necessary to cover large, catastrophic losses that will ruin you financially. The example earlier of an auto accident that injures a heart surgeon would bring you such ruin because you would be held responsible for those losses. Consequently, you would want high dollar amounts of liability coverage on your auto insurance.

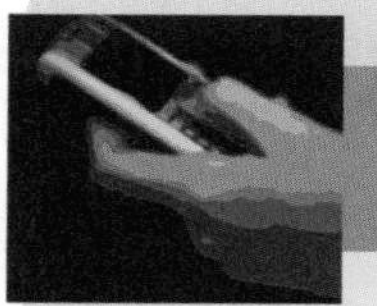

Instant Message

Buy—Don't Be Sold—Insurance

Always remember that your goal is to "buy" the insurance you need at a fair price. Do not let yourself be "sold" more or less insurance coverage than you need at excessive prices. Visit www.insquote.com and www.quotesmith.com once you have decided what insurance you need.

Step 5: Evaluate and Adjust the Program The final step in risk management entails periodic review of your risk-management efforts. The risks people face in their lives change continually. Therefore, no risk-management plan should be put in place and then ignored for long periods of time. For certain exposures, such as ownership of an automobile, an annual review

Renters need home insurance, too.

is appropriate. For areas involving life insurance, a review should occur about once every three to five years or whenever family structure and employment situations change. The necessary adjustments should be implemented promptly to reflect changes over your life cycle. Many people stick with existing policies that no longer fit their needs (too little or too much coverage) simply because they buy once and ignore their insurance needs for years.

CONCEPT CHECK 10.1

1. Distinguish between pure risk and speculative risk.
2. Explain the distinctions between risk and odds.
3. Describe the five steps of risk management.
4. Based on likelihood of loss and severity of loss, explain why one is more important when deciding whether to buy insurance.

Understanding How Insurance Works

2 LEARNING OBJECTIVE
Explain basic insurance terms and the relationship between risk and insurance.

insurance Mechanism for transferring and reducing pure risk through which a large number of individuals share in the financial losses suffered by members of the group as a whole.

premium Comparatively small, predictable fee with which individuals or companies can replace an uncertain—and possibly large—financial loss.

insurance policy Contract between the person buying insurance (the insured) and the insurance company (the insurer).

Insurance is a mechanism for transferring and reducing pure risk through which a large number of individuals share in the financial losses suffered by members of the group as a whole. Insurance protects each individual in the group by replacing an uncertain—and possibly large—financial loss with a certain but comparatively small fee. This fee, called the **premium,** has four components:

- The individual's share of the group's losses
- Insurance company reserves set aside to pay future losses
- A proportional share of the expenses of administering the insurance plan
- An allowance for profit (when the plan is administered by a profit-seeking company)

Insurance premiums are assessed on an annual or semiannual basis. You generally will be charged an extra amount if you choose to make the payments monthly.

The **insurance policy** is the contract between the person buying insurance (the **insured**) and the insurance company (the **insurer**). It contains language that describes the rights and responsibilities of both parties. Most people do not take the time to read and understand their insurance policies. As a result, insurance remains one of the least understood purchases people make. You can do a much better job of managing your risks if you understand the basic terms and concepts used in the field of insurance.

Hazards Make Losses More Likely to Occur

A **hazard** is any condition that increases the probability that a peril will occur. Driving under the influence of alcohol represents an especially dangerous hazard. Three types of hazards exist:

- A **physical hazard** is a particular characteristic of the insured person or property that increases the chance of loss. An example of a physical hazard is high blood pressure in a person covered by health insurance.
- A **morale hazard** exists when a person is indifferent to a peril. For example, a morale hazard exists if the insured party, knowing that theft insurance will pay for the loss, becomes careless about locking doors and windows.
- A **moral hazard** exists when an insured person wants a peril to occur so that he or she can collect on an insurance policy.

Instant Message

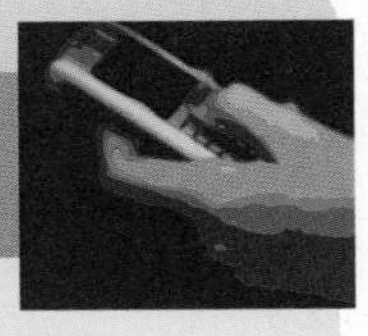

Can Your Insurance Company Honor Its Promises?

Insurance companies must have the financial strength to pay losses as promised. You can assess your company's financial strength at http://www.standardandpoors.com by clicking on "Ratings" and then "Insurance."

Insurance companies often limit or deny coverage if a loss occurs as a result of a morale or moral hazard.

Only Certain Losses Are Insurable

Certain minimum requirements must be met for a loss to be considered insurable—in particular, the loss must be fortuitous, financial, and personal. **Fortuitous losses** are unexpected in terms of both their timing and their magnitude. A loss caused by a lightning strike and fire to your home is fortuitous; a loss caused by a decline in the market value of your home is not because it is reasonable to expect home values to rise and fall over time. A **financial loss** is any decline in the value of income or assets in the present or future. Financial losses can be measured objectively in dollars and cents. When you become sick, you suffer as a result of the discomfort, inconvenience, lost wages, and medical bills. Insurance will cover only the lost wages and medical bills, however, because these losses—but not the others—can be objectively measured. Finally, **personal losses** can be directly suffered by specific individuals or organizations rather than society as whole.

The Principle of Indemnity Limits Insurance Payouts

The **principle of indemnity** states that insurance will pay *no more* than the actual financial loss suffered. For example, an automobile insurance policy will pay only the actual cash value of a stolen automobile. This principle prevents a person from gaining financially from a loss. Furthermore, it does not guarantee that insured losses will be totally reimbursed. Every policy includes **policy limits,** which specify the maximum dollar amounts that will be paid under the policy. These limits explain why there is no such thing as "full coverage" insurance—there is always the potential that a loss will exceed the limits on a policy. As a result, insurance purchasers must carefully select policy limits sufficient to cover their potential losses.

principle of indemnity Insurance will pay *no more* than the actual financial loss suffered.

policy limits Specify the maximum dollar amounts that will be paid under the policy.

Factors That Reduce the Cost of Insurance

Some specific features of insurance policies can lower your premiums without significantly reducing the protection offered. These features include deductibles, coinsurance, hazard reduction, and loss reduction.

Deductibles are requirements that you pay an initial portion of any loss. For example, automobile collision insurance often includes a \$200 deductible. With such a policy, the first \$200 of loss to the car must be paid by the insured. The insurer then pays the remainder of the loss, up to the limits of the policy. You usually have a choice of deductible amounts.

deductibles Requirements that the policyholder pays an initial portion of any loss.

Coinsurance is a method by which the insured and the insurer share proportionately in the payment for a loss. For example, health insurance policies commonly require that the insured pay 20 percent of a loss and the insurer pay the remaining 80 percent. Substantial premium reductions can be realized through coinsurance, but you must be prepared to pay your share of losses. The following *deductible and coinsurance reimbursement formula* can be used to determine the amount of a loss that will be reimbursed when the policy includes a deductible and a coinsurance clause:

coinsurance Method by which the insured and the insurer share proportionately in the payment for a loss.

$$R = (1 - CP)(L - D) \qquad (10.1)$$

where

R = Reimbursement
CP = Coinsurance percentage required of the insured
L = Loss
D = Deductible

As an example, assume you have a health insurance policy with a $100 deductible per hospital stay and a 20 percent coinsurance requirement. If the hospital bill is $1350, the reimbursement will be $1000, calculated as follows:

$$\begin{aligned} R &= (1.00 - 0.20)(\$1350 - \$100) \\ &= (0.80)\ (\$1250) \\ &= \$1000 \end{aligned}$$

Hazard reduction is action taken by the insured to reduce the probability of a loss occurring. Insurance companies often offer reduced premiums to insureds who practice hazard reduction—for example, to nonsmokers.

Loss reduction is action taken by the insured to lessen the severity of loss if a peril occurs. Smoke alarms and fire extinguishers in the home are examples of loss reduction efforts. These items will not prevent fires, but their use may lead to less severe damage. Many property insurers offer reduced premiums to insureds who practice loss reduction.

The Essence of Insurance

Insurance consists of two basic elements: the reduction of risk and the sharing of losses. When you buy insurance, you exchange the uncertainty of a potentially large financial loss for the certainty of a fixed insurance premium, thereby reducing your

Did You Know?...

How to Read an Insurance Policy

Insurance policies do not invite casual reading. Consequently, many people fail to thoroughly examine their policies until a loss occurs, only to find that they had misunderstood the terms of the agreement. You can avoid such problems by systematically reading a policy before you purchase it, focusing on eight points:

1. **Perils covered.** Some policies list only the perils that are covered; others cover all perils except those listed. The definition of certain perils may differ from that used in everyday language.
2. **Property covered.** Like perils, the property covered under a policy may be listed individually, or only the excluded property may be listed. When the property is listed individually, any new acquisitions must be added to the policy.
3. **Types of losses covered.** Three types of property losses can occur: (a) the loss of the property itself, (b) extra expenses that may arise because the property is rendered unusable for a period of time, and (c) loss of income if the property was used in the insured's work.
4. **People covered.** Insurance policies may cover only certain individuals. This information usually appears on the first page of the policy but may be changed subsequently in later sections.
5. **Locations covered.** Where the loss occurs may have a bearing on whether it will be covered. It is especially important to know which locations are not covered.
6. **Time period of coverage.** Policies are generally written to cover specific time periods. Restrictions may exclude coverage during specific times of the day or certain days of the week or year.
7. **Loss control requirements.** Insurance policies often stipulate that certain loss control efforts must be maintained by the insured. For example, coverage for a vehicle may be denied if the owner knowingly allows it to be driven by an unlicensed person.
8. **Amount of coverage.** All insurance policies specify the maximum amount the insurer will pay for various types of losses.

The information on these eight points may be spread throughout a policy. In fact, coverage that appears to be provided in one location actually may be denied elsewhere. Carefully review the entire policy to determine the protection it provides. If necessary, telephone the salesperson or company to obtain clarification.

risk. Risk is reduced for the insurer as well through the **law of large numbers:** As the number of members in a group increases, predictions about the group's behavior become increasingly more accurate. This greater accuracy decreases uncertainty and, therefore, risk.

To illustrate, consider a city of 100,000 households in which the probability of a fire striking a household is 1 in 1000, or 0.1 percent. Thus, 100 home fires are likely to occur each year in this community. If we focus on groups of 100 households at a time, we cannot predict very accurately whether a fire will strike a house in a given group. Some groups might have two or three fires, while others might experience none. If we combine all the households into one group, however, we can more accurately predict that 100 fires will occur (100,000 × 0.001). Even if 103 fires occurred, our prediction would be in error by only a small percentage. Insurance companies, which may have millions of customers, can be even more accurate in their group predictions.

Individual insurance purchasers benefit regardless of whether they actually suffer a loss because of the reduction of risk. This is the essence of insurance. Reduced risk gives one the freedom to drive a car, own a home, and plan financially for the future with the knowledge that some unforeseen event will not result in financial disaster.

law of large numbers As the number of members in a group increases, predictions about the group's behavior become increasingly accurate.

insurance agent Representative of an insurance company authorized to sell, modify, service, and terminate insurance contracts.

binder Temporary insurance contract replaced later by written policy.

underwriting Insurer's procedure for deciding which insurance applicants to accept.

Who Sells Insurance

Sellers of insurance, called **insurance agents,** represent one or more insurance companies. They have the power to enter into, change, and cancel insurance policies on behalf of these companies. Two types of insurance agents exist: independent agents and exclusive agents.

Did You Know?...

How Companies Select Among Insurance Applicants

The purchase of insurance begins with an offer by the purchaser in the form of a written or oral policy application. The insurer typically issues a temporary insurance contract, called a **binder,** which is replaced at a later date with a written policy. The application then goes through a process of **underwriting**—that is, the insurer's procedure for deciding which insurance applicants to accept. To describe the process of underwriting, it is necessary to first understand how insurance rates are set.

An **insurance rate** is the price charged for each unit of insurance coverage. Rates represent the average cost of providing coverage to various **classes of insureds;** these classes consist of insureds who share similar characteristics. For example, automobile insurance policyholders may be classified by age, gender, marital status, and driving record, as well as by the make and model of vehicle that they drive.

When underwriters receive an application, they assign the applicant to the appropriate class. They then determine whether the rates established for that class are sufficient to provide coverage for that applicant. Underwriters divide insurance applicants into four groups:

- *Preferred* applicants have lower-than-average loss expectancies and may qualify for lower premiums.
- *Standard* applicants have average loss expectancies for their class and pay the standard rates.
- *Substandard* applicants have higher-than-average loss expectancies and may be charged higher premiums and have restrictions placed on the types or amounts of coverage they may purchase.
- *Unacceptable* applicants have loss expectancies that are much too high and are rejected.

It is common for insurance companies to use an applicant's credit report to provide information used in underwriting. (This is another reason for maintaining good credit and for making sure your credit bureau files are accurate!) You can save money by confirming with your agent that you have been placed in the proper class for premium-determination purposes. Verifying that you are in the proper class is also important because a claim may be denied if premiums were based on an inappropriate classification.

Table 10.2 Summary of Homeowner's Insurance Policies

	HO-1 (Basic Form)	HO-2 (Broad Form)	HO-3 (Special Form)
Perils covered (descriptions are given below)	Perils 1–11	Perils 1–18	All perils except those specifically excluded for buildings; perils 1–18 on personal property (does not include glass breakage)
Property coverage/limits			
House and any other attached buildings	Amount based on replacement cost, minimum $15,000	Amount based on replacement cost, minimum $15,000	Amount based on replacement cost, minimum $20,000
Detached buildings	10 percent of insurance on the home (minimum)	10 percent of insurance on the home (minimum)	10 percent of insurance on the home (minimum)
Trees, shrubs, plants, etc.	5 percent of insurance on the home, $500 maximum per item	5 percent of insurance on the home, $500 maximum per item	5 percent of insurance on the home, $500 maximum per item
Personal property	50 percent of insurance on the home (minimum)	50 percent of insurance on the home (minimum)	50 percent of insurance on the home (minimum)
Loss of use and/or additional living expense	10 percent of insurance on the home	20 percent of insurance on the home	20 percent of insurance on the home
Credit card, forgery, counterfeit money	$1000	$1000	$1000

Liability coverage/limits (for all policies)		**Special limits of liability**
Comprehensive personal liability	$100,000	For the following classes of personal property, special limits apply on a per-occurrence basis (e.g., per fire or theft): money, coins, bank notes, precious metals (gold, silver, etc.), $200; computers, $5000; securities, deeds, stocks, bonds, tickets, stamps, $1000; watercraft and trailers, including furnishings, equipment, and outboard motors, $1000; trailers other than for watercraft, $1000; jewelry, watches, furs, $1000; silverware, goldware, etc., $2500; guns, $2000.
No-fault medical payments	$1000	
No-fault property damage	$500	

List of perils covered

1. Fire, lightning
2. Windstorm, hail
3. Explosion
4. Riots
5. Damage by aircraft
6. Damage by vehicles owned or operated by people not covered by the homeowner's policy
7. Damage from smoke
8. Vandalism, malicious mischief
9. Theft
10. Glass breakage
11. Volcanic eruption
12. Falling objects (external sources)
13. Weight of ice, snow, sleet
14. Collapse of building or any part of building (specified perils only)
15. Leakage or overflow of water or steam from a plumbing, heating, or air-conditioning system
16. Bursting, cracking, burning, or bulging of a steam or hot water heating system, or of appliances for heating water
17. Freezing of plumbing, heating, and air-conditioning systems and home appliances
18. Injury to electrical appliances and devices (excluding tubes, transistors, and similar electronic components) from short circuits or other accidentally generated currents

Note: This table describes the standard policies. Specific items differ from company to company and from state to state. When you want a limit that exceeds the standard limit for your company, you usually can increase the limit by paying an additional premium.

HO-4 (Renter's Contents Broad Form)	**HO-6 For Condominium Owners)**	**HO-8 (For Older Homes)**
Perils 1–9,11–18	Perils 1–18	Perils 1–11
10 percent of personal property insurance on additions and alterations to the apartment	$1000 on owner's additions and alterations to the unit	Amount based on actual cash value of the home
Not covered	Not covered (unless owned solely by the insured)	10 percent of insurance on the home (minimum)
10 percent of personal property insurance, $500 maximum per item	10 percent of personal property insurance, $500 maximum per item	5 percent of insurance on the home, $500 maximum per item
Chosen by the tenant to reflect the value of the items, minimum $6000	Chosen by the homeowner to reflect the value of the items, minimum $6000	50 percent of insurance on the home (minimum)
20 percent of personal property insurance	40 percent of personal property insurance	20 percent of insurance on the home
$1000	$1000	$1000

Table 10.3 Personal Property Checklist: Living Room

Item	**Date Purchased**	**Purchase Price**	**Actual Cash Value**	**Replacement Cost**
Furniture				
Sofa	8/03	$ 750	$ 375	$ 950
Chair	11/01	250	100	375
Lounger	12/04	575	300	695
Ottoman	12/04	100	50	120
Bookcase	4/06	275	225	300
End table (2)	7/07	300	250	300
Appliances				
TV	1/07	550	500	600
DVD	6/06	400	300	400
Wall clock	7/01	60	10	100
Furnishings				
Carpet	6/00	375	50	600
Painting	12/04	125	225	225
Floor lamp	4/02	150	50	225
Art (three items)	10/06	600	600	800
Table lamp	4/02	75	40	100
Table lamp	5/06	125	100	135
Throw pillows	7/03	45	20	60
	TOTAL	$4755	$3195	$5985

(e) To whom and how much will David's medical protection pay?

(f) How much reimbursement will David receive for his car?

(g) How much will David be required to pay out of his own pocket?

David Smith's Accident: Who Pays What?

Coverage	David's Policy	Ashley's Policy
Liability (limits)		
Bodily injury		
Ashley		
Fran		
Cecilia		
Medical payments (limits)		
David		
Ashley		
Fran		
Cecilia		
Collision coverage (limits)		
David's car		
Ashley's car		
David's out-of-pocket expenses		
Fran's bodily injury		
Excess property damage losses		
Collision insurance deductible		
TOTAL		

Decision-Making Cases

Case 1

The Princes' Auto Insurance Is Not Renewed

Mark and Katrina Prince of Jacksonville, Florida, face a crisis. Their automobile insurance company has notified them that their current coverage expires in 30 days and will not be renewed. Both Mark and the Princes' younger son had minor, at-fault accidents during the past year. Their children are otherwise good drivers, as are both parents. The Princes are confused because they know families whose members have much worse driving records but still have insurance.

(a) Explain to Mark and Katrina why their policy might have been canceled.

(b) Use the box on page 283 to give Mark and Katrina some pointers on how to save money on their new policy.

Case 2

Abigail Contemplates a New Homeowner's Insurance Policy

Abigail Elizabeth Proctor of Bedford, Oregon, recently bought a home for $200,000. The previous owner had a $160,000 HO-1 policy on the property, and Abigail can simply pay the premiums to keep the same coverage in effect. Her insurance agent called her and cautioned that she would be better off to upgrade the policy to an HO-2 or HO-3 policy. Abigail has turned to you for advice. Use the information in Table 10.2 to advise her.

(a) What additional property protection would Abigail have if she purchased an HO-2 policy?

(b) What additional property protection would Abigail have if she purchased an HO-3 policy?

(c) What property protection would remain largely the same whether Abigail had an HO-1, HO-2, or HO-3 policy?

(d) Advise Abigail on what differences in liability protection, if any, exist among the three policies.

Case 3

A Student Buys Insurance for a Used Car

Makiko Iwanami, a student from Osaka, Japan, is in one of your classes. She is considering the purchase of a used car and has been told that she must buy automobile insurance to register the car and obtain license plates. Makiko has come to you for advice, and you have decided to focus on three aspects of automobile insurance.

(a) Explain how liability insurance works in the United States. Advise Makiko about which liability insurance limits she should select.

(b) Makiko is especially impressed that automobile insurance includes medical payments coverage because she has no health insurance. Explain why the medical payments coverage does not actually solve her health insurance problem, and describe the type of coverage it provides.

(c) Makiko plans to pay cash for the car and doesn't want to spend more than $3000. Outline the coverage provided by collision insurance and factors that might make such coverage optional for Makiko.

Case 4
An Argument About the Value of Insurance

You have been talking to some friends about insurance. One young married couple in the group believes that insurance is really a waste of money in most cases. They argue, "The odds of most bad events occurring are so low that you need not worry." Furthermore, they say, "Buying insurance is like pouring money down a hole; you rarely have anything to show for it in the end." Based on what you have learned from this chapter, how might you argue against this couple's point of view?

Case 5
The Hernandezes Consider Additional Liability Insurance

Victor and Maria's next-door neighbor, Jasmine Saunders, was recently sued over an automobile accident and was held liable for $437,000 in damages. Jasmine's automobile policy limits were 100/300/50. Because of the shortfall, she had to sell her house and move into an apartment. Victor and Maria are now concerned that a similar tragedy might potentially befall them. They have a homeowner's policy with $100,000 in comprehensive personal liability coverage, an automobile policy with 50/100/25 limits, and a small ($100,000) professional liability policy through Maria's employer.

(a) How might Victor and Maria more fully protect themselves through their homeowner's and automobile insurance policies?

(b) What additional benefits would they receive in buying an umbrella liability policy?

Case 6
The Johnsons Decide How to Manage Their Risks

The financial affairs of the Johnsons have become much more complicated since we began following them in Chapter 2. Both Harry ($275 per month) and Belinda ($300 per month) have been given raises at work. They have purchased a $125,000 condominium that has added about $400 per month to their housing expense. They have purchased a used car for $3200, adding about $120 per month to their expenses. As a result of these changes, Harry and Belinda realize that they now face greater risks in their financial affairs. They have decided to review their situation with an eye toward managing their risks more effectively. Use Table 10.1, their net worth and income and expense statements at the end of Chapter 3, and other information in this chapter to answer the following questions:

(a) What are Harry and Belinda's major sources of risk from home and automobile ownership, and what is the potential magnitude of loss from each?

(b) Given the choices listed in step 3 of Table 10.1, how should the Johnsons handle the sources of risk listed in part a?

On the 'Net

Go to the Web pages indicated to complete these exercises. You can also go to the *Garman/Forgue* website at college.hmco.com/business/students for an expanded list of exercises. Under General Business, select the title of this text. Click on the Internet Exercises link for this chapter.

1. Visit the website for the Insurance Information Institute at http://www.iii.org/individuals/auto/a/stateautolaws/, where you will find a summary of the automobile insurance requirements in each state. Determine the minimum automobile insurance liability limits in your state. How do these minimums compare with those in other states? How well insured do you feel someone would be if they carried only these minimums?
2. Visit the website for the National Association of Insurance Commissioners, where you will find a map at http://www.naic.org/state_web_map.htm through which you can link to your state insurance regulator's website. If available in your state, obtain an insurance buyer's guide for automobile and homeowner's insurance that describes policy provisions and compares insurance rates. Use these rate comparisons to select two automobile insurance companies that would be appropriate for your needs. Write or telephone the companies to obtain specific premium quotations for the desired insurance protection. Do the same for single-family dwelling, condominium, or renter's insurance, depending on your circumstances.
3. Visit the website for the Insurance Institute for Highway Safety at http://www.iihs.org/ratings/default.aspx. For your own vehicle and one or two you would like to own, check how the vehicles stack up against the competition in terms of injury protection.

Visit the Garman/Forgue website ...

@college.hmco.com/business/students

Under General Business, select *Personal Finance 9e*. There, among other valuable resources, you will find a complete glossary, ACE questions, links to help you complete the chapter exercises, and links to other personal finance sites.

CHAPTER 11

Managing Health Expenses

You Must Be Kidding, Right?

Amber Parker is a 32-year-old married mother with two children, ages 3 and 4. She worked out of her home as a medical transcriptionist for a local hospital. Her employer offered a medical care plan that Amber had chosen from her menu of employment benefits. Last year Amber suffered severe head injuries in a bicycling accident. Amber's wounds have healed and she has regained her ability to speak but is not yet able to walk on her own or use her hands and arms very well. Amber is recuperating at home but requires a daily paid caregiver to assist with her personal needs. Her children now go to daycare, and it may be 5 years before she can work again. Which of the following aspects of her injury were covered by Amber's medical care plan?

A. Her hospital stay and surgery

B. Her at-home custodial care

C. The cost of daycare for her children

D. Her lost income

The answer is A. Having a medical care plan is a must, but your protection is incomplete until you have addressed the need for rehabilitation and custodial care and for the potential lost income from a period of disability!

LEARNING OBJECTIVES

After reading this chapter, you should be able to:

1 **Identify** ways that people can manage the financial burdens resulting from illness or injury.

2 **Distinguish** among the types of protection for direct medical expenses.

3 **Describe** the general benefits and limitations of medical care plans.

4 **Explain** how to protect yourself from the expenses for long-term care.

5 **Develop** a plan for protecting your income when you cannot work due to disability.

What Do You Recommend?

Danielle DiMartino is a 43-year-old single mother with two children, ages 10 and 14. Her 10-year-old daughter has a history of ear infections that require doctor's office visits four or five times per year. Danielle's 71-year-old mother lives with the family for financial reasons; she has hereditary high blood pressure and high cholesterol as well as diabetes. Danielle's mother has enrolled in Medicare Parts A and B.

Danielle's employer sponsors a medical care plan to cover the company's workers, their spouses, and their dependents. Danielle has four options: (1) the basic HMO managed by a local university medical school/hospital with no additional cost for Danielle, but with additional cost of $122 per month to cover her children, (2) a health insurance plan with a PPO at that same medical center for an additional cost of $245 per month, (3) a traditional health insurance plan that provides access to virtually all medical care providers in her community for $455 per month, and (4) a high-deductible plan with a $5000 deductible at no additional cost. Danielle's employer offers no disability income or long-term care group plan. She does receive 10 sick days per year, which can accumulate to 60 days if not taken. Danielle has accumulated 30 days.

What would you recommend to Danielle DiMartino on the subject of managing health expenses regarding:

1. Choosing among the four alternatives available to her?
2. Danielle's concerns about providing for her mother's health care needs?
3. How Danielle can cover her long-term care and disability income risk?

FOR HELP with studying this chapter, visit the Online Student Center:

www.college.hmco.com/pic/garman9e

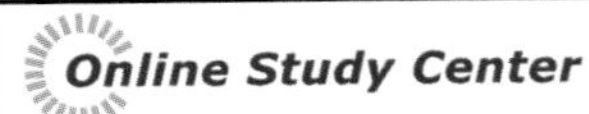

Few things in life are more important than your good health. When illness or injuries do strike, three possible issues may affect your finances. First, the direct cost of the required medical care, such as the cost of hospital stays, surgeries, and visits to the doctor's office, will have to be paid. Second, you will need to address the cost of your rehabilitation and custodial care. Nursing home care is an example of custodial care. Third, you will need to manage despite the loss of income that occurs when anyone who is employed cannot work due to illness or injury. This chapter looks at the ways you can address these three concerns.

group health plan Sold collectively to an entire group of people rather than to individuals, such as the group health care policies offered by employers.

Addressing the Financial Burdens of Illness or Injury

1 LEARNING OBJECTIVE
Identify ways that people can manage the financial burdens resulting from illness or injury.

On average, more than $7500 is spent on health care for each American each year. About 85 percent of Americans are covered by a medical care plan that will pay a portion of these costs. Those without a plan must pay even more.

You can obtain protection as an individual or as a member of a group. A **group health plan** is sold collectively to an entire group of people rather than to individuals. The medical care plan offered by many companies is an example of a group plan.

Each of the three types of losses resulting from illness or injury can be addressed in multiple ways. Of course, you can pay all of your own expenses. That is not always practical or smart. We provide a summary of your options here and in Table 11.1.

Instant Message

Group Health Plans Are Best

Participating in a group plan is desirable for three reasons: First, group health coverage costs less than an individual plan. Second, employers often pay all or the major portion of the cost. Third, people who have existing health problems are less likely to be rejected because of their condition.

1. Covering Your Direct Medical Care Costs

Direct medical care can be covered by an HMO, traditional health insurance, or a high-deductible health care plan (each is defined later). These three types of plans can cover as much as 90 to 100 percent of one's costs and comprise the plans typically offered by employers. Purchased individually, these plans can cost $400 or more per month for an individual and $700 or more for family coverage. Low-income individuals and families may qualify for **Medicaid,** a government health care program funded jointly by the federal and state governments. Finally, people age 65 or over can enroll in the **Medicare** program, which is the federal government's medical care program for the elderly.

Instant Message

Three Ways to Obtain Medical Care Benefits

Medical benefits can come from three sources. First, your employer might provide them as an employee benefit. Second, you might qualify for a government program. Three, you can buy protection as an individual.

2. Covering Your Rehabilitative and Custodial Care Costs

The elderly, people with chronic disease, and accident victims often have needs that go beyond direct medical care. At one extreme is the need for a stay in a nursing home and at the other might be a short period of time during which a patient receives rehabilitation. Medical care plans tend to cover only "medically necessary" care, not these rehabilitation and custodial needs. **Long-term care insurance** provides reimbursement for costs associated with intermediate-term and custodial care in a nursing facility or at home. Medicaid also provides protection here but only for low-income/low-wealth individuals. Those in the greatest need for assistance tend to be those in the middle-income range. They lack the financial resources to pay for nursing home care (perhaps $5000 per month) and have too high of an income to qualify for Medicaid.

3. Covering Your Lost Income

Anyone with a job can lose income when they become sick or are injured. Many employers offer sick days and other time off that can be used as necessary. Some employers may provide a disability income insurance plan that will replace a portion of income for a period of time. The employee may be required to pay all or a portion of the premium for such coverage. If your employer does not offer a plan, you can buy one on your own.

Workers who are eligible can collect **Social Security Disability Income Insurance** benefits if their disability is total (meaning they cannot work at any job) and will last one year (or until death if expected within one year). The amount of these benefits is based on the worker's average lifetime earnings and, thus, might be lower than necessary to fully support young workers. Finally, older workers who have built up considerable funds in a tax-sheltered retirement account may be able to utilize those funds to replace lost income when disabled.

Social Security Disability Income Insurance Under this government program, eligible workers can collect some income for up to one year if their disabilities are total, meaning that they cannot work at any job.

Did You Know?...

Top 3 Financial Missteps in Managing Health Expenses

1. Going unprotected for health care when changing jobs
2. Duplicating employer-provided health care protection with your spouse
3. Ignoring the need for protection of income during a period of disability

CONCEPT CHECK 11.1

1. List three ways that group health plans are better than individually purchased plans.
2. Identify the five mechanisms available to help people pay for direct medical care costs.
3. Explain why someone might want to purchase long-term care insurance.
4. Explain how someone might replace the income lost due to illness or injury.

Sources of Protection from Direct Medical Care Costs

2 LEARNING OBJECTIVE
Distinguish among the types of protection for direct medical expenses.

A **medical care plan** is a generic name for any program that pays or provides reimbursement for direct medical care expenditures. When a medical plan is available as an employee benefit, the employer typically pays the cost for the worker (and possibly other members of the worker's immediate family) for the lowest-cost plan the employer

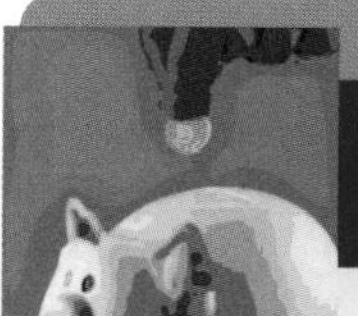

Good Money Habits in Managing Health Expenses

Make the following your money habits in managing health expenses:

1. Always maintain coverage for direct health care expenses.
2. When changing employers, consider continuing your medical care plan coverage using rights established through the COBRA law.
3. Working people should sign up for an employer-sponsored premium conversion plan and a flexible spending account for health care spending, when available, to save money on taxes.
4. If you are a frequent user of health care, reduce spending on deductibles and coinsurance by choosing an HMO or PPO.
5. Take advantage of employer-sponsored long-term disability income insurance or consider purchasing protection individually.
6. Regularly reevaluate your need for long-term care insurance against your resources for providing such care on your own.

Table 11.1 Types of Protection from Health-Related Expenses

	Type of Expense				
	Direct Medical Care			Rehabilitative and Custodial Care	Lost Income
Provider of Coverage?	Health maintenance organizations (HMOs) Medicare for those age 65 and over Medicaid for low-income/low-wealth individuals	Traditional health insurance Medicare for those age 65 and over Medicaid for low-income/low-wealth individuals	Consumer-driven health insurance plans	Long-term care insurance Medicaid for low-income/low-wealth individuals	Disability income insurance Social Security for eligible workers and their families
Services Covered?	Provide hospital, surgical, and medical services directly through their own hospital and physicians or under contract with such providers	Reimburses or pays for hospital, surgical, medical, and other health care costs	Reimburse or pay for hospital, surgical, medical, and other health care costs that exceed a high deductible of $5000 or more	Reimburses for costs associated with custodial care (not direct medical care)	Provides a monthly income to replace that lost when the insured is unable to work due to accident or injury
Payment Mode?	Charge a monthly fee on a prepaid basis	Charges monthly premiums for the insurance coverage	Charge monthly premiums for the insurance coverage	Charges monthly or annual premiums	Charges a monthly premium
Purchased By?	Individuals or by employers as an employee benefit	Individuals or by employers as an employee benefit	Individuals or by employers as an employee benefit	Individuals	Individuals or by employers as an employee benefit

offers. Employees can choose a higher-priced option or add family members to the coverage by paying an additional charge. New employees generally must make a choice among the available plans within the first few days of being hired.

Health Maintenance Organizations

health maintenance organizations (HMOs) Provide a broad range of health care services for a set monthly fee on a prepaid basis.

Health maintenance organizations (HMOs) provide a broad range of health care services for a set monthly fee on a prepaid basis. For the specific monthly fee, HMO members receive a wide array of health care services, including hospital, surgical, and preventive medical care. Some HMO plans require a small copayment of $5 to $20 for each office visit or prescription. A goal of HMOs is to catch problems early, thereby reducing the probability of subsequent high-cost medical treatment. HMO services are available to both groups and individuals.

The monthly fee charged by an HMO is based on the medical services that the average plan member would tend to use. HMOs do not put dollar limits on how much health care can be used. Instead, they list the types of medical care they will provide under the contract. HMOs are one of several types of **managed care plans.** Such

New employees must typically choose from among offered health care plans soon after being hired.

plans seek to control the conditions under which health care can be obtained. Examples of controls include preapproval of hospital admissions, restrictions on which hospital or doctor can be used, and mandates regarding the type of procedures that will be employed to treat a specific medical problem.

HMO subscribers are assigned a **primary-care physician** by the HMO or choose one from an approved list. The primary-care physician usually must order or approve referrals to specialized health care providers (for example, a cardiologist) within or outside the HMO. If the HMO itself does not provide a particular type of care, it refers the patient to a local hospital or clinic for those services. One HMO variation is the **individual practice organization (IPO),** a structure in which the HMO contracts with—rather than hires—groups of physicians. These physicians maintain their own offices in various locations around town and serve as the primary-care physicians and specialists for the HMO.

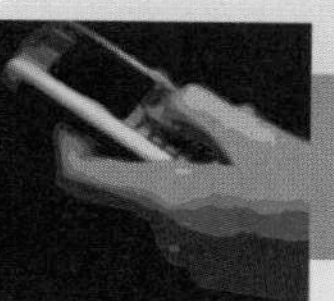

Instant Message

Making Changes in Your Group Plan

When you work for an employer that offers a group health plan, you must wait until the next **open-enrollment period** to make changes in coverage or switch among alternative plans. Open-enrollment periods occur once each year and last for about one month. Open-enrollment period requirements are generally waived for such family changes as births, adoptions, divorce, and marriage.

Traditional Health Insurance

Health insurance provides protection against financial losses resulting from illness and injury. It may cover hospital, surgical, and other medical expenditures. These coverages can be purchased separately, but most consumers and employers prefer **comprehensive health insurance** because it combines these protections into a single policy with policy limits of $1 million or more. Unlike with HMOs, where you are prepaying for health care in advance, health insurance is based on the concept of reimbursement for losses, with the patient choosing the type of care based on the advice of his or her physician. For this reason, health insurance plans are often referred to as **indemnity plans** because they compensate the insured for the cost of care received.

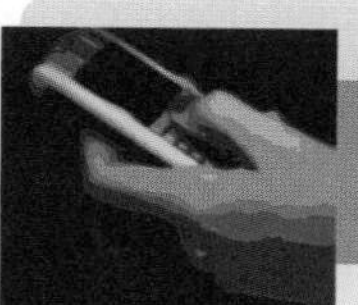

Instant Message

The Difference Between Health Insurance and HMOs

Health insurance pays for or reimburses you for your care. HMOs actually provide your care.

Health insurance plans often identify a **preferred provider organization (PPO).** A PPO is a group of medical care providers (doctors, hospitals, and other health care providers) who contract with a health insurance company to provide services at a discount. This discount is then passed along to the policyholders in the form of reductions or elimination of deductibles and coinsurance requirements if they choose the PPO providers for their medical care.

Consider the case of Dru Cameron, who works for a large marketing firm in Charlotte, North Carolina. Her firm's health insurance plan has contracted with a PPO representing a local university's teaching hospital and its affiliated physicians. Because Dru chose the university hospital for treatment of a broken ankle, she saved $150 on the $250 deductible and did not have to pay the usual 20 percent coinsurance share of office visit charges. She gave up the right to go to her family doctor, who is not a PPO member, although she could still see that physician for other health care needs in the future.

A **provider-sponsored network (PSN),** also called a **provider-sponsored association** is a group of cooperating physicians and hospitals who have banded together to offer a health insurance contract. Such networks operate primarily in rural areas, where access to HMOs may be limited. As a group, the members of the PSN coordinate and deliver health care services and manage the insurance plan financially. They contract with outside providers for medical services that are not available through members of the group.

health insurance Provides protection against financial losses resulting from illness and injury.

indemnity plan Health insurance based on reimbursement for losses with the type of care chosen by patients based upon their physicians' advice.

preferred provider organization (PPO) Group of medical care providers (doctors, hospitals, and other health care providers) who contract with a health insurance company to provide services at a discount.

consumer-driven health care Approach to medical care that assumes that knowledgeable and informed patients/employees will spend their own money more carefully than they would spend an employer's or health plan's funds.

Consumer-Driven Health Care

Consumer-driven health care is a term describing an approach to medical care that is different than that of typical HMOs and traditional health insurance. With these two latter approaches, consumers pay very little out of their own pocket for their medical care and, thus, have little incentive to minimize health care spending. The principle behind **consumer-driven health care** is that knowledgeable and informed patients/employees

Instant Message

Use the Internet to Check the Quality of Your Health Care Providers

The National Committee for Quality Assurance maintains a website that provides its ratings of HMOs, hospitals, clinics, and physicians (http://www.ncqa.org).

will spend their own money more carefully than they would spend an employer's or health plan's funds. Therefore, consumer-driven plans require higher out-of-pocket spending by consumers so that they will shop around, compare prices, pick and choose among options, and all the other things consumers normally do when making expensive purchases.

Consumer-driven plans are based upon a **high-deductible health care plan** that can either be traditional health insurance or an HMO. Deductibles can start at $1100 ($2200 for a family) but can be as high as $5000 per year. The plans will have an out-of-pocket limit of $5500 for an individual or $11,000 for a family per year. High-deductible plans have lower premiums than other plans because workers pay a larger portion of health care bills. Employers like the plans for this reason. But people who must buy their own health care plan might find the lower premiums attractive as well.

The question, then, is how to afford the high out-of-pocket cost when medical care is needed. The answer is with a **health savings account (HSA)** or a **health reimbursement account (HRA).** An HSA is a tax-deductible savings account into which individuals and/or their employers can deposit tax-sheltered funds for use to pay medical bills including deductibles and other out-of-pocket costs. The maximum annual deposit is either the annual deductible under their high-deductible plan or $2900 for an individual or $5800 for a family plan, whichever is lower. An HRA consists of funds set aside by employers to reimburse employees for qualified medical expenses. Thus, the employer helps employees pay their medical bills.

high-deductible health care plan Can either be traditional health insurance or an HMO that follows the consumer-driven health care philosophy by charging relatively high deductibles.

health savings account (HSA) Tax-deductible savings accounts into which individuals or employers can deposit tax-sheltered funds to pay medical bills.

health reimbursement account (HRA) Funds that employers set aside to reimburse employees for qualified medical expenses.

CONCEPT CHECK 11.2

1. Distinguish between HMOs and traditional health insurance.
2. Identify two benefits of selecting a preferred provider organization when seeking health care.
3. Explain the linkage between high-deductible health care plans and health savings accounts (HSAs) and health reimbursement accounts (HRAs).

Did You Know?...

How Medicare Differs from Medicaid

Medicare is funded by means of the Medicare payroll tax. This tax is paid by both workers and employers, much like the Social Security tax. Its beneficiaries include people age 65 and older who are eligible for Social Security retirement benefits, federal civilian employees age 65 and older who retired after 1982, people who are eligible for Social Security disability benefits, and individuals with kidney disorders that require kidney dialysis treatments. Medicare is divided into two parts. **Medicare Part A** is the hospitalization portion of the program; it requires no premium. **Medicare Part B** is the supplementary medical expense insurance portion for outpatient care, doctor office visits, or certain other services of the Medicare program; it requires payment of a monthly premium.

Eligibility for Medicaid is based on household income and net worth. The health services provided through this program generally include hospital, surgical, and medical care. In some states, dental care for children may be covered as well. A key feature of Medicaid is its coverage of custodial long-term and nursing home care. Elderly who have "spent down" their assets on long-term care expenses may be eligible to receive Medicaid reimbursement for a portion of their nursing home costs.

Advice from a Pro...

Be Smart When Shopping for an Individual Plan

Shopping for an individual medical care plan (a plan that is not provided through a group) requires a comparison of the many options available. You should focus your attention on three areas: (1) the cost, (2) the company, and (3) the plan itself.

The Cost

A sound health insurance plan, when purchased outside of a group, can easily cost more than $600 per month for a typical family of four. Obviously, comparison shopping is essential. When you apply for an individual medical care plan, the company's decision whether to accept you is based on a number of underwriting factors, including your age, gender, occupation, family and personal health history, and physical condition. Each of these factors has a bearing on the likelihood of health-related expenditures and, therefore, the cost.

Medical information bureaus (similar to credit bureaus) maintain files on insurance applicants.* Both medical and nonmedical information is maintained in these files. If you are charged more or turned down for credit or insurance because of information in such a file, you should know your consumer rights. If you were denied coverage or charged extra, you have the right to be told that the information came from a medical information bureau. You can then request a copy of the report to verify the accuracy of the information.

The Company

It is important to choose a financially sound health care company. Wise financial planners always ask about the percentage of premiums collected by an insurance company that is subsequently paid out to reimburse the losses of the participants. The **claims ratio (payout ratio)** formula is

$$\text{Claims ratio} = \frac{\text{losses paid}}{\text{premiums collected}} \quad (11.1)$$

Top companies typically have claims ratios that exceed 90 percent. At the other extreme are companies (especially those that sell hospital indemnity and dread disease insurance by mail, over the telephone, or through newspaper inserts) that have claims ratios of less than 25 percent. The lower the claims ratio, the lower the return (the actual benefits) to the policyholder on the premium dollar paid.

The Plan

The smart way to compare medical care plans is to set some criteria for judging whether a policy provides the needed coverage. The plans that do provide the needed coverage (and have high claims ratios) can then be compared on a price basis. No plan should be purchased "sight unseen." If an agent or company will not allow you to study a plan for a few days, buy your policy elsewhere.

Holly Hunts
Montana State University

*To obtain a copy of your report ($8 or free within 30 days of an adverse report), write the Medical Information Bureau at P.O. Box 105, Essex Station, Boston, MA 02112; call (617) 426-3660 for an application; or visit www.mib.com.

Making Sense of Your Medical Plan Benefits

3 LEARNING OBJECTIVE
Describe the general benefits and limitations of medical care plans.

You can save yourself considerable confusion, delay, and money if you understand your health plan benefits before illness or injury strikes. If you have group plan, you will receive a **certificate of insurance** that outlines your benefits. If you have purchased a plan on your own, you should become familiar with your health insurance policy or your HMO contract. Here are some questions to ask yourself and background information to understand what you find in these documents.

medical information bureaus Similar to credit bureaus, these sources provide medical information to insurance companies.

certificate of insurance Paper or booklet that outlines group health insurance benefits.

What Types of Care Are Covered?

The typical medical care plan covers hospital room and board expenses, surgical procedures both as an inpatient and outpatient, prescription drugs, diagnostic tests, visits to the doctor's office, and many other aspects of health care. Dental and vision care are generally not covered. You can buy separate **dental expense insurance**

Instant Message

What If Your Employer Does Not Offer a Plan?

A high-deductible plan in conjunction with a health savings account can be a low-cost option for people who do not have access to a medical care plan through their job. The monthly premium might be about $200.

(possibly as a group plan through your employer) to provide reimbursement for dental care expenses. Orthodontic treatment is typically excluded. High deductibles and coinsurance requirements and low policy limits can make dental plans less beneficial than they might appear. **Vision care insurance** provides reimbursement for eye examinations and purchase of glasses and contact lenses. Vision care insurance is typically written on a group basis as an employee benefit. For an individual, vision care insurance is probably not a good buy because the highest expenses for eye care arise out of diseases and injuries to the eyes, which would be covered under basic medical care plans.

Health plans contain provisions that exclude coverage for certain **preexisting conditions.** These are medical conditions or symptoms that were known to the participant or diagnosed within a certain time period, usually one or two years, before the effective date of the plan. Preexisting conditions can be excluded for a period of time after a plan goes into effect or, possibly, permanently. Group plans exclude fewer preexisting conditions than individual plans. Plans may also dictate waiting periods for specific types of expenses. For example, maternity benefits often have a one-year waiting period.

preexisting conditions Medical conditions or symptoms that the plan participant knew about or had been diagnosed within a certain time period before the plan effective date.

Who Is Covered?

Medical care plans can be written to cover an individual, a family, or a group. Few misunderstandings arise when an individual is the focus of the coverage, but family policies can be more complex. Generally, a family consists of a parent or parents and dependent children. Are children who are born while the plan is in effect automatically covered from the moment of birth? What about stepchildren? At what age are children no longer covered? These questions must be answered to ensure that all family members receive adequate protection.

Did You Know?...

It Is a Bad Idea to Be Young and Uninsured

Many college students lose their medical care coverage when they graduate because they are no longer eligible as a family member under a parent's plan. You might be tempted to go without coverage for a time because of its high cost, you expect to have a job soon that will provide coverage, or you are healthy. This latter reason is problematic because young people do get sick or are injured. For example, your car insurance will cover only a small portion of your medical bills if you are seriously injured in an accident that you cause. So what should you do?

1. Try to stay on a parent's plan. Some states require companies to allow you to do this for a few months. If it is an option via a plan's COBRA provisions, you would need to pay the premium.
2. Buy short-term health insurance. Coverage for less than $100 per month is available. These plans are not as comprehensive as you might like, but they do provide help.
3. Buy a high-deductible plan. For people in a low tax bracket, an HSA is not much benefit, but the high-deductible plan can pay for catastrophic situations.

Going without health insurance has an added risk. If you develop a serious medical condition while uninsured, it will be considered a preexisting condition and make coverage difficult or impossible to obtain in the future. Bottom line ... stay covered.

The question of who is covered under a group plan is similarly important. All group members are usually covered, but new members may have to endure a waiting period before receiving protection. If the group includes the employees of a business, different protection may be offered for full-time and part-time employees. The family of the group member may be covered, but, once again, the definition of "family" must be understood.

Did You Know?...

About Supplemental Health Plans

Accident and dread disease health insurance is often purchased by people who have no other medical care plan or fear that their medical care plan will fall short of their needs. **Accident insurance** pays a specific amount per day—for example, $100 for a hospital stay arising out of an accident—or a specific amount for the loss of certain limbs or body parts—for example, $2000 for the loss of a finger or an arm. **Dread disease insurance** provides reimbursement for medical expenses arising out of the occurrence of a specific disease, such as cancer. These plans are typically highly overpriced and provide benefits much less generous than implied in sales promotions. Since the average daily cost for a hospital stay is more than $1200, these policies cover very little.

When Does Coverage Begin and End?

Individual and group medical care plans are usually written on an annual basis. An annual plan beginning on January 1 will start at 12:00 A.M. that day and end at 11:59 P.M. on December 31. Any illness that begins during the year will be covered. But will coverage continue if the plan expires while you are in the hospital? The answer is usually yes. Similarly, a surgical procedure performed after a plan expires but for an illness or injury for which treatment was originally begun during the plan period may be covered.

Health care plans must be renewed each year. If you are in a group plan, you can renew your participation during the plan's open-enrollment period. Renewal of individual plans is handled in one of three ways. **Optionally renewable policies** may be canceled or changed by the plan provider but only at the time of expiration and renewal, often with 30 days' notice. **Guaranteed renewable policies** must be continued in force as long as the policyholder pays the required premium. Premiums may change but only if the change applies to an entire class of participants rather than to an individual participant. Guaranteed renewability is recommended for medical care plans and long-term care insurance. **Noncancelable policies** must be continued in force without premium changes up to age 65 as long as the participant pays the required premium. Noncancelable policies are recommended when buying disability income insurance.

guaranteed renewable policies Must be continued in force as long as the policyholder pays the required premium.

Did You Know?...

How to Avoid Duplication of Employee Health Care Benefits

Dual-income households often have overlapping health care benefits. For example, both Harry and Belinda Johnson's employers provide partially subsidized family health insurance plans as employee benefits. The Johnsons chose to be covered under Belinda's policy because it provides more protection and is less expensive. Belinda's coverage is fully paid for and she can add Harry to the plan for $125 per month.

Harry's employer offers a flexible approach toward providing employee benefits. Employees are provided with $800 per month to be used for any of the employee benefits available from a menu of benefits offered by the employer. If Harry chose his employer's medical care plan, he would need to pay $375 of the $800 for this benefit. He could use the remaining $425 for life insurance, dental insurance, disability income insurance, or an additional contribution into his 401(k) plan. Harry has decided to forgo his health insurance and will pay the extra $125 to be covered under Belinda's plan. As a result, he has $675 ($800 − $125) available for other options. Harry decided to sign up for disability and dental expense insurance and have the remainder go into his 401(k) plan.

How Much Must You Pay Out of Your Own Pocket?

Medical care plans contain provisions that specify the level of payments for covered expenses.

Deductibles **Deductibles** are clauses in medical care plans that require you to pay an initial portion of medical expenses annually before receiving reimbursement. A deductible of $200 per year, for example, would mean that the patient must pay the first $200 of the medical costs for the year. Family plans warrant special attention. Generally, they include a deductible for each family member (again, perhaps $200 per year) with a maximum family deductible (perhaps $500 per year). Once the deductible payments for individual family members reach the maximum family deductible ($500 in this example), further individual deductibles will be waived.

Copayments A **copayment,** which is a variation of a deductible, requires you to pay a specific dollar amount each time you have a specific covered expense item. A copayment is often required for visits to the doctor's office and prescription drugs. For example, you might have to pay $25 for each prescription, with the insurer paying the remainder. A copayment differs from a deductible in that it might require that you pay $35 for each office visit even after the deductible is met.

Coinsurance A **coinsurance clause** requires you to pay a proportion of any loss suffered. The typical share is 80/20, with the insurer paying the larger percentage. Usually, a coinsurance cap limits the annual out-of-pocket payments required of the patient when meeting the coinsurance. The following example illustrates how a deductible of $250 and an 80/20 coinsurance provision with a $1000 coinsurance cap work together to determine the coverage for an $8760 health care bill. Because the deductible is the responsibility of the insured party, the patient pays the first $250. The coinsurance ratio is applied to the remaining $8510 ($8760 − $250) until the portion paid by the patient reaches the coinsurance cap. Thus, $1000 is covered by the insured and $4000 by the insurer. The additional expenses of $3510 ($8510 − $1000 − $4000) are covered 100 percent by the insurance company up to the overall limits of coverage (perhaps $100,000). In this example, the insured party will pay $1250 ($250 deductible + $1000 coinsurance) and the insurer will pay $7510 ($4000 coinsurance + $3510 remaining charges).

Instant Message

Mental Health Is Treated Differently

Under many health care plans, mental health care has lower policy limits, perhaps $1000 per year; higher copayments; and higher coinsurance requirements, perhaps 50 percent/50 percent. Some states have prohibited this differential treatment.

Instant Message

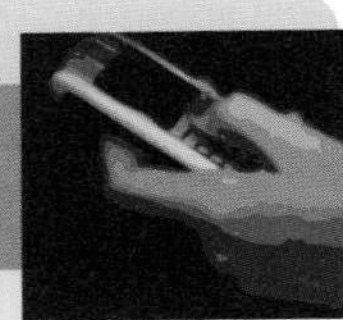

Health Care Plans Have a Grace Period

Health plans contain provisions for a grace period (typically 30 days), which prevents the lapse of a policy if a payment is late. The policy remains fully in force during the grace period but only if the insured pays the premium before the end of the grace period.

Instant Message

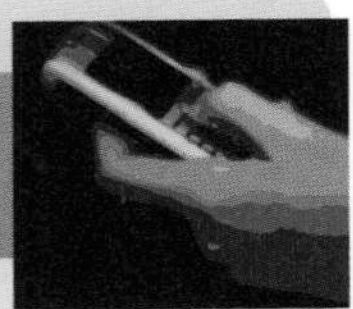

Health Care Reform Is Coming!

Several states, including Massachusetts, Vermont, and California, are at the forefront of efforts to make sure that all citizens are covered by a medical care plan. The goal is to make health care available and affordable for all.

Policy Limits Policy limits specify the maximum dollar amounts that a health insurance plan will pay to reimburse a covered loss. To illustrate policy limits for a health insurance plan, we will consider the case of Karl Gruenfeld, an unmarried electrician from Las Vegas, New Mexico.

- **Item limits** specify the maximum reimbursement for a particular health care expense. Karl's policy contains a $75 maximum per X ray. Karl suffered a heart attack and had X-ray expenses of $840 (seven sets of X rays at $120 each). The policy will pay $525 (7 × $75) of this expense, and Karl must pay the remaining $315.

deductibles Clauses in medical care plans that require you to pay an initial portion of medical expenses annually before receiving reimbursement.

copayment A variation of a deductible, requires you to pay a specific dollar amount each time you use your benefits for a specific covered expense item.

- **Episode limits** specify the maximum payment for health care expenses arising from a single episode of illness or injury, with each episode being considered separately. Karl's policy contains an episode limit of $25,000 for all covered expenses. After his heart attack, Karl was hospitalized for two weeks and incurred $31,223 in medical charges (including the covered portion of the X rays). His policy will pay $25,000 of these charges. One month later, Karl suffered burns in a cooking accident at his home and was hospitalized for two days, incurring hospital care costs of $4310. His policy will pay these expenses in full because the second hospitalization is considered a separate episode.
- Disputes may also center on whether a recurrence of an illness represents a separate episode. A **recurring clause** clarifies conditions under which a recurrence of an illness is considered a continuation of the first episode or a separate episode. If the recurrence is considered a separate episode, the deductible must be paid, but reimbursement will be available up to the full episode limit. If the recurrence is considered a continuation of the original episode, the second deductible will not apply, but the loss may exceed the episode limit.
- **Annual limits** specify the maximum payment for covered expenses occurring within one year. Consider Karl's heart attack and burn hospitalizations. If his policy had contained a $50,000 annual limit, Karl would have used $29,310 ($25,000 + $4310) of this amount and would have only $20,690 ($50,000 − $29,310) remaining for the year.
- A **lifetime** or **aggregate limit** places an overall maximum on the total amount of reimbursement available under a policy. If Karl's policy has an aggregate limit of $500,000, no more than $500,000 will be reimbursed for all medical expenses that Karl incurs during the life of the policy.

Coordination of Benefits A **coordination-of-benefits clause** prevents you from collecting insurance benefits that exceed the loss suffered. Such a clause designates the order in which plans will pay benefits if multiple plans apply to a loss. The primary plan is the first applied to any loss when more than one plan provides coverage. If it fails to reimburse 100 percent of the loss, then any secondary (or excess) plans will be applied in order until the loss is fully paid or until benefits are exhausted, whichever occurs first.

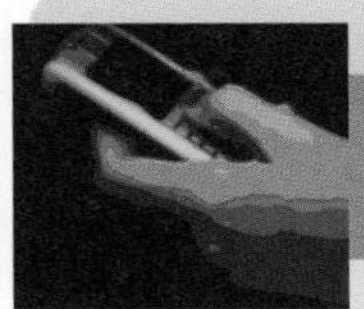

Instant Message

HMOs Do Not Have Dollar Limits

HMO plans generally do not have maximum policy limits specified in dollars. Instead, they limit the health care services they will provide for a specified diagnosis.

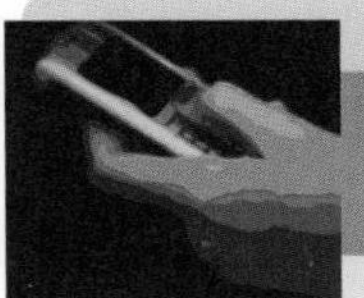

Instant Message

Know Your Limits

Aggregate dollar limits are always higher than time period limits, which are in turn higher than episode limits. A policy with high aggregate limits may seem attractive, but it may not be a good buy if the episode limits are too low. Analyze each limit separately to determine whether it provides sufficient protection.

lifetime/aggregate limit Places an overall maximum on the total amount of reimbursement available under a policy.

coordination-of-benefits clause Prevents you from collecting insurance benefits that exceed the loss suffered by noting the order in which plans will pay if you are covered by multiple plans.

CONCEPT CHECK 11.3

1. What are preexisting conditions and how do they affect coverage under health plans?
2. Distinguish among a deductible, a copayment, and coinsurance.
3. Explain COBRA rights and portability rights that apply when you leave a job that has a group medical care plan.
4. Distinguish among item limits, episode limits, time period limits, and aggregate limits as used in medical care plans.
5. Distinguish among optionally renewable, guaranteed renewable, and noncancelable health care plans.
6. List three ways you can save on taxes when paying for health care or a health care plan.

Did You Know?...

The Tax Consequences of Managing Health Expenses

The Internal Revenue Code allows three principal avenues for reducing income taxes when you spend your own money on medical care premiums and health care expenses:

1. Many employees may save on taxes when they use **premium conversion plans** to pay their health care insurance premiums. With premium conversion, the employee's share of the premiums is paid with pre-tax dollars; those amounts are not included when the employer reports the employee's income to the IRS.
2. Many employers offer **flexible spending arrangements,** allowing employees to place a portion of their salary into an account that is used to pay some of their health care expenditures, including employee-paid health plan premiums. Flexible spending accounts are a "use it or lose it" proposition. Thus, you should set aside only an amount that you are sure you will use.
3. Health care expenditures (including a portion of certain long-term care insurance premiums) can be used as itemized deductions on one's income tax return. Only the amount that exceeds 7.5 percent of the adjusted gross income is deductible. Self-employed people may deduct (as a business expense, not an itemized deduction) the cost of medical expense premiums for themselves and their dependents.

Advice from a Pro...

Maintain Your Medical Care Plan Between Jobs

What happens when you no longer work for an employer that offers a group medical care plan and you want to continue the coverage? You can assert your **COBRA rights** (Consolidated Omnibus Budget Reconciliation Act of 1985). These rules allow you to remain a member of a group health plan for as long as 18 months if you worked for an employer with more than 20 workers. COBRA applies to you and to any of your dependents who had been covered under the employer's plan. COBRA rights apply to your dependents for 36 months. These rights must be exercised within 60 days after the termination of employment, and you must pay the full premiums (including both the employee's and the employer's portions) plus a 2 percent administrative fee.

Eligibility to remain under the group plan eventually will run out. Federal law also mandates a **portability option** that allows you to convert your group coverage to individual coverage within 180 days before COBRA ends, if that is part of the employer's plan originally or as amended. Your individual policy premiums will be higher but the waiting period and preexisting condition provisions will not apply.

Martin Carrigan
The University of Findlay, Ohio

Planning for Long-Term Care

4 LEARNING OBJECTIVE
Explain how to protect yourself from the expenses for long-term care.

Many health care episodes include a period of time when the patient no longer needs skilled medical care but does need assistance to a degree that requires confinement in a nursing home or special help at home. This need is especially prevalent with the extremely elderly and patients with certain conditions such as Alzheimer's disease. Such costs are not covered by HMOs, health insurance, or Medicare because the care is usually considered "not medically necessary" by these providers.

Factors to assess when considering a long-term care policy include the following:

1. **The degree of impairment required for benefits to begin.** Insurance companies use the inability to perform a certain number of **activities of daily living (ADLs)** as a criterion for deciding when the insured becomes eligible for long-term care benefits. Typically, a policy pays benefits when a person cannot perform two or three ADLs without assistance. The ADLs commonly used in this type of decision making are bathing, bladder control, dressing oneself, eating without assistance, toileting (moving on and off the toilet), and transferring (getting in and out of bed). Because bathing is often one of the first ADLs that is lost, a policy that does not list bathing as a criterion makes it more difficult to reach the threshold at which benefits become available.

activities of daily living (ADLs) Insurance companies use the inability to perform a certain number of such activities as a criterion for deciding when the insured becomes eligible for long-term care benefits.

2. **The level of care covered.** The levels of nursing home care are usually categorized three ways. **Skilled nursing care** is intended for people who need intensive care, meaning 24-hour-a-day supervision and treatment by a registered nurse, under the direction of a doctor. **Intermediate care** is appropriate for people who do not require around-the-clock nursing but who are not able to live alone. **Custodial care** is suitable for many people who do not need skilled nursing care but who nevertheless require supervision (for example, help with eating or personal hygiene). Insurance companies' definitions of these levels of care may differ and must be considered when policies are evaluated. Although the largest expenses related to long-term care result from a stay in a nursing home, many people are able to remain in their homes with the assistance of visiting nurses, therapists, and even housekeepers. Long-term care policies can be written to cover such in-home care.

skilled nursing care Intended for prople who need intensive care, meaning 24-hour-a-day supervision and treatment by a registered nurse, under the direction of a doctor.

3. **The person's age.** The younger the person when the policy is purchased, the lower the premium as the odds of needing care increase with age. The trade-off lies between buying young and paying premiums for many years versus waiting to purchase a policy, at which time it may be difficult to afford coverage because of preexisting conditions and consequently high policy costs.
4. **The benefit amount.** Long-term care plans are generally written to provide a specific dollar benefit per day of care. If the cost per day for nursing homes in your geographic area is typically $140, you might buy a policy for $110 per day, thereby coinsuring for a portion of the expenses.
5. **The benefit period.** Although it is possible to buy a policy with lifetime benefits, this option can be very expensive. The average nursing home stay is about two and one-half years. A policy with a three-year limit might cost one-third less than a policy with a lifetime benefit period.
6. **The waiting period.** Policies can pay benefits from the first day of nursing home care or they can include a waiting period. Selecting a 30-day or 90-day waiting period can significantly reduce premiums.
7. **Inflation protection.** If a policy is purchased prior to age 60, the buyer faces a significant risk in that inflation may render the daily benefit woefully inadequate when care is ultimately needed. Some policies increase the daily benefit by 4 or

Did You Know?...

Workers' Comp Pays If You Are Hurt on the Job

If you are injured on the job or become ill as a direct result of your employment, state law requires your employer to pay any resulting medical costs. **Workers' compensation insurance** covers employers for liability losses for injury or disease suffered by employees that result from employment-related causes. The benefits to the employee include health care, recuperative care, replacement of lost income, and, if necessary, rehabilitation. Thus, workers' compensation insurance covers the full range of health-related losses. Because only those losses resulting from work-related accidents are covered and benefits are limited, workers' compensation can only supplement your total health insurance plan.

benefit amount Long-term care plans are generally written to provide a specific dollar benefit per day of care.

benefit period Length of time that the individual for whom a policy is written would likely need the care.

5 percent per year to adjust for inflation, but this protection adds considerably to the premium. The younger your age when a policy is purchased, the more you need inflation protection.

CONCEPT CHECK 11.4

1. Describe the protections provided by long-term care insurance.
2. Distinguish between the benefit period and the waiting period for a long-term care policy.
3. List three aspects of long-term care insurance that affect the cost of a policy.

Protecting Your Income During Disability

5 LEARNING OBJECTIVE
Develop a plan for protecting your income when you cannot work due to disability.

A number of resources are available for income protection during a period of disability. Many U.S. workers have sick-pay benefits that can help ease the burden of a short period of disability, such as four weeks. Some employers offer group disability income insurance, although typically the coverage lasts for only a short term (less than two years). In addition, many pension plans provide benefits to workers who become disabled while still employed. Such benefits plans, however, fall far short of fully meeting the needs of young and middle-age workers, who may have accumulated only a small amount of retirement funds.

A young person with no dependents might need more disability insurance than life insurance.

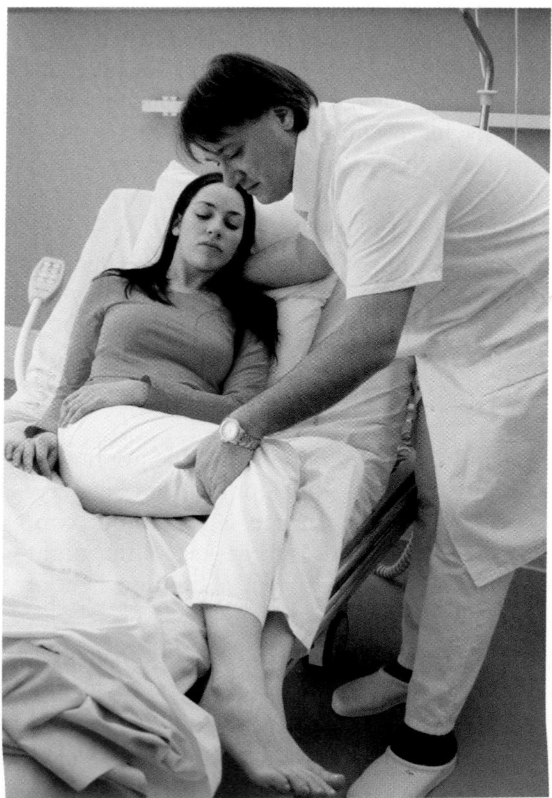

Disability income insurance replaces a portion of the income lost when you cannot work because of illness or injury. Although it is probably the most overlooked type of insurance, it is vitally important for all workers. For example, a 22-year-old without dependents would probably need no life insurance but would likely need disability insurance to support himself during a period of disability.

disability income insurance Replaces a portion of the income lost when you cannot work because of illness or injury.

Social Security disability income insurance is designed to help replace a portion of the lost income of eligible disabled workers. Benefits begin after a five-month waiting period and the disability must be total. That is, the recipient must not be able to engage in any substantial, gainful activity. Social Security disability income protection may provide more than $20,000 annually in tax-free income to the family of a fully insured disabled worker. See Appendix B at the end of the book or the *Garman/Forgue* website for an illustration of how to estimate these benefits, or visit www.ssa.gov/top10.html.

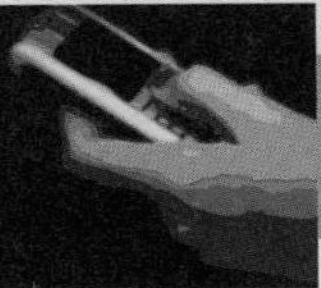

Instant Message

Disability Income or Life Insurance?

At age 22, a person's chances of becoming disabled for at least three months are seven times greater than his or her chances of dying. Disability income insurance is more important for young, single adults than life insurance.

Level of Need

The first question to ask when contemplating disability income insurance is, "How much protection do I need?" The dollar limits on disability income policies are written either in increments of $100 per month or as a percentage of monthly income. Most companies limit policy coverage to 60 to 80 percent of the insured's after-tax earnings.

Decision-Making Worksheet

Determining Disability Income Insurance Needs

The determination of disability insurance needs begins with your current monthly after-tax income. From this figure, subtract the amounts you would receive from Social Security disability and other sources of disability income. The resulting figure will provide an estimate of extra coverage needed.

Decision Factor		Example	Your Figures
1.	Current monthly after-tax income	$2100	_____
2.	Minus previous established disability income protections		
	(a) Monthly Social Security disability benefits	750	_____
	(b) Monthly benefit from employer-provided disability insurance	600	_____
	(c) Monthly benefit from private disability insurance	_____	_____
	(d) Monthly benefit from other government disability insurance	_____	_____
	Total Subtraction	−1350	_____
3.	Estimated monthly disability income insurance needs	$ 750	_____

Determining the amount of protection needed is challenging because some sources of help may not actually be available for all disabilities. A less severe disability that does not qualify for Social Security disability income insurance may create a need for more disability insurance than a more severe disability that does qualify for Social Security. And employer-based disability benefits tend to cover short-term, but not long-term, disability. It is smart to complete the calculations in the Decision-Making Worksheet, "Determining Disability Income Insurance Needs" (page 313). You can use the figure obtained in the worksheet as a starting point when shopping for disability income insurance protection.

Important Disability Income Insurance Policy Provisions

Once you have estimated your level of need, you can begin your search for a disability income insurance policy. Look first for the major policy provisions, discussed in the following paragraphs, that meet your needs. Be aware, however, that disability income insurance policies are very complicated. Do not rely on the verbal assurances of the agent selling the policy. Do your own analysis and, if necessary, seek the advice of a financial planner.

Waiting Period The **waiting period (elimination period)** in a disability income policy is the time period between the onset of the disability and the date that disability benefits begin. Because disability income benefits are paid monthly, the first check will not arrive until 30 days after the end of the waiting period.

own-occupation policy Provides benefits if you can no longer perform the occupation you had at the time you became disabled.

any-occupation policy Provides full benefits only if you cannot perform any occupation.

residual clause of disability income policy Feature of own-occupation policies that allows for some reduced level of disability income benefits when a partial—rather than full—disability strikes.

Benefit Period The **benefit period** in a disability income policy is the maximum period of time for which benefits will be paid. It begins when the elimination period ends. The benefit period is usually stated in years but may instead state a specific age when benefits will cease. Most disability income policies will not pay past age 65.

Degree of Disability Policies can be written on an "own-occupation" or "any-occupation" basis. An **own-occupation policy** will provide benefits if you can no longer perform the occupation you had at the time you became disabled. An **any-occupation policy** will provide full benefits only if you cannot perform any occupation. In effect, an any-occupation policy is an income replacement policy, as it makes up a portion of the difference between what you were earning prior to becoming disabled and what you can earn while disabled. Own-occupation policies are more generous and, therefore, cost more. Some policies provide own-occupation coverage during the first two years of a disability, then switch to an any-occupation basis with income replacement for the remaining years of the benefits. Such **split-definition policies** are likely to provide benefits for rehabilitation and retraining at insurance company expense.

A **residual clause** is a feature of own-occupation policies that allows for some reduced level of disability income benefits when a partial—rather than full—disability occurs. Consider the case of Françoise LaDeux, a criminal lawyer in Providence, Rhode Island, who purchased a disability policy offering a benefit of $3000 per month. Françoise later developed multiple sclerosis and was forced to cut back her workload by 50 percent, thereby taking a 50 percent pay cut. Her disability policy had a residual clause, so she received $1500 (0.50 × $3000) per month during her disability.

Instant Message

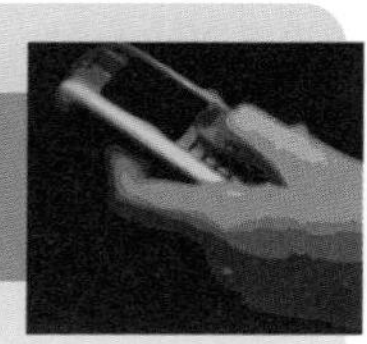

Life Insurance Premiums While Disabled

When you buy life insurance, make sure the policy allows you to waive making premiums when you are disabled.

Did You Know?...

How to Affordably Manage Health-Related Risk

Recall from Chapter 10 that it is smart to insure against the losses you cannot afford and handle more affordable losses on your own. This large-loss principle should be your guide for health-related risks as well. Here is how to apply it:

1. If you do not have access to a health care plan at work and have limited resources to buy a medical care plan on your own, you can use a high-deductible health care plan in conjunction with a health savings account (HSA) (see page 304). This will affordably protect you against catastrophic direct medical costs.
2. Select a long benefit period for both your disability income and long-term care insurance needs. For an equivalent dollar amount, you can buy many more years of protection by extending the waiting period only slightly as illustrated graphically here.

For $X you might buy a plan with a short waiting period (WP) and a short benefit period (BP):

WP	BP	Coverage Has Run Out

Even better, for the same $X you might buy plan with a slightly longer waiting period (WP) and a much longer benefit period (BP):

WP	BP	Coverage Has Run Out

Social Security Rider If you have figured your disability income insurance needs assuming that you would receive Social Security benefits, you will find yourself with inadequate protection if your Social Security application is denied. To provide an extra dollar amount of protection if you fail to qualify for Social Security disability benefits (70 percent of all applicants are rejected), a **Social Security rider** may be added to your policy. Consider the case of Karen Gifford, a florist from Urbana, Illinois. Karen determined that her disability insurance needs would be $1400 per month after assuming that she would receive $1000 from Social Security if she were to become disabled. She could have purchased a $2400-per-month policy and removed all uncertainty, but the premium would have been more than she could afford. Instead, she bought a $1400 policy with a $1000 Social Security rider for a premium savings of 30 percent.

Social security rider Provides an extra dollar amount of protection if you fail to qualify for Social Security disability benefits (70 percent of all applicants are rejected).

Cost-of-Living Adjustments You might want to seek out policies with a cost-of-living clause, which will increase your benefit amount to keep up with inflation. You might also consider buying a policy that limits benefits to a percentage of income rather than a specific dollar amount per month. With such a policy, your potential monthly benefit would increase automatically as your income increases.

CONCEPT CHECK 11.5

1. Explain how you determine your level of need for disability income insurance.
2. Identify the major policy provisions to consider when purchasing disability income insurance.
3. Distinguish between any-occupation and own-occupation disability income insurance plans.
4. Describe how you might adjust the waiting period on a disability income insurance policy in order to affordably obtain a longer benefit period.

What Do You Recommend Now?

Now that you have read the chapter on medical care planning, what do you recommend to Danielle DiMartino in the case at the beginning of the chapter regarding:

1. Choosing among the four alternatives available to her?
2. Danielle's concerns about providing for her mother's health care needs?
3. How Danielle can cover her long-term care and disability income risk?

Big Picture Summary of Learning Objectives

1 Identify ways that people can manage the financial burdens resulting from illness or injury.

Health-related losses include the cost of direct medical care, the cost of rehabilitation and custodial care, and the lost income when one is ill or injured. Protection from the costs of direct medical care is provided by a medical care plan. Long-term care insurance can protect you from rehabilitation and custodial care costs. Disability income insurance can replace income lost while disabled.

2 Distinguish among the types of protection for direct medical expenses.

HMOs, traditional health insurance, and consumer-driven health plans address the need for direct medical care. HMOs provide medical care on a prepaid basis. Health insurance will reimburse you or pay your medical bills directly. Consumer-driven health care plans require that consumers pay a higher portion of the costs out of pocket. Health savings accounts provide a tax-sheltered way to save up the funds to pay these costs. Health reimbursement accounts allow an employer to help pay these costs for an employee.

3 Describe the general benefits and limitations of medical care plans.

Health care policies contain language that outlines coverage in general and, more important, describes the limitations and conditions that determine the level of protection afforded under the plan. Some of the more important plan provisions include what types of care are covered, who is covered under the plan, and the time period for the coverage. Important limitations on coverage include deductibles and copayments, coinsurance requirements, and policy limits.

4 Explain how to protect yourself from the expenses for long-term care.

Long-term care insurance provides a per-day dollar reimbursement when the insured person must stay in a nursing home or other long-term care facility. It is not designed to provide medical care protection, as that coverage is available through other plans such as an HMO, private insurance, or Medicare/Medicaid. Medicaid does provide long-term care benefits, but Medicare does not.

5 Develop a plan for protecting your income when you cannot work due to disability.

Disability income insurance replaces a portion of the income lost when you cannot work as a result of illness or injury. The amount you need is equal to your monthly after-tax income less any benefits to which you are entitled (for example, Social Security). By selecting among various policy provisions, you can tailor a policy that fills any gaps in your existing disability protection.

Let's Talk About It

1. Are you covered by a medical care plan? If so, what do you see as the largest potential for losses if you become ill or injured? How well do you understand the plan?

2. HMO plans and health insurance plans take different approaches to health care. What are the major differences between the two types of plans? Which plan would you prefer for your own health care protection?
3. Are you covered by a long-term care insurance plan? What would happen if you became so incapacitated that such care was necessary? What could you do?
4. Are you covered by disability income insurance? What would happen if you were unable to work for two or three years because of illness or injury?

Do the Numbers

1. Christina Haley of Rockford, Illinois, age 61, recently suffered a severe stroke. She was in intensive care for 12 days and was hospitalized for 18 more days. After being discharged from the hospital, she spent 45 days in a nursing home for medically necessary nursing and rehabilitative care. Christina had a comprehensive health insurance plan through her employer. The policy had a $1000 deductible, a $50,000 episode limit, and a $250,000 aggregate limit with a 80/20 coinsurance clause with a $2000 coinsurance cap. Christina's policy covered the medically necessary services performed in a nursing home setting. Her total medical bill was $125,765.
   (a) How much of Christina's expenses were paid by her insurance policy?
   (b) How much did Christina pay?
2. Michael Howitt of Berkley, Michigan, recently had his gallbladder removed. His total bill for this event, which was his only health care expense for the year, came to $13,890. His health insurance plan has a $500 annual deductible and an 80/20 coinsurance provision. The cap on Michael's coinsurance share is $2000.
   (a) How much of the bill will Michael pay?
   (b) How much of the bill will be paid by Michael's insurance?

Financial Planning Cases

Case 1
A New Employee Ponders Disability Insurance

Jim Napier of Indiana, Pennsylvania, recently took a new job as a manufacturer's representative for an aluminum castings company. While looking over his employee benefits materials, he discovered that his employer would provide 10 sick days per year, and he can accumulate these to a maximum of 60 sick days if any go unused in a given year. In addition, his employer provides a $1000-per-month, short-term, one-year total disability policy. When he called the employee benefits office, Jim found that he might qualify for $500 per month in Social Security disability benefits if he became unable to work. Jim earns a base salary of $2000 per month and expects to earn about that same amount in commissions, for an average after-tax income of $3100 per month. After considering this information, Jim became understandably concerned that a disability might destroy his financial future.

(a) What is the level of Jim's short-term, one-year disability insurance needs?
(b) What is the level of Jim's long-term disability insurance needs?
(c) Help Jim select from among the important disability insurance policy provisions to design a disability insurance program tailored to his needs.

Case 2
A CPA Selects a Medical Care Plan

Your friend Taliesha Jackson of Stillwater, Oklahoma, recently changed to a new job as a CPA in a moderate-size accounting firm. Knowing that you were taking a personal finance course, she asked your advice about selecting the best health insurance plan. Her employer offered five options. In addition, she could open a flexible spending arrangement and pay any premiums she must pay through a premium conversion plan:

- **Option A:** A comprehensive health insurance plan with a $500 annual deductible and an 80 percent/20 percent coinsurance clause with a $2000 out-of-pocket limit. The policy has a $500,000 lifetime limit. Taliesha must pay $60 per month toward this plan.
- **Option B:** Same as option A except that a PPO is associated with the plan. If Taliesha agrees to have services provided by the PPO, her annual deductible drops to $100 and the coinsurance clause is waived. As an incentive to get employees to select option B, Taliesha's employer will provide dental expense insurance worth about $40 per month.
- **Option C:** A comprehensive health insurance plan with a $200 annual deductible and a 90 percent/10 percent coinsurance clause with a $1000 out-of-pocket limit. The major medical policy has a $1 million lifetime limit. Taliesha must pay $150 per month toward the cost of this plan.

- **Option D:** Membership in an HMO. Taliesha will have to contribute $40 extra each month if she chooses this option.
- **Option E:** A consumer-driven health plan at no monthly cost to Taliesha. The annual deductible is $3000. There is a 90 percent/10 percent coinsurance provision. The annual out-of-pocket maximum is $5000. Her employer offers a $1000 health reimbursement account, and if she chooses, Taliesha can set up a health savings account to help her pay her expenses during the year.

(a) To help her make a decision, Taliesha has asked you to list two positive points and two negative points about each plan. Prepare such a list.

(b) Why might Taliesha's employer provide an incentive of dental insurance if she chooses option B?

(c) Which plan would you recommend to Taliesha? Why?

Case 3
The Hernandezes Face the Possibility of Long-Term Care

Victor Hernandez recently learned that his uncle has Alzheimer's disease. While discussing this tragedy with Maria, he realized that two of his grandparents probably had the disease, although no formal diagnosis was ever made. As a result, Victor and Maria have become interested in how they might protect themselves from the financial effects of long-term health care.

(a) What factors should the Hernandezes consider as they shop for long-term care protection?

(b) Victor is still in his 40s. How does his age affect their decisions related to long-term care protection?

Case 4
The Johnsons Consider Buying Disability Insurance

Although Belinda's employer offers a generous employee benefit program, it does not provide disability income protection other than 8 sick days per year, which may accumulate to 20 days if Belinda does not use them. Harry also has no disability income insurance. Although both have worked long enough to qualify for Social Security disability benefits, Belinda has estimated that Harry would receive about $640 and she would receive about $800 per month if they qualified for Social Security. Harry and Belinda realize that they could not maintain their current living standards on only one salary. Thus, the need for disability income insurance has become evident even though they probably cannot afford such protection at this time. In fact, they chose not to purchase the disability waiver of premium option when they purchased their life insurance. Advise them on the following points:

(a) Use the Decision-Making Worksheet on page 313 to determine how much disability insurance Harry and Belinda each need. Use the December salary figures from Table 3.3 on page 69. To determine the amount of taxes and Social Security paid by each, assume that Harry, whose salary represents approximately 42 percent of their total income, paid a comparable percentage of the taxes.

(b) Use the information on pages 314–315 to advise the Johnsons about their selections related to the following major policy provisions:
1. Elimination period
2. Benefit period
3. Residual clause
4. Social Security rider
5. Cost-of-living adjustments

On the 'Net

Go to the Web pages indicated to complete these exercises. You can also go to the *Garman/Forgue* website at college.hmco.com/business/students for an expanded list of exercises. Under General Business, select the title of this text. Click on the Internet Exercises link for this chapter.

1. Visit the website for the National Committee for Quality Assurance at http://www.ncqa.org, where you will find "report cards" on quality and accreditation status of health plans. If you are covered by a health plan, search for information on your plan. If you are not covered or if data are not available on your plan, select a major city and obtain the report on a plan in that city. What information, criteria, and other data in the report might assist you in assessing the quality of any plan?

2. Visit the website for the Social Security Administration and use its online calculator at http://www.ssa.gov/retire2/AnypiaApplet.html to determine whether you are currently eligible to receive Social Security disability insurance benefits if you become disabled and the projected level of those benefits.
3. Visit the website for Yahoo! Finance at http://finance.yahoo.com/insurance and read its discussion of understanding long-term care insurance. How might such protection fit into your risk-management program or that of your family?

Visit the Garman/Forgue website ...

@college.hmco.com/business/students

Under General Business, select *Personal Finance 9e.* There, among other valuable resources, you will find a complete glossary, ACE questions, links to help you complete the chapter exercises, and links to other personal finance sites.

CHAPTER 12

Life Insurance Planning

You Must Be Kidding, Right?

Michelle and Jason Bailey are in their mid-20s and expecting their first child next month. Each earns about $40,000 per year. Currently, they have $20,000 life insurance policies on each of their lives with the other named as the beneficiary. They bought these policies to pay for death-related expenses if tragedy struck. They are thinking about adding another $300,000 each to their protection to replace the income lost if one of them passed away. How much will Michelle and Jason each pay for this additional protection?

A. About $25 per month

B. About $50 per month

C. About $100 per month

D. About $200 per month

The answer is A. Term life insurance for people in their 20s costs about $1 per $1000 of coverage per year. Thus, Michelle and Jason could each buy this insurance for $300 each or about $25 per month. If they chose instead to buy cash-value life insurance, they would likely pay $200 or more each per month. Always buy inexpensive term life insurance to replace the lost income needed by your dependents if you were to pass away!

LEARNING OBJECTIVES

After reading this chapter, you should be able to:

1 **Understand** the reasons why you might need life insurance and calculate the appropriate amount of coverage.

2 **Distinguish** among types of life insurance.

3 **Explain** the major provisions of life insurance policies.

4 **Apply** a step-by-step strategy for implementing a life insurance plan.

What Do You Recommend?

Karen Bridgeman, age 28, and her husband Will, age 30, are planning to start a family in the next year. Both have small cash-value life insurance policies ($25,000 and $50,000, respectively) that their parents purchased when they were children. Karen is a real estate attorney and earns $90,000 per year. She plans to continue working after having a child. Karen's employer offers a 401(k) plan into which she contributes a maximum of 6 percent of her salary each year matched by her employer one-half of 1 percent for each 1 percent that Karen contributes. Her employer does not offer employer-paid life insurance. Will is a high-school teacher and track coach and makes $49,000 per year. His employer pays the full cost of his retirement pension plan. An optional supplemental retirement plan is available into which Will can contribute 5 percent of his salary, but he has not done so as yet. Will has an employer-provided life insurance policy equal to twice his annual salary. Will and Karen have no other life insurance on their lives.

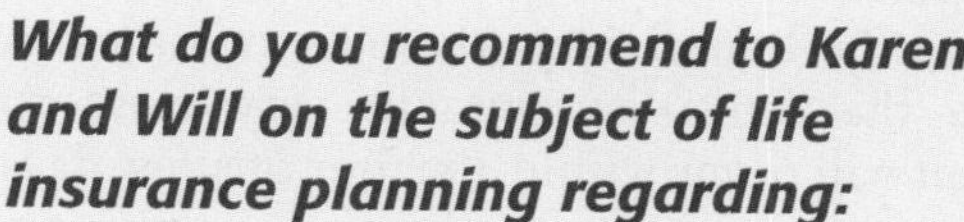

What do you recommend to Karen and Will on the subject of life insurance planning regarding:

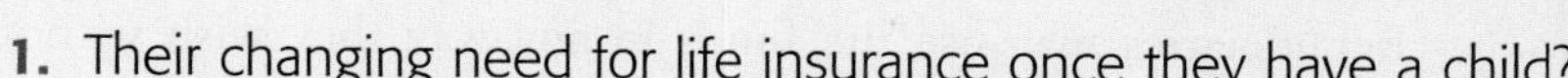

1. Their changing need for life insurance once they have a child?
2. What types of life insurance they should consider and whether they should purchase multiple policies?
3. Coordinating their retirement savings and other investments with their life insurance program?
4. Shopping for life insurance?

FOR HELP with studying this chapter, visit the Online Student Center:

www.college.hmco.com/pic/garman9e

Online Study Center

life insurance An insurance contract that promises to pay a dollar benefit to a beneficiary upon the death of the insured person.

Death is certain. Its timing is not. With this uncertainty comes financial risk. Two financial problems arise because you cannot know how long you will live. The first is the **risk of dying too soon.** This is the possibility that you might die before adequately providing for the financial well-being of loved ones, especially your spouse and children. **Life insurance** protects your loved ones against the possibility that you may die too soon. As you will see, term life insurance does this best. The second problem is the **risk of living too long.** This is the possibility that you will outlive your savings during retirement. Life insurance is not the best way to address the living-too-long problem. Instead, you should invest through tax-sheltered retirement savings plans.

Most Americans buy insufficient life insurance coverage. The need for life insurance is greatest in the child-rearing years. As children grow up, they need fewer years of financial support and a breadwinner's need for life insurance levels off and then declines. Eventually, growth in assets, primarily through a retirement plan, replaces the need for life insurance. Americans also tend to buy the wrong type of life insurance—cash-value life insurance—when term insurance costs 85 to 90 percent less. The best approach is to use the money saved by buying term insurance to invest in a tax-sheltered retirement plan. This approach is referred to as "buy term and invest the rest" and should be your mantra for life insurance planning.

How Much Life Insurance Do You Need?

1 **LEARNING OBJECTIVE**
Understand the reasons why you might need life insurance and calculate the appropriate amount of coverage.

The primary reason for buying life insurance is to allow the family members of the deceased to continue with their lives free from the financial burdens that death can bring. Income can be made available for the surviving spouse. Insurance proceeds can safeguard home ownership. College or other educational plans can remain intact. The bottom line? Your life insurance is for your loved ones, not for yourself.

Life insurance is the simplest form of insurance. It protects against only one peril—death. The policy pays out precisely the amount of insurance purchased. If the policy is for $100,000, then the policy will pay the **beneficiary** (the person named in the policy to receive the funds) an amount very close to $100,000. This payment will occur within a matter of a few days once a death certificate is presented to the insurance company. Beneficiaries may use the funds in any way they wish without paying income taxes on the proceeds. However, if the funds are put in the bank or invested in some way, the interest or investment returns will likely be subject to income taxation.

Good Money Habits in Life Insurance Planning

Make the following your money habits in life insurance planning:

1. Calculate your life insurance needs every three years or when major life events occur, such as the birth of a child.
2. Avoid being talked into buying types and amounts of life insurance that you do not need.
3. Shop for term life insurance on the Internet to obtain the lowest possible rates.
4. Employ the principle of "buy term life insurance and invest the rest" with guaranteed renewable or level-premium term life insurance.
5. Contribute the money saved by purchasing term rather than cash-value insurance into your retirement plan.
6. If you decide that you need a cash-value life insurance policy, get one with a guaranteed insurability option.

What Needs Must Be Met?

Financial losses that arise from dying too soon include expenditures for final expenses; the lost income of the deceased; and funds for a readjustment period, debt repayment, and education for children.

Final-Expense Needs **Final expenses** are one-time expenses occurring just prior to or after a death. Probably the largest of these expenses is for the funeral and burial of the deceased, which often cost more than $10,000. Travel expenses for family members to provide emotional support and to attend a funeral can be quite high as can food and lodging expenses for mourners. Severe and costly disruptions of family life can last as long as a month or more. These final expenses are one area of financial loss that is common to people of all ages. Nonetheless, they may not indicate a need for life insurance if existing assets are sufficient.

Income-Replacement Needs Once someone else becomes financially dependent on you, your lost income will be the major financial loss resulting from your premature death. Included in this lost income is the value of any essential employee benefits, such as health plan benefits for your dependents. Dual-earner families depend on both incomes to maintain the desired level of living and should protect both sources of income.

Readjustment-Period Needs Families often need a period of readjustment after the death of a loved one. This period may last for a few years and may have financial consequences that require substantial life insurance proceeds. For example, the death of a parent with young children may require the surviving spouse to forgo employment for a while. Similarly, a surviving employed spouse may need to take time off from a job to obtain further education.

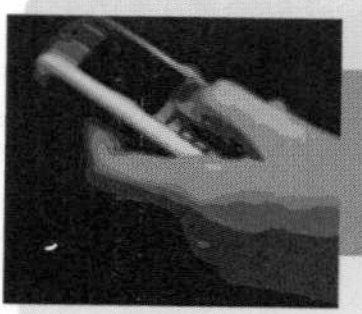

Instant Message

Husbands and Wives Need Their Own Life Insurance Plans

Husbands and wives should integrate their life insurance plans, but both need individual plans. This is true even if one partner makes the bulk of the family income. The cost of replacing the household labor of a stay-at-home spouse should be included in life insurance planning.

Debt-Repayment Needs Many people expect life insurance proceeds to pay off installment loans, personal loans, and the outstanding balance on the home mortgage if a family income provider dies. Actually, a family that has provided adequately for the replacement of lost income probably will not need to make specific insurance provisions for the repayment of debts. It is sometimes helpful, however, to create a plan to pay off all debts other than the mortgage for no other reason than to simplify the financial lives of the survivors. Mortgage debt that was adequately being covered before death will continue to be covered if sufficient life insurance was purchased to replace lost income.

Adequate life insurance can ensure that important financial goals, such as paying for a child's college education, are met should a parent die.

Instant Message

Buying Life Insurance Versus Investing

Most college students will live into their 80s, although about 20 percent will die before retirement. Use life insurance to protect against an early death and investments to prepare for a long life.

College-Expense Needs Many families with small children already have a college savings plan in place. Adequate replacement of lost income should allow for continuation of the plan. Because most families will also use current income to handle expenses when the children are in college, the death of a family income provider may, therefore, impede the ability to meet this need. The solution: Earmark a dollar amount of life insurance proceeds for future college expenses.

Other Special Needs Many families have special needs that must be considered in the life insurance planning process. A family with a disabled child might have special needs if that child is likely to require medical or custodial care as an adult. Wealthier families might need extra life insurance to pay federal estate taxes and state inheritance taxes (covered in Chapter 18).

Government Benefits Can Reduce the Level of Need Widows, widowers, and their dependents may qualify for various government benefits—most notably **Social Security survivor's benefits,** which are paid to a surviving spouse and children. The level of benefits depends on income earned during the lifetime of the deceased that was subject to Social Security taxes. (Details on estimating Social Security benefits are provided in Appendix B and on the *Garman/Forgue* website.) If eligible, a family can receive as much as $25,000 per year, but these benefits generally cease when the youngest child reaches age 18.

Social Security survivor's benefits Government program benefits paid to a surviving spouse and children.

Existing Insurance and Assets Reduce the Level of Need Employers often provide life insurance to their employees as an employee benefit. In addition, many people have existing life insurance that was purchased for them as children or that they purchased previously. These coverages can reduce the need for additional life insurance purchases.

As time passes, individuals and families usually acquire at least a minimal amount of savings and investments. The funds held in savings accounts, certificates of deposit, stocks, bonds, and mutual funds often are specifically earmarked for some special goal, such as retirement, travel, or college for children. In the event of a premature death, they could be used to pay final and readjustment expenses as well as to replace lost income, even though it might be wiser to retain these funds for their originally intended purpose. Pension funds and retirement plans of the deceased, such as 401(k) plans and IRAs (discussed in Chapter 17), may be viewed as resources. Younger families should be wary of using retirement money for living expenses after the death of an income provider, however, as this strategy may jeopardize the surviving spouse's retirement.

Instant Message

Retirees Need Less—Not More—Life Insurance

Life insurance needs typically decrease while assets increase over the course of one's life. At some point, savings and investments should exceed potential losses and eliminate the need for life insurance—especially after age 60.

What Dollar Amount Do You Need?

Determining the magnitude of the possible losses resulting from a premature death can be complicated. Two methods are commonly used: a multiple-of-earnings approach and a needs-based approach. The needs-based approach is more accurate and reflects the changes in family status, income, assets, and age that will occur over your life cycle.

The Multiple-of-Earnings Approach: Easy But Flawed The **multiple-of-earnings approach** estimates the amount of life insurance needed by multiplying your income by some number, such as 5, 7, or 10. Thus, someone with an annual income of $40,000 would need $200,000 to $400,000 in life insurance.

Another multiple-of-earnings approach is to use the interest factors from Appendix Table A.4 for an expected investment rate of return and a given number of years of need. The logic here is that at death, the survivor could invest the funds received from the life insurance policy on the person who has died to provide a flow of income for the number of years desired. For example, a father who wishes to provide his family with income of $40,000 for 20 years at a real rate of return of 4 percent (after inflation and taxes) would need to have about $550,000 ($40,000 × 13.59) of life insurance protection on his life.

The shortcoming of the multiple-of-earnings approach can be seen in the wide range of dollar amounts that result. This approach addresses only one of the factors affecting life insurance needs—income-replacement—and does not take into consideration such factors as age, family situation, and other assets that could cover the lost income.

Did You Know?...

Top 3 Financial Missteps When Protecting Loved Ones Through Life Insurance

People slip up in personal finance when they do the following:

1. Let their life insurance agent convince them how much and what type of life insurance to buy
2. Buy their life insurance during their childbearing years through cash-value life insurance
3. Ignore their changing need for life insurance as their life progresses from young adulthood through retirement

The Needs-Based Approach: A Better Method The **needs-based approach** to estimating life insurance needs considers all of the factors that might potentially affect the level of need. It improves upon the calculations of the multiple-of-earnings approach by including a more accurate assessment of income-replacement needs and incorporates factors that add to and reduce the level of need. The Decision-Making Worksheet, "The Needs-Based Approach to Life Insurance" (page 326), illustrates calculations made via the needs-based approach. You would be wise to calculate your current needs for life insurance and then to revisit those calculations every three years and when changes occur in your family situation or health status.

needs-based approach A superior method of calculating the amount of insurance needed that considers all of the factors that might potentially affect the level of need.

Calculating Life Insurance Needs for a Couple with Small Children

Consider the example of Zoel Raymond, a 35-year-old factory foreman from Holyoke, Massachusetts, who has a spouse (age 30) and three sons (ages 8, 7, and 3 years). Zoel earns $48,000 annually and desires to replace his income for 30 years, at which time his spouse would no longer need to support their children financially. The "Example" column of the Decision-Making Worksheet expands on the situation faced by Zoel.

1. **Final-expense needs.** Zoel estimates his final expenses for funeral, burial, and other expenses at $10,000.
2. **Income-replacement needs.** Zoel's income of $48,000 is multiplied by 0.75 and the interest factor of 17.292. This factor was used because Zoel decided that it would be best to replace his lost income for 30 years or until Mary, his wife, reached age 60 and passed through the Social Security blackout period. Zoel and Mary are moderate-risk investors and believe that she could earn a 4 percent after-tax, after-inflation rate of return on life insurance proceeds. Income-replacement needs based on these conditions amount to $622,512.
3. **Readjustment-period needs.** Mary is a columnist for a local newspaper, earning an annual income of $38,000. Allocating $19,000 for readjustment-period needs would allow her to take a six-month leave of absence from her job or meet other readjustment needs.
4. **Debt-repayment needs.** Zoel and Mary owe $10,000 on various credit cards and an auto loan. They also owe about

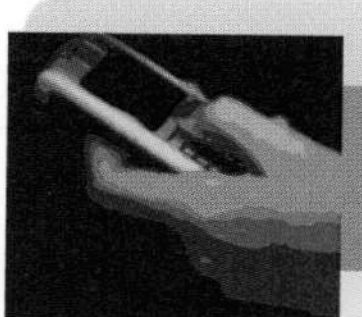

Instant Message

Life Insurance Can Provide a Flow of Future Income

Having the right amount of life insurance will allow your family to invest the proceeds received and then make withdrawals to replace the income you could have provided for them had you lived.

Decision-Making Worksheet

The Needs-Based Approach to Life Insurance

This worksheet provides a mechanism for estimating life insurance needs using the needs-based approach. The amounts needed for final expenses, income replacement, readjustment needs, debt repayment, college expenses, and other special needs are calculated and then reduced by funds available from government benefits and any current insurance or assets that could cover the need. This worksheet is also available on the *Garman/Forgue* website.

Factors Affecting Need	Example	Your Figures
1. Final-expense needs		
Includes funeral, burial, travel, and other items of expense just prior to and after death	$ 10,000	$_____
2. Income-replacement needs		
Multiply 75 percent of annual income* by the interest factor from Appendix Table A.4 that corresponds to the number of years that the income is to be replaced and the assumed after-tax, after-inflation rate of return. ($36,000 × 17.292 for 30 years at a 4% rate of return)	+ 622,512	+_____
3. Readjustment-period needs		
To cover employment interruptions and possible education expenses for surviving spouse and dependents	+ 19,000	+_____
4. Debt-repayment needs		
Provides repayment of short-term and installment debt, including credit cards and personal loans	+ 10,000	+_____
5. College-expense needs		
To provide a fund to help meet college expenses of dependents	+ 75,000	+_____
6. Other special needs	+ 0	+_____
7. Subtotal (combined effects of items 1–6)	+ $736,512	+_____
8. Government benefits		
Present value of Social Security survivor's benefits and other benefits. Multiply monthly benefit estimate by 12 and use Table A.4 for the number of years that benefits will be received and the same interest rate that was used in item 1. ($2725 × 12 × 11.118 for 15 years of benefits and a 4% rate of return)	− 363,558	_____
9. Current insurance assets	− 98,000	_____
10. Life insurance needed	$274,954	$_____

*Seventy-five percent is used because about 25 percent of income is used for personal needs.

$128,000 on their home mortgage. Mary would like to pay off all debts except the mortgage debt if Zoel dies. The mortgage debt would be affordable if Zoel's income was adequately replaced.

5. **College-expense needs.** Zoel estimates that it would currently cost $25,000 for each of his sons to attend the local campus of a public university. If he dies, $25,000 of the life insurance proceeds could be invested for each son. If invested appropriately, the funds would grow at a rate sufficient to keep up with increasing costs of a college education.

6. **Other special needs.** Zoel and Mary do not have any unusual needs related to life insurance planning, so they entered zero for this factor.
7. **Subtotal.** The Raymonds total items 1 through 6 on the worksheet and determine that the family's financial needs arising out of Zoel's death would amount to $736,512. Although this sum seems large to them, they have access to two resources that can reduce this figure, as indicated in items 8 and 9.
8. **Government benefits.** Zoel estimates that his family would qualify for monthly Social Security survivor's benefits of $2725.* These benefits would be paid for 15 years, until his youngest son turns 18. The present value of this stream of benefits is $363,558 (from Appendix Table A.4), assuming a 4 percent return for 15 years.
9. **Current insurance and assets.** Zoel has a $50,000 life insurance policy purchased five years ago. His employer also pays for a group policy equal to his $48,000 gross annual income. Zoel's major assets include his home and his retirement plan. Because he does not want Mary to have to liquidate these assets if he dies, he includes only the $98,000 insurance coverage in item 9.
10. **Life insurance needed.** After subtracting worksheet items 8 and 9 from the subtotal, Zoel estimates that he needs an additional $274,954 in life insurance. This amount may seem like a large sum of insurance, but Zoel can meet this need through term life insurance for as little as $30 per month.

Because Mary earns an income that is about 80 percent of Zoel's, her life insurance needs may be about 20 percent lower. To determine the specific amount, the couple must complete a worksheet for her as well. Next, the Raymonds will need to decide what type of life insurance is best and from whom to buy the additional life insurance needed. These topics are covered later in this chapter.

Calculating Life Insurance Needs for a Young Professional Irene Leech of Rancho Cucamonga, California, recently graduated with a degree in tourism management and has accepted a position paying $43,000 per year. Irene is single and lives with her sister. She owes $14,500 on a car loan and $21,800 in education loans. She has about $7000 in the bank. Among her employee benefits is an employer-paid term insurance policy equal to her annual salary.

Irene has been approached by a life insurance agent who used the multiple-of-earnings approach to suggest that she needs $215,000 in life insurance, or about five times her income. Does she? If you apply the needs-based approach to Irene's situation, you will see the following:

- Irene estimates her burial costs at $8000, which she entered for item 1. Because Irene has no dependents, she needs no insurance for income-replacement needs, readjustment-period needs, college-expense needs, or other special needs.
- Items 2, 3, 5, and 6 in the needs-based approach worksheet on page 326 are zero because Irene has no dependents.
- Irene's survivors will not qualify for any government benefits, so item 8 will also be zero.
- Irene would like to see her $14,500 automobile loan and $21,800 education loans repaid in the event of her death. She feels better knowing that her younger sister could inherit her car free and clear. She entered $36,300 for item 4.
- Irene has combined life insurance and assets of $50,000, so she entered that amount for item 8.

The resulting calculations show that Irene needs *no* additional life insurance ($8000 + $36,300 − $50,000 = −$5,700).

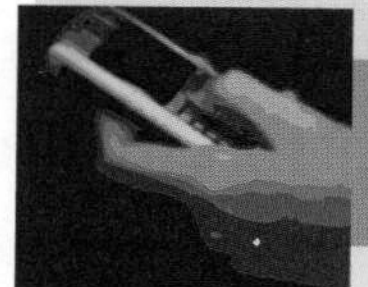

Instant Message

Social Security Survivor Benefits Have a Blackout Period

Once the youngest child reaches age 18, a surviving spouse enters the **Social Security blackout period** and is ineligible for Social Security survivor benefits. The blackout period ends when the surviving spouse reaches age 60. The surviving spouse may then collect survivor's benefits until age 62, and then may begin collecting Social Security retirement benefits based on his or her own or the deceased spouse's retirement account, whichever provides the higher payment.

*Your personal Social Security benefits can be estimated by requesting a Social Security Statement from the Social Security Administration (www.ssa.gov). Appendix B also provides estimates.

The agent suggested that Irene buy now while she is young and rates are low. This, too, is not a smart approach. The lesson here is that you should not buy life insurance simply to lock in low rates. That would be like buying car insurance before you own a car. Unless you have a personal or family-based medical history that might interfere with the purchase of life insurance when needed later, you, like Irene, can wait until family circumstances change to recalculate the need.

CONCEPT CHECK 12.1

1. Distinguish between the dying-too-soon problem and the living-too-long problem and the best ways to address each.
2. List five types of needs that can be addressed through life insurance.
3. Explain why the multiple-of-earnings approach is less accurate than a needs-based approach to life insurance planning.
4. Identify two periods in a typical person's life cycle when the need for life insurance is low and one when it is high.

There Are But Two Basic Types of Life Insurance

2 LEARNING OBJECTIVE
Distinguish among types of life insurance.

term life insurance "Pure protection" against early death; pays benefits only if the insured dies within the time period (term) that the policy covers.

cash-value life insurance Pays benefits at death and includes a savings/investment element that can provide a reduced level of benefits to the policyholder prior to the death of the insured person.

Many people are confused by the wide variety of life insurance plans available. But, in reality, there are only two types of life insurance: term life insurance and cash-value life insurance. **Term life insurance** is often described as "pure protection" because it pays benefits only if the insured person dies within the time period (term) covered by the policy. The policy must be renewed if coverage is desired for another time period. **Cash-value life insurance** pays benefits at death and includes a savings/investment element that can provide benefits to the policyholder prior to the death of the insured person. Thus, it includes a **cash value** representing the value of the investment element in the life insurance policy. Because of its investment aspect, many people automatically believe it is the better option. Cash-value life insurance costs much more than term insurance, however, and there are much better investment options.

Term Life Insurance

face amount Dollar value of protection as listed in the policy and used to calculate the premium.

Term life insurance contracts are most often written for time periods (or terms) of 1, 5, 10, or even 20 years. If the insured survives the specified time period, the beneficiary receives no monetary benefits. Term insurance can be purchased in contracts with face amounts in multiples of $1000, usually with a minimum face amount of $50,000. The **face amount** is the dollar value of life insurance protection as listed in the policy and used to calculate the premium. Variations on term life insurance include decreasing term insurance, guaranteed renewable term insurance, convertible term insurance, and credit (term) life insurance.

Unless otherwise stipulated by the original contract, you must apply for a new contract and may be required to undergo a medical examination to renew the policy. The premium will increase with each renewal, reflecting your increasing age and greater likelihood of dying while the new policy remains in force. If you have a health problem, you may be denied a new policy or be asked to pay even higher premiums. For example, a $100,000 five-year renewable term policy for a man age 25 might have an annual premium of $100; at age 35, the policy might cost $135; and at age 45, it might cost $220. Term policies are much less expensive than cash-value policies at any given age because they do not include a savings/investment element.

Guaranteed Renewable Term Insurance Proving insurability at renewal may be difficult if you develop a health problem during the time period of a term policy. Term life insurance policies, however, are usually written as **guaranteed renewable term insurance.** The guarantee protects you against the possibility of becoming uninsurable. The number of renewals you can make without proving insurability may be limited, and a maximum age may be specified for these renewals (usually 65 or 70 years). Unless you are positive that you will not need a renewal, guaranteed renewable term insurance is recommended.

guaranteed renewable term insurance Protects you against the possibility of becoming uninsurable.

Level-Premium Term Insurance You can partially avoid term insurance premium increases as you grow older by buying **level-premium** (or **guaranteed level-premium) term insurance,** which is a term policy with a long time period (perhaps 5, 10, or 20 years). Under such a policy, the premiums remain constant throughout the entire life of the policy. Premiums charged in early years are higher than necessary to balance out the lower-than-necessary premiums in later years covered by the policy. Premiums on policies written for ten or more years usually remain constant for a five-year interval, then might increase to a new constant rate for another five- or ten-year interval. Such level-premium policies may include a **reenter provision,** requiring proof of good health at the beginning of each five-year interval. If health status changes, the insured must reenter the policy at a higher rate than originally anticipated. Be extremely wary of policies with such a provision, especially if you anticipate needing coverage beyond the initial level-premium interval.

level-premium term insurance Term policy with long term under which premiums remain constant. Also called guaranteed level-premium term insurance.

Decreasing Term Insurance With **decreasing term insurance,** the face amount of coverage declines annually, while the premiums remain constant. The owner chooses an initial face amount and a contract period, after which the face amount of the policy gradually declines (usually each year) to some minimum (such as $50,000) in the last year of the contract. For example, a woman age 35 might buy a 30-year $200,000 decreasing term policy that declines by $5000 each year. The major benefit of decreasing term policies is that they more closely fit changing insurance needs, which typically decline as a person ages.

Convertible Term Insurance **Convertible term insurance** offers the policyholder the option of exchanging a term policy for a cash-value policy without evidence of insurability. Usually, this conversion is available only in the early years of the term policy. Some policies provide for an automatic conversion from term to cash-value insurance after a specific number of years.

convertible term insurance Offers policyholders option of exchanging a term policy for a cash-value policy without evidence of insurability.

There are two ways to convert a term policy to a cash-value policy. First, you can simply request the conversion and begin paying the higher premiums required for the cash-value policy. The savings/investment element of the cash-value policy will begin accumulating as of the date of the conversion. Second, you can pay the company the cash value that would have built up had the policy originally been written on a cash-value basis. Although this lump sum may be a considerable amount, it does represent an asset for the policyholder. Furthermore, the new premiums will be based on your age at the time that you bought the original term policy, which may result in lower premiums.

Instant Message

Buying Life Insurance Through a Group at Work

Unlike with health insurance, group life insurance rates are not lower than individual rates for people in good health. If you have a health condition, you can compare your group rates with what you must pay on your own.

Group Term Life Insurance **Group term life insurance** is issued to people as members of a group rather than as individuals. Most such policies are written for a large number of employees, with premiums being paid in full or in part by the employer. Group life insurance premiums are average rates based on the characteristics of the group as a whole. If you are insured under a group plan, you need not prove your insurability, and you can usually convert the policy to an individual basis without proof of insurability if you leave the group. Such convertibility represents a major benefit for people whose health status makes individual life insurance unaffordable or unattainable.

Credit Term Life Insurance **Credit term life insurance** will pay the remaining balance of a loan if the insured dies before repaying the debt. In essence, it is a decreasing term insurance policy with the creditor named as beneficiary. This product is usually grossly overpriced, and the only people who should consider its purchase are those who are uninsurable because of a serious health condition. Most people are insurable and can obtain term life coverage for a minimal cost, so they do not need credit term life insurance.

Some Forms of Cash-Value Life Insurance Pay a Fixed Return

Cash-value life insurance pays benefits upon the death of the insured and also incorporates a savings/investment element. This cash value belongs to the owner of the policy rather than to the beneficiary (although they can be the same person). While the insured is alive, the owner may obtain the cash value by borrowing from the insurance company or by surrendering and canceling the policy. Cash-value insurance is referred to as **permanent insurance** because it does not need to be renewed and because coverage is maintained for the entire life of the insured. The annual premiums for cash-value policies usually remain constant.

The premiums for cash-value policies are always higher than those for term policies providing the same amount of coverage. This difference arises because only a portion of the premium is used to provide the death benefit; the remainder is used to keep the premium level and to build the cash value. Figure 12.1 illustrates the premium differences between cash-value and term life insurance policies.

Cash-value life insurance actually represents a combination of decreasing term insurance and an investment account that adds up to the face amount of the policy. Figure 12.2 illustrates this concept. Initially, for example, you might have $100,000 of insurance and no savings. Several years later, you might have built up $2000 in savings within the policy. In the event of your death, your beneficiary would collect $100,000,

Figure 12.1

Comparison of Premium Dollars for Life Insurance

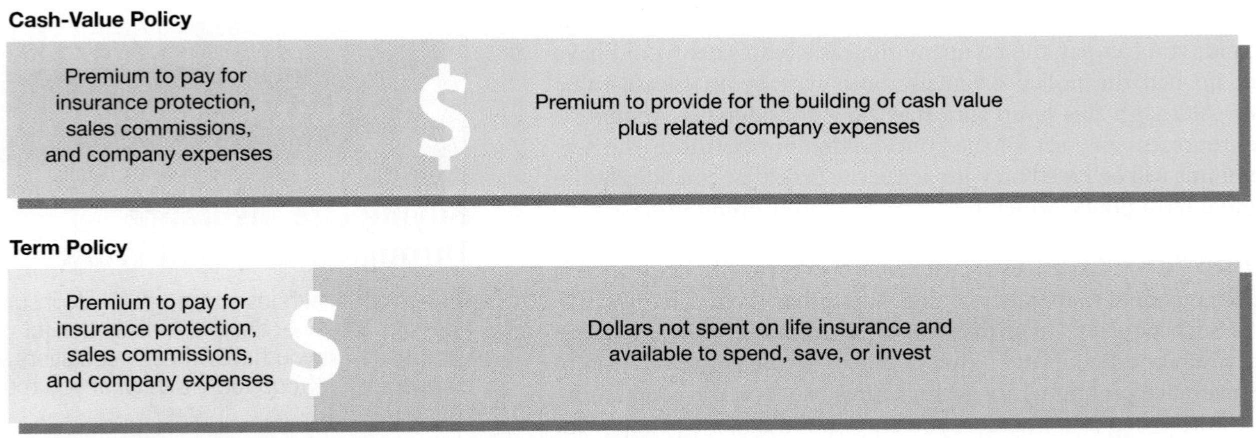

Cash-Value Policy

Premium to pay for insurance protection, sales commissions, and company expenses | $ | Premium to provide for the building of cash value plus related company expenses

Term Policy

Premium to pay for insurance protection, sales commissions, and company expenses | $ | Dollars not spent on life insurance and available to spend, save, or invest

For example, for a 25-year-old female, the annual premium might be $800 for a $100,000 cash-value policy, but only $120 for a $100,000 term policy.

of which $2000 would be your own money. If you lived long enough, the cash value could equal—and might surpass—the $100,000 figure. In effect, your beneficiary would then collect your "savings account" rather than an insurance payment.

Even though the cash value of a life insurance policy accumulates throughout your life, only the face amount of the policy will be paid upon your death. In many ways, cash values represent a kind of forced saving that allows funds to build up while you buy life insurance. Several types of cash-value life insurance are available that pay a fixed rate of investment return.

Whole Life Insurance **Whole**, or **straight, life insurance** is a form of cash-value life insurance that provides lifetime life insurance protection and expects you to pay premiums for life. The policy remains in effect and does not need to be renewed as long as the premiums are paid on time.

whole life insurance Form of cash-value life insurance that provides lifetime life insurance protection and expects the insured to pay premiums for life. Also called straight life insurance.

Limited-Pay Whole Life Insurance **Limited-pay whole life insurance** is whole life insurance that allows premium payments to cease before you reach the age of 100. Two common examples are *20-pay life policies*, which allow premium payments to cease after 20 years, and *paid-at-65 policies*, which require payment of premiums only until the insured turns 65. Although premiums need be paid only for the specified time period, the insurance protection lasts for your entire life. As you might expect, the annual premiums for limited-pay insurance policies are higher than those for whole life insurance policies because the insurance company has fewer years to collect premiums. Limited-pay policies are said to be **paid-up** when the owner can stop paying premiums. An extreme version of limited-pay life insurance is **single-premium life insurance,** in which the premium is paid once in the form of a lump sum.

limited-pay whole life insurance Whole life insurance that allows premium payments to cease before the insured reaches the age of 100.

paid-up Point at which the owner of a whole life policy can stop paying premiums.

Adjustable Life Insurance The three cornerstones of cash-value life insurance are the premium, the face amount of the policy, and the rate of cash-value accumulation. **Adjustable life insurance** allows you to modify any one of these three components, with corresponding changes occurring in the other two. These changes may be made without providing new proof of insurability. For example, you might feel that inflation has increased your need for life insurance. Adjustable life insurance would allow you to increase the face amount. In return, your premiums could increase, the cash-value accumulation could slow, or some combination of the two could apply.

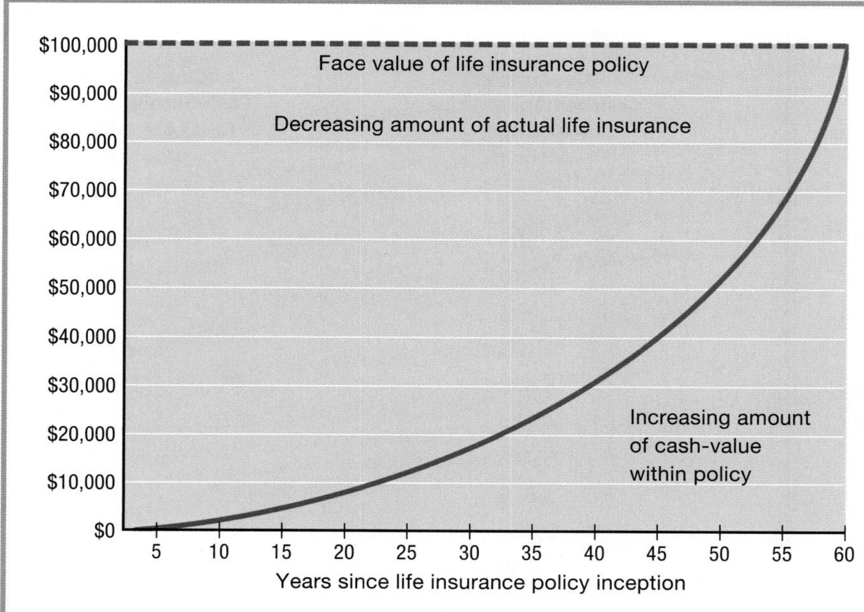

Figure 12.2

The Essence of Cash-Value Life Insurance

The $100,000 death benefit (face value) paid to the beneficiaries comprises a decreasing amount of life insurance and the policyholder's returned built-up cash values.

Modified Life Insurance **Modified life insurance** is whole life insurance for which the insurance company charges reduced premiums in the early years and higher premiums thereafter. The premiums are lower in early years because some of the protection during the early years is provided by term insurance. The period of reduced premiums can vary from one to five years. Modified life insurance is primarily designed for people whose life insurance needs are high (young parents, for example) but who cannot immediately afford the premiums required for a cash-value policy. Because it uses term insurance in the early years, modified life insurance accumulates cash value extremely slowly.

Endowment Life Insurance **Endowment life insurance** pays the face amount of the policy either upon the death of the insured or at some previously agreed-upon date, whichever occurs first. The date of payment, called the endowment date, is commonly some specified number of years after issuance of the policy (for example, 20 or 30 years) or some specified age (such as 65). New endowment policies are no longer being written, however, and this type of policy will be phased out as existing policies "endow" and are converted to cash.

Some Forms of Cash-Value Life Insurance Pay a Variable Return

The rate at which the cash value accumulates in a cash-value policy depends on the rate of return earned. Some forms of cash-value insurance have a guaranteed minimum rate of return, often 4 percent, but pay a higher current rate depending on the success of the investments made by the insurance company with your premiums. Table 12.1 illustrates these rates. An understanding of these policies requires an examination of the premium, the cost of the insurance protection portion, the rate of return on the invested funds, and the company's expense charges.

universal life insurance Provides the pure protection of term insurance and the cash-value buildup of whole life insurance, along with face amount variability, rate of cash-value accumulation, premiums, and rate of return.

Universal Life Insurance **Universal life insurance** provides both the pure protection of term insurance and the cash-value buildup of whole life insurance, along with variability in the face amount, rate of cash-value accumulation, premiums, and rate of return. Initially, the purchaser selects a face amount, and the company quotes an annual

Table 12.1 Cash-Value Buildup—Guaranteed Versus Current Rates

Policy Year	"Guaranteed" Cash-Surrender Value (4.0% rate)	"Current Rate" Cash-Surrender Value (7.6% rate)
1	$ 0	$ 0
2	0	236
3	585	886
4	1,280	1,577
5	1,993	2,377
6	2,723	3,187
7	3,470	4,212
8	4,234	5,258
9	5,016	6,302
10	5,816	7,419
15	10,089	14,748
20	14,738	25,812
25	19,888	39,419

Figures are illustrative for a $50,000 universal life policy; the annual premium is $684.

Advice from a Pro...

Don't Be Fooled by Vanishing-Premium or Return-of-Premium Policies

Life insurance agents often pitch **vanishing-premium life insurance,** which is designed to allow policyholders to cease making premium payments after just a few years. In these plans, cash-value accumulations are used to pay premiums that no longer must be paid. While attractive at first glance, these policies contain a significant hazard. If the growth in cash-value accumulations proves insufficient to pay the premium, the owner of the policy will be billed for the premium shortfall—possibly after many years of having not paid premiums. Always assume any life insurance charge that can be imposed will be imposed.

A similar type of plan is called a **return-of-premium policy.** Here the policy promises to return all the premiums paid if the insured person maintains the policy and lives past a certain number of years—usually 30. These policies cost more so that the extra funds can be invested to provide for the return of premiums. Insurance companies promote these policies as a way to avoid "wasting" your money. In reality, what they are trying to do is entice you to keep the policy in effect for a long time even if you do not need the coverage anymore. Instead buy term insurance and decide for yourself when it is best to drop a policy.

Hyungsoo Kim
University of Kentucky, Lexington, Kentucky

premium. The annual premium goes into the cash-value fund, from which the company deducts the cost of providing the insurance protection and charges for company expenses. As time goes by, the owner of the policy may reduce or increase the premium, with corresponding changes occurring in the insurance protection or amount added to cash value. If premiums drop below the amount necessary to cover the insurance protection and expenses, funds are removed from the cash-value account to cover the shortfall.

Essentially, universal life insurance combines annual term insurance with an investment program. Universal life policies are usually available in initial face amounts of $100,000 or more. The rate of return is tied to some interest rate prevailing in the financial markets or is dictated by the insurance company. The rate of return often exceeds those available under fixed-rate cash-value policies.

Variable Life Insurance **Variable life insurance** allows you to choose the investments made with your cash-value accumulations and to share in any gains or losses. The face amount of your policy and the policy's cash value may rise or fall based on changes in the rates of return on the invested funds. The face amount of the policy usually will not drop below the originally agreed-upon amount, however. Instead, the cash value will fluctuate. If you are unfamiliar with markets for corporate stocks and bonds and mutual funds, however, you should probably avoid variable life insurance. Many variable life insurance policies contain provisions calling for the payment of fees and sales charges before the policyholder can share in any investment returns. Variable life insurance policies should be read and analyzed very carefully before purchase.

Variable-Universal Life Insurance **Variable-universal life insurance** is a form of universal life insurance that gives the policyholder some choice in the investments made with the cash value accumulated by the policy. It is sometimes called **flexible-premium variable life insurance.** The most popular form of cash-value life insurance, it most closely embodies the philosophy of "buy term and invest the difference." Because you select the investment vehicles (a combination of stocks, bonds, or money market mutual funds), you can potentially realize a higher rate of return than is possible under other cash-value policy types. With this flexibility comes the risk of a lower rate of return, of course. As a result, variable-universal life policies usually provide no minimum guaranteed rate of return. Table 12.2 summarizes the features of term life insurance, cash-value insurance with a fixed return, and cash-value insurance with a variable return.

variable-universal life insurance Form of universal life insurance that gives the policyholder some choice in the investments made with the cash value accumulated by the policy. Also called flexible-premium variable life insurance.

Table 12.2 Comparisons of Three Popular Life Insurance Policies

		Cash-Value Life Insurance	
Feature	**Term Insurance**	**Whole Life Insurance**	**Variable Life Insurance**
Cash-value accumulation	None	Fixed rate of accumulation	Variable accumulation as premium and interest rates vary
Rate of return paid on cash accumulations	Not applicable	Fixed	Variable with interest rates in the economy or as specified by company
Face amount	Fixed or declining during term of the policy; changeable at renewal	Fixed	Variable
Premiums	Low with increases at renewal	High and fixed	High but variable within limits
Cost of the death benefit portion	Low, with interest at renewal	Unknown	Known but can vary and may hide some expense charges
Company expense charges	Low but unknown; hidden in premium	Unknown; hidden in premium	Known; may be high

Variable-universal life insurance also carries higher commissions and is more likely to require annual fees than other forms of life insurance. A 2 percent annual fee would change a policy with an annual return of 7 percent on its investments to one with a net 5 percent return. You should also compare the policy's investment component with alternative investments. (Investments are covered in Chapters 13 to 16.)

CONCEPT CHECK 12.2

1. List three similarities and three differences between term life insurance and cash-value life insurance.
2. Explain why the premiums for term insurance are so much lower than those of cash-value life insurance.
3. Describe the benefit of buying guaranteed renewable term insurance.
4. Explain why the amount of "insurance" declines over time under a cash-value life insurance policy.
5. Distinguish between cash-value life insurance with a fixed return and with a variable return.

owner/policyholder Retains all rights and privileges granted by the policy, including the right to amend the policy and the right to designate who receives the proceeds.

Understanding Your Life Insurance Policy

3 LEARNING OBJECTIVE
Explain the major provisions of life insurance policies.

insured Individual whose life is insured

A **life insurance policy** is the written contract between the insurer and the policyholder. It contains all of the information relevant to the agreement. Several parties will be named in the life insurance contract (policy). The **owner,** or **policyholder,** retains all rights and privileges granted by the policy, including the right to amend the policy and the right to designate who receives the proceeds. The **insured** is the person whose life is insured. In addition to the beneficiary, the owner will name a **contingent beneficiary** who will become the beneficiary if the original beneficiary dies before the insured. Although the owner and the insured are often the same person, it is possible for four different people to play all these roles.

Policy Terms and Provisions Unique to Life Insurance

Life insurance policies define the terminology used in the policy and outline the basic provisions of such insurance. This information serves to clarify the meaning of the policy and the protection afforded the insurer and the policyholder.

The Application The **life insurance application** is the policyholder's offer to purchase a policy. It provides information and becomes part of the life insurance policy (the contract). Any errors or omissions in the application may allow the insurance company to deny a request for payment of the death benefit.

Lives Covered Most life insurance policies cover the life of a single person—the insured. It is also possible to cover two or more people with one policy, however. **First-to-die policies** cover more than one person but pay only when the first insured dies. These policies are less costly than separate policies written on each person, but the survivor then has no coverage after the first person dies. An alternative is the **survivorship joint life policy,** which pays when the last person covered dies.

first-to-die policies Cover more than one person but pay only when the first insured dies.

survivorship joint life policy Pays when the last person covered dies.

The Incontestability Clause Life insurance policies generally include an **incontestability clause** that places a time limit—usually two years after issuance of

incontestability clause Places a time limit on the right of the insurance company to deny a claim.

Did You Know?...

How Insurance Policies Are Organized

All insurance policies include five basic components, each of which provides specific information. These five elements, in order of their usual location in the policy, are as follows: declarations, insuring agreements, exclusions, conditions, and endorsements.

- **Declarations** provide the basic descriptive information about the insured person or property, the premium to be paid, the time period of the coverage, and the policy limits. Also included may be promises by the insured to take steps to control the losses associated with a specific peril. For example, a life insurance purchaser may promise not to smoke in exchange for paying a discounted premium. The information in the declarations is used to help determine the premium and for identification purposes.
- **Insuring agreements** are the broadly defined coverages provided under the policy. The insurer makes these promises in return for the premium paid by the insured. For example, in life insurance, the insurer promises to pay the death benefit amount to the beneficiary in the event of the insured's death. In automobile insurance, the insuring agreements will often include definitions of a motor vehicle or insured premises to clarify the promises made.
- **Exclusions** narrow the focus and eliminate specific coverages broadly stated in the insuring agreements. The insurer makes no promise to pay for these exceptions and special circumstances. For example, suicide is commonly excluded during the first two years of a life insurance policy. A common automobile insurance exclusion denies coverage under a family policy if the car is used primarily for business purposes. People who do not understand the exclusions in their policies may believe they are covered for a loss when, in fact, they are not.
- **Conditions** impose obligations on both the insured and the insurer by establishing the ground rules of the agreement. For example, they might include procedures for making a claim after a loss, rules for cancellation of the policy by either party, and procedures for changing the terms of the policy. The insured who fails to adhere to the procedures or obligations described in the conditions may be denied coverage when a loss occurs.
- **Endorsements** (or **riders,** as they are sometimes called in life insurance) are amendments and additions to the basic insurance policy that can both expand and limit coverage to accommodate specific needs. When the terms of an endorsement or rider differ from the terms of the basic policy, the endorsement will be considered valid. Endorsements may be requested at any time during the life of the policy to expand coverage, raise the policy limits, and make other changes.

the policy—on the right of the insurance company to deny a claim. This clause addresses the problems arising out of erroneous statements in the application.

The Suicide Clause Life insurance policies generally include a **suicide clause** that allows the life insurance company to deny coverage if the insured commits suicide within the first few years after the policy is issued. If the specified number of years (usually two) has elapsed, the full death benefit will be paid. If not, only the premiums paid up to that point will be refunded.

insurance dividends Surplus earnings of insurance company when the difference between the total premium charged exceeds the cost to the company of providing insurance.

Cash Dividends **Insurance dividends** are defined by the Internal Revenue Service as a return of a portion of the premium paid for a life insurance policy; they are not considered taxable income. They represent the surplus earnings of the company when the difference between the total premium charged exceeds the cost to the company of providing insurance. Policies that pay dividends are called **participating policies,** and policies that do not pay dividends are called **nonparticipating policies.** Both term and cash-value policies may pay dividends. Owners of participating policies may receive dividends as a cash payment, leave them with the insurance company to earn interest, or use the dividends to purchase small amounts of additional paid-up life insurance.

death benefit Amount that will be paid to beneficiary when the insured dies.

Death Benefit The **death benefit** of a life insurance policy is the amount that will be paid upon the death of the insured person.

The amount of the death benefit may be either higher (due to such items as earned dividends not yet paid or premiums paid in advance) or lower (due to outstanding policy loans or unpaid premiums) than the face amount. Consider a $100,000 participating whole life policy with annual premiums of $1380. If the insured died halfway through the policy year, with an outstanding cash-value loan of $5000 and earned but unpaid dividends of $4000, the death benefit would be $99,690, calculated as follows:

$100,000	Face amount
4,000	Unpaid dividends
+ 690	Premiums paid in advance (one-half year)
$104,690	Subtotal
− 5,000	Outstanding cash-value loan
$ 99,690	Death benefit

Grace Period Prompt payment of the premium is crucial to the continuation of coverage provided by any insurance policy. A **lapsed policy** is one that has been terminated because of nonpayment of premiums. More than one-half of all whole life policies lapse within ten years of being issued. If your life insurance policy lapses, you must prove insurability and pay any missed premiums, plus interest, to be reinstated. Alternatively, you might pay a higher premium for a new policy, reflecting your current age.

grace period Period of time during which an overdue premium may be paid without a lapse of the policy.

To help prevent a lapse, state laws generally require that cash-value and multiyear term policies include a **grace period**—that is, a period of time (usually 30 days following each premium due date) during which an overdue premium may be paid without a lapse of the policy. During the grace period, all provisions of the policy remain intact, but only if payment is made before the grace period ends. Assume, for example, that payment was due but not paid on January 1. If the insured were to die on January 15, the policy could be reinstated as long as payment was made by January 30, given a 30-day grace period. It also may be possible to "buy back" a lapsed cash-value policy by paying any missed premiums and the cash value that would have accumulated while the policy was lapsed.

Multiple Indemnity A **multiple indemnity clause** provides for a doubling or tripling of the face amount if death results from certain specified causes. It is most often used to double the face amount if death results from an accident. Such a clause is often included automatically as part of the policy at no extra cost, but sometimes a charge is assessed. If you are adequately insured, a multiple indemnity clause is unnecessary.

Settlement Options Allow the Beneficiary to Decide How to Receive the Death Benefit

Settlement options are the choices that the life insurance beneficiary or policyholder has in determining how the death benefit payment will be structured. The owner may choose the option before death, or the beneficiary may select the option after the insured's death. Each option's appropriateness depends on the beneficiary's financial situation. The five settlement options are as follows:

settlement options Choices from which the policyholder can choose in how the death benefit payment will be structured.

1. **Lump sum.** The death benefit may be received as a lump-sum cash settlement immediately after death.
2. **Interest income.** The beneficiary can receive the annual interest earned from the death benefit. For example, the beneficiary would receive $4000 each year from a $100,000 death benefit earning 4 percent interest. The $100,000 principal would remain intact and would continue to earn interest until the death of the beneficiary, when it becomes part of his or her estate.
3. **Income of a specific amount.** The beneficiary may receive a specific amount of income per year from the death benefit. Under this option, payments cease when the death benefit and interest are exhausted. For example, a $100,000 death benefit earning 4 percent interest would provide a $15,000 annual income for approximately eight years.*
4. **Income for a specific period.** The beneficiary may receive an income from the death benefit for a specific number of years. For example, a widow with small children may choose to receive an income for 18 years. The insurance company would calculate a level of income that would allow for equal proceeds each year, with all funds, including interest, being exhausted at the end of the 18th year.
5. **Income for life.** The beneficiary may elect to receive an income for life. In such a case, the insurance company would use the life expectancy of the beneficiary to calculate the level of income that would allow for equal annual payments so that funds would be exhausted by the expected date of the beneficiary's death. If the beneficiary lives longer than expected, the income payments would continue.

Policy Features Unique to Cash-Value Life Insurance

Cash-value life insurance policies carry special features that all relate to the cash values built up in the policies.

The Policy Illustration Prior to death, you may cash in the policy for the accumulated cash value, which cancels your insurance coverage, or you may borrow all or part of the cash value. You must repay the amount borrowed with interest, and any amount owed will be subtracted from the face amount of the policy if you die while the debt remains outstanding.

Cash-value life insurance policies generally provide a **policy illustration** that charts the projected growth in the cash value for given rates of return. Two rates are usually quoted: the **guaranteed minimum rate of return** (the minimum rate that, by contract, the company is legally obligated to pay) and the **current rate** (the rate of return recently paid by the company to policyholders). Agents typically emphasize the current rate, perhaps by presenting a table that illustrates the rate of cash-value accumulation resulting from the two rates. Table 12.1 provides an example of such a table. Note the differences in the two cash-value columns in Table 12.1—you can readily understand why the agent would emphasize the current rate. Policy illustrations can easily be made to look much more optimistic than it is reasonable to expect. Only after the policy is in force for perhaps 10 to 20 years can an accurate picture be drawn. For this reason, it is smart to periodically ask your agent for an **in-force illustration** that shows the cash-value

guaranteed minimum rate of return Minimum rate that, by contract, the insurance company is legally obligated to pay.

current rate Rate of return the insurance company has recently paid to policyholders.

*This option and options 4 and 5 are variations of an annuity as covered further in Chapter 17.

status of the policy and projections for the future given the current rate of return at the time of the illustration (rather than the rate used at the inception of the policy).

Policy illustrations can be helpful in many cases, but they can also be written in such a way as to make the policy look better than it really is. Asking a few pertinent questions can help cut through some of the misconceptions:

1. Is the "current rate" illustrated actually the rate paid recently? What was the current rate in each of the past five years?
2. What assumptions have been made regarding company expenses, dividend rates, and policy lapse rates?
3. Does all of my cash value earn a return at the current rate? (If not, the current rate is misleading.)
4. Is the illustration based on the "cash surrender value" or the "cash value"? (The cash surrender value is usually the lower value and reflects what will actually be paid if the policy is cashed in.)

nonforfeiture values Amounts stipulated in a life insurance policy that protect the cash value, if any, in the event that the policyholder chooses not to pay or fails to pay required premiums.

cash surrender value Represents the cash value of a policy minus any surrender charges.

Nonforfeiture Values **Nonforfeiture values** are amounts stipulated in a life insurance policy that protect the cash value, if any, in the event that the policyholder chooses not to pay or fails to pay the required premiums. The policy owner can receive the accumulated cash-value funds in one of three ways. First, he or she may simply surrender the policy and receive the **cash surrender value,** which represents the cash value minus any surrender charges. In reality, the true measure of the cash value of a policy is its cash surrender value (the amount received when the policy is canceled). Second, the policy owner may continue the policy with the original face amount but for a time period shorter than the original policy. Third, the policy may be continued on a paid-up basis, with a new and lower face amount being established based on the amount that can be purchased with the accumulated funds. Table 12.3 illustrates the nonforfeiture values for a paid-at-65 cash-value policy. Note that a cash-value policy has very little cash surrender value unless you have held it for ten years or more.

Policy Loans The owner of a cash-value policy may borrow all or a portion of the accumulated cash value. Interest rates charged for the loan will range from 2 to 8 percent, depending on the terms of the policy. In addition, the interest rate earned on the remaining cash value typically reverts to the guaranteed minimum rate while the loan remains outstanding. As a result, the cash value ultimately accumulated may be significantly reduced.

automatic premium loan Provision allows any premium not paid by the end of the grace period to be paid automatically with a policy loan if sufficient cash value or dividends have accumulated.

An **automatic premium loan** provision allows any premium not paid by the end of the grace period to be paid automatically with a policy loan if sufficient cash value or dividends have accumulated. In the first few years of a policy, this provision may not offer much benefit because cash value and dividends accumulate slowly. Eventually these funds may grow enough to pay premiums for a considerable length of time, thereby effectively preventing the lapse of the policy.

Many life insurance companies make a policy's death benefit available to a terminally ill insured through a **living benefit clause** that allows the payment of all or a portion of the death benefit prior to death if the insured contracts a terminal illness. This allows the policy to offer, in effect, long-term health care protection. These early payments are not cash-value loans, so it is possible to obtain more than the cash value accumulated in the policy. In addition, **viatical companies** specialize in buying life insurance policies from insureds for $0.50 to $0.80 per $1 of death benefit in return for being named beneficiary on the policy.

waiver of premium Sets certain conditions under which an insurance policy would be kept in full force by the company without the payment of premiums.

Waiver of Premium A **waiver of premium** sets certain conditions under which an insurance policy would be kept in full force by the company without the payment of premiums. It usually applies when a policyholder becomes totally and permanently disabled, but it may also apply under other conditions, depending on the policy provisions. In effect, the waiver-of-premium option (for an extra cost) protects against the risk of becoming disabled and being unable to pay premiums. This option can be expensive and may account for as much as 10 percent of the policy premium. If you

Table 12.3 Cash-Value Life Insurance Nonforfeiture Values

(Policyholder can choose A, B, or C.)

	A	B		C
		Period of $10,000 Term Insurance		
Policy Year	Cash or Surrender Value*	Years	Days	Face Value of Term Insurance Paid-up for Life†
0	$ 0	0	0	$ 0
2	0	0	0	0
3	60	2	81	240
4	190	7	35	720
5	310	10	282	1,140
10	1,000	19	351	3,160
15	1,790	22	346	4,900
20	2,690	23	122	6,410
30	4,350	21	228	8,260
35	5,390	20	286	9,140
40	6,520	For life	—	10,000
45	7,110	For life	—	10,000

For a $10,000, paid-at-65, limited-payment, cash-value life insurance policy for a male aged 25; the annual premium is $180.

*The policy has a back-end load that reduces the buildup of cash value in early years.
†Much lower commissions tend to be charged on term insurance policies.

are adequately covered by disability income insurance (see Chapter 11), then you might want to avoid this option.

Guaranteed Insurability The **guaranteed insurability** (or **guaranteed purchase) option** permits the cash-value policyholder to buy additional stated amounts of cash-value life insurance at stated times in the future without evidence of insurability. This option differs from the guaranteed renewability option for term insurance in that it enables the owner to increase the face amount of the policy or to buy an additional policy. The policy might allow the exercise of these options when the insured turns 30, 35, or 40, or when he or she marries or has children. The added cost of this option is nominal and worthwhile.

guaranteed insurability (guaranteed purchase option) Permits the cash-value policyholder to buy additional stated amounts of cash-value life insurance at stated times in the future without evidence of insurability.

CONCEPT CHECK 12.3

1. Distinguish among the owner, the insured, the beneficiary, and the contingent beneficiary of a life insurance policy.
2. Briefly describe each of the five components of all insurance policies.
3. Identify the five settlement options for the payment of the proceeds of a life insurance policy to its beneficiary.
4. Besides taking the cash value as a lump sum, what are four more ways a cash-value policyholder may take the proceeds of the policy at cancellation?
5. Distinguish between an automatic premium loan and a waiver of premium option in a life insurance policy.
6. Explain how guaranteed renewability for term life insurance and guaranteed insurability for cash-value insurance protect insured people who develop serious health conditions.

Step-by-Step Strategies for Buying Life Insurance

4 LEARNING OBJECTIVE
Apply a step-by-step strategy for implementing a life insurance plan.

In a recent year, more than $140 billion of new life insurance was purchased in the United States. Did each individual really need to be covered by life insurance? Was the policy purchased the right one, and was it purchased from a reputable company and agent? Did the buyer pay the right price?

First Ask Whether or Not, and For How Much, Your Life Should Be Insured

Anyone whose death will result in financial losses to others should be covered by life insurance unless other resources are sufficient to cover the losses. At a minimum, there will be final expenses such as for funeral and burial. Beyond that, the need depends on the person's family situation. Parents with minor children almost always need life insurance.

People who generally do not need life insurance include children and people with no dependents who have no desire to leave an estate. People who are sometimes unnecessarily insured include retirees who may have already built up assets sufficient to provide for income for survivors and to cover final expenses. The only way to really know how much additional life insurance you need is through the needs-based calculations covered earlier in this chapter. You should do this yourself and not rely on an insurance agent who has a vested interest in selling you some life insurance.

Did You Know?...

About Life Insurance After Divorce

If you receive income from a former spouse through either alimony or child support, life insurance on that person is advisable. If a policy that was purchased while a couple was married remains in effect, it is wise to keep it. To be certain that the correct beneficiary is named, have that requirement stated in a court order and/or made part of the divorce decree. The custodial parent should then be named as owner of the policy, thereby preventing the noncustodial parent from making any changes in the policy. Noncustodial parents will also need life insurance on their former spouses because they will probably receive custody of the children if the former spouse dies and may need additional income to support them.

Then Properly Integrate Your Life Insurance into Your Overall Financial Planning

Advertising and sales promotion literature for cash-value life insurance often pushes the idea that this type of insurance is a good investment and is appropriate as a retirement savings vehicle. Most independent personal finance experts would disagree strongly. Instead, they typically advise people to take a broader perspective and think of life insurance as just one facet of their plans. Specifically, you should always think in terms of the two longevity risks: the risk of dying too soon and the risk of living too long. Term life insurance most effectively solves the dying-too-soon problem. Investing through tax-sheltered retirement plans most effectively solves the living-too-long problem.

Your need for life insurance will change significantly over the course of your life. So should your life insurance plan. You should reassess your plan every two or three years and any time your family or employment situation changes. Keep these facts in mind:

- During childhood and while single, your need for life insurance is either nonexistent or very small because few, if any, other people rely on you for financial support.
- With marriage comes the increased responsibility for another person, although life insurance needs probably remain low because spouses usually have the potential to support themselves if the other partner were to die.
- The arrival of children, however, triggers a sharp increase in life insurance needs. Children often require as many as 25 years of parental support, during which time they usually have little ability to provide for themselves.
- As children grow older, the number of years of their remaining dependency declines, reducing the need for life insurance.

Did You Know? ...

The Tax Consequences of Protecting Loved Ones Through Life Insurance

Some people consider cash-value life insurance to be a tax-advantaged way to invest for retirement. Life insurance does have some tax-sheltering aspects because the cash value built up in the policy is not subject to income taxes. For a number of other reasons, however, cash-value life insurance does not compare favorably with qualified retirement plans available through your employer or with IRAs (discussed in Chapter 17)

1. The rate of return on cash-value life insurance has historically lagged well behind what can be achieved by a diversified portfolio of stock and bond mutual funds. Mutual funds can be purchased through various tax-sheltered retirement accounts (discussed in Chapters 1, 4, and 17).
2. The commissions and expense charges on cash-value life insurance are much higher than those associated with most no-load mutual funds. This is especially true for index mutual funds. (See Chapter 15.)
3. The premiums paid on life insurance policies cannot be used to reduce taxable income; however, contributions to individual retirement accounts and 401(k) plans do offer this significant advantage.

You should be contributing the maximum amount possible into available tax-sheltered retirement plans before you consider the purchase of cash-value life insurance as a retirement savings vehicle.

- Parents with grown children see a reduced need for life insurance because their retirement investment program will have grown large enough to cover the losses that death might bring.
- Retirement and widowhood reduce the need for life insurance or may even eliminate it altogether.

Figure 12.3 depicts a life insurance and investment plan recommended over an individual's life cycle. This plan is built on two cornerstones: (1) the purchase of term insurance for the bulk of life insurance needs (because term insurance is more flexible than cash-value insurance and provides more protection for each premium dollar) and (2) a systematic, regular investment program. The first type of life insurance to buy is a permanent cash-value policy with a guaranteed insurability option. A $20,000 to $50,000

As a family ages, life insurance needs typically decrease.

Advice from a Pro...

Buy Term and Invest the Rest

The principle behind the strategy "buy term and invest the rest" is simple: If you invest the money difference between the cost of premiums for a term life insurance policy and the cost of premiums for a far more expensive cash-value policy, you will *always* come out ahead financially. To see why, consider the buildup of protection shown in the accompanying table for Seth Cameron, a 30-year-old who is considering life insurance policies. Seth could pay an $870 annual premium to buy a $100,000 whole life policy. Alternatively, he could spend $130 for the first-year premium of a $100,000 five-year renewable term policy and invest the $740 difference ($870 − $130) in a mutual fund account and earn a 5 percent after-tax rate of return.

If Seth dies tomorrow, the policy's beneficiary would receive both the $100,000 in insurance proceeds and the $740 in savings. After five years (age 35), Seth's annual $740 in savings would have grown to $4293; if he dies at that time, the total death benefit would be $104,293. If Seth dies years into the future, the estate is even further ahead because of the growing principal in the account. By age 60, Seth's mutual fund investment would have grown to $58,052. If the fund earned higher than 5 percent annually, the amount would be much greater.

By the time Seth reached age 60, the term insurance premiums would exceed the premiums for the cash-value policy. However, his need for life insurance would presumably be eliminated or greatly reduced at that point. If Seth's children were self-supporting by then, he could probably drop the term insurance policy altogether. Nevertheless, his mutual fund account would remain to provide a financial nest egg of $58,052 or more to his heirs.

With the "buy term and invest the rest" strategy, Seth would have been insured more than 30 years at total premium cost of just $7450. By contrast, the cash-value policy would have required total premiums of $26,100 ($870 × 30) and the policy's cash value at year 30 would be about $44,000.

For "buy term and invest the rest" to work, however, the difference between the term and cash-value policy premiums must, in fact, be invested on a regular basis. Many people say that they will invest this money but then fail to follow through on that promise. You can succeed with a little discipline. The easiest way to ensure that your money is actually invested is to set up an **automatic investment program (AIP)** in which a mutual fund is authorized to withdraw money from your checking account, perhaps monthly, to buy mutual fund shares. When you agree to invest the "difference" automatically, the strategy will work well for you. (See Chapters 13 and 15.)

Jordan Goodman
Moneyanswers.com

Estate Buildup if a Term Life Insurance Buyer Invests the Difference

Age	Premium for Five-Year Renewable Term	Difference (Not Spent on Whole Life)	Total Investment and Earnings* at 5%	Total Estate
30	$ 130	$ 740	$ 740	$100,740
35	150	720	4,293	104,293
40	180	690	9,657	109,657
45	210	660	16,328	116,328
50	240	630	24,668	124,668
55	580	290	35,139	135,139
60			58,052	58,052

*This illustration makes the following assumptions: The whole life policy premium for the same $100,000 in coverage is fixed at $870 every year; the buyer pays the five-year renewable term premium at the beginning of each year; and the difference is invested. Those amounts stay in the investments account all year, as does the previous year's ending balance. Investments earn a compounded 5 percent after-tax annual rate of return. Upon the insured's death, the beneficiary would receive the $100,000 face amount of the term life insurance policy plus the amount built up in the investments account earning 5 percent.

policy is sufficient to cover final expenses, the only permanent need that is present throughout life. The remainder of your life insurance should consist of multiple term insurance policies that you start buying when you begin to have dependents. These should be five- or ten-year, level-premium, guaranteed renewable policies in increments of $100,000 or more. The policies should be layered so that you can drop policies as your need declines. By the time you reach retirement, you will have dropped all your term policies and the cash-value policy can remain to pay final expenses or be cashed in to provide a little retirement income. Of course, this scenario requires that you implement an investment program to save for retirement. Chapters 13 through 17 cover investments in sufficient detail to provide you with the necessary tools to construct this program.

Where and How to Buy Your Life Insurance

The most important feature of any life insurance company is its ability to pay its obligations. The company you choose must have the stability and financial strength to survive for the many years your policy will remain in force. Ratings of the financial strengths of insurance companies are available from A.M. Best Company (www.ambest.com) and Standard & Poor's (www.standardandpoors.com).

You Can Easily Buy Life Insurance Online Smart personal financial managers take a do-it-yourself approach to life insurance. They regularly calculate their needs and decide what types of insurance to buy and cancel in what increments. This allows them to use a **premium quote service** that offers computer-generated comparisons among 20 to 80 different companies. Premium quote services can be found at www.quotesmith.com, www.quotescout.com, and www.accuquote.com. These websites also offer online life insurance needs calculators and a wealth of information on life insurance from an unbiased perspective. In addition, all the major life insurance companies have an online purchase system. Term insurance is easiest to buy this way, but even cash-value insurance can be purchased online.

premium quote service Offers computer-generated comparisons among 20 to 80 different companies.

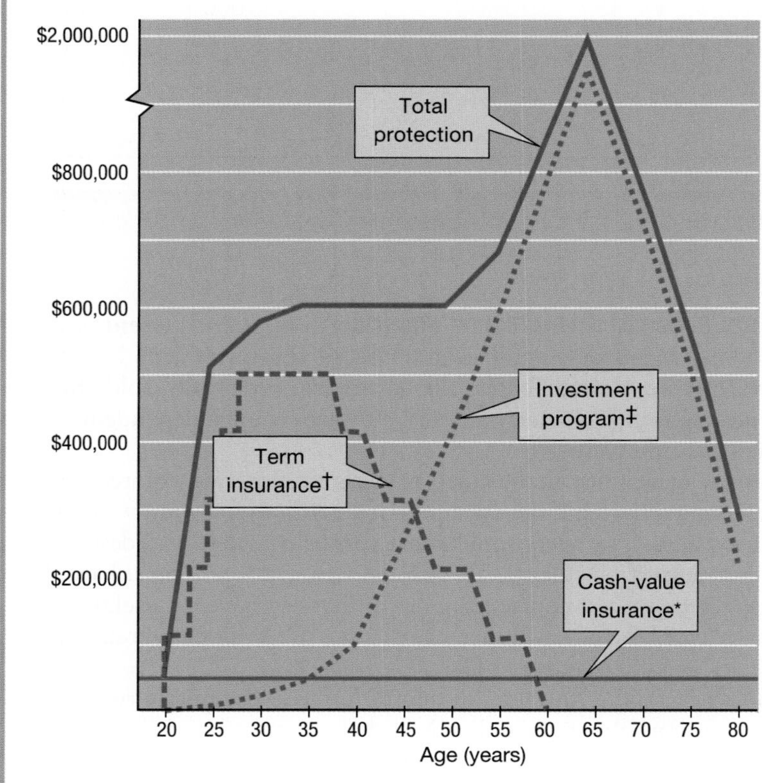

Figure 12.3

Life Insurance and Investment Planning over the Life Cycle

*With a guaranteed insurability option and paid-up at 65.

†Term insurance policies.

††Includes vested employer-sponsored retirement [e.g., 401(k)] plans. (See Chapter 17.)

Did You Know?...

How to Layer Your Term Insurance Policies for $60 per Month

Trying to meet one's life insurance needs with just one or two life insurance policies is not the best way to obtain protection over the life cycle. Life insurance needs fluctuate over one's lifetime, and you will need flexibility. Your life insurance needs are low (burial, debt repayment) until the moment when your first child is born or adopted. Then the need can easily spike up to $200,000 or $500,000 (or more). This need will remain high until the youngest child is approximately ten years old and then will decrease until your retirement age. You can meet the bulk of this need by **layering term insurance policies** so that coverage grows and then can be decreased as your needs change.

An example is provided in the chart below. It assumes that the person is age 25 when a first child is born and age 30 when a last child is born. In this example, the parents buy several level-premium term policies near the birth of the first child, with the policies having differing time periods. They buy another policy when their last child is born and another as the first child gets close to college age. As the children go out on their own, some of the earliest policies expire, thereby reducing the overall amount of insurance as the parents' needs decline.

One benefit of layering is affordability. Based on premium rates for healthy nonsmokers, the cost for the plan illustrated here would never be more than approximately $60 per month.

Age	Buy	Policies in Force at Each Age	Total Coverage at Each Age
25	Policy 1, $100,000, 30 years	#1, #2, #3	$450,000
	Policy 2, $150,000, 25 years		
	Policy 3, $200,000, 20 years		
30	Policy 4, $150,000, 25 years	#1, #2, #3, #4	600,000
35		#1, #2, #3, #4	600,000
40	Policy 5, $50,000, 20 years	#1, #2, #3, #4, #5	650,000
45		#1, #2, #4, #5	450,000
50		#1, #4, #5	300,000
55		#5	50,000
60			0

layering term insurance policies Purchasing level-premium term policies so that coverage grows when you need it most and then can be decreased as your needs change.

insurance agent Representative of an insurance company authorized to sell, modify, service, and terminate insurance contracts.

Or You Can Use a Local Insurance Agent An **insurance agent** is a representative of an insurance company authorized to sell, modify, service, and terminate insurance contracts. In the United States, life insurance is typically sold through exclusive agents who represent only one company, although some independent agents represent more than one company.

The life insurance agent must be qualified to design a program tailored to your specific needs and should understand the dynamics of family relationships, which influence all life insurance needs. The agent should have earned a professional designation, such as chartered life underwriter (CLU). To earn the CLU, an agent must have three years of experience and pass a ten-course program in life insurance counseling. Some agents also may have earned the certified financial planner (CFP) or chartered financial consultant (ChFC) designation (see page 344).

Your agent should be willing to take the time to provide personal service and to answer all of your questions about the policy both before and after you purchase it. Always ask an agent about the first-year commission on any policies you are considering.

In addition, you should check your agent's reputation with your state's insurance and securities investment regulatory agencies.

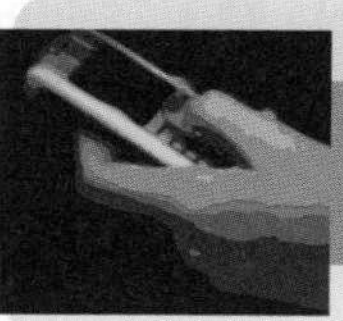

Instant Message

State Insurance Departments Are a Good Consumer Resource

You can find information about life insurance companies through your state's insurance regulatory agency (www.naic.org/state_web_map.htm).

Compare Costs Among Policies The price people pay for life insurance depends on their age, health, and lifestyle. Age is important, of course, because the probability of dying increases with age. A person who has a health problem such as heart disease or diabetes may pay considerably higher rates for life insurance or may not be able to obtain coverage at any price. People with hazardous occupations (police officers) or dangerous hobbies (skydivers) are often required to pay higher life insurance premiums as well. Life insurance companies typically offer their lowest prices to "preferred" applicants whose health status and lifestyle (for example, nonsmokers) suggest longevity. "Standard" and "impaired" applicants would pay more. Because companies differ in how they assign these labels to applicants, you should shop around for the best treatment.

Popular magazines such as *Kiplinger's Personal Finance Magazine*, *Consumer Reports*, and *Money* regularly publish articles that give average or typical premiums for different types of policies. In addition, your state department of insurance may publish life insurance buyer's guides containing price guidelines that may prove useful in selecting companies with the lowest prices. These independent life insurance agents or groups of agents concentrate on marketing term life insurance at the lowest possible rates.

Term life insurance premiums are usually quoted in dollars per $1000 of coverage. Generally, the higher the face amount of the policy, the lower the rate per $1000. For example, a company might sell term life insurance for $1 per $1000 per year when purchased in face amounts of $100,000 or more and for $1.25 per $1000 per year for policies of less than $100,000. Policies with face amounts of $1 million can cost less than $0.50 per $1000 per year for people younger than age 35.

It is easy to pay too much for term life insurance, especially if you do not comparison shop. The rates shown in Table 12.4 represent good values for term insurance. Note that smokers pay much higher premiums than nonsmokers because as a group smokers die ten years earlier than nonsmokers. Men pay more than women because they typically die three years earlier. Table 12.5 lists annual premiums that are near the average required for various types of insurance policies.

Did You Know?...

About Life Insurance Sales Commissions

Sales commissions are paid to the selling insurance agent every year that a life insurance policy remains in force. Very low sales commissions tend to be charged on term insurance policies—perhaps 10 percent or less of the premium if the policy is purchased directly rather than through an agent. Sales commissions typically represent as much as 90 percent of the first-year premium paid for a cash-value life insurance policy. Over the next several years, commissions drop considerably (perhaps to 50, 40, 30, 20, and 10 percent) so that more of the premium builds cash value.

You can buy all types of life insurance policies with low commissions by mail, on the Internet, and through fee-only financial planners and fee-for-service insurance agents. Even policies sold with a low commission rate may have a **surrender charge,** which is a fee assessed if the policyholder withdraws some or all of the cash value accumulated. This charge is often highest in the early years of the policy but may be reduced or eliminated in later years. The policy illustrated in Table 12.1 has a surrender charge, for example. Ask about commissions and surrender charges whenever you shop for life insurance. Be wary of policies that have both high commissions and surrender charges.

Table 12.4 Fair Prices for Term Life Insurance*

(Authors' estimates based on Internet shopping on the major quote services.)

	Nonsmokers		Smokers	
Age	**Male**	**Female**	**Male**	**Female**
18–30	$0.70	$0.67	$1.00	$0.95
35	$0.83	$0.74	$1.25	$1.15
40	$1.08	$1.00	$1.95	$1.60
45	$1.67	$1.60	$2.80	$2.40
50	$2.30	$2.20	$4.00	$3.25

*Multiply the rate by each $1000 of coverage and add $60 for estimated administrative fees. For example, a fair annual premium for a $50,000 policy for a 36-year-old male nonsmoker might be $101.50 ($0.83 × 50 = $41.50; $41.50 + $60 = $101.50).

The cost of insurance measured in dollars per $1000 is not an appropriate decision criterion when attempting to compare term with cash-value insurance or when examining different types of cash-value insurance. Three methods are used to compare similar policies:

1. **Net cost method.** The **net cost** of a life insurance policy equals the total of all premiums to be paid minus any accumulated cash value and accrued dividends. It is calculated for a specific point in time during the life of the policy—for example, at the end of the 10th or 20th year. The net cost is often a negative figure, giving a false impression that the policy will pay for itself. You should ignore net cost calculations provided by a life insurance agent.
2. **Interest-adjusted cost index method.** A **cost index** is a numerical method used to compare the costs of similar plans of life insurance. The **interest-adjusted cost index (IACI)** measures the cost of life insurance, taking into account the interest that would have been earned had the premiums been invested rather than used to buy insurance. The lower the IACI, the lower the cost of the policy. Ask for 5-, 10-, 20-, and 30-year IACI values as well because companies have been known to manipulate their dividend and cash-value accumulations to look especially good at the 20-year point. You should insist on being told the index before you agree to buy a policy, and you should shop elsewhere if the agent refuses, resists, or implies that the index has little value.
3. **Interest-adjusted net payment index method.** The IACI assumes that the policy will be cashed in and surrendered at the end of a certain period (usually 20 years) rather than remaining in force until the death of the insured. If the policy will remain in force until death, you can use the **interest-adjusted net payment index (IANPI)** to effectively measure the cost of cash-value insurance. The lower the IANPI, the lower the cost of the policy.

interest-adjusted net payment index (IANPI) If a policy will remain in force until death, this method allows you to effectively measure the cost of cash-value insurance. The lower the IANPI, the lower the cost of the policy.

Table 12.5 Typical Premiums* for Various Types of Life Insurance (Face Amount $100,000)

	Policy Year							
Policy Type	**1**	**2**	**3**	**5**	**10**	**11**	**20**	**Age 65**
Annual renewable term (guaranteed renewability to age 70)	$80	$81	$82	$83	$90	$92	$110	$2,400
Decreasing term (over 20 years)	160	160	160	160	160	160	160	0
Convertible term (within 5 years)	170	170	170	170	940	940	940	940
Whole life	870	870	870	870	870	870	870	870
Universal life	590	590	590	590	680	730	760	790
Limited-pay life (paid at age 65)	920	920	920	920	920	920	920	0

*Premiums quoted are for a 21-year-old male nonsmoker.

CONCEPT CHECK 12.4

1. List the benefits of buying term and investing the rest.
2. Identify the weaknesses of cash-value life insurance as a mechanism for saving for retirement.
3. Explain how the pattern of one's life insurance program should vary from young adulthood through retirement years.
4. Explain how you can benefit by layering your term insurance policies.

What Do You Recommend Now?

Now that you have read the chapter on protecting loved ones through life insurance, what would you recommend to Karen and Will Bridgeman in the case at the beginning of the chapter regarding:

1. Their changing need for life insurance once they have a child?
2. What types of life insurance they should consider and whether they should purchase multiple policies?
3. Coordinating their retirement savings and other investments with their life insurance program?
4. Shopping for life insurance?

Big Picture Summary of Learning Objectives

1 Understand the reasons why you might need life insurance and calculate the appropriate amount of coverage.

Life insurance is designed to provide protection from the financial losses that result from death. The reasons to purchase life insurance change over the life cycle. The need for this type of protection is nonexistent or very small for children and single adults. Factors affecting life insurance needs include the need to replace income, final-expense needs, readjustment-period needs, debt-repayment needs, college-expense needs, availability of government programs, and ownership of other life insurance and assets. Two methods to calculate life insurance needs are the multiple-of-earnings approach and the needs-based approach. The needs-based approach is the more accurate of the two and should be conducted every three years or whenever your family situation changes.

2 Distinguish among types of life insurance.

Two basic types of life insurance exist: term life insurance and cash-value life insurance. Variations on term life insurance include decreasing term insurance, guaranteed renewable term insurance, convertible term insurance, and credit life insurance. Variations on cash-value insurance include whole life insurance, limited-pay life insurance, and universal and variable life insurance.

3 Explain the major provisions of life insurance policies.

A life insurance policy is a written contract between the insurance purchaser and the insurance company, spelling out in detail the terms of the agreement. When buying life insurance, you should pay attention to the policy's general terms and conditions, the special features of cash-value life insurance, and settlement options.

4 Apply a step-by-step strategy for implementing a life insurance plan.

Life insurance should be purchased to address the dying-too-soon problem. Your investments should manage the living-too-long problem. Addressing these two problems appropriately requires a small amount of cash-value life insurance, high amounts of term insurance while you are raising children, and a sound investment program to prepare for your retirement years. You should not purchase life insurance until you have determined the actual dollar amount and type of policy you need and compared premiums using various life insurance cost indices.

Let's Talk About It

1. What were your feelings about the need for life insurance before you read this chapter? What are they now?
2. Are you covered by life insurance? If so, how much? Do you feel that you are over- or underinsured?
3. Why do you think people persist in buying cash-value life insurance when, in most cases, they would be better off buying term insurance and investing the money saved into a tax-sheltered retirement account?
4. In many married-couple families, one of the spouses is the primary breadwinner and the other focuses more on homemaking duties. In your view, how does such an arrangement affect the approach that should be taken for each spouse in terms of life insurance?
5. Many young people today choose to cohabitate rather than marry (at least for some time period). Should this affect their thinking about life insurance?

Do the Numbers

1. Andrew Blake of Tuscaloosa, Alabama, is single and has been working as an admissions counselor at a university for three years. Andrew owns a home valued at $156,000 on which he owes $135,000. He has a two-year-old vehicle valued at $12,500 on which he owes $8000. He has about $3800 remaining on his student loans. His retirement account has grown to $7800, and he owns some stock valued at $4400. He has no life insurance and is considering buying some. How much should he buy?
2. Kyle and Laura Parker have been married for three years. They recently bought a home costing $212,000 using a $190,000 mortgage. They have no other debts. Kyle earns $42,000 per year and Laura $41,000. Each has a retirement plan valued at approximately $10,000. They recently received a mail offer from their mortgage lender for a mortgage life insurance policy of $190,000. Their only life insurance currently is a $20,000 cash-value survivorship joint life policy. They each would like to provide the other with support for five years if one of them should die. Assuming $10,000 in final expenses, calculate the amount of life insurance they need using the needs-based approach. Assume a 4% interest rate.
3. Lauren Crow of Davis, California, has a $100,000 participating cash-value policy written on her life. The policy has accumulated $4700 in cash value; Lauren has borrowed $3000 of this value. The policy also has accumulated unpaid dividends of $1666. Yesterday Lauren paid her premium of $1200 for the coming year. What is the current death benefit from this policy?

Financial Planning Cases

Case 1
Life Insurance for a Newly Married Couple

Just-married couples sometimes overindulge in the type and amount of life insurance that they buy. John and Nicole Greenwood of Gunnison, Colorado, took a different approach. Both were working and had a small amount of life insurance provided through their respective employee benefit programs: John, $40,000, and Nicole, $50,000. During their discussion of life insurance needs and related costs, they decided that if Nicole completed her master's degree in industrial psychology, she would have better employment opportunities. Consequently, they decided to use money they had available for additional life insurance to pay for Nicole's education. They both feel, however, that they do not want to have inadequate life insurance.

(a) In what way does Nicole's return to school alter the Greenwoods' life insurance needs?

(b) Would you agree that the amount of life insurance provided by the Greenwoods' respective employers is adequate while Nicole is in school? Explain your response.

(c) Summarize how the Greenwoods' life insurance needs might change over their life cycle.

Case 2
Fraternity Members Contemplate Permanent Life Insurance

Zachary Chen is a college student from Santa Ana, California. Soon to graduate, Zachary was approached recently by a life insurance agent, who set up a group meeting for several members of his fraternity. During the meeting, the agent presented six life insurance plans and was very persuasive about the benefits of a universal life insurance plan that his company calls Affordable Life II. Under the plan, the prospective graduate can buy $100,000 of permanent life insurance for a very low premium during the first five years and then pay a higher premium later when income presumably will have increased. Zachary was confused after the meeting, as were his friends. Armed with your knowledge from this personal finance book, you have been asked to respond to some of their questions.

(a) Do you think universal life insurance is a good deal for these people? Why or why not?

(b) How can the individual fraternity members decide how much life insurance they need?

(c) Life insurance cannot be as confusing as the agent made it seem. What clearer explanation would you give to the fraternity members?

(d) What type of life insurance, if any, would you advise for the fraternity brothers?

(e) How would they know if a life insurance policy is offered at a fair price?

Case 3
A Married Couple with Children Address Their Life Insurance Needs

Joseph and Samantha Hensley of Savannah, Georgia, are a married couple in their mid-30s. They have two children, ages five and three, and Samantha is pregnant with their third child. Samantha is a book indexer who earned $15,000 after taxes last year. Because she performs much of her work at home, it is unlikely that she will need to curtail her work after the baby is born. Joseph is a family therapist; he earned $48,000 last year after taxes. Because both are self-employed, Samantha and Joseph do not have access to group life insurance. They are each covered by $50,000 universal life policies they purchased three years ago. In addition, Joseph is covered by a $50,000, five-year guaranteed renewable term policy, which will expire next year. The Hensleys are currently reassessing their life insurance program. As a preliminary step in their analysis, they have determined that Samantha's account with Social Security would yield the family about $1094 per month, or an annual benefit of $13,128, if she were to die. For Joseph, the figure would be $2072 per month, or an annual benefit of $24,864. Both agree that they would like to support each of their children to age 22, but to date they have been unable to start a college savings fund. The couple estimates that it would cost $80,000 to put each child through a regional university in their state as measured in today's dollars. They expect that burial expenses for each spouse would total about $10,000, and they would like to have a lump sum of life insurance clearly marked for paying off their $155,000 home mortgage. They also feel that each spouse would want to take a six-month leave from work if the other were to die.

(a) Calculate the amount of life insurance that Samantha needs based on the information given. Use the Decision-Making Worksheet on page 326 or the *Garman/Forgue* website. Assume a 3 percent rate of return after taxes and inflation and an income need for 22 years because the unborn child will need financial support for that many years.

(b) Calculate the amount of life insurance that Joseph needs based on the information given. Use the Decision-Making Worksheet on page 326 or the *Garman/Forgue* website. Assume a 3 percent rate of return after taxes and inflation and an income need for 22 years because the unborn child will need financial support for that many years.

(c) If Samantha and Joseph purchased term insurance to cover their additional needs, how much more would each need to spend on life insurance?

Case 4
Victor and Maria Hernandez Contemplate Switching Life Insurance Policies

Victor and Maria Hernández have a total of $200,000 in life insurance. Victor has a $50,000 cash-value policy purchased more than 20 years ago when the couple was first married (now with a $16,000 cash value) and a $100,000 group term policy through his employer. Maria has a $50,000 group term insurance policy through her employer. The couple has been approached by a life insurance agent who thinks that they need to change their policy mix because, he says, they are inadequately insured. Specifically, the agent has suggested that Victor cash in his cash-value policy and buy a new variable-universal life insurance policy.

(a) If Victor cashes in his policy, what options would he have when receiving the cash value?

(b) Determine what the $16,000 in cash value in Victor's life insurance policy would be worth in 20 years if that sum were invested somewhere else and earned an 8 percent annual return. (Hint: Use the *Garman/Forgue* website.)

(c) Would cashing in the policy be a wise decision? Why or why not?

(d) As the Hernandezes' children are now grown and out on their own, and both Victor and Maria are employed full time, give general reasons why Victor may need more or less insurance.

(e) Explain why it would be a bad idea for Victor to buy a variable-universal life insurance policy.

Case 5
The Johnsons Change Their Life Insurance Coverage

Harry and Belinda Johnson spend $9 per month on life insurance in the form of a premium on a $10,000, paid-at-65 cash-value policy on Harry. Belinda has a group term insurance policy from her employer with a face amount of $59,400 (1.5 times her annual salary). By choosing a group life insurance plan from his menu of employee benefits, Harry now has $30,900 (his annual salary) of group term life insurance. Harry and Belinda have decided that, because they have no children, they could reduce their life insurance needs by protecting one another's income for only four years, assuming the survivor would be able to fend for himself or herself after that time. They also realize that their savings fund is so low that it would have no bearing on their life insurance needs. Harry and Belinda are basing their calculations on a projected 4 percent rate of return after taxes and inflation. They also estimate the following expenses: $8000 for final expenses, $4000 for readjustment expenses, and $5000 for repayment of short-term debts.

(a) Should the $3000 interest earnings from Harry's trust fund be included in his annual income for the purposes of calculating the likely dollar loss if he were to die? (See the discussions about the Johnsons at the end of Chapter 3.) Explain your response.

(b) Based on your response to the previous question, how much more life insurance does Harry need? Use the Decision-Making Worksheet on page 326 to arrive at your answer.

(c) Repeat the calculations to arrive at the additional life insurance needed on Belinda's life.

(d) How might the Johnsons most economically meet any additional life insurance needs you have determined they may have?

(e) In addition to their life insurance planning, how might the Johnsons begin to prepare for their retirement years?

On the 'Net

Go to the Web pages indicated to complete these exercises. You can also go to the *Garman/Forgue* website at college.hmco.com/business/students for an expanded list of exercises. Under General Business, select the title of this text. Click on the Internet Exercises link for this chapter.

1. Visit the website for QuoteSmith at www.quotesmith.com to obtain a quote for the annual premium on a $200,000 guaranteed renewable, ten-year term policy for you. Then call a life insurance agent in your community to obtain a quote on the same term insurance coverage. How do the term rates quoted by your local agent compare with the rates found over the Internet? Also, ask for the quote on a $100,000 universal life policy with guaranteed insurability and waiver-of-premium options. Ask the agent to explain why the quotes for the two types of policies differ. Analyze his or her response based on what you learned in this chapter.
2. Visit the website for A.M. Best Company at www.ambest.com/ratings and check the ratings for the insurance company recommended by the agent in Exercise 1 as well as the company with the lowest cost for term insurance that you found on the Web. What do the ratings tell you about the relative strengths of those companies?
3. Visit the www.life-line.org website. Click on "Life Insurance" then "How much do I need" and then "Insurance needs calculator." Calculate your current need for life insurance. Then recalculate your need for five years from now given your estimates of your income and family situation.

Visit the Garman/Forgue website...

@college.hmco.com/business/students

Under General Business, select *Personal Finance 9e.* There, among other valuable resources, you will find a complete glossary, ACE questions, links to help you complete the chapter exercises, and links to other personal finance sites.

PART 4

CHAPTER 13 Investment Fundamentals

CHAPTER 14 Investing in Stocks and Bonds

CHAPTER 15 Investing Through Mutual Funds

CHAPTER 16 Real Estate and High-Risk Investments

CHAPTER 13

Investment Fundamentals

You Must Be Kidding, Right?

Twins Laura and Lauren Jackson have worked for the same employer for many years. They have always differed in their investment philosophies toward saving for retirement. Laura invested $5000 for 10 years starting at age 25 and never added any more money to the account. Lauren invested $5000 per year for 20 years starting at age 35 and never contributed more to her account. Assuming that they both earn an 8 percent annual return, how much more money will Laura have accumulated for retirement than Lauren by the time they reach age 65?

A. $144,000 **B.** $235,000 **C.** $494,000 **D.** $729,000

The answer is B, $235,000. Laura's account balance at age 65 is projected at $729,000 and Lauren's is $494,000. Even though Laura saved for only 10 years compared with Lauren's 20 years of saving, Laura's long-term investment approach had her starting to save for retirement early in her working career. Thus, she accumulated 48 percent more money than her sister ($235,000 ÷ $494,000). Starting early on long-term investment goals is a money-winning idea!

LEARNING OBJECTIVES

After reading this chapter, you should be able to:

1. **Explain** how to get started as an investor.
2. **Discover** your own investment philosophy.
3. **Identify** the kinds of investments that match your interests.
4. **Describe** the major factors that affect the rate of return on investments.
5. **Decide** which of the five long-term investment strategies you will utilize.
6. **Create** your own investment plan.

What Do You Recommend?

Jennifer and Julia are sisters, both in their 20s. Jennifer drives a leased BMW convertible, and she makes about $42,000, including tips, as a part-time bartender at two different restaurants. Although she has no employee benefits, she enjoys having flexible work hours so that she can go to the beach and the local nightspots. Currently, Jennifer has $10,000 in credit card debt. She has $1500 in a bank savings account, and two years ago she opened an individual retirement account (IRA) with a $1000 investment in a mutual fund. Her sister Julia drives a paid-for Geo, pays her credit card purchases in full each month, and sacrifices some of her salary by putting $100 per month into her employer's company stock through her 401(k) retirement account. Over the past seven years, the stock price, which was once about $40, has risen to almost $70, and Julia's 401(k) plan is now worth about $16,000. Julia also has invested about $14,000 in aggressive-growth mutual funds, and she plans to use that money for a down payment on a home purchase. She earns $58,000 as a manager of a restaurant, plus she receives an annual bonus ranging from $2000 to $4000 every January that she uses for a spring vacation in Mexico. Julia's employer provides many employee benefits.

What do you recommend to Jennifer and Julia on the subject of investment fundamentals regarding:

1. Getting more money to save and invest?
2. Prerequisites to investing for Jennifer?
3. Portfolio diversification for Julia?
4. Dollar-cost averaging for Jennifer?
5. Investment alternatives for Julia?

FOR HELP with studying this chapter, visit the Online Student Center:

www.college.hmco.com/pic/garman9e

fortable during rising and falling market conditions. They remain secure in the knowledge that they are investing for the long term. Their tactics might include spreading investment funds among several choices and trading some assets perhaps once a year.

People seeking moderate returns consider investing in dividend-paying common stocks, growth and income mutual funds, high-quality corporate bonds, government bonds, and real estate. Over the course of a year, a moderate investor with $1000 could possibly lose $150 and is likely to gain $80 to $100.

aggressive investment philosophy Investors with this philosophy primarily seek capital gains, often with a short time horizon.

Are You an Aggressive Investor? If you choose to strive for a very high return by accepting a high level of risk, you have an **aggressive investment philosophy.** As such, you could be characterized as a risk seeker. Aggressive investors primarily seek capital gains. Many such investors take a short-term approach, remaining confident that they can profit substantially during major upswings in market prices.

People seeking exceptionally high returns consider investing in common stocks of new or fast-growing companies, high-yielding junk bonds, and aggressive-growth mutual funds. Such investors may put their money into limited real estate partnerships, undeveloped land, precious metals, gems, commodity futures, stock-index futures, and collectibles. Devotees of this investment philosophy sometimes do not spread their funds among many alternatives. Also, they may adopt short-term tactics to increase capital gains. For example, aggressive investors might place most of their investment funds in a single stock in the hope that it will rise 10 percent over 90 days, giving an annual yield of more than 40 percent. Those shares could then be sold and the money invested elsewhere.

Investment tactics for aggressive investors are discussed in Chapter 16. Aggressive investors must be emotionally and financially able to weather substantial short-term losses—such as a downward swing in a stock's price of 30 or 40 percent even though they might expect that an upswing in price will occur in the future. Over the course of a year, an aggressive investor with $1000 could possibly lose $300 and could gain $150 or even more.

Should You Take an Active or Passive Investing Approach?

Another aspect of your personal investment philosophy is your level of involvement in investing. That is, do you want to be an active or passive investor?

active investor An investor who wishes to manage her own account by carefully studying the economy, market trends, and investment alternatives; regularly monitoring these factors; and buying and selling three to four times a year, with or without the advice of a professional.

Active Investing An **active investor** carefully studies the economy, market trends, and investment alternatives; regularly monitors these factors; and makes decisions to buy and sell, perhaps three or four or more times a year, with or without the advice of a professional. In addition, because the prices of many investments vary with certain news events, world happenings, and economic and political variables, active investors stay alert. Knowing what is going on in the larger world helps active investors understand when to buy or to sell investments quickly so as to reap profits or reduce losses.

passive investor An investor who does not actively engage in trading securities or monitoring his or her investments; seeks to match the market return via mutual funds or other managed investments in the longer term.

Passive Investing A **passive investor** does not actively engage in trading of securities or spend large amounts of time monitoring his or her investments. Such an individual may make regular investments in securities, such as mutual funds (described in Chapter 15), and his or her assets are rarely sold for short-term profits. Instead, passive investors simply aim to match the returns of the entire market. They ignore "hot" tips and the investment of the day touted in the financial press. They keep their emotions in check, and they earn higher returns than active investors over the long term. Most long-term investors utilize a passive approach.

Once you have clarified your investment philosophy and how involved you want to be as an investor, you will be able to make future investing decisions with confi-

An active investor keeps a close watch on the economy and financial markets.

dence and conviction. You will be able to show patience by following your long-term views rather than make emotional and wrong decisions—in other words, mistakes—about your money. The investments you choose and the returns earned are likely to match your investment philosophy.

CONCEPT CHECK 13.2

1. Summarize your investment philosophy and general approach to tolerance for risk.
2. Indicate whether you view yourself as an active or passive investor, and explain why.

Identify the Kinds of Investments You Want to Make

3 LEARNING OBJECTIVE
Identify the kinds of investments that match your interests.

The investments you choose should match your interests. Before investing, think about lending versus owning, short term versus long term, and how to select investments that are likely to provide your desired potential total return.

Do You Want to Lend or Own?

You can invest money in two ways, by lending or by owning. When you lend your money, you receive some form of IOU and the promise of repayment plus interest. The interest is a form of current income while you hold the investment. Lending investments rarely result in capital gains.

You can lend by depositing money in banks, credit unions, and savings and loan associations (via savings accounts and certificates of deposit) or by lending money to governments (via Treasury notes and bonds as well as state and local bonds), businesses (corporate bonds), mortgage-backed bonds (such as Ginnie Maes), and life insurance companies (annuities). Such lending investments, or **debts,** generally offer both a fixed maturity and a fixed income. With a **fixed maturity,** the borrower agrees to repay the principal to the investor on a specific date. With a **fixed income,** the borrower agrees to pay the investor a specific rate of return for use of the principal. Such investments allow lenders to be fairly confident that they will receive a certain amount of interest income for a specified period of time and that the borrowed funds will eventually be returned. Thus, the return is somewhat assured. No matter how much profit the borrower makes with your funds, the investing lender receives only the fixed return promised at the time of the initial investment.

debts Lending investments that typically offer both a fixed maturity and a fixed income.

fixed maturity Specific date on which borrower agrees to repay the principal to the investor.

fixed income Specific rate of return that borrower agrees to pay the investor for use of the principal (initial investment).

Alternatively, you may invest money through ownership of an asset. Ownership investments are often called **equities.** You can buy common or preferred corporate stock (to obtain part ownership in a corporation) in publicly owned companies, purchase shares in a mutual fund company (which invests your funds in corporate stocks and bonds), put money into your own business, purchase real estate, buy commodity futures (pork bellies or oranges), or buy investment-quality collectibles (such as rare antiques or stamps). Ownership investments have the potential for providing current income; however, the emphasis is usually upon achieving substantial capital gains.

equities Ownership equities such as common or preferred stocks, equity mutual funds, real estate, and so on that focus on capital gains more than on income.

Making Short-, Intermediate-, and Long-Term Investments

If you are investing for a short-term time horizon of less than a year or an intermediate-term of perhaps up to five years, you want to be confident that you preserve the value of what you have. After all, you don't want to lose money in an investment when you need to use that money for a near-term goal, such as college tuition, or be forced to sell an investment because you need cash in a hurry. People with a short or intermediate time horizon require investments that offer some predictability and stability. As a result, these investors are usually more interested in current income than capital gains. If you are investing to achieve long-term goals, by contrast, you want your money to grow, and, therefore, you are likely to keep your money in the same investments for 10 or 15 years. Long-term investors usually invite more risk by seeking capital gains as well as current income. Table 13.1 provides an overview of investment alternatives.

Instant Message

Financial Planning on the Web

To obtain an overall assessment of your financial progress in life and advice on how to achieve your goals, you may want a financial plan. Prices vary from $250 to $500 or more. Check out Fidelity.com, Schwab.com, TrowePrice.com, and Vanguard.com. Answers to specific questions for $50 to $100 may be obtained on the Web and over the telephone from companies such as Myfinancialadvice.com.

Choose Investments for Their Components of Total Return

When investing, you want to select a portfolio of investments that will provide the necessary potential total return through current income and capital gains in the proportions that you desire. One stock might provide an anticipated cash dividend of

Table 13.1 Overview of Investment Alternatives

This chapter provides background information to help you to initially assess which types of investments might best suit your needs. The next three chapters examine details of investment alternatives. After reading those chapters, you will have learned enough about investments to make informed decisions.

- **Stocks.** Shares of ownership in the assets and earnings of a business corporation. Examples: Blue-chip stocks (like Dow Chemical, Exxon Mobil, and General Electric), well-known growth stocks (like Microsoft and McDonald's), lesser-known growth stocks (like American Greeting and Panera Bread), and income stocks (like water and electricity companies).
- **Bonds.** Interest-bearing negotiable certificates of long-term debt issued by a corporation, a municipality (such as a city or state), or the federal government. Examples: U.S. savings bonds, Series EE bonds, corporate bonds, high-yield corporate bonds, municipal bonds, and zero-coupon bonds.
- **Mutual funds.** An investment company that combines the funds of investors who have purchased shares of ownership in it and then invests that money in a diversified portfolio of stocks and bonds issued by other corporations or governments. Examples: Fidelity Growth Fund, Calvert Social Investment, and Vanguard Growth Index.
- **Real estate.** Property consisting of land; all structures permanently attached to that land; and accompanying rights and privileges, such as crop and mineral rights. Examples: residential housing units, commercial properties, residential lots, raw land.
- **High-risk investments.** Alternatives that have the potential for significant fluctuations in return over short time periods, perhaps only days or weeks. Examples: collectibles (baseball cards, posters, sports jerseys, comic books, stamps, rare coins, antiques), precious metals and stones, and options and futures contracts.

1.5 percent and an expected annual price appreciation of 10 percent, for a total anticipated return of 11.5 percent. Another choice offering the same projected total return might be a stock with expected annual cash dividends of 3.5 percent and capital gains of 8 percent.

CONCEPT CHECK 13.3

1. Summarize your personal views on lending or owning investments.
2. Which type of investment return—current income or capital gains—seems more attractive to you? Why?

Risks and Other Factors Affect the Investor's Return

Because of the uncertainty that surrounds investments, people often follow a conservative course in an effort to keep their risk low. Being too conservative when investing means that they also risk not reaching their financial goals. To be a successful investor, you must understand the major factors that affect the rate of return on investments. Being informed, you can then take the appropriate risks when making investment decisions.

4 LEARNING OBJECTIVE
Describe the major factors that affect the rate of return on investments.

Random and Market Risk

Random risk (also called **unsystematic risk**) is the risk associated with owning only one investment of a particular type (such as stock in one company) that, by chance, may do very poorly in the future because of uncontrollable or random factors, such as labor unrest, lawsuits, and product recalls. If you invest in only one stock, its value might rise or fall. If you invest in two or three stocks, the odds are lessened that all of their prices will fall. Such **diversification**—the process of reducing risk by spreading investment money among several investment opportunities—provides one effective method of managing random risk. It results in a potential rate of return on all of the investments that is lower than the potential return on a single alternative, but the

random/unsystematic risk Risk associated with owning only one investment of a particular type (such as stock in one company) that, by chance, may do very poorly in the future due to uncontrollable or random factors that do not affect the rest of the market.

return is more predictable and the risk of loss is lower. Diversification averages out the high and low returns.

Research suggests that you can cut random risk in half by diversifying into as few as five stocks or bonds; you can eliminate random risk by holding 15 or more stocks or bonds. Rational investors diversify so as to reduce random risk.

market risk/systematic risk/undiversifiable risk Risk that the value of an investment may drop due to influences and events that affect all similar investments.

Diversification among stocks or bonds cannot eliminate all risks. Some risk would exist even if you owned all of the stocks in a market because stock (and bond) prices in general move up and down over time. This movement results in **market risk** (also known as **systematic** or **undiversifiable risk**). In this case, the value of an investment may drop due to influences and events that affect all similar investments. Examples include a change in economic, social, political, or general market conditions; fluctuations in investor preferences; or other broad market-moving factors, such as a recession or a terrorist attack.

Market risk is the risk that remains after an investor's portfolio has been fully diversified within a particular market, such as stocks. Over the years, market risk has averaged about 8 percent. As a consequence of this risk, the return on any single securities investment (such as a stock), through no fault of its own, might vary up and down about 8 percent annually. The total risk in an investment consists of the sum of the random risk and the market risk.

Other Types of Investment Risks

A number of other investment risks affect investor returns:

- **Business failure risk. Business failure risk,** also called **financial risk,** is the possibility that the investment will fail, perhaps go bankrupt, and result in a massive or total loss of one's invested funds. Investigate thoroughly before investing. See Chapters 14, 15, and 16.
- **Inflation risk.** Inflation risk may be the most important concern for the long-term investor. **Inflation risk,** also called **purchasing power risk,** is the danger that your money will not grow as fast as inflation and therefore not be worth as much in the future as it is today. Over the long term, inflation in the United States has averaged 3.1 percent annually. Thus, the cumulative effects of inflation diminish your investment return. Historically, common stocks and real estate have reduced inflation risk, as values tend to rise with inflation over several years. However, houses, real estate, and other ownership investments are also subject to **deflation risk.** This is the chance that the value of an investment will decline when overall prices decline.
- **Time risk.** The role of time affects all investments. The sooner your invested money is supposed to be returned to you—the **time horizon** of an investment—the less the likelihood that something could go wrong. The more time your money is invested, the more it is at risk. For taking longer-term risks, investors expect and normally receive higher returns.
- **Business-cycle risk.** As we discussed in Chapter 1, economic growth usually does not occur in a smooth and steady manner. Instead, periods of expansion lasting three or four years are often followed by contractions in the economy, called recessions, that may last about a year. The profits of most industries follow the business cycle. Some businesses do not experience business-cycle risk because they continue to earn profits during economic downturns. Examples are gasoline retailers, supermarkets, and utility companies.
- **Market-volatility risk.** All investments are subject to occasional sharp changes in price as a result of events affecting a particular company or the overall market for similar investments. For example, the value of a single stock, such as that of

Instant Message

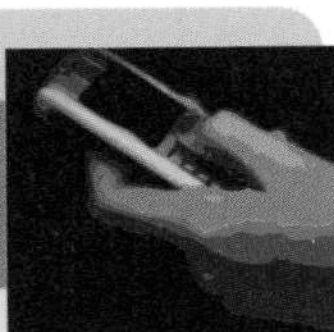

Time Reduces the Risk of Owning Stock

Since 1927 the worst 20-year performance for stocks was a gain of 3 percent. The worst over 10 years was only −1 percent; over 1 year it was −43 percent. The chance of making money during any one year in the stock market over the past 80 years is 66 percent. Over 5 years, the probability increases to 81 percent; over 10 years it rises to 89 percent.

a technology company like Microsoft, might change 10 or even 30 percent in a single day. Also, all technology stocks could decline 2 or perhaps 5 percent if two or three competitors announce poor earnings. In an average year, the price of a typical stock fluctuates up and down by about 50 percent; thus, the price of a stock selling for $30 per share in January might range from $15 to $45 before the end of the following December.

- **Liquidity risk. Liquidity** is the speed and ease with which an asset can be converted to cash. You can convert your savings into cash instantly. You can sell your stocks and bonds in one day, although it may take four days to have the proceeds available in cash. Real estate is *illiquid* because it may take weeks, months, or years to sell.
- **Reinvestment risk.** Reinvestment risk is the risk that the return on a future investment will not be the same as the return earned by the original investment.
- **Marketability risk.** When you have to sell a certain asset quickly, it may not sell at or near the market price. This possibility is referred to as **marketability risk.** Selling real estate in a hurry, for example, may require the seller to substantially reduce the price in order to sell to a willing buyer.

Transaction Costs Reduce Returns

Buying and selling investments may result in a number of transaction costs. Examples include "fix-up costs" when preparing a home for sale, appraisals for collectibles, and storage costs for precious metals. **Commissions** are usually the largest transaction cost in investments. These are fees or percentages of the units or selling price paid to salespeople, agents, and companies for their services—that is, to buy or sell an investment. The commission charged to buy an investment (one commission) and then later sell it (a second commission) is partially based on the value of the transaction. Typical ranges for commissions are as follows: stocks, 1.5 to 2.5 percent (although trades can be made on the Internet for less than $20); bonds, 0 to 2.0 percent; mutual funds, 0 to 8.5 percent; real estate, 4.5 to 7.5 percent; options and futures contracts, 4.0 to 6.0 percent; limited partnerships, 10.0 to 15.0 percent; and collectibles, 15.0 to 30.0 percent. You can increase your investment returns by holding down transaction costs.

commissions Fees or percentages of the selling price paid to salespeople, agents, and companies for their services in buying or selling an investment.

Leverage May Increase Returns

Another factor that can affect return on investment is **leverage**. In the leveraging process, borrowed funds are used to make an investment with the goal of earning a rate of return in excess of the after-tax costs of borrowing. Investing in real estate for its rental income provides an illustration of leverage, as shown in Table 13.2 Assume

leverage Using borrowed funds to invest with the goal of earning a rate of return in excess of the after-tax costs of borrowing.

Table 13.2 Leverage Illustration: Buying Real Estate

	Pay Cash	Use Credit
Purchase price of office building	$300,000	$300,000
Amount borrowed	0	− 270,000
Amount invested	300,000	30,000
Rental income ($2500 per month)	30,000	30,000
Minus tax-deductible interest (6.5%, 30-year loan on $270,000)	− 0	− 17,450
Net earnings before taxes	30,000	12,550
Minus income tax liability (25% bracket)	− 7,500	− 3,137
Rental earnings after taxes	$22,500	$9,413
	÷ 300,000	÷ 30,000
Percentage return on amount invested	7.5%	31.38%

Did You Know?...

The Tax Consequences in Investment Fundamentals

There are some favorable aspects to income taxes to think about when making investments.

1. **After-tax return.** When comparing similar investments, your objective is to earn the best after-tax return. This return is the net amount earned on an investment after payment of income taxes. [See Equation (4.1) on page 122.]
2. **Income versus capital gain.** Current investment income, such as dividends and interest, is taxed at one's marginal tax bracket, likely 25 percent. Capital gains are taxed at special lower rates, likely at 5 or 15 percent.
3. **Tax-deferred investments.** The income and capital gains from investments within employer-sponsored retirement accounts are not subject to income taxes until the funds are withdrawn.
4. **Tax-exempt income.** Income earned from municipal bonds is exempt from income taxes.
5. **Tax-exempt investments.** The income and capital gains from investments within Roth IRA accounts are never subject to income taxes.

that a person can buy a small office building either by making a $30,000 down payment and borrowing $270,000 or by paying $300,000 cash. If the rental income is $30,000 annually ($2500 per month) and the person pays income taxes at a 25 percent rate, a higher return can be obtained using credit to buy the building because the yield would be 31.38 percent versus a 7.5 percent yield when paying cash.

Leverage can prove particularly beneficial when substantial capital gains occur, as this strategy sharply boosts the return on the investment. Assume that at the end of one year, the value of the building described in the previous example has appreciated 7 percent and you could sell it for $321,000 (excluding commission costs). If you had purchased the property for $300,000 cash and then sold it for $321,000, the capital gain on the sale would be 7 percent (the $21,000 return divided by the $300,000 originally invested). If you had bought it using credit, the capital gain would be 70 percent (the $21,000 return divided by the $30,000 originally invested, ignoring transaction costs, taxes, and inflation).

Leverage has a potential negative side as well. In the preceding example, if you used credit to purchase the property, you would need a minimum rental income of $20,479 (using Table 9.4 on page 252, 6½ percent interest on a 30-year loan) just to make the mortgage loan payments. A few months of vacancy or expensive repairs to the building could result in a losing situation. Furthermore, any decline in value would be magnified when you use leverage. You can become financially overextended by using leverage for investments, a factor that you should not ignore.

CONCEPT CHECK 13.4

1. Distinguish between random risk and market risk.
2. Summarize three other risks that may affect investment returns.
3. Explain how transactions costs, leverage, and income taxes increase or decrease investment returns.

Establishing Your Long-Term Investment Strategy

5 LEARNING OBJECTIVE
Decide which of the five long-term investment strategies you will utilize.

Investing is not rocket science! Anyone reading this book and following its recommendations for making long-term investments can become a successful investor. To succeed, you must establish your own long-term investment strategies. Fortunately, this is easy because there are only five strategies to follow, and they all "hang together." And once learned, as the Nike slogan goes, you "Just do it!" And don't forget to start investing as early in life as possible, as illustrated in Figure 13.3 and Table 13.3.

Long-term investors seek growth in the value of their investments that exceeds the rate of inflation. In other words, they want their investments to provide a positive **real rate of return.** This is the return after subtracting the effects of both inflation and income taxes. A long-term investor generally wants to hold an investment as long as it provides a return commensurate with its risk, often for 10 or 15 years or more.

real rate of return Return on an investment after subtracting the effects of inflation and income taxes.

In addition to understanding the overall economic picture (see Chapter 1), long-term investors understand how the **securities markets** (places where stocks and bonds

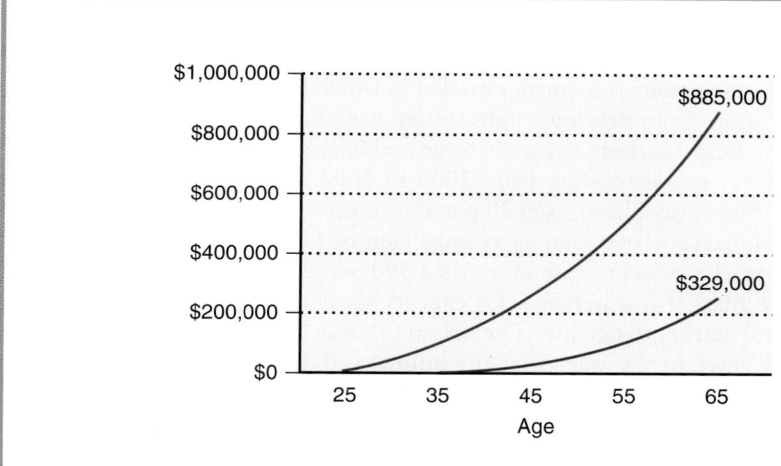

Figure 13.3
A 10-Year Delay in Investing Can Cost You $500,000
Delaying ten years before starting to save $2000 a year in a tax-deferred account that earns a 10 percent return can cost you $500,000. Saving $2000 a year between age 25 and 65 accumulates to $885,000, but if you don't start to save until age 35, you accumulate only $329,000. Thus, the $20,000 that you did not invest between ages 25 and 35 will cost you $556,000 by the time you reach age 65.

Table 13.3 The Wisdom of Starting to Invest Early in Life

	Early Investor*		**Late Investor†**	
Age	**Cumulative Investment**	**Account Value**	**Cumulative Investment**	**Account Value**
30	$ 2,000	$ 2,180	$ 0	$ 0
35	10,000	13,047	0	0
40	20,000	33,121	2,000	2,180
45	0	50,960	10,000	13,047
50	0	78,408	20,000	33,121
55	0	120,641	30,000	64,007
60	0	185,621	40,000	111,529
65	0	285,601	50,000	184,648

Conclusion: $20,000 gets the early investor $285,601; $50,000 gets the late investor only $184,648.

*The early investor invested $2000 at the beginning of every year from ages 30 to 39 (ten years of cumulative investing totaling $20,000), and the funds compounded at 9 percent annually.

†The late investor invested $2000 at the beginning of every year from ages 40 to 64 (25 years of cumulative investing totaling $50,000), and the funds compounded at 9 percent annually.

Did You Know?...

Calculate the Real Rate of Return (After Taxes and Inflation) on Investments

1. **Identify the rate of return before income taxes.** Perhaps you think that a stock will offer a return of 10 percent in one year, including current income and capital gains.
2. **Subtract the effects of your marginal tax rate on the rate of return to obtain the after-tax return.** If you are in the 25 percent federal income tax bracket, the calculation is $(1 - 0.25) \times 0.10 = 0.075 = 7.5$ percent.
3. **Subtract the effects of inflation from the after-tax return to obtain the real rate of return on the investment after taxes and inflation.** If you estimate an annual inflation of 4 percent, the calculation gives 3.5 percent (7.5 percent − 4.0 percent). Thus, your before-tax rate of return of 10 percent provides a real rate of return of 3.5 percent after taxes and inflation.

are traded) are performing as a whole. That is, are the markets moving up, moving down, or remaining stagnant? A securities market in which prices have declined in value by 20 percent or more from previous highs, often over the course of several weeks or months, is called a **bear market.** Since 1926, several bear markets have occurred, with the most recent bear market lasting from 2000 to 2002. In contrast, a **bull market** results when securities prices have risen 20 percent or more over time. Historically, the more than 20 bull markets have seen an average gain of 110 percent. The bull market of the 1990s saw stock prices increase more than 300 percent!

bear market Market in which securities prices have declined in value by 20 percent or more from previous highs, often over the course of several weeks or months.

bull market Market in which securities prices have risen 20 percent or more over time.

A **bull** in the market is a person who expects securities prices to go up; a **bear** expects the general market to decline. The origin of these terms is unknown, but some suggest that they refer to the ways that the animals attack: Bears thrust their claws downward, and bulls move their horns upward. Bear markets last, on average, about 9 months; bull markets average 29 months in length.

Long-Term Investors Understand Market Timing

market timers Long-term investors who pull out of stocks or bonds in anticipation of a market decline or hold back from investing until the market "settles down"—that is, when they expect prices to climb.

Long-term investors must be able to withstand some market volatility, the likelihood of large price swings in their chosen securities. Although they do not like to be described as such, some long-term investors are **market timers.** Market timing entails shifting your money into cash or bonds when you think stocks and stock mutual funds are overpriced and then later reinvesting your money in stocks and stock mutual funds when you think they have gotten cheap. Market timers pull out of stocks or bonds in anticipation of a market decline or hold back from investing until the market "settles down." In this scenario, investors try to "time" their investments, hoping to capture most of the upside of rising stock prices while avoiding most of the downside.

To succeed in timing the market, you need to know just the right time to buy and just the right time to sell. Research shows that most of the market's gains are realized in a few trading days that occur every now and then. If market timers are out of the market on those days, they lose. In times of rising markets, it is very easy for market timers to sell too early and as a result miss out on much larger profits as the bull market continues to push up prices even more. Those who sell after a sudden drop in investment value, a "down market," actually lock in their losses.

Instant Message

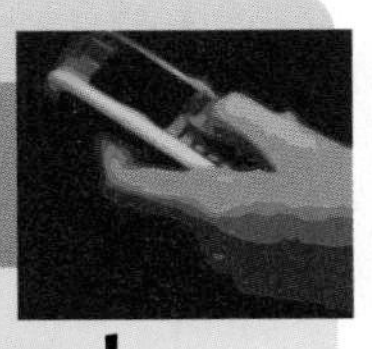

Out of the Market? You Missed a 45% Gain

If you had been out of stocks during the market's ten best days in the past decade, according to Charles Schwab, you would have missed out on 45 percent of the gains.

Very few market timers succeed in simultaneously lowering their risk and raising their returns. In fact, research shows that most of these investors earn returns far worse than the averages, in part because they pay lots of transaction fees. The reality is that market timing increases market risk. Short-term buying and selling is more like gambling than investing. What contributes the most to successful investing is not timing, but time.

Strategy 1: Buy and Hold Anticipates Long-Term Economic Growth

The secret to investment success is benign neglect. Long-term investors need to relax with the confidence and knowledge that investing regularly and not trading frequently will create a substantial portfolio over time. Long-term investors do not follow or react emotionally to the day-to-day changes that occur in the market. Ignore them is the best advice. Because most people are sensitive to short-term losses, daily monitoring could motivate one to make shortsighted buying and selling decisions. Selling high-quality assets in a bear market is a poor strategy because bear markets are so short in duration. It is tough to do, but it is smart to buy more shares when prices are lower during normal market downturns because rising prices in a bull market always follow a bear market. Investors who remain invested in the stock market are rewarded with the opportunity to earn the historic average return of the equities markets, which is 11.4 percent annually.

Most long-term investors use the **buy-and-hold** (also called **buy-to-hold**) approach to investing. That is, they buy a widely diversified mix of stocks and/or mutual funds, reinvest the dividends by buying more stocks and mutual funds, and hold on to those investments almost indefinitely. With this approach, the investor expects that the values of the assets will increase over the long run in tandem with the growth of the U.S. and world economies. The investments may pay some current income as well. The investor's emphasis is on holding the assets through both good and bad economic times with the confidence that their values will go up over the long term. This is a wise strategy.

buy and hold/buy to hold Investment strategy in which investors buy a widely diversified mix of stocks and/or mutual funds, reinvest the dividends by buying more stocks and mutual funds, and hold on to those investments almost indefinitely.

Buy and hold does not mean buy and ignore. Investors are unwise to blindly hold on to an investment for years. Instead, review all holdings at least once a year to make

Short-term buying and selling is more like gambling than investing.

sure that each remains a good investment. Questions to ask: "Is the valuation too high?" "Has the fundamental outlook of the company changed?" "Does this asset still fit my investment plan?" "Would I buy it today?" If necessary, sell the asset.

Strategy 2: Dollar-Cost Averaging Buys at "Below-Average" Costs

dollar-cost averaging/cost averaging Systematic program of investing equal sums of money at regular intervals regardless of the price of the investment.

below-average costs "Averaging" means that you purchase more shares when the price is down and fewer shares when the price is high, so most of your shares are purchased at below-average cost.

Dollar-cost averaging (or **cost averaging**) is a systematic program of investing equal sums of money at regular intervals regardless of the price of the investment. In this approach, the same fixed dollar amount is invested in the same stock or mutual fund at regular intervals over a long time. Since investments generally rise more than they fall, the "averaging" means that you purchase more shares when the price is down and fewer shares when the price is high. Most of the shares are, therefore, purchased at **below-average costs.**

This strategy avoids the risks and responsibilities of investment timing because the stock purchases are made regularly (usually every month) regardless of the price. It also ignores all outside events and short-term gyrations of the market, providing the investor with a disciplined buying strategy. A well-diversified stock mutual fund would be an excellent choice for dollar-cost averaging.

Table 13.4 shows the results of dollar-cost averaging for a stock under varying market conditions. (Commissions are excluded.) As an example, assume that you invest $300 into a stock every three months. Notice that dollar-cost averaging is successful in all three scenarios illustrated.

average share price Calculated by dividing the share price total by the number of investment periods.

Dollar-Cost Averaging in a Fluctuating Market To illustrate the effects of dollar-cost averaging, assume that you first invested funds during the "fluctuating market" shown in Table 13.4. Because the initial price is $15 per share, you receive 20 shares for your investment of $300. Then the market drops—an extreme but easy-to-follow example—and the price falls to $10 per share. When you buy $300 worth of the stock now, you receive 30 shares. Three months later, the market price rebounds to $15 and you invest another $300, receiving 20 shares. The price then drops and rises again.

You now own 120 shares, thanks to your total investment of $1500. The **average share price** is calculated by averaging the amounts paid for the investment: Simply divide the share price total by the number of investment periods. In this example, the

Table 13.4 Dollar-Cost Averaging for a Stock or Mutual Fund Investment

	Fluctuating Market			Declining Market			Rising Market		
	Regular Investment	Share Price	Shares Acquired	Regular Investment	Share Price	Shares Acquired	Regular Investment	Share Price	Shares Acquired
	$300	$15	20	$300	$15	20	$300	$6	50
	300	10	30	300	10	30	300	10	30
	300	15	20	300	10	30	300	12	25
	300	10	30	300	6	50	300	15	20
	300	15	20	300	5	60	300	20	15
Totals	$1,500	$65	120	$1,500	$46	190	$1,500	$63	140
	Average share price: $13.00 ($65 ÷ 5)*			Average share price: $9.20 ($46 ÷ 5)*			Average share price: $12.60 ($63 ÷ 5)*		
	Average share cost: $12.50 ($1500 ÷ 120)†			Average share cost: $7.89 ($1500 ÷ 190)†			Average share cost: $10.71 ($1500 ÷ 140)†		

*Sum of share price total ÷ number of investment periods.
†Total amount invested ÷ total shares purchased.

Advice from a Pro...

Buy Shares of Stock Directly Using a Dividend-Reinvestment Plan

More than 1000 well-known companies allow investors to purchase shares of stock directly from them without the assistance of a stockbroker and then to continue to invest on a regular basis without paying brokerage commissions. Such a program is known as a **dividend-reinvestment plan (DRIP).** You simply sign up with the company, agreeing to buy a certain number of shares and to reinvest cash dividends into more shares of stock for little or no transaction fees. Investors' accounts are credited with fractional shares, too.

Wal-Mart is illustrative. It requires a minimum investment of $250, and continuing investments of $50 thereafter. The enrollment fee is $20 plus $0.10 per share. Most companies will buy back shares for a transaction fee of only $10. Companies offering DRIPs include Ameritech, ExxonMobil, Home Depot, Tenneco, Wal-Mart, McDonalds, and Sears. For a list of companies offering direct purchases, see the Securities Transfer Association at www.netstockdirect.com or the Direct Stock Purchase Plan Clearinghouse at www.dripinvestor.com/clearinghouse/home.asp.

Buying shares regularly through a DRIP is a great example of dollar-cost averaging. It allows you to take advantage of fluctuating stock prices by purchasing on a regular basis at below-average costs.

Linda Gorham
Berklee College of Music, Boston, Massachusetts

average share price is $13 ($65 ÷ 5). The **average share cost,** a more meaningful figure, is the actual cost basis of the investment used for income tax purposes. It is calculated by dividing the total amount invested by the total shares purchased. In this example, it is $12.50 ($1500 ÷ 120). Based on the recent price of $15 per share, each of your 120 shares is worth on average $2.50 ($15 − $12.50) more than you paid for it. Thus, your gain is $300 (120 × $2.50; or $15 × 120 = $1800, $1800 − $1500 = $300).

average share cost Actual cost basis of the investment used for income tax purposes, calculated by dividing the total amount invested by the total shares purchased.

Dollar-Cost Averaging in a Declining Market Markets may also decline over a time period. The "declining market" columns in Table 13.4 (representing a prolonged bear market of 15 months) show purchases of 190 shares for increasingly lower prices that eventually reach $5 per share at the bottom of the business cycle. In a declining market, if you keep investing using dollar-cost averaging, you will purchase a large volume of shares. If you sell when the market is down substantially, you will not profit. In this example, you have purchased 190 shares at an average cost of $7.89, and they now have a depressed price of $5. Selling at this point would result in a substantial loss of $550 [$1500 − (190 × $5)]. Dollar-cost averaging requires that you continue to invest if the longer-term prospects suggest an eventual increase in price.

Dollar-Cost Averaging in a Rising Market During the "rising market" in Table 13.4, you continue to invest but buy fewer shares. The $1500 investment during the bull market bought only 140 shares for an average cost of $10.71. In this rising market, you profit because your 140 shares have a recent market price of $20 per share, for a total value of $2800 (140 × $20).

Almost anyone can profit in a rising market. If you use dollar-cost averaging over the long term, you will continue to buy in rising, falling, and fluctuating markets. The overall result will be that you buy more shares when the cost is down, thereby lowering the average share cost to below-average prices. The totals in Table 13.4, for example, reveal an overall investment of $4500 ($1500 + $1500 + $1500) used to purchase 450 shares (120 + 190 + 140) for an average cost of $10 per share ($4500 ÷ 450). With the recent market price at $20, you will realize a long-term gain of $4500 ($20 current market price × 450 shares = $9000; $9000 − $4500 invested = $4500 gain). Note that the dollar-cost averaging method would remain valid if the time interval for investing were monthly, quarterly, or even semiannually; benefits are derived from the regularity of investing.

Dollar-Cost Averaging Offers Two Advantages First, it reduces the average cost of shares of stock purchased over a relatively long period. Profits occur when prices for an investment fluctuate and eventually go up. Although this approach does not eliminate the possibility of loss, it does limit losses during times of declining prices. Profits accelerate during rising prices. Second, dollar-cost averaging dictates investor discipline. This strategy of investing is not particularly glamorous, but it is the only approach that is almost guaranteed to make a profit for the investor. It takes neither brilliance nor luck, just discipline. People who invest through individual retirement accounts (IRAs), employee stock ownership programs, and 401(k) retirement plans (discussed in Chapter 17) enjoy the benefits of dollar-cost averaging when they invest regularly.

Strategy 3: Portfolio Diversification Reduces Portfolio Volatility

Owning too much of any one investment creates too great a financial risk. Experts advise that you never keep more than 10 percent of your assets in one investment, including your employer's stock. Many workers who did not diversify properly have seen their retirement funds disappear or be drastically reduced in value when their employers' stocks plunged in price.

portfolio diversification Practice of selecting a collection of different asset classes of investments (such as stocks, bonds, mutual funds, real estate, and cash) that are chosen not only for their potential returns but also for their dissimilar risk-return characteristics.

Diversification is the single most important rule in investing. **Portfolio diversification** is the practice of selecting a collection of different asset classes of investments (such as stocks, bonds, mutual funds, real estate, and cash) that are chosen not only for their potential returns but also for their dissimilar risk-return characteristics.

The goal of portfolio diversification is to create a collection of investments that will provide an acceptable level of return and an acceptable exposure to risk. This outcome can be achieved because asset classes typically react differently to economic and marketplace changes. The major benefit of having a diversified portfolio is that when one asset class performs poorly, there is a good chance that another will perform well, and vice versa.

For example, you might buy a number of mutual funds, perhaps including a balanced fund, an asset-allocation fund, a life-cycle fund, and an aggressive-growth fund. Similarly, you could invest in three or four stocks within an industry group, instead of just one, and then invest in several industry groups, plus invest in a bond mutual fund and a certificate of deposit.

Diversification reduces portfolio volatility while averaging out an investor's return. (See Figure 13.4.) Diversification lowers the odds that you will lose money investing and increases the odds that you will make money.

Strategy 4: Asset Allocation Keeps You in the Right Investment Categories at the Right Time

Research shows that more than 90 percent of returns earned by long-term investors result from having one's assets allocated in a diversified portfolio. Most of the return comes not from specific investments but rather is derived from owning the right asset categories at the right time.

asset allocation Form of diversification in which investor decides on proportions of an investment portfolio that will be devoted to various categories of assets.

Asset allocation, a form of diversification, is deciding on the proportions of your investment portfolio that will be devoted to various categories of assets. Asset allocation helps preserve capital by selecting assets so as to protect the entire portfolio from negative events while remaining in a position to gain from positive events. This strategy helps control your exposure to risk.

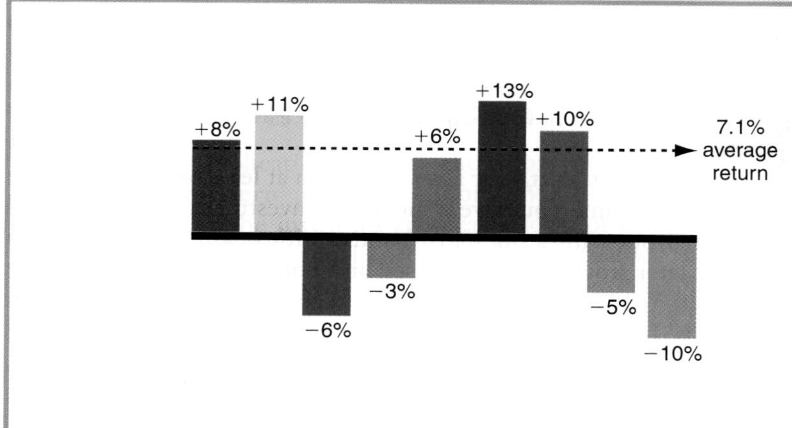

Figure 13.4

Diversification Averages Out an Investor's Return

The chart at the left represents a hypothetical mix of winning and losing investments after one year. The investment on the far left, for instance, increased in value 8 percent; another declined 10 percent. While some investments lost value, over the year those losses were offset with the gains of others, and the overall portfolio earned a 7.1 percent average return.

To achieve an appropriate mix of growth, income, and stability in your portfolio, you need a combination of three investments: (1) stocks and/or stock mutual funds *(equities)*, (2) bonds (*debt*), and (3) *cash* (or cash equivalents like Treasury securities). Asset allocation requires that you keep your equities, debt, and cash at a fixed ratio for long time periods, occasionally rebalancing the allocations, perhaps quarterly or annually, so as to continue to meet your investment objectives.

Your allocation proportions and investment choices need to reflect your age, income, family responsibilities, financial resources, risk tolerance, goals, retirement plans, and investment time horizon. You need not change the proportions of your asset allocation until your broad investment goals change—possibly not for another five or ten years. When your investment objectives change, perhaps because of marriage, birth of a child, child graduating from college, loss of employment, divorce, or death of a spouse, you will need to change your asset allocation as well.

Figure 13.5 illustrates model portfolios that reflect varying degrees of risk tolerance and time horizons. A young, risk-tolerant, long-term investor with an aggressive investment philosophy might have a portfolio that is 100 percent in equities because equities offer the highest return over the long term and

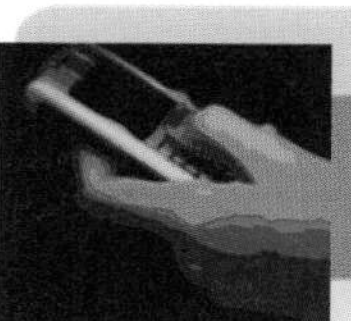

Instant Message

Asset Allocation Rules of Thumb

Consider these two rules of thumb to guide the stock and bond allocation of your portfolio:

1. The percent to invest in equities is 110 minus your age, multiplied by 1.25. For example, if you are 40 years old, calculate as follows: 110 − 40 = 70; 70 × 1.25 = 87.5. Therefore, a 40-year old investor is advised to maintain a portfolio where 87.5 percent of the assets are in equities and 12.5 percent in bonds (or cash equivalents).
2. The percent to invest in equities is found by subtracting your age from 120. Put the resulting number in the form of the percentage of your portfolio to invest in stocks. Put the remainder in bonds. So if you are age 30, put 90 percent (120 − 30) in stocks and 10 percent in bonds. Every year, subtract your age from 120 again and rebalance your portfolio as needed.

Did You Know?...

Employers Offer Automatic Portfolio Rebalancing

Employees who participate in their employer-sponsored retirement plan may have access to services to automatically rebalance their retirement assets. Instead of being a do-it-yourself investor, a worker can sign up for the services of a **limited managed account.** Once you have decided on your preferred asset allocation and signed a contract with a vender approved by your employer, the company sells and buys your mutual fund assets on your behalf to adjust your portfolio back to your specific standards. Your professional money manager does this on a quarterly basis for an annual fee of as little as $150.

Advice from a Pro...

When to Sell an Investment

It is time to sell an investment when one of the following conditions has been met:

- Something significant about the company's business or its earnings has changed dramatically for the worse since you bought the company's stock.
- The stock is doing so well that it is overvalued, and the share price is much higher than what you believe the company is worth.
- The investment is performing poorly and causing you undue anxiety. The great financier Bernard Baruch advised, "Sell down to the level where you are sleeping well."
- You need cash for a worthwhile purpose, and this investment appears the most fully priced.
- The investment no longer fits your situation or goals, and you have a more promising place to invest your money.

Reynolds Griffith
Stephen F. Austin State University

fees range from $150 to $300 annually. Monte Carlo simulations are frequently used in retirement planning, which is discussed in Chapter 17. Many employers offer free or low-cost access to MPT software as an employee benefit.

CONCEPT CHECKS 13.5

1. Distinguish between bull and bear markets, making sure to indicate the likely duration of each.
2. Summarize why smart people conclude that it is impossible to beat the average stock market returns, and then note why some market timers try anyway.
3. Explain the concept of dollar-cost averaging including why one invests at below-average costs.
4. Summarize what the buy-and-hold strategy is all about, and describe how portfolio diversification fits into that investment strategy.
5. What is asset allocation and why does it work?

Creating Your Own Investment Plan

6 LEARNING OBJECTIVE
Create your own investment plan.

investment plan An explanation of your investment philosophy and your logic on investing to reach specific goals.

The steps in the investment planning process are summarized in Table 13.5. To create an **investment plan,** which is an explanation of your investment philosophy and your logic on investing to reach specific goals, see the illustrated plan for Jessica Shipp in Figure 13.8. You can begin creating your own investment plan, using Figure 13.8 as a model, by identifying your financial goals and explaining your investment philosophy.

Table 13.6 lists investments for various investment time horizons. (Terms new to you are explained in the chapters that follow.) What are the time horizons for your investment goals? Are you building up an amount for a down payment on a home, cre-

Table 13.5 The Steps in the Investment Planning Process

Steps	Chapter in Which Topic Is Covered
Identify your long- and short-term goals reflecting your age, income, family responsibilities, financial resources, and desires.	1, 3, 13, 17
Determine your investment philosophy.	13
Determine current amount of investment assets.	3, 13
Estimate how much money you need to accumulate.	1, 13, 17
Determine how much time you have.	1, 13, 17
Calculate how much you can regularly invest.	1, 3, 17
Learn about investment alternatives.	13, 14, 15, 16
Select investments and invest.	13, 14, 15, 16, 17
Identify what could stop you from succeeding.	1, 3, 13, 17
Rebalance investment portfolio regularly.	13, 17
Monitor your investments.	13, 17
Change asset allocations only when investment objectives change.	13, 17

ating a college fund for a child, or putting away money for retirement? Or are all three time horizons relevant? Keep in mind why you are investing and proceed accordingly. Now calculate the numbers. How much money do you need to achieve each goal, and by when? What is the total of your current investment assets? Do the math.

Figure 13.9 provides insight about possible investment choices, describing the major characteristics of each. This shows how each might be used to help achieve your financial goals. Don't be overwhelmed because these investment choices are explained in the following chapters. You *will* learn how to make informed investment decisions for yourself.

To accelerate investment decision making, take a pencil and delete some investment choices that do not appeal to you or match your investment philosophy. Do this by reviewing Tables 13.5 and 13.6 and Figure 13.9. You will be left with alternatives that better fit your investment goals, philosophy, and time horizon. Now you have an investment plan. All that remains is to put your plan into action. That means filling out forms to open an investment account, writing checks for your first investing dollars, and overseeing your investments. These topics are examined in the chapters that follow.

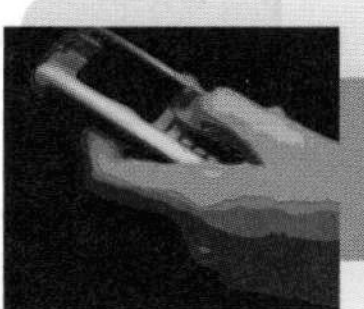

Instant Message

Jessica Shipp's Investment Goal Math

Jessica wants to save $200 a month to be used as a down payment on a new vehicle. If she invests $200 a month that earns 4 percent interest for four years, how much will she have accumulated? Answer: She will have about $10,200, and this includes $9600 of Jessica's money and $600 in interest.

CONCEPT CHECK 13.6

1. **Review Tables 13.5 and 13.6 and Figures 13.8 and 13.9, and record in writing an investment plan to fund your retirement, presumably one of your own long-term goals.**

(b) Would you recommend active or passive investing for her, and why?

(c) Should Jennifer be a lender or owner?

(d) Identify three risks to her retirement investments that Jennifer should try to avoid, and explain how she can avoid them.

(e) Select two of the five recommended investment strategies to recommend to Jennifer, and explain why she should follow them.

(f) If Jennifer's $50,000 and her $1000 monthly investment grow at 8 percent annually for 25 years, how much money will she have accumulated? Use Appendix Table A.1 and Appendix Table A.3 or the *Garman/Forgue* website.

Case 3

Victor and Maria Hernandez Try to Catch Up on Their Investments

The expenses associated with sending two children through college prevented Victor and Maria Hernandez from adding substantially to their investment program. Now that their younger son, Brian, has completed school and is working full time, they would like to build up their investments quickly. Victor is 47 years old and wants to retire early, perhaps by age 60. In addition to the retirement program at his place of employment, Victor believes that their investment portfolio, currently valued at $70,000, will need to triple to $210,000 by retirement time. He and Maria realize that they will have to sacrifice a lot of current spending to save and invest for retirement.

(a) What rate of return is needed on the $70,000 portfolio to reach their goal of $210,000 (assuming no additional contributions)? Use the *Garman/Forgue* website or Appendix Table A.1.

(b) Victor and Maria think they will need a total of $400,000 for a retirement financial nest egg. Therefore, they will need to create an additional sum of $190,000 through new investments. Assuming an annual return of 8 percent, how much do the Hernandezes need to invest each year to reach their goal of $190,000? Use Appendix Table A.3 or visit the *Garman/Forgue* website.

(c) If they assume a 6 percent annual return, how much do the Hernandezes need to invest each year to reach their goal of $190,000? Use Appendix Table A.3 or the *Garman/Forgue* website.

Case 4

The Johnsons Start an Investment Program

Harry and Belinda's finances have improved in recent months, even though they have incurred new debts for an automobile loan and a condominium. The improvement has occurred because they cut back their spending on discretionary items (clothing, food, and entertainment) and because Harry also received a sizable increase in salary after changing employers. His new job as an assistant designer at Medical Facilities Inc. pays $6000 more than his other job. The new job is also closer to home, reducing Harry's commuting time. The Johnsons have decided to forgo some current spending to concentrate on getting a solid investment program under way while they have two incomes available. They are willing to accept a moderate amount of risk and expect to invest between $200 and $400 per month over the next five years. Assuming that they have an adequate savings program, respond to the following questions:

(a) In what types of investments (choose only two) might the Johnsons place the first $2000? (Review Figures 13.2, 13.5, and 13.9 for ideas and available options, and consider the types of investment risks inherent in each choice.) Give reasons for your selections.

(b) In what types of investments might they place the next $4000? Why?

(c) What types of investments should they choose for the next $10,000? Why?

(d) If inflation is 4 percent, what would their earnings be for the year if they earn 8 percent on a $400 monthly investment? Calculate the projected earnings using the *Garman/Forgue* website.

On the 'Net

Go to the Web pages indicated to complete these exercises. You can also go to the *Garman/Forgue* website at college.hmco.com/business/students for an expanded list of exercises. Under General Business, select the title of this text. Click on the Internet Exercises link for this chapter.

1. Visit the website for the Motley Fool at http://www.fool.com/school/13steps/13steps.htm. Read the article discussing its 13 steps to "foolish" investing. Which of the 13 steps were you aware of before reading this chapter? Which did you become aware of after reading this chapter and the article?

2. Visit the website for investment beginners at About.com at http://beginnersinvest.about.com/od/assetallocation1/a/aa102404.htm to read its article on asset allocation. Identify the asset allocation percentages with which you would feel most comfortable now. How might your views change in five years? Twenty years?
3. Visit the website for Investopedia and read its article on the risk pyramid at http://www.investopedia.com/articles/basics/03/050203.asp. Contrast your risk tolerance for short-term and long-term investing after reading the article. Did your views change after reading the article? If so, in what ways?

Visit the Garman/Forgue website ...

@college.hmco.com/business/students

Under General Business, select *Personal Finance 9e*. There, among other valuable resources, you will find a complete glossary, ACE questions, links to help you complete the chapter exercises, and links to other personal finance sites.

CHAPTER 14

Investing in Stocks and Bonds

You Must Be Kidding, Right?

Brothers Ricky and Marvin Morton differ in investment philosophies—Marvin is conservative and Ricky holds a moderate investing outlook. Their father left each of them $100,000 when he died ten years ago, and Ricky invested in common stocks while Marvin invested in corporate bonds. After ten years, how much more money is Ricky likely to have in his account than Marvin?

A. $97,000 **B.** $163,000 **C.** $260,000 **D.** $357,000

The answer is A, $97,000. In U.S. securities markets, one could typically expect to obtain a long-term average annual return of 10 percent on common stocks compared with 5 percent on corporate bonds. Thus, a common stock portfolio that returned 10 percent annually would accumulate to $260,000 in ten years while a bond portfolio earning 5 percent annually over the same time period would grow to $163,000. Dividing $97,000 ($260,000 − $163,000) by $163,000 reveals that Ricky's willingness to accept more risk by investing in common stocks may provide him with a balance bigger than his brother's by a whopping 60 percent!

LEARNING OBJECTIVES

After reading this chapter, you should be able to:

1. **Explain** how stocks and bonds are used as investments.
2. **Classify** common stocks according to their major characteristics.
3. **Describe** fundamental and numerical ways to evaluate stock values.
4. **Determine** whether an investment's potential rate of return is sufficient.
5. **Use** the Internet to evaluate common stocks in which to invest.
6. **Summarize** how stocks are bought and sold.
7. **Describe** how to invest in bonds.

What Do You Recommend?

Caitlin Diaz, age 42, is a senior Web designer for a communications company in Lansing, Michigan. She earns $92,000 annually. From her salary, Caitlin contributes $200 per month to her 401(k) retirement account, through which she invests in the company's stock. Caitlin is divorced and has custody of her three children, 10-year-old twins and a 12-year-old. Her ex-husband pays $1500 per month in child support. Caitlin and her former spouse contribute $3000 each annually to a college fund for their children. Over the past 15 years, Caitlin has built a $300,000 stock portfolio after starting by investing the proceeds of a $50,000 life insurance policy following the death of her first husband. Currently, her portfolio is allocated 40 percent into preferred stocks (paying 4.5 percent), 30 percent into cyclical, blue-chip common stocks (P/E ratio of 18), 10 percent into Treasury bonds (paying 5.2 percent), 10 percent into municipal bonds (paying 3.7 percent), and 10 percent into AAA corporate bonds (paying 5.6 percent). Today's comparable corporate bonds pay 5 percent. Caitlin's total return in recent years has been about 6 percent annually. Her investment goals are to have sufficient cash to pay for her children's education and to retire in about 18 years.

What do you recommend to Caitlin on the subject of stocks and bonds regarding:

1. Investing for retirement in 18 years?
2. Owning blue-chip common stocks and preferred stocks rather than other common stocks given Caitlin's investment time horizon?
3. The wisdom of owning municipal bonds rather than corporate bonds?
4. The likely selling price of her corporate bonds, if sold today?
5. Investments that might be appropriate to fund her children's education?

FOR HELP with studying this chapter, visit the Online Student Center:

www.college.hmco.com/pic/garman9e

To earn a larger return than offered by conservative investments, you must accept more risk. Historically, common stocks for example have earned substantially more than cash savings, often twice as much. When you invest in stocks and bonds, you can increase returns significantly while increasing risk only slightly. These investments belong in everyone's investment portfolio because they provide opportunities for conservative, moderate, and aggressive investors alike.

Buying individual stocks and bonds is risky for investors because the rate of return and value of these securities fluctuate up and down over time. Accordingly, investors often choose to invest in stocks and bonds indirectly through mutual funds, the subject of Chapter 15. Because stocks and bonds are the basic securities used in the world of investing, you need to understand how they are used. When wisely selected, they are excellent choices for long-term investors.

The Role of Stocks and Bonds in Investments

1 LEARNING OBJECTIVE
Explain how stocks and bonds are used as investments.

Individual investors provide the money corporations use to create sales and earn profits. The investor shares in those profits. A **corporation** is a state-chartered legal entity that can conduct business operations in its own name. A **public corporation** is one that issues stock purchased by individuals and traded in stock markets. The ability to sell shares of ownership to investors offers a corporation the opportunity to develop into a firm of considerable size. It can continue to exist even as ownership of its shares changes hands. AT&T, for example, has issued more than 4 million shares of stock.

start-up capital Funds initially invested in a business enterprise.

securities Negotiable instruments of ownership or debt, including common stock, preferred stock, and bonds.

A corporation's financial needs may vary over time. To begin its operations, a new corporation needs **start-up capital** (funds initially invested in a business enterprise). During its life, a corporation may need additional money to grow. To raise capital and finance its goals, it may issue three types of **securities** (negotiable instruments of ownership or debt): common stock, preferred stock, and bonds, which we mentioned in Chapter 13.

Good Money Habits in Investing in Stocks and Bonds

Make the following your money habits in investing in stocks and bonds:

1. Include stocks and bond or mutual funds that own stocks and bonds in your investment portfolio.
2. Use fundamental analysis to determine a company's basic value before investing in a stock.
3. Resist putting money into so-called hot stocks.
4. Invest part of the conservative portion of your portfolio in TIPS (Treasury Inflation-Protected Securities) to beat inflation.
5. Use zero-coupon bonds to help fund a child's education and your retirement.

Common Stock

Stocks are shares of ownership in the assets and earnings of a business corporation. Each stock investor is a part owner (albeit very small) in a corporation. **Common stock** is the most basic form of ownership of a corporation. For the investor, stocks represent potential income because the investor own a piece of the future profits of the company. Investors have two expectations: (1) the corporation will be profitable enough that income will exceed expenses, thereby allowing the firm to pay **cash dividends** (a share of profits distributed in cash) and (2) the **market price** of a share of stock, which is the current price that a buyer is willing to pay a willing seller, will increase. Stocks require a low minimum investment. Common stocks pay annual returns about twice as high as preferred stocks and bonds. Investors expect to earn annual returns of 10 percent or higher.

Each person who owns a share of stock—called a **shareholder** or **stockholder**—has a proportionate interest in the ownership (a very small slice) and, therefore, in the assets and income of the corporation. This **residual claim** means that common stockholders have a right to share in the income and assets of a corporation after higher-priority claims are satisfied. These higher-priority claims include interest payments to those who own company bonds and preferred stocks.

Stockholders have a **limited liability,** as their responsibility for business losses is limited to the amount invested in the shares of stock owned. These amounts may be small or large, but the most the shareholder can lose is the original amount invested. If the corporation becomes bankrupt, the common stockholder's ownership value consists of the amount left per share after the claims of all creditors are satisfied first.

Each common stockholder has **voting rights:** the proportionate authority to express an opinion or choice in matters affecting the company. Stockholders vote to elect the company's **board of directors.** This group of individuals sets policy and names the principal officers of the company, **management,** who run the firm's day-to-day operations. The number of votes cast by each shareholder depends on the number of shares he or she owns. Stockholders attend an annual meeting or vote by **proxy**—shareholders' written authorization to someone else to represent them and to vote their shares at a stockholder's meeting.

voting rights Proportionate authority to express an opinion or choice in matters affecting the company.

Preferred Stock

Preferred stock is a type of fixed-income ownership security in a corporation. Owners of a preferred stock receive a fixed dividend per share that corporations are required to distribute before any dividends are paid out to common stockholders. They receive no extra income from the stock other than their fixed dividend, even when the firm is highly profitable. The regular dividend payments appeal to retired investors and others who desire a reliable stream of income. While the income stream may be consistent, the market price of preferred stock is sensitive to interest rates. Preferred stockholders rarely have voting privileges.

preferred stock Type of fixed-income ownership security in a corporation that pays fixed dividends.

Sometimes a corporation decides not to pay dividends to preferred stockholders because it lacks profits or simply because it wants to retain and reinvest all of its earnings. When the board of directors votes to skip *(pass)* making a cash dividend to preferred stockholders, holders of **cumulative preferred stock** must be paid that dividend before any future dividends are distributed to the common stockholders. For example, assume that a company passes on the first two quarterly dividends of \$2.25 each to preferred stockholders, who expect to receive \$9 each year (\$2.25 × 4 quarters). If the company prospers and wants to give a cash dividend to its common stockholders in the third quarter, it must first pay the passed \$4.50 to the cumulative preferred stockholders. Furthermore, the usual third-quarter cash dividend of \$2.25 has to be made to the preferred stockholders before the common stockholders can receive any dividends. In the case of **noncumulative preferred stock,** the preferred stockholders would have no claim to previously skipped dividends. **Convertible preferred stock,** a unique security occasionally sold by companies, can be exchanged at the option of the stockholder for a specified number of shares of common stock.

cumulative preferred stock Preferred stock for which dividends must be paid, including any skipped dividends, before dividends go to common stockholders.

convertible preferred stock Can be exchanged at the option of the stockholder for a specified number of shares of common stock.

Bonds

Individuals who want to invest by loaning their money can do so by buying bonds and becoming a creditor (again very small) of the business. As we noted in Chapter 13, a **bond** is an interest-bearing negotiable certificate of long-term debt issued by a corporation, the U.S. government, or a municipality (such as a city or state). Bonds are basically IOUs. Corporations and governments often use the proceeds from bonds to finance expensive construction projects and to purchase costly equipment.

With bonds, investors lend the issuer a certain amount of money—the **principal**—with two expectations: (1) they will receive regular interest payments at a fixed rate of return for many years, and (2) they will get their principal returned at some point in the future, called the **maturity date.** The regular pattern of dividends appeals to those who desire a reliable stream of income. The market price of bonds is sensitive to interest rates.

principal Face amount of a bond, or price originally paid for a bond.

maturity date Date upon which the principal is returned to the bondholder.

An Illustration of Stocks and Bonds: Running Paws Cat Food Company

To better understand how a corporation finances its goals by issuing common and preferred stock while also paying returns for stockholders, consider the example of Running Paws Cat Food Company. When reading through the example, imagine that the numbers have many more zeros to better visualize a company the size of Google or Microsoft.

Running Paws Is Born Running Paws began as a small family business in Lincoln, Nebraska, started by Linda Webtek. She developed a wonderful recipe for cat food and sold the product through a local grocery store. As sales increased, Linda decided to incorporate the business, expand its operations, and share ownership of the company with the public by asking people to invest in the company's future. Running Paws issued 10,000 shares of common stock at $10 per share. Three friends each bought 2500 shares, and Linda signed over the cat food recipe and equipment to the corporation itself in exchange for the remaining 2500 shares. At that point, Running Paws had $75,000 in working capital (7500 shares sold at $10 each), equipment, a great recipe, and a four-person board of directors. Each of the directors worked for the firm, although they paid themselves very low salaries.

Running Paws Begins to Grow The sales revenues of a corporation like Running Paws are used to pay (1) expenses, (2) interest to bondholders, (3) taxes, (4) cash dividends to preferred stockholders, and (5) cash dividends to common stockholders, in that order. If money is left over after items 1 and 2 are paid, the corporation has earned a **profit.** If funds are available after item 3 is paid, the company has an **after-tax profit.** The average corporation pays out 40 to 60 percent of its after-tax profit in cash dividends to stockholders. The remainder, called **retained earnings,** is left to accumulate and finance the company's goals—often expansion and growth. In its early years, Running Paws retained all of its profits and distributed no dividends.

profit Money left over after a firm pays all expenses and interest to bondholders.

after-tax profit Money left over after a firm has paid expenses, bondholder interest, and taxes.

retained earnings Money left over after firm has paid expenses, bondholder interest, taxes, preferred stockholder dividends, and common stockholder dividends.

Common stockholders, such as the stockholders of Running Paws Cat Food Company, are not guaranteed dividends. However, most profitable companies do pay common stockholders a small dividend on a quarterly basis until increased earnings justify paying out a higher amount. Given that Running Paws retained all its earnings, you might wonder why people would invest in such a company. Two reasons explain the attraction. First, as a company becomes more efficient and profitable, cash dividends to common stockholders may not only begin but also become significant. Second, the market price of the stock may increase sharply as more investors become interested in the future profitability of a growing company. Common stock constitutes a share of ownership, thus as the company grows, the price of its common stock follows suit.

Increasing sales meant more production for Running Paws. Soon more orders were coming in from Chicago than the firm could handle. After three years, the owners of Running Paws decided to expand once again. They wanted to borrow an additional $100,000, but their business was so new and its future so uncertain that lenders demanded an extremely high interest rate. To raise the needed funds, the owners decided to issue 5000 shares of preferred stock at $20 per share, promising to pay a cash dividend of $1.80 per share annually, providing a 9 percent yield to investors. The preferred stock was sold to outside investors, but the original investors retained control of the company through their common stock.

Running Paws Becomes a National Company Following its pattern of expanding into new markets, Running Paws soon developed additional lines of cat food that sold well. With the proceeds from the sale of preferred stock, and after a new plant in Brooklyn, New York, opened, the income of the four-year-old business finally exceeded expenses, and it had a profit of $13,000. The board of directors declared the promised preferred stock dividend of $9000 (5000 preferred shares × $1.80) but no dividend for common stockholders. In the following year, net profits after taxes amounted to $28,000. Once again the board paid the $9000 dividend to preferred stockholders but retained the remainder of the profits to finance continued expansion and improved efficiency.

Then one of the original partners wanted to exit the business and needed to sell her 2500 shares of stock, for which she had originally paid $25,000. Because Running Paws was beginning to show some profits, two other private investors recommended by a local stockbroker made offers to purchase her shares. The shares were sold at $16 per share, with 1500 shares going to one investor and 1000 shares to another investor. Thus, this original investor gained $15,000 in price appreciation ($16 × 2500 = $40,000; $40,000 − $25,000 = $15,000) when she sold out. (The corporation did not profit from this transaction.) Now five owners of the common stock, including the two new ones, voted for the board of directors, with each share representing one vote.

During the sixth year, the company's sales again increased and its earnings totaled $39,000. This time the board voted $9000 for the preferred stockholders and $5000 ($0.50 per share) for the common stockholders but retained the remaining $25,000. With the $5000 distribution, the common stockholders finally began to receive cash dividends.

Even with its success, Running Paws faced another decision. To distribute its products nationally would require another $400,000 to $500,000 for expansion costs. After much discussion, the board voted to sell additional shares of stock and issue some bonds.

The company planned to sell 10,000 shares of common stock at $25 per share. This would dilute the owners' proportion of ownership by half. Common stockholders, however, have a **preemptive right** to purchase additional shares before new shares are offered to the public. Thus, each current stockholder retained the legal right to maintain proportionate ownership by being allowed to purchase more shares.

preemptive right Common stockholders hold this right to purchase additional shares before a firm offers new shares to the public.

Bonds were sold, too. Running Paws issued 200 $1000 bonds with a coupon rate of 8 percent. After several months, all of the new stock and bond shares were sold. After brokerage expenses, the company netted more than $190,000 from the bonds to help finance the expansion. On the stock sales, various local stockbrokers took selling commissions totaling $16,000, leaving $234,000 available for the company to use for expansion. These and other investors will follow the progress of Running Paws and

Did You Know?...

How Stock Dividends and Stock Splits Work

A **stock dividend** is a dividend paid in the form of securities instead of cash. For example, a company's board of directors might declare a 10 percent stock dividend to stockholders who currently own shares. In this case, if you owned 100 shares, the company would send you 10 more shares. A stock dividend has no effect on price because the owners retain their same proportional ownership in the company.

A **stock split** occurs when the shares of stock owned by existing shareholders are divided into a larger number of shares. A reverse stock split results in a smaller number of shares. For example, a two-for-one split—say, from $80 to $40 per share—will reduce the value of each share by 50 percent. Thus twice as many shares are available but each is worth only half as much as before. The company will cut the dividend by 50 percent as well. Management splits shares to change the stock price, often lowering it in an effort to open up trading to a greater number of investors. Investors often are more attracted to a stock that is selling at $40 rather than at $80 or $120. Stock splits are seen as an indicator that management expects better profits in the years ahead.

buy and sell shares accordingly. The company will not benefit from this trading. Running Paws and its shareholders will benefit from a rising stock price because ownership in a growing company becomes increasingly valuable. If Running Paws continues to prosper, its board of directors might work toward having its stock listed on a regional stock exchange (discussed later in this chapter) to facilitate trading of shares and to further enhance the company's image.

CONCEPT CHECK 14.1

1. Distinguish between common stocks and bonds.
2. How do public corporations use stocks and bonds?
3. Why do individuals invest in stocks and bonds?

The Major Characteristics of Common Stocks

2 **LEARNING OBJECTIVE** Classify common stocks according to their major characteristics.

A first and easy step in evaluating stock issues is to examine the major characteristics of stock classifications. Here you determine which ones match your investment goals.

Match Your Investment Choices Using P/E Ratio and Beta

multiple Another term for P/E ratio.

trailing P/E ratio Calculated using recently reported earnings, usually from the previous four quarters.

projected P/E ratio Because investors need to look to the future rather than the past, this measure divides price by projected earnings over the coming four quarters. Also known as forward price/earnings ratio.

earnings yield Inverse of the P/E ratio; helps investors more clearly see investment expectations.

Price/Earnings Ratio The **price/earnings ratio (P/E ratio)** is the current market price of a stock divided by earnings per share over the past four quarters. This ratio is the primary means of valuing a stock. It demonstrates how expensive the stock is versus the company's recently reported earnings, by revealing how much you are paying for each $1 of earnings. The P/E ratio is also referred to as a stock's **multiple.** For example, if the market price of a share of Running Paws stock is currently $25 and the company's EPS is $1.60, the P/E ratio will be 16 ($25 ÷ $1.60 = 15.6, which rounds to 16). This value can also be called a 16-to-1 ratio or a P/E ratio of 16. The P/E ratios of many corporations are widely reported on the Internet and in the financial section of newspapers. Stocks with low P/E ratios tend to have higher dividend yields, less risk, lower prices, and slower earnings growth.

To assess a company's financial status, you could compare that firm's P/E ratio with the P/E ratios for other similar stocks. The P/E ratios for corporations typically range from 5 to 25. The typical market average P/E is about 18, although it varies for different industries. Financially successful companies that have been paying good dividends through the years might have a P/E ratio ranging from 7 to 10. Rapidly growing companies would likely have a much higher P/E ratio—15 to 25. Speculative companies might have P/E ratios of 40 or 50 because they have low earnings now but anticipate much higher earnings in the future. Firms that are expected to have strong earnings growth generally have a high stock price and a correspondingly high P/E ratio. The standard P/E ratio is, in fact, called a **trailing P/E ratio** measure because it is calculated using recently reported earnings, usually from the previous four quarters. Investors need to focus on future prospects when analyzing the value of a stock. A **projected P/E** or **forward price/earnings ratio** divides price by projected earnings over the coming four quarters, an estimate available via online stock quote providers. The **earnings yield,** which is the inverse of the P/E ratio [Running Paws' earnings yield is 6.4 percent ($1.60 ÷ $25)], helps investors think more clearly about expectations for investments.

Use Beta to Compare a Stock to Similar Investments Beta is a number widely used by investors to predict future stock prices. The **beta value** (or **beta coefficient**) is a measure of an investment's volatility compared with a broad market index for similar investments. For large-company stocks, the S&P 500 Stock Index often serves as a benchmark. The average for all stocks in the market has arbitrarily been assigned a beta of +1.0, and a beta greater than 1.0 indicates higher-than-market volatility.

beta/beta value/beta coefficient A measure of stock volatility; that is, how much the stock price varies relative to the rest of the market.

Beta reports the relative history of an investment's up-and-down price changes. Most individual stocks have positive betas between 0.5 and 2.0. A beta of less than 1.0 (0.0 to 0.9) indicates that the stock price is less sensitive to the market. This is because the price moves in the same direction as the general market, but not to the same degree. A beta of more than +1.0 to +2.0 (or higher) indicates that the price of the security is more sensitive to the market because its price moves in the same direction as the market but by a greater percentage. Higher betas mean greater risk relative to the market. A beta of zero suggests that the price of the stock is independent of the market, much like that of a risk-free U.S. Treasury security. You may look up betas for stocks at www.investor.reuters.com/stockEntry.aspx?target-/stocks and www.finance.yahoo.com/?u.

Income Stocks

A company whose stock is classified as an **income stock** characteristically may not grow too quickly, but year after year it pays a cash dividend higher than that offered by most companies. It does so because the firm has fairly high earnings and chooses to retain only a small portion of the earnings. To declare high cash dividends regularly, a company has to have a steady stream of profits. Stocks issued by telephone, electric, and gas utility companies fit this profile and are labeled income stocks. Investors in these companies usually are not very concerned with the **P/E ratio** or the growth potential of the price of the stock. The betas of such stocks are often less than 1.0. Individuals who desire some income from their portfolio are often attracted to income stocks.

income stock A stock that may not grow too quickly, but year after year it pays a cash dividend higher than that offered by most companies.

Growth Stocks

The term **growth stock** describes the stock of a company that offers the promise of much higher profits tomorrow and has a consistent record of relatively rapid growth in earnings in all economic conditions. The return to investors from growth stocks comes primarily from increases in share prices. Such stocks typically pay low or no dividends because most of their earnings are retained to maintain company growth.

Well-Known Growth Stocks Stocks of companies that are leaders in their fields, that dominate their markets, and that have several consecutive years of above-industry-average earnings are considered **well-known growth stocks.** Investor awareness of such corporations is widespread, and expectations for continued growth are high. The P/E ratio is high, too. Many growth stocks have a glamorous reputation that improves or declines sharply in conjunction with the overall market and, therefore, have betas of 1.5 or more. Investors like well-known growth stocks because they typically pay some dividends and offer a good opportunity for price appreciation. In the past, well-known growth stocks have included those offered by Microsoft, Oracle, eBay, Coca-Cola, Intel, Cisco, Nike, and Wal-Mart.

Lesser-Known Growth Stocks Because some **lesser-known growth stocks** are not as popular with investors, the P/E ratios for such firms are generally lower (although still high) than those of the more glamorous growth stocks. Often such firms represent regional businesses with strong earnings or companies that may be the third or fourth leading firm in an industry. In recent years, lesser-known growth stocks have included Quality Systems, Longs Drug Stores, and Urban Outfitters. Their betas are usually 1.5 or more.

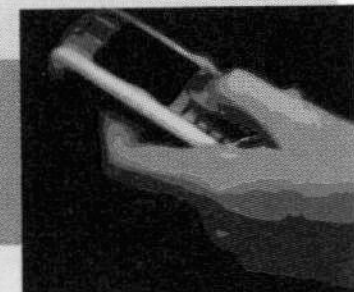

Instant Message

Keep an Eye on Local Investment Situations

According to Peter Lynch, the highly successful former manager of the Fidelity Magellan Fund, amateur investors have an advantage over the large investors. Three to five years before analysts really start to follow such developments, local people can be among the first to see the industry in which they work start to turn around. They also may see nearby businesses with bright futures.

Value Stocks

A **value stock** is one that tends to trade at a low price relative to its company fundamentals (dividends, earnings, sales, and so on) and thus is considered undervalued by a value investor. A **value investor** believes that the market isn't always efficient and that it is possible to find companies trading for less than they are worth. Value stocks often operate within industries that benefit from a growing economy. Stocks that have a relatively high dividend yield, low price/sales ratio, and/or low P/E ratio are classified as value stocks. The low valuations that value stocks enjoy are often a result of some type of bad news (poor earnings report, bad press, legal issues, and so on). Although their stock prices may have changed, some past examples of value stocks have included General Motors, General Electric, DuPont, Merck, Citigroup, and AT&T.

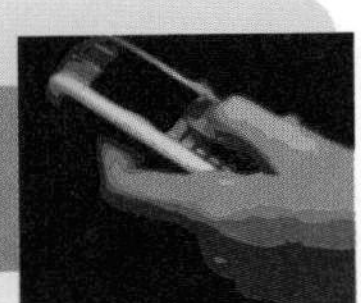

Instant Message

Penny Stocks Are Fraught with Frauds

A **penny stock** is one that sells for less than $1 per share. These often are new companies with erratic sales, few profits, and only some hope of success. Penny stocks are sometimes sold over the telephone by high-pressure salespeople to unsophisticated investors. Legitimate stocks or not, these are very speculative investments.

Speculative Stocks

The term **speculative stock** describes the stock of a company that has a potential for substantial earnings at some time in the future. These stocks are considered speculative because those earnings may never be realized. A speculative stock may have a spotty earnings record or is so new that no earnings pattern has emerged. Investors in these companies accept some risk because they expect the companies to be highly profitable in the future. They hope that the company will make a new discovery, invent a new product, or generate valuable information that later may push up the price of the stock, creating substantial capital gains.

Examples of speculative companies include computer graphics firms, Internet applications firms, small oil exploration businesses, genetic engineering firms, and some pharmaceutical manufacturers. For these firms, the P/E ratio fluctuates widely in tandem with the company's fortunes, and beta values exceeding 2.0 are common. For every speculative company that succeeds, many others do poorly or fail altogether.

Tech Stocks

Tech stocks are those in the technology sector. Technology firms are dominant in the stock market and include firms that offer technology-based products and services, biotechnology, Internet services, network services, wireless communications, and more. Some are large blue-chip firms, such as Microsoft and Cisco Systems, while most are speculative ventures, such as Human Genome Sciences and Cognus Corporation.

Blue-Chip Stocks

The term **blue-chip stock** suggests a company that has been around for a long time, has a well-regarded reputation, dominates its industry (often with annual revenues of $1 billion or more), and is known for being a solid, relatively safe investment. Typically, blue-chip companies have a history of both good earnings and consistent cash dividends, and they grow at approximately the same rate as the overall economy. The term comes from poker, in which the highest chip denomination is colored blue.

Did You Know?...

Most Stocks Are Cyclical and Some Are Countercyclical

The term **cyclical stock** describes the stock of a company whose profits are greatly influenced by changes in the economic business cycle. Such companies operate in consumer-dependent industries, such as automobiles, housing, airlines, retailing, and heavy machinery. The market prices of cyclical stocks mirror the general state of the economy and reflect the various phases of the business cycle. During times of prosperity and economic expansion, corporate earnings rise, profits grow, and stock prices climb; during a recession, these measures decline sharply. The stock of many firms characterized as blue-chip, income, growth, value, or speculative stocks can be described as cyclical stocks. Cyclical stocks have a beta of about 1.0.

A stock with a beta that is less than 1.0 or even a negative beta is called a **countercyclical** (or **defensive**) **stock** because it exhibits price changes contrary to movements in the business cycle. These stocks perform well even in an environment characterized by weak economic activity and sliding interest rates. Cigarette smokers, for example, do not quit during a recession, and people usually continue to go to movies, consume soft drinks, purchase cat and dog food, buy electric utility service, and go grocery shopping. The prices of countercyclical stocks remain steady during an economic recession.

Blue-chip stock shares are widely held by individual investors, mutual funds, and pension plans. The earnings of blue-chip companies (whose stocks are usually considered income stocks or well-known growth stocks) are expected to increase at a consistent but unspectacular rate because these highly stable firms are the leaders in their industries. Examples of such stocks are Wal-Mart, Coca-Cola, Berkshire Hathaway, and Exxon Mobil. Investing in such companies is considered much less risky than investing in other types of firms.

Large-Cap, Small-Cap, and Midcap Stocks

A company's size classification in the stock market is based on its **market capitalization.** This is the total value of a company's common stock shares determined at its current market price. **Large-cap stocks** are those of firms that have issued $3 billion to $4 billion (or more) of stocks. Most are considered blue-chip companies, too. Examples include Texaco, Microsoft, Time Warner, and General Foods. Stocks of midsize and smaller firms often outperform large-cap stocks.

Midcap stocks are the stocks of those remaining companies that are quite substantial in terms of capitalization—perhaps $750 million to $3 billion in size—but not among the very largest firms. Examples include Wendy's and Starbucks. A **small-cap stock** is stock of a company that has a capitalization of less than $750 million. **Microcaps** are firms with less than $100 million in capitalization, and perhaps as little as $10 million. When the smaller firms achieve substantial increases in sales and earnings, their stock prices typically jump quite sharply.

CONCEPT CHECK 14.2

1. Distinguish between income stocks and growth stocks.
2. Explain how a value stock might or might not differ from a blue-chip stock or a tech stock.
3. Explain how a stock with a beta of 1.0 differs from ones with a beta of 1.2 and 2.5.

How to Evaluate Stock Values

3 **LEARNING OBJECTIVE**
Describe fundamental and numerical ways to evaluate stock values.

How do you know whether buying a particular stock is a good idea? Or when you should sell shares that you hold? To get answers, first use fundamental research analysis. Second, understand that evaluating stocks is largely about earnings. Third, use numerical measures to evaluate stock values. And fourth, use beta values to compare a stock to similar investments.

Use Fundamental Analysis to Evaluate Stocks

fundamental analysis School of thought in market analysis that assumes each stock has an intrinsic (or true) value based on its expected stream of future earnings.

The premise underlying **fundamental analysis** is that each stock has an intrinsic (or true) value based on its expected stream of future earnings. Most professional stock analysts and investors take this approach to investing as they research economic, corporate, and industry financials. Fundamental analysis suggests that you can identify some stocks that will outperform others. The fundamental approach presumes that a stock's basic value is largely determined by current and future earnings trends, expected levels of interest rates, industry outlook, and management's expertise. The aim is to seek out sound stocks—perhaps even unfashionable ones—that are priced below what they ought to be.

technical analysis Method of evaluating securities that uses statistics generated by market activity, such as past prices and volume, over time to determine when to buy or sell a stock.

An opposing and minority view on valuing common stocks is advocated by proponents of **technical analysis,** often newsletter authors. This method of evaluating securities analyzes statistics generated by market activity, such as past prices and volume. Technical analysts do not attempt to measure a security's intrinsic value but instead use charts, graphs, mathematics, and software programs to identify and predict future price movements. Technical analysis has proved to be of little value, although some novice investors may find technical analysts' logic appealing.

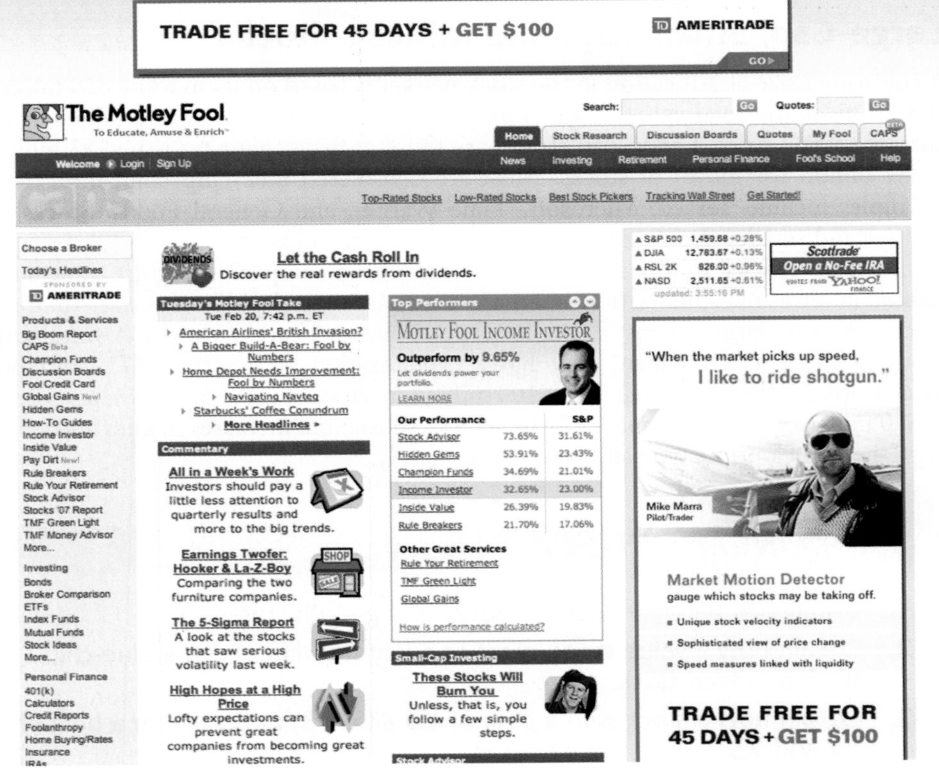

There are numerous websites that offer fundamental and technical analysis of stocks. The Motley Fool does so with a sense of humor.

Corporate Earnings Are Most Important

Corporate earnings are the profits a company makes during a specific time period. If a company cannot generate earnings now or in the future, stock market analysts and investors are not going to be impressed. As people reach this conclusion, there quickly will be more sellers than buyers of the company's common stock, and that will depress the stock's market price. Here are some numerical indicators of earnings.

corporate earnings The profits a company makes during a specific time period indicate to many analysts whether to buy or sell a stock.

Earnings per Share

A company's **earnings per share (EPS)** is annual profit divided by the number of outstanding shares. It indicates the income that a company has available, on a per-share basis, to pay dividends and reinvest as retained earnings. The EPS is a measure of the firm's profitability on a common-stock-per-share basis, and it is helpful because investors can use it to compare financial conditions of many companies. The EPS is reported in the business section of many newspapers.

In our example, assume that, next year after payment of $9000 in dividends to preferred stockholders, Running Paws had a net profit of $32,000. With 20,000 shares of stock, the company's EPS would be $1.60 ($32,000 ÷ 20,000).

earnings per share (EPS) A firm's profit divided by the number of outstanding shares; analysts follow EPS because it indicates the income that a company has available to pay dividends and reinvest as retained earnings—used to compare stocks across the board.

Price/Sales Ratio

The **price/sales ratio (P/S ratio)** indicates the number of dollars it takes to buy a dollar's worth of a company's annual revenues. The P/S is obtained by dividing a company's total market capitalization by its sales for the past four quarters. For example, if Running Paws Cat Food Company's common stock currently sells for $25 per share and 20,000 shares of the company's stock are outstanding, its total capitalization is $500,000. If company revenues (sales of cat food) were $750,000 over the past year, the stock's P/S would be 0.67 ($500,000 ÷ $750,000). Stock analysts suggest investors avoid companies with a P/S greater than 1.5 and favor those having a P/S of less than 0.75. Many investors ignore the P/S, but it works better than the highly acclaimed P/E ratio in predicting which companies provide the best return, as explained in James P. O'Shaughnessy's *What Works on Wall Street.*

price/sales ratio (P/S ratio) Tells the number of dollars it takes to buy a dollar's worth of a company's annual revenues; calculated by dividing company's total market capitalization by its sales for the past four quarters.

Numerical Measures to Evaluate Stock Prices

Several other numerical measures are used to evaluate stock performance. These numbers are readily available to investors on the Internet. Here are some numerical indicators that will help you assess future stock prices.

Cash Dividends

Stocks usually pay dividends. Cash dividends are distributions made in cash to holders of stock. They are the current income that you receive while you own shares in the company. The firm's board of directors usually declares a dividend on a quarterly basis (four times per corporate year), typically at the end of March, June, September, and December. Dividends are ordinarily paid out of current earnings, but, in the event of unprofitable times (low earnings or none), the money might come from cash reserves held by the company. Occasionally, a company will borrow to pay the dividend so as to maintain its reputation of consistently paying dividends. Later profits can be used to repay any funds borrowed for this purpose.

Dividends per Share

The **dividends per share** measure translates the total cash dividends paid out by a company to common stockholders into a per-share figure. For example, Running Paws might elect to declare a total cash dividend of $8000 for the year to common stockholders. In that case, cash dividends per share would amount to $0.40 ($8000 ÷ 20,000 shares).

dividends per share Translates the total cash dividends paid out by a company to common stockholders into a per-share figure.

Dividend Payout Ratio

The **dividend payout ratio** is the dividends per share divided by earnings per share. It helps you judge the likelihood of future dividends. For example, imagine that Running Paws Cat Food Company earned $32,000 (after paying preferred stockholders), paid out a cash dividend of $8000 to company stockholders, and retained the remaining $24,000 to facilitate growth of the company. In

dividend payout ratio Dividends per share divided by earnings per share; helps judge likelihood of future dividends.

this case, the dividend payout ratio equals 0.25 (\$8000 ÷ \$32,000). For that year, Running Paws paid a dividend equal to 25 percent of earnings. Newer companies usually retain most, if not all, of their profits to facilitate growth. An investor interested in growth would, therefore, seek a company with a low payout ratio. The lower the payout ratio, the greater the likelihood that the company will grow, resulting in capital gains for investors.

dividend yield Cash dividend to an investor expressed as a percentage of the current market price of a security.

Dividend Yield The **dividend yield** is the cash dividend paid to an investor expressed as a percentage of the current market price of a security. For example, the \$0.40 cash dividend of Running Paws divided by the current \$25 market price for its stock reveals a dividend yield of 1.6 percent (\$0.40 ÷ \$25). Growth and speculative companies typically pay little or no cash dividends, so they have limited dividend yields. Such companies are attractive to investors who are interested in capital gains.

book value/shareholder's equity Net worth of a company, determined by subtracting total liabilities from assets.

Book Value **Book value** (also known as **shareholder's equity**) is the net worth of a company, which is determined by subtracting the company's total liabilities from its assets. It theoretically indicates a company's worth if its assets were sold, its debts were paid off, and the net proceeds were distributed to the investors who own the outstanding shares of common stock.

book value per share Reflects the book value of a company divided by the number of shares of common stock outstanding.

Book Value per Share The **book value per share** reflects the book value of a company divided by the number of shares of common stock outstanding. Running Paws has a net worth of \$230,000, which, when divided by 20,000 shares, gives a book value per share of \$11.50.

Often little relationship exists between the book value of a company and its earnings or the market price of its stock. A stock's price usually exceeds its book value per share. The reason is that stockholders bid up the stock price because they anticipate earnings and dividends in the future and expect the market price to rise even more. When the book value per share exceeds the price per share, the stock may truly be underpriced.

price-to-book ratio (P/B ratio) Current stock price divided by the per-share net value of a firm's plant, equipment, and other assets (book value); helps investors identify stocks that are value rich. Also called market-to-book ratio.

Price-to-Book Ratio The **price-to-book ratio (P/B ratio),** also called the **market-to-book ratio,** identifies firms that are asset rich, such as many banks, brokerage firms, and insurance companies. The P/B ratio is the current stock price divided by the per-share net value of the company's plant, equipment, and other assets (book value). It tells you the premium that you are paying for the net assets of the company.

Did You Know...

About Employee Stock Options

Many employers give stock options to attract and retain employees. An **employee stock option (ESO)** is a gift, like a bonus, from an employer to an employee that allows employees to benefit from the appreciation of their employer's stock without putting any money down. The company gives the employee the right and opportunity to "exercise" the option by buying the stock sometime in the future at an "exercise" or "striking" price established when the option was given. If the company prospers, when the employee eventually decides to exercise the options, the current share price may be much higher than the exercise price, thus allowing the employee to buy the shares at a considerable discount.

requires an initial deposit (perhaps as little as $100) and specifies that full settlement is due to the brokerage firm within three business days after a buy or sell order has been given. After each transaction, your account is debited or credited and written confirmation is immediately forwarded to you. All brokers offer such services.

Discount Brokers Many investors use **discount brokers** because they charge commissions to execute trades that are often 30 to 80 percent less than the fees charged by full-service brokers. These brokers feature low commissions because they have lower overhead and may offer fewer customer services. That is, they focus on a single function: efficiently executing orders to buy and sell securities. Some discount brokerage firms do not conduct research or provide investment advice. Transactions can be completed online as well as via a toll-free telephone number; investors can also obtain price quotes, check the status of their accounts, and transfer funds online or by phone. Discounters include Ameritrade, Scottrade, E*Trade, ShareBuilder, and BUYandHOLD.

discount brokers Charge commissions to execute trades that are often 30 to 80 percent less than the fees charged by full-service brokers, but also offer fewer services.

Online brokers (also called **Internet** or **electronic brokers**) have reduced the cost of executing a trade to perhaps $20 or even $10 because their primary business is online trading. Online **day trading** occurs when an investor buys and sells stocks quickly throughout the day with the hope that the price will move enough to cover transaction costs and earn some profits. Day traders do not own stocks overnight. Transactions are executed online because they can be done quickly with low commissions. Day trading is a risky practice. One of billionaire Warren Buffett's commandments for getting ahead in personal finance states, "You will lose money if you trade stocks actively."

online brokers Such brokers, also called Internet or electronic brokers, have reduced the cost of executing a trade to perhaps $20 or even $10 because their primary business is online trading.

day trading Occurs when an investor buys and sells stocks quickly throughout a day with the hope that prices will move enough to cover transaction costs and earn some profits.

Did You Know?...

Regulations Protect Against Investment Fraud

Public trust is vital to the success of the securities industry; without it, consumers will not invest. Regulation of securities markets aims to provide investors with accurate and reliable information about securities, maintain ethical standards, and prevent fraud against investors. This regulation occurs at four levels:

1. The **Securities and Exchange Commission (SEC),** a federal government agency, focuses on ensuring disclosure of information about securities to the investing public and on approving the rules and regulations employed by the organized securities exchanges. The SEC requires registration of listed securities with appropriate and updated information. It also prohibits manipulative practices, such as using insider information for illegal personal gain or causing the price of a security to rise or fall for false reasons. All states require registration of securities sold within their states, and they, too, regulate the securities industry.
2. The Financial Industry Regulatory Authority (FINRA) and other self-regulatory organizations enforce standards of conduct for their members and their member organizations. They dictate rules for listing and for trading securities.
3. Individual brokerage firms have established standards of conduct for brokers that govern how they deal with investors.
4. The U.S. Congress decides when investors need more federal laws. Congress created a limited insurance program to protect the investing public. Although investment losses are not covered, the Security Investors Protection Corporation (SIPC) protects investors when an SEC-registered brokerage firm goes bankrupt. Each of an investor's accounts at a brokerage firm is protected against financial loss as a result of unreturned securities and cash up to a total of $500,000, but no more than $100,000 in cash.

general (full-service) brokerage firms Offer a full range of services to customers, including investment advice and research.

Full-Service General Brokerage Firms A traditional **general brokerage firm** offers a full range of services to customers, including investment information and advice; research reports on companies, industries, general economic trends, and world events; an investment newsletter; recommendations to buy, sell, or hold stocks; execution of securities transactions by humans and online; and margin loans. Investors receive monthly statements summarizing all of the transactions in their account and commissions, dividends, and interest. Commissions and fees are higher than those of discount and online brokers; however, investors can discuss their investments with a qualified professional.

Advice from a Pro...

Check Your Stockbroker's Background

You can check the background of a stockbroker or a brokerage firm via the Financial Industry Regulatory Authority (www.finra.org and click on FINRA BrokerCheck). Some investors neglect to investigate a stockbroker or firm and lose money as a result. The broker may abscond with the investor's funds; at other times, the investor receives poor advice. Don't let it happen to you!

Allen Martin
California State University–Northridge

Broker Commissions and Fees

Brokerage firms receive a commission on each securities transaction to cover the direct expenses of executing the transaction and other overhead expenses. They have established fee schedules that they use when dealing with any except the largest investors. The fees reflect a commission rate that declines as the total value of the transaction increases. For example, in lieu of a minimum commission charge of $25, a brokerage firm might charge 2.8 percent on a transaction amounting to less than $800, 1.8 percent on transactions between $800 and $2500, 1.6 percent on amounts between $2500 and $5000, and 1.2 percent on amounts exceeding $5000.

Transaction costs are based on sales of **round lots,** which are standard units of trading of 100 shares of stock and $1000 or $5000 par value for bonds. An **odd lot** is an amount of a security that is less than the normal unit of trading for that particular security; for stocks, any transaction less than 100 shares is usually considered to be an odd lot. When brokerage firms buy or sell shares in odd lots, they may charge a fee of 12.5 cents (called an **eighth**) per share on the odd-lot portion of the transaction, which is called the **differential.**

round lots Standard units of trading of 100 shares of stock and $1000 or $5000 par value for bonds.

odd lot An amount of a security that is less than the normal unit of trading for that particular security; for stocks, any transaction less than 100 shares is usually considered to be an odd lot.

The payment of commissions can quickly reduce the return on any investment. A purchase commission of 2 percent added to a sales commission of another 2 percent, for example, means that the investor has to earn a 4 percent yield just to pay the transaction costs. Brokerage commissions typically range from $25 to 3 percent of the value of the transaction. The easiest way to hold down investing costs is to find a brokerage firm that charges low commissions.

How to Order Stock Transactions

Hundreds of millions of shares of securities are traded daily on the stock markets in the United States. Every trade brings together a buyer and a seller to complete the transaction at a given price.

The Process of Trading Stocks Assume you instruct brokerage firm A to purchase a certain number of shares at a specific price. The firm relays the buy order to its representative, who coordinates trading. Because the brokerage firm has a seat on the exchange, the buy order is then given to the brokerage firm's contact person at the exchange—a **floor broker.** This broker contacts a **specialist,** a person on the floor of the exchange who handles trades of that particular stock in an effort to maintain a fair and orderly market. The buy order is then filled, either by taking shares from the specialist's own inventory or by matching it with another investor's sell order.

floor broker Brokerage firm's contact person at an exchange.

specialist Person on floor of an exchange who handles trades of a particular stock in an effort to maintain a fair and orderly market.

Matched or Negotiated Stock Price Securities prices are either matched or negotiated.

Matched Price On the organized stock exchanges, a match must occur between the buyer's price and the seller's price for a sale to take place. Therefore, a specialist could hold a specific order for a few minutes, a few hours, or even a week before making a match. With actively traded issues, a transaction is completed in just a few minutes. A slower-selling security can be traded more quickly if an investor is willing to accept the current market price (as discussed later).

Negotiated Price. In the over-the-counter market, the final transaction price is negotiated because two prices are involved. The **bid price** is the highest price anyone has declared that he or she wants to pay for a security. Thus, it represents the amount a brokerage firm is willing to pay for a particular security. The **ask price** is the lowest price anyone will accept at that time for a particular security. Thus, it represents the amount for which another brokerage firm is willing to sell a particular security. The **spread** represents the difference between the bid price at which a broker/dealer will buy shares and the higher ask price at which the broker/dealer will sell shares. The spread can be as little as 5 cents per share, but it can range from 10 to 20 cents for OTC stocks. In addition to paying the ask price, investors typically pay a nominal sales commission to their stockbroker for executing the transaction.

bid price Declared highest price anyone wants to pay for a security.

ask price Declared lowest price that anyone is willing to accept to sell a security.

spread Represents difference between bid price at which a broker/dealer will buy shares and higher ask price at which the broker/dealer will sell shares.

If a buyer does not want to pay the asking price, he or she instructs the stockbroker to offer a lower bid price, which may or may not be accepted. If it is refused, the buyer might cancel the first order and raise the bid slightly in a second order in the hope that the owner will sell the shares at that price. Otherwise, the buyer may have to pay the full ask price to complete the deal. OTC trades usually occur at prices somewhere between the bid and ask figures.

Types of Stock Orders

Basically, there are only two types of orders—buy and sell. The stockbroker will buy or sell securities according to prescribed instructions in a process called **executing an order.** Those instructions can place constraints on the prices at which those orders are carried out. Following are examples of instructions that may accompany stock orders:

Market Order. A **market order** instructs the stockbroker to execute an order at the prevailing market price—that is, the current selling price of the stock. A stockbroker can generally conduct the desired transaction within a few minutes. The floor broker tries to match the instructions from many investors with the narrow range of prices available from the specialist. Traders on the floor of the stock market typically shout and signal back and forth as part of this effort to match buyers and sellers. Most trades are market orders.

market order Instructs the stockbroker to execute an order at the prevailing market price—that is, the current selling price of the stock.

Limit Order. A **limit order** instructs the stockbroker to buy or sell a stock at a specific price. It may include instructions to buy at the best possible price but not above a specified limit, or to sell at the best possible price but not below a specified limit. A limit order provides some protection against buying a security at a price higher than desired or selling at a price deemed too low. The stockbroker transmits the limit order to the specialist. The order is executed if and when the specified price (or better) is reached and all other previously received orders on the specialist's book have been considered.

limit order Instructs the stockbroker to buy or sell a stock at a specific price.

A disadvantage for buyers who place a limit order is that they might miss an excellent opportunity. For example, assume you place a limit order with your stockbroker to buy 100 shares of Running Paws common stock at $60.50 or lower. You have read in the newspaper that the stock has recently been selling at $61 and $61.25, and you hope to save $0.50 to $1.00 on each share. On that same day, the company announces publicly that it plans to expand into the dog food area for the first time. Investor confidence in the new sales effort pushes the price up to $70. If you had given your stockbroker a market order instead, you would have purchased 100 shares of Running Paws at perhaps

\$61.50, which would have given you an immediate profit of \$850 (\$70 − \$61.50 = \$8.50; \$8.50 × 100 shares = \$850) on an initial investment of \$6150 (\$61.50 × 100).

A disadvantage for sellers placing a limit order is that it could result in no sale if the price drops because of negative news. Assume that you bought stock at \$50 that is currently selling at \$58 and that you have placed a limit order to sell at a price of no less than \$60 so as to take your profit. The price could creep up to \$59 and then fall back to \$48, however. In this event, you did not sell the securities because the limit order was priced too high, and they are now worth less than what you originally paid for them. A limit order is best used when you expect great fluctuations in the price of a stock and when you buy or sell infrequently traded securities on the over-the-counter market. Limit orders account for about one-third of all trades.

stop order Instructs a stockbroker to sell your shares of stock at the market price if a stock declines to or goes below a specified price.

Stop Order (Stop-Loss Order). A **stop order** instructs a stockbroker to sell your shares of stock at the market price if a stock declines to or goes below a specified price. It is often called a **stop-loss order** because the investor uses it to protect against a sharp drop in price and thus to stop a loss. The specialist executes the order as soon as the stop-order price is reached and a buyer is matched at the next market price.

As an example of how to stop a loss, assume you bought 100 shares of Running Paws stock at \$70. You are nervous about the company's entry into the competitive dog food business, however, and you fear that it might lose money. As a consequence, you place a stop order to sell your shares if the price drops to \$56, thereby limiting your potential loss to 20 percent (\$70 − \$56 = \$14; \$14 ÷ \$70 = 0.20). Some months later, you read in the financial section of your newspaper that even after six months Running Paws still has less than 1 percent of the dog food market. You call your stockbroker, who informs you that the price of Running Paws stock dropped drastically in response to the article, which was published in the previous day's *Wall Street Journal*. The broker reports that all of your shares were sold at \$55, that the current price is \$49, and that the sales transaction notice is already in the mail to your home. The stop order cut your losses to slightly more than 20 percent (\$70 − \$55 = \$15; \$15 ÷ \$70 = 21.4 percent) and saved an additional loss of \$6 (\$55 − \$49) per share. Thus, the stop order limited your loss to \$1500 [(100 × \$70 = \$7000) − (100 × \$55 = \$5500)] instead of \$2100 [(100 × \$70 = \$7000) − (100 × \$49 = \$4900)].

You can use a stop order to protect your profits, too. Assume you bought 100 shares of Alpo Dog Food Company at \$60 per share, which now has a current selling price of \$75. Your paper profit is \$1500 (\$75 − \$60 = \$15; \$15 × 100 shares = \$1500), less commissions. To protect part of that profit, you place a stop order with your stockbroker to sell at \$65 if the price drops that low. If your stock is sold, you will have a real profit of \$500 (\$65 − \$60 = \$5; \$5 × 100 shares = \$500). If Alpo Dog Food stock climbs in price instead, perhaps in response to the bad news about Running Paws, the stop order would have cost you nothing. If the price does climb, you might replace the stop order with one having a higher price to lock in an even greater amount of profit.

Time Limits. Investors have several ways to place time limits on their orders to buy or sell stocks. A **fill-or-kill order** instructs the stockbroker to buy or sell the stock at the market price immediately or else cancel the order. A **day order** is valid only for the remainder of the trading day during which it was given to the brokerage firm. Unless otherwise indicated, any order received by a stockbroker is assumed to be a day order. A **week order** remains valid until the close of trading on Friday of the current week. A **month order** is effective until the close of trading on the last business day of the current month. An **open order,** also called a **good-til-canceled (GTC) order,** remains valid until executed by the stockbroker or canceled by the investor. If you give an order longer than a week in duration, you should carefully monitor events and then alter the order if the situation changes substantially.

Did You Know?...

The Tax Consequences of Investing in Stocks and Bonds

The government encourages investing through tax policies that favor investors.

- Money invested in qualified tax-sheltered retirement plans accumulates tax free, thereby avoiding current income taxes on interest, dividends, and capital gains for many years. As a result, balances can build up more quickly than funds in traditional investment accounts. Income taxes must be paid on such money when it is eventually withdrawn.
- Taxes are low on dividend income. Funds put into regular investment accounts represent "after-tax money" (you earn an income, you pay taxes on that income, and then you invest some of the remaining money). Taxes are due on any interest, dividends, and capital gains in the year in which the income is received. Interest is taxable at the investor's marginal tax rate. Dividend income is taxed at a maximum rate of 15 percent for most people; a 5 percent rate applies to lower-income taxpayers.
- Capital gains taxes are low. No tax liability is incurred for any capital gains until the stock, bond, mutual fund, real estate, or other investment is sold. When you sell an investment, such as a stock, the gain or loss is calculated by analyzing what you paid for the investment plus broker commissions and loads minus the selling price minus commissions or redemption fees. Short-term gains (for investments held for one year or less) are taxed at the same rates as ordinary income. Long-term gains (for investments held at least a year and a day) are taxed at special rates: The federal rate is 15 percent, but taxpayers in the 10 to 15 percent tax brackets pay a long-term capital gains tax of 5 percent. The long-term capital gain rate for collectibles such as stamps and coins is 28 percent.
- Capital losses can be used to offset capital gains or even your regular income. See Chapter 4.

Margin Buying and Selling Short Are Risky Trading Techniques

For investors interested in taking on additional risk, there are two advanced trading techniques, and both involve using credit: buying stocks on margin and selling short. Buying stocks on margin involves using a line of credit from a stockbroker, thereby enabling the investor to effectively control many more shares with a small amount of cash. Investors who sell shares of stock short are actually selling shares they do not own.

Margin Trading Is Buying Stocks on Credit Some investors open a margin account with a brokerage firm in addition to their cash account so they can buy securities using credit. Opening a **margin account** requires making a substantial deposit of cash or securities ($2000 or more) and permits the purchase of other securities using credit granted by the brokerage firm. Using a margin account to purchase securities, or **margin buying,** allows the investor to apply leverage that magnifies returns. In essence, the investor borrows money from the brokerage firm to buy more stocks and bonds than would be possible with his or her available cash. Both brokerage firms and the Federal Reserve Board regulate the use of credit to buy securities.

The **margin rate** is the percentage of the value (or equity) in an investment that is not borrowed. In recent years, it has ranged from 25 to 40 percent. Thus, if the margin rate is 40 percent, you can buy securities by putting up only 40 percent of the total price and borrowing the remainder from the brokerage firm. The securities purchased, as well as other securities in the margin account, are used as collateral. Margin lending is financed at competitive interest rates.

margin account Account at a brokerage firm that requires a substantial deposit of cash or securities and permits the purchase of other securities using credit granted by the brokerage firm.

margin buying Using a margin account to buy securities; allows the investor to apply leverage that magnifies returns—or losses.

margin rate Set by the Fed, percentage of the value (or equity) in an investment that is not borrowed—recently 25 to 40 percent.

Buying on Margin Can Increase Returns. Buying on margin is commonly used to increase the individual's return on investment. For example, assume that Greenfield Computer Company common stock is selling for $80 per share. You want to buy 100 shares, requiring a total expenditure of $8000. Using your margin account, you will make a cash payment of $3200 (0.40 × $8000), with the brokerage firm lending you the difference of $4800 ($8000 − $3200). For the sake of simplicity, we will omit commissions from this example and assume that the brokerage firm lends the funds at 10 percent interest. Thus, your equity (market value minus amount borrowed) in the investment is $3200. If, as illustrated in Table 14.2, the price of Greenfield stock increases from $80 to $92 at the end of a year, you can sell your investment for proceeds of $9200, minus the amount invested ($3200), the amount borrowed ($4800), and the cost of borrowing ($4800 × 0.10 = $480), for a return of $720. Because you invested equity of only $3200 to obtain a profit of $720, you have earned a return of 22.5 percent ($720 ÷ $3200). If you had put up the entire $8000 and not bought on margin, your return on investment would have been only 15 percent ($9200 − $8000 = $1200; $1200 ÷ $8000 = 0.15). In this way, you can use credit to increase the rate of return on your own investment. Those with an aggressive investment philosophy might buy on margin because it gives them the opportunity to obtain a higher rate of return.

Table 14.2 How Buying on Margin Affects Investment Returns

	Cash Transaction	Margin Transaction
Price of stock rises (from $80 to $92 per share)		
Buy 100 shares at $80 (amount invested)	−$8,000	−$3,200
Sell 100 shares at $92 (proceeds)	9,200	9,200
Net proceeds	$1,200	$6,000
Minus amount borrowed	—	−4,800
Net	$1,200	$1,200
Minus cost of borrowing	—	−480
Return	$1,200	$720
Yield (return ÷ amount invested)	+15.0%	+22.5%
Price of stock declines (from $80 to $70 per share)		
Buy 100 shares at $80 (amount invested)	−$8,000	−$3,200
Sell 100 shares at $70 (proceeds)	7,000	7,000
Net proceeds	−$1,000	$3,800
Minus amount borrowed	—	−4,800
Net	−$1,000	−$1,000
Minus cost of borrowing	—	−480
Return	−$1,000	−$1,480
Yield (return ÷ amount invested)	−12.5%	−46.25%
Price of stock declines (from $80 to $60 per share)		
Buy 100 shares at $80 (amount invested)	−$8,000	−$3,200
Sell 100 shares at $60 (proceeds)	6,000	6,000
Net proceeds	−$2,000	$2,800
Minus amount borrowed	—	−4,800
Net	−$2,000	−$2,000
Minus cost of borrowing	—	−480
Return	−$2,000	−$2,480
Yield (return ÷ amount invested)	−25.0%	−77.5%

Buying on Margin Can Increase Losses. If the price of a security bought on margin declines, however, leverage can work against you, as Table 14.2 also illustrates. For example, if the price of the Greenfield stock bought at \$80 dropped to \$70 after a year, you would lose \$10 per share on the 100 shares, for a total loss of \$1000. Your proceeds from selling the stock would be only \$7000. If you bought the stock on 40 percent margin, these proceeds are offset by the cost of the investment (\$3200), the margin loan from the broker (\$4800), and interest on the loan (\$480), for a total deduction of \$8480 and a net loss of \$1480 (\$7000 − \$8480). Thus, a loss of \$1480 on an investment of \$3200 is a negative return of 46.25 percent (−\$1480 ÷ \$3200). The same \$10 loss per share (from a price of \$80 to \$70 per share) would have been a negative loss of only 12.5 percent if the stocks were not bought on margin (\$7000 − \$8000 = −\$1000; −\$1000 ÷ \$8000 = −0.125). Similarly, the example cited in Table 14.2 shows the magnitude of the loss due to a \$20 decline in value as a negative return of 77.5 percent, compared with a loss of only 25 percent if the investor had not bought on margin.

Did You Know?...

How to Determine a Margin Call Stock Price

To determine the price at which a margin call for a stock will occur, use the formula given in Equation (14.3). This formula also appears on the *Garman/Forgue* website.

$$\text{Margin call stock price} = \frac{\text{amount owed broker} \div (1 - \text{margin call requirement})}{\text{number of shares bought}} \quad (14.3)$$

$$\$64 = \frac{\$4800 \div (1 - 0.25)}{100}$$

Substituting the figures from the Running Paws text example, the investor will receive a margin call if the stock price dropped below \$64, as equity at this point is 25 percent.

A Margin Call Makes Matters Even Worse. When the price of a stock declines to the point where the investor's equity is less than the required percentage, the brokerage firm will make a telephone call to the investor. A representative of the firm will tell the investor to immediately either put up more collateral (money or other stocks) or face having the investment liquidated. This procedure is known as a **margin call.** If the investor fails to put up the additional cash or securities to maintain a required level of equity in the margin account, the broker will sell the securities at the market price, resulting in a sharp financial loss to the investor. The investor is required to repay the broker for any losses. The margin call concept protects the broker that has loaned money on securities.

margin call If a stock price declines to the point that the investor's equity is less than the required percentage, a representative of the brokerage firm makes a phone call and tells the investor to either put up more money or securities or face having the position bought on margin liquidated.

For example, in Table 14.2, the 100 shares of Greenfield priced at \$80 were originally valued at \$8000, consisting of investor's equity of \$3200, or 40 percent (\$3200 ÷ \$8000), and \$4800 borrowed from the brokerage firm. Assume that the stock price drops to \$60 per share, resulting in a current market value of \$6000 for the investment. Because the investor still owes \$4800, his or her equity has dropped to \$1200 (\$6000 − \$4800), which is now only 20 percent of the value of the securities (\$1200 ÷ \$6000), rather than the required 40 percent. The broker, operating with a 25 percent margin requirement, will immediately make a margin call and demand that funds or collateral be added to the account to bring the equity up to a minimum of 25 percent. In this example, to maintain a 25 percent margin, an additional \$300 (\$6000 × 0.25 = \$1500; \$1500 −\$1200 = \$300) would be required.

Selling Short Is Selling Stocks Borrowed from Your Broker

Buying a security with the hope that it will go up in value—the goal of most investors—is called **buying long.** You might suspect, however, that the price of a security will drop. You can earn profits when the price of a security declines by **selling short.** In this trading technique, investors sell securities they do not own (borrowing them from a broker) and later buy the same number of shares of the security at a lower price (returning them to the broker). Thus, the investor earns a profit on the transaction. Brokerage firms require an investor to maintain a margin account when selling short

buying long Buying a security (especially on margin) with the hope that the stock price will rise.

selling short Investors selling securities they do not own (borrowing them from a broker) and later buying the same number of shares of the security at a lower price (returning them to the broker).

because it provides some assurance that the investor can repay the firm for the borrowed stock, if necessary. As a result, some or all of an investor's funds deposited in a margin account are effectively tied up during a short sale. Many brokers hold the proceeds of a short sale, without paying interest, until the customer **covers the position** by buying it back for delivery to the broker.

covering a position When an investor using a margin account buys back securities sold short or sells securities bought long.

An Example of Short Selling. As an example, suppose you believe that the price of Greenfield stock will drop substantially over the next several months. You have heard that some top managers of the company may resign and that competitors are expected to introduce newer products. Accordingly, you instruct your broker to sell 100 shares of Greenfield at \$80 per share (\$80 × 100 = \$8000). In this illustration, assume that you have a 40 percent margin requirement, which means you have committed \$3200 (0.40 × \$8000). The shares are actually borrowed by the broker from another investor or another broker. Several months later, Greenfield announces lower profits because of strong competition, and the share price drops to \$70. Now you instruct your broker to buy 100 shares at the new price and use the purchased shares to repay the borrowed shares. You gain a profit of \$1000 (\$8000 − \$7000), ignoring commissions, providing a return of 31.3 percent (\$1000 ÷ \$3200).

Using Margin to Sell Short. A very small price drop can provide big profits for the short-term investor who sells short *and* uses margin-buying techniques. As an example, imagine that you sell 100 shares of a \$10 stock with a 40 percent margin requirement. The committed funds amount to \$400 (0.40 × \$1000). Even if the price of the stock declines by only \$1, you still earn a significant profit: 100 shares sold at \$10 equals \$1000, minus 100 shares bought at \$9 equals \$900, for a profit of \$100 and a return of 25 percent (\$100 ÷ \$400). The price could decline in just a day or two. This possibility of a fast, high return explains the allure of such investments.

Almost unlimited losses can occur with the use of margin to sell short if the price rises rather than falls. If the \$10 stock soars to \$22, for example, the loss will exceed the original investment: 100 shares sold at \$10 equals \$1000, minus 100 shares bought at \$22 equals \$2200, for a loss of \$1200 and a negative return of 550 percent (\$2200 ÷ \$400). When the price of a security rises, short sellers are subject to margin calls.

Only a small proportion of investors sell stocks short because this approach is so risky. Selling short and buying on margin are techniques to be used only by sophisticated investors. Rydex Investments and ProFunds sell short index mutual funds, allowing market timers to profit during bear markets.

Did You Know?...

Top 3 Financial Missteps of Investing in Stocks and Bonds

People slip up in investing in stocks and bonds when they do the following:

1. Seek to invest in just one stock that promises to make them a lot of money
2. Neglect to carefully research investment choices
3. Hold onto a lousy investment too long instead of cutting losses by selling it

CONCEPT CHECK 14.6

1. Summarize the differences among discount, online, and full-service brokers.
2. Distinguish between round lot and odd lot broker's commissions.
3. Summarize the differences among types of stock orders: market, limit, and stop order.
4. Explain what buying on margin is and how it can go wrong for an investor.
5. Explain what selling short is and how it can go wrong for an investor.

Investing in Bonds

7 LEARNING OBJECTIVE

Describe how to invest in bonds.

Investment-grade bonds offer investors a reasonable certainty of regularly receiving the periodic income (interest) and retrieving the amount originally invested (principal). Bonds are usually issued at a **par value** (also known as **face value**) of $1000. An investor typically earns a low to moderate return on bond investments, an appropriate yield when compared with the higher total returns earned on riskier stocks and stock mutual funds. Fewer than 800 of the 23,000 largest U.S. companies that issue bonds meet the highest investment-grade rating standards. Owning some bonds (or bond mutual funds) along with stocks and cash diversifies an investment portfolio. The Bond Market Association (http://www.investinginbonds.com/) sponsors a bond website.

investment-grade bonds Offer investors a reasonable certainty of regularly receiving periodic income (interest) and retrieving the amount originally invested (principal).

par value/face value Some multiple of $1000 that is printed on a bond when issued and repaid at maturity.

Speculative-grade bonds pay a high interest rate. These are often called **junk bonds,** and they are long-term, high-risk, high-interest-rate corporate (or municipal) IOUs issued by companies (or municipalities) with poor or no credit ratings. The interest rates paid investors on junk bonds are 3.5 to 8 percent higher than those of Treasury bonds. Also called **high-yield bonds,** they carry investment ratings that are below traditional investment grade and carry a higher default risk. The **default rate** on high-quality bonds is less than 1 percent. The default rate on junk bonds over time has ranged from a low of 2 percent to a whopping 31 percent. For more information, see Bond Pickers (www.bondpickers.com) or www.defaultrisk.com or search Google using "high-yield bond offerings."

speculative-grade bonds Long-term, high-risk, high-interest-rate corporate (or municipal) IOUs issued by companies (or municipalities) with poor or no credit ratings. Also called junk bonds or high-yield bonds.

default rate Percentage of bonds that do not repay principal at maturity and sometimes cease interest payments in the interim.

Individual investors often avoid buying individual junk bonds because of the substantial financial risk involved with owning too few investments. Instead, they reduce risk by diversifying their investments through a "high-yield income" bond mutual fund (see Chapter 15) that has junk bonds in its portfolio.

Corporate, U.S. Government, and Municipal Bonds

Three types of bonds are available: corporate bonds, U.S. government securities, and municipal government bonds.

Corporate Bonds **Corporate bonds** are interest-bearing certificates of long-term debt issued by a corporation. They represent a needed source of funds for corporations. The dollar value of newly issued bonds is three times the dollar value of newly issued stocks. Because of tax regulations, corporations often finance major projects by issuing long-term bonds instead of selling stocks. One reason they do so is that payments of dividends to common and preferred stockholders are not tax deductible for corporations, unlike interest paid to bondholders. State laws require corporations to make bond interest payments on time. Therefore, companies in financial difficulty are required to pay bondholders before paying any short-term creditors.

corporate bonds Interest-bearing certificates of long-term debt issued by a corporation.

Compared with other bonds, corporate bonds pay the highest interest rates. The default risk varies with the issuer. To help you in appraising the risks and potential rewards of bond investments, independent advisory services, such as Moody's Investors Service and Standard & Poor's, grade bonds for credit risk. These firms publish unbiased ratings of the financial conditions of corporations and municipalities that issue bonds. A **bond rating** represents the opinion of an outsider on the quality—or creditworthiness—of the issuing organization. It reflects the likelihood that the issuing organization will be able to repay its debt. Ratings for each bond issue are continually reevaluated, and they often change after the original security has been sold to the public. Investors have access to measures of the **default risk** (or **credit risk**), which is the uncertainty associated with not receiving the promised periodic interest payments and the principal amount when it becomes due at maturity. Bond rating directories are available in large libraries and online.

bond rating An impartial outsider's opinion of the quality—or creditworthiness—of the issuing organization.

default risk/credit risk Uncertainty associated with not receiving the promised periodic interest payments and the principal amount when it becomes due at maturity.

Table 14.3 shows the bond ratings used by Moody's and Standard & Poor's. The higher the rating, the greater the probable safety of the bond and the lower the default risk. The lower the rating of the bond, the higher the stated interest rate or the effec-

Table 14.3 Summary of Bond Ratings

Ratings		
Moody's	**Standard & Poor's**	**Interpretation of Ratings**
Aaa Aa A	AAA AA A	High investment quality suggests ability to repay principal and interest on time. Aaa and AAA bonds are generally referred to as "gilt-edged" because issuers have demonstrated profitability over the years and have paid their bondholders their interest without interruption; thus, they carry the smallest risk.
Baa Ba	BBB BB B	Medium-quality investments that adequately provide security to principal and interest. They are neither highly protected nor poorly secured; thus, they may have some speculative characteristics.
B Caa Ca	CCC CC C	Lack characteristics of a desirable investment and investors have decreasing assurance of repayment as the rating declines. Elements of danger may be present regarding repayment of principal and interest.
C	DDD DD D	In default with little prospect of regaining any investment standing.

Note: Bonds rated Baa and higher by Moody's and BBB and higher by S&P are investment-grade quality; Ba, BB, and lower-rated bonds are junk bonds.

tive interest rate. When bonds are reduced in price from their face amount, more risk is involved. Higher ratings denote confidence that the issuer will not default and, if necessary, that the bond can readily be sold before its maturity date. Investment-grade corporate bonds may provide returns as much as 1.5 percentage points higher than the returns available on comparable U.S. Treasury securities.

U.S. Government Bills, Notes, and Bonds U.S. Treasury securities are the world's safest investment because the government has never defaulted on its debt. U.S. Treasury securities are backed by the "full faith, credit, and taxing power of the U.S. government," and this all but guarantees the timely payment of principal and interest.

U.S. government securities are classified into two groups: (1) Treasury bills, notes, and bonds and (2) federal agency issue notes, bonds, and certificates. Treasury bills, notes, and bonds are collectively known as **Treasury securities,** or **Treasuries.** The federal government uses these debt instruments to finance the public national debt. Treasury securities have excellent liquidity and are simple to acquire and sell. Previously issued marketable Treasury securities are bought and sold in securities markets through brokers. New issues can be purchased online using the Treasury Direct Plan (www.savingsbonds.gov).

Treasury securities Known as Treasuries, securities issued by the U.S. government, including bills, notes, and bonds.

The interest rates on federal government securities are lower than those on corporate bonds because they are virtually risk free. The possibility of default is near zero. Individuals with a conservative investment philosophy are often attracted to the certainty offered by U.S. government securities. Investors can purchase Treasury securities through their bank or broker or directly from the Treasury. Investors often buy Treasury issues to protect a portion of their assets and to diversify their portfolios. Although interest income is subject to federal income taxes, interest earned on Treasury securities is exempt from state and local income taxes.

Treasury Bills, Notes, and Bonds **Treasury bills,** or **T-bills,** are short-term U.S. government securities issued with maturities of a year or less. They are sold at a discount from their face value (par). The difference between the original purchase price and what the Treasury pays you at maturity, the gain or "par," is interest. This interest is exempt from state and local income taxes but is reported as interest income on your federal tax return in the year the Treasury bill matures. Stated as an interest rate, the return on such investments is called a **discount yield.** For example, if you buy a $10,000 26-week Treasury bill for $9750 and hold it until maturity, your interest will be $250. An investor can hold a bill until maturity or sell it before it is due.

Treasury bills Known as T-bills, U.S. government securities with maturities of one year or less.

discount yield Difference between the original purchase price of a T-bill and what the Treasury pays you at maturity—the gain, or "par," is interest.

When a bill matures, the proceeds can be reinvested into another bill or redeemed and the principal will be deposited into the investor's checking or savings account.

A **Treasury note** or **bond** is a fixed-principal, fixed-interest-rate government security issued for an intermediate term or long term. Notes are issued for two, three, five, or ten years and bonds have a maturity of more than ten years. Notes and bonds exist only as electronic entries in accounts. The interest rate is higher than the rates for T-bills because the lending period is longer. Owners of Treasury notes and bonds receive interest payments every six months, which is reported as interest income on their federal tax return in the year received. When the security matures, the investor is repaid the principal. Investors can hold a note or bond until maturity or sell it.

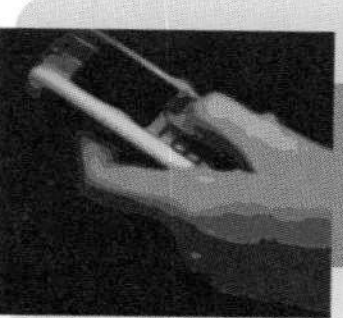

Instant Message

Reinvestment Risk

As we noted in Chapter 13, **reinvestment risk** is the risk that the return on a future investment will not be the same as the return earned by the original investment. This term is often heard in the context of bonds during periods of falling interest rates when the coupon payments are reinvested at less than the yield to maturity at the time of purchase.

I bonds are nonmarketable savings bonds backed by the U.S. government that pay an earnings rate that is a combination of two rates: a fixed interest rate that is set when the investor buys the bond and a semiannual variable interest rate tied to inflation that protects the investor's purchasing power. They are sold at face value, such as $50 for a $50 bond. Interest stops accruing 30 years after issue, and I bonds pay off only when redeemed. If you redeem an I bond within the first five years, you will forfeit the three most recent months' interest; after five years, you will not be penalized. The maximum purchase allowed in one calendar year is $30,000. All earnings on savings bonds are exempt from both state and local income taxes, while federal taxes can be deferred until the bonds are either redeemed or reach final maturity. I bonds cashed in to pay education expenses are tax exempt.

TIPS, also known as **Treasury Inflation-Protected Securities,** are marketable Treasury bonds whose principal increases with inflation and decreases with deflation. These inflation-indexed $1000 bonds are the only investment that guarantees that the investor's return will outpace inflation. TIPS bonds are sold in terms from 5 to 30 years, and interest is paid to TIPS owners every six months until they mature. The interest rate is set when the security is purchased, and the rate never changes. The principal is adjusted every six months according to the rise and fall of the consumer price index (CPI); if inflation occurs and the CPI rises, the principal increases. The government sends the interest payment on the new principal to the investor's account.

The fixed interest rate on TIPS is applied to the inflation-adjusted principal; so if inflation occurs throughout the life of a TIPS security, every interest payment will be greater than the one before it. The amount of each interest payment is determined by multiplying the inflation-adjusted principal by one-half the interest rate. The inflation-adjusted amount added to the principal on a TIPS bond every six months is taxable, even though the investor does not receive the money until the bond matures. Thus, TIPS bonds pay "phantom taxable interest income," like **zero-coupon bonds** (described on page 422), so the investor pays federal income taxes on the interest earned each year. The investor uses other funds to pay the taxes on that income.

When TIPS mature, the federal government pays the inflation-adjusted principal (or the original principal if it is greater). Investors can hold a TIPS bond until it matures or sell it before it matures. The interest on TIPS bonds can be excluded from federal income tax when the bond owner pays tuition and fees for higher education in the year the bonds are redeemed.

U.S. government savings bonds are nonmarketable, interest-bearing bonds. **Series EE savings bonds** are issued at a sharp discount from face value and pay no annual interest, and they may be redeemed at full value upon maturity. For example, a $100 savings bond might be purchased for half of its face amount, $50. The interest, compounded semiannually, accumulates within the bond itself, and the return to the investor comes from redeeming the bond at its stated face value at the maturity date. Interest on Series EE bonds is exempt from state and local taxes. There is no federal income tax liability on the interest at redemption if the proceeds are used to fund the

Treasury note/Treasury bond Fixed-principal, fixed-interest-rate government security issued for an intermediate term or long term. Notes mature in ten years or less; bonds mature in more than ten years.

I bonds Nonmarketable savings bonds backed by the U.S. government that pay an earnings rate that combines two rates: a fixed interest rate set when the investor buys the bond and a semiannual variable interest rate tied to inflation that protects the investor's purchasing power.

Treasury Inflation-Protected Securities (TIPS) Marketable Treasury bonds whose value increases with inflation. These inflation-indexed $1000 bonds are the only investment that guarantees that the investor's return will outpace inflation.

zero-coupon bonds (zeros or deep discount bonds) Municipal, corporate, and Treasury bonds that are issued at a sharp discount from face value and pay no annual interest but are redeemed at full face value upon maturity.

U.S. government savings bonds Nonmarketable, interest-bearing bonds issued by the U.S. Treasury.

Series EE savings bonds Nonmarketable, interest-bearing bonds issued by the federal government that are issued at a sharp discount from face value and pay no annual interest, and they may be redeemed at full value upon maturity.

child's college education. (**Series HH savings bonds** [no longer sold] were issued at par and acquired only by exchanging Series EE bonds. Interest on Series HH bonds is exempt from state and local taxes.)

Federal Agency Debt Issues More than 100 different bonds, notes, and certificates of debt are issued by various federal agencies that are government sponsored but stockholder owned. Examples of these agencies include Government National Mortgage Association (Ginnie Mae), Federal National Mortgage Association (Fannie Mae), and Student Loan Marketing Association (Sallie Mae). Ginnie Mae and Fannie Mae buy mortgage loans from lenders, thereby supplying them with more cash to make loans. Each security represents interest in a pool of mortgages that are sold to institutions and investors in units of $25,000 (they can also be purchased in smaller units through a mutual fund). When homeowners make their monthly mortgage payments to Ginnie Mae, part of the principal and interest is passed to investors.

The assets and resources of the issuing agency back these agency issues. Although the federal government does not guarantee the debt issued by such agencies, investors nevertheless believe it would step in if an agency faced default. Agency issues are not as widely publicized as Treasury securities, yet they often pay a yield that is three-quarters of a percentage point higher than the yield for comparable-term Treasury securities because of their somewhat higher degree of risk.

municipal government bonds (munis) Long-term debts (bonds) issued by local governments (cities, states, and various districts and political subdivisions) and their agencies. Interest from munis, also known as tax-free bonds or tax-exempt bonds, is exempt from federal income tax.

Municipal Government Bonds As we discussed in Chapter 4, **municipal government bonds** (also called **munis**) are long-term debts issued by local governments (cities, states, and various districts and political subdivisions) and their agencies. Their proceeds are used to finance public improvement projects, such as roads, bridges, and parks, or to pay ongoing expenses. Moody's Bond Record rates some 20,000 munis, and twice as many unrated securities exist. Bonds range in quality from AAA-rated state highway bonds to unrated securities issued by local governmental parking authorities.

The investor's interest income on municipal bonds is not subject to federal income taxes. This is because the U.S. Constitution requires that municipal bond interest be exempt from federal income tax. Because the interest income is tax free, municipal bonds are also known as **tax-free bonds** or **tax-exempt bonds.** Interest income on munis also is exempt from state and local income taxes when the investor lives in the state that issued the bond.

Municipal bonds offer a lower stated return than other bonds. However, if your marginal tax rate is higher than 25 percent, it generally makes economic sense to invest in municipal bonds because the after-tax return on a muni might be higher than that of a corporate bond. To compare the after-tax returns of investments, see page 122.

Capital gains on the sale of munis are taxable. Such gains may be realized when bonds are bought at a discount and then sold at a higher price or redeemed for full value at maturity. Bonds bought at a premium also may appreciate to produce a gain.

Unique Characteristics of Bond Investing

Bonds have certain characteristics that distinguish them from other investment alternatives.

coupon rate/coupon/coupon yield/stated interest rate Interest rate printed on the certificate when the bond is issued.

Coupon Rate The bond's **coupon rate** (also known as the **coupon, coupon yield,** or **stated interest rate)** is the interest rate printed on the certificate when the bond is issued. It reflects the total annual fixed rate of interest that will be paid. For example, Leslie Geradine Sherman, a retired teacher from Laramie, Wyoming, bought a 20-year, $1000 Running Paws Cat Food Company bond last week with a coupon rate of 7 percent that promises to pay her $70 in interest annually (bonds pay interest in two semiannual installments—$35 in this instance). A disadvantage of bonds is that the investment does not provide the automatic benefit of compounding of interest; therefore, investors have no choice but to find other places to invest interest payments.

Serial or Sinking Fund The coupon rate of a bond remains the same until the maturity date, when the face amount is due and the debt is required to be paid off (or **retired**). Corporate bonds often mature in 20 to 30 years. Occasionally, bonds are retired serially; that is, each bond is numbered consecutively and matures according to a prenumbered schedule at stated intervals. These investments are known as **serial bonds.** Many bonds include a **sinking fund** through which money is set aside with a trustee each year for repayment of the principal portion of the debt. The details about each bond issue are contained in its **indenture.** This written, legal agreement between a group of bondholders (representing each bondholder) and the debtor describes the terms of the debt by setting forth the maturity date, interest rate, and other factors.

Secured or Unsecured Bonds are issued as either secured or unsecured. A corporation issuing a **secured bond** pledges specific assets as collateral in the indenture or has the principal and interest guaranteed by another corporation or a government agency. In the event of default, the trustee could take legal action to seize and sell such assets. In the event of bankruptcy, the claims of secured creditors are paid first.

An **unsecured bond** (or **debenture**) does not name collateral as security for the debt and is backed only by the good faith and reputation of the issuing agency. Although secured bonds might appear safer than unsecured bonds, this assumption may not be true. The strong financial reputations of many large corporations enable them to offer unsecured bonds that are safer than the secured bonds of many other companies. All federal government bonds are unsecured and are backed by the U.S. government.

Registered and Issued By law, all bonds issued now are **registered bonds.** This provides for the recording of the bondholder's name so that checks or electronic funds transfers for payment of interest and principal can be safely forwarded when due. The Internal Revenue Service is notified of the payments as well. A registered bond can be transferred only when the registered owner endorses the transaction.

Book Entry All bonds today are issued in **book-entry form,** which means that certificates are not issued. Instead, an account is set up in the name of the issuing organization or the brokerage firm that sold the bond, and interest is paid into this account when due. In the past, all corporations issued **bearer bonds** (also called **coupon bonds** because owners redeemed the coupons for interest). Some of these older bonds are still traded today.

Callable An issuer might desire to exercise a **call option** when interest rates drop substantially. For example, assume a company issues bonds paying a $90 annual dividend (9 percent coupon rate). When interest rates drop perhaps to 7 percent, the 9 percent bonds may represent too high a cost for borrowing to the corporation. If the bonds have a **callable** feature, according to dates and terms detailed in the indenture, the issuer can redeem the bonds before the maturity date. In such a case, the issuer repurchases the bond at par value or by paying a premium, often one year's worth of interest. Approximately 80 percent of long-term bonds are classified as callable.

serial bonds Bonds that are retired serially; that is, each bond is numbered consecutively and matures according to a prenumbered schedule at stated intervals.

sinking fund Bond feature through which money is set aside with a trustee each year for repayment of the principal portion of the debt at maturity.

indenture Written, legal agreement between bondholders and debtor that describes terms of the debt by setting forth the maturity date, interest rate, and other details.

secured bond Pledges specific assets as collateral in indenture or has the principal and interest guaranteed by another corporation or government agency.

unsecured bond/debenture Does not name collateral as security for debt; backed only by the good faith and reputation of the issuing agency.

registered bond Bondholder's name is recorded so that checks or electronic funds transfers for payment of interest and principal can be safely forwarded when due.

book-entry form Bond certificates aren't issued; rather, account is set up in name of the issuing organization or the brokerage firm that sold the bond, and interest is paid into this account when due.

call option Stipulation in an indenture that allows issuer to repurchase the bond at par value or by paying a premium, often one year's worth of interest. Bonds are thus callable.

Advice from a Pro...

Zero-Coupon Bonds Pay Phantom Interest

Zero-coupon bonds (also called **zeros** or **deep discount bonds**) are municipal, corporate, and Treasury bonds that pay no annual interest. They are sold to investors at sharp discounts from their face value and may be redeemed at full value upon maturity. For example, a 7 percent, $1000 zero-coupon bond to be redeemed in the year 2025 might sell today for $258. Zeros pay no current income to investors, so investors do not have to be concerned about where to reinvest interest payments. The semiannual interest accumulates within the bond itself, and the return to the investor comes from redeeming the bond at its stated face value at the maturity date. In this manner, zeros operate much like Series EE savings bonds and T-bills. The maturity date for a zero could range from a few months to as long as 30 years.

Parents often invest in zero-coupon bonds to help pay for their children's college education, and they wisely establish ownership of the zeros in the child's name. The phantom income "paid" to the child is generally so small that little, if any, income taxes are due.

Treasury zeros, unlike other zeros, are not callable. People planning for retirement buy zeros because they know exactly how much will be received at maturity. Even though the investor receives no interest money until maturity, the investor still pays income taxes every year on the interest that accumulates within the bond. Investors can avoid income taxes altogether by buying zeros in a qualified tax-sheltered retirement plan account.

Elizabeth Dolan
University of New Hampshire

Evaluating Bond Prices and Returns

Factors that affect bond prices and returns to the investor include interest rates, premiums and discounts, current yield, and yield to maturity.

Interest Rate Risk Results in Variable Value A bond's price, or its value on any given day, is affected by a host of factors. These include its type, coupon rate, availability in the marketplace, demand for the bond, prices for similar bonds, the underlying credit quality of the issuer, and the number of years before it matures. Most important, the price also varies because of fluctuations in current **market interest rates** in the general economy. The state of the economy and the supply and demand for credit affect market interest rates. These are the current long- and short-term interest rates paid on various types of corporate and government debts that carry similar levels of risk.

market interest rates Current long- and short-term interest rates paid on various types of corporate and government debts that carry similar levels of risk.

interest rate risk Risk that interest rates will rise and bond prices will fall, thereby lowering the prices on older bond issues.

fixed yield Interest income payment remains the same regardless of bond's price.

variable value Because interest rates change, bonds may trade at a premium (more than face value) or at a discount (less than par) so that the yield equals the current yield for bonds with similar maturities and risk levels.

Long-term rates are largely set by bond investors' buying and selling decisions, primarily based on their expectations of future inflation. Short-term interest rates are manipulated by the Federal Reserve Board, which is popularly known as the Fed. When the economy slows, the Fed often lowers the interest rates on short-term Treasury issues in an attempt to stimulate economic activity by making borrowing cheaper. When inflation rises, the Fed often raises interest rates.

As we noted in Chapter 13, **interest rate risk** is the risk that interest rates will increase and bond prices will fall, thereby lowering the prices on older bond issues. This decline in value ensures that an older bond and a newly issued bond will offer potential investors approximately the same yield. Bonds generally have a **fixed yield** (the interest income payment remains the same) but a **variable value.** For example, assume that you buy a 20-year, $1000 bond with a stated annual interest rate of 8 percent, or an annual return of $80 ($1000 × 0.08). If interest rates in the general economy jump to 10 percent after one year, no one will want to buy your bond for $1000 because it pays only $80 per year. If you want to sell it at that time, the price of the bond will have to be lowered, perhaps to \$800 [Equation (14.4), the *bond-selling price formula*, shows the calculation involved].

$$\text{Bond selling price} = \frac{\text{annual interest income in dollars}}{\text{current market interest rate}} \qquad (14.4)$$

Conversely, if interest rates on newly issued bonds slip to 6 percent after one year, the price of your bond will increase sharply (perhaps to \$1333). This occurs because investors will be willing to pay a **premium** (a sum of money paid in addition to a regular price) to own your bond paying 8 percent when other rates are only 6 percent. Remember that bond yields and prices move in opposite directions—as one goes up, the other goes down.

premium A sum of money paid in addition to a regular price.

Bond prices are most volatile in the following circumstances: (1) when bonds are sold at less than face value when first issued, (2) when the stated rate is low, and (3) when the bond maturity time is long. The investor who holds a bond to maturity might ignore such information, but the person considering selling before maturity might be shocked to see price swings of 20 percent or more, as illustrated on page 424. A person with a moderate or aggressive investment philosophy might regard such rapid price changes as opportunities.

Premiums and Discounts When a bond is first issued, it is sold in one of three ways: (1) at its face value (the value of the bond stated on the certificate and the amount the investor will receive when the bond matures), (2) at a discount below its face value, or (3) at a premium above its face value. After a bond is issued, its market price changes in order to provide a competitive effective rate of return for anyone interested in purchasing it from the original bondholder.

As an example, assume that Running Paws Cat Food Company decided to issue 20-year bonds at 8.8 percent. While the bonds were being printed and prepared for sale, the market interest rate on comparable bonds rose to 9 percent. In this instance, Running Paws will sell the bonds at a slight discount to provide a competitive return. Discounts and premiums on bonds reflect changing interest rates in the economy and the number of years to maturity.

Current Yield The **current yield** equals the bond's fixed annual interest payment divided by its bond price. It is a measure of the current annual income (the total of both semiannual interest payments in dollars) expressed as a percentage when divided by the bond's current market price. When you buy a bond at par, its current yield equals its coupon yield. For example, a bond with a 5.5 percent coupon yield purchased at par for \$1000 has a current yield of 5.5 percent. As bond prices fluctuate because of interest rate changes and other factors, the current yield also changes. For example, if Leslie paid \$940 for a \$1000 bond paying \$55 per year, the bond's current yield is 5.85 percent, as shown by the *current yield formula*, Equation (14.5).

current yield Equals the bond's fixed annual interest payment divided by its bond price.

$$\begin{aligned}\text{Current yield} &= \frac{\text{current annual income}}{\text{current market price}} \qquad (14.5)\\ &= \frac{\$55}{\$940}\\ &= 5.85\%\end{aligned}$$

A bond's current yield is based on the purchase price, not on the prices at which it later trades. The current yields for many bonds based on that day's market prices are available online and are published in the financial section of many newspapers.

The total return on a bond investment consists of the same components as the return on any investment: current income and capital gains. In Leslie's case, she will receive \$1000 at the maturity date (20 years from now), even though she paid only \$940 for the bond; therefore, her anticipated total return (or effective yield) will be

Did You Know?...

How Far Bond Prices Will Move When Interest Rates Change

On any given day, the major determinant of bond prices is the prevailing level of interest rates in the economy. Figure 14.4 illustrates the price changes for bonds when interest rates rise or fall. Rising interest rates reduce bond prices and falling rates increase bond prices. The longer the time until maturity of a bond, the more sensitive the price to interest rate changes. Thus, prices for long-term bonds fluctuate much more dramatically than those for short-term securities.

Figure 14.4
Price Changes for Bonds

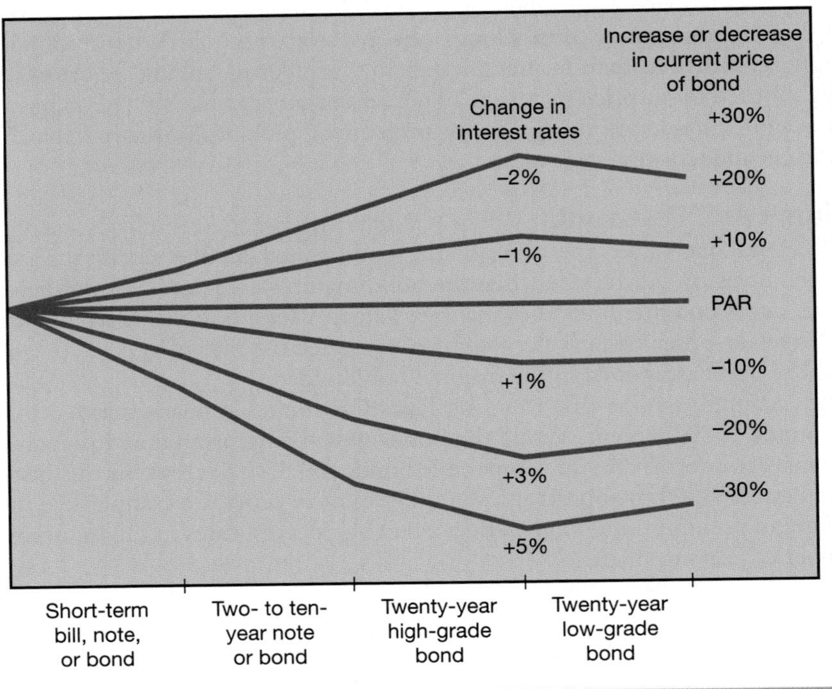

higher than the 5.85 percent current yield. How much higher is accurately revealed by the yield to maturity (discussed next).

yield to maturity (YTM) Total annual effective rate of return earned by a bondholder on a bond if the security is held to maturity—takes into consideration both the price at which the bond sold and the coupon interest rate to arrive at effective rate of return.

Yield to Maturity **Yield to maturity (YTM)** is the total annual effective rate of return earned by a bondholder on a bond if the security is held to maturity. The YTM is the internal rate of return on cash flows of a fixed-income security. The YTM reflects both the current income and any difference if the bond was purchased at a price other than its face value spread over the life of the bond. The market price of a bond equals the present value of its future interest payments and the present value of its face value when the bond matures. Three generalizations can be made about the yield to maturity:

1. If a bond is purchased for exactly its face value, the YTM is the same as the coupon rate printed on the certificate.

Did You Know?...

How to Estimate the Selling Price of a Bond After Interest Rates Have Changed

Bond prices are influenced partially by supply and demand but mostly by the cost of money. If you paid \$1000 for a 20-year, 7 percent bond and then were forced to sell it after interest rates on comparable bonds had increased to 9 percent, you would lose more than \$200. You can estimate the selling price of an existing bond (assuming it is more than a few years from maturity) after interest rates change by using the bond-selling price formula given in Equation (14.4) on page 423.

Using Equation (14.4), the selling price equals \$777.78 (\$70 ÷ 0.09) for the preceding example. If you bought the bond for \$1000, you will lose \$222.22 if you sell it for \$777.78. If interest rates drop to 5.5 percent instead of increasing, however, you could sell your 7 percent bond at a profit of \$272.72 (\$70 ÷ 0.055 = \$1272.72; \$1272 − \$1000 = \$272.72). If you keep the bond until maturity, the issuer is obligated to retire it for \$1000. An online financial calculator or brokerage firm can perform exact calculations of selling prices.

2. If a bond is purchased at a premium, the YTM will be lower than the coupon rate.
3. If a bond is purchased at a discount, the YTM will be higher than the coupon rate.

For example, because Leslie bought her 20-year bond with a coupon rate of 5.5 percent at a discount for \$940, her yield to maturity must be greater than the coupon rate because she will receive \$60 more than she paid for the bond when she receives the \$1000 at maturity. Exactly how much greater can be determined by calculating an approximate yield to maturity when contemplating a bond purchase because bonds that seem comparable may have different YTMs. The *yield to maturity (YTM) formula*, Equation (14.6), which is duplicated on the *Garman/Forgue* website, factors in the approximate appreciation when a bond is bought at a discount or at a premium:

$$\text{YTM} = \frac{I + [FV - CV)/N]}{(FV + CV)/2} \tag{14.6}$$

where

I = Interest paid annually in dollars
FV = Face value
CV = Current value (price)
N = Number of years until maturity

If Leslie paid \$940 for a 20-year bond with a 5.5 percent coupon rate, the YTM is calculated as follows:

$$\begin{aligned}\text{YTM} &= \frac{\$55 + [(\$1000 - \$940)/20]}{(\$1000 + \$940)/2} \\ &= \frac{\$58}{\$970} \\ &= 5.98\%\end{aligned}$$

If you plan to buy and hold a bond until its maturity, you should compare YTMs instead of current yields when considering a purchase because YTMs fairly represent

Instant Message

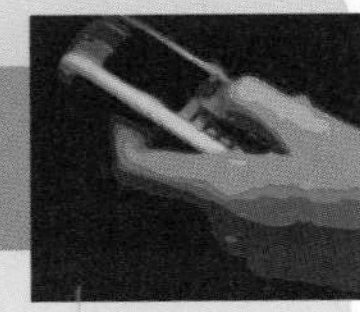

Check Bond Performance Online

BondInfo (http://www.nasdbondinfo.com/asp/bond_search.asp) is where you will find bond indexes and tools to gauge overall market direction and to measure the performance of corporate bond holdings against the broader market of more than 30,000 corporate bonds.

all factors. The current yield on a bond is not an effective measure of the total annual return to the investor; in fact, the fewer years until maturity, the worse an indicator it becomes. As just calculated, Leslie's 20-year bond with a coupon rate of 5.5 percent and a current yield of 5.85 percent has a YTM of 5.98 percent. If the same bond had been purchased with only 10 years until maturity, the YTM would be 6.29 percent; with 5 years until maturity, the YTM would be 6.90 percent; and with 2 years until maturity, the YTM would be 8.76 percent. Exact YTMs are online and listed in detailed bond tables available at large libraries and at brokers' offices.

Six Decisions for Bond Investors Individuals interested in investing in bonds can review resources on the website of The Bond Market Association (http://www.investinginbonds.com/). It offers a free, searchable database of the latest corporate, government, municipal, and mortgage-backed bond issues and prices. Bond investors must make six decisions:

1. **Decide on credit quality.** Consider Treasury/agency, investment-grade corporate and municipal, and below investment-grade corporate and municipal.
2. **Decide on maturity.** Consider the time schedule of your financial needs: short, medium or long term. Bonds with a short maturity have the lowest current yield but excellent price stability. Medium maturity bonds pay close to the higher rates earned on long-term bonds and enjoy much greater price stability.
3. **Determine the after-tax return.** Assuming equivalent risk, choose the bond that provides the better after-tax return because tax-exempt securities may offer a higher after-tax return than taxable alternatives. To compare the after-tax return of investments, see page 122.
4. **Select the highest yield to maturity.** Given similar bond securities with comparable risk, maturity, and tax equivalency, investors are wise to choose the one that offers the highest yield to maturity, as calculated by Equation (14.6).
5. **Consider selling.** When interest rates have dropped, consider selling because you can profit when rate decreases push up the value of your bond. Consider selling also if the bond rating has seriously slipped because it could mean greater risk and possible default.
6. **Think about investing in bond mutual funds.** Consider whether it is smarter to invest in bond mutual funds rather than individual bonds. This topic is examined in Chapter 15.

CONCEPT CHECK 14.7

1. Distinguish between investment- and speculative-grade bonds.
2. Give some reasons why individuals often invest in corporate bonds rather than Treasuries.
3. Summarize the differences among Treasury bonds, I bonds, and TIPS bonds.
4. Explain what interest rate risk is and tell what calculation individuals considering bond investments avoid that problem when buying an existing bond.

What Do You Recommend Now?

Now that you have read the chapter on stocks and bonds, what do you recommend to Caitlin Diaz in the case at the beginning of the chapter regarding:

1. Investing for retirement in 18 years?
2. Owning blue-chip common stocks and preferred stocks rather than other common stocks given Caitlin's investment time horizon?
3. The wisdom of owning municipal bonds rather than corporate bonds?
4. The likely selling price of her corporate bonds, if sold today?
5. Investments that might be appropriate to fund her children's education?

Big Picture Summary of Learning Objectives

1 Explain how stocks and bonds are used as investments.

Individual investors provide the money corporations use to create sales and earn profits. The investor shares in those profits.

2 Classify common stocks according to their major characteristics.

Common stocks may be broadly classified as either income or growth stocks. Other terms used to describe stocks are *blue chip*, *value*, *speculative*, and *tech*. Market capitalization is used to classify large-cap, midcap, and small-cap stocks.

3 Describe fundamental and numerical ways to evaluate stock values.

The investor studies certain fundamental factors, such as the company's sales, assets, earnings, products or services, markets, and management, to determine a company's basic value. To do so, investors examine several revealing ratios such as price/earnings, price/sales, and dividend payout, as well as revealing numbers such as book value per share. Individuals also estimate the value of a company by using beta to compare its history and expected future profitability with those of competing stocks.

4 Determine whether an investment's potential rate of return is sufficient.

Estimating and calculating returns on a potential investment involve using beta to estimate the level of risk of the investment, estimating the market risk, calculating the required rate of return, calculating the potential rate of return on the investment, and comparing the required rate of return with the potential rate of return on the investment.

5 Use the Internet to evaluate common stocks in which to invest.

Individuals begin evaluating stocks by setting criteria for a stock investment. This may involve using stock-screening software; obtaining security analysts' research reports, annual reports, 10-K reports, and prospectuses; acquiring economic and stock market data; and using portfolio-tracking services.

6 Summarize how stocks are bought and sold.

Securities transactions require the use of a licensed broker serving as a middleman between the seller and the buyer. You can buy or sell securities through an online or human stockbroker who works for a brokerage firm that has access to the securities markets. Many individuals use discount and online brokers rather than full-service brokers. Types of stock orders include market, limit, and stop orders. Buying on margin and selling short are risky trading techniques.

7 Describe how to invest in bonds.

Investment-grade bonds offer a reasonable certainty of regularly receiving the periodic income (interest) and retrieving the amount originally invested (principal). Junk bonds are available, too. Corporate bonds usually pay higher returns than government bonds. Interest-rate risk results in variable value in bond investments.

CHAPTER 15

Investing Through Mutual Funds

You Must Be Kidding, Right?

Twins Amanda and Daniel invest in mutual funds. Amanda majored in finance. For more than 20 years she invested in managed funds, counting on intelligent professional financial advisers to select the winning companies more often than not. Daniel majored in English; he invested in unmanaged index funds that achieve the same return as a particular market index by buying and holding all or a representative selection of securities in the index. After 20 years of investing, what is the likelihood that Amanda's investment portfolio balance will be better than Daniel's?

A. 10% **B.** 20% **C.** 30% **D.** 40%

The answer is B or A but never C or D. Managed mutual funds generally do not earn returns for investors that exceed the overall market indexes. The fact is, the average mutual fund manager earns a lower return at least 80 percent of the time. In most years, only 10 percent beat the market averages. Finding a mutual fund investment manager who can consistently beat the market is very challenging!

LEARNING OBJECTIVES

After reading this chapter, you should be able to:

1. **Describe** the features, services, and advantages of investing in mutual funds.
2. **Differentiate** mutual funds by investment objectives, types, and characteristics.
3. **Summarize** the fees and charges involved in buying and selling mutual funds.
4. **Establish** strategies to evaluate and select mutual funds that meet your investment goals.

What Do You Recommend?

David and Sarah Gent, a couple in their early 30s, have a 2-year-old child, and they enjoy living in a moderately priced downtown apartment. David, a librarian section manager, earns $44,000 annually. Sarah earns $59,000 as a merchandise buyer for a specialty store. They are big savers: Together they have been putting $1000 to $2000 per month into certificates of deposit, and the couple now has a portfolio balance worth $120,000 paying about 4 percent annually. The Gents are conservative investors and want to retire in about 20 years.

What would you recommend to David and Sarah on the subject of investing through mutual funds regarding:

1. Redeeming their certificates of deposit and investing their retirement money in mutual funds?
2. Investing in growth and income mutual funds instead of income funds?
3. Buying no-load rather than load funds?
4. Buying life-cycle mutual funds instead of balanced mutual funds?
5. Buying mutual funds through their employers' 401(k) retirement accounts?

FOR HELP with studying this chapter, visit the Online Student Center:

www.college.hmco.com/pic/garman9e

Most investors prefer to avoid stocks and bonds because of the high financial risk associated with owning too few investments. The average investor usually cannot accumulate a portfolio diversified enough to minimize the risk linked to the failure of a single holding. Investors often also lack the ability and time required to research individual securities and manage such a portfolio. To avoid these problems, many people invest *in* the stock and bond markets *through* mutual funds, which typically buy hundreds of different stocks and bonds. Mutual funds make it easy and convenient for investors to open an account and continue investing. Half of all households invest through mutual funds. The investor in mutual funds, using common sense and a little knowledge of the world of investments, can obtain very good returns.

Why Invest in Mutual Funds?

1 LEARNING OBJECTIVE

Describe the features, services, and advantages of investing in mutual funds.

mutual fund Investment company that pools funds by selling shares to investors and makes diversified investments to achieve financial goals of income or growth, or both.

A **mutual fund** is an investment company that pools funds obtained by selling shares to investors and makes investments to achieve the financial goal of income or growth, or both. Mutual funds invest in a diversified portfolio of stocks, bonds, short-term money market instruments, and other securities or assets.

The fund might own common stock and bonds in such companies as General Motors, IBM, Sears, or Running Paws Cat Food Company (our example from Chapter 14). The combined holdings are known as a **portfolio,** as we noted in Chapter 13 and as shown graphically in Figure 15.1. The mutual fund company owns the investments it makes and the mutual fund investors own the mutual fund company. Unlike corporate shareholders, holders of mutual funds have no say in running the company, although they have equity interest in the pool of assets and a residual claim on the profits.

Net Asset Value

net asset value (NAV) Per-share value of a mutual fund.

One measure of the investor's claim on assets is the net asset value. The **net asset value (NAV)** is the price one pays (excluding any transaction costs) to buy a share of a mutual fund; it is the per-share value of the mutual fund. It is calculated by summing the values of all the securities in the fund's portfolio, subtracting liabilities, and then dividing by the total number of shares outstanding.

Figure 15.1
How a Mutual Fund Works

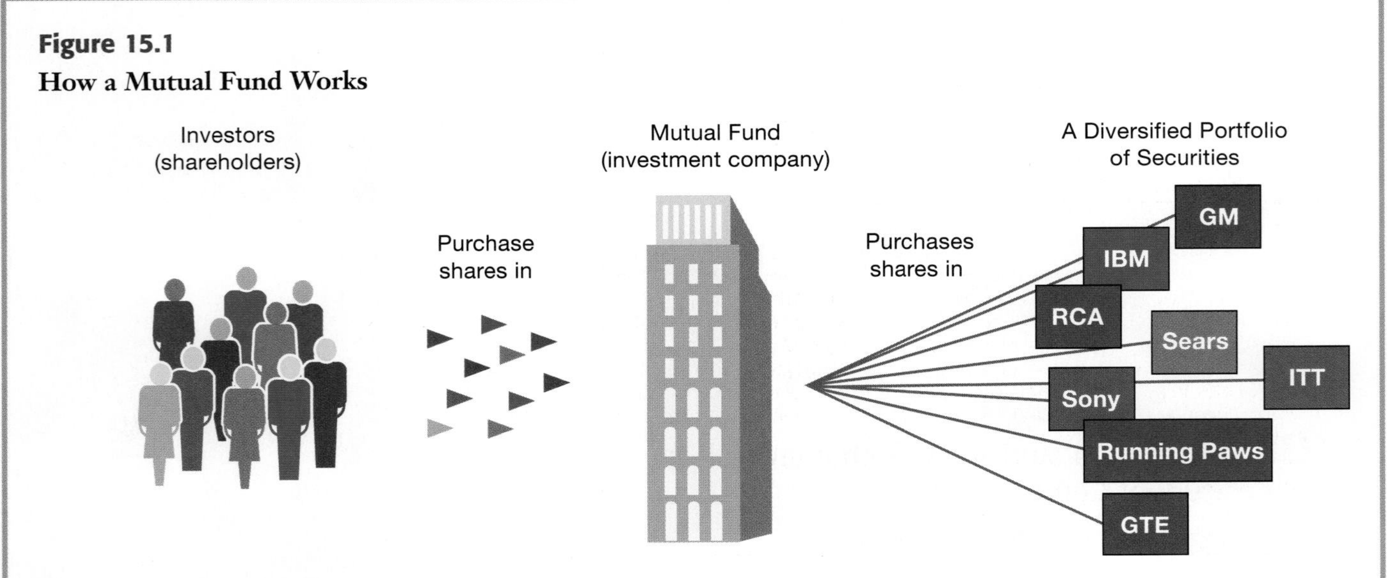

$$\text{Net asset value} = \frac{\text{market value of assets} - \text{market value of liabilities}}{\text{number of shares}} \quad (15.1)$$

For example, a mutual fund has 10 million shares outstanding, a portfolio worth \$100 million, and its liabilities are \$5 million. The net asset value of a single share is

$$\text{Net asset value} = \frac{\$100{,}000{,}000 - \$5{,}000{,}000}{10{,}000{,}000} = \frac{\$95{,}000{,}000}{10{,}000{,}000} = \$9.50 \text{ per share}$$

The NAV rises or falls to reflect changes in the market value of the investments held by the mutual fund company. This value is calculated daily after the major U.S. stock exchanges close, and a new NAV is posted in the financial media. If the assets held in a mutual fund increase in value, the NAV will rise. For example, if a mutual fund owns IBM and General Electric common stocks and the prices of those stocks increase, the increased value of the underlying securities is reflected in the NAV of fund shares. The increase in NAV due to rising portfolio values is price appreciation. When investors sell shares at a net asset value higher than that paid when they purchased the shares (after transaction costs), they will have a capital gain.

Good Money Habits in Mutual Funds

Make the following your money habits when investing through mutual funds:

1. Match your investment philosophy and financial goals to a mutual fund's objectives.
2. Invest only in no-load mutual funds that have low expenses and have no or a low 12b-1 fee.
3. Get the right mix of asset classes in your long-term fund investments and learn to love consistency.
4. Sign up for automatic reinvestment of your mutual fund dividends.
5. Invest regularly through your employer's retirement plan.
6. Rebalance your portfolio at least once a year.

Dividend Income and Capital Gains

A **mutual fund dividend** is income paid to investors out of profits that the mutual fund has earned from its investments. The dividend represents both ordinary income dividend distributions and capital gains distributions. **Ordinary income dividend distributions** occur when the fund pays out dividend income and interest (monthly, quarterly, or annually) it has received from securities it owns. **Capital gains distributions** represent the net gains (capital gains minus capital losses) that a fund realizes when it sells securities that were held in the fund's portfolio. Mutual funds distribute capital gains once a year, even though the gains occur throughout the year whenever securities are sold at a profit. When a fund pays out these distributions, the NAV drops by the amount paid. Figure 15.2 illustrates theses sources of mutual fund returns.

mutual fund dividend Income paid to investors out of profits earned by the mutual fund from its investments.

Sources of Investor Returns from Owning a Share in a Mutual Fund		
Current Income (returns received while you own a share)		Capital Gains (returns received when you sell your share)
Ordinary Dividend Income Distributions	Capital Gains Distributions	
The mutual fund receives dividends from the stocks and interest from the bonds it holds in its portfolio. These are passed on to you every three months (quarterly).	The mutual fund occasionally sells stocks and bonds in its portfolio. When it receives more from the sale than it paid for the securities, it achieves a capital gain. The gains are passed along to you each year (annually).	When you sell your share in the mutual fund, you receive the NAV of the share at its current market price. If that price is higher than the price you paid at purchase, you have a capital gain due to the increase in NAV. Your capital gain will be reduced by transaction costs.

Figure 15.2
Sources of Investor Returns from Owning Mutual Fund Shares

Advantages of Investing Through Mutual Funds

open-end mutual funds Issue redeemable shares that investors purchase directly from the fund (or through a broker for the fund).

The type of mutual fund that is the focus in this chapter is an **open-end mutual fund.** Accounting for more than 90 percent of all funds, open-end mutual funds issue redeemable shares that investors purchase directly from the fund (or through a broker for the fund) instead of purchasing from investors on a stock market. They are always ready to sell new shares of ownership and to buy back previously sold shares at the fund's current NAV. Open-end mutual funds, numbering more than 8100, outnumber companies listed on the New York Stock Exchange (approximately 2800). Mutual funds offer a number of advantages to investors.

Diversification Mutual funds are broadly diversified in financial markets. They might own several hundred different securities, and all are represented in a single mutual fund share. The individual with $500 or $5000 to invest could never obtain such diversification. A diversified portfolio reduces the risk if a company or sector fails. **Random risk,** or **nonsystematic risk,** as we discussed in Chapter 13, is reduced. Recall that random risk arises when one owns only one investment of a particular type (such as stock in one company) that, by chance, may do very poorly in the future due to uncontrollable or random factors. Many investors find it easier to achieve diversification through ownership of mutual funds that own stocks and bonds rather than picking and then owning individual stocks and bonds.

Affordability Individuals can invest in mutual funds with relatively low dollar amounts for initial purchases, such as $250 or $1000. Subsequent purchases can be as little as $50.

Professional Management Many investors lack the knowledge, time, and commitment to worry about which of their stocks and bonds to buy and sell. Mutual fund investors like the fact that professional investment advisers registered with the Securities and Exchange Commission manage their investment portfolio. The fund management company may control many millions or billions of dollars of assets. The **fund investment advisers** have access to the best research, and they select, buy, sell, and monitor the performance of the securities purchased; they oversee the portfolio. Investment advisers use the most current information, analytical tools, and investment techniques available. Fund investment advisers (money managers, securities analysts, and traders) share the same investment objective as the individual investor: to make money by increasing the net asset value of the mutual fund.

fund investment advisers Have access to the best research; they select, buy, sell, and monitor the performance of the securities purchased; thus, they oversee the portfolio.

Liquidity Mutual funds have good **liquidity,** a term we discussed in Chapters 5 and 13. You can very easily convert mutual fund shares into cash without loss of value because the investor sells (**redeems**) the shares back to the investment company. To do so, individuals simply pick up the telephone or go online. The price the investor gets depends upon the value of the portfolio and the resulting NAV.

redeems When an investor sells shares.

Low Transaction Costs Because mutual funds trade in large quantities of shares, they pay far less in brokerage commissions than individual investors. Lower transaction costs result in higher returns for investors. Individuals purchase mutual fund shares from the fund itself (or through a broker for the fund) instead of from other investors on a secondary market, such as the New York Stock Exchange or NASDAQ stock market. Shares bought and sold are at the NAV plus any fees and charges that the fund imposes, and these are often low. While some funds charge significant fees on purchases and redemptions, individuals need not invest in them.

Uncomplicated Investment Choices Selecting a mutual fund is easier than selecting specific stocks or bonds. Mutual funds state their investment objectives, allowing investors to select funds that almost perfectly match their own objectives.

Did You Know?...

Mutual Fund Disadvantages

There are some disadvantages for mutual fund investors:

1. **Performance is often lower than the market.** Despite having intelligent professionals make investment decisions for mutual funds, they often do not deliver annual returns higher than the stock market averages, such as the S&P 500. It is hard for a mutual fund to beat the market averages (an index has no transaction costs) when the fund has to pay administrative and brokerage expenses, particularly over many years.
2. **Diversification may not really exist.** Mutual funds that specialize in particular segments of investments, such as biotechnology, Southeast Asia, or precious metals, are not diversified across asset classifications. They may have a diversified investment portfolio of 50 precious metals companies within that sector, but **market risk** exists because stock prices move up and down over time due to influences and events that affect all similar investments.
3. **Costs can be high.** While individual investors can choose among thousands of mutual funds for the net asset value, some funds charge substantial commissions and fees on purchases and sales. These can run from 2 to 8.5 percent. Mutual fund investors pay annual management fees regardless of how the fund performs, and some funds have "hidden fees." And although these are not out-of-pocket expenses, they reduce the NAV.

Identifying mutual funds that meet certain investment criteria can be done easily using mutual fund screening software. This topic is examined later in this chapter.

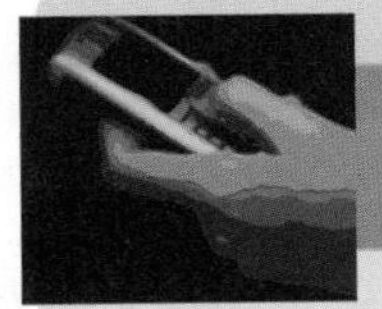

Instant Message

Reasons Why People Invest in Mutual Funds

Individuals invest in mutual funds to (1) obtain diversification in their investment portfolio, (2) employ the services of investment professionals, (3) earn an attractive rate of return that matches their investment philosophy and meets their investment goals, and (4) enjoy the conveniences of mutual fund investing.

Unique Mutual Fund Services

Mutual funds offer a number of valuable services that are unique to this type of investment and that are helpful and appealing to investors.

Convenience Mutual funds are extremely convenient for investors. Funds make it easy to open an account and invest in and sell shares. Fund prices are widely quoted. Services include toll-free telephone numbers, detailed records of transactions, and various checking and savings alternatives. Funds handle all the paperwork and record keeping, including accounting for fractional shares, so it is simple for investors to calculate taxable gains and losses when shares are sold.

Ease of Buying and Selling Shares Opening an account with a mutual fund company is just as simple as opening a checking account. After sending the fund your initial investment, you can easily buy more shares. Any number of shares can be sold at any time, or you can simply ask that a specific dollar amount be taken out by selling the appropriate number of shares. Each share is redeemed at the closing price—that is, the NAV—at the end of the trading day. Shares can be bought and sold by communicating with the company via telephone, wire, fax, mail, or online.

Check Writing and Electronic Transfers Mutual funds often offer interest-earning money market mutual funds in which investors can accumulate cash, accept dividends, or hold their money while making decisions about investing. They can write checks from money market funds. A money market fund invests exclusively in cash and cash equivalents. Investors can electronically transfer funds to and from mutual funds and banks.

automatic reinvestment When investors choose to automatically reinvest any interest, dividends, and capital gains payments to purchase additional fund shares.

exchange privilege Permits mutual fund shareholders to easily swap shares on a dollar-for-dollar basis for shares in another mutual fund within a mutual fund family. Also called switching, conversion, or transfer privilege.

exchange fees Small amount charged to move money among funds within a mutual fund family.

mutual fund family Investment management company that offers a number of different funds to the investing public, each with its own investment objectives or philosophies of investing.

beneficiary designation Allows fund holder to name one or more beneficiaries so that the proceeds bypass probate proceedings if the original shareholder dies.

Distribution of or Automatic Reinvestment of Income and Capital Gains Unlike most other investments, mutual funds allow investors to choose to receive interest, dividends, and capital gains payments or have them automatically reinvested to purchase additional fund shares (often without paying any commissions). This is **automatic reinvestment,** and it produces the same effects as the compounding of interest because the investor earns money on past earnings. Fractional shares are acquired as needed. Automatic reinvestment is one of the most appealing aspects of mutual funds for investors. Most shareholders reinvest their mutual fund income as this keeps all their capital fully invested because it is wise to do so, as illustrated in Figure 15.3.

Telephone and Internet Exchange Privileges An **exchange privilege** (also called a **switching, conversion,** or **transfer privilege**) permits mutual fund shareholders to easily swap shares on a dollar-for-dollar basis for shares in another mutual fund within a mutual fund family. Telephone and online transfers from one fund to another, such as moving money from a domestic stock fund to a Taiwan international fund, can be accomplished at no cost or for only a small charge, typically $5 or $10 per transaction, called an **exchange fee.** A **mutual fund family,** and there are more than 400 (see http://biz.yahoo.com/p/fam/a-b.html), is an investment management company that offers a number of different funds to the investing public, each with its own investment objectives.

Beneficiary Designation When opening a mutual fund account, the investor is given the opportunity to complete a form to designate a beneficiary in case of the investor's death. A **beneficiary designation** enables the shareholder to name one or more beneficiaries so that the proceeds go to them without going through probate. The delays and expenses of probate are discussed in Chapter 18.

Automatic Investment Funds often allow investors to make periodic monthly or quarterly payments using money automatically transferred from their bank

Figure 15.3

The Wisdom of Automatic Dividend Reinvestment

Reinvesting income greatly compounds share ownership. Figure 15.3 illustrates the positive results obtained by reinvesting dividends. The initial $10,000 investment in Vanguard's S&P 500 Index Fund grew to $110,897 over 20 years, instead of $66,931, because of the reinvestment of dividends. According to Standard & Poor's Dave Guarino, "Automatic reinvestment of dividends is one of the most overlooked ways of accumulating wealth. In addition to the benefits of compounding, it also provides a mechanism to dollar-cost average investments."

Source: Data copyright © 2007 Standard & Poor's, a dvision of the McGraw-Hill Companies, Inc. Reprinted with permission.

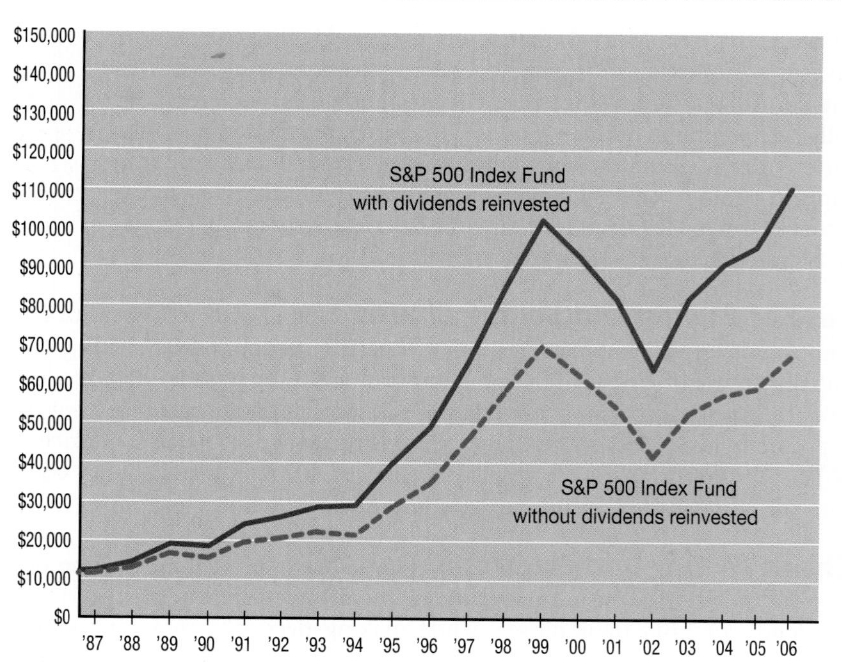

accounts or paychecks to the mutual fund company. You can invest as little as $25 monthly or quarterly. You can change your investment selections without penalty by contacting the fund. This is an example of dollar-cost averaging. By regularly investing in mutual funds, you can build a substantial portfolio of assets over time.

Effortless Establishment of Retirement Plans Mutual funds are perhaps the best option available to people saving for retirement through 401(k) plans and IRAs (topics examined in Chapter 17). An employee can direct his employer to transfer a specified dollar amount from every paycheck to a mutual fund to buy shares for a 401(k) plan; individuals can buy shares for their IRA accounts, too.

Multiple Income Withdrawal Options Mutual funds offer **withdrawal options** (also called **systematic withdrawal plans**) to shareholders who want to receive income on a regular basis from their mutual fund investments. Once enrolled in a withdrawal plan, the minimum withdrawal amount is $50. The fund forwards the amounts to you (or to anyone you designate) at regular intervals (monthly or quarterly). You can make regular withdrawals by (1) taking a set dollar amount each month, (2) cashing in a set number of shares each month, (3) taking the current income as cash, or (4) taking a portion of the asset growth.

withdrawal options/systematic withdrawal plans Arrangements with a mutual fund company for shareholders who want to receive income on a regular basis from their mutual fund investments.

Did You Know?...

Other Investment Companies

The Investment Company Act of 1940 distinguishes among investment companies. Open-end mutual funds are by far the most widely owned investment companies. Four other types exist:

1. **Closed-end mutual fund. Closed-end mutual funds** issue a limited and fixed number of shares at inception and do not buy them back. These companies operate with a fixed amount of capital. Closed-end shares are bought and sold on a stock exchange or in the over-the-counter market. After the original issue is sold, the price of a share depends primarily on the supply and demand in the market rather than the performance of the investment company assets. Closed-end shares are actively traded like common stocks and bonds, primarily on the New York Stock Exchange.
2. **Real estate investment trusts.** A special kind of closed-end investment company is a **real estate investment trust (REIT).** REITs invest in a portfolio of assets as defined in the trust agreement, such as properties, like office buildings and shopping centers (called an equity REIT), or mortgages (a mortgage REIT). Hybrid REITs invest in both. REITs have no predetermined life span. REIT shares are traded on stock exchanges, although many are illiquid investments.
3. **Unit investment trusts.** A **unit investment trust (UIT)** is a closed-end investment company that makes a one-time public offering of only a specific, fixed number of units. A UIT buys and holds an unmanaged fixed portfolio of fixed-maturity securities, such as municipal bonds, for a period of time. This could be a few months or perhaps 50 years. Each unit represents a proportionate ownership interest in the specific portfolio of perhaps 10 to 50 securities. Sold by brokers for perhaps $250 to $1000 a unit, there is no trading of these securities, although brokers may repurchase and resell them.
4. **Exchange-traded fund.** An **exchange-traded fund (ETF)** is a basket of passively managed securities structured like an index fund (described elsewhere in this chapter) as it owns all or a representative set of securities that duplicate the performance of a market segment or index. There are ETFs for the S&P 500, called Spiders; the Dow Jones Industrial Average, called Diamonds; and Qubes based on the NASDAQ 100. ETF prices are set by market forces since they are listed on securities markets [primarily on the American Stock Exchange (AMEX)] and traded throughout the day by brokers. One in four investors have ETFs in their portfolios, likely because of the extremely low costs. *Enhanced* ETFs are available that track an index but overweigh companies with the greatest potential; that's a "managed ETF."

CONCEPT CHECK 15.1

1. Explain how net asset value is calculated and how it is used by mutual funds.
2. List five advantages of investing in mutual funds.
3. Summarize some possible disadvantages of mutual fund investing.
4. Name five services that are unique to mutual funds.

Fund Objectives, Types, and Characteristics

2 LEARNING OBJECTIVE
Differentiate mutual funds by investment objectives, types, and characteristics.

managed funds Each fund's professional managers constantly evaluate and choose securities to buy or sell, using a specific investment approach.

Most mutual funds are **managed funds,** meaning that professional managers are constantly evaluating and choosing securities using a specific investment approach. On a daily basis, active managers select the stocks and bonds in which to invest and sell them when they deem appropriate. The managers earn a fee for their services, and ultimately their choices are responsible for the performance of the fund. Often, however, investing in a managed mutual fund is not the best choice for investors. Index funds are unmanaged, and they are often the best choice for investors; they are discussed later in the chapter.

Before investing in any specific mutual fund, decide whether the fund's investment objectives are a good fit for you. The Securities and Exchange Commission requires funds to disclose their investment objective. Mutual funds may be classified in one of three categories: income, growth, and growth and income. Each type has different features, risks, and reward characteristics. The name of a fund gives a clue to its objectives.

Income Objective

A mutual fund with an income objective invests in securities that pay regular income in dividends or interest. One key to earning a good return is to buy a fund that has low expenses.

Money Market Funds Mutual fund companies and brokerage firms offer **money market funds.** They invest in highly liquid, relatively safe securities with very short maturities (always less than one year), such as certificates of deposit, government securities, and commercial paper (i.e., short-term obligations issued by corporations). You can write checks or use an ATM card to access a money market fund account. Issuers keep the NAV (the price of each share of the fund) at $1.

As we discussed in Chapter 5, money market funds (and there are more than 1000 of them) pay a higher rate of return than accounts offered through banks and credit unions. While money market funds are not insured by a federal agency, they are considered extremely safe. **Tax-exempt money market funds** limit their investments to tax-exempt municipal securities with maturities of less than 90 days. The earnings are tax free to investors. **Government securities money market funds** appeal to investors' concerns about safety by investing solely in Treasury bills and other short-term securities backed by the U.S. government.

tax-exempt money market funds Funds that limit their investments to tax-exempt municipal securities with maturities of 90 days or less.

government securities money market funds Appeal to investor concerns about safety by investing solely in U.S. Treasury bills and other short-term securities backed by the U.S. government.

Bond Funds **Bond funds** (also called **fixed-income funds**) aim to earn current income higher than a money market fund without incurring undue risk by investing in a portfolio of bonds and other investments, such as preferred stocks and common stocks that pay high dividends. They do not ignore capital gains, however. Bond fund prices fluctuate with changing interest rates. Bond funds are categorized by what they own and the maturities of their portfolio holdings.

- **Short-term corporate bond funds** invest in securities maturing in 1 to 5 years.
- **Short-term U.S. government bond funds** invest in Treasury issues maturing in 1 to 5 years.
- **Intermediate corporate bond funds** invest in investment-grade corporate securities with 5- to 10-year maturities.
- **Intermediate government bond funds** invest in Treasuries with 5- to 10-year maturities.
- **Long-term corporate bond funds** specialize in investment-grade securities maturing in 10 to 30 years.
- **Long-term U.S. government bond funds** invest in Treasury and zero-coupon bonds with maturities of 10 years or longer.
- **Mortgage-backed funds** invest in mortgage-backed securities issued by agencies of the U.S. government, such as Ginnie Mae (GNMA).
- **Junk bond funds** invest in high-yield, high-risk corporate bonds.
- **Municipal bond (tax-exempt) funds** invest in municipal bonds that provide tax-free income. Both investment-grade and high-yield municipal bond funds exist.
- **Single-state municipal bond funds** invest in debt issues of only one state.
- **World bond funds** invest in debt securities offered by foreign corporations and governments.

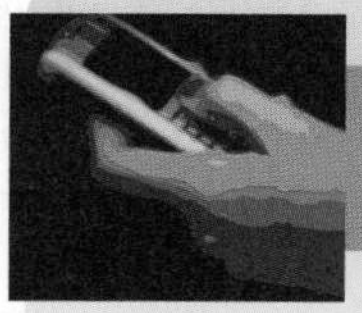

Instant Message

Invest in Bond Funds Rather Than Bonds

There are three advantages for people investing in bond funds rather than bonds: (1) Bond funds are more liquid because shares can be readily sold; (2) bond funds provide cost-effective diversification because shares are inexpensive (perhaps $10, $20, or $40 a share) compared with buying a single bond for $1000, $5000, or $10,000; (3) bond funds (but not bonds) automatically reinvest interest and other income.

Growth Objective

A mutual fund that has a growth objective seeks capital appreciation. It invests in the common stock of companies that have above average growth potential, firms that may not pay a regular dividend but have the potential for large capital gains. Growth funds carry a fair amount of risk exposure, and this is reflected in substantial price volatility.

Aggressive growth funds (also known as **maximum capital gains funds**) seek the greatest long-term capital appreciation. Also known as **capital appreciation funds,** they make investments in speculative stocks with volatile price swings. They may employ high-risk investment techniques, such as borrowing money for leverage, short selling, hedging, and options. Lots of buying and selling occurs to enhance returns.

aggressive growth funds Make investments in speculative stocks with volatile price swings, seeking the greatest long-term capital appreciation possible. Also known as maximum capital gains funds and capital appreciation funds.

Did You Know?...

Stable-Value Funds Available in Employer-Sponsored Retirement Plans

Stable-value funds are primarily available through employer-sponsored retirement plans. This is a different breed of fund. Stable-value funds get their name in part because they buy an insurance policy designed to allow the fund to redeem shares at a stable price regardless of overall market prices. This gives investors some assurance that the fund will be able to maintain the net asset value of the portfolio. Stable-value funds invest in high-quality, intermediate-term investments, including **guaranteed investment contracts (GICs)** offered by insurance companies. A GIC guarantees the owner a fixed or floating interest rate for a predetermined period of time, and the return of principal is guaranteed.

growth funds Seek long-term capital appreciation by investing in common stocks of companies with higher-than-average revenue and earnings growth, often the larger and well-established firms.

growth and income funds Invest in companies that have a high likelihood of both dividend income and price appreciation; less risk-oriented than aggressive growth funds or growth funds.

value funds Specialize in stocks that are fundamentally sound whose prices appear to be low (low P/E ratios) based on the logic that such stocks are currently out of favor and undervalued by the market.

Growth funds seek long-term capital appreciation by investing in the common stocks of companies with higher-than-average revenue and earnings growth, often the larger and well-established firms. Such companies (like Wal-Mart, Microsoft, and Coca-Cola) tend to reinvest most of their earnings to facilitate future growth.

Growth and income funds invest in companies that have a high likelihood of both dividend income and price appreciation.

Value funds specialize in stocks that are fundamentally sound and whose prices appear to be low (low P/E ratios), based on the logic that such stocks are currently out of favor and undervalued by the market.

Midcap funds invest in the stocks of midsize companies with a market capitalization of less than $1 billion that are expected to grow rapidly.

Small-cap funds (or **small company growth funds**) invest in lesser-known companies with a market capitalization of less than $500 million that offer strong potential for growth.

Microcap funds invest in high-risk companies with a market capitalization of less than $300 million.

Sector funds concentrate their investment holdings in one or more industries that make up a targeted part of the economy that is expected to grow, perhaps very rapidly, such as energy, biotechnology, health care, and financial services.

Regional funds invest in securities listed on stock exchanges in a specific region of the world, such as the Pacific Rim, Australia, or Europe.

Precious metals and gold funds invest in securities associated with gold, silver, and other precious metals.

Global funds invest in growth stocks of companies listed on foreign exchanges as well as in the United States, usually multinational firms.

International funds invest only in foreign stocks throughout the world.

Emerging market funds seek out stocks in countries whose economies are small but growing. Fund prices are volatile because these countries tend to be less stable politically.

Advice from a Pro...

Invest Only "Fun Money" Aggressively

People with a moderate or conservative investment philosophy may have the occasional urge to invest aggressively in a speculative mutual fund or other security. Once the investor has his or her financial plan in place, taking on more risk is acceptable—but *only* within the limits of the individual's "fun money." **Fun money** is a sum of investment money that you can afford to lose without doing serious damage to your total portfolio.

Resolve to trade with a specific sum, such as $5000, or perhaps no more than 2 or 3 percent of your portfolio. Decide mentally that if and when the money is gone, it has been spent on an activity that you enjoyed trying, but accept that the money lost is lost forever. In particular, avoid the temptation to "throw good money after bad" in trying to recover your losses. Speculative investing is not much different from gambling but, if armed with information, you might avoid losing 100 percent of your fun money. The biggest danger of fun-money investing is that you might be successful. Success can give you the confidence—albeit perhaps false confidence—that you are a great investor. While you might be the next Warren Buffet, such success is likely to tempt you to aggressively invest even more of the assets in your total portfolio. That approach can result in disaster.

Investing in aggressive growth mutual funds for some might be a lot of fun, particularly when the amount of money at stake is small. Over time, you will be best served by pursuing a disciplined investing plan with a focus on diversification. As financial columnist Jane Bryant Quinn observes, "The money you really need for life is better off in broadly diversified mutual funds, where a mistake is not forever."

Robert O. Weagley
University of Missouri–Columbia

Did You Know?...

Quant Funds

Charles Schwab, Janus, and other investment companies offer **quant funds (quantitative funds)** to investors. Computers make the buy and sell decisions based strictly on constant crunching of hundreds or thousands of numbers according to the criteria they are programmed to monitor. Why? Only people, not computers, have bad days in making investment decisions.

Vanguard quant funds look for the best growth prospects and lowest valuations. Schwab likes rapid earnings. Janus prefers stock movement volatility.

Growth and Income Objective

A mutual fund that has a combined growth and income objective seeks a balanced return made up of current income and capital gains. Such funds heavily invest in common stocks. They seek a return not as low as offered by funds with an income objective but not as high as that offered by funds with a growth objective. They invite less risk than growth funds.

Growth and income funds invest in companies expected to show average or better growth and pay steady or rising dividends.

Equity-income funds invest in well-known companies with a long history of paying high dividends as they emphasize income and capital preservation.

Socially conscious funds invest in companies that meet some predefined standard of moral and ethical behavior. Criteria could be progressive employee relations, strong records of community involvement, an excellent record on environmental issues, respect for human rights, and safe products (as well as no "sinful" products such as tobacco, guns, alcohol, gambling). See www.socialinvest.org for examples.

Balanced funds (or **hybrid funds**) keep a set mix of stocks and bonds, often 60 percent stocks and 40 percent bonds, in order to earn a well-balanced return of income and long-term capital gains. **Blend funds** invest in a combination of stocks and money market securities, but no fixed-income securities, such as bonds.

Asset allocation funds invest in a mix of assets (usually stocks, bonds, and cash equivalents and sometimes international assets, gold, and real estate), and they buy and sell regularly to reduce risk while trying to outperform the market. The asset mix may be based on risk tolerance (aggressive, moderate, and conservative).

Life-cycle funds are asset allocation funds that offer investors premixed portfolios of stocks, bonds, and cash that investors of a certain age and risk tolerance might prefer. These are targeted to people in their 30s, 40s, 50s, 60s, and 70s. They are also known as **target retirement funds.** Life-cycle funds shift assets from aggressive to moderate to conservative securities as the retirement target approaches. They seek to first grow and then preserve the portfolio assets. This is a no-hassle, "buy-and-forget" way to invest.

Mutual fund funds earn a return by investing in other mutual funds. This provides extensive diversification, but expenses and fees are higher than average.

socially conscious funds Invest in companies that meet some predefined standard of moral and ethical behavior.

balanced funds Keep a set mix of stocks and bonds, often 60 percent stocks and 40 percent bonds, in order to earn a well-balanced return of income and long-term capital gains.

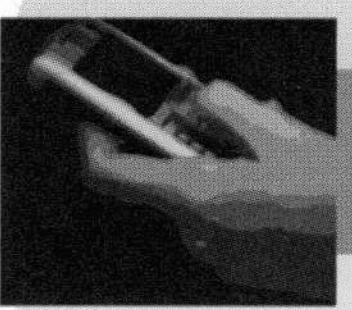

Instant Message

Index Funds Are Unmanaged

An **index fund** is a mutual fund whose investment objective is to achieve the same return as a particular market index by buying and holding all or a representative selection of securities in it. An S&P 500 index fund would effectively mirror the companies in the index, which are primarily large-cap U.S. stocks. A Russell 2000 Index Fund invests in the 2000 small-cap stocks in the index. Index funds offer a guarantee that the investor will get the same return that the market obtains.

Index funds are called **unmanaged funds** because their managers do not evaluate or select individual securities. Being unmanaged, annual management fees are extremely low, perhaps only 0.20 to 0.30 percent. Both index funds and ETFs follow market benchmarks, and ETF management fees often are lower. The returns achieved by actively managed stock funds typically trail the stock market averages by about 1.5 percentage points per year.

Burton Malkiel, professor of economics at Princeton University, says that very few individual investors or fund managers will do better than the indexes. "It's like looking for a needle in a haystack." He recommends that investors buy the haystack.

CONCEPT CHECK 15.2

1. How can investors use a money market fund?
2. Distinguish among income, growth, and growth and income funds.
3. Distinguish between asset allocation and life-cycle funds.
4. Explain why investors like index mutual funds.

Fees and Charges of Mutual Fund Investing

3 **LEARNING OBJECTIVE**
Summarize the fees and charges involved in buying and selling mutual funds.

Individuals who invest through mutual funds pay transaction costs that often are less than those associated with buying individual stocks, bonds, and cash equivalent securities. Mutual fund investors do pay certain fees and charges for the benefits of diversification, professional management, liquidity, check writing, and record keeping. Funds also pay their operating expenses out of fund assets, and this means that investors indirectly pay these costs.

Shareholder fees are charged directly to investors for specific transactions, such as purchases, redemptions, or exchanges. **Annual fund operating expenses** are the normal operating costs of the business that are deducted from fund assets before earnings are distributed to shareholders. The fees and charges associated with investing in mutual funds are many, and they can be confusing; some can be avoided.

Did You Know?...

Top 3 Financial Missteps in Mutual Fund Investing

People slip up in mutual fund investing when they do the following:

1. Buy funds with high fees and expenses
2. Withdraw dividends rather than reinvesting
3. Chase performance by investing in "hot" funds

Load and No-Load Funds

All mutual funds are classified as either load or no-load funds. This refers to whether or not they assess a sales charge, or load, when shares are purchased. Table 15.1 shows the basic fund classes.

Load Funds Always Charge Transaction Fees Funds that levy a sales charge for purchases are called **load funds.** Load funds are generally *sold* by stock brokerage firms, banks, and financial planners rather than marketed directly to investors by a mutual fund company. The load is the commission used to compensate brokers.

This commission, also called a **front-end load,** typically amounts to 3 to 8.5 percent of the amount invested; this reduces the amount available to purchase fund shares. For example, assume that you and a salesperson have discussed the investment potential of the Conglomerate Cat and Dog Food Mutual Fund and you decide to invest $10,000. Because this load fund charges a commission of 8.5 percent (the maximum permitted by the Securities and Exchange Commission), the salesperson receives $850 ($10,000 × 0.085). As a result, only $9150 of your money is actually available to purchase shares. Such a commission is much higher than stock transaction costs, which are usually 0.25 percent to 2 percent of the security's purchase price.

The sales charge may be shown either as the stated commission or as a percentage of the amount invested. The **stated commission** (8.5 percent in our example) is always somewhat misleading. In contrast, the **percentage of the amount invested** is a more accurate figure because it is based on the actual money invested and working. A stated commission of 8.5 percent actually amounts to 9.3 percent of the amount invested: $10,000 − $9150 = $850; $850 ÷ $9150 = 9.3%. If you

shareholder fees Charged directly to investors for specific transactions, such as purchases, redemptions, or exchanges.

annual fund operating expenses Normal operating costs of the business that are deducted from fund assets before shareholders receive earnings.

load funds Mutual funds that always charge a "load" or sales charge upon purchase; the load is the commission used to compensate brokers.

front-end load A sales charge paid when an individual buys an investment, reducing the amount available to purchase fund shares.

Table 15.1 Load Fund Share Classes

A single mutual fund company may offer more than one class of shares to investors: Class A, B, or C. Realize that Classes A, B, and C all are the same fund. Each class invests in the same investment portfolio of securities and has the same investment objectives but has different shareholder distribution arrangements and services, resulting in dissimilar fees and expenses and therefore performance results. To determine which class of shares suits your needs, use the Mutual Fund Expense Analyzer of NASD (National Association of Securities Dealers) (http://apps.nasd.com/investor_Information/ea/nasd/mfetf.aspx) and the U.S. Securities and Exchange Commission's Mutual Fund Cost Calculator (http://www.sec.gov/investor/tools/mfcc/mfcc-intsec.htm). Investors in no-load funds can avoid most of these charges, although some no-load funds do assess 12b-1 fees and back-end loads.

Share Class	Characteristics	Who Should Invest?
A	Front-end load (usually modest); small 12b-1 fee; low annual expenses	Long-term investors
B	No front-end load; substantial back-end loads up to ten years; maximum12b-1 fees; substantial annual expenses; might convert to Class A shares with a lower 12b-1 fee after a set period of time	Should be avoided as too expensive
C	Low front-end load; small back-end load; modest 12b-1 fee; highest annual expenses	Short-term investors; better than Class B shares

want to invest a full $10,000 in this load fund, you will need to pay out $10,930 [$10,930 − ($10,930 × 8.5%) = $10,000]. Investments of $10,000 or more often receive a discount on the load (see the "Breakpoints on Load Funds" box).

So-called **low-load funds** may carry a sales charge of perhaps 1 to 3 percent. These funds may also be sold by brokers and are sold via mail and sometimes through mutual fund retailers located in shopping centers. About half of all mutual funds levy a load.

No-Load Funds A **no-load mutual fund** sells shares at the net asset value without the addition of sales charges. These mutual fund companies let people purchase shares directly from the mutual fund company without the services of a broker, banker, or financial planner. Interested investors simply seek out advertisements for these funds in financial newspapers, magazines, and the Internet and make contact through toll-free telephone numbers, online, or mail. The SEC does allow funds to be called "no-load" even though they assess a "service fee" of 0.25 percent or less when shares are purchased.

Some No-Load Funds Assess 12b-1 Fees A **12b-1 fee** (named for the SEC rule that permits the charge) is an annual charge deducted by the fund company from a fund's assets to compensate underwriters and brokers for fund sales as well as to pay for advertising, marketing, distribution, and promotional costs. A 12b-1 fee is also known as a **distribution fee.** For load funds, these charges also pay for **trailing commissions,** which is compensation paid to salespeople for months or years in the future.

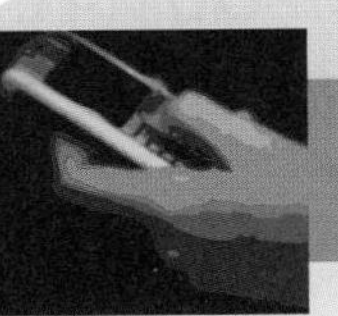

Instant Message

No-Load Mutual Fund Investors Avoid Bad Brokers

No-load mutual fund investors do not have to deal with persuasive salespeople, potentially bad financial advice, and outrageous sales commissions.

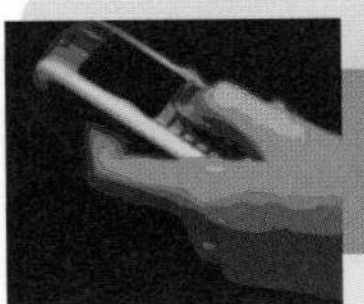

Instant Message

Breakpoints on Load Funds

The investment levels required to obtain a reduced sales load are referred to as **breakpoints,** and these start at $10,000. Funds are not required to offer breakpoints in the fund's sales load, but if they exist they must be disclosed. You have to ask how a fund establishes breakpoint discounts. NASD's Mutual Fund Breakpoint search tool (http://tools1.nasd.com/nbst/) can help you determine whether you are entitled to breakpoint discounts.

Although the funds do not call 12b-1 fees "loads" because they are not charged up front, they have the same effect as loads—that is, they reduce the investor's return.

These **hidden fees** decrease a shareholder's earning power each year without being described as a sales commission. A 12b-1 fee is actually a "perpetual sales load" because it is assessed on the initial investment as well as on reinvested dividends, every year, forever. The SEC caps 12b-1 fees at 0.75 percent, although it permits a 0.25 percent "service fee," which brings the total cap to 1 percent. Some funds stop assessing 12b-1 fees after four to eight years.

Some No-Load Funds Assess Deferred Load and Redemption Fees Approximately 60 percent of no-load mutual funds (and many load funds) assess additional fees for transactions, such as deferred load and redemption charges. A **deferred load,** also known as a **back-end load,** is a sales commission that is imposed only when shares are sold. Deferred loads are often on a sliding scale. The fee may decline 1 percentage point for each year the investor owns the fund. For example, a fund might charge a 6 percent fee if an investor redeems the shares within one year of purchase, and then the fee declines on an annual basis, until it reaches zero after six years.

deferred load/back-end load A sales commission that is imposed only when shares are sold; often charges are on a sliding scale, with the fee dropping 1 percentage point per year that the investor stays in the fund.

A **redemption charge** (or **exit fee**) is similar to a deferred load, although often it is much lower; it is used to reduce excessive trading of fund shares. The fee is usually 1 percent of the value of the shares redeemed. It disappears after the investment has been held for six months or a year. Long-term investors should not shy away from funds with redemption fees that disappear after a year.

redemption charge/exit fee Similar to a deferred load but often much lower; used to reduce excessive trading of fund shares.

Disclosure of Fees in Standardized Expense Table

The SEC requires that a mutual fund's prospectus include a **standardized expense table** within its first three pages that describes and illustrates in an identical manner the effects of all of its fees and other expenses. (See Table 15.2.) This description must estimate the hypothetical total costs that a mutual fund investor would pay on a $1000 investment that earns 5 percent annually and is withdrawn after ten years. All figures must be adjusted to reflect the effects of loads and fees. Also look for the fund's **expense ratio,** the expense per dollar of assets under management. Some mutual funds are much more efficient than others, and the expense ratio could range from 0.2 percent to more than 4 percent. Expense ratios average 1.45 percent for diversified stock funds and 0.40 percent for index funds.

standardized expense table SEC-required information that describes and illustrates mutual fund charges in an identical manner so that investors can accurately compare the effects of all of a fund's fees and other expenses relative to other funds.

expense ratio Expense per dollar of assets under management.

What's Best: Load or No Load? Low Fee or High Fee?

The sales commissions charged by load funds indisputably reduce total returns as illustrated in Table 15.3. When investment results are adjusted to account for the effects of sales charges, no-load mutual funds have an initial advantage because the investor has more money at work. In general, the shorter the time period you own the shares, the greater the negative impact of loads on the total return for the mutual fund investor. Up-front load charges are costly to the investor in the short run (less than five years), whereas annual 12b-1 charges are very costly over the long run.

If you pay 1 percent per year in 12b-1 fees for a mutual fund in which you invest for ten years, you will be giving up nearly 10 percent of your investment amount in trailing commissions. Yikes! You would be well advised to invest in a load fund rather than pay 12b-1 assessments if you plan to own the fund for more than five years.

Independent research has found that over five-year periods, lower-cost funds always deliver returns better than those offered by higher-cost funds. Even a small difference in fees can seriously affect long-term returns. For example, a

Table 15.2 Mutual Fund Fee Table Required by Federal Law

This illustrative mutual fund fee table is hypothetical, and the estimated expenses are based on the U.S. Securities and Exchange Commission's Mutual Fund Cost Calculator (www.sec.gov/investor/tools/mfcc/get-started.htm).

Shareholder Fees		Annual Fund Operating Expenses	
A Maximum Sales Charge (Load) Imposed on Purchases (as a percentage of offering price)	4.5%	G Management Fee	0.52%
		H Distribution (12b-1) Fee	0.25%
		I Other Expenses	0.20%
B Maximum Deferred Sales Charge (Load)	None		
		J Total Annual Fund Operating Expenses (Expense Ratio)	0.97%
C Maximum Sales Charge (Load) on Reinvested Dividends	None	K **Example** This example is intended to help an investor compare the cost of investing in different funds. The example assumes a $10,000 investment in the fund for one, three, five, and ten years and then a redemption of all fund shares at the end of those periods. The example also assumes that an investment returns 5 percent each year and that the fund's operating expenses remain the same. Although actual costs may be higher or lower, based on these assumptions an investor's estimated expenses would be:	
D Redemption Fee	None	1 year	$547
E Exchange Fee	None	3 years	$754
F Annual Account Maintenance Fee	None	5 years	$977
		10 years	$1,617

Source: *Guide to Understanding Mutual Funds,* copyright © by the Investment Company Institute (www.ici.org). Reprinted with permission.

Table 15.3 Effect of Loads and Fees on Mutual Fund Returns (Estimated figures based on a $10,000 investment and assuming a 10 percent gain each year.)

Years	No-Load*	3% Front-end Load	8.5% Front-end Load	5.5% Front-end Load with 0.25% 12b-1	5% Back-end Load with 1% 12b-1†
>1	$10,890	$10,560	$ 9,960	$10,260	$10,280
3	12,900	12,500	11,800	12,150	12,230
5	15,320	14,860	14,020	14,380	14,460
7	18,170	17,620	16,620	18,000	16,930
10	23,470	22,770	21,480	21,200	20,200

*1 percent annual management fee.

† A declining redemption fee of 5 percent the first year that goes to zero after the fifth year.

Did You Know?...

The Total Long-Term Returns for Stock Mutual Funds Are Roughly the Same

Data from the Investment Company Institute reveal that the type of stock mutual fund in which you invest over the long term makes very little difference. Over 10 or 20 years, the average annual returns for different types of diversified stock funds (growth, domestic equity, growth and income, equity income, and balanced) converge around 11 percent (11.2 percent, according to Ibbotson Associates). The only secret to obtaining such a good return is to remain patient and keep investing. Returns over one, three, and five years vary widely, but over the long term, the returns of major categories of diversified stock mutual funds are roughly the same.

Instant Message

Keep Your Mutual Fund Costs Low

John C. Bogle, who started the no-load mutual fund powerhouse Vanguard, says in *The Little Book of Commonsense Investing* that the costs of the average managed mutual fund is 2.5 percent, while the classic index fund's cost is 0.2 percent. Over time compounding costs greatly reduce compounding returns.

$50,000 portfolio earning an 8 percent annual return would grow to $176,182 in 20 years with a 1.5 percent management fee. By comparison, over the same time span it would grow to $193,484 with a 1.0 percent fee and to $212,393 with a 0.5 percent fee. Over 30 years, the returns with these fee rates would be $330,718, $380,613, and $437,748, respectively. The negative effects of high fees on long-term returns are enormous.

The investor would be wise to invest in no-load fee mutual funds that have low management fees. "If you pick your own funds, sales charges [and loads] are a total waste of money," observes Fred W. Frailey, editor of *Kiplinger's Personal Finance Magazine*.

CONCEPT CHECK 15.3

1. Give three examples of fees and charges associated with load funds.
2. Which is better for most investors, load or no-load fund?
3. Summarize the effects of loads on investment returns.

Selecting Funds in Which to Invest

4 LEARNING OBJECTIVE
Establish strategies to evaluate and select mutual funds that meet your investment goals.

Selecting mutual funds in which to invest is usually a do-it-yourself effort. A tremendous amount of objective information is available to help potential investors evaluate and select funds. To explain the process of selecting funds, let's follow Jessica Shipp's decision making. She is in sales and earns $51,000 annually; she lives in Sacramento, California. Figure 15.4 illustrates the process of selecting mutual fund investments, and Table 15.4 contains performance data for a number of large-cap mutual funds from *Consumer Reports* magazine.

Review Your Investment Philosophy and Investment Goals

Jessica began by reviewing her investment philosophy and financial goals. These topics were examined in Chapter 13. Jessica has a moderate investment philosophy, and

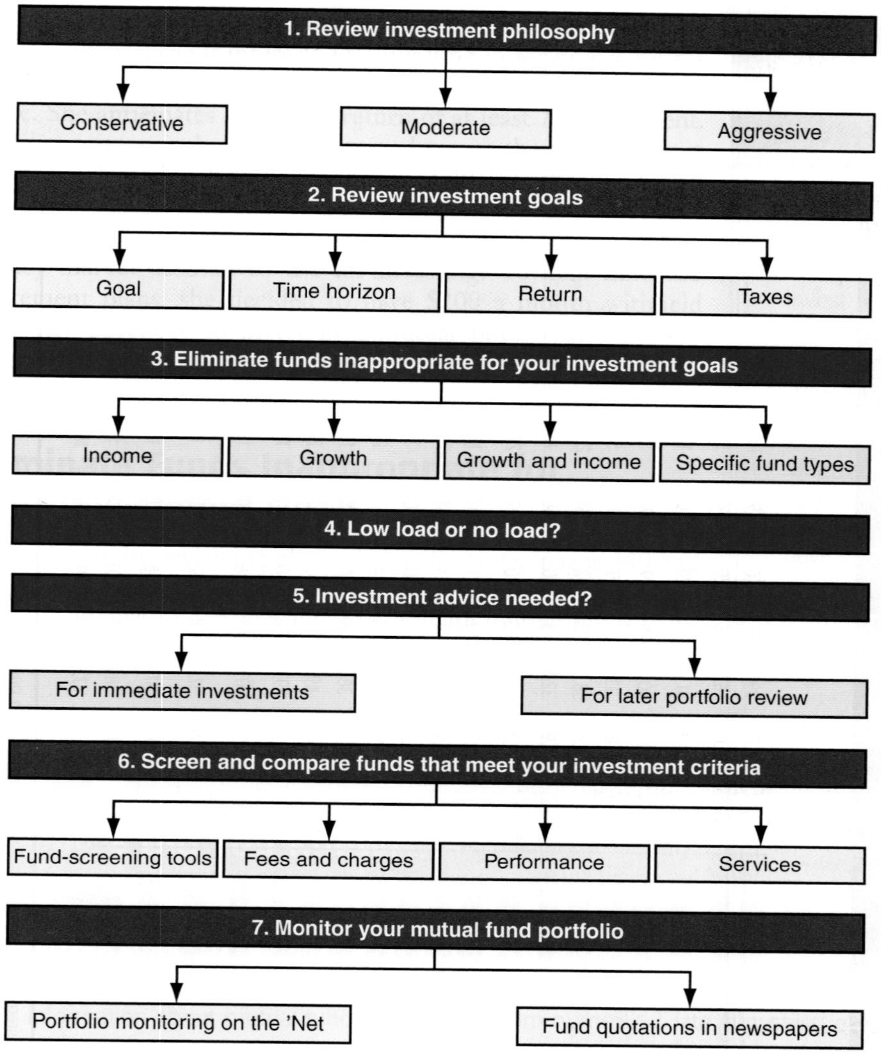

Figure 15.4
Process of Selecting Mutual Fund Investments

1. Review investment philosophy
- Conservative
- Moderate
- Aggressive

2. Review investment goals
- Goal
- Time horizon
- Return
- Taxes

3. Eliminate funds inappropriate for your investment goals
- Income
- Growth
- Growth and income
- Specific fund types

4. Low load or no load?

5. Investment advice needed?
- For immediate investments
- For later portfolio review

6. Screen and compare funds that meet your investment criteria
- Fund-screening tools
- Fees and charges
- Performance
- Services

7. Monitor your mutual fund portfolio
- Portfolio monitoring on the 'Net
- Fund quotations in newspapers

Capital Strategies Community Investment Fund is a mutual fund that provides returns through socially oriented investment vehicles. The fund fosters economic development in America's underserved communities, including victims of Hurricane Katrina.

CHAPTER 16

Real Estate and High-Risk Investments

You Must Be Kidding, Right?

Friends Richard Belisle and Nicholas Stevenson both have aggressive investment philosophies. Richard invests primarily in residential real estate, and Nicholas invests in commodities futures contracts. As longtime investors, they consider themselves experts, but occasionally each has experienced financial losses. What are the odds that the typical investor will make money investing in commodities futures contracts?

A. 50%

B. 30%

C. 20%

D. 10%

The answer is D. Ninety percent of individual investors in futures contracts lose money. Funds used for these investments should be only those that one can afford to lose!

LEARNING OBJECTIVES

After reading this chapter, you should be able to:

1 **Demonstrate** how you can make money investing in real estate.

2 **Calculate** the right price to pay for real estate and how to finance your purchase.

3 **Assess** the disadvantages of investing in real estate.

4 **Summarize** the risks and challenges of investing in collectibles, precious metals, and gems.

5 **Explain** why options and futures are high-risk investments.

What Do You Recommend?

Jamie Day, a 37-year-old marketing manager for a large corporation in Long Beach, California, earns $110,000 per year. She saves about $1800 each month beyond her contributions to her employer's 401(k) retirement plan. To date, Jamie has been investing her 401(k) plan money primarily in aggressive stock mutual funds and the remainder in her employer's company stock. She has found excellent success investing in the mutual funds within the plan, and her investments have grown at a healthy pace through the years. Her total 401(k) holdings are worth $260,000.

Ever since her grandfather gave her some stocks as a child, Jamie has loved investing—and she has enjoyed a good track record with her efforts. Jamie is an active trader, often trading every three or four weeks, primarily in the oil, technology, and prescription drug industries. Every year she has some losses as well as gains. Her private portfolio is currently worth $160,000. Jamie has never bought or sold options or futures contracts, but her stockbroker suggested that she consider them. Jamie also has a friend who owns several residential rental properties who has asked her to consider investing as her partner in her next real estate venture.

What would you recommend to Jamie on the subject of real estate and high-risk investments regarding:

1. Investing in real estate?
2. Putting some of her money in a high-risk investment, like collectibles?
3. Investing in options and futures contracts?

FOR HELP with studying this chapter, visit the Online Student Center:

www.college.hmco.com/pic/garman9e

A home tends to accomplish more than just putting a roof over your head. It is also an investment because housing values increase over the long term. But real estate investing is not the same as buying a home in which to live. Investing in real estate can provide you extra income now and give a boost to your future retirement plans. But to do so you have to do a lot of things right. Real estate is not rocket science, but investors must know a lot about taxes, financing, insurance, community economics, and dealing with difficult tenants. Real estate investments are complex, and they are much riskier than investing in mutual funds and stocks.

high-risk/speculative investments Present potential for significant fluctuations in return, sometimes over short time periods.

You also might consider owning tangible assets such as collectibles, precious metals, and gems for their investment potential. Or you may be attracted to options and futures contracts investments. All these are referred to as **high-risk** (or **speculative) investments** because they have the potential for significant fluctuations in return, sometimes over short time periods. They are suitable only for investors with a moderate-to-aggressive investment philosophy.

Making Money Investing in Real Estate

1 LEARNING OBJECTIVE
Demonstrate how you can make money investing in real estate.

"Anyone can get rich investing in real estate." This may be true, but it may not be the whole truth. It sounds too easy when successful real estate investors tell their stories: "My rental properties freed me from having a full-time job." "I have more income now than when I was in the rat race working." "I fixed up and sold three homes and now I own seven." "I can pay off all my mortgages in 13 years and never lift a finger again."

real estate Property consisting of land, all structures permanently attached to that land, and accompanying rights and privileges, such as crops and mineral rights.

Real estate is property consisting of land, all structures permanently attached to that land, and accompanying rights and privileges, such as crops and mineral rights. A real estate investment is termed **direct ownership** when an investor holds actual legal title to the property. For example, you can invest directly as an individual or jointly with other investors to buy properties designed for residential living, such as houses, duplexes, apartments, mobile homes, and condominiums. You also could invest in commercial properties designed for business uses, such as office buildings, medical centers, gasoline stations, and motels. You might buy raw land or residential lots, although they are extremely risky.

Good Money Habits in Real Estate and High-Risk Investments

Make the following your money habits when investing in real estate and high-risk investments:

1. Consider the disadvantages before investing in real estate.
2. Invest only in real estate properties that have a positive cash flow.
3. Finance real estate investments with conventional mortgages, not mortgages with adjustable interest terms.
4. Use the discounted cash-flow method to help determine the right price to pay.
5. If you put money into high-risk assets, limit your investment to no more than 10 percent of your portfolio.

Current Income and Capital Gains

Following are two key questions for real estate investors:

- Can you make current income while you own?
- Can you profit with capital gains when you sell the property?

The most important consideration for real estate investors is whether the rental income will be sufficient to make a profit. If you invest in a property and you are paying out more than the rental income coming in, you face three risks: (1) whether you can afford to continue paying out that money every month, (2) whether the price on the property will increase, and (3) whether the property actually will sell for more than what you paid for it.

To measure the current income in a real estate market, investors can begin by using the **price-to-rent ratio.** This numerical relationship might range from 11 to 26 depending upon local market conditions—meaning how high housing prices are. The larger the number, the less likely the investor can make money. In San Diego, California, a condominium renting for \$1500 a month might sell for the sky-high price of \$390,000 for a ratio of 21.7 (12 × \$1500 = \$18,000; \$390,000 ÷ \$18,000 = 21.7), while a similar one in Dallas, Texas, might cost only \$165,000 for a ratio of 9.17

(12 × \$1500 = \$18,000; \$165,000 ÷ \$18,000 = 9.17). Buying property with a high ratio will provide a profit only with a future increase in the value of the property.

Investors also calculate the **rental yield** on properties. This is a computation of how much income the investor might pocket from rent each year before mortgage payments as a percentage of the purchase price. Most properties yield about 4 percent of income annually, although the rental yield may be as little as 1 or 2 percent and as high as 8 or 9 percent. Less expensive properties often offer higher yields. The formula assumes half of rental income goes for expenses (other than debt repayment).

rental yield A computation of how much income the investor might pocket from rent each year (before mortgage payments) as a percentage of the purchase price; divide the annual rent by 2 and then divide by the purchase price.

$$\text{Rental yield} = \frac{(\text{rent} \div 2)}{\text{purchase price}} \quad \textbf{(16.1)}$$

	Example A	Example B
Purchase price	\$500,000	\$150,000
Annual rent	36,000	26,000
Yield	3.6%	8.67%

Current Income Results from Positive Cash Flow

In real estate investing, current income takes the form of positive cash flow. For an income-producing real estate investment, you pay operating expenses out of rental income. If the property has a mortgage (a common occurrence), payments toward the mortgage principal and interest also must be made out of rental income. Operating expenses such as vacancies, taxes, mortgage payments, and repairs may eat up half of rental income.

The amount of rental income you have left after paying all operating expenses is called **cash flow.** The amount of cash flow—obtained by subtracting any cash outlays from the cash income—depends on the amount of rent received, the amount of expenses paid, and the amount necessary to repay the mortgage debt. Investors usually prefer a positive cash flow to a negative cash flow because any shortages represent out-of-pocket expenses for the investor.

cash flow Amount of rental income you have left after paying all operating expenses.

Many real estate investments will not generate a positive cash flow, even though they may offer the likelihood of high potential returns through price appreciation. Investors might manage a negative cash flow for a few years while waiting for capital gains to later materialize when selling the property.

Price Appreciation Leads to Capital Gains

The capital gain earned in a real estate investment comes from **price appreciation.** It is the amount above ownership costs for which an investment is sold. In real estate, ownership costs include the original purchase price as well as expenditures for any capital improvements made to a property prior to sale. **Capital improvements** are costs incurred in making changes in real property, beyond maintenance and repairs, that add to its value. Paneling a living room, adding a new roof, and putting up a fence represent capital improvements. **Repairs** are expenses (usually tax deductible against an investor's cash-flow income) necessary to maintain the value of the property. Repainting, mending roof leaks, and fixing plumbing are examples of repairs.

capital improvements Costs incurred in making value-enhancing changes (beyond maintenance and repair) in real property.

repairs Usually tax-deductible expenses necessary to maintain property value.

As an example, assume that Andrew Webb, an unmarried schoolteacher from Fayetteville, Arkansas, bought a small rental house as an investment five years ago for \$120,000 in cash that he received as an inheritance. He fixed some roof leaks (repairs) for \$1000 and then added a new shed and some kitchen cabinets (capital improvements) at a cost of \$10,000 before selling the property this year for \$160,000. As a

Did You Know?...

What to Do Before Investing in Real Estate

1. Set up a limited liability corporation to own your real estate investments as it protects your personal assets in case someone injured on your rental property sues you.
2. Hire an accountant experienced in real estate investing.
3. Line up financing options before searching for properties.
4. Hire an inspector to inspect the physical condition of the property.
5. Hire a licensed contractor for plumbing, electrical, and expensive repair jobs rather than doing them yourself.
6. Consider hiring a management company to tend to your property; the cost is 5 to 10 percent of rental income.
7. Set aside $5000 as a contingency fund for unanticipated property problems.
8. Consider investing in properties only in locales where there are thriving businesses located near good schools, supermarkets, and public transportation.

result, Andrew happily realized a capital gain of $30,000 ($160,000 minus the $120,000 purchase price minus $10,000 in capital improvements).

Residential real estate values can generally be expected to increase 3 percent annually, about the rate of inflation, or a little above. In some markets, prices might jump 10 percent or more in one year and perhaps continue rising for two or three more years. Prices can decline, too, as even in hot regional real estate markets prices in individual neighborhoods may decline. Prices can drop 10 or 20 percent in one year. In markets in which real estate is hard to sell (too many properties on the market and too few buyers), perhaps because of job losses in a slow regional economy, residential housing prices might decline 2 or 3 percent annually for a long time.

If you cannot forecast the future of what you invest in, such as price appreciation on a property in a local housing market, you are speculating. Using a mortgage loan invites more risk. While price appreciation is where the big profits are in real estate investing, you can reduce risk by investing in property for which the expected rental income exceeds projected mortgage payments, property taxes, and maintenance costs.

Leverage Can Increase an Investor's Return

As we noted in Chapter 13, **leverage** involves using borrowed funds to make an investment with the goal of earning a rate of return in excess of the after-tax costs of borrowing. Lenders allow investors to borrow from 75 to 95 percent of the price of a property.

Suppose that Andrew, instead of paying cash for the house, had made a down payment of $25,000 and borrowed the remainder. What effect would this borrowing have on his return? In the first instance, Andrew paid $120,000 cash for the property and earned a 25 percent return on his investment ($30,000 ÷ $120,000) over the five-year period, or roughly 5 percent per year. In the second situation, using leverage, he would have an apparent return of 120 percent ($30,000 ÷ $25,000), or roughly 24 percent per year. The true return would be lower because of mortgage payments, interest expenses, property taxes, and repairs but would still be a double-digit return.

loan-to-value ratio Measures the amount of leverage in a real estate investment project by dividing the total amount of debt by the market price of the investment.

The **loan-to-value ratio** measures the amount of leverage in a real estate investment project. It is calculated by dividing the amount of debt by the value of the total original investment. For example, because his down payment was $25,000 on the $120,000 property, Andrew had a loan-to-value ratio of 79 percent ($95,000 ÷ $120,000), or 79 percent leverage.

Did You Know?...

Top 3 Financial Missteps in Real Estate and High-Risk Investment Investing

People slip up in real estate and high-risk investment when they do the following:

1. Failing to factor in income lost due to vacancies and collection costs for tenants who do not pay
2. Not setting enough money aside for maintenance, repairs, unanticipated capital improvements, and rising real estate taxes
3. Assuming that real estate prices will go up and interest rates will not increase

Beneficial Tax Treatments

The U.S. Congress, through provisions in the Internal Revenue Code, encourages real estate investments by giving investors five special tax treatments. The first three may increase the real estate investor's income while the last two may enhance capital gains.

1. Depreciation Is Tax Deductible Investors in real estate become successful by understanding the "numbers" of real estate investing. For example, assume that Jisue Han, a lawyer from Huntsville, Alabama, invested $200,000 in a residential building ($170,000) and land ($30,000). She rents the property to a tenant for $24,000 per year. You might think that Jisue has to pay income taxes on the entire $24,000 in rental income. Wrong. IRS regulations allow taxpayers to deduct depreciation from rental income. **Depreciation** represents the decline in value of an asset over time due to normal wear and tear and obsolescence. A proportionate amount of a capital asset representing depreciation may be deducted against income each year over the asset's estimated life. Land cannot be depreciated.

Jisue can deduct an equal part of the building's cost over the estimated life of the property. IRS guidelines provide that residential properties may be depreciated over 27.5 years while nonresidential properties are allowed 39 years. Jisue calculates (from Table 16.1) the amount she can annually deduct from income to be $6182 ($170,000 ÷ 27.5). Table 16.1 shows the effects of depreciation on her income taxes, assuming Jisue pays income taxes at a combined federal and state rate of 36 percent. In this example, the depreciation deduction lowers taxable income on the property from $24,000 to $17,818 ($24,000 − $6182) and increases the return on the investment to 8.79 percent.

depreciation Decline in value of an asset over time due to normal wear and tear and obsolescence.

2. Interest Is Tax Deductible Real estate investors incur many business expenses in attempting to earn a profit: interest on a mortgage, real estate taxes, insurance, utilities, capital improvements, and repairs. The largest of these costs often is the interest expense, as properties are often purchased with a mortgage loan. Table 16.2 illustrates the effect of interest expenses on income taxes. Assume Jisue borrowed $175,000 to purchase her $200,000 property. After deducting annual depreciation of $6182 and interest expenses of $13,050, her taxable income is reduced to $4768. Because her income tax liability is only $1716, Jisue's after-tax return of $9234 yields 36.94 percent on her leveraged investment.

Table 16.1 Effect of Depreciation on Income Taxes and Return

			Without Depreciation	With Depreciation
Total amount invested	$200,000	Gross rental income	$24,000	$24,000
Cost of land	− 30,000	Less annual depreciation expense	0	6,182
Cost of rental building	$170,000	Taxable income	24,000	17,818
Depreciation for 27.5 years	$ 6,182	Income taxes (36 percent combined federal and state tax rate)	8,640	6,414
		After-tax return	$15,360	$17,586
		After-tax yield (divide return by $200,000)	7.68%	8.79%

Table 16.2 Additional Effect of Interest Paid on Income Taxes on Return

Gross rental income	$24,000
Less annual depreciation deduction	− 6,182
Subtotal	$17,818
Less interest expense for the year (7.5 percent mortgage loan)	− 13,050
Taxable income	$ 4,768
Cash flow after paying interest ($24,000 − $13,050)	10,950
Less income tax liability (0.36 × $4,768)	− 1,716
After-tax return ($10,950 − $1,716)	$ 9,234
After-tax yield [$9,234 ÷ ($200,000 − $175,000)]	36.94%

Tax laws permit investors to deduct interest expenses (with the amount of the deduction allowed depending on the investor's marginal tax bracket). The interest deduction gives Jisue a cash flow after paying mortgage interest of $10,950 ($24,000 − $13,050). In essence, the $13,050 in interest is paid with $4698 ($13,050 × 36 percent combined federal and state income tax rate) of the money that was not sent to the federal and state governments and $8352 ($13,050 − $4698) of Jisue's money.

3. Rental Income Tax Regulations on Vacation Homes If you rent out your vacation property for 14 or fewer days during the year, you can pocket the income tax-free, regardless of how much you charge. The IRS does not want to hear about this gain. The home is considered a personal residence, so you can deduct mortgage interest and property taxes just as you would for your principal residence.

Renting a vacation home for more than 14 days turns the endeavor into a business, and you must report all rental income. You also can deduct rental expenses up to the level of rental income you report. When your adjusted gross income (AGI) is less than $100,000, a maximum of $25,000 of rental-related losses may be deducted each year to offset income from *any* source, including your salary. The $25,000 limit is gradually phased out as your AGI moves between $100,000 and $150,000. This ability to shelter income from taxes represents a terrific benefit for people who invest in real estate on a small scale.

4. Capital Gains Are Taxed at Reduced Rates Capital gains on real estate are realized through price appreciation. For most taxpayers, long-term capital gains are taxed at a rate of 15 percent, and taxpayers in the 10 to 15 percent tax brackets pay a long-term capital gains tax of 5 percent. (See Chapter 4.)

5. Tax-Free Exchanges Another special tax treatment results when a real estate investor trades equity in one property for equity in a similar property. If none of the people involved in the trade receives any other form of property or money, the transaction is considered a **tax-free exchange.** If one person receives some money or other property, only that person has to report the extra proceeds as a taxable gain. For example, assume you bought a residential rental property five years ago for $220,000 and today it is worth much more money. You trade it with your friend by giving $10,000 in cash for your friend's $280,000 single-family rental home. Your friend needs to report only the $10,000 as income this year. In contrast, you do not need to report your long-term gain, $50,000 ($280,000 − $10,000 − $220,000), until you actually sell the new property.

tax-free exchange Arises when a real estate investor trades equity in one property for equity in a similar property and no other forms of property or money change hands.

Did You Know?...

About Real Estate Seminars

Infomercials and Internet ads tout the money to be make after attending seminars with names such as the Enlightened Millionaire Institute, The Real Estate Goddess, Carlton Sheets, and Ron LeGrand. Inspirational! Spiritual! Motivating! Practical! The seminars offer advice on marketing and deal making and sell participants books, tapes, additional seminars, and personal mentoring for thousands of dollars more.

Beginner real estate entrepreneurs are encouraged to pursue "no money down" and "little money down" schemes to make a quick fortune buying and selling real estate. The basic idea is to buy "distressed properties" at no more than 70 percent of their value from motivated sellers (such as after a death, divorce, foreclosure notice, or bankruptcy) by persuading them to do what may not be in their best interest.

Those sitting in weekend-long real estate seminars at a hotel meeting room with 400 people or a convention center with thousands of other novices (read that as "suckers") listening to get-rich gurus can cost each attendee big bucks, $599 to $5000. Real estate investing is very competitive, as investors may own one in four homes in a community.

If real estate seminars lead to novices making great profits, why aren't all local real estate agents rich? And retired in Hawaii? Seminar promoters are the ones who are making money off these schemes. For a critique of the real estate seminar industry, see John T. Reed's views (http://www.johntreed.com/Reedgururating.html) and the Australian Securities and Exchange Commission (http://www.asic.gov.au/fido/fido.nsf/byheadline/Investment+seminars+homepage?openDocument).

CONCEPT CHECK 16.1

1. What are the two key questions for real estate investors?
2. Distinguish between the price-to-rent ratio and the rental yield as measures of current income.
3. Give an example of how leverage can increase an investor's yield in real estate.
4. Explain how two beneficial tax treatments are helpful to real estate investors.

discounted cash-flow method Effective way to estimate the value or asking price of a real estate investment based on after-tax cash flow and the return on the invested dollars discounted over time to reflect a discounted yield.

Pricing and Financing Real Estate Investments

2 LEARNING OBJECTIVE
Calculate the right price to pay for real estate and how to finance your purchase.

Sure ways to go wrong in a real estate investment are to pay too much for the property and finance it incorrectly.

Pay the Right Price

The **discounted cash-flow method** is an effective way to estimate the value or asking price of a real estate investment. It emphasizes after-tax cash flow and the return on the invested dollars discounted over time to reflect a discounted yield. Software programs are available to calculate the discounted cash flows. You also can use Appendix Table A.2, as illustrated in Table 16.3.

Prices typically decline as the inventory of houses for sale goes up.

Table 16.3 Discounted Cash-Flow to Estimate Price

	After-Tax Cash Flow	Present Value of $1 at 10 Percent*	Present Value of After-Tax Cash Flow
1 year	$ 4,000	0.909	$ 3,636
2 years	4,200	0.826	3,469
3 years	4,400	0.751	3,304
4 years	4,600	0.683	3,142
5 years	4,800	0.621	2,981
Sell property	$265,000	0.621	164,565
Present value of property			$181,097

*From Appendix Table A.2.

Instant Message

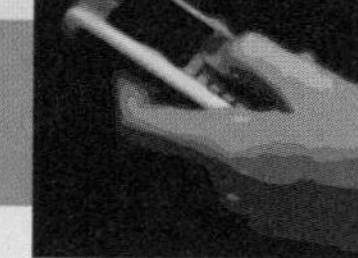

Find Information on Home Prices

To find prices on homes where you live, check out www.realtor.org and http://www.huduser.org/.

To see how this method works, assume that you require an after-tax rate of return of 10 percent on a condominium advertised for sale at $200,000. You estimate that rents can be increased each year for five years. After all expenses are paid, you expect to have after-tax cash flows of $4000, $4200, $4400, $4600, and $4800 for the five years. Assuming some price appreciation, you anticipate selling the property for $265,000 after all expenses are incurred. How much should you pay now to buy the property?

Table 16.3 explains how to answer this question. Multiply the estimated after-tax cash flows and the expected proceeds of $265,000 to be realized on the sale of the property by the present value of a dollar at 10 percent (the required rate of return). Add the present values together to obtain the total present value of the property—in this case, $181,097. The asking price of $200,000 is too high for you to earn an after-tax return of 10 percent. Your choices are to negotiate the price down, accept a return of less than 10 percent, hope that the sale price of the property will be higher than

$265,000 five years from now, or consider another investment. The discounted cash-flow method provides an effective way to estimate real estate values because it takes into account the selling price of the property, the effect of income taxes, and the time value of money.

Financing a Real Estate Investment

Borrowing to finance a real estate investment is more expensive than borrowing to buy one's own home, often 0.5 to 1.5 percent percentage points above the rate for customary homebuyers. There is more risk because the investor does not live in the property. The minimum down payment for investors is often 20 or 25 percent. Most investors finance real estate investments with conventional fixed-rate, fixed-term mortgage loans.

To make a smaller down payment and get a lower mortgage rate, some real estate investors buy a home, live in it for a year, and then rent it out as an investment. Another way to finance a real estate investment is through **seller financing** (or **owner financing**). This occurs when a seller is willing to self-finance a loan by accepting a promissory note from the buyer who makes monthly mortgage payments. No lending agency is involved. Investing buyers pay higher interest rates for seller financing. The seller may accept little or no down payment in exchange for an even higher interest rate, perhaps 1½ to 2½ percent above conventional mortgage rates. Owner-financed deals can be transacted very quickly.

A popular way to start in real estate investing is to purchase **sweat equity property.** With this approach, you seek a property that needs repairs but has good underlying value. You buy this fixer-upper at a favorable price and "sweat" by spending many hours cleaning, painting, and repairing it to rent or sell at a profit.

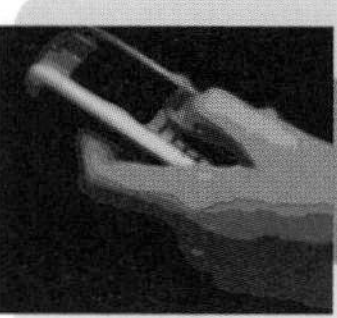

Instant Message

Own Real Estate Indirectly

In an indirect investment in real estate, a trustee, not the investor, holds actual legal title to the property. Examples are real estate syndicates, limited partnerships, and **real estate investment trusts (REITs),** which we discussed in Chapter 15. REITs typically specialize in a segment of the real estate market, such as shopping centers, apartment buildings, or medical offices. Investors can obtain information on these alternatives from brokerage firms.

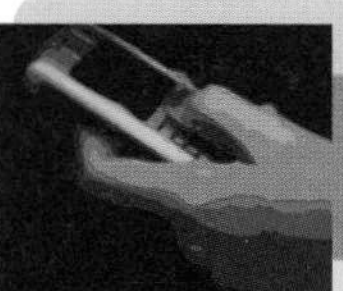

Instant Message

Adjustable-Rate Mortgage Loans Are Risky

It is risky to buy real estate by financing it with an adjustable-rate mortgage loan (see Chapter 9). When rates begin to rise—and they eventually will—the higher rates mean the investor is forced to write bigger and bigger monthly checks to the lender.

CONCEPT CHECK 16.2

1. Summarize how the discounted cash-flow method helps determine the right price to pay for a real estate investment.
2. List three ways to finance a real estate investment, and tell why a conventional mortgage might be safer than another financing method.

seller financing/owner financing
When seller self-finances a buyer's loan by accepting a promissory note from buyer, who makes monthly mortgage payments at a slightly higher rate.

Disadvantages of Real Estate Investing

3 LEARNING OBJECTIVE
Assess the disadvantages of investing in real estate.

Real estate investing can be very profitable. But it does have some significant disadvantages.

- **Business risk.** It is quite possible to lose money in real estate investments. A local recession can depress prices. Zoning changes can slash housing values. Some property values simply decline, and so do rents. Rents will not keep up with costs in communities in which industries and jobs are moving elsewhere or in deteriorating neighborhoods.
- **Complexity.** Real estate investments require much more investigation than do most other investments. Numerous assumptions about financial details in the future also must be made.

Did You Know?...

Timesharing Is Not an Investment

Timesharing is the joint ownership or lease of vacation property through which the principals occupy the property individually for set periods of time. Timesharing is not an investment, although it is promoted as a way to simultaneously invest and obtain vacation housing. For $5000 to $20,000, buyers can purchase one or more weeks' use of luxury vacation housing furnished right down to the salt-and-pepper shakers. Timeshare owners pay an annual maintenance fee of perhaps $100 to $300 for each week of ownership.

With **deeded timesharing,** the buyer obtains a legal title or deed to limited time periods of use of real estate. Purchasers become secured creditors who are guaranteed continued use of the property throughout any bankruptcy proceedings. They also really own their week (or two) of the property.

Most timeshares are sold without a deed. **Non-deeded timesharing** is a legal right-to-use purchase of a limited, preplanned timesharing period of use of a property. It is a long-term lease, license, or club membership permitting use of a hotel suite, condominium, or other accommodation, and the right to use expires in 20 to 25 years. It does not grant legal real estate ownership interest to the purchaser. If the true owner of the property—the developer—goes bankrupt, problems abound. Creditors can lock out the timeshare purchasers (technically they are tenants) from the premises.

It is very hard to sell a timeshare. A survey from the Resort Property Owners Association says that the average timeshare unit languishes on the market for 4.4 years before being sold. At any point in time, 60 percent of all timeshares are up for sale. Timeshare sellers rarely receive more than 50 percent of their original investment in the sale. If you are interested in such property for vacation purposes, buy a deeded timeshare. Timeshare commissions are 25 percent of the price.

- **Large initial investment.** Direct investment in real estate generally requires many thousands of dollars, often with an initial outlay of $15,000, $30,000, or $50,000.
- **Lack of diversification.** So much capital is required in real estate investing that spreading risk is almost impossible.
- **Dealing with tenants.** Someone has to screen rental applicants for their credit histories, criminal records, work references, and experience with previous landlords. State laws may make it impossible to evict a deadbeat tenant for several months. Picking the wrong tenants can quickly turn a real estate property into a financial loss.
- **Time-consuming management demands.** Managing a real estate investment requires time for conducting regular inspections of the property, dealing with insurance companies, making repairs, and collecting overdue rents.
- **Low current income.** Expenses may reduce the cash-flow return to less than 2 percent or even generate a net loss in a given year.
- **Unpredictable costs.** Estimating costs is problematic. Investors cannot control increasing real estate tax assessments or when a central air-conditioning unit might break down.
- **Interest rate risk.** As we noted in Chapter 13, when interest rates rise, fewer people can afford to buy homes, and this puts downward pressure on prices and rents.
- **Legal fees.** The services of a real estate attorney will be needed to help handle the real estate purchase, sale, building inspections, zoning issues, tenant problems, insurance disputes, and any liability issues.
- **Illiquidity.** Real estate is expensive, and the market for investment property is much smaller than the securities market. As a result, it is common to experience trouble in selling. It may take months or even a year or more to find a buyer, arrange the financing, and close the sale of a real estate investment.

- **High transfer costs.** Substantial transfer costs, often representing 6 to 7 percent of the property's sale price, plus money for fix-up costs, may be incurred when real estate is bought or sold.

CONCEPT CHECK 16.3

1. Summarize why illiquidity, transfer costs, and unpredictable costs are disadvantages in real estate investing.
2. Do you think you could successfully deal with tenants and the time-consuming management demands required in real estate investing? Why or why not?

Investing in Collectibles, Precious Metals, and Gems

4 LEARNING OBJECTIVE
Summarize the risks and challenges of investing in collectibles, precious metals, and gems.

Investors usually think of assets as something they would like to own for the long term. When investing in collectibles, precious metals, and gems, the investor owns illiquid real assets, not intangible items represented by pieces of paper. While an asset may be bought for its long-term investment potential, a profit might be earned in the short term. A speculator buys in the hope that someone else will pay more for an asset in the not-too-distant future. Speculators often buy or sell in expectation of profiting from market fluctuations. If you put money into these illiquid assets, limit such speculative investing to no more than 10 percent of your portfolio.

Collectibles

collectibles Cultural artifacts that have value because of their beauty, age, scarcity, or popularity, such as antiques, stamps, rare coins, art, baseball cards, and so on.

Collectibles are cultural artifacts that have value because of their beauty, age, scarcity, or popularity. They include baseball cards, posters, sports memorabilia, guns, photographs, paintings, ceramics, comic books, watches, lunchboxes, matchbooks, glassware, spoons, stamps, rare coins, art, rugs, cars, and antiques. The collectible markets are fueled by nostalgia, limited availability, and "what is hot to own today."

Making a Profit on Collectibles Is Not Easy A key to success in collectibles is to invest in quality—the higher the better. Although buying collectibles can be fun and easy, turning a profit may not. The only return on collectibles occurs through price appreciation, and you must sell to realize a profit. That could be hard for you to do if the collectibles give you pleasure.

Items that are almost certain to lose value include those that are mass-produced and marketed as collectibles or limited editions. Another risk is the wholesale-to-retail price spread. Prices on collectibles vary greatly from item to item and year to year. Markets are fickle. If the investor needs to convert the asset to cash, a sale may take days, weeks, or months, and the seller may be forced to accept a lower price. The collectibles industry is rife with forgeries, scams, and frauds, particularly in sports memorabilia.

Buying and Selling Collectibles on the 'Net You can buy collectibles on the Internet, using eBay for example, purchasing in minutes what you might never have found after searching for years in magazines, junk shops, flea markets, and auctions. Buying collectibles on the Internet is efficient and convenient, and it is easy to compare products and prices. It's hard to inspect them before purchase, however. Search Google for "collectibles." This is a very risky way to invest!

Did You Know?...

The Tax Consequences of an Income-Producing Real Estate Investment

When you are considering a real estate investment, you use the investment amount (purchase price or down payment) to begin the process of estimating the likely rate of return. This calculation may then be compared with other investment alternatives. Because some of the many assumptions in real estate calculations could be incorrect, caution is warranted in real estate analyses.

The following table shows five-year estimates for a hypothetical residential property in Bozeman, Montana, with a purchase price of $200,000. The building will be purchased with a $150,000 mortgage loan, so the buyer has to make a $50,000 down payment plus pay $8000 in closing costs. The gross rental income of $18,000 annually is projected to rise at an annual rate of 5 percent, vacancies and unpaid rent at 10 percent, real estate taxes at 7 percent, insurance at 8 percent, and maintenance at 10 percent. Virtually the entire payment for the 30-year, $150,000, 8 percent, fixed-rate mortgage loan is assumed to be interest during these early years. For income tax purposes, the land is valued at $20,000, and the building is depreciated over 27.5 years. The amount of annual straight-line depreciation is calculated to be $6546 ($200,000 − $20,000 = $180,000; $180,000 ÷ 27.5 = $6546).

Note (in line D) how challenging it is to earn current income from rental properties. During the first year, the total cash-flow loss is projected to be $2808. However, because the income tax laws permit depreciation (line E, $6546) to be recorded as a real estate investment expense,

Estimates for a Successful Real Estate Investment

	Year				
	1	2	3	4	5
A. Gross rental income	$ 18,000	$18,900	$ 19,845	$ 20,837	$ 21,879
Less vacancies and unpaid rent	1,800	1,890	1,985	2,084	2,188
B. Projected gross income	$ 16,200	$17,010	$ 17,860	$ 18,753	$ 19,691
C. Less operating expenses					
Principal and Interest (*P* + *I*)	$ 13,208	$13,208	$ 13,208	$ 13,208	$ 13,208
Real estate taxes (*T*)	2,600	2,782	2,977	3,185	3,408
Insurance (*I*)	800	864	933	1,008	1,089
Maintenance	2,400	2,640	2,904	3,194	3,513
Total operating expenses	$ 19,008	$ 19,494	$ 20,022	$ 20,595	$ 21,218
D. Total cash flow (negative)	$(2,808)	$(2,484)	$(2,162)	$(1,842)	$(1,527)
E. Less depreciation expense	6,546	6,546	6,546	6,546	6,546
F. Taxable income (or loss) (D − E)	$(9,354)	$(9,030)	$(8,708)	$(8,388)	$(8,073)
G. Annual tax savings (30 percent marginal rate)	2,806	2,709	2,612	2,516	2,422
H. Net cash-flow gain (or loss) after taxes (G − D)	$ (2)	$ 225	$ 450	$ 674	$ 895

even though it is not an out-of-pocket cost, the total taxable loss (line F) is projected to be $9354. This loss can be deducted on the investor's income tax returns. Because the investor pays a 30 percent combined federal and state income tax rate, the loss results in a first-year annual tax savings of $2806. Therefore, instead of sending the $2806 to the government in taxes, the investor can use that amount to help pay the operating expenses of the investment. Consequently, the net cash-flow income (line D) of $2808 is reduced by tax savings (line G) of $2806 to result in a net cash-flow gain after taxes of $2 ($2808 – $2806).

Assume that the property appreciates in value at an annual rate of 6 percent and will be worth $267,645 (line K) in five years ($200,000 × 1.06 × 1.06 × 1.06 × 1.06 × 1.06). If it is sold at this price, a 6 percent real estate sales commission of $16,059 ($267,645 × 0.06) would reduce the net proceeds to $251,586 ($267,645 – $16,059).

Now we can calculate the **crude annual rate of return** on the property, as shown in the second table. A crude rate of return is a rough measure of the yield on amounts invested that assumes that equal portions of the gain are earned each year. The total return in this example was substantial. The investor made out-of-pocket cash investments of $50,000 for the down payment and $8000 in closing costs, and we subtract the accumulated net cash flow (line N) of $2242 (adding all the numbers across line H because the investor already has received that money) for a total investment (line O) of $55,758. The investor has a capital gain (line M) of $76,316. After dividing to determine the before-tax total return (line R) to obtain 137 percent, the crude annual rate of return (line S) is 27.4 percent annually over the five years (137 percent ÷ 5 years).

Crude Rate of Return on a Successful Real Estate Investment

I.	**Taxable cost**	
	Purchase price ($50,000 down payment; $150,000 loan)	$200,000
	Closing costs	8,000
	Subtotal	208,000
J.	Less accumulated depreciation	32,730
	Taxable cost (adjusted basis)	$ 175,270
	Proceeds (after paying off mortgage)	
K.	Sale price	$ 267,645
	Less sales commission	16,059
	Net proceeds	$251,586
L.	Less taxable cost (J)	175,270
M	Taxable proceeds (capital gain)	$ 76,316
	Amount invested	
	Down payment	$ 50,000
	Closing costs	8,000
N.	Less accumulated net cash-flow gains	(2,242)
O.	Total invested	$ 55,758
	Crude annual rate of return	
P.	Total invested	$ 55,758
Q.	Taxable proceeds (capital gain from M)	$ 76,316
R.	Before-tax total return ($ 76,316 ÷ $55,758)	137%
S.	Crude before-tax annual rate of return (137 percent ÷ 5 years)	27.4%

Selling collectibles at a profit is not a sure thing.

Gold and Other Metals

There is an allure to owning gold. It is beautiful to look at, hold, and own. Gold is a uniquely private, personal, and portable way to hold some genuine wealth. People around the world occasionally invest some of their assets in gold to preserve capital, reasoning that if their national economies crash they will be able to trade gold even if their country's paper currency is devalued. The prices of gold tend to increase in times of economic and political turmoil, war, and high inflation because investors fear a future that may be worse than today, perhaps a lot worse. Some other metals have a similar appeal to investors.

gold bullion A refined and stamped weight of precious metal.

Gold Bullion **Gold bullion** is often thought of as the large gold "bricks" that weigh about 28 pounds that people imagine are stored in Fort Knox. Each is worth more than $100,000. The term simply means a refined and stamped weight of precious metal. Gold bullion is traditionally purchased and traded in 1- and 10-ounce gold bars. Gold is expensive to own. There are fees for refining, fabricating, and shipping bullion. A sales charge of 5 to 8 percent is common. There are storage costs. When gold is sold, the bank or dealer buying it from an investor may insist on reassaying its quality, yet another cost for the investor. The investor may also need to purchase insurance against fire and theft.

Gold Bullion Coins Some costs of investing in gold can be avoided by those wanting to take physical possession of gold bullion itself by owning modern

gold bullion coins, each containing 1 troy ounce (31.15 grams) of pure gold issued by the various world mints. The most popular coins are the South African Krugerrand, Canadian Maple Leaf, and U.S. American Eagle. Other gold bullion coins are available, including the Great Britain Sovereign, Australian Kangaroo Nugget, and Chinese Panda. Minimum orders are 10 coins, and commissions are 2 to 4 percent when buying and selling. These gold bullion coins have total liquidity worldwide.

gold bullion coins Various world mints issue these coins, which contain 1 troy ounce (31.15 grams) of pure gold.

Gold Stocks and Mutual Funds People usually do not invest in gold because it does not pay interest or dividends. Also, gold has been in a bear market for most of the past 25 years, government central banks have tons of stored bullion that they could sell (which would depress prices), and almost no one recommends gold as an investment.

Promoters (and that is the correct term because traders only make money when something sells) always tell investors that they are crazy not to participate in the "ongoing gold boom." They are confident that economic conditions today are similar to the 1970s when gold prices moved from $38 to more than $800. Investors deeply worried about the future, instead of owning gold, often find it more convenient to put some of their assets in the cash of the world's two safest currencies, the U.S. dollar and the euro.

Investors wanting to capitalize on world crises and rising gold prices may invest in the stocks of gold mining companies and in mutual funds that own gold companies. You may have heard of the Homestake Gold Mine, one of the early enterprises associated with the Gold Rush of 1876 in the northern Black Hills of what was then Dakota Territory. There are a handful of gold mining companies in the United States and dozens around the world. When there is turmoil in the world and people are fearful about the future, the prices of gold stocks rise, including gold mutual funds and gold exchange-traded funds (ETFs). Search Google for information, and you will find many scams.

Silver, Platinum, Palladium, Rhodium Some less popular metals also appeal to some investors. Silver, platinum, palladium, and rhodium are metals used industrially and occasionally in jewelry. The values of these metals rise and fall with changes in demand. An investor might reason that since palladium is used in auto production that when China's demand for vehicles increases substantially the price of the metal will soar.

Did You Know?...

Scams Abound in Collectibles, Precious Metals, and Gems

The average investor can't tell a diamond from cubic zirconium or a Monet from a Manet. The values of collectibles, gold, other precious metals, and precious gems rely in part upon the authority of "experts" who purport to determine their worth, and such blind trust invites risk for potential investors. When an asset does not generate a readily quantifiable return (such as rent, interest, or dividends), its value is determined by supply and demand—and rumors. Scams and frauds abound with these investments, as promoters and telemarketers tell tales about skyrocketing prices and high profit potentials to encourage their purchase. Collectibles, precious metals, and gems are not wise choices for the casual investor.

CONCEPT CHECK 16.5

1. Distinguish between a call and a put for the options investor.
2. Summarize two ways a person with a conservative investment philosophy can profit in options.
3. Explain how a speculative options investor can lose a lot of money.
4. Offer reasons why futures contracts are not appropriate for the average investor.

What Do You Recommend Now?

Now that you have read the chapter on real estate and high-risk investments, what do you recommend to Jamie regarding:

1. Investing in real estate?
2. Putting some of her money in a high-risk investment, like collectibles?
3. Investing in options and futures contracts?

Big Picture Summary of Learning Objectives

1 Demonstrate how you can make money investing in real estate.

The key questions for real estate investors are: "Can you make current income while you own the property?" and "Can you profit with capital gains when you sell the property?" To help find answers, investors calculate the price-to-rent ratio and rental yield. Leverage enhances real estate returns, and the IRS offers investors five beneficial tax treatments, including depreciation and tax-deductible interest.

2 Calculate the right price to pay for real estate and how to finance your purchase.

The discounted cash-flow method is an effective way to estimate the value or asking price of a real estate investment. It takes into account the selling price of the property, the effect of income taxes, and the time value of money. There are many ways to finance a real estate investment, although a conventional mortgage loan is the most popular.

3 Assess the disadvantages of investing in real estate.

There are many disadvantages in real estate investing: large initial investment, lack of diversification, dealing with tenants, low current income, unpredictable costs, illiquidity, and high transfer costs.

4 Summarize the risks and challenges of investing in collectibles, precious metals, and gems.

When investing in collectibles, precious metals, and gems, the investor owns illiquid real assets, not intangible items represented by pieces of paper. The investor's only return comes from price appreciation, as they do not pay interest or dividends. While prices are set by supply and demand, promoters hype these high-risk investments. Changing investor tastes and rumors also influence prices.

5 Explain why options and futures are high-risk investments.

Derivatives, such as options and futures, are instruments used by market participants to trade or manage more easily the asset upon which these instruments are based. While all types of investors can profit in options, only "speculators" with an aggressive investment philosophy should consider trading in futures. Most investors in derivatives lose money, and losses can accumulate quickly.

Let's Talk About It

1. Assume you have $30,000 in cash. Give reasons why you might want to invest that money in a real estate

investment. Offer two reasons why others might not be willing to invest in real estate.

2. The text describes several disadvantages of real estate investments. Identify two that might stop you from investing in real estate. Identify ways to circumvent those two obstacles.
3. Explain why timeshares should never be considered an investment. What are some reasons why people buy timeshares?
4. What percentage of your portfolio do you think should be invested in high-risk investments? Explain.
5. Both options and futures are high-risk investments. Identify one that seems like an unwise idea, and explain why it is unappealing.

Do the Numbers

1. Justin Nicholas, an electrician from Great Bend, Kansas, is interested in the numbers of real estate investments. He has reviewed the figures in Table 16.2 and is impressed with the potential 36.9 percent return after taxes. Justin is in the 25 percent marginal tax bracket. Answer the following questions to help guide his investment decisions:
   (a) Substitute Justin's 25 percent marginal tax bracket in Table 16.2, and calculate the taxable income and return after taxes.
   (b) Why does real estate appear to be a favorable investment for Justin?
   (c) What one factor might be changed in Table 16.2 to increase Justin's return?
   (d) Calculate the after-tax return for Justin, assuming that he bought the property and financed it with a 7 percent, $170,000 mortgage with annual interest costs of $11,175.
2. Elizabeth Bennett, a caterer from New Orleans, Louisiana, is considering buying a vacation condominium apartment for $265,000 in Park City, Utah. Elizabeth hopes to rent the condo to others to keep her costs down. Answer the following questions to help Elizabeth with her decisions:
   (a) Elizabeth's $210,000, 30-year mortgage loan costs $16,766 annually (from Table 9.4 on page 252). She figures that $1020 of her $1397 monthly mortgage payment will go for interest. On top of that are monthly expenses for property taxes ($140), homeowner's insurance ($80), and homeowner's association fee ($100). These amounts total $1717 a month. Which of these costs will be tax deductible?
   (b) If Elizabeth is in the 30 percent combined federal and state marginal tax bracket, how much less in taxes will she pay if she buys this condo?
   (c) Given that she should would like to personally use the condo for vacations totaling 10 to 12 days per year, how many days will Elizabeth have to rent it out before she would become eligible to deduct rental losses from her taxes?
   (d) Because Park City is primarily a winter ski resort, few condo renters can be found in the off season; therefore, Elizabeth is concerned about qualifying to deduct rental losses. Assuming she could rent the condo for $400 per day, summarize the IRS-approved rental alternative she could use to generate some tax-free income. Calculate the maximum amount of money Elizabeth could obtain using that plan.
   (e) Figure Elizabeth's annual net out-of-pocket cost to buy the condominium and rent it out minimally for tax-free income. List the costs and total on an annualized basis. Next, deduct the savings on income taxes as well as the presumed rental for the number of IRS-allowed days.
   (f) Using the figure derived in part (e), what would Elizabeth's out-of-pocket cost per day be to use the condo herself if she stayed there ten days each year? Fifteen days each year?

Financial Planning Cases

Case 1
Real Estate or Stocks?

Junhee Chang, a senior research analyst in Austin, Texas, has bought and sold high-technology stocks profitably for years. Lately some of her stock investments have done poorly, including one company that went bankrupt. Emily, a longtime friend at work, has suggested that the two of them invest in real estate together because property values in some neighborhoods have been rising. Emily has looked at three small office buildings and some residential duplexes as possible investments.

(a) Contrast the wisdom of investing in commercial office buildings versus the attraction of investing in residential properties.
(b) List three of the advantages associated with real estate investments.
(c) List three things that can go wrong for real estate investors.

Case 2
From Real Estate to Options and Futures

Brandon Williams and Jason Richardson, longtime partners in Berkeley, California, have bought and sold real estate properties for ten years. They have profited on every transaction and now have a portfolio of real estate worth about $4.7 million, on which they owe only $2.9 million. Jason has read about investing in options and futures contracts, and last week he talked with a stockbroker about the possibilities.

(a) Offer some reasons why Jason might gain by investing $100,000 or $200,000 in options and futures contracts.

(b) List some of the risks of options trading for Brandon and Jason.

(c) From an investor's point of view, contrast trading in futures contracts with buying highly leveraged real estate.

Case 3
Victor and Maria Consider Hedging an Investment with Puts

Victor and Maria Hernandez invested in 200 shares of Pharmacia Corporation common stock at $93 per share. They purchased the stock because the company is testing a new drug that may represent a significant medical breakthrough. The stock's value has already risen $8 in three months, in anticipation of the U.S. Food and Drug Administration's approval of the new drug. Many observers believe that the price of the stock could reach $120 if the drug is successful. If it does not prove to be the breakthrough anticipated, the price of the stock could drop back to the $85 range, or even lower. The Hernandezes are optimistic but feel that they should hedge their position a bit. As a result, they have decided to purchase two nine-month Pharmacia 100-share puts for $3 per share at a striking price of $93 per share. Ignore commissions when answering the following questions.

(a) What price would the Pharmacia stock need to reach for the Hernandezes to break even on their investment?

(b) How much would the Hernandezes gain if they sold the stock for $102 six months from now?

(c) How much would the return be as a percentage on an annualized basis?

(d) If the price of the stock dropped to $85 in six months, how much would the Hernandezes lose?

Case 4
The Johnsons Consider a Real Estate Investment

Harry and Belinda Johnson are considering purchasing a residential income property as an investment. The Johnsons want to achieve an after-tax total return of 10 percent. They are considering a property with an asking price of $190,000 that should produce $27,000 in gross rental income and $15,000 in net operating income.

(a) Calculate the present value of after-tax cash flow for the property, assuming that the after-tax cash-flow numbers are $8000 for the first year, $8400 for the second year, $8800 for the third year, $9200 for the fourth year, and $9600 for the fifth year, and that the selling price of the property will be $220,000 in five years. Prepare your information in a format similar to Table 16.3, using Appendix Table A.2 or the *Garman/Forgue* website to discount the future after-tax cash flows to their present values.

(b) Give the Johnsons your advice on whether they should invest in the property at its current price of $190,000.

On the 'Net

Go to the Web pages indicated to complete these exercises. You can also go to the *Garman/Forgue* website at college.hmco.com/business/students for an expanded list of exercises. Under General Business, select the title of this text. Click on the Internet Exercises link for this chapter.

1. Visit the website for the Chicago Board of Trade (www.cbot.com). In its Education section, use the tutorials and glossary to answer the following questions:
   (a) What is a futures contract?
   (b) What is the difference between a stock market and a futures exchange?
   (c) Browse the site further to learn about the commodities that are traded on the CBOT.
2. Visit the website for Investopedia.com. Search "reducing risk with options" at www.investopedia.com. There you will see an article on how option investing can serve to reduce risk. When might investors want to use options in their investment portfolios?

Visit the Garman/Forgue website...

@college.hmco.com/business/students

Under General Business, select *Personal Finance 9e*. There, among other valuable resources, you will find a complete glossary, ACE questions, links to help you complete the chapter exercises, and links to other personal finance sites.

PART 5

CHAPTER 17 Retirement Planning

CHAPTER 18 Estate Planning

CHAPTER 17

Retirement Planning

You Must Be Kidding, Right?

Lindsey Jones is 27 years old, and she recently took a new job. Lindsey had accumulated $6000 in her previous employer's 401(k) retirement plan, and she withdrew it to pay for her wedding. How much less money will Lindsey have at retirement at age 67 if she could have earned 9 percent on the $6000?

A. $6000 **B.** $24,000 **C.** $48,000 **D.** $188,000

The answer is D. Spending retirement money for discretionary purposes, instead of keeping it in a tax-deferred account where it can compound for many years, is unwise. The lesson is to keep your retirement money where it belongs!

LEARNING OBJECTIVES

After reading this chapter, you should be able to:

1. **Recognize** that you are solely responsible for funding your retirement and must sacrifice some current spending and invest for your future lifestyle.
2. **Estimate** your Social Security retirement income benefit.
3. **Calculate** your estimated retirement savings needs in today's dollars.
4. **Understand** why you should save for retirement within tax-sheltered retirement accounts.
5. **Distinguish** among the types of employer-sponsored retirement plans.
6. **Explain** the various types of personally established tax-sheltered retirement accounts.
7. **Recognize** that professional investment advice for retirement assets is available, including Monte Carlo simulations.
8. **Describe** techniques for living in retirement without running out of money.

What Do You Recommend?

Maryanne Johnson, age 32, worked for a previous employer for eight years. When she left that job, Maryanne left her retirement money (now worth $90,000) in that employer's defined-contribution plan. After getting divorced and remarried four years ago, she has been working as an assistant food services manager for a large convention center in Indianapolis, Indiana, earning $80,000 per year. Maryanne contributes $267 each month (4 percent of her salary) to her account in her employer's 401(k) retirement plan. Her current employer provides a 100 percent match for the first 4 percent of Maryanne's salary contributions. Today, Maryanne's 401(k) account balance is $21,000. Her investments are equally divided among three mutual funds: a growth fund, a value fund, and an S&P index fund.

Maryanne's husband, Bob, is permanently disabled, and most of his medical expenses are paid for through Maryanne's health benefits at work. Bob receives $1000 per month in disability insurance benefits, and he earns about $5000 per year as a freelance cartoonist. Maryanne is hoping that she and Bob can retire when she is age 55.

What do you recommend to Maryanne and Bob on the subject of retirement and estate planning regarding:

1. The major steps in the process to determine the amount of Maryanne and Bob's retirement savings goal?
2. How Bob's net income could be invested in a personal tax-sheltered retirement account?
3. The kinds of investment accounts into which they might put additional money over the next 23 years if they determined they needed $1 million to meet their retirement savings goal?
4. The investment strategies that Maryanne and Bob might follow for accumulating their retirement funds?

FOR HELP with studying this chapter, visit the Online Student Center:

www.college.hmco.com/pic/garman9e

Today's Americans are healthier, are better educated, will live longer, and have higher expectations than their counterparts from earlier generations. Your view may include retiring to a comfortable and happy life with little stress and lots of leisure. Enjoying financial security during your retirement years is not a matter of luck, as it takes planning and action. You must invest money you save during your working years, and do so wisely. Then when you no longer want to work or are unable, all your money can work for you.

To invest for your future lifestyle in retirement, you simply sacrifice some current spending. By starting early and contributing regularly, you can turn small monthly investments into hundreds, then thousands, and eventually millions of dollars over the years. You can have a lot of fun investing, but realize that building assets for retirement is serious business. While compiling this seemingly enormous sum may seem like an impossible proposition today, you can, and you need to do it.

retirement The time in life when the major sources of income change from earned income (such as salary or wages) to employer-based retirement benefits, private savings and investments, income from Social Security, and perhaps part-time employment.

Retirement Planning Is Your Responsibility

1 LEARNING OBJECTIVE

Recognize that you are solely responsible for funding your retirement and must sacrifice some current spending and invest for your future lifestyle.

Retirement is the time in life when the major sources of income change from earned income (such as salary or wages) to employer-based retirement benefits, private savings and investments, income from Social Security, and perhaps part-time employment. (See Figure 17.1.) Planning for retirement has changed dramatically in recent years. Yesterday's employer-provided pensions were commonly a reward for 30-plus years of working for one employer, but they are no longer widely available. Instead, most employers today offer "voluntary" retirement plans to which employees may or may not choose to contribute.

As a result, both the responsibility of investing funds for retirement and the risk of making poor investments with these funds has been shifted from the employer to the employee. You cannot count on your boss in retirement. You must accept the fact that you—and only you—are solely responsible for meeting your retirement needs.

On the day when your regular full-time paycheck stops, you are retired. If you have not saved enough money to enjoy the lifestyle you prefer, you will have to lower your level of living, continue working part time, or do both. Many of today's retirees continue to work part time because they need to supplement their retirement income, enjoy working, and want an employer's subsidized health care benefits. Others continue working simply because they must do so to survive. You may choose to save and invest for your retirement, or you can work forever.

Financial planners say that people need 80 to 100 percent of their pre-retirement gross income (along with Social Security) to meet their expenses in retirement and maintain their lifestyle. This amount includes what you have to pay in income taxes. Achieving this goal will be a big challenge, but it is one you can meet successfully. As the American Savings Education Council says, "You have the power to choose today how you will spend your retirement tomorrow."

To prepare for a financially successful retirement, you must build a sufficient amount of savings and investments to sup-

Good Money Habits in Retirement Planning

Make the following your money habits in retirement planning:

1. Save early and often by beginning early in life to invest in mutual funds through tax-sheltered retirement accounts and continuing to invest every year.
2. Take enough risk to increase the likelihood that you will have enough money in retirement.
3. Save within an employer-sponsored retirement plan at least the amount required to obtain the full matching contribution from your employer.
4. Diversify your investments and limit company stock to no more than 10 percent of your portfolio.
5. Contribute to Roth IRA and traditional IRA accounts to supplement your employer-sponsored plans.
6. Keep your hands off your retirement money. Do not borrow it. Do not withdraw it. When changing employers, roll over the funds into the new employer's plan or a rollover IRA.

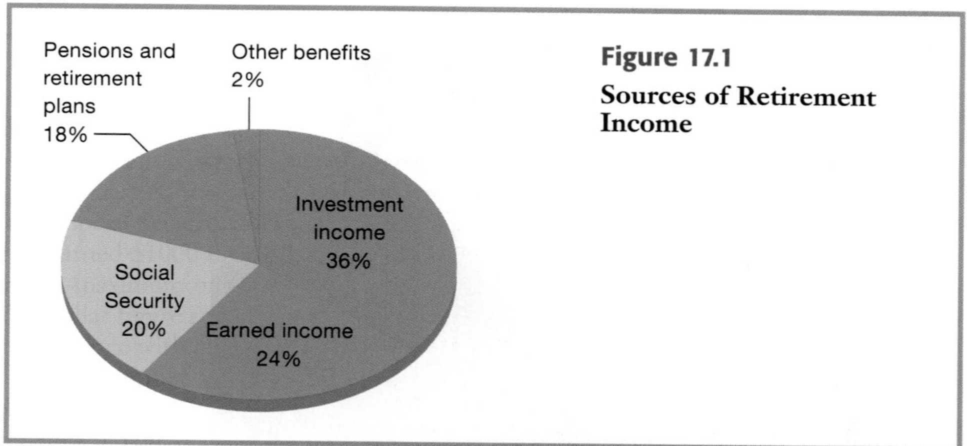

Figure 17.1
Sources of Retirement Income

plement other sources of income in retirement, such as monthly checks from the **Social Security Administration (SSA).** To succeed in this endeavor, during your 30 or 40 years in the workforce you must select among the various retirement plans and accounts that are available to you and adequately fund them through regular and consistent savings. You must make sound investment decisions regarding your retirement assets. You are advised to start early to save and invest for retirement and to continue this effort throughout your working years. You can then let the magical powers of compounding fully fund your needs and wants during the latter third of your life.

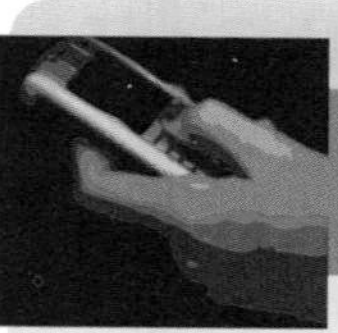

Instant Message

Cost of Delaying Saving for Retirement

Making steady contributions of $3000 every year to a tax-sheltered retirement account earning 8 percent annually for 30 years will accumulate to $340,000. Delaying 10 years before beginning to save accumulates only $137,000.

CONCEPT CHECK 17.1

1. Summarize why retirement planning has changed in recent years and has now become each individual's responsibility.
2. List some financial planning actions that individuals must do during their working life to prepare for retirement.
3. Comment on the cost of delaying saving for retirement.

Federal Insurance Contributions Act (FICA) Act that authorizes Social Security and Medicare tax withdrawals from employee paychecks; amounts withheld go into Social Security trust fund accounts, which pay benefits to current retirees.

Understanding Your Social Security Retirement Income Benefits

2 LEARNING OBJECTIVE
Estimate your Social Security retirement income benefit.

The Social Security program has become the most successful and popular domestic government program in U.S. history. Funding for Social Security benefits comes from a compulsory payroll tax split equally between employee and employer. Social Security taxes withheld from wages are called **FICA taxes** (named for the Federal Insurance Contributions Act). The amounts withheld are put into the Social Security trust fund accounts from which benefits are paid to current program recipients.

CHAPTER 18

Estate Planning

You Must Be Kidding, Right?

Michael and Jessica have two children. In addition, Michael has a child from his previous marriage to Ashley. Unfortunately, one day a big bus hit and killed Michael. The assets in his IRA and 401(k) accounts amount to $700,000. Who is likely to get the $700,000 now that Michael has died?

A. First wife, Ashley

B. Second wife, Jessica

C. Children of first or second wife

D. Michael's mother

The answer is D, Michael's mother. Why? If Michael was like many unmarried guys starting a career who designate their mothers as the beneficiary, his mom will get all the money if he neglected to change the beneficiary and designate either of his wives or his children on his retirement accounts. And his first wife, Ashley, would get all the money if, when Michael married Jessica, he failed to fill out the form to change the beneficiary designation to his second wife. As you can see, estate planning, like designating beneficiaries, is not just for old people!

LEARNING OBJECTIVES

After reading this chapter, you should be able to:

1 **Identify** the ways that your estate can be transferred through contracts and a will.

2 **Determine** how trusts can be used to transfer assets and reduce estate taxes.

3 **Summarize** the benefits of preparing advance directive documents.

4 **List** the questions and documents needed to simplify the settlement and transfer of your estate.

5 **Explain** the potential impact of estate and inheritance taxes.

What Do You Recommend?

Orlando Molina, age 34, the ballet master at a professional ballet company, recently remarried after being single for several years. He shares custody of his son with his first wife. Orlando married into a ready-made family: Giselle, his new wife, who was divorced from her husband two years ago, has two children, Jamie and Jon. Like many married couples, Orlando and Giselle, who is a modern dance choreographer, have a variety of financial assets. These include bank accounts, money market accounts, mutual fund accounts, 401(k) plans, Roth IRAs, and whole life insurance policies. They also plan to buy a larger home in the near future. Soon after they returned from their honeymoon, Orlando's father, who is only 56 years of age, had a serious stroke. Despite undergoing physical therapy, he is now in a nursing home and likely will reside there for the remainder of his life. The financial and emotional impacts of the elder Mr. Molina's illness have forced Orlando and Giselle to talk about some delicate financial circumstances in their own family.

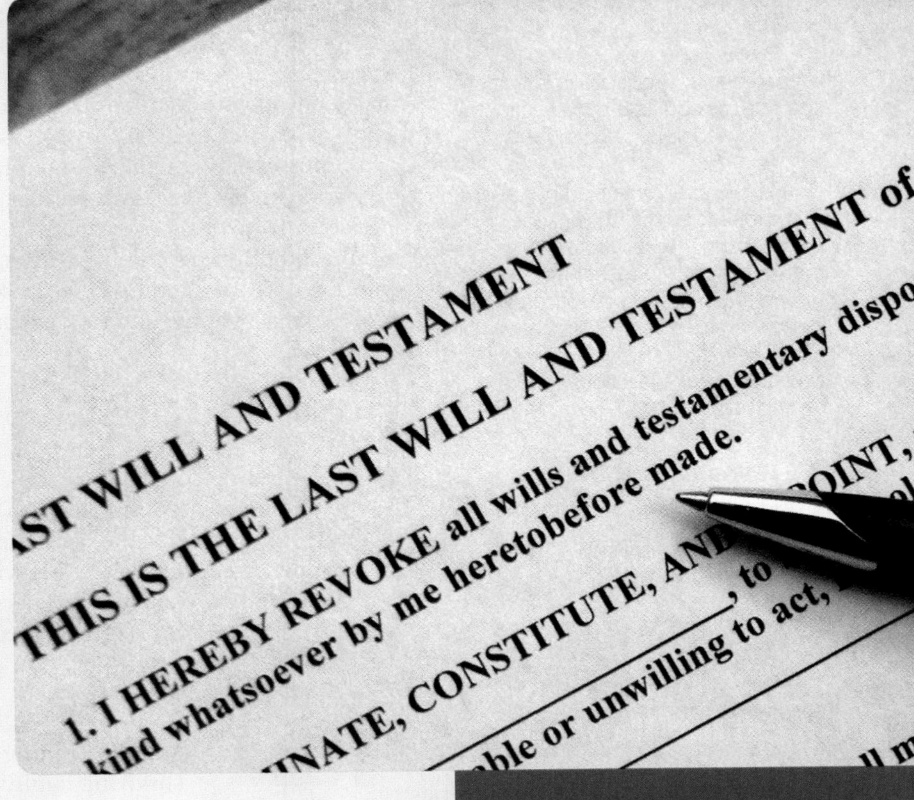

What do you recommend to Orlando and Giselle on the subject of estate planning regarding:

1. Beneficiary designations for their financial assets?
2. Joint ownership of their home, vehicles, and other property?
3. Making a will?
4. Establishing guardianship for the children?
5. Using advance directive documents to avoid a situation like that confronting Orlando's father?
6. Establishing trusts for their children?

FOR HELP with studying this chapter, visit the Online Student Center:

www.college.hmco.com/pic/garman9e

You will work hard over the course of your life to build an **estate.** Everyone has an estate. Your estate consist of your worldly possessions and financial wealth less any debts you owe. As this book amply illustrates, you can and should develop and execute plans for spending, for saving, for investing, for pre-retirement asset accumulation, for protection of those assets, and for the spend-down years of retirement. Now is the time to think about your final financial planning task, the plan to transfer your estate to others. College-educated people now in their 20s may have an estate worth $2 million or more at retirement. They will want to avoid having these assets become depleted because of an extended end-of-life hospital stay, mental incapacitation, or a catastrophic health problem. They also will want to have their estate transferred to the desired people and organizations at death.

This book's closing chapter offers guidance in making these transfers through proper estate planning. **Estate planning** comprises the definite arrangements you make during your lifetime that are consistent with your wishes for the administration, disposition, and transfer of your wealth and worldly possessions to your dependents and others when you die. Estate planning takes into consideration the needs of your survivors, making sure the greatest amount of the estate passes to the intended beneficiaries. It involves both financial and legal considerations, and a common goal is to minimize both taxes and legal costs. Protecting and transferring your estate can be an emotional process, and it is both smart and practical to take the fundamental steps while you are young and then update them as your life progresses.

estate planning Definite arrangements made during your lifetime that are consistent with your wishes for the administration, disposition, and transfer of your wealth and worldly possessions to your dependents and others when you die.

probate court Special court specifically charged to conduct the distribution of assets of people who have died.

probate Court-supervised process that allows creditors to present claims against an estate and ensures the transfer of a decedent's assets to the rightful beneficiaries according to a properly executed and valid will or, when no will exists, to the people, agencies, or organizations required by state law.

How Your Estate Is Transferred

1 LEARNING OBJECTIVE
Identify the ways that your estate can be transferred through contracts and a will.

The deceased person cannot "walk away" from his or her debts when death occurs. Before any money is distributed to heirs, state law requires that all of the deceased's creditors be notified of the death, usually by posting a notice in a local newspaper. In this manner, creditors can collect what they are owed from the estate. Surviving relatives have no personal obligation to repay the decedent's creditors for debts that exceed the assets of the estate.

Good Money Habits in Estate Planning

Make the following your money habits in estate planning:

1. Every three years or whenever your family situation changes, review the beneficiary and ownership designations in your life insurance policies, retirement plans, bank accounts, and other assets to make certain they will transfer the property according to your wishes.
2. Always have both an up-to-date will and a letter of last instructions and revise them as major life events occur.
3. Prepare and regularly update advance directive documents so others can make the right decisions for you if you become incapacitated.
4. Once a year, discuss with your spouse or significant other your family's financial and estate plans.
5. Be positive that certain family members or friends know where you keep financial records, advance directives, your will, and an estate planning checklist.

Probate

When planning for the disposal of your estate, realize that your surviving family members do not conduct the distribution of your assets after death. The distributions are either set up by you before your death or conducted by a **probate court**—a special court that is specifically charged to conduct the distribution of assets of people who have died. **Probate** is a court-supervised process that allows creditors to present claims against an estate and ensures the transfer of a decedent's assets to the rightful beneficiaries according to a properly executed and valid will or, when no will exists, to the people, agencies, or organizations required by state law.

Probate and Nonprobate Property

Figure 18.1 illustrates the different ways that your property can be distributed after your death. **Nonprobate property,** which does not go through probate, includes assets transferred to survivors by contract (such as naming a beneficiary for your retirement plan or with bank accounts owned with another person through joint tenancy with right of survivorship). Trusts (discussed in the next section) can also be used to transfer assets outside of probate.

The remaining probate property goes through the court-supervised probate process of publicly administering the disposition of an estate. A decedent's **probate property** consists of what

Figure 18.1

How Your Estate Is Distributed

YOUR ENTIRE ESTATE

Your nonprobate property is transferred at your death before your estate goes through probate court. These transfers can be implemented:	Your probate property is transferred by the probate court in accordance with:
By contracts you set up before death, such as: ▪ Beneficiary designations in life insurance and retirement plans ▪ Assets owned by joint ownership with rights of survivorship ▪ Payable-at-death clauses in bank accounts **By setting up trusts that designate who will receive the property at your death** ▪ Living trusts established while you are still alive ▪ Testamentary trusts designed to take effect at your death	**Your wishes as outlined in your will** **OR** **If you have no will, the intestate succession laws in your state**

the decedent owned individually and totally in his or her name, as well as the value of assets jointly owned through tenancy in common. In the latter case, the heirs will receive the deceased's share, but not the co-owner's share. In some states, the decedent's half of community property owned with a spouse is included in a person's estate. Avoiding probate may save some costs (the probate process can charge a fee based on the net worth of the deceased) and time and maintain privacy (the probate process is public). Also, the probate process can take between 4 and 18 months.

The proceeds of life insurance if payable to the estate of the deceased—exactly the wrong thing to do—(instead of being payable directly to beneficiaries) are included in one's estate as well. While the beneficiary does not have to pay income taxes on the life insurance proceeds, the amount is included in a person's estate for federal estate tax purposes if the deceased, while alive, retained any ownership interest, such as the right to change beneficiaries or to borrow against any cash value of the policy. Assigning ownership of the policy to someone else, such as the beneficiary, prior to death solves this problem.

Transfer Your Estate by Contracts

Described next are three ways to transfer by contract most or all of one's estate. (Trusts are a special form of contract that is discussed later in this chapter.) Transferring your estate by contract is an easy do-it-yourself project. You just have to take a few minutes of time to fill out the appropriate forms.

1. Transfers by Beneficiary Contract Designation The forms one fills out to open investment accounts or title certain assets often require a named beneficiary. Examples are IRAs, 401(k) plans, Keogh plans, bank and credit union accounts, stock brokerage accounts, mutual funds, and life and disability income insurance policies. A **beneficiary** is a person or organization designated to receive a benefit. A **beneficiary designation** is a legal form signed by the owner of an asset providing that the property goes to a certain person or organization in the event of the owner's death. The form also contains a place to designate a **contingent** (or **secondary**) **beneficiary** in case the first-named beneficiary has died. If no one has been named as beneficiary for a particular asset or if that person and a named contingent beneficiary have died, the property will go to one's estate and to probate court for distribution.

Retirement plan administrators are required by the Employee Retirement Income Security Act (ERISA) to pay benefits in the plan to the beneficiaries identified in the

beneficiary designation Legal form signed by the owner of an asset providing that the property goes to a certain person or organization in the event of the owner's death.

contingent beneficiary The beneficiary in case the first-named beneficiary has died; also called the secondary beneficiary.

.com, Kiplinger's WILLPower, LegalZoom, and Quicken WillMaker.*

If you die with a valid will, the probate court will transfer or distribute your property according to your wishes. A person who inherits or is entitled by law or by the terms of a will to inherit some asset is called an **heir.** A will that is properly drafted,

one can make minor changes to a will.

heir Person who inherits or is entitled by law or by the terms of a will to inherit some asset.

*Visit www.courttv.com/people/wills to see some wills of famous people.

plan documents. Some people leave retirement savings to parents or siblings and never update the forms. If the employee dies without changing the beneficiary, an ex-spouse might inherit all of the plan assets, even if state law views his children as the rightful heirs.

children or grandchildren that relate to the behavior of those assets?

Do the Numbers

1. Christopher Marcos, of Compton, California, died recently without a valid will. His probate estate for federal estate tax purposes was $3.2 million. Christopher's wife, Amanda, and three children were his only survivors. Answer the following questions, assuming that Christopher's state of residence followed the typical guidelines of division (one-half for the spouse with the children equally splitting the remainder):
   (a) What will be the proportional division of assets for the wife and children?
   (b) What dollar amount will be inherited by Amanda?
   (c) If Amanda now dies without a will, what will be the proportional division of assets, assuming that she has no other children?
   (d) If Amanda has personal assets (beyond her inheritance from Christopher) that have a fair market value of $400,000, when she dies, how much will her estate total?
   (e) Assuming Amanda's estate paid $15,000 for her funeral expenses, $14,000 for probate costs, and $180,000 to pay off the remaining debts and mortgages, what was Amanda's taxable estate?
2. Laura Kim of Southington, Connecticut, lives with her elderly grandmother, Haejeong. Her grandmother owns two profitable auto parts stores that are worth millions. Because current law has the federal estate tax going to zero in 2010, the pair is wondering how these taxes might affect Haejeong's estate. Laura hopes that her grandmother, who is in excellent health, lives at least another 20 years. If she doesn't, the federal estate tax will apply in all years except 2010. If Haejeong's probate estate is valued at $3.5 million, calculate the following:
   (a) The amount of the federal estate tax if she dies in 2008 (exclusion is $2 million; 45 percent tax rate)
   (b) The amount of the federal estate tax if she dies in 2010 (zero taxes)

Financial Planning Cases

Case 1
A Couple Considers the Ramifications of Dying Intestate

Melissa Merryweather of Savannah, Georgia, is a 34-year-old police detective earning $58,000 per year. She and her husband, Joshua, have two children in elementary school. They own a modestly furnished home and two late-model cars. Melissa also owns a snowmobile. Both spouses have 401(k) retirement accounts through their employers, and their employers also provide them with $50,000 group term life policies. Melissa also has a $50,000 term life policy of her own. The couple has about $5000 in their joint checking account. Neither has a will.

(a) List four negative things that could happen if either Melissa or Joshua were to die without a will.
(b) What would be the most important negative consequence of not having a will if both Melissa and Joshua were to die together in an accident?
(c) Which assets could be jointly owned so that they will automatically transfer to the other spouse if either Melissa or Joshua dies?
(d) What qualities should Melissa and Joshua look for when naming the executors of their wills?
(e) Once they have completed and signed their wills, where should the Merryweathers keep the original documents and any copies?

Case 2
A Lottery Winner Practices Estate Planning

Your good friend and next-door neighbor, Brandon, has just announced that he has the sole winning ticket in the $7 million lottery drawing of last week. Brandon is 60 years old and divorced. He has two adult children (Nicole and Heather) and four grandchildren. Recognizing that you are not an attorney, and knowing that your friend needs personal finance advice, offer some estate planning suggestions regarding the following points:

(a) Assume that Brandon's taxable estate now amounts to $7,200,000 and after the $2,000,000 exclusion, his remaining estate could be taxed at 20 percent. If he died tomorrow, how much would he owe? Give him that figure while offering him a single piece of advice.
(b) Name two types of trusts that Brandon might consider to reduce his eventual estate taxes and summarize what those trusts might help him accomplish.
(c) Offer some suggestions on how Brandon might use life insurance to avoid estate taxes.
(d) Offer Branson some suggestions for things he might want to put into his letter of last instructions.

Case 3
Victor and Maria Update Their Estate Plans

Since retiring earlier this year, Victor and Maria have found that their assets amount to approximately $800,000, made up of the following: Victor's half-interest in their home

($90,000), his tax-sheltered pension plan ($144,000), his stock ($56,000), his personal property ($50,000), Maria's half-interest in their home ($90,000), the inherited home from her mother ($120,000), her tax-sheltered pension plan ($112,000), the present value (obtained from Victor's employer) of the survivors benefits under her husband's defined-benefit pension plan ($60,000), personal property ($50,000), and her zero-coupon bonds ($28,000).

(a) Offer the Hernandezes advice about how each might establish a durable power of attorney.

(b) Should both Victor and Maria have living wills and medical powers of attorney? Why or why not?

(c) Victor purchased his $100,000 term life insurance policy through his employer, and he has been paying on his privately purchased $50,000 whole life insurance policy for many years (which now has a cash value of $30,000). Maria is listed as the beneficiary on both policies. Assuming that Victor owns both policies, what advice can you offer regarding ownership of the two policies?

(d) After adding up the value of the estate, what is the likelihood of having to pay federal estate taxes if Victor dies?

(e) Offer Victor and Maria some suggestions on how to ease the transfer of assets to their adult children and grandchildren while avoiding estate taxes.

Case 4
Belinda Johnson Helps Her Uncle Plan His Estate

Belinda Johnson has been approached by her uncle, Ryan Lawrence, who seeks advice about planning his estate. She has been handling some of Ryan's investments, and he trusts her judgment on financial matters. Ryan has a net worth of $2,340,000. At age 54, he is concerned about preparing his finances so that as much as possible of his estate will go to his heirs according to his wishes. Ryan has no will but has written down some of his ideas. He has no wife or children but wants to be able to provide for his mother, four nephews, Belinda, and a disabled sister.

(a) What is the first action Ryan should take in planning his estate?

(b) Why might an irrevocable living trust be a good idea for Ryan in providing for his mother and sister?

(c) What other types of trusts might Ryan use in his estate planning?

On the 'Net

Go to the Web pages indicated to complete these exercises. You can also go to the *Garman/Forgue* website at college.hmco.com/business/students for an expanded list of exercises. Under General Business, select the title of this text. Click on the Internet Exercises link for this chapter.

1. Visit the website for Legacy Writer at www.legacywriter.com. Click on "Living Wills," where you can begin the process of developing a living will and other advance directives. Finishing the process will require payment of a fee, but for this exercise simply answer the questions asked. After doing so, is an advance directive something you would consider? Why or why not?
2. Upon death, a person's will can become a public document through the probate process. Visit the Court TV website at http://www.courttv.com/archive/legaldocs/newsmakers/wills/, where the wills of some famous people have been posted. Select a person whose will interests you. Identify one of the estate planning techniques outlined in this chapter that were used by that person.
3. Visit the website for the Internal Revenue Service at http://www.irs.gov/formspubs/article/0,,id=112782,00.html, where you can find information on the federal gift and estate tax. Is this a tax you ever expect to pay? What are your views on this tax as an appropriate way to provide revenue to support government operations?

Visit the Garman/Forgue website...

@college.hmco.com/business/students

Under General Business, select *Personal Finance 9e.* There, among other valuable resources, you will find a complete glossary, ACE questions, links to help you complete the chapter exercises, and links to other personal finance sites.

APPENDIXES

APPENDIX A Present and Future Value Tables

APPENDIX B Estimating Social Security Benefits

APPENDIX C Glossary

Appendix A

Present and Future Value Tables

Many problems in personal finance involve decisions about money values at varying points in time. These values can be directly and fairly compared only when they are adjusted to a common point in time. Chapter 1 introduced the basic time value concepts. This appendix offers more details about the time value of money. In addition, it provides tables listing the future and present value of $1 with which to make calculations.

Four assumptions must be made to eliminate unnecessary complications:

1. Each planning period is one year long.
2. Only annual interest rates are considered.
3. Interest rates are the same during each of the annual periods.
4. Interest is compounded and continues earning a return in subsequent periods.

Tables of present and future values can be constructed to make these adjustments. **Future values** are derived from the principles of compounding the dollar values ahead in time. **Present values** are derived by discounting (which is the inverse of compounding) the dollar values and transferring them to an earlier point in time.

It is usually unnecessary to precisely identify whether the interest is paid/received at the *beginning* of a period or at the end of a period, or to know whether interest compounds daily or quarterly instead of annually. (These calculations require even more tables.) The following present and future value tables assume that money is accumulated, received, paid, compounded, or whatever at the *end* of a period. The tables can be used to compute the mathematics of personal finance with high certainty and to confirm (or reject as inaccurate) what people tell you about financial matters.

The most significant task is to find the correct table. Accordingly, each table is clearly described here, and illustrations of its use appear on the facing page where possible. In addition, the appropriate mathematical equation is shown and can be easily solved using a calculator.

Illustrations Using Table A.1: Future Value of a Single Amount ($1)

To use Table A.1 on page A-5, locate the future value factor for the time period and the interest rate.

1. You invest $500 at a 15 percent rate of return for 12 years. How much will you have at the end of that 12-year period?

   The future value factor is 5.350; hence, the solution is $500 × 5.350, or $2675.

2. Property values in your neighborhood are increasing at a rate of 5 percent per year. If your home is presently worth $90,000, what will its worth be in 7 years?

   The future value factor is 1.407; hence, the solution is $90,000 × 1.407, or $126,630.

3. You need to amass $40,000 in the next 10 years to make a balloon payment on your home mortgage. You have $17,000 available to invest. What annual interest rate must be earned to realize the $40,000?

   $40,000 ÷ $17,000 = 2.353. Read down the periods (n) column to 10 years and across to 2.367 (close enough), which is found under the 9 percent column. Hence, the $17,000 invested at 9 percent for 10 years will grow to a future value of slightly more than $40,000.

4. An apartment building is currently valued at $160,000, and it has been appreciating at 8 percent per year. If this rate continues, in how many years will it be worth $300,000?

   $300,000 ÷ $160,000 = 1.875. Read down the 8 percent column until you reach 1.851 (close enough to 1.875). This number corresponds to a period of 8 years. Hence, the $160,000 property appreciating at 8 percent annually will grow to a future value of $300,000 in slightly more than 8 years.

5. You have the choice of receiving a down payment from someone who wants to purchase your rental property as $15,000 today or as a personal note for $25,000 payable in 6 years. If you could expect to earn 8 percent on such funds, which is the better choice?

   The future value factor is 1.587; hence, the future value of $15,000 at 8 percent is $15,000 × 1.587, or $23,805. Thus, it would be better to take the note for $25,000.

6. How much will an automobile now priced at $20,000 cost in 4 years, assuming an annual inflation rate of 5 percent?

   Read down the 5 percent column and across the row for 4 years to locate the future value factor of 1.216. Hence, the solution is $20,000 × 1.216, or $24,320.

7. How large a lump-sum investment do you need now to have $20,000 available in 5 years, assuming a 10 percent annual rate of return?

   The $20,000 future value is divided by 1.611 (10 percent at 5 years), resulting in a current lump-sum investment of $12,415.

8. You have $5000 now and need $10,000 in 9 years.What rate of return is needed toreach that goal?

   Divide the future value of $10,000 by the present value of the lump sum of $5000 to obtain a future value factor of 2.0. In the row for 9 years, locate the future value factor of 1.999 (very close to 2.0). Read up the column to find that an 8 percent return on investment is needed.

9. How many years will it take your lump-sum investment of $10,000 to grow to $16,000, given an annual rate of return of 7 percent?

Divide the future value of $16,000 by the present value of the $10,000 lump sum to compute a future value factor of 1.6; look down the 7 percent column to find 1.606 (close enough). Read across the row to find that an investment period of 7 years is needed.

An alternative approach is to use a calculator to determine the future value, *FV*, of a sum of money invested today, assuming that the amount remains in the investment for a specified number of time periods (usually years) and that it earns a certain rate of return each period. The equation is

$$FV = PV\,(1.0 + i)^n \qquad \textbf{(A.1)}$$

where

FV = *Future Value*
PV = *Present Value* of the investment
i = *Interest* rate per period
n = *Number* of periods the PV is invested

Table A.1 Future Value of a Single Amount ($1 at the End of *n* Periods)
(Used to Compute the Compounded Future Value of a Known Lump Sum)

n	1%	2%	3%	4%	5%	6%	7%	8%	9%	10%	11%	12%	13%	14%	15%	16%	17%	18%	19%	20%
1	1.0100	1.0200	1.0300	1.0400	1.0500	1.0600	1.0700	1.0800	1.0900	1.1000	1.1100	1.1200	1.1300	1.1400	1.1500	1.1600	1.1700	1.1800	1.1900	1.2000
2	1.0201	1.0404	1.0609	1.0816	1.1025	1.1236	1.1449	1.1664	1.1881	1.2100	1.2321	1.2544	1.2769	1.2996	1.3225	1.3456	1.3689	1.3924	1.4161	1.4400
3	1.0303	1.0612	1.0927	1.1249	1.1576	1.1910	1.2250	1.2597	1.2950	1.3310	1.3676	1.4049	1.4429	1.4815	1.5209	1.5609	1.6016	1.6430	1.6852	1.7280
4	1.0406	1.0824	1.1255	1.1699	1.2155	1.2625	1.3108	1.3605	1.4116	1.4641	1.5181	1.5735	1.6305	1.6890	1.7490	1.8106	1.8739	1.9388	2.0053	2.0736
5	1.0510	1.1041	1.1593	1.2167	1.2763	1.3382	1.4026	1.4693	1.5386	1.6105	1.6851	1.7623	1.8424	1.9254	2.0114	2.1003	2.1924	2.2878	2.3864	2.4883
6	1.0615	1.1262	1.1941	1.2653	1.3401	1.4185	1.5007	1.5869	1.6771	1.7716	1.8704	1.9738	2.0820	2.1950	2.3131	2.4364	2.5652	2.6996	2.8398	2.9860
7	1.0721	1.1487	1.2299	1.3159	1.4071	1.5036	1.6058	1.7138	1.8280	1.9487	2.0762	2.2107	2.3526	2.5023	2.6600	2.8262	3.0012	3.1855	3.3793	3.5832
8	1.0829	1.1717	1.2668	1.3686	1.4775	1.5938	1.7182	1.8509	1.9926	2.1436	2.3045	2.4760	2.6584	2.8526	3.0590	3.2784	3.5115	3.7589	4.0214	4.2998
9	1.0937	1.1951	1.3048	1.4233	1.5513	1.6895	1.8385	1.9990	2.1719	2.3579	2.5580	2.7731	3.0040	3.2519	3.5179	3.8030	4.1084	4.4355	4.7854	5.1598
10	1.1046	1.2190	1.3439	1.4802	1.6289	1.7908	1.9672	2.1589	2.3674	2.5937	2.8394	3.1058	3.3946	3.7072	4.0456	4.4114	4.8068	5.2338	5.6947	6.1917
11	1.1157	1.2434	1.3842	1.5395	1.7103	1.8983	2.1049	2.3316	2.5804	2.8531	3.1518	3.4785	3.8359	4.2262	4.6524	5.1173	5.6240	6.1759	6.7767	7.4301
12	1.1268	1.2682	1.4258	1.6010	1.7959	2.0122	2.2522	2.5182	2.8127	3.1384	3.4985	3.8960	4.3345	4.8179	5.3503	5.9360	6.5801	7.2876	8.0642	8.9161
13	1.1381	1.2936	1.4685	1.6651	1.8856	2.1329	2.4098	2.7196	3.0658	3.4523	3.8833	4.3635	4.8980	5.4924	6.1528	6.8858	7.6987	8.5994	9.5964	10.6993
14	1.1495	1.3195	1.5126	1.7317	1.9799	2.2609	2.5785	2.9372	3.3417	3.7975	4.3104	4.8871	5.5348	6.2613	7.0757	7.9875	9.0075	10.1472	11.4198	12.8392
15	1.1610	1.3459	1.5580	1.8009	2.0789	2.3966	2.7590	3.1722	3.6425	4.1772	4.7846	5.4736	6.2543	7.1379	8.1371	9.2655	10.5387	11.9737	13.5895	15.4070
16	1.1726	1.3728	1.6047	1.8730	2.1829	2.5404	2.9522	3.4259	3.9703	4.5950	5.3109	6.1304	7.0673	8.1372	9.3576	10.7480	12.3303	14.1290	16.1715	18.4884
17	1.1843	1.4002	1.6528	1.9479	2.2920	2.6928	3.1588	3.7000	4.3276	5.0545	5.8951	6.8660	7.9861	9.2765	10.7613	12.4677	14.4265	16.6722	19.2441	22.1861
18	1.1961	1.4282	1.7024	2.0258	2.4066	2.8543	3.3799	3.9960	4.7171	5.5599	6.5436	7.6900	9.0243	10.5752	12.3755	14.4625	16.8790	19.6733	22.9005	26.6233
19	1.2081	1.4568	1.7535	2.1068	2.5270	3.0256	3.6165	4.3157	5.1417	6.1159	7.2633	8.6128	10.1974	12.0557	14.2318	16.7765	19.7484	23.2144	27.2516	31.9480
20	1.2202	1.4859	1.8061	2.1911	2.6533	3.2071	3.8697	4.6610	5.6044	6.7275	8.0623	9.6463	11.5231	13.7435	16.3665	19.4608	23.1056	27.3930	32.4294	38.3376
21	1.2324	1.5157	1.8603	2.2788	2.7860	3.3996	4.1406	5.0338	6.1088	7.4002	8.9492	10.8038	13.0211	15.6676	18.8215	22.5745	27.0336	32.3238	38.5910	46.0051
22	1.2447	1.5460	1.9161	2.3699	2.9253	3.6035	4.4304	5.4365	6.6586	8.1403	9.9336	12.1003	14.7138	17.8610	21.6447	26.1864	31.6293	38.1421	45.9233	55.2061
23	1.2572	1.5769	1.9736	2.4647	3.0715	3.8197	4.7405	5.8715	7.2579	8.9543	11.0263	13.5523	16.6266	20.3616	24.8915	30.3762	37.0062	45.0076	54.6487	66.2474
24	1.2697	1.6084	2.0328	2.5633	3.2251	4.0489	5.0724	6.3412	7.9111	9.8497	12.2392	15.1786	18.7881	23.2122	28.6252	35.2364	43.2973	53.1090	65.0320	79.4968
25	1.2824	1.6406	2.0938	2.6658	3.3864	4.2919	5.4274	6.8485	8.6231	10.8347	13.5855	17.0001	21.2305	26.4619	32.9190	40.8742	50.6578	62.6686	77.3881	95.3962
26	1.2953	1.6734	2.1566	2.7725	3.5557	4.5494	5.8074	7.3964	9.3992	11.9182	15.0799	19.0401	23.9905	30.1666	37.8568	47.4141	59.2697	73.9490	92.0918	114.4755
27	1.3082	1.7069	2.2213	2.8834	3.7335	4.8223	6.2139	7.9881	10.2451	13.1100	16.7386	21.3249	27.1093	34.3899	43.5353	55.0004	69.3455	87.2598	109.5893	137.3706
28	1.3213	1.7410	2.2879	2.9987	3.9201	5.1117	6.6488	8.6271	11.1671	14.4210	18.5799	23.8839	30.6335	39.2045	50.0656	63.8004	81.1342	102.9666	130.4112	164.8447
29	1.3345	1.7758	2.3566	3.1187	4.1161	5.4184	7.1143	9.3173	12.1722	15.8631	20.6237	26.7499	34.6158	44.6931	57.5755	74.0085	94.9271	121.5005	155.1893	197.8136
30	1.3478	1.8114	2.4273	3.2434	4.3219	5.7435	7.6123	10.0627	13.2677	17.4494	22.8923	29.9599	39.1159	50.9502	66.2118	85.8499	111.0647	143.3706	184.6753	237.3763
40	1.4889	2.2080	3.2620	4.8010	7.0400	10.2857	14.9745	21.7245	31.4094	45.2593	65.0009	93.0510	132.7816	188.8835	267.8635	378.7212	533.8687	750.3783	1051.668	1469.772
50	1.6446	2.6916	4.3839	7.1067	11.4674	18.4202	29.4570	46.9016	74.3575	117.3909	184.5648	289.0022	450.7359	700.2330	1083.657	1670.704	2566.215	3927.357	5988.914	9100.438

Illustrations Using Table A.4: Present Value of Series of Equal Amounts (an Annuity of $1 per Period)

To use this table, locate the present value factor for the time period and the interest rate.

1. You are entering into a contract that will provide you with an income of $1000 at the end of the year for the next 10 years. If the annual interest rate is 7 percent, what is the present value of that stream of payments?

   The present value factor is 7.024; hence, the solution is $1000 × 7.024, or $7024.

2. You expect to have $250,000 available in a retirement plan when you retire. If the amount invested yields 8 percent and you hope to live an additional 20 years, how much can you withdraw each year so that the fund will just be liquidated after 20 years?

   The present value factor for 20 years at 8 percent is 9.818. Hence, the solution is $250,000 ÷ 9.818, or $25,463.

3. You have received an inheritance of $60,000 that you invested so that it earns 9 percent. If you withdraw $8000 annually to supplement your income, in how many years will the fund run out?

   Solving for n, $60,000 ÷ $8000 = 7.5. Scan down the 9 percent column until you find a present value factor close to 7.5, which is 7.487. The row indicates 13 years; thus, the fund will be depleted in approximately 13 years with $8000 annual withdrawals.

4. A seller offers to finance the sale of a building to you as an investment. The mortgage loan of $280,000 will be for 20 years and requires an annual mortgage payment of $24,000. Should you finance the purchase through the seller or borrow the funds from a financial institution at a current rate of 10 percent?

   $280,000 ÷ $24,000 = 11.667. Scan down the periods (n) column to 20 years and then read across to locate the figure closest to 11.667, which is 11.470. The column indicates 6 percent; thus, seller financing offers a lower interest rate.

5. You have the opportunity to purchase an office building for $750,000 with an expected life of 20 years. Looking over the financial details, you see that the before-tax net rental income is $90,000. If you want a return of at least 15 percent, how much should you pay for the building?

   The present value factor for 20 years at 15 percent is 6.259, and $90,000 × 6.259 = $563,310. Thus, the price is too high for you to earn a return of 15 percent.

An alternative approach is to use a calculator to determine the present value, *PV*, of a stream of payments. The equation is

$$PV = \frac{[1.0 - 1.0\ /\ (1.0 + i)^n] \times A}{i} \tag{A.4}$$

where

PV = *Present Value* of the investment
i = *Interest* rate per period
n = *Number* of periods the PV is invested
A = *Amount* of the annuity

Table A.4 Present Value of a Series of Equal Amounts (an Annuity of $1 Received at the End of Each Period)
(Used to Compute the Discounted Present Value of a Stream of Income Payments)

n	1%	2%	3%	4%	5%	6%	7%	8%	9%	10%	11%	12%	13%	14%	15%	16%	17%	18%	19%	20%
1	0.9901	0.9804	0.9709	0.9615	0.9524	0.9434	0.9346	0.9259	0.9174	0.9091	0.9009	0.8929	0.8850	0.8772	0.8696	0.8621	0.8547	0.8475	0.8403	0.8333
2	1.9704	1.9416	1.9135	1.8861	1.8594	1.8334	1.8080	1.7833	1.7591	1.7355	1.7125	1.6901	1.6681	1.6467	1.6257	1.6052	1.5852	1.5656	1.5465	1.5278
3	2.9410	2.8839	2.8286	2.7751	2.7232	2.6730	2.6243	2.5771	2.5313	2.4869	2.4437	2.4018	2.3612	2.3216	2.2832	2.2459	2.2096	2.1743	2.1399	2.1065
4	3.9020	3.8077	3.7171	3.6299	3.5460	3.4651	3.3872	3.3121	3.2397	3.1699	3.1024	3.0373	2.9745	2.9137	2.8550	2.7982	2.7432	2.6901	2.6386	2.5887
5	4.8534	4.7135	4.5797	4.4518	4.3295	4.2124	4.1002	3.9927	3.8897	3.7908	3.6959	3.6048	3.5172	3.4331	3.3522	3.2743	3.1993	3.1272	3.0576	2.9906
6	5.7955	5.6014	5.4172	5.2421	5.0757	4.9173	4.7665	4.6229	4.4859	4.3553	4.2305	4.1114	3.9975	3.8887	3.7845	3.6847	3.5892	3.4976	3.4098	3.3255
7	6.7282	6.4720	6.2303	6.0021	5.7864	5.5824	5.3893	5.2064	5.0330	4.8684	4.7122	4.5638	4.4226	4.2883	4.1604	4.0386	3.9224	3.8115	3.7057	3.6046
8	7.6517	7.3255	7.0197	6.7327	6.4632	6.2098	5.9713	5.7466	5.5348	5.3349	5.1461	4.9676	4.7988	4.6389	4.4873	4.3436	4.2072	4.0776	3.9544	3.8372
9	8.5660	8.1622	7.7861	7.4353	7.1078	6.8017	6.5152	6.2469	5.9952	5.7590	5.5370	5.3282	5.1317	4.9464	4.7716	4.6065	4.4506	4.3030	4.1633	4.0310
10	9.4713	8.9826	8.5302	8.1109	7.7217	7.3601	7.0236	6.7101	6.4177	6.1446	5.8892	5.6502	5.4262	5.2161	5.0188	4.8332	4.6586	4.4941	4.3389	4.1925
11	10.3676	9.7868	9.2526	8.7605	8.3064	7.8869	7.4987	7.1390	6.8052	6.4951	6.2065	5.9377	5.6869	5.4527	5.2337	5.0286	4.8364	4.6560	4.4865	4.3271
12	11.2551	10.5753	9.9540	9.3851	8.8633	8.3838	7.9427	7.5361	7.1607	6.8137	6.4924	6.1944	5.9176	5.6603	5.4206	5.1971	4.9884	4.7932	4.6105	4.4392
13	12.1337	11.3484	10.6350	9.9856	9.3936	8.8527	8.3577	7.9038	7.4869	7.1034	6.7499	6.4235	6.1218	5.8424	5.5831	5.3423	5.1183	4.9095	4.7147	4.5327
14	13.0037	12.1062	11.2961	10.5631	9.8986	9.2950	8.7455	8.2442	7.7862	7.3667	6.9819	6.6282	6.3025	6.0021	5.7245	5.4675	5.2293	5.0081	4.8023	4.6106
15	13.8651	12.8493	11.9379	11.1184	10.3797	9.7122	9.1079	8.5595	8.0607	7.6061	7.1909	6.8109	6.4624	6.1422	5.8474	5.5755	5.3242	5.0916	4.8759	4.6755
16	14.7179	13.5777	12.5611	11.6523	10.8378	10.1059	9.4466	8.8514	8.3126	7.8237	7.3792	6.9740	6.6039	6.2651	5.9542	5.6685	5.4053	5.1624	4.9377	4.7296
17	15.5623	14.2919	13.1661	12.1657	11.2741	10.4773	9.7632	9.1216	8.5436	8.0216	7.5488	7.1196	6.7291	6.3729	6.0472	5.7487	5.4746	5.2223	4.9897	4.7746
18	16.3983	14.9920	13.7535	12.6593	11.6896	10.8276	10.0591	9.3719	8.7556	8.2014	7.7016	7.2497	6.8399	6.4674	6.1280	5.8178	5.5339	5.2732	5.0333	4.8122
19	17.2260	15.6785	14.3238	13.1339	12.0853	11.1581	10.3356	9.6036	8.9501	8.3649	7.8393	7.3658	6.9380	6.5504	6.1982	5.8775	5.5845	5.3162	5.0700	4.8435
20	18.0456	16.3514	14.8775	13.5903	12.4622	11.4699	10.5940	9.8181	9.1285	8.5136	7.9633	7.4694	7.0248	6.6231	6.2593	5.9288	5.6278	5.3527	5.1009	4.8696
21	18.8570	17.0112	15.4150	14.0292	12.8212	11.7641	10.8355	10.0168	9.2922	8.6487	8.0751	7.5620	7.1016	6.6870	6.3125	5.9731	5.6648	5.3837	5.1268	4.8913
22	19.6604	17.6580	15.9369	14.4511	13.1630	12.0416	11.0612	10.2007	9.4424	8.7715	8.1757	7.6446	7.1695	6.7429	6.3587	6.0113	5.6964	5.4099	5.1486	4.9094
23	20.4558	18.2922	16.4436	14.8568	13.4886	12.3034	11.2722	10.3711	9.5802	8.8832	8.2664	7.7184	7.2297	6.7921	6.3988	6.0442	5.7234	5.4321	5.1668	4.9245
24	21.2434	18.9139	16.9355	15.2470	13.7986	12.5504	11.4693	10.5288	9.7066	8.9847	8.3481	7.7843	7.2829	6.8351	6.4338	6.0726	5.7465	5.4509	5.1822	4.9371
25	22.0232	19.5235	17.4131	15.6221	14.0939	12.7834	11.6536	10.6748	9.8226	9.0770	8.4217	7.8431	7.3300	6.8729	6.4641	6.0971	5.7662	5.4669	5.1951	4.9476
26	22.7952	20.1210	17.8768	15.9828	14.3752	13.0032	11.8258	10.8100	9.9290	9.1609	8.4881	7.8957	7.3717	6.9061	6.4906	6.1182	5.7831	5.4804	5.2060	4.9563
27	23.5596	20.7069	18.3270	16.3296	14.6430	13.2105	11.9867	10.9352	10.0266	9.2372	8.5478	7.9426	7.4086	6.9352	6.5135	6.1364	5.7975	5.4919	5.2151	4.9636
28	24.3164	21.2813	18.7641	16.6631	14.8981	13.4062	12.1371	11.0511	10.1161	9.3066	8.6016	7.9844	7.4412	6.9607	6.5335	6.1520	5.8099	5.5016	5.2228	4.9697
29	25.0658	21.8444	19.1885	16.9837	15.1411	13.5907	12.2777	11.1584	10.1983	9.3696	8.6501	8.0218	7.4701	6.9830	6.5509	6.1656	5.8204	5.5098	5.2292	4.9747
30	25.8077	22.3965	19.6004	17.2920	15.3725	13.7648	12.4090	11.2578	10.2737	9.4269	8.6938	8.0552	7.4957	7.0027	6.5660	6.1772	5.8294	5.5168	5.2347	4.9789
40	32.8347	27.3555	23.1148	19.7928	17.1591	15.0463	13.3317	11.9246	10.7574	9.7791	8.9511	8.2438	7.6344	7.1050	6.6418	6.2335	5.8713	5.5482	5.2582	4.9966
50	39.1961	31.4236	25.7298	21.4822	18.2559	15.7619	13.8007	12.2335	10.9617	9.9148	9.0417	8.3045	7.6752	7.1327	6.6605	6.2463	5.8801	5.5541	5.2623	4.9995

Appendix B

Estimating Social Security Benefits

The Social Security Administration (SSA) provides basic benefits for your retirement, for a period of disability, or for your survivors. To qualify, you must have earned the number of credits required for each benefit program. Once you qualify, the level of benefits received is based on your income in years past that was subject to the Federal Insurance Contributions Act (FICA) taxes, commonly known as Social Security taxes. Benefits increase each year based on a cost of living adjustment (COLA) announced by the SSA each October for the following year. Over the past ten years, COLA adjustments have averaged 2.6 percent. The discussion and Table B.1 provide the authors' estimates of Social Security benefits for 2008 for various income levels using calculators found at http://www.ssa.gov/planners/calculators.htm. The amounts are for a 30-year-old worker but would not differ significantly for workers ten years older or younger.

Social Security Retirement Benefits

To qualify for Social Security retirement benefits, any worker born after 1928 must have earned 40 credits of coverage. As noted in the text, it is possible to receive a maximum of four credits per year. In 2007 a worker would earn one credit for each $1000 of income subject to Social Security taxes (this figure is adjusted upward each year for inflation). Dependent children, spouses caring for dependent children, and retired spouses at age 62 (including former spouses if the marriage lasted at least ten years) may also collect benefits based on the eligibility of the retired worker.

You can use Table B.1 to estimate a person's Social Security retirement benefits in today's dollars, assuming the retiree worked steadily, received average pay raises, and retired at the full-benefit retirement age. If more than one person would receive a benefit under the retiree's account (retiree and spouse, for example), the amount of the second person's benefit would be one-half of the retiree's benefit, giving a couple a total benefit 50 percent higher than the individual figure listed in Table B.1.

Social Security Disability Benefits

Social Security will pay disability benefits to an insured worker, dependent children up to age 18 (or 19 if the child is still in high school), a spouse caring for a dependent child who is younger than age 16 or disabled, and a spouse (even if divorced, but not remarried, provided that the marriage lasted ten years) age 62 or older. The benefit amount depends on two factors. The first factor is the eligibility of the disabled worker. To qualify for disability benefits, workers need at least 40 credits of coverage under Social Security, with at least 20 of the credits attained in the previous ten years (depending on year of birth). A worker younger than age 31 must have attained at least six credits or one more than one-half of the total credits possible after age 21, whichever is greater. (For example, a 26-year-old worker would have five years, or 20 credits, possible and would need ten credits of coverage.) The second factor affecting benefit levels is the predisability income of the covered individual that was subject to the FICA tax.

You can use Table B.1 to estimate an individual's Social Security disability benefits, assuming the disabled person worked steadily and received average pay raises. To obtain figures more specific than those given in Table B.1, contact the Social Security Administration to obtain your Social Security Statement as described in Chapter 17 or log on to http://www.ssa.gov/mystatement/ or http://www.ssa.gov/planners/calculators.htm.

Social Security Survivors Benefits

Social Security will pay benefits to surviving children younger than age 18 (or 19 if the child is still in high school), to a surviving spouse (even if divorced from the deceased, but not remarried) caring for surviving children who are younger than age 16, and to a surviving spouse (even if divorced, if the marriage lasted at least ten years) age 60 or older. Two factors are important in such cases. The first factor is the eligibility of the covered worker. The deceased worker who has accrued at least 40 credits of coverage is considered to be "fully insured." Workers who have earned at least as many credits of coverage as years since turning age 21 will be fully insured as well. Other individuals may be considered "currently insured" if they have earned six credits of coverage out of the previous 13 possible calendar credits. The survivors of currently insured workers receive limited types of benefits compared with those available to fully insured workers. The second factor is the covered worker's level of earnings, as indicated in Table B.1.

You can use Table B.1 to estimate monthly survivors benefits from Social Security in today's dollars for eligible surviving family members. The table assumes that the deceased worker worked steadily and received average pay raises.

Table B.1 Estimates* of Social Security Benefits for the Three Major Social Security Programs

	Current Annual Earnings					
	$25,000	**$35,000**	**$45,000**	**$55,000**	**$70,000**	**$90,000**
Monthly Retirement Benefits at Age 67 in Today's Dollars						
Per month	$ 1,092	$ 1,367	$ 1,642	$ 1,831	$ 2,025	$ 2,282
Per year	$13,104	$16,404	$19,704	$21,972	$24,300	$ 27,284
As a percentage of income	52.4%	46.9%	43.8%	40.0%	34.7%	30.4%
Monthly Retirement Benefits at Age 67 in Future Dollars						
Per month	$ 4,034	$ 5,021	$ 6,007	$6,882	$ 7,576	$ 8,501
Per year	$48,408	$60,252	$72,084	$82,584	$90,912	$102,012
Monthly Disability Benefits If You Became Disabled in 2008						
Individual benefit per month	$ 993	$ 1,234	$ 1,467	$ 1,700	$ 1,896	$ 2,117
Individual benefit per year	$11,916	$14,808	$17,604	$20,400	$22,752	$ 25,404
As a percentage of income	47.7%	42.3%	39.1%	37.1%	32.5%	28.2%
Maximum family benefit per month	$ 1,688	$ 2,091	$ 2,494	$ 2,890	$ 3,223	$ 3,599
Maximum family benefit per year	$20,256	$25,092	$29,928	$34,680	$38,676	$ 43,188
Monthly Survivors Benefits If You Died in 2008						
Individual benefit per month†	$ 766	$ 952	$ 1,136	$ 1,307	$ 1,449	$ 1,623
Individual benefit per year	$ 9,192	$11,424	$13,632	$15,684	$17,388	$ 19,476
As a percentage of income	36.7%	32.6%	30.3%	28.5%	24.8%	21.6%
Maximum family benefit per month	$ 1,687	$ 2,360	$ 2,722	$ 3,081	$ 3,384	$ 3,788
Maximum family benefit per year	$20,244	$28,320	$32,664	$36,972	$40,608	$ 45,456

* Authors' estimates in today's dollars for a 30-year-old worker using Social Security Administration website calculators.
†A surviving spouse age 65 or older would receive a retirement benefit approximately one-third higher than these figures.

Glossary

above-the-line deductions Adjustments subtracted from gross income whether taxpayer itemizes deductions or not.

abstract Detailed written history of the ownership of a piece of property.

acceleration clause Part of a credit contract stating that after a specific number of payments are unpaid (often just one), the loan is considered in default and all remaining installments are due and payable upon demand of the creditor.

accident insurance Pays a specific amount per day—for example, $100 for a hospital stay arising out of an accident—or a specific amount for the loss of certain limbs or body parts.

account reconciliation Comparing your records with your bank's records, checking the accuracy of both sets of records, and identifying any errors.

acquisition fee Pays for a credit report, application fee, and other paperwork, either in cash or included in the gross cap cost.

active investor An investor who wishes to manage her own account by carefully studying the economy, market trends, and investment alternatives; regularly monitoring these factors; and buying and selling three to four times a year, with or without the advice of a professional.

activities of daily living (ADLs) Insurance companies use the inability to perform a certain number of such activities as a criterion for deciding when the insured becomes eligible for long-term care benefits.

actual cash value (of personal property) Represents the purchase price of the property less depreciation.

add-on interest method Interest is calculated by applying an interest rate to the amount borrowed times the number of years to arrive at the total interest to be charged.

add-on loans/flipping Occurs when you refinance or rewrite a loan for a larger amount before it has been completely repaid.

adjustable life insurance Allows the owner of a policy to modify one of the three cornerstones of cash-value policies—the premium, the policy face amount, and the rate of cash-value accumulation—with corresponding changes occurring in the other two.

adjustable-rate mortgage (ARM)/variable-rate mortgage Mortgage in which the borrower's interest rate fluctuates according to some index of interest rates based on the rising or falling cost of credit in the economy—thus transferring interest rate risk to the borrower.

adjusted capitalized cost (adjusted cap cost) Subtracting the capitalized cost reductions from the gross capitalized cost.

adjusted gross income (AGI) Gross income less any exclusions and adjustments.

adjustments to income Allowable subtractions from gross income.

adoption tax credit A nonrefundable income tax credit of up to $11,390 based on qualifying costs of the adoption of a child.

advance medical directive Statement of medical preferences, including designation of surrogate decision maker if patients become unable to make medical decisions for themselves in case of coma, dementia, or brain death.

affinity card Standard bank credit cards with the logo of a sponsoring organization imprinted on the face of the card.

after-tax dollars Money on which employee has already paid taxes.

after-tax money Funds put into regular investment accounts; subject to income taxes.

after-tax profit Money left over after a firm has paid expenses, bondholder interest, and taxes.

after-tax yield Percentage yield on taxable investment after subtracting effects of federal income taxes.

aggressive growth funds Make investments in speculative stocks with volatile price swings, seeking the greatest long-term capital appreciation possible. Also known as maximum capital gains funds and capital appreciation funds.

aggressive investment philosophy Investors with this philosophy primarily seek capital gains, often with a short time horizon.

all-risk (open-perils) policies Cover losses caused by all perils other than those that the policy specifically excludes.

alpha statistic Quantifies the difference between an investment's expected return and its actual recent performance (outperforming or underperforming) given its risk; positive values indicate better-than-market performance.

alternative dispute resolution programs Industry- or government-sponsored programs that provide an avenue to resolve disputes outside the formal court system.

alternative minimum tax (AMT) Tax rate (26 or 28 percent) triggered for people with excessive deductions.

amortization Loan repayment method in which part of the payment goes to pay interest and part goes to repay principal. Extra payments toward principal shorten the life of the loan and decrease total amount of interest paid.

amortization schedule List that shows all the monthly payments, the portions that will go toward interest and principal, and the debt remaining after each payment is made throughout the life of the loan.

annual fees Charges levied against cardholders for the privilege of having an open account but that are not included in the advertised APR.

annual fund operating expenses Normal operating costs of the business that are deducted from fund assets before shareholders receive earnings.

annual limits Specify the maximum payment under a medical care plan for covered expenses occurring within one year.

annual percentage rate (APR) The cost of credit on a yearly basis as a percentage rate.

annual percentage yield (APY) Return on total interest received on $100 deposit for 365-day period, given institution's simple annual interest rate and compounding frequency.

annual report Legally required yearly report about financial performance, activities, and prospects sent to major stockholders and made available to the general public.

annuitant Person covered by an annuity who is to receive the benefits.

annuity A stream of payments to be received in the future.

any-occupation policy Provides full benefits only if you cannot perform any occupation.

appraisal fee Fee charged for a professionally prepared estimate of the fair market value of the real estate property by an objective party.

aptitudes The natural abilities and talents that individuals possess.

arbitration Dispute resolution process in which a neutral third party hears (or reads) claims made and positions taken by the parties to the dispute and then issues a ruling that is binding on one or both parties.

"as is" Way for seller to get around legal requirements for warranties; buyer takes all risk of nonperformance or other problems despite any salesperson's verbal assurances.

ask price Declared lowest price that anyone is willing to accept to sell a security.

assessed value Price that local authorities place on your home as used to calculate property taxes.

asset Property owned by a taxpayer for personal use or as an investment that has monetary value.

asset allocation Form of diversification in which investor decides on proportions of an investment portfolio that will be devoted to various categories of assets.

asset allocation funds Invest in a mix of assets (usually stocks, bonds, and cash equivalents and sometimes international assets, gold, and real estate); they buy and sell regularly to reduce risk while trying to outperform the market.

asset management account (AMA, central asset accounts, or all-in-one account) Multiple-purpose, coordinated package that gathers most monetary asset management [illegible] a unified account and reports activit[illegible] monthly statement to the client.

asset-to-debt ratio Compares total assets with total liabilities.

assumable mortgage Buyer pays the seller a down payment generally equal to the seller's equity in the home and takes responsibility for the mortgage loan payments for the remaining term of the seller's existing mortgage loan.

ATM cards Allow deposits and withdrawals into an account and transfers among checking and savings accounts using a PIN at an ATM.

ATM transaction fee Payments levied each time an ATM is used.

automatic enrollment plan Plan in which the employer withholds up to 6 percent (and sometimes more) of an employee's salary and places it into a defined-contribution retirement plan account.

automatic funds transfer agreement Agreement whereby the amount necessary to cover a bad check will be transmitted from your savings account to your checking account.

automatic investment program (AIP) Agreement by which a mutual fund is authorized to withdraw money from your checking account, perhaps monthly, to buy mutual fund shares.

automatic overdraft loan agreement Arrangement whereby the amount necessary to cover a bad check will be automatically loaned to you by your bank or charged to your Visa or MasterCard account as a cash advance.

automatic premium loan Life insurance policy provision that allows any premium not paid by the end of the grace period to be paid automatically with a policy loan if sufficient cash value or dividends have accumulated.

automatic reinvestment When investors choose to automatically reinvest any interest, dividends, and capital gains payments to purchase additional fund shares.

automobile bodily injury liability Occurs when a driver or car owner is held legally responsible for bodily injury losses that other people, including pedestrians, suffer.

automobile insurance Combines the liability and property insurance coverages that most car owners and drivers need into a single-package policy.

automobile medical payments insurance Insurance that covers bodily injury losses suffered by the driver of the insured vehicle and any passengers, regardless of who is at fault.

automobile property damage liability Occurs when a driver or car owner is held legally responsible for damage to others' property.

average daily balance Sum of the outstanding balances owed each day during the billing period divided by the number of days in the period.

average share cost Actual cost basis of the investment used for income tax purposes, calculated by dividing the total amount invested by the total shares purchased.

average share price Calculated by dividing the share price total by the number of investment periods.

average-balance account Checking account for which service fees are assessed if the account's average daily balance drops below a certain level during specified time.

average tax rate Proportion of total income paid in income taxes.

back-end ratio Compares the total of all monthly PITI expenditures plus auto loans and other debts with gross monthly income.

balance sheet (or net worth statement) Snapshot of assets, liabilities, and net worth on a particular date.

bad check A check written for which there were insufficient funds in the account.

balance transfer Full or partial payment on the balance of one credit card using a cash advance from another.

balanced funds Keep a set mix of stocks and bonds, often 60 percent stocks and 40 percent bonds, in order to earn a well-balanced return of income and long-term capital gains.

balloon automobile loan A loan that has a low monthly payment similar in amount to that required if the vehicle had been leased and with a large final payment similar in amount to the residual value under a lease.

bank credit card account Open-ended credit account with a financial institution that allows the holder to make purchases almost anywhere.

Bank Insurance Fund (BIF) of the Federal Deposit Insurance Corporation (FDIC) Federal agency that insures deposits in federally chartered banks against loss up to $100,000 per account.

bankruptcy Constitutionally guaranteed right that permits people (and businesses) to ask a court to find them officially unable to meet their debts.

basic (homeowner's insurance) form (HO-1) Named-perils policy that covers 11 property-damage–causing perils and provides three areas of liability-related protection: personal liability, property damage liability, and medical payments.

basic liquidity ratio Number of months you could meet expenses using only monetary assets if all income ceases.

basic retirement benefit/primary insurance amount Amount of Social Security benefits a worker would receive at his or her full-benefit retirement age, which is 67 for those born after 1960.

bear market Market in which securities prices have declined in value by 20 percent or more from previous highs, often over the course of several weeks or months.

below-average costs "Averaging" means that you purchase more shares when the price is down and fewer shares when the price is high, so most of your shares are purchased at below-average cost.

beneficiary A person or organization designated to receive a benefit.

beneficiary designation Legal form signed by the owner of an asset providing that the property goes to a certain person or organization in the event of the owner's death.

benefit amount Long-term care plans are generally written to provide a specific dollar benefit per day of care.

benefit period Length of time that the individual for whom a policy is written would likely need the care.

best buy Product or service that, in the buyer's opinion, represents acceptable quality at a fair or low price for that quality level.

beta/beta value/beta coefficient A measure of stock volatility; that is, how much the stock price varies relative to the rest of the market.

bid price Declared highest price anyone wants to pay for a security.

billing cycle Time from one billing date to the next for a credit account.

billing/closing/statement date The last day for which any transactions are reported on the credit statement.

binder Temporary insurance contract replaced later by written policy.

biweekly mortgage GEM that calls for payments of half of the normal payment to be made every two weeks; the borrower thus makes 26 payments a year and reduces the principal amount by one full payment each year; this reduces the mortgage term to about 20 years on a 30-year mortgage.

blank endorsement Check that shows only the payee's signature on the back, making it a bearer instrument that anyone can cash.

board of directors Individuals who set policy and name the principal officers of the company.

bond A debt instrument issued by an organization that promises repayment at a specific time and the right to receive regular interest payments during the life of the bond; from investor's standpoint, a loan that the investor makes to a government or a corporation.

bond funds These fixed-income funds aim to earn current income higher than a money market fund without incurring undue risk by investing in a portfolio of bonds and other low-risk investments that pay high dividends and offer capital appreciation.

bond rating An impartial outsider's opinion of the quality—or creditworthiness—of the issuing organization.

book value per share Reflects the book value of a company divided by the number of shares of common stock outstanding.

book value/shareholder's equity Net worth of a company, determined by subtracting total liabilities from assets.

book-entry form Bond certificates aren't issued; rather, account is set up in name of the issuing organization or the brokerage firm that sold the bond, and interest is paid to the bondholder when due.

bounce protection agreement Bank will honor checks written against insufficient funds up to a certain limit and charge customer for each check written.

breakeven price Price at which the cost of a contract is negated by a profit (or the cost is reduced by hedging a loss).

breakpoints Investment levels required to obtain a reduced sales load; start at $10,000.

broad (homeowner's insurance) form (HO-2) Named-perils policy that covers 18 property-damage–causing perils and provides protection from three liability-related exposures.

broker/dealer Financial intermediary that not only buys and sells securities but also makes a market in one or more of the stocks listed on the OTC.

broker's commission Largest selling cost in selling a home; these commissions often amount to 6 percent of the selling price of the home.

brokered certificates of deposit CDs purchased through a stock brokerage firm.

budget Paper or electronic document used to record both planned and actual income and expenditures over a period of time.

budget estimates Projected dollar amounts to receive or spend in a budgeting period.

budget exceptions When budget estimates differ from actual expenditures.

budget variance Difference between amount budgeted and actual amount spent or received.

bull market Market in which securities prices have risen 20 percent or more over time.

bump-up CDs Allow savers to bump up interest rate once if rates rise and to add up to 100 percent of initial deposit whenever desired.

bunching deductions For taxpayers who do not meet floor for itemizing deductions every year, strategy of prepaying expenses in one year so that itemizing works every other year.

business cycle/economic cycle Business cycles can be depicted as a wavelike pattern of rising and falling economic activity; the phases of the business cycle include expansion, peak, contraction (which may turn into recession), and trough.

business-cycle risk The chance that an economic downturn will affect an investment's value.

buy and hold/buy to hold Investment strategy in which investors buy a widely diversified mix of stocks and/or mutual funds, reinvest the dividends by buying more stocks and mutual funds, and hold on to those investments almost indefinitely.

buyer's agent Serves as the buyer's representative in the real estate negotiations and transaction.

buyer's orders Written offer that names a specific vehicle and all charges; only sign such offers after the salesperson and sales manager have signed *first*.

buying long Buying a security (especially on margin) with the hope that the stock price will rise.

call option Gives option holder the right to buy the optioned asset from the option writer at the striking price at any time before the expiration date.

canceled check A check that has been paid to the payee and returned to the writer as a record that the check has been paid.

capital accumulation The process of building wealth.

capital gain Increase in the value of an initial investment (less costs) realized upon the sale of the investment.

capital gains distributions Represent the net gains (capital gains minus capital losses) that a fund realizes when it sells securities that were held in the fund's portfolio.

capital improvements Costs incurred in making value-enhancing changes (beyond maintenance and repair) in real property.

capital loss Decrease in paper value of an initial investment; only realized if sold.

capitalized cost reductions (cap cost reductions) Monies paid on the lease at its inception, including any down payments, trade-in values, or rebates.

card registration service Firm that will notify all companies with which you have debit and credit cards if your cards are lost or stolen.

card verification value The three- or four-digit code on the signature strip on the back of credit cards.

career fairs University-, community- and employer-sponsored events for job seekers to meet with many employers quickly to screen potential employers.

career goal Identifying what you want to do for a living, whether a specific job or field of employment.

career planning Finding employment that will use your interests and abilities and that will support you financially.

cash account A brokerage account that requires an initial deposit (perhaps as little as $100) and specifies that full settlement is due to the brokerage firm within three business days after a buy or sell order has been given.

cash advance The use of a credit card to obtain cash rather than to make a purchase.

cash advance (or convenience) checks A check-equivalent way to take a cash advance on a credit card.

cash basis Only transactions involving actual money received or money spent are recorded.

cash dividend Cash profits that a firm distributes to stockholders.

cash flow Amount of rental income you have left after paying all operating expenses.

cash loan Credit situation in which the borrower receives cash and then uses it to make purchases, pay off other loans, or make investments.

cash surrender value Represents the cash value of a life insurance policy minus any surrender charges.

cash value Represents the value of the investment element in a cash-value life insurance policy.

cash-balance plan Defined-benefit plan funded solely by an employer that gives each participant an interest-earning account credited with a percentage of pay on a monthly basis.

cash-flow calendar Budget estimates for monthly income and expenses.

cash-flow statement (or income and expense statement) Summary of all income and expense transactions over a specific time period.

cashier's checks A check made out to a specific party and drawn on the financial institution's account itself; thus, it is backed by the institution's finances.

cash-value life insurance Pays benefits at death and includes a savings/investment element that can provide a reduced level of benefits to the policyholder prior to the death of the insured person.

catch-up provision Permits workers age 50 or older to contribute an additional $5000 to most employer-sponsored plans ($1000 limit on IRA accounts).

certificate of deposit (CD) An interest-earning savings instrument purchased for a fixed period of time.

certificate of insurance Paper or booklet that outlines group health insurance benefits.

certified check Personal check on which your financial institution imprints the word *certified*, signifying that the account has sufficient funds to cover its payment.

Chapter 7 of the Bankruptcy Act—Immediate Liquidation Plan (straight bankruptcy) Provides for the liquidation of assets with proceeds applied to paying off excusable debts to the degree possible.

Chapter 13 of the Bankruptcy Act—(wage earner or regular income plan) Designed for individuals with regular incomes who might be able to pay off some or all of their debts given certain court protections.

chargeback The amount of the transaction is charged back to the business where the transaction originated in the case of a dispute or challenge by the cardholder.

checking accounts At depository institutions, allow depositors to write checks against their deposited funds, which transfer funds to other people and organizations.

chronological format Résumé that provides your information in reverse order, with most recent first.

city indexes Comparing wages and cost of living for various employment locations.

claims adjuster Person designated by the insurance company to assess whether the loss is covered and to determine the dollar amount that the company will pay.

claims/payout ratio Percentage of premiums collected by an insurance company that is subsequently paid out to reimburse the losses of the participants.

classes of insureds Consist of insureds who share similar characteristics.

cleared A check that has been paid by your bank to the entity to which it was written.

cliff vesting Schedule under which employee is fully vested within three years of employment.

closed-end lease/walkaway lease Agreement in which the lessee pays no charge if the end-of-lease market value of the vehicle is lower than the originally projected residual value.

closed-end mutual funds Funds that issue a limited and fixed number of shares at inception and do not buy them back; after purchase, fund shares trade at market prices.

closing Meeting to transfer ownership on a piece of real property.

closing costs Include fees and charges other than the down payment and may vary from 2 to 10 percent of the mortgage loan amount.

COBRA rights (Consolidated Omnibus Budget Reconciliation Act of 1985) Allow you to remain a member of a group health plan for as long as 18 months if you worked for an employer with more than 20 workers.

co-branded credit card Arrangement in which consumer product companies contract with banks or other financial institutions to offer credit cards.

codicil Legal instrument with which one can make minor changes to a will.

coinsurance Method by which th the insurer share proportionately i for a loss.

collateral An asset pledged in a credit account so that the lender may seize the asset should the borrower fail to repay as agreed.

coinsurance clause Requires insured to pay a proportion of any loss suffered.

collectibles Cultural artifacts that have value because of their beauty, age, scarcity, or popularity, such as antiques, stamps, rare coins, art, baseball cards, and so on.

college savings plan Program that allows after-tax contributions to a designated beneficiary to pay college costs; allows tax-free growth and tax-free withdrawals for beneficiary's college costs.

collision insurance Reimburses insureds for losses to their vehicles resulting from a collision with another car or object or from a rollover.

commercial bank Corporation chartered under federal and state regulations to offer consumer financial services.

commissions Fees or percentages of the selling price paid to salespeople, agents, and companies for their services in buying or selling an investment.

common stock Most basic form of ownership of a corporation.

community property Arrangement in which most of the money and property acquired during a marriage are legally considered the joint property of both spouses.

community property laws In cases of divorce, assumes that the surviving spouse owns half of everything that both partners earned during the marriage, no matter how much was actually contributed by either partner and even if only one spouse held legal title to the property.

comparison shopping Process of comparing products or services to find the best buy.

compounding When interest on an investment itself earns interest.

comprehensive automobile insurance Protects against property damage losses to an insured vehicle caused by perils other than collision and rollover.

comprehensive health insurance Insurance that combines protections against various medical perils into a single policy with policy limits of $1 million or more.

conditional sales contracts/financing leases A type of contract used when purchasing goods with an installment loan; title does not pass to buyer until last installment payment has been made.

conditions Impose obligations on both the insured and the insurer by establishing the ground rules of the agreement.

condominium Form of ownership with the owners holding legal title to their own housing unit among many with common grounds and facilities owned by the developer or homeowner's association.

condominium form (HO-6) Named-perils policy protecting condominium owners from the three principal losses they face.

conservative investment philosophy (risk aversion) Investors with this philosophy accept very little risk and are generally rewarded with relatively low rates of return for seeking the twin goals of a moderate amount of current income and preservation of capital.

consumer credit Nonbusiness debt that consumers use for expenditures other than home mortgages.

consumer finance company/small loan company Firm that specializes in making relatively small secured or unsecured loans that require monthly installment payments.

consumer price index (CPI) A broad measure of changes in the prices of all goods and services purchased for consumption by urban households.

consumer statement Your version of a credit issue that shows up on your credit report when the credit bureau refuses to drop a disputed claim.

consumer-driven health care Approach to medical care insurance with high deductibles that assumes that knowledgeable and informed patients/employees will spend their own money more carefully than they would spend an employer's or health plan's funds.

contents replacement-cost protection Option sometimes available in homeowner's insurance policies (including the renter's form) that pays the full replacement cost of any personal property.

contingency clauses Specify that certain conditions must be satisfied before a contract is binding.

contingent beneficiary Person who becomes the beneficiary if the primary beneficiary dies before the insured.

continuous-debt method Approach for determining your debt limit that asks whether you are able to get completely out of debt every four years (except for a mortgage loan).

contraction A period of negligible economic growth or even a decline in economic activity; unemployment rises and both companies and individuals stop spending.

contributory plan The most common type of employee-sponsored defined-contribution retirement plan; accepts employee as well as employer contributions.

conventional mortgage A fixed-rate, fixed-term, fixed-payment mortgage loan.

convertible preferred stock Can be exchanged at the option of the stockholder for a specified number of shares of common stock.

convertible term insurance Offers policyholders option of exchanging a term policy for a cash-value policy without evidence of insurability.

cooperative (co-op) Form of ownership in which owner holds a share of the corporation that owns and manages a group of housing units as well as common grounds and facilities; co-op owners pay a monthly management fee to an independent entity that carries out activities similar to those that homeowner associations do for condo owners.

coordination-of-benefits clause Prevents you from collecting insurance benefits that exceed the loss suffered by noting the order in which plans will pay if you are covered by multiple plans.

copayment A variation of a deductible, requires you to pay a specific dollar amount each time you use your benefits for a specific covered expense item.

corporate bonds Interest-bearing certificates of long-term debt issued by a corporation.

corporate earnings The profits a company makes during a specific time period indicate to many analysts whether to buy or sell a stock.

corporation State-chartered legal entity that can conduct business operations in its own name.

corpus/trust estate/trust fund Assets put into a trust.

cosigner Individual who agrees to pay a debt if the original borrower fails to do so.

cost index A numerical method used to compare the costs of similar plans of life insurance.

countercyclical (defensive) stock Exhibits price changes contrary to movements in the business cycle; performs well even during weak economic activity and sliding interest rates.

counteroffer Legal offer to sell (or buy) a home at a different price and perhaps with different conditions from those outlined in the original offer.

coupon rate/coupon/coupon yield/stated interest rate Interest rate printed on the certificate when the bond is issued.

cover letter A letter of introduction sent to a prospective employer to get an interview.

coverage A—liability insurance Liability insurance for automobiles that covers insureds when they are responsible for others' losses.

coverage B—medical payments insurance Covers bodily injury losses suffered by the driver of the insured vehicle and any passengers regardless of who is at fault.

coverage C—uninsured and underinsured motorist insurance Coverage that an insured can purchase as part of automobile insurance that covers the insured in an accident with an uninsured or underinsured driver at fault.

coverage D—physical damage insurance Provides protection against losses caused by damage to your car from collision, theft, and other perils.

Coverdell education savings account (education savings account or education IRA) After-tax investments made to pay future education costs for a child younger than age 18; growth and withdrawals are tax free.

covered option Option for a security that the writer owns and thus the writer can settle any call options contract with relatively little risk.

covering a position When an investor using a margin account buys back securities sold short or sells securities bought long.

credit A term used to describe an arrangement in which goods, services, or money is received in exchange for a promise to repay at a future date.

credit agreement Contract that stipulates repayment terms for credit cards.

credit application Form or interview that provides information about your ability and willingness to repay debts.

credit bureau Firm that collects and keeps records of many borrowers' credit histories.

credit card blocking Hotels or other service providers use a credit card number to secure reservations and charge the anticipated cost of services.

credit card liability Amount that cardholder must pay in the case of a lost or stolen card; capped at $50.

credit cards Cards that allow repeated use of credit as long as the consumer makes regular monthly payments.

credit counseling agency (CCA) Agency that can arrange payment schedules with unsecured creditors for overly indebted consumers and can provide individuals with credit counseling.

credit disability insurance Repays an outstanding credit balance if the borrower becomes disabled.

credit history Continuing record of a person's credit usage and repayment of debts.

credit investigation Process in which creditor compares information on your application with your credit report as reported by credit agencies.

credit life insurance/credit disability insurance/credit unemployment insurance Grossly overpriced insurance offered to make credit payments in the event that the borrower dies or becomes disabled or unemployed.

credit limit Maximum outstanding debt that a lender will allow on an open-ended credit account.

credit rating Lender's evaluation of the applicant's creditworthiness.

credit receipt Written evidence of any items returned that notes the specific amount and date of the transaction.

credit repair company (credit clinic) Firm that offers to help improve or fix a person's credit history for a (usually hefty) fee.

credit report Information compiled by a credit bureau from merchants, utility companies, banks, court records, and creditors about your payment history.

credit scoring (risk scoring) system Statistical measure used to rate applicants based on various factors deemed relevant to creditworthiness and the likelihood of repayment.

credit statement The monthly bill on a credit card account showing the charges and payments made, minimum payment required and due date among other information; also called a periodic statement.

credit term life insurance Pays the remaining balance of a loan if the insured dies before repaying the debt.

credit union (CU) Member-owned, not-for-profit federally insured financial institutions that provide checking, savings, and loan services to members.

crude annual rate of return A rough measure of the yield on amounts invested (usually in real estate) that assumes that equal portions of the gain are earned each year.

cumulative preferred stock Preferred stock for which dividends must be paid, including any skipped dividends, before dividends go to common stockholders.

current income Money received while you own an investment; usually received regularly as interest, rent, or dividends.

current rate Rate of return a life insurance company has recently paid to policyholders.

current yield Equals the bond's fixed annual interest payment divided by its bond price.

currently insured status Requires workers to earn six credits in the most recent three years; provides for some survivors or disability benefits but no retirement benefits.

custodial account An account opened by an adult in the name of a child younger than age 14 under the provisions of the Uniform Gifts to Minors Act (or Uniform Transfers to Minors Act).

custodial care Suitable for many people who do not need skilled nursing care but who nevertheless require supervision (for example, help with eating or personal hygiene).

cyclical stock Describes the stock of a company whose profits are greatly influenced by changes in the economic business cycle, usually a consumer-oriented stock.

damage deposit Amount given in advance to a landlord to pay for repairing rental space beyond the damage expected from normal wear and tear.

day trading Occurs when an investor buys and sells stocks quickly throughout a day with the hope that prices will move enough to cover transaction costs and earn some profits.

dealer holdback/dealer rebate Dealer incentive in which the manufacturer allows dealers to hold back a percentage of invoice price, thereby providing the dealer with additional profit on the vehicle.

dealer sticker price Includes additional charges tacked on by the dealer as an attempt to generate additional revenue.

death benefit Amount that will be paid to beneficiary when the insured dies.

debit cards A plastic card that, when used with a PIN number, allows you to withdraw funds or transfer funds among accounts as well as make purchases via point-of-sale (POS) terminals at retail outlets.

debit collection agency Firm that specializes in collecting debts that the original lender could not collect.

debt limit Overall maximum you believe you should owe based on your ability to meet repayment obligations.

debt management plan (DMP) Arrangement whereby consumer provides one monthly payment (usually somewhat smaller than the total of previous credit payments) that is distributed to all creditors.

debt payments-to-disposable income method Percentage of disposable personal income available for regular debt repayments aside from set obligations.

debt payments-to-disposable income ratio Divides monthly disposable personal income into monthly debt repayments.

debt service-to-income ratio Compares dollars spent on gross annual debt with gross annual income.

debt-consolidation loan A loan taken out to pay off several smaller debts.

debts (investments) Lending investments that typically offer both a fixed maturity and a fixed income.

debt-to-equity ratio Ratio of your consumer debt to your assets.

declarations Provide the basic descriptive information about the insured person or property, the premium to be paid, the time period of the coverage, and the policy limits.

declining-balance method Interest calculation method in which interest is assessed during each billing period (usually each month) based on the outstanding balance of the installment loan that billing period.

decreasing term insurance Policy with an annually decreasing face amount of coverage but constant premiums.

deductibles Clauses in medical care plans that require you to pay an initial portion of medical expenses annually before receiving reimbursement.

deed Written document used to convey real estate ownership.

deed restrictions Rules placed on the homeowner's use of a property by local government or a homeowner's association.

deeded timesharing Buyer obtains a legal title or deed to limited time periods of use of real estate and becomes a secured creditor who really does own a time period of habitation.

default Situation in which borrower has failed to make a principal or interest payment when due or has failed to meet any other credit contract requirement.

default rate (on credit cards) A high APR that is assessed whenever a borrower fails to uphold certain rules of the account, such as making on-time payments or staying within the specified credit limit.

default rate (on bonds) Percentage of bonds that do not repay principal at maturity and sometimes cease interest payments in the interim.

default risk/credit risk Uncertainty associated with not receiving the promised periodic interest payments and the principal amount on bonds when it becomes due at maturity.

deferred annuity Annuity plan in which annuitants pay premiums during their working lives, then take income payments at some future date, such as retirement.

deferred load/back-end load A sales commission that is imposed only when shares are sold; often charges are on a sliding scale, with the fee dropping 1 percentage point per year that the investor stays in the fund.

deficiency balance Occurs when money raised by sale of repossessed collateral doesn't cover the amount owed on the debt plus any repossession expenses.

deficit/net loss The result on a cash-flow statement when expenditures exceed income.

defined-benefit retirement plan Employer-sponsored retirement plan that pays lifetime monthly annuity payments to retirees based on a predetermined formula.

defined-contribution plan A retirement plan designed to provide a lump-sum at retirement; it is distinguished by its "contributions"—the total amount of money put into each participating employee's individual account. (Also called *salary reduction plan.*)

deflation Involves generally falling prices across business sectors.

deflation risk Chance that the val[illegible] investment will decline when o[illegible] decline.

demand deposits Another term for checking accounts, demand deposit funds must be always accessible to customers.

dental expense insurance Provides reimbursement for dental care expenses.

Department of Veterans Affairs (VA) Promotes home ownership among military veterans (active-duty, reserve, and National Guard veterans may qualify) by providing insurance against default.

deposit insurance Insures deposits, both principal amounts and accrued interest, up to $100,000 per account for most accounts ($200,000 for retirement accounts).

depository institutions Organizations licensed to take deposits and make loans.

depreciation Decline in value of an asset over time due to normal wear and tear and obsolescence.

derivative/derivative security A financial instrument that people trade in order to more easily manage the underlying asset upon which these instruments are based that can be used to reduce risk or take on additional risk.

direct deposit Having paychecks electronically sent from employer into your bank account.

direct ownership Results when investor holds actual legal title to real estate property.

direct sellers Companies that market insurance policies through salaried employees, mail-order promotions, newspapers, the Internet, and even vending machines.

disability benefits Substantially reduced benefits paid to employees who become disabled prior to retirement.

disability income insurance Replaces a portion of the income lost when you cannot work because of illness or injury.

discharged debts Debts (or portions thereof) that are excused as a result of a bankruptcy.

disclosure statement Government-required written notice of users' rights and responsibilities in using electronic money management, including receipts for ATM transactions.

discount bonds (zeroes) Bonds that pay no interest that are bought below face value which grow to face value at maturity.

discount brokers Charge commissions to execute trades that are often 30 to 80 percent less than the fees charged by full-service brokers, but also offer fewer services.

discount method of calculating interest Interest is calculated based on discount rate multiplied by the amount borrowed and by number of years to repay. Interest is then subtracted from the amount of the loan and the difference is given to the borrower. In this method, interest is paid up-front before the borrower receives the amount borrowed.

discount yield Difference between the original purchase price of a T-bill and what the Treasury pays you at maturity—the gain, or "par," is interest.

discounted cash-flow method Effective way to estimate the value or asking price of a real estate investment based on after-tax cash flow and the return on the invested dollars discounted over time to reflect a discounted yield.

discretionary income Money left over after necessities such as housing and food are paid for.

disposable (personal) income Amount of income remaining after taxes and withholding.

disposition fee Charge assessed when lessee turns in a vehicle at end of lease and lessor must prepare it for resale.

diversification Process of reducing risk by spreading investment money among several investment opportunities.

dividend Portion of a company's earnings that the firm pays out to shareholders.

dividend payout ratio Dividends per share divided by earnings per share; helps judge likelihood of future dividends.

dividend yield Cash dividend to an investor expressed as a percentage of the current market price of a security.

dividends per share Translates the total cash dividends paid out by a company to common stockholders into a per-share figure.

dollar-cost averaging/cost averaging Systematic program of investing equal sums of money at regular intervals regardless of the price of the investment.

domestic-relations order/court order acceptable for processing QDRO for public-sector employees.

down payment Portion of the purchase price of an item or property that is not borrowed.

dread disease insurance Provides reimbursement for medical expenses arising out of the occurrence of a specific disease, such as cancer.

due-on-sale clause Requires that the mortgage loan be fully paid off if the home is sold. It can impose a burden on the seller because it prohibits a buyer from assuming the mortgage loan.

dunning letters Notices that make insistent demands for repayment.

durable power of attorney Document that appoints someone, called an attorney-in-fact, to handle your legal or business matters and sign your name to documents if illness prevents you from doing so yourself.

early termination charge Charge if lessee turns car in before the end of lease period.

early termination payoff Total amount lessee would need to repay if ending the lease agreement early; includes both early termination charge and unpaid lease balance.

earned income Compensation for performing personal services, such as salaries, wages, tips, and net earnings from self-employment.

earned income credit A refundable income tax credit for workers whose income falls below a certain threshold.

earnest money Funds given to a real estate seller as a deposit to hold the property until a purchase contract can be negotiated.

earnings per share (EPS) A firm's profit divided by the number of outstanding shares; analysts follow EPS because it indicates the income that a company has available to pay dividends and reinvest as retained earnings—used to compare stocks across the board.

earnings yield Inverse of the P/E ratio; helps investors more clearly see investment expectations.

economic growth A condition of increasing production (business spending) and consumption (consumer spending) in the economy and hence increasing national income.

effective marginal tax rate The total marginal rate reflects all taxes on a person's income, including federal, state, and local income taxes as well as Social Security and Medicare taxes.

electronic benefits transfer cards (EBTs) Government cards to pay military personnel and provide Social Security and other government payments.

electronic funds transfers (EFTs) Electronic fund transfers among various accounts or to and from other people and businesses.

electronic money management Transactions conducted without using paper documents.

emergency fund Saving enough money to cover living expenses (perhaps 70 percent of gross income) for three to six months in case of financial emergency.

employee benefit Compensation for employment that does not take the form of wages, salaries, commissions, or other cash payments.

Employee Retirement Income Security Act (ERISA) Regulates employer-sponsored plans by calling for proper plan reporting and disclosure to participants in defined-contribution, defined-benefit, and cash-balance plans.

employee stock option (ESO) Gift, like a bonus, from employer to employees that allows employees to benefit from employer's stock appreciation without putting any money down.

employee stock-ownership plan (ESOP) Benefit plan in which employers make tax-deductible gifts of company stock into trusts, which are then allocated into employee accounts.

employment agency Firm that locates employment for certain types of employees.

endorsement Process of writing on the back of a check to legally transfer its ownership.

endorsements/riders Amendments and additions to the basic insurance policy that can both expand and limit coverage to accommodate specific needs.

endowment life insurance Pays the face amount of the policy either upon the death of the insured or at some previously agreed-upon date (the endowment date), whichever occurs first.

envelope system Placing exact amounts into envelopes for each budgetary purpose.

episode limits Specify the maximum payment for health care expenses arising from a single episode of illness or injury, with each episode being considered separately.

equities Ownership equities such as common or preferred stocks, equity mutual funds, real estate, and so on that focus on capital gains more than on income.

equity Amount by which value of personal assets (excluding primary residence) exceeds debts.

equity (real estate) Dollar value of the home in excess of the amount owed on it.

equity-income funds Invest in well-known companies with a long history of paying high dividends as they emphasize income and capital preservation.

escrow account Special reserve account at a financial institution in which funds are held until they are paid to a third party—for example, for home insurance and for property taxes.

estate Consists of your worldly possessions and financial wealth less any debts you owe.

estate planning Definite arrangements made during your lifetime that are consistent with your wishes for the administration, disposition, and transfer of your wealth and worldly possessions to your dependents and others when you die.

estimated taxes Amounts of quarterly tax payments forwarded to the IRS by people who are self-employed or who receive a substantial income from a source that does not withhold payroll taxes.

excess mileage charge Type of end-of-lease charge attached to closed-end lease agreements if vehicle has been driven more miles than specified in the original contract.

exchange fees Small amount charged to move money among funds within a mutual fund family.

exchange privilege Permits mutual fund shareholders to easily swap shares on a dollar-for-dollar basis for shares in another mutual fund within a mutual fund family. Also called switching, conversion, or transfer privilege.

exchange-traded fund (ETF) Basket of passively managed securities structured like an index fund; owns all or a representative set of securities that duplicate the performance of a market segment or index.

exclusion amount The value of assets that may be transferred to heirs without incurring an estate tax.

exclusions Income not subject to federal taxation.

exclusions (insurance) Narrow the focus and eliminate specific coverages broadly stated in the insuring agreements.

exclusive insurance agents Represent only one insurance company for a specific type of insurance.

executor/personal representative Person responsible for carrying out the provisions of a will and managing the assets until the estate is passed on to heirs.

exemption (or personal exemption) Legally permitted amount deducted from AGI based on number of people that taxpayer's income supports.

expansion phase Phase of the business cycle when economic activity is increasing, unemployment is falling, prices may rise, businesses are investing in capital equipment, and consumption is on the upswing.

expense ratio Expense per dollar of assets under management.

expenses Total expenditures made in a specified time.

exposures Sources of pure risk.

express warranty Any verbal or written warranty.

extended warranty/service contract/maintenance agreement/buyer protection plan Agreement between the seller and buyer of product to repair or replace covered product components for some specified time period; purchased separately from product itself.

face amount Dollar value of protection as listed in a life insurance policy and used to calculate the premium.

Fair Credit Billing Act (FCBA) Helps people who wish to dispute billing errors on revolving credit accounts.

Fair Credit Reporting Act (FCRA) Requires that credit reports contain accurate, relevant, and recent information and that only bona fide users be permitted to review a file for approved purposes.

Fair Debt Collection Practices Act (FDCPA) Prohibits third-party debt collection agencies from using abusive, deceptive, or unfair practices to collect past-due debts.

fair market value Amount a willing buyer would pay to a willing seller for a charitable item; also, the price that a buyer would likely pay for a home based on comparisons with other home sales in the area.

family auto policy (FAP) Covers vehicle owners, relatives living in their households, and people who have the owners' permission to drive the vehicle.

FDIC's Savings Association Insurance Fund (SAIF) Insures deposits in savings banks up to $100,000 per account.

federal estate tax Assessed against a deceased person's estate before property (real estate, stocks and bonds, business interests, and so on) is transferred to heirs or assigned according to terms of a will or state intestacy laws.

federal funds rate The rate that banks charge one another for overnight loans; set by the Federal Reserve Board.

Federal Housing Administration (FHA) An arm of the U.S. Department of Housing and Urban Development (HUD) that insures loans that meet its standards to encourage home ownership.

Federal Insurance Contributions Act (FICA) Act that authorizes Social Security and Medicare tax withdrawals from employee paychecks; amounts withheld go into Social Security trust fund accounts, which pay benefits to current retirees.

Federal Reserve Board (Fed) An agency of the federal government commonly referred to as the *Fed*, it regularly reports its decisions and opinions about the direction of monetary policy via setting the federal funds rate.

FICO score Method using complex statistical models that correlate certain borrower characteristics with the likelihood of repayment.

file To report formally to the IRS your income earned and your tax liability for the year.

filing status Description of a taxpayer's marital status on last day of tax year (December 31).

final expenses One-time expenses occurring just prior to or after a death.

finance charge Total dollar amount paid to use credit.

financial goals Specific objectives addressed by planning and managing finances.

financial literacy Knowledge of facts, concepts, principles, and technological tools that are fundamental to being smart about money.

financial loss Any decline in the value of income or assets in the present or future.

financial planner An investment professional who evaluates the personal finances of an individual or family and recommends strategies to set and achieve long-term financial goals.

financial planning The process of developing and implementing a coordinated series of financial plans to help achieve financial success.

financial ratios Calculations designed to simplify evaluation of financial strength and progress.

financial records Documents that evidence financial transactions.

financial responsibility Means that you are accountable for your future financial well-being and that you strive to make wise personal financial decisions.

financial risk Possibility that an investment will fail to pay a return to the investor.

financial services industry Companies that provide monetary asset management and other services.

financial statements Compliations that show financial conditions, including balance sheets and cash-flow statements.

financial strategies Preestablished action plans implemented in specific situations.

first-to-die policies Cover more than one person but pay only when the first insured dies.

fixed expenses Expenses that recur at fixed intervals.

fixed income Specific rate of return that borrower agrees to pay the investor for use of the principal (initial investment).

fixed maturity Specific date on which borrower agrees to repay the principal to the investor.

fixed yield Interest income payment remains the same regardless of bond's price.

fixed-rate loans Loans for which the interest rate will not change over the life of the loan.

fixed-time deposits/CDs Specify a period (usually 6 months to 5 years) that the savings *must* be left on deposit; early withdrawals carry a penalty.

fizbo For sale by owner (FSBO).

flat-fee brokers Charge a flat fee for their services rather than a percentage-based commission.

flexible benefit plan An employer-sponsored plan that gives the employee a choice of selecting either cash or one or more qualifying nontaxable benefits; also known as a cafeteria plan.

flexible spending account (FSA) or expense reimbursement account Allows employees to fund qualified medical or dependent expenses on pretax basis by reducing take-home salary.

flexible spending arrangements Employer-offered programs that allow employees to have money diverted from their IRS-reported income into accounts that pay medical, dental, vision, or other allowable expenses using pretax dollars.

floater policies Provide all-risk protection for accident and theft losses to movable property regardless of where the loss occurs.

floor broker Brokerage firm's contact [illegible] an exchange.

foreclosure Process in which th[illegible] the borrower to prove default and [illegible] to order the sale of the property to [illegible]

fortuitous losses Losses that are unexpected in terms of both their timing and their magnitude.

401(k) plan Defined-contribution plan designed for employees of private corporations.

403(b) plan Defined-contribution plan designed for eligible employees of not-for-profit institutions, such as colleges, hospitals, and religious organizations.

457 plans Defined-contribution plan for state and local governments and non-church controlled tax-exempt organizations. Only employees (not employers) make contributions into the plan.

front-end load A sales charge paid when an individual buys an investment, reducing the amount available to purchase fund shares.

front-end ratio Compares the total annual PITI expenditures for housing with the loan applicant's gross annual income to assess the borrower's ability to pay the mortgage.

full warranty Warranty that meets three stringent promises: product must be fixed at no cost to buyer within reasonable time, owner will not have to undertake an unreasonable task to return product for repair, and defective product will be replaced with a new one or the buyer's money will be returned if product cannot be fixed.

full-benefit retirement age Age at which a retiree is entitled to full Social Security benefits; 67 for those born in 1960 or later.

fully insured Social Security status Requires 40 credits and provides workers and their families with benefits under the retirement, survivors, and disability programs; once status is earned, it cannot be taken away even if the eligible worker never works again.

functional format Résumé that emphasizes career-related experiences.

fund investment advisers Have access to the best research; they select, buy, sell, and monitor the performance of the securities purchased; thus, they oversee the portfolio.

fund screener/fund-screening tool Permits investors to screen all of the mutual funds in the market to gauge performance.

fundamental analysis School of thought in market analysis that assumes each stock has an intrinsic (or true) value based on its expected stream of future earnings.

future value The valuation of an asset projected to the end of a particular time period in the future.

futures contract Type of exchange-traded standardized forward contract that specifies the size of the contract, quality of product to be delivered, and delivery date.

"gap" insurance Pays off the remainder of a totaled vehicle after an accident loan if the insurance payment is insufficient to do so.

garnishment Court-sanctioned procedure by which a portion of debtors' wages are set aside by their employers to pay debts.

general (full-service) brokerage firms Offer a full range of services to customers, including investment advice and research.

generic products Goods that carry store brands or are sold under a general commodity name such as "whole-kernel corn" rather than a brand name, such as Del Monte.

gold bullion coins Various world mints issue these coins, which contain 1 troy ounce (31.15 grams) of pure gold.

gold bullion A refined and stamped weight of precious metal.

good-faith estimate Lender's list of all the costs associated with the loan, including the annual percentage rate, application and processing fees, closing costs, and any other charges that must be paid when the deal is legally consummated.

goods and services dispute Asserts that charges were for faulty, damaged, shoddy, defective, or poor-quality goods and services and cardholder made a good-faith effort to try to correct the problem with the merchant.

government securities money market funds Appeal to investor concerns about safety by investing solely in U.S. Treasury bills and other short-term securities backed by the U.S. government.

grace period (on credit accounts) Time period between the posting date of a transaction and the payment due date during which no interest accrues.

grace period (for interest earning accounts) Period (in days) for which deposits or withdrawals can be made without any penalty.

grace period (in life and health insurance) Period of time during which an overdue premium may be paid without a lapse of the policy.

graduated vesting Schedule under which employees must be at least 20 percent vested after two years of service and gain an additional 20 percent of vesting for each subsequent year until, at the end of year six, the account is fully vested.

graduated-payment mortgage Mortgage in which borrower pays smaller-than-normal payments in the early years but payments gradually increase to larger-than-normal payments in later years.

grantor/settler/donor/trustor Creator of a trust.

gross capitalized cost (gross cap cost) Includes vehicle price plus cost of any extra features such as insurance or maintenance agreements.

gross domestic product (GDP) The nation's broadest measure of economic health, it reports how much economic activity (all goods and services) has occurred within the U.S. borders during a given period.

gross income All income in the form of money, goods, services, and/or property.

group health plan Sold collectively to an entire group of people rather than to individuals, such as the group health care policies offered by employers.

group term life insurance Issued to people as members of a group (such as a company's employees) rather than as individuals.

growing-equity mortgage (GEM) Meant for people who design their loan in advance to reduce interest costs by paying off the mortgage loan early.

growth and income funds Invest in companies that have a high likelihood of both dividend income and price appreciation; less risk-oriented than aggressive growth funds or growth funds.

growth funds Seek long-term capital appreciation by investing in common stocks of companies with higher-than-average revenue and earnings growth, often the larger and well-established firms.

guaranteed insurability (guaranteed purchase option) Permits the cash-value policyholder to buy additional stated amounts of cash-value life insurance at stated times in the future without evidence of insurability.

guaranteed minimum rate of return Minimum rate that, by contract, the insurance company is legally obligated to pay.

guaranteed renewable policies Must be continued in force as long as the policyholder pays the required premium.

guaranteed renewable term insurance Protects you against the possibility of becoming uninsurable.

guardian Person responsible for caring for and raising any child under the age of 18 and for managing the child's estate.

habitability Suitability for use as a dwelling.

harassment Illegal bullying, such as rent increases, eviction, or utility shutoff.

hazard Any condition that increases the probability that a peril will occur.

health care plan An employee benefit designed to pay all or part of the employee's medical expenses.

health care proxy Legal document that appoints another person to make health care decisions if the writer of the proxy is rendered medically incapable of making his or her wishes known.

health insurance Provides protection against financial losses resulting from illness and injury.

health maintenance organizations (HMOs) Provide a broad range of health care services for a set monthly fee on a prepaid basis.

health reimbursement account (HRA) Funds that employers set aside to reimburse employees for qualified medical expenses.

health savings account (HSA) Tax-deductible savings accounts into which individuals or employers can deposit tax-sheltered funds to pay future medical bills.

hedge fund Global company beyond the regulations of the U.S. Securities and Exchange Commission that uses unconventional (and sometimes very risky) investment strategies.

heir Person who inherits or is entitled by law or by the terms of a will to inherit some asset.

high-balling Sales tactic in which dealer offers a trade-in allowance that is much higher than the vehicle is worth.

high-deductible health care plan A plan that requires individuals pay a higher deductible to cover medical expenses before insurance plan payments begin; chosen to save money on premiums.

high-risk/speculative investments Present potential for significant fluctuations in return, sometimes over short time periods.

home equity line of credit Use of home equity as collateral for a line of credit.

home inspection Conducted to ensure that the home is physically sound and that all operating systems are in proper order.

home warranty insurance Operates much like a service contract on existing homes.

homeowner's association Organization of condo owners that is responsible for enforcing bylaws, managing common grounds and facilities, and holding insurance on buildings.

homeowner's fee Fee charged to condo owners to provide for association activities and facilities.

homeowner's general liability protection Applies when you are legally liable for another person's losses, other than those that arise out of use of vehicles or your professional duties.

homeowner's insurance Combines liability and property insurance coverages that homeowners and renters typically need into single-package policies.

homeowner's no-fault medical payments protection Pays for bodily injury losses that others suffer regardless of who was at fault.

homeowner's no-fault property damage protection Pays for property losses of others for which a homeowner wishes to assume responsibility.

I bonds Nonmarketable savings bonds backed by the U.S. government that pay an earnings rate that combines two rates: a fixed interest rate set when the investor buys the bond and a semiannual variable interest rate tied to inflation that protects the investor's purchasing power.

identity theft When someone else uses your personal information to run up debt in your name or access your financial accounts.

image statement A type of bank statement for which you receive a photocopy of checks written and deposits you had made rather than the actual document.

immediate annuity Annuity, often funded by a lump sum from the death benefit of a life insurance policy or lump sum from a defined-contribution plan, that begins payments one month after purchase.

implied warranty/warrant of merchantability/warranty of fitness Product sold is warranted to be suitable for sale (warranty of merchantability) and to work effectively (a warranty of fitness) whether or not a written warranty exists.

impulse buying Buying without fully considering priorities and alternatives.

income Total payments received over a specified time period.

income stock A stock that may not grow too quickly, but year after year it pays a cash dividend higher than that offered by most companies.

incontestability clause Places a time limit on the right of the insurance company to deny a claim.

indemnity plan Health insurance based on reimbursement for losses with the type of care chosen by patients based upon their physicians' advice.

indenture Written, legal agreement between bondholders and debtor that describes terms of the debt by setting forth the maturity date, interest rate, and other details.

independent insurance agents Independent businesspeople who act as third-party links between insurers and insureds.

index fund Mutual fund that seeks to achieve the same return as a particular market index by buying and holding all or a representative selection of securities in it.

index of leading economic indicators (LEI) A composite index reported monthly by the Conference Board that collects relevant economic data for business, governments, and individuals' use.

indexed A procedure used by the Social Security Administration to adjust the earnings during one's working years to reflect increases in average wages for all workers over time; used in the process of calculating SSA benefits.

indexing Yearly adjustments to tax brackets that reduce inflation's effects on tax brackets.

individual account Has one owner who is solely responsible for the account and its activity.

individual practice organization (IPO) HMO structure in which the HMO contracts with—rather than hires—groups of physician.

individual retirement account (IRA) Non-employer-based retirement accounts in which earnings off the account are allowed to accumulate tax free.

inflation A steady and sustained rise in general price levels across economic sectors; measured by the changing cost over time of a "market basket" of goods and services that a typical household might purchase.

inflation risk/purchasing power risk Danger that your money will not grow as fast as inflation and therefore not be worth as much in the future as it is today.

in-force illustration Shows the policy's cash-value status and projections for the future given the current rate of return at the time of the illustration (rather than the rate used at the inception of the policy).

inheritance tax Tax assessed by the decedent's state of residence on beneficiaries who receive inherited property (only eight states have this tax).

initial public offerings (IPOs) New issues of stocks or bonds; the primary market for securities.

insolvent Carrying a negative net worth.

installment credit (closed-end credit) Credit arrangement in which the borrower must repay the amount owed plus interest in a specific number of equal payments.

installment purchase agreements/collateral installment loans/chattel mortgage loans A type of contract used when purchasing goods with an installment loan; title of property passes to buyer when contract is signed.

installment-certain annuity Provides monthly payments for the rest of the life of the annuitant with a guarantee that if the person dies before receiving a specific number of payments, the beneficiary will receive a certain number of payments for a particular time period.

insurance Mechanism for transferring and reducing pure risk through which a large number of individuals share in the financial losses suffered by members of the group as a whole.

insurance agent Representative of an insurance company authorized to sell, modify, service, and terminate insurance contracts.

insurance claim Formal request to the insurance company for reimbursement for a covered loss.

insurance companies Financial institutions that provide property, liability, health, life, and other insurance products, as well as monetary asset services.

insurance dividends Surplus earnings of insurance company when the difference between the total premium charged exceeds the cost to the company of providing insurance.

insurance policy Contract between the person buying insurance (the insured) and the insurance company (the insurer).

insurance rate Price charged for each unit of insurance coverage.

insured Individual whose life is insured.

insuring agreements Broadly defined coverages provided under the policy.

interest The price of borrowing money.

interest inventories Scaled surveys that assess career interests and activities.

interest rate risk Risk that interest rates will rise and bond prices will fall, thereby lowering the prices on older bond issues.

interest-adjusted cost index (IACI) Measures the cost of life insurance, taking into account the interest that would have been earned had the premiums been invested rather than used to buy insurance.

interest-adjusted net payment index (IANPI) If a policy will remain in force until death, this method allows you to effectively measure the cost of cash-value insurance. The lower the IANPI, the lower the cost of the policy.

interest-earning checking account Any account on which you can write checks that pays interest.

interest-only mortgage Mortgage in which the borrower pays only the interest on the mortgage in monthly payments for a fixed term, then either refinances the principal, pays off the principal, or starts paying the higher monthly payment with the principal payments added in.

interest-rate caps Limit the amount by which the interest rate can increase in an ARM.

interests Long-standing topics and activities that engage your attention.

intermediate care Appropriate for people who do not require around-the-clock nursing but who are not able to live alone.

intermediate-term goals Financial targets that can be achieved within one to five years.

Internal Revenue Code Laws governing income tax collection in the United States.

Internal Revenue Service (IRS) Government agency charged with collecting income taxes.

intestate When a person dies without a legal will.

investing Putting saved money to work so that it makes you even more money.

investment (capital) assets Tangible and intangible items acquired for their monetary benefits.

investment assets-to-total assets ratio Compares investment asset value with net worth.

investment banking firms Intermediaries between companies issuing new stocks and bonds and the investing public.

investment philosophy Investor's [illegible] erance for risk in investments, [illegible] conservative, moderate, or aggressive, given the investor's financial goals.

investment plan An explanation of your investment philosophy and your logic on investing to reach specific goals.

investment risk The possibility that the yield on an investment will deviate from its expected return.

investment-grade bonds Offer investors a reasonable certainty of regularly receiving periodic income (interest) and retrieving the amount originally invested (principal).

investments Assets purchased with the goal of providing additional income from the asset itself.

invoice price/seller's cost Reflects the price the dealer has been billed from the manufacturer.

irrevocable charitable remainder trust (CRT) Trust that pays you and/or your survivors tax-advantaged income while you are alive, and then the designated charity eventually receives the corpus of the CRT when you (and your spouse, if so arranged) die.

irrevocable living trust Arrangement in which the grantor permanently gives up ownership and the right to control of the property, to change the beneficiaries, and to change the trustees.

IRS 20 percent withholding rule Rollover penalty that applies if a participant in a retirement plan takes direct possession of the funds.

IRS tax table Used to figure income tax for taxable incomes up to $100,000.

item limits Specify the maximum reimbursement for a particular health care expense.

itemized deductions Tax-deductible expenses.

job interview Formal meeting between employer and potential employee to discuss job qualifications and suitability.

joint account Has two or more owners, each of whom has legal rights to the funds in the account.

joint and survivor benefit/survivor's benefit Annuity whose payments continue to a surviving spouse after the participant's death; often equals at least 50 percent of participant's benefit.

joint tenancy with right of survivorship/joint tenancy Most common form of joint ownership, especially for husbands and wives, in which each person owns the whole of the asset, such as a bank account or home, and can dispose of it without the approval of the other owner(s).

joint-and-survivor annuity Provides monthly payments for as long as one of the two people—usually a husband and wife—is alive.

Keogh Tax-deferred retirement account designed for self-employed and small-business owners.

kiddie tax rule Applies the parents' marginal tax rate to unearned income of a child under age 18 who has such income in excess of $1700 for the year.

land contract/contract for deed Brings greater risk for the buyer because all terms in the contract (including payment of the debt) must be satisfied before transfer of title will occur.

lapsed policy Policy that has been terminated because of nonpayment of premiums.

large-loss principle A basic rule of risk management that encourages us to insure the losses that we cannot afford and assume the losses that we can reasonably afford.

law of large numbers As the number of members in a group increases, predictions about the group's behavior become increasingly accurate.

layering term insurance policies Purchasing multiple level-premium term policies so that coverage grows when you need it most and then can be decreased as your needs change.

LEAP Long-term Equity AnticiPation Security; an option with a much longer term than traditional stock or index options.

lease In this context, a contract specifying both tenant and landlord legal responsibilities.

leasing Renting a product while ownership title remains with lease grantor.

lemon laws State laws that provide guidelines for arbitrators to use to order a dealer's buyback of a "lemon" as defined under the law—commonly a car that has been in the shop four or more times to fix the same problem.

lender buy-down mortgage Mortgage in which base interest rate is set for the loan that is perhaps 0.5 percentage points higher than the interest rate for a conventional mortgage. For the first year, the borrower pays a rate 2 percentage points below the base rate. In the second year, the rate is 1 point below the base rate. In the third and future years, the base rate is charged.

letter of last instructions Nonlegal instrument that may contain suggestions and recommendations regarding funeral and burial instructions, organ donation wishes, material to be included in the obituary, contact information for relatives and friends, and other information useful to the survivors, such as the location of important documents.

level-premium term insurance Term policy with long term under which premiums remain constant. Also called guaranteed level-premium term insurance.

leverage Using borrowed funds to invest with the goal of earning a rate of return in excess of the after-tax costs of borrowing.

liabilities What you owe.

liability insurance Protection from financial losses suffered when you are held liable for others' losses.

lien Legal right to take and hold property or to sell it in the event the borrower (mortgagor) defaults on the loan.

life insurance An insurance contract that promises to pay a dollar benefit to a beneficiary upon the death of the insured person.

life insurance application Policyholder's offer to purchase a policy.

life-cycle funds/target retirement funds Asset allocation funds that offer investors premixed portfolios of stocks, bonds, and cash that investors of a certain age and risk tolerance might prefer.

lifeline banking accounts Offer access to minimal financial services that every consumer needs.

lifestyle trade-offs Weighing the demands of particular jobs with your social and cultural preferences.

lifetime/aggregate limit Places an overall maximum on the total amount of reimbursement available under a policy.

limit order Instructs the stockbroker to buy or sell a stock at a specific price.

limited liability Common shareholders' responsibility for business losses is limited to the amount invested in the shares of stock owned.

limited managed account A company that buys and sells an investor's mutual fund assets to adjust the portfolio to specified standards (called rebalancing).

limited warranty Any warranty that offers less than the three conditions for full warranty.

limited/special power of attorney Allows someone to act in your behalf for a single transaction or limited time period, such as a real estate agent signing your name at a closing if you are unable to attend the closing yourself.

limited-pay whole life insurance Whole life insurance that allows premium payments to cease before the insured reaches the age of 100.

liquidity Speed and ease with which an asset can be converted to cash.

listed Refers to housing that is under contract with the seller and the broker.

listing agent The party with whom the seller signs the listing agreement; listing agent advertises the property, shows it to prospective buyers, and assists the seller in negotiations.

listing agreement Agreement that brokers require homeowners to sign that permits the broker to list the property exclusively or with a multiple-listing service.

living benefit clause Allows the payment of all or a portion of the death benefit prior to death if the insured contracts a terminal illness.

living trust A trust that takes effect while the grantor is still alive.

load funds Mutual funds that always charge a "load" or sales charge upon purchase; the load is the commission used to compensate brokers.

loan Consumer credit that is repaid in equal amounts over a set period of time.

loan commitment/loan preapproval Lender's promise to grant a loan.

loan origination fee Fees (often 1 point) that a lender might charge for the paperwork associated with the processing of the mortgage loan application.

loan preapproval Oral commitment from a bank or credit union agreeing to furnish credit for a purchase; lets buyers know how much they can borrow and at what interest rate.

loan-to-value (LTV) ratio Measures the amount of leverage in a real estate purchase or investment project by dividing the total amount of debt by the market price of the property.

long-term care insurance Provides reimbursement for costs associated with intermediate-term and custodial care in a nursing facility or at home.

long-term gain/or loss A profit or loss on the sale of an asset that has been held for more than a year.

long-term goals Financial targets to achieve more than five years in the future.

long-term liability Debt that comes due in more than one year.

loss control Designing specific mechanisms to reduce loss frequency and loss severity.

loss frequency Refers to the likely number of times that a loss might occur over a period of time.

loss severity Describes the potential magnitude of loss due to a peril.

low-balling An attempt to raise an already negotiated price when it comes time to finalize the written contract.

low-load funds Carry sales charges of perhaps 1 to 3 percent; sold by brokers, via mail, and sometimes through mutual fund retailers located in shopping centers.

lump-sum distribution When all of the funds are removed from a retirement account at one time, usually "rolled over" into another qualified plan.

managed care plans Plans that seek to control the conditions under which health care can be obtained.

managed funds Each fund's professional managers constantly evaluate and choose securities to buy or sell, using a specific investment approach.

management Individuals who run the firm's day-to-day operations.

manufactured housing Fully or partially factory-built housing units transported to home site for final assembly.

manufacturer's suggested retail price (MSRP)/sticker price Suggested initial asking price.

margin account Account at a brokerage firm that requires a substantial deposit of cash or securities and permits the purchase of other securities using credit granted by the brokerage firm.

margin buying Using a margin account to buy securities; allows the investor to apply leverage that magnifies returns—or losses.

margin call If a stock price declines to the point that the investor's equity is less than the required percentage, a representative of the brokerage firm makes a phone call and tells the investor to either put up more money or securities or face having the position bought on margin liquidated.

margin rate Set by the Fed, percentage of the value (or equity) in an investment that is not borrowed—recently 25 to 40 percent.

marginal cost The additional (marginal) cost of one more incremental unit of some item.

marginal tax bracket (MTB)/marginal tax rate One of six income-range segments at which income is taxed at increasing rates.

marginal tax rate The tax rate at which your last dollar earned is taxed.

marginal utility The extra satisfaction derived from gaining one more incremental unit of a product or service.

marital deduction Allows an estate to pass on an unlimited amount of assets to a surviving spouse free of estate taxes.

market interest rates Current long- and short-term interest rates paid on various types of corporate and government debts that carry similar levels of risk.

market making Occurs when a broker/dealer provides a continuous market in a security by maintaining an inventory to sell to other brokerage firms and stands ready to buy reasonable quantities of the same security or securities at market prices.

market order Instructs the stockbroker to execute an order at the prevailing market price—that is, the current selling price of the stock.

market price Current price that a buyer is willing to pay a willing seller for a share of stock.

market risk/systematic risk/undiversifiable risk Risk that the value of an investment may drop due to influences and events that affect all similar investments.

market timers Long-term investors who pull out of stocks or bonds in anticipation of a market decline or hold back from investing until the market "settles down"—that is, when they expect prices to climb.

marketability risk The chance that, if you need to sell your investment quickly, you may not get your full asking price—you might have to sell at a discount.

market-volatility risk The extent to which an asset's returns vary over time.

matching contributions Employer programs that match employees' 401(k) contributions up to a particular percentage.

maturity date Date upon which the principal is returned to the bondholder.

maximum taxable yearly earnings (MTYE) The maximum amount to which the FICA tax is applied.

mediation Procedure in which a neutral third party works with parties involved in a dispute to arrive at a mutually agreeable solution.

Medicaid A government health care program for low-income people funded jointly by the federal and state governments.

medical care plan Generic name for any program that pays or provides reimbursement for direct medical care expenditures.

medical information bureaus Similar to credit bureaus, these sources provide medical information to insurance companies.

Medicare The federal government's medical care program for the elderly.

Medicare Part A Hospitalization portion of the program; it requires no premium.

Medicare Part B Supplementary medical expense insurance portion for outpatient care, doctor office visits, or certain other services.

mentor Experienced person who offers advice to a less experienced person.

minimum payment The lowest amount a borrower may repay in a given month to avoid penalties.

minimum-balance account Checking account that requires customers to keep a certain minimum amount for a specified time period to avoid fees.

mobile homes Fully factory-assembled housing units that are designed to be towed on a frame with a trailer hitch.

moderate investment philosophy Investors with this philosophy accept some risk as they seek capital gains through slow and steady growth in investment value along with current income.

modern portfolio theory (MPT) Goal is to identify the investor's acceptable level of risk tolerance and then find an optimal portfolio of assets that will have the highest expected returns for that level of risk.

modified life insurance Whole life insurance for which the insurer charges smaller premiums in the early years and higher premiums thereafter.

monetary asset (cash) management How you handle your monetary assets.

monetary assets Cash and low-risk, near-cash items that can quickly be converted into cash.

money factor Measures the rent charge portion of lease payment; lessors must disclose true credit (money factor) costs. Also known as lease rate or lease factor.

money market account Interest-earning accounts that pay relatively high interest rates and offer limited check-writing privileges.

money market deposit account (MMDA) Government-insured money market account in a depository institution with minimum-balance requirements and tiered interest rates.

money market mutual fund (MMMF) Money market account in a mutual fund rather than at a depository institution.

money order A checking instrument bought for a particular amount.

Monte Carlo analysis Technique that performs a large number of trial runs of a particular portfolio mix of investments, called simulations, to find an optimal allocation for a particular investor's goals and risk tolerance.

morale hazard Arises when a person is indifferent to a peril, such as being careless about preventing a loss.

mortgage broker Individual or company that acts as an intermediary between borrowers and lenders.

mortgage insurance Insures the difference between the amount of down payment required by an 80 percent LTV ratio and the actual, lower down payment.

mortgage interest tax credit A nonrefundable income tax credit of up to $2000 for persons who borrow money to buy a home under certain state and local government programs.

mortgage loan Loan to purchase real estate in which the property itself serves as collateral.

mortgage lock-in Agreement that includes a lender's promise to hold a certain interest rate for a specified period of time, such as 60 days.

mortgage refinancing New mortgage is obtained to pay off and replace an existing mortgage, usually at a lower interest rate.

multiple Another term for P/E ratio.

multiple indemnity clause Provides for a doubling or tripling of the face amount if death results from certain specified causes.

multiple-listing (open-listing) service An information and referral network among real estate brokers allowing properties listed with a particular broker to be shown by all brokers.

multiple-of-earnings approach estimating the amount of life insur by multiplying income by some number, such as 5, 7, or 10.

municipal government bonds (munis) Long-term debts (bonds) issued by local governments (cities, states, and various districts and political subdivisions) and their agencies. Interest from munis, also known as tax-free bonds or tax-exempt bonds, is exempt from federal income tax.

mutual fund ask price Price at which an investor can purchase a mutual fund's shares; current NAV per share plus sales charges.).

mutual fund bid price Same as NAV (net asset value).

mutual fund dividend Income paid to investors out of profits earned by the mutual fund from its investments.

mutual fund family Investment management company that offers a number of different funds to the investing public, each with its own investment objectives or philosophies of investing.

mutual fund Investment company that pools funds by selling shares to investors and makes diversified investments to achieve financial goals of income or growth, or both.

mutual fund funds Earn a return by investing in other mutual funds, providing extensive diversification and higher-than-average expenses and fees.

mutual savings bank (MSB) Depositors own these financial institutions and share in earnings from deposits and housing and consumer loans.

naked option Speculative option that the writer does not own thus exposing the writer to unlimited risk (if selling a call) or substantial risk (if selling a put).

named-perils policies Cover only losses caused by perils that the policy specifically mentions.

NASDAQ National Association of Securities Dealers Automated Quotations system, which provides instantaneous information on securities offered by more than 3200 domestic and foreign companies.

NCUSIF The credit union checking and savings account program.

need Item thought to be necessary.

needs-based approach A superior method of calculating the amount of insurance needed that considers all of the factors that might potentially affect the level of need.

negative amortization Occurs when monthly payments are actually smaller than necessary to pay interest on the loan, which will result in a rising principal loan balance.

negotiating/haggling Process of discussing actual terms of agreement with a seller, usually on higher-priced items.

net asset value (NAV) Per-share value of a mutual fund.

net cost A misleading way to compare several life insurance policies, the net cost equals the total of all premiums to be paid minus any accumulated cash value and accrued dividends.

net surplus Amount remaining after all budget classification deficits are subtracted from those with surpluses.

net worth What's left when you subtract liabilities from assets.

new-vehicle buying service No-fee organization that arranges discount purchases for new-car buyers who are referred to nearby participating automobile dealers that have agreed to charge specific discount prices.

no-load mutual funds Funds that allow investors to purchase shares directly at the net asset value without the addition of sales charges.

nominal income Also called money income, it is income that has not been adjusted for inflation and decreasing purchasing power.

noncancelable policies Must be continued in force without premium changes up to age 65 as long as the participant pays the required premium.

noncontributory plan An employer-sponsored defined-contribution retirement plan in which only the employer makes contributions.

noncumulative preferred stock Preferred stock that gives stockholders no claim to previously skipped dividends.

nondeeded timesharing Legal right-to-use purchase of a limited, preplanned timesharing period of use of a property; does not grant legal real estate ownership interest to the purchaser.

nonforfeiture values Amounts stipulated in a life insurance policy that protect the cash value, if any, in the event that the policyholder chooses not to pay or fails to pay required premiums or wishes to cash in the policy.

noninstallment credit Single-payment, open-ended credit and service credit arrangements.

nonparticipating policies Policies that don't pay insurance dividends.

nonprobate property Does not go through probate; includes assets transferred to survivors by contract (such as beneficiaries listed on retirement accounts and bank accounts held with another person).

nonrefundable tax credit Credit that can reduce your tax liability only to zero.

notary fees Fees charged by a public official authorized to authenticate signatures for contracts, deeds, affidavits, and so on.

odd lot An amount of a security that is less than the normal unit of trading for that particular security; for stocks, any transaction less than 100 shares is usually considered to be an odd lot.

older home form (HO-8) Named-perils policy that provides actual-cash-value protection on the dwelling, which may be more valuable than a new home.

online brokers Such brokers, also called Internet or electronic brokers, have reduced the cost of executing a trade to perhaps $20 or even $10 because their primary business is online trading.

open-end lease Agreement in which lessee must pay any difference between projected residual value of vehicle and actual market value at the end of the lease period.

open-end mutual funds Issue redeemable shares that investors purchase directly from the fund (or through a broker for the fund).

open-ended (revolving) credit Arrangement in which credit is extended in advance of any transaction so that borrowers do not need to reapply each time they need to use credit.

open-enrollment period Period during which employees can make changes in coverage or switch among alternative health plans.

opportunity cost The opportunity cost of any decision is the value of the next best alternative that must be forgone.

option Contract to buy or sell a financial asset at a specified point in the future at a specified price.

option holder Person who buys and then owns an option contract.

option premium Price of an option contract.

option writer Agrees to sell an option contract that promises either to buy or to sell a specified asset for a fixed striking price.

optionally renewable policies May be canceled or changed by the plan provider, but only at the time of expiration and renewal.

ordinary income dividend distributions Occur when the fund pays out dividend income and interest (monthly, quarterly, or annually) it has received from securities held in the fund.

organized exchanges Actual physical location for a market, at which some securities prices are set by open outcry. Organized exchanges are quickly merging with electronic markets.

overindebted When one's excessive personal debts make repayment difficult and cause financial distress.

over-the-counter (OTC) marketplace Electronic marketplace for securities transactions.

overwithholding Occurs when employees have their employers withhold more in estimated taxes than the tax liability ultimately due the government.

owner/policyholder Retains all rights and privileges granted by the policy, including the right to amend the policy and the right to designate who receives the proceeds.

own-occupation policy Provides benefits if you can no longer perform the occupation you had at the time you became disabled.

paid-up Point at which the owner of a whole life policy can stop paying premiums.

par value/face value Some multiple of $1000 that is printed on a bond when issued and repaid at maturity.

participating policies Policies that pay insurance dividends.

partnership theory of marital rights Presumes that wedded couples intend to share their fortunes equally, thus, property acquired during the marriage and titled in the name of only one partner (other than property acquired by gift or inheritance) becomes the property of both spouses.

passive investor An investor who does not actively engage in trading securities or monitoring his or her investments; seeks to match the market return via mutual funds or other managed investments in the longer term.

pawnshop Lender that offers small single-payment loans for short time periods in return for an item of personal property that serves as collateral.

payable-at-death designation Status granted to individuals who are not joint tenants and who might need to access accounts without going through probate—the deceased signs the designation before death and the designee simply presents a death certificate to access the accounts.

payday lenders Businesses that grant credit by honoring a personal check but agree not to deposit the check for a week or longer (until payday).

payment caps Limit the amount by which the payment can vary on an ARM.

payroll withholding An employer takes a certain amount from an employee,s income as a prepayment of an individual,s tax liability for the year and sends that amount to the IRS

peak Point in the business cycle when economic activity is at its highest.

penny stocks Stocks that sell for less than $1 per share and often are issued by new companies with erratic sales, few profits, and only some hope of success.

Pension Benefit Guaranty Corporation (PBGC) ERISA-established watch-dog organization that insures defined-benefit (but not defined-contribution) pension plans to guarantee certain minimum benefits to eligible workers whose employers' plans are not financially sound enough to pay their obligations.

pension Sum of money paid regularly by a former employer as a retirement benefit.

peril Any event that can cause a financial loss.

periodic rate The APR for a charge account divided by the number of billing cycles per year (usually 12).

periodic statements Consumer-protecting recaps that show all transfers to and from accounts, fees charged, and opening and closing balances.

periodic tenancy Type of lease that provides for residency week to week, month to month, or some other set period and that can be terminated by either party upon advance notice.

permanent insurance Alternate name for cash-value insurance, so named because the insurance remains in effect for the insured's entire life.

personal auto policies (PAPs) Policies that cover all property and bodily injury liability losses resulting from an accident until the limit is reached.

personal finance The study of personal and family resources considered important in achieving financial success; it involves how people spend, save, protect, and invest their financial resources.

personal inflation rate Inflation's effect on a particular person's purchasing power. For example, inflation pushes up the cost of borrowing, so monthly car payments and home mortgage rates increase when the personal inflation rate rises.

personal injury protection (PIP) Medical payments coverage for the driver and any passengers for bodily injury losses as well as possibly lost wages and rehabilitation expenses common in no-fault accident states.

personal line of credit Form of open-ended credit in which the lender allows the borrower access to a prearranged revolving line of credit.

personal losses Losses that specific individuals or organizations suffer rather than society as whole suffering the losses.

personal values The principles, standards, or qualities that you consider desirable.

physical hazard A particular characteristic of the insured person or property that increases the chance of loss.

PITI Elements of a monthly real estate payment consisting of principal, interest, real estate taxes, and homeowner's insurance.

planned buying Thinking through all the details of a purchase from the initial desire to buy to your satisfaction after the purchase.

point/or interest point Fee equal to 1 percent of the total mortgage loan amount.

policy illustration Charts the projected growth in the cash value for given rates of return.

policy limits Specify the maximum dollar amounts that will be paid under the policy.

portability option Allows you to convert your group medical care coverage to individual coverage within 180 days before COBRA ends.

portability Upon termination of employment, employees with portable benefits can keep their savings in tax-sheltered accounts by transferring retirement funds from employer's account directly to another account without penalty.

portfolio diversification Practice of selecting a collection of different asset classes of investments (such as stocks, bonds, mutual funds, real estate, and cash) that are chosen not only for their potential returns but also for their dissimilar risk-return characteristics.

portfolio tracking Automatically updates the value of your portfolio after you enter the symbols of the stocks you own and the number of shares held.

portfolio Collection of investments assembled to meet your investment goals.

posting date The date at which a credit card transaction is actually charged to the card holder's account.

potential rate of return Determined by adding anticipated income (from dividends, interest, rents, or other sources) to future value of investment and then subtracting investment's original cost.

preapproved credit card offers Firms find and send prescreened creditworthy individuals applications that become active accounts upon the individual signing the application.

preemptive right Common stockholders hold this right to purchase additional shares before a firm offers new shares to the public.

preexisting conditions Medical conditions or symptoms that the plan participant knew about or had been diagnosed within a certain time period before the plan effective date.

preferred employer Identifying employers that would suit you best.

preferred provider organization (PPO) Group of medical care providers (doctors, hospitals, and other health care providers) who contract with a health insurance company to provide services at a discount.

preferred stock Type of fixed-income ownership security in a corporation that pays fixed dividends.

premium A sum of money paid in addition to a face amount for a bond; comparatively small, predictable fee for insurance with which individuals or companies can replace an uncertain—and possibly large—financial loss.

premium conversion plans Employees can pay their share of insurance premiums with pretax dollars; such pretax paid expenses come off of total income reported to the IRS.

premium quote service Offers computer-generated comparisons among 20 to 80 different companies.

prepaid educational service plan Type of qualified tuition program that allows purchase of a child's future college education at today's prices, locking in tuition prices.

prepayment fee/penalty (mortgages) Charge set to discourage buyers from continually refinancing their home loans, this is a mortgage contract clause that charges 1 to 3 percent of the original mortgage loan if the mortgage is paid off prematurely.

prepayment penalty Special charge assessed to the borrower for paying off a loan early.

present value The current value of an asset (or stream of assets) that will be received in the future; also known as discounted value.

preservation of capital An investment goal that means the investor does not want to risk any principal or original investment; risk averse.

preshopping research Gathering information before actually beginning to interact with sellers.

prestige cards Bank credit cards whose names are often associated with a precious metal ("gold," "silver," "platinum"); require users to possess higher credit qualifications and offer enhancements such as free traveler's checks and higher credit limits.

pretax dollars Money income that has not been taxed by the government.

pretax income Income before taxes are calculated.

pretax money Investing with pretax money to a tax-sheltered retirement account comes out of your earnings before income taxes are calculated, thus gaining an immediate elimination of part of your income tax liability for the current year.

price/earnings ratio (P/E ratio) Widely followed measure of stock value that is calculated by dividing the current market price of a stock by earnings per share over the past four quarters.

price/sales ratio (P/S ratio) Tells the number of dollars it takes to buy a dollar's worth of a company's annual revenues; calculated by dividing company's total market capitalization by its sales for the past four quarters.

price-to-book ratio (P/B ratio) Current stock price divided by the per-share net value of a firm's plant, equipment, and other assets (book value); helps investors identify stocks that are value rich. Also called market-to-book ratio.

price-to-rent ratio Measures the current income in a real estate market; multiply the monthly rent by 12 and then divide the property price by this figure. The higher the number, the less likely you are to make money.

primary-care physician HMO-assigned doctor who usually must order or approve referrals to specialized health care providers.

prime rate Key measure of interest rates in the economy; its fluctuations drive th
rates for all types of variable-rate c

principal The original amount invested; or total amount owed on a credit account not including interest.

principle of indemnity Insurance will pay *no more* than the actual financial loss suffered.

private mortgage insurance Mortgage insurance obtained from a private company rather than a government agency.

probate Court-supervised process that allows creditors to present claims against an estate and ensures the transfer of a decedent's assets to the rightful beneficiaries according to a properly executed and valid will or, when no will exists, to the people, agencies, or organizations required by state law.

probate court Special court specifically charged to conduct the distribution of assets of people who have died.

professional abilities Job-related activities that you can perform physically, mentally, artistically, mechanically, and financially.

professional liability insurance/malpractice insurance Protects individuals and organizations that provide professional services when they are held liable for their clients' losses.

professional networking Making and using contacts with individuals, groups, and other firms to exchange career information.

professional shopper In exchange for a fee based on the sticker price, will find the best available price from a nearby dealer and finalize the sale or, for a lower price, will provide easily comparable information to buyer so that buyer can finalize purchase.

profile prospectus/fund profile Describes the mutual fund, its investment objectives, and how it tries to achieve its objectives in lay terms rather than the legal language used in a regular prospectus.

profit Money left over after a firm pays all expenses and interest to bondholders.

profit-sharing plan Employer-sponsored plan that allocates some of the employer profits to employees in the form of end-of-year cash or common stock contributions to employees' 401(k) accounts.

progressive income tax Tax rate increases as taxable income increases.

projected P/E ratio Because investors need to look to the future rather than the past, this measure divides price by projected earnings over the coming four quarters. Also known as forward price/earnings ratio.

promissory note Written installment loan contract that spells out the terms of the loan.

property insurance Protection from financial losses resulting from the damage to or destruction of your property or possessions.

prospectus Highly legalistic information presented by a firm to the SEC and to the public with any new issue of stock; this disclosure statement describes the experience of the corporation's management, the company's financial status, any anticipated legal matters that could affect the company, and potential risks of investing in the firm.

provider-sponsored network (PSN) Group of cooperating physicians and hospitals who have banded together to offer a health insurance contract. Also known as provider-sponsored association.

proxy Shareholders' written authorization to allow someone else to represent them and to vote their shares at a stockholder's meeting.

public corporation Corporation that issues stock purchased by individuals and traded in stock markets.

purchase contract/sales contract Formal legal document that outlines the actual agreement that results from the real estate negotiations.

purchase loan/sales credit Credit situation in which the consumer makes a purchase on credit with no cash transferring from the lender to the borrower.

purchase offer/offer to purchase Written offer to purchase real estate.

purchasing power Measure of the goods and services that one's income will buy.

pure risk Exists when there is no potential for gain, only the possibility of loss.

put option Gives option holder the right to sell the optioned asset to the option writer at the striking price at any time before the option expires.

qualified domestic-relations order (QDRO) Establishes the rights of an alternate payee to receive all or a portion of a participant's retirement plan benefits upon divorce or as soon as the participant leaves a private-sector job or reaches retirement age—must be court approved.

qualified retirement accounts IRS-approved retirement savings programs.

qualified tuition (Section 529) program Provides tax-sheltering when saving for a child's education.

quant funds (quantitative funds) In quant funds, computers make the buy and sell decisions based strictly on constant crunching of many numbers according to the criteria they are programmed to monitor.

random/unsystematic risk Risk associated with owning only one investment of a particular type (such as stock in one company) that, by chance, may do very poorly in the future due to uncontrollable or random factors that do not affect the rest of the market.

rate of return/yield Total return on an investment expressed as a percentage of its price.

real estate Property consisting of land, all structures permanently attached to that land, and accompanying rights and privileges, such as crops and mineral rights.

real estate broker (agent) Person licensed by a state to provide advice and assistance, for a fee, to buyers or sellers of real estate. Real estate brokers who are members of the National Association of Realtors often use the registered trademark of Realtor® to describe themselves.

real estate investment trust (REIT) Special kind of closed-end mutual fund that invests in a portfolio of assets, such as properties, like office buildings and shopping centers, or mortgages.

real estate property taxes Taxes assessed by local government agencies on the value of real estate to pay for schools and municipal services.

real estate transfer taxes Community-assessed taxes paid by the seller and also sometimes by the buyer based on the purchase price of the home or the equity the seller has in the home.

real income Income measured in constant prices relative to some base time period. It reflects the actual buying power of the money you have as measured in constant dollars.

real rate of return Return on an investment after subtracting the effects of inflation and income taxes.

rebate A partial refund of a purchase price offered as an inducement to buy.

recession A recurring period of decline in total output, income, employment and trade, usually lasting from six months to a year and marked by widespread contractions in many sectors of the economy.

record date Date that an issuer establishes to determine who is eligible to receive a dividend or distribution.

record keeping Recording sources and amounts of dollars earned and spent.

recurring clause Clarifies conditions under which a recurrence of an illness is considered a continuation of the first episode or a separate episode.

redeems When an investor sells shares.

redemption charge/exit fee Similar to a deferred load but often much lower; used to reduce excessive trading of fund shares.

redress Process of righting a wrong.

reenter provision Clause in a level-premium term policy that requires proof of good health at regular intervals.

refundable tax credit Credit that reduces taxes to below zero and the excess is refunded to taxpayer.

registered bond Bondholder's name is recorded so that checks or electronic funds transfers for payment of interest and principal can be safely forwarded when due.

regressive income tax As income rises, tax rate decreases.

reinvestment risk Risk that the return on a future investment will not be the same as the return earned by the original investment.

release Insurance document affirming that the dollar amount of the loss settlement is accepted as full and complete reimbursement.

remainder beneficiaries Parties named in the trust who are to receive the corpus upon termination of the trust agreement.

rent Payment received in return for allowing someone to use your real estate property, such as land or a building.

rental reimbursement coverage Provides a rental car when the insured's vehicle is being repaired after an accident or has been stolen.

rental yield A computation of how much income the investor might pocket from rent each year (before mortgage payments) as a percentage of the purchase price; divide the annual rent by 2 and then divide by the purchase price.

renter's contents broad form (HO-4) Named-perils policy that protects the insured from losses to the contents of a rented dwelling rather than the dwelling itself.

rent-to-own programs Provide a mechanism for buying an item with little or no down payment by renting it to the borrower for a period of time after which the borrower owns the merchandise.

repairs Usually tax-deductible expenses necessary to maintain property value.

replacement-cost requirement Stipulates that a home *must* be insured for 80 percent of its replacement value (some companies require 100 percent) in order for any loss to be fully covered.

repossession/foreclosure Legal proceeding by which the lender seizes an asset.

residual claim Common stockholders have a right to share in the income and assets of a corporation after higher-priority claims are satisfied.

residual clause of disability income policy Feature of own-occupation policies that allows for some reduced level of disability income benefits when a partial—rather than full—disability strikes.

residual value Projected value of leased asset at end of lease time period.

restrictive endorsement Uses the phrase *For deposit only* written on the back along with signature, authorizing the financial institution to accept the check only as an account deposit.

résumé Summary record of your education, training, experience, and other qualifications.

retail credit cards Allow customers to make purchases on credit at any of the outlets of a particular retailer.

retained earnings Money left over after firm has paid expenses, bondholder interest, taxes, preferred stockholder dividends, and common stockholder dividends.

retirement The time in life when the major sources of income change from earned income (such as salary or wages) to employer-based retirement benefits, private savings and investments, income from Social Security, and perhaps part-time employment.

retirement plan contribution credit/saver's tax credit Program to encourage low-income individuals to save for retirement, this tax credit ranges from 10 to 50 percent of every dollar they contribute to an IRA or employer-sponsored retirement plan up to $2000.

retirement savings goal/retirement nest egg Total amount of accumulated savings and investments needed to support desired retirement lifestyle.

return-of-premium policy Very expensive policy that promises to return all the premiums paid if the insured person maintains the policy and lives past a certain number of years—usually 30.

reverse mortgage/home-equity conversion loan Allows a homeowner older than age 61 to continue living in the home and to borrow against the equity in a home that is fully paid for and to receive the proceeds in a series of monthly payments, often over a period of 5 to 15 years or for life.

revocable living trust Grantor maintains the right to change the trust's terms or cancel it at any time, for any reason, during his or her lifetime.

revolving savings fund Variable budgeting tool that places funds in savings to cover large irregular or higher-than-usual expenses.

right of escheat Law by which, in the absence of a will, an estate transfers to the state if no surviving legal heirs exist.

risk Uncertainty about the outcome of a situation or event.

risk avoidance Refraining from owning items or engaging in activities that expose you to possible financial loss.

risk management Diversifying financial resources and ensuring you can handle large unexpected expenses.

risk management (in insurance) Process of identifying and evaluating purely risky situations to determine and implement appropriate management.

risk premium Amount that risk-averse investors require for taking on a riskier investment rather than a risk-free investment like U.S. government securities. The riskier the investment, the greater the premium demanded.

risk reduction Includes mechanisms, such as insurance, that reduce the overall uncertainty about the magnitude of loss.

risk retention Consciously accepting that some risks simply arise in the course of one's life and consciously retaining that risk.

risk tolerance An investor's ability and willingness to weather changes in security prices, that is, to weather market risk.

risk transfer Paying someone else, such as an insurance company, to accept the risk in your place and to reimburse you for any financial loss.

rollover Action of moving assets from one tax-sheltered account to another tax-sheltered account or to an IRA within 60 days of a distribution.

rollover IRA IRA opened to accept rollover funds.

rollover mortgage Consists of a series of short-term loans for two- to five-year time periods but with total amortization spread over the usual 25 to 30 years. The loan is renewed for each time period at prevailing market interest rates.

rollover penalty Penalty assessed by IRS if owner of qualified retirement plan does not follow IRS rollover regulations.

Roth individual retirement account (IRA) Investments made with after-tax money; the investment returns on such accounts is allowed to grow tax free, and withdrawals are also tax free.

round lots Standard units of trading of 100 shares of stock and $1000 or $5000 par value for bonds.

rule of 72 A formula for figuring the number of years it takes to double the principal using compound interest; simply divide the interest rate that the money will earn *into* the number 72.

rule of 78s method/sum of the digits method for calculating prepayment penalties A common method of calculating the prepayment penalty on a loan.

salary reduction plan Qualified plan in which contributed income is not included in an employee's salary.

sales finance company Seller-related lender whose primary business is financing sales for its parent company.

saver credit A credit of 50 percent of the amount contributed to a qualified retirement plan applies if adjusted gross income does not exceed $31,000 on a joint return or $15,500 for singles.

savings Income not spent on current consumption.

savings account Account that provides an accessible source of emergency cash and a temporary holding place for extra funds that will earn some interest.

savings banks (savings and loan associations—S&Ls) Financial institutions that pay depositors a slightly higher interest rate and focus primarily on savings and providing mortgage and consumer loans.

Savings Incentive Match Plan for Employees IRA (SIMPLE IRA) Defined-contribution retirement plan for employees of firms with fewer than 100 employees.

second mortgage An additional loan on a residence besides the original mortgage, usually at a higher interest rate because in case of default, the first mortgage is paid first.

Section 529 Plan Provides a tax-free way to save for college.

secured bond Pledges specific assets as collateral in indenture or has the principal and interest guaranteed by another corporation or government agency.

secured loan Loan that is backed by collateral or a cosigner.

securities Negotiable instruments of ownership or debt, including common stock, preferred stock, and bonds.

Securities and Exchange Commission (SEC) Federal government agency that ensures full disclosure of securities information to the investing public and approves rules and regulations employed by the organized securities exchanges.

securities exchange/stock market Market where agents of buyers and sellers can find each other easily by providing an orderly, open plan to trade securities.

securities market index Measures the average value of a number of securities chosen as a sample to reflect the behavior of a more general market, for example, the Dow Jones Industrial Average, the S&P 500, and so on.

security deposit Amount, often equal to the last month's rent payment, that landlords usually charge to ensure that tenants do not move without paying their rent.

security's street name Securities certificates kept in the brokerage firm's name instead of the name of the individual investor.

self-directed In defined-contribution plans, employees control the assets in their account—how often to make contributions to the account, how much to contribute, how much risk to take, and how to invest.

seller financing/owner financing When seller self-finances all or a portion of the buyer's purchase by accepting a promissory note from buyer.

selling agent Any real estate agent who seeks out buyers for a home. Listing agen[illegible] this role, but any real estate agent c[illegible] buyers to whom to sell a property.

selling short Investors selling securities they do not own (borrowing them from a broker) and later buying the same number of shares of the security at a lower price (returning them to the broker).

separable property Property wholly owned by one spouse; the property either belonged to one spouse before marriage or was received by that person as a gift or an inheritance during the marriage.

serial bonds Bonds that are retired serially; that is, each bond is numbered consecutively and matures according to a prenumbered schedule at stated intervals.

Series EE savings bonds Nonmarketable, interest-bearing bonds issued by the federal government that are issued at a sharp discount from face value and pay no annual interest, and they may be redeemed at full value upon maturity.

service credit Credit that public utilities, physicians, dentists, and other service providers extend to clients or users.

settlement options Choices from which the life insurance policyholder and/or beneficiary can choose in how the death benefit payment will be structured.

share draft account A checking account at a credit union.

shared-appreciation mortgage The lender offers an interest rate about one-third less than the market rate. In exchange, the lender gains the right to receive perhaps one-third of any appreciation in the home's value when the home is sold or ten years after the time of the loan.

shareholder fees Charged directly to investors for specific transactions, such as purchases, redemptions, or exchanges.

short-term (current) liability Obligation paid off within one year.

short-term gain/loss A profit or loss on the sale of an asset that has been held for one year or less.

signature card Identification used to verify the signatures of the owners of an account.

simplified employee pension—individual retirement account (SEP-IRA) Intended for taxpayers with self-employment income and owners of small businesses, contributions are tax deductible and funds grow tax deferred.

single-family dwelling Housing unit that is detached from other units.

single-payment loans Credit arrangement in which the full principal and interest amount is repaid at a specified future date.

single-premium life insurance Premium is paid once in the form of a lump sum; often used to pay for final expenses.

sinking fund Bond feature through which money is set aside with a trustee each year for repayment of the principal portion of the debt at maturity.

skilled nursing care Intended for people who need intensive care, meaning 24-hour-a-day supervision and treatment by a registered nurse, under the direction of a doctor.

skills format Résumé that emphasizes your aptitudes and qualities.

small-claims court State courts in which civil matters are often resolved without attorney assistance.

Social Security Administration (SSA) U.S. government agency that distributes checks to survivors and disabled workers—our national "safety net" funded by employee and employer contributions.

Social Security blackout period Once the youngest child reaches 18, the surviving spouse cannot collect Social Security survivors' benefits again until age 60.

Social Security credits Accumulated quarterly credits to qualify for Social Security benefits obtained by paying FICA taxes.

Social Security Disability Income Insurance Under this government program, eligible workers can collect some income for up to one year if their disabilities are total and expected to last one year or until death.

Social Security rider Provides an extra dollar amount of protection if you fail to qualify for Social Security disability benefits (70 percent of all applicants are rejected).

Social Security Statement The SSA periodically sends this document to all workers; it includes records of earnings history, records of how much workers and their employers have paid in Social Security taxes, and estimates of current and future benefits.

Social Security survivor's benefits Government program benefits paid to a surviving spouse and children of a deceased worker.

socially conscious funds Invest in companies that meet some predefined standard of moral and ethical behavior.

special (homeowner's insurance) form (HO-3): Provides open-perils protection (except for the commonly excluded perils of war, earthquake, and flood) for four types of property losses.

special endorsement Additional information, such as "Pay to the order of (name)," that creates a two-party check; such checks are very difficult to cash.

special needs trust Provides disabled beneficiary with lifelong access to supplemental and emergency funds to cover expenses that public assistance does not.

specialist Person on floor of an exchange who handles trades of a particular stock in an effort to maintain a fair and orderly market.

speculative risk Exists in situations that offer potential for gain as well as for loss. Investments involve speculative risk.

speculative-grade bonds Long-term, high-risk, high-interest-rate corporate (or municipal) IOUs issued by companies (or municipalities) with poor or no credit ratings. Also called junk bonds or high-yield bonds.

spending Amount of cash flow used in consuming goods and services now.

split-definition policy Provides benefits for rehabilitation and retraining at insurance company expense.

spousal consent requirement Federal law that protects surviving rights of spouse or ex-spouse to retirement or pension benefits unless the person signs a waiver of those rights.

spousal IRA Account set up for spouse who does not work for wages; offers tax-deferred growth and tax deductibility.

spread Represents difference between bid price at which a broker/dealer will buy shares and higher ask price at which the broker/dealer will sell shares.

springing power of attorney "Jumps" into effect when a specified event occurs, usually mental incapacitation or disability.

standard deduction Fixed amount that all taxpayers may subtract from their adjusted gross income if they do not itemize their deductions.

standard deviation A measure of a security's or mutual fund's volatility; also known as beta.

standard of living Material well-being and peace of mind that individuals or groups earnestly desire and seek to attain, to maintain if attained, to preserve if threatened, and to regain if lost.

standardized expense table SEC-required information that describes and illustrates mutual fund charges in an identical manner so that investors can accurately compare the effects of all of a fund's fees and other expenses relative to other funds.

start-up capital Funds initially invested in a business enterprise.

statement savings account (passbook savings account) Savings account that permits frequent deposits or withdrawals of funds without fees as long as client maintains minimum balance.

stay An order in bankruptcy court that temporarily prevents all creditors from recovering claims arising from before the start of the bankruptcy proceeding.

stock brokerage firms Licensed financial institutions that specialize in selling and buying stocks, bonds, and other investments for investors.

stock dividend Dividend paid in the form of stock shares instead of cash.

stock option Security that gives the holder the right to buy or sell a specific number of shares (normally 100) of a certain stock at a specified (striking) price before a specified expiration date.

stock split Occurs when stock shares owned by existing shareholders are divided into a larger number of shares.

stockbroker/account executive Professional who is licensed to buy and sell securities on behalf of the brokerage firm's clients.

stockholder/shareholder Each person who owns a share of a company's stock holds a proportionate interest in firm ownership (a very small slice) and, therefore, in the assets and income of the corporation.

stocks Shares of ownership in a business corporation's assets and earnings.

stock-screening tools Enable you to quickly sift through vast databases of hundreds of companies to find those that best suit your investment objectives.

stop order Instructs a stockbroker to sell your shares of stock at the market price if a stock declines to or goes below a specified price.

stop-payment order Notifying your bank not to honor a check when it's presented for payment.

stored-value card Usually gift cards that have magnetic strips or bar codes that encrypt the amount of money stored via the card.

straight annuity Provides lifetime payments for the life of the annuitant only.

subleasing An arrangement in which the original tenant leases the property to another tenant.

subordinate budget Detailed listing of planned expenses within a single budgeting classification.

subprime market Market that serves higher-risk credit applicants at higher interest rates.

subrogation rights Allow an insurer to take action against a negligent third party (and that party's insurance company) to obtain reimbursement for payments made to an insured.

suicide clause Allows the life insurance company to deny coverage if the insured commits suicide within the first few (usually two) years after the policy is issued.

super NOW account Government-insured money market account offered through depository institutions.

surplus/net gain/net income Income that exceeds total expenditures.

surrender charge A fee assessed if the policyholder withdraws some or all of the cash value accumulated.

survey Professional study undertaken to certify the specific boundaries of a lot.

survivorship joint life policy Pays when the last person covered dies.

sweat equity property Property that needs repairs but that has good underlying value; an investor buys the property at a favorable price and fixes it up to rent or sell at a profit.

sweeps Computer programs that check various subaccounts in an AMA and adjust balances in and out of the MMMF to ensure the highest interest rates.

take-home pay/disposable income Pay received after employer withholdings for taxes, insurance, and union dues.

tangible (use) assets Personal property used to maintain your everyday lifestyle.

tax avoidance Reducing tax liability through legal techniques.

tax balance due Money you must pay to the IRS if withholding and quarterly payments are insufficient to cover tax liability.

tax credit Dollar-for-dollar decrease in tax liability; also known as credit.

tax deferred Interest, dividends, or capital gains that are allowed to grow without taxes until distributions are taken.

tax evasion Deliberately, willfully, and illegally hiding income, falsely claiming deductions, or otherwise cheating the government out of taxes owed.

tax losses Paper losses that may not represent actual losses created when deductions generated from an investment exceed income from the investment.

tax planning Seeking legal ways to reduce, eliminate, or defer income taxes.

tax rate schedules Equations to figure taxes for returns with taxable incomes above $100,000.

tax refund Amount the IRS sends back to taxpayer if withholding and estimated payments exceed tax liability.

taxable income Income upon which income taxes are levied.

tax-deferred compounding Tax-free growth of tax-deferred investments.

taxes Compulsory government-imposed charges levied on citizens and their property.

tax-exempt income Income that is totally and permanently free of taxes.

tax-exempt money market funds Funds that limit their investments to tax-exempt municipal securities with maturities of 90 days or less.

tax-free exchange Arises when a real estate investor trades equity in one property for equity in a similar property and no other forms of property or money change hands.

tax-sheltered income Income exempt from income taxes in the current year but that will be subject to taxation in a later tax year.

tax-sheltered investments Investments that yield returns that are tax advantaged.

tax-sheltered retirement accounts Retirement account for which all earnings from the invested funds are not subject to income taxes.

tax-sheltered retirement plan Employer-sponsored, defined-contribution retirement plans including 401(k) plans and similar 403(b) and 457 plans.

teaser rate Low interest rate that lenders sometimes use to lure buyers; these rates will be low for the first year or so and then will rise to more realistic rates.

technical analysis Method of evaluating securities that uses statistics generated by market activity, such as past prices and volume, over time to determine when to buy or sell a stock.

10-K report A firm's financial statements and activity details for any publicly traded company appear in this mandatory report sent to the SEC annually.

tenancy by the entirety Restricted to property held between a husband and a wife; under this arrangement, no one co-owner can sell or dispose of his or her portion of an asset without the permission of the other.

tenancy for a specific time Type of lease that provides for residency for a specific period of time—usually one year.

tenancy in common A form of joint ownership in which two or more parties own the asset, but each retains control over a separate piece of the property rights.

term life insurance "Pure protection" against early death; pays benefits only if the insured dies within the time period (term) that the policy covers.

testamentary trust Becomes effective upon death of the grantor according to the terms of the grantor's will or a revocable living trust. Such trusts can provide money or asset management after the grantor's death for the heirs' benefit.

testator Writer of a will and owner of the estate.

tiered interest Common feature of NOW accounts that pays lower interest on smaller deposits and higher interest on larger balances.

tiered pricing Lending practice whereby those with best credit scores are offered better terms than those with less-than-perfect scores.

time deposits Savings accounts that financial institutions expect to remain on deposit for an extended period.

time horizon The period of time for which an investor is willing to invest; the longer the term, the higher return investors expect.

time value of money (TVM) A method by which one can compare cash flows across time, either as what a future cash flow is worth today (present value) or what an investment made today will be worth in the future (future value).

timesharing Joint ownership or lease of vacation property through which the principals occupy the property individually for set periods of time.

title Legal right of ownership interest to real property.

title insurance Protects the lender's interest if the title search is later found faulty.

title search An examination of local government records to ensure that the seller of a piece of property is the legal owner and that there are no liens or other claims outstanding.

total income Compensation from all sources.

total return Income an investment generates from current income and capital gains.

towing coverage Pays the cost of having a disabled vehicle transported for repairs.

trade-off Giving up one thing for another.

traditional (regular) IRA Account that offers tax-deferred growth; the initial contribution may be tax deductible for the year that the IRA was funded.

trailing commission Compensation paid to salespeople for months or years in the future.

trailing P/E ratio Calculated using recently reported earnings, usually from the previous four quarters.

transaction date Date on which a credit cardholder makes a purchase (or receives a credit).

transaction fees Charges levied against cardholders per use of the card but that are not included in the APR advertised.

travel and entertainment (T&E) cards Credit cards that allow holders to make purchases at numerous businesses but that require the holder to repay the entire balance charged within 30 days.

traveler's checks Financial instruments issued by extremely large institutions that are accepted virtually anywhere in the world upon countersignature.

Treasury bills Known as T-bills, U.S. government securities with maturities of one year or less.

Treasury Inflation-Protected Securities (TIPS) Marketable Treasury bonds whose value increases with inflation. These inflation-indexed $1000 bonds are the only investment that guarantees that the investor's return will outpace inflation.

Treasury note/Treasury bond Fixed-principal, fixed-interest-rate government security issued for an intermediate term or long term. Notes mature in ten years or less; bonds mature in more than ten years.

Treasury securities Known as Treasuries, securities issued by the U.S. government, including bills, notes, and bonds.

trough The point in the business cycle when economic activity is at its lowest point.

trust Legal arrangement between you as the creator of the trust and the trustee, the person designated to faithfully and wisely manage any assets in the trust to your benefit and to the benefit of your heirs.

trustee Financial institution, bank, or trust company that has fiduciary responsibility for holding plan assets and that invests the money in various securities; person charged with carrying out the trust for the benefit of the grantor(s) and heirs.

trustee-to-trustee rollover Retirement funds go directly from the previous employer's trustee to the trustee of the new account, with no payment to the employee occurring.

Truth in Lending Act (TIL) Requires lenders to disclose to credit applicants both the interest rate expressed as an annual percentage rate (APR) and the finance charge.

12b-1 fees/distribution fees Annual fees that some "no-load" fund companies deduct from a fund's assets to compensate salespeople and pay other expenses; they decrease the amount of money available for investment.

2006 Pension Protection Act Prohibits companies from requiring that employees buy company stock to qualify for matching contributions.

U.S. government savings bonds Nonmarketable, interest-bearing bonds issued by the U.S. Treasury.

umbrella (excess) liability insurance Catastrophic liability policy that covers liability losses in excess of those covered by any underlying homeowner's, automobile, or professional liability policy.

unearned income Investment returns in the form of rents, dividends, capital gains, interest, or royalties.

underwriting Insurer's procedure for deciding which insurance applicants to accept.

unfair discrimination Making distinctions among individuals based on unfair criteria when granting credit.

uniform settlement statement Lists all of the costs and fees to be paid at the closing.

unit investment trust (UIT) Closed-end investment company that makes a one-time public offering of only a specific, fixed number of units; once the UIT closes, it becomes an unmanaged fund that is somewhat illiquid.

universal default Situation in which credit companies assign much higher rates to accounts because credit report rechecks indicate repayment problems in one or more other accounts with any lender.

universal life insurance Provides the pure protection of term insurance and the cash-value buildup of whole life insurance, along with face amount variability, rate of cash-value accumulation, premiums, and rate of return.

unmanaged fund Fund with very low management fees since managers do not evaluate or select individual securities; ETFs and index funds are examples.

unsecured bond/debenture Does not name collateral as security for debt; backed only by the good faith and reputation of the issuing agency.

unsecured loan/signature loan Loan granted based solely on borrower's good creditworthiness.

"upside down" Situation in which you owe more on the vehicle than its current market value.

use-it-or-lose-it rule An IRS regulation requiring that unspent dollars in a flexible spending account at the end of a calendar year be forfeited, unless the employer allows a three-month grace period for spending the funds.

usury laws/small loan laws Laws that stipulate state-mandated maximum amounts, interest rates, and credit-related fees for different types of loans.

utility A highly personalized concept that expresses how much satisfaction each person will obtain from any particular decision.

value funds Specialize in stocks that are fundamentally sound whose prices appear to be low (low P/E ratios) based on the logic that such stocks are currently out of favor and undervalued by the market.

values Fundamental beliefs about what is important, desirable, and worthwhile.

vanishing-premium life insurance Designed to allow policyholders to cease making premium payments after just a few years.

variable annuity Annuity whose value rises and falls like mutual funds and pays a limited death benefit via an insurance contract. Not as efficient as a mutual fund; costs are high for little return.

variable expenses Expenses over which you have substantial control.

variable interest rate cards Have rates that change monthly or annually according to general changes in the economy as a whole.

variable life insurance Allows you to choose the investments made with your cash-value accumulations and to share in any gains or losses.

variable value Because interest rates change, bonds may trade at a premium (more than face value) or at a discount (less than par) so that the yield equals the current yield for bonds with similar maturities and risk levels.

variable-rate (adjustable-rate) loans Loans for which the interest rate varies with the monthly payment going up or down, allowing the loan to be paid off by the original end date.

variable-rate certificates of deposit (or adjustable-rate CDs) Financial instruments that pay an interest rate that tracks general interest rates in the economy.

variable-universal life insurance Form of universal life insurance that gives the policyholder some choice in the investments made with the cash value accumulated by the policy. Also called flexible-premium variable life insurance.

vesting Ensures that a retirement plan participant has the right to take full possession of all employer contributions and earnings if employee is dismissed, resigns, or retires.

viatical companies Firms that specialize in buying life insurance policies from insureds for $0.50 to $0.80 per $1 of death benefit in return for being named beneficiary on the policy.

vision care insurance Provides reimbursement for eye examinations and purchase of glasses and contact lenses.

volatility A mutual fund's (or any security's) tendency to rise or fall in price over time.

voting rights Proportionate authority to express an opinion or choice in matters affecting the company.

waiting period Long-term care and disability income policies can pay benefits from the first day of a triggering event or they can include a waiting period. Premiums drop with longer waiting periods.

waiver of premium Sets certain conditions under which an insurance policy would be kept in full force by the company without the payment of premiums.

want Item not necessary but desired.

warranty Sellers' assurances that goods are as promised and that certain steps will be taken to rectify problems if they arise.

whole life insurance Form of cash-value life insurance that provides lifetime life insurance protection and expects the insured to pay premiums for life. Also called straight life insurance.

will Written document in which a person tells how his or her remaining assets should be given away after death; without a will, the property will be distributed according to state probate law.

withdrawal options/systematic withdrawal plans Arrangements with a mutual fund company for shareholders who want to receive income on a regular basis from their mutual fund investments.

workers' compensation insurance Covers employers for liability losses for injury or disease suffered by employees that result from employment-related causes.

work-style personality Your own ways of working with and responding to job requirements, surroundings, and associates.

yield to maturity (YTM) Total annual effective rate of return earned by a bondholder on a bond if the security is held to maturity—takes into consideration both the price at which the bond sold and the coupon interest rate to arrive at effective rate of return.

zero-coupon bonds (zeros or deep discount bonds) Municipal, corporate, and Treasury bonds that are issued at a sharp discount from face value and pay no annual interest but are redeemed at full face value upon maturity.

zero-sum game Situation in which the wealth of all investors remains the same; the trading simply redistributes the wealth among those traders. Each profit must be offset by an equivalent loss; therefore, the average rate of return for all investors in futures is zero.

Index

Note: Boldface type indicates key terms that are defined in text.

AARP. *See* American Association of Retired Persons
Abilities, professional, 34
About.com, 383
Abstract, 239
Accident insurance, 307
Account reconciliation, 142
Ackley, Dennis R., 497
Active investor, 360
Activities of daily living (ADL), 311
ACY. *See* **Approximate compound yield**
Add-on method of interest, 200–201
Adjustable life insurance, 331
Adjusted capitalized cost (adjusted cap cost), 217
ADL. *See* **Activities of daily living**
Adoption tax credit, 112
Advance medical directive, 530–531
After-tax dollars, 118
After-tax money, 498
After-tax yield, 122
Aggressive growth mutual fund, 441
AGI. *See* **Income, adjusted gross**
AIP. *See* **Automatic investment program**
Alhabeeb, M. J., 192
Allowance, 152
All-risk (open-perils) insurance, 277
Alpha statistic, 397
Alternative dispute resolution programs, 226
A.M. Best Company, 350
AMA. *See* **Asset management account**
American Association of Retired Persons (AARP), 519
American Savings Education Council, 488
Amortization, 200, 250
  effects, 251
  negative, 254
  schedule, 250
AMT. *See* **Tax, higher alternative minimum**
Anderson, Jan D., 292
Annual percentage rate (APR), 162, 179
Annual percentage yield (APY), 143
Annual report, 402
Annuitant, 514
Annuity, 18, 514
  deferred, 515
  future value of, 17
  immediate, 514
  installment-certain, 514
  joint-and-survivor, 515
  present value of, 18
  straight, 514
  variable, 515
Appraisal fee, 239
Approximate compound yield (ACY), 400
APR. *See* **Annual percentage rate**
Aptitudes, 34
APY. *See* **Annual percentage yield**
Arbitration, 226
"As is," 219
Ask price, 411
Assessed value, 241
Asset allocation, 372–374
  rules of thumb, 373
  sharpe ratio of, 374
Asset management account (AMA), 147
Assets, 65, 104
  increasing, 67
  investment (capital), 65, 66
  monetary/liquid/cash equivalent, 65, 132
  tangible (use), 65
  transferring, 524, 535
Asset-to-debt ration, 74
Assumable mortgage, 255
ATM cards, 148
ATM transaction fee, 148
Attorney
  fees, 238
  hiring, 249
Automatic enrollment retirement plan, 500
Automatic funds transfer agreement, 140, 141
Automatic investment program (AIP), 342
Automatic overdraft loan agreement, 140, 141
Automatic premium loan, 338
Automatic rebalancing of portfolio, 373, 374
Automatic reinvestment, 438
Average share cost, 371
Average share price, 370

Back-end load mutual fund, 446
Back-end ratio, 245
Bad checks, 140
Balance statement, 64, 90
  components of, 65–66
  sample, 66–67, 68, 69
Balance transfer, 186
Balloon automobile loan, 218
Bank Insurance Fund (BIF), 134
Bank, mutual savings (MSB), 134
Bankrate.com, 205, 243
Bankruptcy, 177–178
Bankruptcy Act
  Chapter 7 of, 178–179
  Chapter 13 of, 178
Banks, commercial, 134
Basic ratio of liquidity, 74
Bear market, 368, 475
Beneficial Finance Corporation (BFC), 173
Beneficiaries, remainder, 528
Beneficiary designation form, 499, 523
Benign neglect, 369
Best buy, 215
Beta value, 391, 397–398
BFC. *See* Beneficial Finance Corporation
Bid price, 411
BIF. *See* **Bank Insurance Fund**
Biweekly mortgage, 255
Blink (Gladwell), 52
Blogs, investment, 404
Bloomberg, 402
Blue-chip stock, 392–393
Bogle, John C., 448
Bond(s), 359, 363, **373, 387**
  bearer, 421
  callable, 421
  corporate, 417–418
  coupon rate, 420–421
  default rate on, 417
  funds, 440–441
  government savings, 119, 122, 144
  high-yield, 417
  I, 419
  indenture, 421
  investment-grade, 417
  junk, 417
  maturity date, 387
  municipal, 122, 123, **420**
  par value of, 417
  price changes for, 424, 425
  principal of, 387
  rating, 417, 418
  registered, 421
  secured, 421
  serial, 421
  Series EE savings, 119, 144, 419
  Series HH savings, 420
  Series I savings, 119
  speculative-grade, 417
  tax-free, 420
  unsecured, 421
  variable value of, 422
  zero-coupon, 419, 422
Bond Market Association, 426
Bondinfo, 426
Book value, 396
Book-entry form, 421
Bounce protection agreement, 140
Breakpoints, 445
Brokered certificate of deposit, 141
Budget, 78, 90
  analyses, 88
  balancing, 354
  controls, 85
  deficits, 88
  envelope system, 86
  estimates, 79, **80,** 82, 83
  exceptions, 86
  missteps in planning, 85
  problems, 93
  rules for successful, 84

Budget *(cont.)*
sample, 81
subordinate, 85
variance, 86
Bull market, 364
Bump-up certificate of deposit, 141
Bureau of Labor Statistics Consumer Price Index, 29
Business cycle, 7
Business Cycle Dating Committee, 7
Business-cycle risk, 364
"Buy term and invest the rest," 342
Buy-and-hold investing, 369
Buyer protection plan, 219
Buyer's order, 225
Buyer's real estate broker (agent), 247
Buying long, 415

Cafeteria plan. *See* **Flexible benefit plan**
Call option, 421, 477, 479
Campolo, Anthony J., 107
Canceled checks, 137
Capital
accumulation, 60
assets, 65, 66
improvements, 463
loss, 104, 356
preservation of, 359
start-up, 386
Capital gain, 104, 356, 360
distributions, 435
Capitalized cost reductions (cap cost reductions), 217
Car purchase contract, 204–205
Card registration service, 150
Career, 32
advancement tips, 45
fairs, 46
goal, 33, 39
planning, 55
Career planning, 32, 33
changes to, 39
financial missteps in, 34
Carrigan, Martin, 310
Cash, 373
account, 407
basis, 67
flow, 463
surplus, 71
Cash advance, 184
checks, 186
Cash equivalent assets, 65, 132
Cash-balance retirement plan, 504–505
Cash-flow calendar, 82, 84
Cash-flow statement, 65, 67–68, 70–71, 90
sample, 71–72, 73
Cashier's checks, 137
CCAs. *See* **Credit counseling agencies**
CD. *See* **Certificate of deposit**
Central asset accounts, 147
Certificate of deposit (CD), 131, **139,** 141
brokered, 141
bump-up, 141
interest rates on, 141
laddering, 141
uninsured, 141
variable-rate, 141
Certificate of insurance, 305
Certified checks, 137, 138
Certified financial planner (CFP), 344
Certified Financial Planner Board of Standards, 24
CFP. *See* Certified financial planner
Chapter 7 of Bankruptcy Act, 178–179
Chapter 13 of Bankruptcy Act, 178
Charity, gifts to, 108–109
Chartered financial consultant (ChFC), 344
Chartered life underwriter (CLU), 344
Check register, 135
Checking account, 135
average-balance, 138
costs/penalties on, 139
free, 136
interest-earning, 136
minimum-balance, 138
minimum-balance requirements, 136, 138
options, 155–156
share draft, 136
tiered interest, 136
Checks
bad, 140
canceled, 137
cashier's, 137
certified, 137, 138
cleared, 137
endorsement, blank, 140
endorsement, restrictive, 139, **140**
endorsement, special, 140
image statements, 137
stop-payment order on, 137
substitute, 137
traveler's, 137, 138
Chex Systems, 140
ChFC. *See* Chartered financial consultant
Chicago Board of Trade, 484
Child and dependent care credit, 112
Child tax credit, 112
Children, money sense and, 152
Chronological format résumé, 46, 48
City indexes, 41
Claims adjuster, 293
Claims ratio, 305
Classified job advertisements, 38, 46
Cleared checks, 137
Cliff vesting, 502
"CliffsNotes," 535
Closed-end leasing, 217
Closed-end mutual fund, 439
CLU. *See* Chartered life underwriter
CNN Money, 459
COBRA. *See* **Consolidated Omnibus Budget Reconciliation Act of 1985**
Codicil, 525
Coinsurance, 273, 308
COLA. *See* Cost of living adjustment
Collectibles, 471
College savings plan, 119
College-expense needs, 324, 326
Collegiate Funding Services, 166
Collision insurance, 285
Commissions, 365, 446
life insurance, 345
stated, 444
trailing, 445
Common stock, 386–387, 427
Community property, 146, 528
laws, 528
Comparison shopping, 215, 227
Compound interest, 2, 14, **15**
Comprehensive insurance, 285
Comprehensive personal liability insurance, 289
Computer banking service, 156
Conditional sales contracts, 198
Condominium, 234, 235, **278**
buying, 381
Conference Board, 29
Consolidated Omnibus Budget Reconciliation Act of 1985 (COBRA), 310
Consumer confidence index, 8
Consumer finance company, 173
Consumer Handbook on Credit Protection, 181
Consumer Information Center, 210
Consumer price index (CPI), 9–10
Consumer protection regulations, 149–150
Consumer Reports, 210, 229, 448
Consumer Reports Buying Guide, 210
Consumer statement, 171
Contents replacement-cost protection, 282
Contingency clauses, 247
Contingent beneficiary, 523
Continuous-debt method, 165
Contraction, 7
Contributory retirement plan, 500
Controlling overspending, 85
Convenience, price of, 209
Conventional mortgage, 253
Cooperative, 234
Copayments, 308
Corporate earnings, 395
Corporation, 386
board of directors, 387
management, 387
public, 386
Corpus, 528
Cost
below-average, 370
of buying home, 238, 243–244, 260
closing, 237
marginal, 12, 27
opportunity, 11, 27, **116**
seller's, 221
Cost of living adjustment (COLA), A-12
Costs/benefits, 35
Countercyclical stock, 393
Counteroffer, 246–247
Court TV, 537
Cover letter, 49
sample, 50
Coverdell education savings account, 119, 144
Covered option, 477
"Covering a position," 416

CPI. *See* **Consumer price index**
Credit, 160
agreement, 168
application, 167
building/maintaining, 160, 170
bureau, 168
common sources of consumer, 179
consumer, 184
disability insurance, 191
divorce and, 172
downside of, 161–162
free, 161
good uses of, 160–161
history, 167, 242
home-equity line of, 185, 256
installment, 184
investigation, 168
life insurance, 191
limit, 184
missteps with, 167
noninstallment, 184
obtaining, 167
open-ended, 184
personal line of, 184–185
rating, 168
repair company, 177
report, 46, **168,** 170
reputation, 169–171
score, 242, 248
scoring, 168
service, 185
transactions, 86
Credit cards, 148, 160, 184
affinity, 186
annual fees, 190
average daily balance, 195
bank, 185–186
billing date, 191
blocking, 160
calculating balance on, 195
chargeback, 195
closing, 187
co-branded, 186
debt, 192
default rate, 189
due date, 192
features of, 203
fixed-rate, 190
grace period, 192–193
liability, 190
minimum payment, 185, 193–194
missteps with, 185
periodic rate, 195
posting date, 192
preapproved, 190
prestige, 186
prime rate, 189–190
principle, 185
receipt, 194
retail, 186
secured, 190
statement, 191, 193
stolen, 204
teaser rate, 187
transaction date, 192
transaction fee, 190
travel and entertainment, 186
universal default, 189
variable interest rate, 189–190
verification value, 162
withholding payment to, 196
Credit counseling agencies (CCAs), 177
Credit union (CU), 134
Crude annual rate of return on real estate, 473
CU. *See* **Credit union**
Cude, Brenda, 162, 214
Current income, 356
Current yield, 423
Currently insured, 491, A-13
Custodial account, 144
Custodial care, 311
Cyclical stock, 393

Dalbar, 359
Damage deposit, 232
Day orders, 412
Day trading, 409
Debit card, 135, 148
Debt, 362
collection agencies, 176
consolidation, 173, 180
credit card, 192
discharged, 177
getting out of excessive, 176–177
limit, 163, 165, 179
payments, 164
student loan, 166
Debt management plan (DMP), 177
Debt payments-to-disposable income ratio, 75, 163
Debt service-to-income ratio, 75
Debt-consolidation loan, 161
Debt-repayment needs, 323–324, 325–326
Debt-to-equity ratio, 165, 176
Decision-making grid, 224, 225
Decision-Making Worksheet, 40
Decker, Lorraine, 534
Declining market, 371
Declining-balance method of interest, 200
Deductibles, 220, **273, 308**
Deductions
above-the-line, 106
bunching, 124
increasing itemized, 124
itemized, 107
miscellaneous, 109–110
standard, 106–107
Deed
of bargain and sale, 239
quitclaim, 238
restrictions, 235
special warranty, 238
warranty, 238
Default risk, 417
Deferred annuity, 515
Deferred compounding tax, 118
Deferred income tax, 498
Deferred load mutual fund, 446
Deferred tax, 118
Deficiency balance, 175
Deficit, 67
budget, 88
Defined contribution retirement plan, 500–501
Defined-benefit retirement plan, 502–503
Defined-contribution retirement plan, 117
Deflation risk, 364
Demand deposit savings account, 138
Dental expense insurance, 305
Dental expenses, 107–108
Department of Veterans Affairs (VA), 240
Depository institutions, 134
Depreciation, 465
Derivative, 476
Differential, 410
Direct deposit, 149
Direct ownership, 462
Disability benefits, 504
Disclosure statement, 149
Discount bonds, 144
Discount brokers, 409
Discount method of interest, 202
Discount yield, 418
Discounted cash-flow method, 467–469
Discounted value. *See* **Present value**
Discretionary income, 80
Disposable personal income, 75, 80, 163
Diversification, 363
Dividend, 356
cash, 386, 388, 395
mutual fund, 435
payout ratio, 395–396
per share, 395
stock, 389
yield, 396
DJIA. *See* Dow Jones Industrial Average
DMP. *See* **Debt management plan**
"Do not resuscitate order," 531
Dolan, Elizabeth, 422
Dollar-cost averaging investing, 370–372
Domestic-relations order, 493
Domestic-relations order, qualified (QDRO), 493
Donee, 528
Dow Jones Industrial Average (DJIA), 405
Down payment, 237
Dread disease insurance, 307
Driving, 270
Due-on-sale clause, 255
Dunning letters, 196
Durable power of attorney, 530

Earned income, 101
Earned income credit (EIC), 112
Earnest money, 246
Earnings per share (EPS), 395
eBay, 471
EBT. *See* **Electronic benefits transfer cards**
ECOA. *See* Equal Credit Opportunity Act
Economic cycle. *See* **Business cycle**
Economic growth, 6

Economic Review, 157
Economy Policy Institute, 94
EDGAR. *See* Electronic Data Gathering and Retrieval
Edmunds, 212
Education
training, 35
value of additional, 42
EFTs. *See* **Electronic funds transfers**
EIC. *See* **Earned income credit**
Eighth, 410
Electronic benefits transfer cards (EBT), 148
Electronic Data Gathering and Retrieval (EDGAR), 402
Electronic Funds Transfer Act, 155
Electronic funds transfers (EFTs), 148
Electronic money management, 147, **148**–150, 155
Emergency fund, 143
Emergency savings, 74
Employee benefit, 19
future value of, 42–43
market value of, 42
tax-free, 105
Employee Retirement Income Security Act (ERISA), 500
Employee stock option (ESO), 396
Employee stock-ownership plan (ESOP), 505
Employer
matching contributions, 22, **118**
preferred, 38
staff opinions on, 51
Employer-sponsored retirement plan, 500
Employment
agency, 49
rights, 43–44
trends, 36–37
Employment Report, 8
Endorsement checks
blank, 140
restrictive, 139, **140**
special, 140
EPS. *See* **Earnings per share**
Equal Credit Opportunity Act (ECOA), 168
Equity, 165, 250, 362, 373
ERISA. *See* **Employee Retirement Income Security Act**
Escrow account, 240
ESO. *See* **Employee stock option**
ESOP. *See* **Employee stock-ownership plan**
Estate buildup, 342
Estate planning, 522
checklist for, 532
do it yourself, 527
on internet, 530
missteps in, 533
steps in, 531
for unmarried couples, 530
Estimated tax, 102
ETF. *See* **Exchange-traded fund**
Evaluating stocks, 394–397, 427
Exchange fee, 438
Exchange privilege, 438
Exchange-traded fund (ETF), 439
gold, 475
Exclusion amount, 533
Exclusions, 104–105
Exclusive insurance agent, 276
Executor, 526
Exemptions, 110
Expansion, 7
Expense reimbursement account, 117
Expenses, 67
dental, 107–108
fixed, 68, 70
job, 109
medical, 107–108
variable, 68, 70–71
Experiences, 34–35
Exposures, 269
Express warranty, 219, 220
Extended warranty, 219

Fair Credit and Charge Card Disclosure Act (FCCCDA), 188
Fair Credit Billing Act (FCBA), 161, **195**
Fair Credit Reporting Act (FCRA), 170, 171
Fair Debt Collection Practices Act (FDCPA), 176
Fair Isaac and Company, 169
Fair market value, 109, 241
Family auto policy insurance, 283
Fannie Mae. *See* Federal National Mortgage Association
FCBA. *See* **Fair Credit Billing Act**
FCCCDA. *See* Fair Credit and Charge Card Disclosure Act
FCRA. *See* **Fair Credit Reporting Act**
FDCPA. *See* **Fair Debt Collection Practices Act**
FDIC. *See* **Federal Deposit Insurance Corporation**
Federal Consolidation Loans, 166
Federal Deposit Insurance Corporation (FDIC), 134, 139
Federal estate tax, 533
Federal funds rate, 10
Federal Housing Administration (FHA), 240
Federal Insurance Contributions Act (FICA), 489
tax rate of, 490, A-12
Federal National Mortgage Association (Fannie Mae), 245, 420
Federal Reserve Bank of Chicago, 157
Federal Reserve Board, 10, 181, 229
Federal Trade Commission, 171
Federation of Tax Administrators, 129
FICA. *See* **Federal Insurance Contributions Act**
Fidelity Magellan Fund, 392
Filing status, 107
Filing tax, 101
Fill-or-kill orders, 412
Final expenses, 322, 325
Finance charge, 161
Financial behavior, examples of poor, 24
Financial calculator, 18
Financial disagreements, 151
Financial goals, 61
intermediate term, 79
long term, 78
prioritizing, 79
reachable, 82
short term, 79
Financial happiness, 5
Financial literacy, 4, 7
Financial planner, 24
choosing, 25
commission only, 25
fee-based, 25
fee-offset, 25
fee-only, 25
professional certifications, 26
Financial planning, 32, **60,** 62–63
good money habits in, 61
process, 60
Financial Planning Association, 29
Financial progress, assessing, 76
Financial ratios, 72, 74, 90
Financial records, 76, 77–78, 90
Financial responsibility, 4
Financial risk, 356, 364, 372
Financial services industry, 133
Financial software, 87
Financial statements, 64
Financial strategies, 63
Financial success, 5, 27
building blocks of, 6
Financing options, 216
First-to-die life insurance, 335
Fixed expenses, 68, 70
Fixed income, 362
Fixed maturity, 362
Fixed yield, 422
Fizbo, 258
Flat-fee real estate broker (agent), 247
Flexible benefit plan, 19, 117
Flexible premium variable life insurance, 333–334
Flexible spending account (FSA), 20, 117
Floor broker, 410
Foreclosure, 175, 249
Form 1040, 114–115
Form 1040X, 113
Form 1099, 101
Form 8822, 101
Form W-2, 101, 103
Fortuitous loss, 273
401(k) retirement plan, 3, **117,** 487, **501**
cashing out, 45
"net pay" numbers of, 498
403(b) retirement plan, 501
457 retirement plan, 501
Fox, Jonathan, 479
Free credit, 161
Front-end load, 444
Front-end ratio, 245
FSA. *See* **Flexible spending account**
Full warranty, 219
Fully insured, 491, A-13
Fulmer, Caroline S., 37
Fun money, 442

Functional format résumé, 46, 48
Fund investment advisors, 436
Fund screener, 453
Future value (FV), 15, A-2
  of employee benefit, 42–43
  of lump sum, 16–17
  of series of equal amounts, A-8, A-9
  of single amount, A-3, A-4, A-5
Futures contract, 480, 483–484
  leverage in, 481
Futures market, 480
  speculators in, 480–481
FV. *See* **Future value**

Gain
  capital, 104, 356, 360, **435**
  long-term, 104
  short-term, 104
"Gap" insurance, 213
Garnishment, 175
GDP. *See* **Gross domestic product**
General brokerage firm, 410
Generic products, 208, 209
Ginnie Mae. *See* Government National Mortgage Association
Gladwell, Malcolm, 52
Gold bullion, 474
  coins, 474–475
Gold Rush of 1876, 475
Good cop–bad cop, 224
Good-faith estimate, 248
Goods and service dispute, 196
Good-til-cancelled orders, 412
Gorham, Linda, 371
Government National Mortgage Association (Ginnie Mae), 420
Grace period, 143
Graduated mortgage, 254
Graduated vesting, 502
Grantor, 528
Greninger, Sue Alexander, 493
Griffith, Reynolds, 376
Gross capitalized cost (gross cap cost), 217
Gross domestic product (GDP), 8
Gross income, 104
Group term life insurance, 329–330
Growing-equity mortgage, 255
Growth stock, 391
Guaranteed investment contracts (GICs), 441
Guaranteed renewable term life insurance, 329
Guardian, 526

Habitability, 233
Harassment, 233
Hazard, 272
  reduction, 273
Health care plan, 19, 301
  annual limits, 309
  benefit amount, 311
  benefit period, 311
  consumer-driven, 303–304
  coordination of benefits clause, 309
  coverage of, 306–307
  episode limit, 309
  flexible spending arrangements for, 310
  group, 300
  guaranteed renewable policies, 307
  high-deductible, 20, 304
  item limits, 308
  lifetime limit, 309
  noncancellable policies, 307
  open enrollment period, 303
  optionally renewable policies, 307
  policy limits, 308–309
  premium conversion, 310
  recurring clause, 309
  selecting, 317–318
Health care proxy, 531
Health expenses
  managing, 301
  types of protection from, 302
Health insurance. *See* **Health care plan**
Health maintenance organizations (HMOs), 302–303
  goal of, 302
Health reimbursement account (HRA), 304
Health savings accounts (HSAs), 20, 118, **304**
Hedge fund, 480
Heir, 525
HFC. *See* Household Finance Corporation
High-balling, 222
HMOs. *See* **Health maintenance organizations**
Home, buying
  costs, 238, 243–244, 260
  missteps in, 242
  steps in, 243, 260
Home inspection, 239
Home, selling, 258–259
  aspects of, 260
Home warranty insurance, 240
Home-equity conversion loan, 256
Home-equity installment loan, 256
Homeowner's association, 234
Homeowner's fee, 234
Homeowner's general liability protection, 277
Homeowner's insurance, 241
Homeowner's insurance, 241, **276**
  basic form (HO-1), 277
  broad form (HO-2), 277
  buying, 278–282
  condominium form (HO-6), 278
  older home form (HO-8), 278
  renter's contents broad form (HO-4), 277
  replacement-cost requirement in, 278–279
  special form (HO-3), 277
  summary of, 280–281
  types of, 277–278
Homeowner's no-fault medical payments protection, 277
Homeowner's no-fault property damage protection, 277
Homestake Gold Mine, 475
Hope Scholarship credit, 112
Household Finance Corporation (HFC), 173
HRA. *See* **Health reimbursement account**
HSAs. *See* **Health savings accounts**
Hunts, Holly, 305
Hyungsoo, Kim, 333

IACI. *See* **Interest-adjusted cost index**
IANPI. *See* **Interest-adjusted net payment index**
Identity theft, 162
Immediate annuity, 514
Implied warranty, 219
Impulse buying, 208, 209
Income, 67, 68, 108
  adding up actual, 88
  adjustments to, 105–106
  assessing benefits of second, 44
  current, 356
  discretionary, 80
  disposable personal, 75, 80, 163
  earned, 101
  fixed, 362
  gross, 104
  nominal, 9
  nontaxable, 128
  postponing, 123–124
  pretax, 118
  real, 9
  stocks, 391
  tax deferred, 498
  taxable, 98, 128
  tax-exempt, 13, 42
  tax-sheltered, 13
  total, 101
  unearned, 101
Income, adjusted gross (AGI), 106, 466
Income-and-expense statement. *See* **Cash-flow statement**
Income-replacement needs, 323, 325
Indemnity plans, 303
Independent insurance agent, 276
Indexing, 99
Individual account, 146
Individual practice organization (IPO), 303
Individual retirement account (IRA), 3, **119, 506**
  rollover, 503
  Roth, 119, 144, 507
  spousal, 507
  traditional, 119, 506–507
Inflation, 8
  impact of, 10
  measuring, 9–10
Inflation risk, 364
Inheritance tax, 533
Initial public offerings (IPOs), 408
Insolvent, 66
Inspector, 248–249
Installment purchase agreements, 198
Installment-certain annuity, 514
Insurance, 272. *See also* **Health care plan**
  accident, 307
  all-risk (open-perils) policies, 277
  binder, 275

Insurance *(cont.)*
- **cash-value, 331**
- **certificate of, 305**
- **claim, 293**
- college students and, 291
- **companies, 135**
- comprehensive personal liability, 289
- **dental expense, 305**
- **deposit, 134**
- **direct sellers, 276**
- **dread disease, 307**
- essence of, 274–275
- **floater policies, 290**
- **"gap," 213**
- **home warranty, 240**
- how to read, 274
- **liability, 268, 277**
- **long-term care, 300**
- **mortgage,** 239–**240**
- **named-perils policies, 277**
- **policy limits, 273**
- **premium, 272**
- **professional liability/malpractice, 289**
- **property, 268,** 276–277
- **rate, 275**
- saving money on, 290
- **single-premium, 331**
- **Social Security Disability Income, 301, 313**
- **title, 239**
- **umbrella liability, 289**–290, 291
- **underwriting, 275**
- **"upside down," 213**
- **vision care, 306**

Insurance agent, 275, 292–293, **344**
- **exclusive, 276**
- **independent, 276**

Insurance, automobile, 282
- **bodily injury liability, 282**
- buying, 286, 288
- **collision, 285**
- **comprehensive, 285**
- designing, 294
- **family auto policy, 283**
- **medical payments, 284**
- **personal auto policy, 283**
- **physical damage, 285**
- policy limits, 284
- **property damage liability, 283**
- **rental reimbursement coverage, 285**
- summary of, 283
- **towing coverage, 285**
- types of, **282**
- **underinsured motorist, 285**
- **uninsured motorist, 285**

Insurance, disability income, 313, 318
- **any-occupation policy, 314**
- **benefit period, 314**
- **cost of living adjustments, 315**
- **own-occupation policy, 314**
- provisions of, 314–315
- **residual clause, 314**
- **social security rider, 315**
- **split definition policy, 314**
- **waiting period, 314**

Insurance, homeowner's, 241, **276**
- **basic form (HO-1), 277**
- **broad form (HO-2), 277**
- buying, 278–282
- **condominium form (HO-6), 278**
- **older home form (HO-8), 278**
- **renter's contents broad form (HO-4), 277**
- **replacement-cost requirement in, 278**–279
- **special form (HO-3), 277**
- summary of, 280–281
- types of, 277–278

Insurance Information Institute, 297

Insurance Institute for Highway Safety, 297

Insurance, life, 322
- **adjustable, 331**
- after divorce, 340
- **application, 335**
- **beneficiary, 322**
- buying online, 343
- **cash surrender value, 338**
- **cash-value, 328**
- commissions, 345
- comparisons of, 334
- **contingent beneficiary, 334**
- **convertible term, 329**
- **credit term, 330**
- **current rate, 337**
- **death benefit, 336**
- **decreasing term, 329**
- **dividends, 336**
- **endowment, 332**
- **face amount, 328**
- fair prices for, 346
- **first-to-die, 335**
- **flexible premium variable, 333**–334
- **grace period, 336**
- **group term, 329**–330
- **guaranteed insurability option, 339**
- **guaranteed minimum rate of return, 337**
- **guaranteed renewable term, 329**
- **incontestability clause, 335**–336
- **in-force illustration, 337**
- **lapsed, 336**
- **layering term, 344**
- **level-premium term, 329**
- **limited pay whole, 331**
- **living benefit clause, 338**
- **modified, 332**
- **multiple indemnity clause, 336**
- **multiple-of-earnings approach, 324**–325
- **needs-based approach, 325,** 326
- **net cost of, 346**
- **nonforfeiture values, 338,** 339
- **nonparticipating policies, 336**
- organization of, 335
- **paid-up, 331**
- **participating policies, 336**
- **pay-at-60 policies, 331**
- **permanent, 330**
- **policy illustration, 337**–338
- **policyholder, 334**
- **premium quote service for, 343**
- premiums for, typical, 346
- provisions of, 347
- **return-of-premium policy, 333**
- **settlement options, 337**
- **suicide clause, 336**
- **surrender charge, 345**
- **survivorship joint, 335**
- switching, 349–350
- tax consequences of, 341
- **term, 328**
- **20-pay policies, 331**
- types of, 347
- **universal, 332**
- **vanishing premium, 333**
- **variable, 333**
- **variable-universal, 333**–334
- **waiver of premium, 338**–339
- **whole, 331**
- for young professional, 327–328

Insured, 272, 334
- **classes of, 275**

Insurer, 272

Interest, 10, 161, 253, **356**
- **add-on method of, 200**–201
- on CD, 141
- **compound,** 2, 14, **15**
- **declining-balance method of, 200**
- **discount method of, 202**
- on mortgage loan, 253
- negotiating, 222
- **rate risk, 422**
- **simple formula for, 14**

Interest tax credit mortgage, 112

Interest-adjusted cost index (IACI), 346

Interest-adjusted net payment index (IANPI), 346

Interest.com, 205

Interest-only mortgage, 254

Interests, 34
- **inventories, 34**

Internal Revenue Code, 98, 465

Internal Revenue Service (IRS), 21, **98,** 537

Intestate, 527, 536

Investing, 354
- **buy-and-hold, 369**
- **dollar-cost averaging, 370**–372
- early in life, 367
- goals, 451
- missteps in, 375
- software programs for, 375

Investment(s), 5
- **assets-to-total ratio, 75**
- **banking firms, 408**
- catching up on, 382
- **high-risk,** 363, **462**
- passive, 125
- **potential rate of return for, 398**
- real estate, 125
- **risk, 357,** 397–398
- scams, 404
- setting criteria for, 400–401
- **tax-sheltered, 118**
- **time horizon of, 364,** 374
- when to sell, 376

Investment (capital) assets, 65, 66

Investment Company Institute, 448
Investment philosophy, 358, **359,** 380
  aggressive, 360, 429–430
  conservative, 359
  moderate, 359–360
Investment plan, 376–377, 380
  steps in, 377, 378, 379
Investment risk, 357, 397–398
Investopedia, 383, 484
Investor
  active, 360
  getting started as, 380
  passive, 360–361
  value, 392
Invoice price, 221
IPO. *See* **Individual practice organization**
IPOs. *See* **Initial public offerings**
IRA. *See* **Individual retirement account**
Irrevocable living trust, 529
IRS. *See* **Internal Revenue Service**
Itemized deductions, 107

J. K. Lasser's Your Income Tax, 110
Job interview, 51
  common mistakes in, 53
  evaluating, 53
  over meal, 53
  preparing for, 52
  telephone, 52–53
Job opportunities, 46–49
  Internet and, 49
  keeping track of, 47
Job, temporary, 35
Johnson, Alena C., 88
Joint account, 146
Joint and survivor benefit, 504
Joint tenancy, 146, 524
Joint-and-survivor annuity, 515
Jordan, Ronald R., 241

Kelley Blue Book, 212, 229
Keogh retirement plan, 509
Keynes, John Maynard, 116
Kiddie tax, 125, 144
Kiplinger.com, 431
Kiplinger's Personal Finance Magazine, 82, 94, 453
Kratzer, Constance Y., 241

Land contract, 255
Lansing, Steve, 500
Large-cap stock, 393
Large-loss principle, 271
Law of large numbers, 275
Lawrence, Frances C., 123
Leading economic indicators, index of (LEI), 8
LEAP. *See* **Long-term Equity AnticiPation Security**
Leasing, 216, 232–233
  acquisition fee, 217
  closed-end, 217
  disposition fee, 217
  early termination charge, 217
  early termination payoff, 218
  open-end, 217
Legacy Writer, 537
LEI. *See* **Leading economic indicators, index of**
Lemon laws, 226
Lender buy-down mortgage, 254
Lesser-known growth stock, 391–392
Letter of last instructions, 526–527
Level-premium term life insurance, 329
Leverage, 365–366, **464**
  in futures contracts, 481
Liabilities, 65
  decreasing, 67
  insurance, 268, 277
  limited, 387
  long term, 66
  short-term (current), 66
Liability, tax, 110–111
Lien, 197, 249
Life planning issues, 64
Lifeline banking account, 136, 152
Life-line.org, 350
Lifestyle trade-offs, 35–36
Lifetime learning credit, 112
Limit orders, 411–412
Limited liabilities, 387
Limited managed account, 373
Limited pay whole life insurance, 331
Limited power of attorney, 530
Limited warranty, 219
Liquid assets, 65, 132
Liquidity, 74, 132, 436
  basic ratio of, 74
  risk, 365
Listing agreement, 258
Listing real estate broker (agent), 247
The Little Book of Commonsense Investing (Bogle), 448
Living trust, 528
Load mutual fund, 444, 445
Loan(s), 160
  acceleration clause, 197
  automatic premium, 338
  balloon automobile, 218
  cash, 197
  collateral for, 197
  commitment, 248
  consumer, 172
  cosigner on, 197
  debt-consolidation, 161
  finance charge on, 199–202
  fixed interest rate, 198
  home-equity conversion, 256
  home-equity installment, 256
  preapproval, 211
  prepayment penalty, 201
  purchase, 197
  secured, 197
  unsecured, 197
  variable-rate, 198
Loan-to-value ratio (LTV), 239, 464–465
Long term liabilities, 66
Long-term care insurance, 300
Long-term Equity AnticiPation Security (LEAP), 478
Long-term gain, 104
Long-term loss, 104
Loss
  capital, 104, 356
  casualty/theft, 109
  control, 270
  financial, 273
  fortuitous, 273
  frequency, 269, 270
  long-term, 104
  personal, 273
  reduction, 273
  severity, 269, 270
  short-term, 104
  tax, 125
Lotteries, state, 15
Lottery winner, 536
Low-balling, 224
Low-load mutual fund, 445
Lown, Jean, 153
LTV. *See* **Loan-to-value ratio**
Lump sum distribution, 503
Lynch, Peter, 392

Maintenance agreement, 219
Managed funds, 440
Manufactured housing, 234–235
Manufacturer's suggested retail price (MSRP), 211
Margin account, 413
Margin buying, 413, 414, 415
Margin call, 415
Margin rate, 413
Marginal utility, 12
Marital deduction, 533
Market
  bear, 368, 475
  bull, 364
  capitalization, 393
  conditions, 364
  declining, 371
  interest rates, 422
  making, 408
  order, 411
  rising, 371–372
  risk, 364, 398, 437
  timers, 368
Marketability risk, 365
Market-volatility risk, 364–365
Martin, Allen, 410
Matching contribution retirement plan, 501
Maximum taxable yearly earnings (MTYE), 490
Mediation, 226
Medicaid, 300
Medical information bureaus, 305
Medicare, 300
  Part A, 304
  Part B, 304
  tax, 490
Microcap stock, 393
Midcap stock, 393
MMDA. *See* **Money market deposit account**
MMMF. *See* **Money market mutual fund**
Modern portfolio theory (MPT), 375
Modified life insurance, 332

Retained earnings, 388
Retirement age, full-benefit, 491
Retirement benefit, basic, 491
Retirement fund, target-date, 509
Retirement plan, 21
  automatic enrollment, 500
  cash-balance, 504–505
  catch-up provision, 501
  computer software for, 511
  contribution credit, 502
  contributory, 500
  defined contribution, 500–501
  defined-benefit, 502–503
  employer-sponsored, 500
  403(b), 501
  457, 501
  Keogh, 509
  matching contribution, 501
  missteps in, 510
  mutual funds and, 458
  noncontributory, 500
  profit-sharing, 505
  qualified, 500
  salary reduction, 500
  self directed, 501
  tax consequences in, 514
  tax-sheltered, 21, 340, **498,** 507
  "voluntary," 488
  women and, 490
Retirement plan, 401(k), 3, **117,** 487, **501**
  cashing out, 45
  "net pay" numbers of, 498
Retirement savings contribution credit, 113
Retirement savings goal, 494
  estimating, 495
Return on investment, 22
Return-of-premium policy life insurance, 333
Reverse mortgage, 256
Revocable living trust, 529
Revolving savings fund, 84
Rhodium, 475
Right of escheat, 527
Rising market, 371–372
Risk, 268
  avoidance, 270
  business-cycle, 364
  default, 417
  deflation, 364
  of dying too soon, 322, 340
  estimating, 269–270
  financial, 356, 364, 372
  handling, 270–271
  inflation, 364
  interest rate, 422
  investment, 357, 397–398
  liquidity, 365
  of living too long, 322, 340
  market, 364, 398, 437
  marketability, 365
  market-volatility, 364–365
  premium, 357, 358
  pure, 268, 357
  random, 363, 436
  reduction, 271
  reinvestment, 365, 419
  retention, 270
  sources of, 269
  speculative, 268, 357
  time, 364
  tolerance, 358
  transfer, 270–271
Risk management, 60, 268–272
  evaluating/adjusting, 271–272
  process, 269
Rollover IRA, 503
Rollover mortgage, 254
Rollover penalty, 503
Roth IRA, 119, 144, 507
Round lots, 410
Rule of 72, 17, 22
Rule of 78s, 201
"Rule of three," 215
Running Paws Cat Food Company, 388–390, 395–396, 397, 399–400
Russell 3000 Index, 405

SAIF. *See* **Savings Association Insurance Fund**
Salary reduction retirement plan, 500
Sales finance company, 172
Sallie Mae. *See* Student Loan Marketing Association
Saver credit, 113
Savings, 5, 354
Savings account, 138
  benefits of, 154
  costs/penalties on, 139
  demand deposit, 138
  statement, 138–139
  time deposit, 138
Savings Association Insurance Fund (SAIF), 134
Savings calculator, 143
Savings Incentive Match Plan for Employees IRA (SIMPLE IRA), 501
SEC. *See* **Securities and Exchange Commission**
Second mortgage, 256
Secured loan, 197
Securities, 354, 358, **367, 386**
  exchange, 405
  market index, 404
  transactions, 408
  Treasury, 418
Securities and Exchange Commission (SEC), 25, 404, **409**
Security analysts' research reports, 402, 403
Security deposit, 232, 233
Security Investors Protection Corporation (SIPC), 409
Security's street name, 407
Self directed retirement plan, 501
Seller financing, 255, 259, **469**
Selling real estate broker (agent), 247
Selling short, 415–416
  example of, 416
Separable property, 528
SEP-IRA. *See* **Simplified employee pension—individual retirement account**
Series EE savings bonds, 119, 144, 419
Series HH savings bonds, 420
Series I savings bonds, 119
Shareholders, 386
  common, 388, 389
  fees, 444
  preemptive right of, 389
Short-term gain, 104
Short-term (current) liabilities, 66
Short-term loss, 104
Sick-pay benefits, 312
Sideline business, 107
Signature card, 146
Silver, 475
Simple formula for interest, 14
SIMPLE IRA. *See* **Savings Incentive Match Plan for Employees IRA**
Simplified employee pension—individual retirement account (SEP-IRA), 509
Single-family dwelling, 233–234
Single-premium insurance, 331
Singletary, Michelle, 10, 526
Sinking fund, 421
SIPC. *See* Security Investors Protection Corporation
Skilled nursing care, 311
Skills format résumé, 46, 49
Small-cap stock, 393
Small-claims court, 226
Social Security
  blackout period, 327
  credits, 491, A-13
  currently insured, 491, A-13
  Disability Income Insurance, 301, 313
  estimation of, 491–493, 516, A-13, A-14
  fully insured, 491, A-13
  future of, 491
  length of work requirements for, 492
  not insured, 491
  qualifying for, 490–491
  Statement, 493, A-13
  Survivor's benefits, 324, A-13, A-14
  traditionally insured, 491
Social Security Administration (SSA), 319, **489,** 519, A-12
  contacting, A-13
Social Security Disability Income Insurance, 301, 313
Socially conscious mutual fund, 443
S&P. *See* Standard and Poor's 500 Index
Special needs trust, 529
Specialist, 410
Speculative risk, 268, 357
Speculative stock, 392
Spending, 60
Split, 389
Spousal consent requirement, 504
Spousal IRA, 507
Spread, 411
Springing power of attorney, 530
SRI Consulting, 94
SSA. *See* **Social Security Administration**
Standard deviation, 453
Standard of living, 5

Standard and Poor's 500 Index (S&P), 405
Standardized expense table, 446
Stated commissions, 444
Stay, 178
Stock(s), 354, 363, **386**
  ask price of, 411
  average share cost, 371
  average share price, 370
  bid price of, 411
  blue-chip, 392–393
  brokerage firms, 135
  calculating rate of return of, 397–400
  common, 386–387, 427
  countercyclical, 393
  cyclical, 393
  dividend, 389
  evaluating, 394–397, 427
  fundamental analysis of, 394
  growth, 391
  how to order, 410–412
  income, 391
  large-cap, 393
  lesser-known growth, 391–392
  looking up price of, 406–407
  market price of, 386
  matched/negotiated price of, 410–411
  microcap, 393
  midcap, 393
  multiple, 390
  online calculators for, 401
  option, 476
  penny, 392
  preferred, 387
  screening tools, 401–402, 431
  small-cap, 393
  speculative, 392
  split, 389
  spread of, 411
  tech, 392
  technical analysis of, 394
  using Internet to evaluate/select, 400–407
  value, 392
  well-known growth, 391
Stock orders
  day, 412
  fill-or-kill, 412
  good-til-cancelled, 412
  limit, 411–412
  market, 411
  month, 412
  open, 412
  stop, 412
  time limits on, 412
  week, 412
Stockbroker, 407
  checking background of, 410
  commissions/fees, 410
Stop orders, 412
Stored-value cards, 148
Straight annuity, 514
Strong Interest Inventory, 34
Student Loan Marketing Association (Sallie Mae), 420
Stuhlman, Donald, 194
Subleasing, 233
Subprime market, 248
Subrogation rights, 284
Substitute checks, 137
Super NOW account, 145
Surplus, 67
Surplus/deficit formula, 71
Survivorship joint life insurance, 335
Sweat equity property, 469
Sweeps, 147

T. Rowe Price, 510
Take-home pay, 80
Tangible (use) assets, 65
Tax(es), 98, 108
  avoidance, 116
  avoiding overpayment of, 126
  balance due, 113
  calculating, 102, 126
  consequences of investing in real estate, 472–473
  consequences of life insurance, 341
  consequences of mutual fund investing, 454
  consequences in retirement planning, 514
  credits, 111–112
  credits, nonrefundable, 112
  credits, refundable, 112
  deferred, 118
  deferred compounding, 118
  deferred income, 498
  estimated, 102
  evasion, 116
  federal estate, 533
  filing, 101
  free withdrawals, 499
  inheritance, 533
  keeping records of, 109
  kiddie, 125, 144
  liability, 110–111
  losses, 125
  Medicare, 490
  missteps in managing, 126
  planning, 98
  progressive, 98, 99, 126
  real estate property, 241
  real estate transfer, 259
  reducing, 116, 123
  refund, 113
  regressive, 98
  table, 98, 111
Tax bracket, marginal (MTB), 98
Tax free withdrawal, 499
Tax, higher alternative minimum (AMT), 111
Tax rate
  average, 100
  FICA, 490, A-12
  schedules, 98, 106
Tax rate, marginal, 12–13, 27, **98,** 99, 126
  determining, 100
  effective, 13, 100
Taxable income, 98, 128
Tax-deferred growth, 22
Tax-exempt income, 13, 42
Tax-free exchange, 466
Tax-sheltered income, 13
Tax-sheltered retirement plan, 21, 340, **498,** 507
T-bill. *See* **Treasury bill**
Tech stock, 392
"Ten Things Every Spouse Should Know," 534
10-K report, 402, 403
Tenancy
  in common, 146
  by entirety, 146
  for specific time, 233
Tenant rights, 233
Term life insurance, 328
Testamentary trust, 528
Testator, 525
Tiered pricing, 168
TIL. *See* **Truth in Lending Act**
Time deposit savings account, 138
Time risk, 364
Time value of money, 14
Timesharing, 470
TIPS. *See* **Treasury Inflation-Protected Securities**
Title, 238
  search, 239
Total income, 101
Total return, 356
Towing coverage insurance, 285
Trade-in vehicle, 212
  negotiating, 222
Trade-off, 4
Traditional IRA, 119, 506–507
Traditionally insured, 491
Trailing commissions, 445
Trailing price/earnings ratio, 390
Transfer risk, 270–271
Transportation reimbursement plan, 117
Traveler's checks, 137, 138
Treasury bill (T-bill), 357, 358, 398, **418**
  discount yield of, 418
Treasury Direct Plan, 418
Treasury Inflation-Protected Securities (TIPS), 419
Treasury note, 419
Trough, 7
Trust, 527, **528**
  irrevocable living, 529
  living, 528
  revocable living, 529
  special needs, 529
  testamentary, 528
Trust, irrevocable charitable remainder (CRT), 529
Trustee, 500, 528
Trustee-to-trustee rollover, 503
Truth in Lending Act (TIL), 161, **198**
12b-1 fee, 445–446
20-pay life insurance, life, 331
20-percent withholding rule, 503
2006 Pension Protection Act, 505, 510

UIT. *See* **Unit investment trusts**
Umbrella liability insurance, 289–290, 291
Underinsured motorist insurance, 285
Unearned income, 101

Unfair discrimination, 168
Uniform settlement statement, 249
Uninsured certificate of deposit, 141
Uninsured motorist insurance, 285
Unit investment trusts (UIT), 439
United States Bankruptcy Trustee, 178
Universal life insurance, 332
Unmanaged mutual fund, 443
Unsecured loan, 197
"Upside down" insurance, 213
U.S. Department of Housing and Urban Development, 245, 264
U.S. Department of Labor, 519
U.S. Treasury Department, 431
Use-it-or-lose-it rule, 117
Usury laws, 162

VA. *See* **Department of Veterans Affairs**
Vacation homes, 466
Value Line, 404
Value stock, 392
Values, 35, 60
Vanguard, 448, 459
Vanishing premium life insurance, 333
Variable annuity, 515
Variable expenses, 68, 70–71
Variable life insurance, 333
Variable-rate certificate of deposit, 141
Variable-rate loan, 198
Variable-rate mortgage, 254
Variable-universal life insurance, 333–334
Vesting, 501–**502,** 505
  cliff, 502
  graduated, 502
Viatical companies, 338
Viorst, Judith, 151
Vision care insurance, 306
Voluntary repossession, 176
"Voluntary" retirement plan, 488
Voting rights, 387

Want, 208
Warranty, 219
  express, 219, 220
  extended, 219
  of fitness, 219
  full, 219
  implied, 219
  limited, 219
  of merchantability, 219
Weagley, Robert O., 442
Web portals, 87
Week orders, 412
Well-known growth stock, 391
Whole life insurance, 331
Will, 524, **525**–527, **535**
  software for, 525
Wilshire 5000 Index, 405
Withdrawal, 498, 508
  tax free, 499
Wolff, Dana, 45
Work-style personality, 39
  worksheet, 40

Xerox, 479

Yahoo! Finance, 319, 431
Yield, 356
  current, 423
  discount, 418
  dividend, 396
  earnings, 390
  fixed, 422
  long term rates of, 357
  rental, 463
Yield to maturity (YTM), 424–**426**
Your Federal Income Tax: For Individuals, 110, 129

Zero-sum game, 481

My Personal Financial Planner

A PERSONAL APPLICATION OF FINANCIAL PLANNING CONCEPTS AND TOOLS FROM

Personal Finance

NINTH EDITION

E. Thomas Garman
Virginia Tech University

Raymond E. Forgue
University of Kentucky

HOUGHTON MIFFLIN COMPANY BOSTON NEW YORK

Contents

PREFACE VII

SECTION ONE – FINANCIAL PLANNING 1

Worksheet 1—Tracking The Economy *2*

Worksheet 2—Calculating The Future Value Of A Lump Sum *3*

Worksheet 3—Calculating The Future Value Of An Annuity *4*

Worksheet 4—Calculating The Present Value Of A Lump Sum *5*

Worksheet 5—Calculating The Present Value Of An Annuity *6*

Worksheet 6—Comparing Salary Offers In Two Different Cities *7*

Worksheet 7—Assessing The Benefits Of A Second Income *8*

Worksheet 8—My Balance Sheet *9*

Worksheet 9—My Cash-Flow Statement *11*

Worksheet 10—My Financial Ratios *13*

Worksheet 11—My Financial Records *15*

Worksheet 12—My Financial Goals *17*

Worksheet 13—Determining Monthly Budget Amounts For My Nonmonthly Expenses *18*

Worksheet 14—My Revolving Savings Fund *19*

Worksheet 15—My Budget *20*

Worksheet 16—My Budget Category Ledger Worksheets *22*

SECTION TWO – MONEY MANAGEMENT 23

Worksheet 17—My Sources Of Taxable Income *24*

Worksheet 18—Estimating My Income Tax Liability *25*

Worksheet 19—Determining Whether I Should File For A Refund *26*

Worksheet 20—Strategies To Reduce My Income Tax Liability *27*

Worksheet 21—Selecting A Checking Account That Meets My Needs *28*

Worksheet 22—Reconciling My Checking Account *29*

Worksheet 23—Comparing My Credit Card Options *31*

Worksheet 24—The Effect Of Taking On Additional Debt On My Financial Ratios *32*

Worksheet 25—Monthly Installment Loan Payment Calculator *33*

Worksheet 26—My Credit Card Accounts Inventory *34*

Worksheet 27—My Installment Loan Inventory *35*

Worksheet 28—My Student Loan Inventory *36*

Worksheet 29—My Top Priority Motor Vehicle Features 37
Worksheet 30—Comparing Vehicle Purchase Contracts 38
Worksheet 31—Should I Lease Or Buy A Vehicle? 39
Worksheet 32—Should I Take A New Vehicle Rebate Or Low-Rate Financing Offer? 40
Worksheet 33—Decision-Making Worksheet For A Major Product Purchase 41
Worksheet 34—Sample Product Or Service Complaint Letter 42
Worksheet 35—Should I Rent Or Buy Housing? 43
Worksheet 36—Monthly Mortgage Payment Calculator 44
Worksheet 37—Estimating Home Buying And Closing Costs 45
Worksheet 38—Should I Refinance My Mortgage? 46
SECTION THREE – INCOME AND ASSET PROTECTION 47
Worksheet 39—My Insurance Inventory 48
Worksheet 40—My Home Inventory 51
Worksheet 41—My Comparison Of Auto Insurance Providers 52
Worksheet 42—Determining My Disability Income Insurance Needs 54
Worksheet 43—Determining My Life Insurance Needs 55
Worksheet 44—Layering Term Insurance Policies 56
SECTION FOUR – INVESTMENTS 57
Worksheet 45—My Readiness-To-Invest Checklist 58
Worksheet 46—My Investment Philosophy 59
Worksheet 47—My Preferred Long-Term Investment Strategies 60
Worksheet 48—My Investment Goals And Time Horizons 61
Worksheet 49—Comparing Taxable And Tax-Free Income 62
Worksheet 50—My Preferences Among Stocks 63
Worksheet 51—Comparing Stocks As Investments 64
Worksheet 52—My Preferences Among Bonds 65
Worksheet 53–The Current Yield On My Bond Investment 66
Worksheet 54—The Current Market Price Of My Bond Investment 67
Worksheet 55—The Real Return On My Investments 68
Worksheet 56—The Yield To Maturity Of My Bond 69
Worksheet 57—My Mutual Fund Preferences 70
Worksheet 58—Comparing Mutual Funds As Investments 71
Worksheet 59—Calculating The Return On Mutual Fund Investments 72
Worksheet 60—Evaluating The Performance (Gain Or Loss) Of My Investments 73

SECTION FIVE – RETIREMENT AND ESTATE PLANNING 74

Worksheet 61—My Estimated Retirement Savings Goal In Today's Dollars *75*

Worksheet 62—Questions To Ask About Your Employer's Retirement Plan *76*

Worksheet 63—My Will, Letter Of Last Instructions, And Advance Directive Documents *78*

Worksheet 64—My Assets To Be Transferred By Beneficiary Designations *79*

Preface

All the financial knowledge you will gain from your study of personal finance will be of little use if you do not put it into practice. *My Personal Financial Planner* takes all of the major financial planning tools from *Personal Finance*, Ninth Edition, and makes them real for you, and in a genuinely meaningful and personal way. We have converted the tools into forms, calculators, and worksheets that you can use for years to come to develop your own financial plans and successfully manage your own financial life. We want you to be truly successful in your personal finances *throughout* your life. Reading *Personal Finance* will give you a big head start. Using *My Personal Financial Planner* will give you additional support because it will personalize your own finances for you.

My Personal Financial Planner is organized according to the five-part structure of *Personal Finance*.

► **Financial Planning** We first deal with the basics of financial planning. Here you will prepare your own financial statements, calculate your financial ratios, and be able to make almost any type of time value of money calculation imaginable.

► **Money Management** The second section of the workbook focuses on money management and covers income taxes, banking, credit, and the purchase of vehicles and a home. Using these worksheets will save you literally thousands of dollars in taxes, bank fees, interest, and dollars not spent for "big-ticket" items that you buy. That's real money, and these savings will help you along on your road to financial success.

► **Income and Asset Protection** The third section focuses on income and asset protection, specifically on insurance as the primary mechanism for that protection. These worksheets will help you buy the right insurance coverage and make the most of your insurance dollar. If you don't waste money, it is yours to keep for spending, saving, or investing.

► **Investments** The fourth section of the workbook covers investments. It walks you though the subject of investments using worksheets and forms to help you clarify your thinking about investing successfully for your future. It gives you the tools you absolutely must put in place in your investment program so that you will build the wealth you will need to reach your most ambitious financial goals.

► **Retirement and Estate Planning** The fifth section of *My Personal Financial Planner* focuses on retirement and estate planning. Here you will be able to set in motion–early in your full-time working career--the steps to build the multi-million dollar financial nest egg for a secure retirement. Yes, you can build that kind of financial success. To do so, you must start early and sacrifice some spending so you can save and invest to support your future lifestyle. This section of worksheets and forms also will help you prepare for the distribution of your estate in ways that meet your desires. There are some simple steps that you can take, and the forms and worksheets will guide you along that path.

We encourage you to make use of this special workbook as you study *Personal Finance*. Your efforts will help you visualize and really understand the practical aspects of what you are learning while you read *Personal Finance*. Your efforts will make that knowledge richer and deeper, and totally personal to you. That's what *personal* in *Personal Finance* is all about! The forms and worksheets in *My Personal Financial Planner* will aid in your success in class, but more than that they will improve your genuine personal financial success throughout your lifetime.

Note: Many of the worksheets in this workbook including interactive calculators can also be found by visiting the *Garman/Forgue* website, college.hmco.com/business/students. Under General Business, select *Personal Finance 9e*.

SECTION ONE

Financial Planning

This section of your workbook focuses on the basics of the study of personal finances and begins your efforts in financial planning. Each worksheet will allow you to think through a decision or perform calculations related to a specific area of personal financial management in a way that has direct benefit to you.

Worksheet 1	Tracking the Economy
Worksheet 2	Calculating the Future Value of a Lump Sum
Worksheet 3	Calculating the Future Value of an Annuity
Worksheet 4	Calculating the Present Value of a Lump Sum
Worksheet 5	Calculating the Present Value of an Annuity
Worksheet 6	Comparing Salary Offers in Two Different Cities
Worksheet 7	Assessing the Benefits of a Second Income
Worksheet 8	My Balance Sheet
Worksheet 9	My Cash-Flow Statement
Worksheet 10	My Financial Ratios
Worksheet 11	My Financial Records
Worksheet 12	My Financial Goals
Worksheet 13	Determining Monthly Budget Amounts for My Nonmonthly Expenses
Worksheet 14	My Revolving Savings Fund
Worksheet 15	My Budget
Worksheet 16	My Budget Category Ledger Worksheets

WORKSHEET 1—TRACKING THE ECONOMY

The success of your personal financial plans will depend on your understanding of the current state of the economy as measured by several key statistics. You will also want to be able to predict the movement of those statistics over the next one or two years. This worksheet will provide a way for you to record these key statistics for reference as you make your financial plans. For each statistic, we have included a website that will provide the information you will need. Your forecasts can also be based on your reading of economic news in your local newspaper, weekly news magazines, and financial periodicals such as the *Wall Street Journal*. (Use with *Personal Finance*, Ninth Edition, pages 6-10.)

Tracking the Economy Worksheet

Key economic statistic	Current data	Your forecast for one year from now	Your forecast for two years from now
Inflation rate—consumer price index (www.bls.gov)			
Inflation rate—producer price index (www.bls.gov)			
Federal funds rate (www.federalreserve.gov)			
30-year mortgage interest rate (www.bankrate.com)			
1-year certificate of deposit rate (www.bankrate.com)			
5-year certificate of deposit rate (www.bankrate.com)			
T-bill constant maturity rate (www.treasurydirect.gov)			
Index of leading economic indicators (www.globalindicators.org)			
Rate of change in the gross domestic product (www.bea.doc.gov)			

WORKSHEET 2—CALCULATING THE FUTURE VALUE OF A LUMP SUM

One of the most common questions that people ask about their investments and savings is "How much money will I have in *x* years?" An example might be someone who earns a bonus at work and wants to save it for five years. In personal finance language, he or she wants to know the future value of a lump sum. This worksheet can be used in conjunction with Table A.1 in the Appendix in your text to answer this question if you know the amount to be invested, the time period, and the rate of return or interest on the investment. An interactive calculator that performs this same procedure can be found on the *Garman/Forgue* website. (Use with *Personal Finance*, Ninth Edition, pages 14-18.)

Future Value of a Lump-Sum Worksheet

(A) Lump sum to be invested or saved	(B) Time period that the funds will be invested	(C) Rate of return on the invested funds	(D) Factor from Table A.1 that corresponds to items B and C	(E) Future value (A x D)

WORKSHEET 3—CALCULATING THE FUTURE VALUE OF AN ANNUITY

Another common question that people ask about their investments is "How much money will I have in *x* years if I put a certain amount away each year?" An example might be someone who puts $3,000 into an IRA account each year. In personal finance language, this person wants to know the future value of an annuity. This worksheet can be used in conjunction with Table A.3 in the Appendix in your text to answer this question if you know the amount to be invested, the time period, and the rate of return or interest on the investment. An interactive calculator that performs this same procedure can be found on the *Garman/Forgue* website. (Use with *Personal Finance*, Ninth Edition, pages 14–18.)

Future Value of an Annuity Worksheet

(A) Amount to be invested or saved each year (the annuity)	(B) Time period that the funds will be invested	(C) Rate of return on the invested funds	(D) Factor from Table A.3 that corresponds to items B and C	(E) Future value (A x D)

WORKSHEET 4—CALCULATING THE PRESENT VALUE OF A LUMP SUM

Another common question that people ask about their investments and savings is "How much money will I have to put away now to reach some goal?" An example might be someone wanting to save for a down payment on a home in five years. In personal finance language, he or she wants to know the present value of a lump sum. This worksheet can be used in conjunction with Table A.2 in the Appendix in your text to answer this question if you know the amount to be invested, the time period, and the rate of return or interest on the investment. An interactive calculator that performs this same procedure can be found on the *Garman/Forgue* website. (Use with *Personal Finance*, Ninth Edition, pages 14-18.)

Present Value of a Lump-Sum Worksheet

(A) Lump sum needed	(B) Time period that the funds will be invested	(C) Rate of return on the invested funds	(D) Factor from Table A.2 that corresponds to items B and C	(E) Present value (A x D)

WORKSHEET 5—CALCULATING THE PRESENT VALUE OF AN ANNUITY

Another question that people ask about their investments and savings is "How much money will I need to save so that withdrawing a certain amount each year will allow the money to last *x* years?" An example might be someone who wants to know how large a retirement fund she or he would need to ensure that the money would last 20 years given a certain rate of withdrawal. In personal finance language, the person wants to know the present value of an annuity. This worksheet can be used in conjunction with Table A.4 in the Appendix in your text to answer this question if you know the amount to be invested, the time period, and the rate of return or interest on the investment. An interactive calculator that performs this same procedure can be found on the *Garman/Forgue* website. (Use with *Personal Finance*, Ninth Edition, pages 14-18.)

Present Value of an Annuity Worksheet

(A) Amount of money annuity to be received or withdrawn each year	(B) Time period that the funds will be withdrawn	(C) Rate of return on the invested funds	(D) Factor from Table A.4 that corresponds to items B and C	(E) Present value (A x D)

WORKSHEET 6—COMPARING SALARY OFFERS IN TWO DIFFERENT CITIES

Comparing salary offers from two different cities can be difficult because the cost of living varies across the United States. You can use this worksheet and data from cityrating.com's website to adjust offers you might receive from prospective employers. An interactive calculator that performs this same procedure can be found on the *Garman/Forgue* website. (Use with *Personal Finance*, Ninth Edition, pages 41-42.)

Comparing Salary Offers Worksheet

(A) City	(B) Salary offer	(C) Estimate of the value of employee benefits	(D) Total compensation package	(E) Cost of Living Index*	(F) Salary adjusted for the cost of living (D/E)

*http://www.cityrating.com/costofliving.asp.

WORKSHEET 7—ASSESSING THE BENEFITS OF A SECOND INCOME

While a second income might appear to be a way to get ahead financially, there are some considerations that may diminish the benefits. The second income will be taxed at the household's marginal tax rate, and there are additional expenses for meals, transportation, child care, and other considerations. This worksheet can provide you with a better estimate of the actual contribution of a second income. An interactive calculator that performs this same procedure can be found on the *Garman/Forgue* website. (Use with *Personal Finance*, Ninth Edition, page 44.)

Decision-making worksheet	**Assessing the benefits of a second income**	
	Example	**Your figures**
1. Second income		
Annual earnings	$30,000.00	
Value of benefits	$300.00	
Total	$30,300.00	
2. Expenses		
Federal income taxes*	$7,500.00	
State/local income taxes†	$1,800.00	
Social Security taxes	$2,295.00	
Transportation and commuting	$2,000.00	
Child care	$3,200.00	
Lunches out	$1,000.00	
Work wardrobe	$1,200.00	
Other work-related expenses	$300.00	
Take-out food for supper	$1,200.00	
Guilt complex purchases	$600.00	
Total	$21,095.00	
3. Net value of second income		
Total second income	$30,300.00	
Total second income expenses	$21,095.00	
Net amount of second income	$9,205.00	
*Your federal marginal tax rate.	25.00%	
†Your state/local marginal tax rate.	6.00%	

WORKSHEET 8—MY BALANCE SHEET

A balance sheet provides a snapshot look at your financial status as of a particular date. The result is an accurate assessment of your net worth. You can use this worksheet to determine your assets, liabilities, and resulting net worth. If you complete a worksheet like this once per year, you will see an ongoing picture of your financial progress. An interactive calculator that performs this same procedure can be found on the *Garman/Forgue* website. (Use with *Personal Finance*, Ninth Edition, pages 64-67.)

My Balance Sheet

Date: ______ **Your Name:** ______

Assets

Monetary assets

Cash ______
Checking account #1 ______
Checking account #2 ______
Savings account #1 ______
Savings account #2 ______
Savings account #3 ______
Certificate of deposit #1 ______
Certificate of deposit #2 ______
Money market account ______
Other ______
Total monetary assets ______

Tangible assets

Vehicle #1 ______
Vehicle #2 ______
Home #1 ______
Home #2 ______
Clothing ______
Furniture ______
Entertainment electronics ______
Home appliances & equipment ______
Computer equipment ______
Computer software ______
Jewelry ______
Recreation items ______
Personal property ______
Other tangible assets ______

Total tangible assets ______

Investment assets

Stocks ______
Bonds ______
Mutual fund #1 ______
Mutual fund #2 ______
Retirement account(s) ______
Life ins. cash value(s) ______
Collectibles ______
Other investment assets ______
Total investment assets ______

Total Assets ______

Liabilities

Short-term liabilities

Credit card #1 ______
Credit card #2 ______
Credit card #3 ______
Credit card #4 ______
Medical debts ______
Past due utilities ______
Past due rent ______
Personal loans ______
Other ______
Other ______
Total short-term liabilities ______

Long-term liabilities

Vehicle loan #1 ______
Vehicle loan #2 ______
Home mortgage #1 ______
Home mortgage #2 ______
Student loan(s) ______
Furniture loans ______
Computer loans ______
Home appliance loans ______
Personal loans ______
Other ______
Other ______
Total long-term liabilities ______

Total Liabilities ______

Net Worth ______

WORKSHEET 9—MY CASH-FLOW STATEMENT

The key to getting ahead financially is to spend less than you earn. As a college student, that might be difficult, but ignoring the reality of your cash flows in and out is no solution. You can start by keeping track of your spending and income for one month. Then use this worksheet to summarize your spending and income into a cash-flow statement for the month. Assembling your statements over the course of a year will enable you to construct an annual statement. An interactive calculator that performs this same procedure can be found on the *Garman/Forgue* website. (Use with *Personal Finance*, Ninth Edition, pages 67-72.)

My Cash-Flow Statement

Month: ________ **Your Name:** ______________________________

Income

Wages #1 (gross) ________
Wages #2 (gross) ________
Interest income ________
Dividend income ________
Sales commissions ________
Tips ________
Gifts ________
Other ________
Other ________
Total income ________

Expenditures

Fixed expenses

Rent/mortgage payment ________
Home insurance ________
Car insurance ________
Vehicle loan #1 ________
Vehicle loan #2 ________
Medical insurance ________
Life insurance ________
Student loan payments ________
Savings #1 ________
Savings #2 ________
Savings #3 ________
Retirement fund ________
Other ________
Other ________
Total fixed expenses ________

Variable expenses

Federal income tax ________
State income tax ________
Social Security tax ________
Food (home) ________
Food (away) ________

Variable expenses (continued)

Food (entertain) ________
Entertainment ________
Electricity ________
Natural gas ________
Water/sewer ________
Garbage collection ________
Cable TV ________
Local telephone ________
Long distance ________
Cell phone ________
Medical ________
Clothing ________
Gifts ________
Personal care ________
Personal allowances ________
Gasoline ________
Vehicle maintenance ________
Education expenses ________
Other ________
Miscellaneous ________
Total variable expenses ________

Total expenditures ________

Surplus/Deficit ________

WORKSHEET 10—MY FINANCIAL RATIOS

The information contained in your balance sheet and your cash-flow statement is a valuable tool for keeping track of and understanding your personal finances. It is also important to use several financial ratios to bring your financial status and behavior into clear focus. The information for these ratios can be found in your balance sheet and cash-flow statement from Worksheets 7 and 8. The ratios are provided below. An interactive calculator that performs these same procedures can be found on the *Garman/Forgue* website. (Use with *Personal Finance*, Ninth Edition, pages 72-76.)

The **basic liquidity ratio** tells how many months you could afford to maintain your current level of spending if all income ceased. A common rule of thumb for this ratio is three months.

Basic Liquidity Ratio

(A) Monetary assets	(B) Monthly expenses	(C) Basic liquidity ratio (A/B)

The **asset-to-debt ratio** tells whether you are solvent; your assets exceed your liabilities. An asset-to-debt ratio of more than 1.0 indicates that you are solvent and have a positive net worth.

Asset-to-Debt Ratio

(A) Total assets	(B) Total debt	(C) Asset-to-debt ratio (A/B)

The **debt service-to-income ratio** compares your total annual debt payments (including home mortgage debt) with your gross annual income. A debt service-to-income ratio in excess of 0.36 indicates that you are carrying too much debt.

Debt Service-to-Income Ratio

(A) Annual debt repayments	(B) Gross income	(C) Debt service-to-income ratio (A/B)

The **debt payments-to-disposable income ratio** compares your monthly nonmortgage debt payments to your monthly disposable income. A debt service-to-disposable income ratio in excess of 0.16 indicates that you are carrying too much nonmortgage debt.

Debt Payments-to-Disposable Income Ratio

(A) Monthly nonmortgage debt payments	(B) Disposable income	(C) Debt payments-to-disposable income ratio (A/B)

The **investment assets-to-total assets ratio** provides a good indicator of the degree to which investment assets make up your total assets. The higher the ratio, the more you are on your way to achieving real wealth.

Investment Assets-to-Total Assets Ratio

(A) Investment assets	(B) Total assets	(C) Investment assets-to-total assets ratio (A/B)

The **savings ratio** indicates the level of your savings compared to your after-tax income. Many financial planners recommend a savings ratio of 10 to 12 percent.

Savings Ratio

(A) Annual savings	(B) After-tax income	(C) Savings ratio (A/B)

WORKSHEET 11—MY FINANCIAL RECORDS

As an effective personal financial planner, you will want to have a system for storing your important documents and records. These documents should be both accessible and secure. It is often wise to keep copies in a file cabinet so they can be accessible and originals in a safe-deposit box, home safe, or other secure location. (Use with *Personal Finance*, Ninth Edition, pages 76-77.)

Financial Records Worksheet

	Location (indicate copy or original document)		
Item	**Home file**	**Safe-deposit box**	**Other**
Financial statements			
Balance sheets for past several years			
Cash-flow statements for current and past year			
Written goal statements			
Budgets for current and past year			
Credit control sheet			
Cash-flow calendar for current year			
Personal documents			
Birth certificate			
Social Security card			
Marriage certificate			
Divorce documents			
Health history			
Record of alimony paid or received			
Record of child support paid or received			
Passport			
Banking and credit documents			
Checking and saving account contracts			
Checking and saving account statements			
Certificates of deposit			
Money market/asset management account statements			
Loan agreements/contracts			
Credit card monthly statements			
Insurance documents			
Automobile insurance policies			
Homeowners insurance policies			
Home inventory			
Health insurance policy or plan description			
Life insurance policies			
Cash value life insurance annual statements			
Insurance claims records			

Item	Home file	Safe-deposit box	Other
Home ownership records			
Deed and title documents			
Mortgage contract			
Home repair records			
Home improvement records			
Home owner's warranty contract			
Annual escrow account statements			
Annual mortgage interest statements			
Vehicle ownership records			
Vehicle titles			
Vehicle lease agreements			
Vehicle warranty contracts			
Major repair records and receipts			
Tax documents			
Federal, state, and local returns for past three years			
Older federal, state, and local returns			
Record of work-related child care expenses			
Record of flexible spending accounts			
W-4 forms and pay stubs			
Record of all correspondence with the IRS			
Investment documents			
Brokerage account agreements			
Brokerage account statements			
Mutual fund account contracts			
Employer defined-benefit plan documents			
Employer defined-contribution plan documents			
IRA and Keogh plan documents			
Mutual fund account statements			
Stock dividends reports			
Inventory and appraisals of collectibles			
Estate planning documents			
Wills and letters of last instructions			
List of joint-ownership designations for bank accounts and other assets			
Living wills and durable powers of attorney			
Financial and medical power of attorney documents			
Trust account agreements and statements			

WORKSHEET 12—MY FINANCIAL GOALS

Financial goals must be specific in terms of dollar amounts, time, and the interim short-term goals that will lead to their achievement. Effective financial planners write their goals down. This worksheet provides a mechanism for you to compile your goals. You then can build your monthly savings needed to reach the goals into your budget (see Worksheet 14). An interactive calculator that performs this same procedure can be found on the *Garman/Forgue* website. (Use with *Personal Finance*, Ninth Edition, pages 78-79.)

My Financial Goals Worksheet

(A) Describe the goal	(B) Dollar amount required	(C) Deadline date	(D) Date to start saving	(E) Number of months to save (E – D)	(F) Monthly savings amount (from Web calculator)

WORKSHEET 13—DETERMINING MONTHLY BUDGET AMOUNTS FOR MY NONMONTHLY EXPENSES

Allowing for nonmonthly expenses is one of the most difficult aspects of budgeting for people who are new to the task. You might have expenses for college tuition, auto insurance, vehicle maintenance, and other items that occur some months and not others. Your best approach is to determine an equivalent monthly amount for each and then include it as a budgeted amount every month. You then can carry over any unspent amounts from month to month to build up a fund to pay the expense in the month that it does occur. The worksheet below can be used to identify these expenses and their monthly allocation. (Use with *Personal Finance*, Ninth Edition, pages 80-82.)

Determining Monthly Budget Amounts for My Nonmonthly Expenses Worksheet

(A) Expense item	(B) Estimated annual expense	(C) Number of months	(D) Estimate monthly allocation (B/C)
Automobile insurance		12	
Homeowners insurance		12	
Life insurance		12	
Other irregular insurance expenses		12	
School tuition		12	
School books and supplies		12	
Other irregular education expenses		12	
Vehicle license renewal and tax		12	
Vehicle maintenance		12	
Vehicle repairs		12	
Other irregular vehicle expenses		12	
Vacations		12	
Holiday gifts		12	
Real estate taxes		12	
Home repair and maintenance		12	
Other irregular housing expenses		12	
Other		12	
Other		12	
Other		12	

WORKSHEET 14—MY REVOLVING SAVINGS FUND

Over the course of a year you will have certain months where an unusually large expenditure might need to be made. Perhaps it will be for a vacation, payment of school expenses, holiday gifts, or insurance premiums. A revolving savings fund provides a mechanism for setting aside funds for these events. Worksheet 14 builds on Worksheet 13 to provide you with the total amounts you would need to set aside monthly and the cumulative totals that would need to go into your own revolving savings fund. (Use with *Personal Finance*, Ninth Edition, pages 84-85.)

My Revolving Savings Fund Worksheet

(A) Month	(B) Expense item	(C) Amount needed	(D) Deposit into the fund	(E) Withdrawal from the fund	(F) Fund balance
Jan.					
Feb.					
Mar.					
Apr.					
May					
June					
July					
Aug.					
Sept.					
Oct.					
Nov.					
Dec.					
Total					

WORKSHEET 15—MY BUDGET

Spending less than you earn is the way to get ahead financially. But it does not happen automatically. You need to plan your spending and your income so that you can reach your financial goals. Such a plan is called a budget. The basic idea would be to prepare a budget for a month based on the cash-flow statement for the previous month that you prepared in Worksheet 8. In addition, your budget should be based on the cash-flow statement and your goals list you prepared in Worksheet 11 and provide a monthly allocation for your nonmonthly expenses such as insurance. Then you would put the budget into action. Once the month is over you can prepare a new cash-flow statement for that month. Finally, you would prepare a new budget for the next month based on what you learned from living out the first month's budget. This may sound like quite a bit of work, but the payoff from developing these sound financial habits will pay off handsomely in the coming years. An interactive calculator that performs this same procedure can be found on the *Garman/Forgue* website. (Use with *Personal Finance*, Ninth Edition, pages 79-85.)

My Budget

Month: ________ **Your Name:** ____________________

Income

Wages #1 (gross)	______
Wages #2 (gross)	______
Interest income	______
Dividend income	______
Sales commissions	______
Tips	______
Gifts	______
Other	______
Other	______
Total income	______

Expenditures

Fixed expenses

Rent/mortgage payment	______
Home insurance	______
Car insurance	______
Vehicle loan #1	______
Vehicle loan #2	______
Medical insurance	______
Life insurance	______
Student loan payments	______
Savings #1	______
Savings #2	______
Savings #3	______
Retirement fund	______
Other	______
Other	______
Total fixed expenses	______

Variable expenses

Federal income tax	______
State income tax	______
Social Security tax	______
Food (home)	______
Food (away)	______
Food (entertain)	______
Entertainment	______
Electricity	______
Natural gas	______
Water/sewer	______
Garbage collection	______
Cable TV	______
Local telephone	______
Long distance	______
Cell phone	______
Medical	______
Clothing	______
Gifts	______
Personal care	______
Personal allowances	______
Gasoline	______
Vehicle maintenance	______
Education expenses	______
Other	______
Miscellaneous	______
Total variable expenses	______

Total expenditures ______

Net gain (loss) ______

WORKSHEET 16—MY BUDGET CATEGORY LEDGER WORKSHEETS

Budgeting entails more than simply preparing a budget. You also have to use the budget to monitor and control spending. To do so, you must have some type of recording or ledger system that allows you to keep track of how you are doing in each budget category as the month progresses. Worksheet 15 provides an example ledger sheet you can use. You could set up a page like this in a small spiral notebook—one page for each of your budget categories. (Use with *Personal Finance*, Ninth Edition, pages 79-85.)

My Budget Category Ledger Worksheets

Budget category and amount budgeted for the month (example: groceries $150)		
(A) Date	**(B) Expenditure amount**	**(C) Balance remaining (previous balance remaining – item B)**
Initial budgeted amount plus any carry over from previous month		$150
Total		

SECTION TWO

Money Management

This section of your workbook focuses on managing money, credit, and spending. Each worksheet will allow you to think through a decision or perform calculations related to a specific area of personal financial management in a way that has direct benefit to you.

Worksheet 17 My Sources of Taxable Income

Worksheet 18 Estimating My Income Tax Liability

Worksheet 19 Determining Whether I Should File for a Refund

Worksheet 20 Strategies to Reduce My Income Tax Liability

Worksheet 21 Selecting a Checking Account That Meets My Needs

Worksheet 22 Reconciling My Checking Account

Worksheet 23 Comparing My Credit Card Options

Worksheet 24 The Effect of Taking on Additional Debt on My Financial Ratios

Worksheet 25 Monthly Installment Loan Payment Calculator

Worksheet 26 My Credit Card Accounts Inventory

Worksheet 27 My Installment Loan Inventory

Worksheet 28 My Student Loan Inventory

Worksheet 29 My Top Priority Motor Vehicle Features

Worksheet 30 Comparing Vehicle Purchase Contracts

Worksheet 31 Should I Lease or Buy a Vehicle?

Worksheet 32 Should I Take a New Vehicle Rebate or Low-Rate Financing Offer?

Worksheet 33 Decision-Making Worksheet for a Major Product Purchase

Worksheet 34 Sample Product or Service Complaint Letter

Worksheet 35 Should I Rent or Buy Housing?

Worksheet 36 Monthly Mortgage Payment Calculator

Worksheet 37 Estimating Home Buying and Closing Costs

Worksheet 38 Should I Refinance My Mortgage?

WORKSHEET 17—MY SOURCES OF TAXABLE INCOME

It is smart to keep track of your various income sources throughout the tax year so that you will not forget to report them to the Internal Revenue Service. Omitted income could possibly result in an IRS audit, and penalties may be assessed on top of the income taxes actually owed.

Use the worksheet below to record all income sources. Record the names of the income sources in the spaces provided. Record the amounts in the appropriate spaces. (Use with *Personal Finance*, Ninth Edition, pages 101-106).

Sources of Income Worksheet

Type of Income	Source 1 ________	Source 2 ________	Source 3 ________	Source 4 ________	Source 5 ________
Salary	$	$	$	$	$
Wages	$	$	$	$	$
Tips	$	$	$	$	$
Commissions	$	$	$	$	$
Bonuses	$	$	$	$	$
Scholarship for room, board, and other living expenses	$	$	$	$	$
Grants and the value of tuition reductions received for teaching or other services	$	$	$	$	$
Business income	$	$	$	$	$
Capital gains	$	$	$	$	$
Interest and dividends	$	$	$	$	$
Alimony	$	$	$	$	$
Other income	$	$	$	$	$
Other income	$	$	$	$	$

WORKSHEET 18—ESTIMATING MY INCOME TAX LIABILITY

Taxable income is calculated by taking the taxpayer's gross income, subtracting any adjustments to income, subtracting either the standard deduction or total itemized deductions, and subtracting the amount permitted for the number of exemptions allowed. The amount of taxable income is then used to determine the taxpayer's liability via the tax tables or tax-rate schedules combined with the appropriate filing status. Use the worksheet below to determine an estimate of your income tax liability (for either last year or next year).

Go on line to obtain the amounts for standard deduction, exemption value, and tax tables or tax rate schedules, as well as possible adjustments to income and itemized deductions. Perhaps use figures from Quicken Taxes (quicken.com), YahooFinance Tax Center (finance.yahoo.com/taxes), CCH (finance.cch.com), or Internal Revenue Service (irs.gov).

Record your figures in column C. Step 1: Record your gross income. Step 2: Record any adjustments to gross income. Step 3: Subtract Step 2 from Step 1. Step 4: Record amount of standard deduction or total of itemized deductions. Step 5: Subtract Step 4 from Step 3. Step 6: Record the value of an exemption. Step 7: Subtract Step 6 from Step 5. Step 8: Record tax liability from appropriate tax table or tax rate schedule. Step 9: Record amount of any tax credits. Step 10: Subtract Step 9 from Step 8. An interactive calculator that performs this same procedure can be found on the *Garman/Forgue* website. (Use with *Personal Finance*, Ninth Edition, pages 101-115.)

Income Tax Liability Worksheet

(A) Steps	(B) Instructions	(C) Your figures
Step 1	Record your gross income.	
Step 2	Record any adjustments to gross income.	
Step 3	Subtract Step 2 from Step 1; the result is your adjusted gross income (AGI).	
Step 4	Record amount of standard deduction or total of itemized deductions.	
Step 5	Subtract Step 4 from Step 3; the result is a subtotal.	
Step 6	Record the total value of your exemptions.	
Step 7	Subtract Step 6 from Step 5; the result is taxable income.	
Step 8	Record tax liability from appropriate tax table or tax rate schedule; result is your final tax liability (if you do not have any tax credits to subtract).	
Step 9	Record amount of any tax credits.	
Step 10	Subtract Step 9 from Step 8; the result is your final tax liability.	

WORKSHEET 19—DETERMINING WHETHER I SHOULD FILE FOR A REFUND

You must file a federal income tax return each year if your income meets certain thresholds based on your filing status. But what if you are not required to file a return? Should you file a return? The answer is yes if you have a refund coming, that is, if you had more taxes withheld from your paychecks than you ultimately owed. (Use with *Personal Finance*, Ninth Edition, pages 101-115.)

There are four steps in determining whether you should file so you can obtain your federal income tax refund. Step 1: Calculate an estimate of your tax liability, as shown in Step 10 in Worksheet 18. Step 2: Add up the total amounts withheld for federal income taxes. Step 3: Calculate your refund due or amount owed. Step 4: File for a refund if you are due a refund.

Should I File for a Refund Worksheet

Step 1: My estimated tax liability is $_______________ (from Step 10 in Worksheet 18).

Step 2: The total amounts withheld for federal taxes is $_____________ (from the total of the amounts in column B below).

(A) Income sources	(B) Amounts withheld for federal income taxes
	$
	$
	$
	$
	$
	$
Total	$

Step 3: Calculate your refund due or amount owed.

The total amount withheld (from Step 2)	$_____________
Add total amount of tax credits (from Step 3)	$_____________
Subtotal	$_____________
Subtract your estimated tax liability (from Step 1)	$_____________
Calculate the refund due you or the amount you owe	$_____________

Step 4: File for a refund if you are due a refund.

To obtain your refund, you must file a federal income tax return. If you also have had state or city income taxes withheld, you may follow the same step-by-step process to determine if you are owed a refund from your state or city. If so, file appropriate tax forms to claim any refund amounts due from those governments.

WORKSHEET 20—STRATEGIES TO REDUCE MY INCOME TAX LIABILITY

There are several ways to reduce your income tax liability. For each of the strategies below that are of interest to you, identify what one characteristic you like about it, and note which strategies you might follow during your tax-paying life. (Use with *Personal Finance*, Ninth Edition, pages 116-125.)

Income Tax Reduction Strategies Worksheet

Tax reduction strategy	**Note one characteristic I like about the strategy. (Only comment below if the strategy is of interest to you.)**	**Checkmark each strategy I might follow.**
Investing with pretax income		
Deferring taxes on investment income		
Premium conversion account		
Flexible spending account		
Defined-contribution retirement account		
Individual Retirement Account (IRA)		
Roth IRA		
Coverdell education savings account		
Qualified tuition (Section 529) program		
Government savings bonds		
Municipal bonds		
Income shifting		
Postpone income		
Bunch deductions		
Saver credit		
Take all legal deductions		
Buy and manage a real estate investment		
Other		

WORKSHEET 21—SELECTING A CHECKING ACCOUNT THAT MEETS MY NEEDS

With the low interest rates prevalent today and the high fees that accompany many checking accounts, it is important to choose an account that fits your personal usage patterns. Worksheet 21 provides a way for you to analyze your checking account usage patterns and to estimate the costs associated with various options available to you to ensure that you have chosen the right account. In Step 1 you will identify the ways that you use a checking account. If you currently have a checking account, you can use your past two or three monthly statements to estimate the answers to the questions asked. If you currently do not have a checking account, you can make your best estimate of the answers.

Step 2 provides a way for you to estimate the costs associated with various accounts that are available to you at your current or other financial institutions. Your answers should be based on the usage patterns you identified in Step 1. If you currently have a checking account, you should go back to your account statements over the past two or three months to determine the amounts. You can use the three right columns to record the likely interest and fees associated with other account options. A financial institution that wants your business would be happy to help you estimate these items on the basis of your usage patterns as outlined in Step 1. The goal is to choose an account that has the lowest overall cost given your usage patterns. (Use with *Personal Finance*, Ninth Edition, pages 135-139.)

Comparing Checking Account Options Worksheet

Step 1—My checking account usage patterns

How many checks do or will I write per month? ______________
How many ATM transactions do or will I perform each month? ______________
What is the lowest dollar balance I will likely have in my account each month? ______________
What is the highest dollar balance I will likely have in my account each month? ______________
What is the average dollar balance I will typically have in my account each month? ______________
Will I conduct my checking account on-line? ______________
Will my paycheck be electronically deposited into my checking account? ______________

Step 2—Net earnings (or costs) on my checking account

	Current account	**Account option #1**	**Account option #2**	**Account option #3**
Name of financial institution				
Type (name) of account				
Item				
A. Monthly interest or dividends earned				
Fees				
ATM usage fees (charged by my bank)				
Total per-check transaction fees				
Monthly account maintenance fee				
Overdraft fees				
On-line access fees				
Low-balance fees				
Other fees				
B. Total fees				
C. Net earnings or costs (A – B)				

WORKSHEET 22—RECONCILING MY CHECKING ACCOUNT

You should reconcile your checking account each month. Reconciling is the process of comparing your records with those on your monthly account statement. The goals are to make sure that your account balance is accurate, to correct and update your records, and to check the monthly statement for errors the bank may have made. Worksheet 22 provides a form you can use for this reconciliation process.

In Step 1, record the balance shown on your account statement. In Step 2, total all outstanding deposits. In Step 3, subtract the Step 2 result from the Step 1 figure. In Step 4, total all outstanding checks or debits to your account. In Step 5, subtract the Step 4 result from Step 3 figure. The result is the up-to-date statement balance.

In Step 6, record the current balance in your checkbook register. In Step 7, total all credits to your account that you had not previously recorded. In Step 8, record any interest payments into your account as shown on your monthly account statement. In Step 9, add the results from Steps 6, 7, and 8. In Step 10, total any debits from your account that were not previously recorded in your checkbook register. In Step 11, record any fees charged to your account as indicated on your monthly account statement. In Step 12, subtract the results for Step 10 and Step 11 from Step 9. The result is your up-to-date check register balance. The results for Step 5 and Step 12 should agree. If they do not, you will need to determine where an error may have occurred. An interactive calculator that performs this same procedure can be found on the *Garman/Forgue* website. (Use with *Personal Finance*, Ninth Edition, page 142.)

Checking Account Reconciliation Worksheet for Month/Year ____________________

Step

#1 Balance shown on statement $______

Outstanding deposits (by date) — Amt.

____________________ $______
____________________ $______
____________________ $______

#2 Total outstanding deposits $______

#3 Adjusted statement balance (#1 + #2) $______

Outstanding checks/debits (by check # or date) — Amt.

____________________ $______
____________________ $______
____________________ $______
____________________ $______
____________________ $______
____________________ $______
____________________ $______
____________________ $______
____________________ $______
____________________ $______
____________________ $______
____________________ $______
____________________ $______
____________________ $______
____________________ $______

#4 Total outstanding checks $______

#5 Up-to-date statement balance (#3 – #4) $______

Step

#6 Balance shown in check register $______

Credits not recorded in check register — Amt.

____________________ $______
____________________ $______
____________________ $______
____________________ $______

#7 Total credits not recorded $______

#8 Interest received as shown on statement $______

#9 Adjusted check register balance (#6 + #7 + #8) $______

Checks/debits not recorded in check register — Amt.

____________________ $______
____________________ $______
____________________ $______
____________________ $______
____________________ $______
____________________ $______
____________________ $______
____________________ $______

#10 Total debits not recorded $______

#11 Account fees $______

#12 Up-to-date check register balance [#9 – (#10 + #11)] $______

WORKSHEET 23—COMPARING MY CREDIT CARD OPTIONS

All credit card offers are not alike. In addition to the obvious differences in APRs and annual fees, there are a number of other features of cards that distinguish among appropriate and inappropriate offers, given your likely usage patterns. Worksheet 23 allows you to summarize several offers side by side for easy analysis and selection. (Use with *Personal Finance*, Ninth Edition, pages 185-197.)

Comparing My Credit Card Options Worksheet

Card feature	Card #1	Card #2	Card #3
Type of card (VISA, MC, AMEX, etc.)			
Company/bank offering the card			
Introductory APRs Purchases Cash advances Balance transfers			
Subsequent APRs Purchases Cash advances Balance transfers			
Default APRs Purchases Cash advances Balance transfers			
If APRs are variable, what base rate is used?			
If APRs are variable, what percentage is added to the base rate to arrive at the APR? Purchases Cash advances Balance transfers			
Annual fee			
Method of computing the balance			
Grace period for purchases			
Minimum finance charge			
Transaction fees Purchases Cash advances Balance transfers			
Additional fees Over-the-limit fee Late payment fee Bounced check fee			

WORKSHEET 24—THE EFFECT OF TAKING ON ADDITIONAL DEBT ON MY FINANCIAL RATIOS

Two key financial ratios can provide additional insights into the affordability of taking on additional debt. Worksheet 24 builds on Worksheet 10 to provide those insights. (Use with *Personal Finance*, Ninth Edition, pages 163-166.)

The **debt service-to-income ratio** compares your total annual debt payments (including home mortgage debt) with your gross annual income. A debt service-to-income ratio in excess of 0.36 indicates that you are carrying too much debt. What if you were to take on more debt? How would your debt service-to-income ratio change from what you calculated in Worksheet 10?

The **debt payments-to-disposable income ratio** compares your monthly nonmortgage debt payments to your monthly disposable income. A debt service-to-disposable income ratio of 0.16 or more indicates that you are carrying too much nonmortgage debt. What if you were to take on more debt? How would your debt payments-to-disposable income ratio change from what you calculated in Worksheet 10? An interactive calculator that performs these same procedures can be found on the *Garman/Forgue* website.

The Effect of Taking on Additional Debt on My Financial Ratios Worksheet

Debt service-to-income ratio

(A) Current annual debt repayments	(B) Gross income	(C) Current debt service-to-income ratio (A/B)	(D) New annual debt repayments	(E) New debt service-to-income ratio (D/B)

Debt payments-to-disposable income ratio

(A) Current monthly nonmortgage debt payments	(B) Disposable income	(C) Current debt payments-to-disposable income ratio (A/B)	(D) New monthly nonmortgage debt repayments	(E) New debt payments-to-disposable income ratio (D/E)

WORKSHEET 25—MONTHLY INSTALLMENT LOAN PAYMENT CALCULATOR

Whenever you apply for an installment loan, you will be faced with a number of options regarding the amount to borrow, the APR of the loan, and the time period of the loan. Changes in any one of these factors will result in a different monthly payment on the loan for principal and interest. This worksheet can be used in conjunction with Table 7.1 on page 199 in your text to calculate the monthly payment for loans with differing factors. An interactive calculator that performs this same procedure can be found on the *Garman/Forgue* website. (Use with *Personal Finance*, Ninth Edition, pages 198-199.)

Monthly Installment Loan Payment Calculation Worksheet

(A) Loan	(B) Time period of the loan in months	(C) APR of the loan	(D) Factor from Table 7.3 that corresponds with (B) and (C)	(E) Amount borrowed	(F) Amount borrowed (E) divided by 1,000	(G) Monthly payment (D x F)
#1						
#2						
#3						
#4						
#5						
#6						

WORKSHEET 26—MY CREDIT CARD ACCOUNTS INVENTORY

The typical American with a credit card has an average of seven open accounts. Accounts stay open even if not used for several years. Worksheet 26 provides a quick way for you to list your accounts and the information needed to contact the lender in case the card is lost or stolen, there is an error on your monthly statement, or if you change your address. These numbers can be found on your monthly statement or the website for the issuing financial institution. (Use with *Personal Finance*, Ninth Edition, pages 185-197.)

My Credit Card Accounts Inventory

	Name of card	Issuing financial institution	Account number	Usual due date	Phone number to notify if lost or stolen	Phone number to notify of a billing error	Phone number to notify of a change of address
Card #1							
Card #2							
Card #3							
Card #4							
Card #5							
Card #6							
Card #7							
Card #8							
Card #9							
Card #10							

WORKSHEET 27—MY INSTALLMENT LOAN INVENTORY

Have you taken out a loan for a vehicle, vacation, or other purpose? How many loans other than student loans (see Worksheet 28) do you have outstanding? Worksheet 27 provides a handy way to list all your loans. It gives you a clear picture of your outstanding installment debts. The information needed to complete this inventory can be found in your monthly statements or original loan contracts. (Use with *Personal Finance*, Ninth Edition, pages 197-202.)

My Installment Loan Inventory

	Name and address of lender	Reason for the loan	Original loan amount	Monthly payment	Due date	Payoff date
Loan #1						
Loan #2						
Loan #3						
Loan #4						
Loan #5						
Loan #6						

WORKSHEET 28—MY STUDENT LOAN INVENTORY

Do you have any outstanding student loans? Worksheet 28 provides a handy way to list each of your student loans along with relevant information about the source of the funds, lender, amount owed, loan costs, and so on. When you graduate, you may be able to consolidate all your loans into one to receive a lower APR. This worksheet will help you get started in that process. (Use with *Personal Finance*, Ninth Edition, pages 197-202.)

My Student Loan Inventory

Loan feature	Loan #1	Loan #2	Loan #3	Loan #4
Program through which loan was obtained				
Interest deferred? (yes/no)				
If interest is deferred, when must payments begin?				
Source/lender				
Current APR				
Current loan balance				
Maximum number of years to repay				
Approximate monthly payment (see Table 7.3 in text or Worksheet 25)				

WORKSHEET 29—MY TOP PRIORITY MOTOR VEHICLE FEATURES

The number of options available on vehicles today is almost limitless. Before you begin shopping for a vehicle, it is wise to think through the options that you desire and assign a priority level to each. Worksheet 29 provides a mechanism for this task by listing many common features so you can use a checkmark to assign each to one of three priority levels: 1 for essential features, 2 for highly desirable features, and 3 for "nice to have" features. Features that are not desired can be left unchecked. Blank rows are included for you to include additional features that you might desire. (Use with *Personal Finance*, Ninth Edition, pages 208-210.)

My Vehicle Features Worksheet

Vehicle feature	Priority Level		
	1	2	3
Adjustable steering column			
Side-impact air bags			
Air conditioning			
Satellite radio			
Four-wheel antilock brakes			
Automatic transmission			
Central power locking system			
CD player/changer			
Cruise control			
All-wheel drive			
Four-wheel drive			
Power windows			
Rear-window defroster			
Sun/moon roof			
Theft-deterrent system			
Advanced sound system			
DVD player			
Power adjustable seating			
Heated seats			
Remote keyless entry			
Removable rear seating			
Luggage rack			
GPS system			
Towing package			
High gas mileage rating			
Daytime running lights			
Power mirrors			
Integrated child seat			

WORKSHEET 30—COMPARING VEHICLE PURCHASE CONTRACTS

Buying a vehicle can be a very complicated process. There are so many variables that many people simply focus on one or two aspects such as the monthly payment or the trade-in value. This can be a recipe for a bad deal because the profit that a dealer might give up on one aspect can be more than made up for on another. Worksheet 30 provides a handy place to record all of the terms for several purchase contracts from three dealers. The worksheet allows you to see the full picture and make accurate comparisons. (Use with *Personal Finance*, Ninth Edition, pages 210-225.)

Vehicle Purchase Contract Worksheet

Contract provision	Dealer #1	Dealer #2	Dealer #3
Vehicle sticker price			
Vehicle invoice price (estimated)			
Dealer offer price			
Trade-in value offered by dealer			
APR by source of financing			
Manufacturer			
Dealer			
Your own arrangement			
Is there a rebate? (If so, complete Worksheet 32.)			
Down payment			
Amount borrowed			
Length of loan			
Monthly payment			
Warranty provisions			
Miles/years			
Service contract provisions			
Miles			
Coverage (drive train, bumper to bumper?)			
Cost			
Cost of dealer option package			
Cost of gap insurance			

WORKSHEET 31—SHOULD I LEASE OR BUY A VEHICLE?

The worksheet below can be used to compare leasing and borrowing to buy a vehicle. Remember that the cost of credit is the finance charge—the extra that you pay because you borrowed. In the example below, the finance charge on the loan is $1,950. Your lender will be able to tell you the finance charge on any vehicle loan offer you are considering.

Leases also carry costs, but they are hidden in the contract, and some remain unknown until the end of the lease period. These items, which are indicated by an asterisk (*) below, are negotiable and are defined in the text. Ask the dealer for the amount of each of these costs. Then complete the worksheet and compare the dollar cost of leasing with the finance charge on a loan for the same time period.

In Step 1, total all the monthly lease payments as outlined in the contract. In Step 2, record other charges for which you will be responsible (note that you cover the residual value of the vehicle by returning or buying the vehicle at the end of the lease period). Step 3 is the total for Steps 2 and 3. In Step 4, record the adjusted capitalized cost (capitalized cost less items such as a trade-in and down payment) as indicated in your contract. Step 5 is the result of subtracting Step 4 from Step 1. In Step 6, record the finance charge on the loan you would arrange to buy the vehicle instead of leasing. The lower of items in Step 5 and Step 6 is the better arrangement. In the example, the $1,950 finance charge is lower than the $2,400 additional cost of leasing. This means that you should borrow to buy the vehicle rather than obtain it with a lease.

To make the comparison accurately, you must know the underlying price of the car if you were purchasing it. Often you are not told this value with a lease arrangement, so you must negotiate a price for the vehicle before mentioning the lease option. An interactive calculator that performs this same procedure can be found on the *Garman/Forgue* website. (Use with *Personal Finance*, Ninth Edition, pages 216-219.)

Vehicle Lease Versus Buy Worksheet

Step	(A) Example	(B) Your figures
1. Monthly lease payments (36 payments of $275, for example)	$9,900	
2. Plus acquisition fee* (if any) • Plus disposition charge* (if any) • Plus estimate of excess mileage charges* (if any) • Plus projected residual value of the vehicle	+ 300 + 300 + 0 + 4,500	
3. Amount for which you are responsible under the lease (#1 + #2)	**$15,000**	
4. Adjusted capitalized cost*—the capitalized cost* after taking capitalized cost reductions*	– 12,600	
5. Dollar cost of leasing (#3 – #4)	$2,400	
6. Finance charge for loan you arrange to purchase rather than lease the vehicle	**$1,950**	

WORKSHEET 32—SHOULD I TAKE A NEW VEHICLE REBATE OR LOW-RATE FINANCING OFFER?

Ads for new vehicles often offer either a low APR loan or a cash rebate of $1,000 to $3,000 (or more) off the price of the car. Which alternative is better when you can arrange your own financing? You can't simply compare the dealer APR to the APR that you arranged on your own.

To compare the two APRs accurately, you must add the opportunity cost of the forgone rebate to the finance charge of the dealer financing. The worksheet below provides an example (column A) of this process for an offer with a $3,000 rebate versus a loan of $12,000 with a 2.9 percent APR for three years with a $907 finance charge.

In Step 1, record the dollar value of the rebate offered. In Step 2, add the rebate amount to the finance charge that would be required by the loan obtained via the low-rate financing offer. Step 3 requires that you use the *n*-ratio formula (7.2) in your text (page 200) to recalculate the low-rate finance APR. In Step 4, record the APR for the best loan you can arrange on your own through your bank or credit union. The lower of the values obtained in Steps 3 and 4 is the better deal. In the example below, the financing that you could arrange on your own is more attractive. In fact, any loan that carries an APR lower than 10.9 percent compares favorably with the dealer-arranged 2.9 percent financing in this case. An interactive calculator that performs this same procedure can be found on the *Garman/Forgue* website. (Use with *Personal Finance*, Ninth Edition, pages 211-212.)

New Vehicle Rebate or Low-Rate Financing Offer Worksheet

Step	(A) Example	(B) Your figures
1. Determine the dollar amount of the rebate.	$ 3,000	
2. Add the rebate amount to the finance charge for the dealer financing (dollar cost of credit).	+ 907 = $ 3,907	
3. Use the *n*-ratio APR formula from Chapter 7 (Equation 7.3 on page 193) to calculate an adjusted APR for the dealer financing.	10.9%	
4. Write in the APR that you arranged on your own.	6.5%	

WORKSHEET 33—DECISION-MAKING WORKSHEET FOR A MAJOR PRODUCT PURCHASE

Making a major purchase decision can be a difficult task. It sometimes helps to put some numbers to the decision. For example, price might represent 50 percent of the importance you place on the various criteria. Worksheet 33 allows you to calculate a total weighted score for up to three different models of a product. In Step 1 (column A), assign weights to the criteria. Then in Step 2, give each model a score for each criterion on a ten-point scale (columns B, D, and F). For Step 3, calculate the weighted scores for each of the criteria for each model (columns C, E, and G). Finally, in Step 4, total up the weighted scores for each model. The one with the highest total weighted score will stand above the others on the criteria you have chosen. An interactive calculator that performs this same procedure can be found on the *Garman/Forgue* website. (Use with *Personal Finance*, Ninth Edition, pages 224-225.)

Decision-Making Worksheet for a Major Product Purchase

		Model 1		Model 2		Model 3	
Criteria	**(A) (Step 1) Decision weight**	**(B) (Step 2) Score 1***	**(C) (Step 3) Weighted score 1 (A x B)**	**(D) (Step 2) Score 2***	**(E) (Step 3) Weighted score 2 (A x D)**	**(F) (Step 2) Score 3***	**(G) (Step 3) Weighted score 3 (A x F)**
Price							
Durability							
Features							
Warranty							
Styling							
Other							
Other							
(Step 4) Total							

*Using a ten-point scale where 10 is the highest score.

WORKSHEET 34—SAMPLE PRODUCT OR SERVICE COMPLAINT LETTER

The final step in wise buying is to evaluate your decision. Sometimes this evaluation results in a desire to complain or seek redress for some deficiency in the product or service you purchased. A simple "I don't like . . ." is not usually sufficient to correct the problem. Instead, a letter containing all the specifics of the problem and the remedy desired is likely to get action. Worksheet 34 provides a sample letter you can use whenever seeking redress of a deficient product or service. (Use with *Personal Finance*, Ninth Edition, pages 225-226.)

Sample Product or Service Complaint Letter

(Your address)
(Your city, state, zip code)

(Date)

(Name of contact person)
(Title)
(Company name)
(Street address)
(City, state, zip code)

Dear (contact person):

On (date), I purchased (or had repaired) a (name of the product with the serial or model number or service performed). I made this purchase at (location, date, and other important details of the transaction).

Unfortunately, your product (or service) has not been satisfactory because (state the problem).

Therefore, to resolve the problem, I request that you (state the specific action you want).

Enclosed are copies (copies, *not* originals) of my records (receipts, guarantees, warranties, canceled checks, contracts, model and serial numbers, and any other documents).

I look forward to your reply and a resolution to my problem and will wait (set a time limit) before seeking third-party assistance.

Please contact me at the above address or by telephone (home or office numbers with area codes).

Sincerely,

(Your name)

(Your account number)

WORKSHEET 35—SHOULD I RENT OR BUY HOUSING?

This worksheet can be used to help you estimate whether you would be better off renting housing or buying over the first year of a home purchase. An interactive calculator that performs this same procedure can be found on the *Garman/Forgue* website. (Use with *Personal Finance*, Ninth Edition, pages 232-236.)

Should I Rent or Buy Housing Worksheet

	(A) Example amounts (from text)		**(B) Your figures**	
	Rent	**Buy**	**Rent**	**Buy**
Step 1—Annual cash-flow considerations				
Annual rent ($800/month) or mortgage payments ($740.95/month)*	$12,000	$11,496		
Property and liability insurance	360	725		
Private mortgage insurance	N/A	0	N/A	
Real estate taxes	0	3,000		
Maintenance	0	600		
Other housing fees	0	1,800		
Less interest earned on funds not used for down payment (at 4%)	– 1,440	N/A		N/A
Net cash-flow cost for the year	$10,920	$17,621		
Step 2—Tax and appreciation considerations				
Less principal† repaid on the mortgage loan	N/A	– 1,464	N/A	
Plus tax on interest earned on funds not used for down payment (25% marginal tax bracket)	240	N/A		N/A
Less tax savings due to deductibility of mortgage interest‡ (25% marginal tax bracket)	N/A	– 2,508	N/A	
Less tax savings due to deductibility of real estate property taxes (25% marginal tax bracket)	N/A	– 750	N/A	
Less appreciation on the dwelling (2.5% annual rate)	N/A	– 4,500	N/A	
Step 3—Net cost for the year (Step 1 +/– Step 2)	$12,580	$8,399		

*Calculated using Table 9.4 in your text.

†Calculated according to the method illustrated in Table 9.2 in your text or in Worksheet 36.

‡Mortgage interest tax savings equal total mortgage payments minus principal repaid multiplied by the marginal tax rate.

WORKSHEET 36—MONTHLY MORTGAGE PAYMENT CALCULATOR

Whenever you apply for a mortgage loan you will be faced with a number of options regarding the amount to borrow, the APR of the loan, and the time period of the loan. Changes in any one of these factors will result in a different monthly payment for principal and interest. This worksheet can be used in conjunction with Table 9.4 on page 252 in your text to calculate the monthly payment for mortgage loans with differing factors. An interactive calculator that performs this same procedure can be found on the *Garman/Forgue* website. (Use with *Personal Finance*, Ninth Edition, pages 249-253.)

Monthly Mortgage Loan Payment Calculation Worksheet

(A) Mortgage loan	(B) Time period of the loan in years	(C) Interest rate of the loan	(D) Factor from Table 9.3 that corresponds with (B) and (C)	(E) Amount borrowed	(F) Amount borrowed (E) divided by 1,000	(G) Monthly payment (D x F)
#1						
#2						
#3						
#4						
#5						
#6						

WORKSHEET 37—ESTIMATING HOME BUYING AND CLOSING COSTS

Buying a home requires that you carefully consider all of the costs associated with the mortgage used to make the purchase. These costs include all payments made at the closing and then all of the monthly expenditures, as well. Worksheet 37 provides a way for you to record the costs for your mortgage in a handy summary form. Most of the information can be obtained from the "good faith estimate" that lenders must provide when you apply for a mortgage loan. (Use with *Personal Finance*, Ninth Edition, pages 236-242.)

Estimating Home Buying and Closing Costs Worksheet

Home buying costs	**At closing**	**Monthly**
Down payment		
Points		
Loan application fee		
Principal and interest†		
Property taxes	*	
Homeowner's insurance	**	
Mortgage insurance		
Loan origination fee		
Title search		
Title insurance (to protect lender)		
Title insurance (to protect buyer)		
Attorney's fee		
Credit reports		
Recording fees		
Appraisal fee		
Termite and radon inspection fees		
Survey fee		
Notary fee		
Subtotal		
Less amount owed by seller	*	
Subtotal		
Warranty insurance (optional)		
Total		

*Would be received from seller, who legally owes these taxes, and then deposited in escrow account.

**Would be paid to escrow account.

†Calculated using Table 9.4 in your text or Worksheet 36.

WORKSHEET 38—SHOULD I REFINANCE MY MORTGAGE?

In times of low interest rates, many people wonder whether they should take out a new loan to pay off their current high-rate mortgage to take advantage of the lower current rates. Such an action is referred to as a mortgage refinancing.

Worksheet 38 provides a way for you to decide whether it is financially advantageous to refinance a mortgage. Note that the worksheet is only applicable if you are borrowing only the current outstanding loan balance for the same number of years as are remaining on the current loan.

In Step 1, record the current monthly payment on your mortgage for principal and interest only (not taxes and insurance). In Step 2, record the monthly payment for principal and interest only (not taxes and insurance) on the new mortgage. In Step 3, subtract Step 2 from Step 1 and multiply by 12 to obtain your annual mortgage payment reduction. In Step 4, estimate the number of years you remain living in the home. In Step 5, determine how much you could save if you placed the monthly mortgage payment reduction into a savings account. You will have to estimate the interest rate after taxes that could be achieved on this account. In Step 6, record any prepayment penalties for paying off your current loan early. In Step 7, record the total of all up-front costs for the new loan including points and other fees. In Step 8, determine the future value if you would instead invest the up-front costs into a savings account rather than use them to refinance. Again, you will have to estimate the interest rate after taxes that could be achieved on this account.

In Step 9, subtract the results of Step 5 from the results of Step 8. The result is an estimate of the net savings from refinancing the mortgage.

In the example, it would appear that refinancing would benefit the owner. An interactive calculator that performs this same procedure can be found on the *Garman/Forgue* website. (Use with *Personal Finance*, Ninth Edition, page 257.)

Should I Refinance My Mortgage? Worksheet

(A) Step	(B) Example	(C) Your figures
1. Current monthly payment	$954	
2. New monthly payment	840	
3. Annual saving (Step 1 – Step 2 x 12)	1,368	
4. Additional years you expect to live in the house	4	
5. Future value of an account balance after 4 years if the annual savings were invested at 3% after taxes (using Appendix A.3)	5,723	
6. Prepayment penalty on current loan (if any)	1,202	
7. Points and fees for new loan	2,404	
8. Future value of an account balance after 4 years if the prepayment penalty and closing costs ($4,200) had been invested instead at 3% after taxes (using Appendix A.1)	4,059	
9. Net saving after 48 months (Step 5 – Step 8)	$1,664	

SECTION THREE

Income and Asset Protection

This section of your workbook focuses on efforts to protect your property and income from loss. Each worksheet will allow you to think through a decision or perform calculations related to a specific area of personal financial management in a way that has direct benefit to you.

Worksheet 39 My Insurance Inventory

Worksheet 40 My Home Inventory

Worksheet 41 My Comparison of Auto Insurance Providers

Worksheet 42 Determining My Disability Income Insurance Needs

Worksheet 43 Determining My Life Insurance Needs

Worksheet 44 Layering Term Insurance Policies

WORKSHEET 39—MY INSURANCE INVENTORY

As your financial life gets more complicated and you own more possessions, your need for insurance protection also increases. Most Americans are covered by five major types of insurance: life, health, automobile, homeowner's, and disability income. The details of each of these protections are contained in the actual insurance policies. It helps to have the basic information about all your policies in one place for handy reference. Worksheet 39 provides an insurance inventory you can use for this purpose. (Use with *Personal Finance*, Ninth Edition, pages 268-348.)

My Insurance Inventory Worksheet

Insurance Inventory Worksheet for ______________________________

Do you have life insurance? If so, complete the following for each policy.	Policy limits (face amount)	Annual premium	Beneficiary	Term or cash value policy?	If cash value, what is the current cash value?
Company: Policy #: Agent: Contact Info:					
Company: Policy #: Agent: Contact info:					
Company: Policy #: Agent: Contact info:					

Are you covered by any health care plans? If so, complete the following.	Is it an HMO? What is its name?	Or is it traditional insurance? What company?	If insurance, what is the aggregate limit?	Does an employer pay all or a portion of the premium?	Do you or a parent or guardian pay part of the premium? If so, how much?
Company: Policy or plan #: Agent: Contact info:					
Company: Policy or plan #: Agent: Contact info:					

Do you have disability income insurance? If so, complete the following.	Amount of monthly premium?	Annual premium?	Waiting period?	Maximum benefit period?
Company: Policy #: Agent: Contact info:				
Company: Policy #: Agent: Contact info:				

Do you have automobile insurance on the vehicles you drive? Describe the vehicles covered including the VIN number. Also complete the following.	What are the liability limits? ($/$/$)	Collision deductible? (N/A if no collision)	"Other than collision" deductible?	Under- or uninsured motorist limits?	Medical payment (PIP) limits?
Description and VIN: Company: Policy or plan #: Agent: Contact info:					
Description and VIN: Company: Policy or plan #: Agent: Contact info:					

Are you covered by homeowner's or renter's insurance? Which form (HO-1, HO-2, etc.)? If so, complete the following.	Limit on dwelling?	Limit on personal property?	Personal liability limit?	Deductible amount?	Annual premium?
Form: Company: Policy #: Agent: Contact info:					

WORKSHEET 40—MY HOME INVENTORY

Making an inventory of, and placing a value on, all the contents of your home are time-consuming but important tasks. Should some or all of these assets be stolen or lost in a fire or natural disaster, providing a copy of a home inventory worksheet to your insurance company can greatly aid the process of filing a claim. An interactive calculator that calculates actual cash values can be found on the *Garman/Forgue* website. Worksheet 40 provides a form you can use for this purpose. (Use with *Personal Finance*, Ninth Edition, pages 268-269)

Home Inventory Worksheet

Date inventory prepared: ______________________

Items	Item description	Date purchased	Purchase price	Actual cash value	Replace-ment cost
Living room					
			$	$	$
			$	$	$
			$	$	$
			$	$	$
Dining room					
			$	$	$
			$	$	$
			$	$	$
Kitchen					
			$	$	$
			$	$	$
			$	$	$
Bedrooms					
			$	$	$
			$	$	$
			$	$	$
Hallways					
			$	$	$
			$	$	$
Home office					
			$	$	$
			$	$	$
Bathroom					
			$	$	$
			$	$	$
Garage, attic, basement, and storage					
			$	$	$
			$	$	$
Other items					
			$	$	$
			$	$	$

WORKSHEET 41—MY COMPARISON OF AUTO INSURANCE PROVIDERS

The premium required for automobile insurance varies considerably from company to company and from driver to driver. Automobile insurance definitely is one of those areas where it pays to shop around. Worksheet 41 provides a mechanism for recording automobile insurance premium quotations from insurers. (Use with *Personal Finance*, Ninth Edition, pages 282-288.)

Auto Insurance Comparison Worksheet

Coverage type	Coverage limits or amount of deductible	Company 1 premium for each component	Company 2 premium for each component	Company 3 premium for each component
A. Liability insurance				
Bodily injury	$_____/$_____	$_____	$_____	$_____
Property damage	$_____/$_____	$_____	$_____	$_____
B. Medical payment/personal injury protection				
Medical payments	$_____/$_____	$_____	$_____	$_____
PIP (no-fault states)	$_____/$_____	$_____	$_____	$_____
C. Uninsured/underinsured motorist protection				
Uninsured motorist	$_____/$_____	$_____	$_____	$_____
Underinsured motorist	$_____/$_____	$_____	$_____	$_____
D. Physical damage protection				
Collision coverage	$_____ deductible	$_____	$_____	$_____
Comprehensive	$_____ deductible	$_____	$_____	$_____
Total premium		$_____	$_____	$_____
Plus surcharges		$_____	$_____	$_____
Less discounts		$_____	$_____	$_____
Final total premium		$_____	$_____	$_____

WORKSHEET 42—DETERMINING MY DISABILITY INCOME INSURANCE NEEDS

Disability income insurance is one of the most overlooked forms of insurance, yet is especially vital for young workers who have not established retirement funds or Social Security earnings histories which can provide support in times of disability. Worksheet 42 can be used to estimate the monthly dollar amount of your disability income insurance needs.

The determination of disability insurance needs begins with your current monthly after-tax income. From this figure, subtract the amounts you would receive from Social Security disability and other sources of disability income. The resulting figure would provide an estimate of the extra coverage needed. You should also consult with your employer to determine the provisions of any disability income insurance protection that is provided as an employee benefit. An interactive calculator that performs this same procedure can be found on the *Garman/Forgue* website. (Use with *Personal Finance*, Ninth Edition, pages 312-315.)

Disability Income Insurance Needs Worksheet

	Example	Your figures
1. Current monthly after-tax income	$2,100	$_________
Minus previous established disability income protections		$_________
2. Estimated monthly Social Security benefits (See Appendix B or use the Benefits Estimator on the Social Security Administration website, www.ssa.gov.)	–$750	$_________
3. Monthly benefit from employer-provided disability insurance	–$600	$_________
4. Monthly benefit from private disability insurance		$_________
5. Monthly benefit from other government disability insurance		$_________
6. Reduction of monthly life insurance premiums due to waiver of premiums on these policies		$_________
7. Total currently established disability income protections (total of Step 2 through Step 6)	$1,350	$_________
8. Estimated monthly disability income insurance needs. (Step 1 – Step 7)	$ 750	$_________

WORKSHEET 43—DETERMINING MY LIFE INSURANCE NEEDS

Life insurance needs vary considerably over the life cycle. They are low for single adults, peak when becoming a parent for the first time, and then slowly decline as the children grow up. Thus, it is important to recalculate your needs every three to five years or when a major life transition occurs such as marriage, parenthood, divorce, death of a spouse or child, or major change in your level of income.

Worksheet 43 can be used to calculate your life insurance needs using the needs approach outlined in your textbook. An interactive calculator that performs this same procedure can be found on the *Garman/Forgue* website. (Use with *Personal Finance*, Ninth Edition, pages 325-328.)

My Life Insurance Needs Worksheet

Factors affecting need	**Example**	**Your figures**
1. Income-replacement needs Multiply 75 percent of annual income by the interest factor from Appendix A.4 that corresponds with the number of years that the income is to be replaced and the assumed after-tax, after-inflation rate of return.* ($36,000 x 17.292 for 30 years at a 4% rate of return)	$ 622,512	$_________
2. Final-expense needs Includes funeral, burial, travel, and other items of expense just prior to and after death.	+ 10,000	+_________
3. Readjustment-period needs Covers employment interruptions and possible education expenses for surviving spouse and dependents.	+ 19,000	+_________
4. Debt-repayment needs Provides repayment of short-term and installment debt, including credit cards and personal loans.	+ 10,000	+_________
5. College-expense needs Provides a fund to help meet college expenses of dependents.	+ 75,000	+_________
6. Other special needs	+ 0	+_________
7. Subtotal (combined effects of items 1–6)	$ 736,512	+_________
8. Government benefits Present value of Social Security survivor's benefits and other benefits. Multiply monthly benefit estimate by 12 and use Appendix A.4 for the number of years that benefits will be received and the same interest rate that was used in item 1. ($2,725 x 12 x 11.118 for 15 years of benefits and a 4% rate of return)	– 363,558	–_________
9. Current insurance assets	– 98,000	–_________
10. Life insurance needed	$ 274,954	_________

*Seventy-five percent is used because about 25 percent of income is used for personal needs.

WORKSHEET 44—LAYERING TERM INSURANCE POLICIES

Trying to meet one's life insurance needs with just one or two life insurance policies is not the best method of obtaining protection over the life cycle. This is because life insurance needs fluctuate over one's lifetime. The bulk of this need can be met by layering term insurance policies so that coverage grows and then automatically decreases as needs change.

Worksheet 44 can be used to set up your term insurance layers. The worksheet also provides an example you can use as a model. The example assumes that the person is age 25 when the first child is born and age 30 when the last child is born. In this example, the person buys several level premium term policies near the birth of the first child with the policies having differing time periods. Then the person buys another policy when the last child is born and another as the first child gets close to college age. Then as the children go out on their own, some of the earliest policies expire thereby reducing the overall amount of insurance as needs decline. One benefit of layering is affordability. On the basis of premium rates for healthy nonsmokers, the cost for the illustrated plan would never be more than approximately $50 per month. (Use with *Personal Finance*, Ninth Edition, page 344.)

Term Insurance Layering Worksheet

Example						
	Buy			**Policies in force at that age**	**Total coverage at that age**	**Monthly premium required**
Age	**Policy**	**Face amount**	**Years in force**			
25	#1 #2 #3	$100,000 $150,000 $200,000	30 years 25 years 20 years	#1, #2, #3	$450,000	$38
30	#4	$150,000	25 years	#1, #2, #3, #4	$600,000	$48
35				#1, #2, #3, #4	$600,000	$54
40	#5	$50,000	20 years	#1, #2, #3, #4, #5	$650,000	$60
45				#1, #2, #4, #5	$450,000	$58
50				#1, #4, #5	$300,000	$50
55				#5	$50,000	$20
60				None	$0	$0
Your Plan						
25						
30						
35						
40						
45						
50						
55						
60						

SECTION FOUR

Investments

This section of your workbook focuses on investing. Each worksheet will allow you to think through a decision or perform calculations related to a specific area of personal financial management in a way that has direct benefit to you.

Worksheet 45	My Readiness-to-Invest Checklist
Worksheet 46	My Investment Philosophy
Worksheet 47	My Preferred Long-Term Investment Strategies
Worksheet 48	My Investment Goals and Time Horizons
Worksheet 49	Comparing Taxable and Tax-Free Income
Worksheet 50	My Preferences Among Stocks
Worksheet 51	Comparing Stocks as Investments
Worksheet 52	My Preferences Among Bonds
Worksheet 53	The Current Yield on My Bond Investment
Worksheet 54	The Current Market Price of My Bond Investment
Worksheet 55	The Real Return on My Investments
Worksheet 56	The Yield to Maturity of My Bond
Worksheet 57	My Mutual Fund Preferences
Worksheet 58	Comparing Mutual Funds as Investments
Worksheet 59	Calculating the Return on Mutual Fund Investments
Worksheet 60	Evaluating the Performance (Gain or Loss) of My Investments

WORKSHEET 45—MY READINESS-TO-INVEST CHECKLIST

Before you embark on an investment program, make sure you are ready. Give yourself a readiness grade of A, B, C, D, or F for each of the following prerequisites to investing. Make note of things you can do to improve your readiness to invest and set dates for completion. And begin investing as soon as you can! (Use with *Personal Finance*, Ninth Edition, pages 354-355.)

Readiness-to-Invest Worksheet

Prerequisite to investing	**Your current readiness grade**	**Things I will do to improve my readiness to invest**	**Expected completion date**
Balance your budget			
Continue a savings plan			
Establish sufficient credit card maximum limits			
Carry adequate insurance to protect against major catastrophes			
Establish investment goals			
Other prerequisites			

WORKSHEET 46—MY INVESTMENT PHILOSOPHY

Before embarking on an investment plan, you need to understand your own approach to investing. Your ability to handle investment risk greatly influences your personal investment philosophy. Successful investors follow their philosophy. Is your investment philosophy conservative, moderate, or aggressive? Select one philosophy and give your reasons below. (Use with *Personal Finance*, Ninth Edition, pages 357-361.)

1. My investment philosophy is

 ____

2. My willingness to accept investment risk is

 ____

 ____

3. My goals in terms of investment returns are

 ____

 ____

4. Other things that may characterize my investment philosophy are

 ____

 ____

5. People with my investment philosophy typically consider investing in the following kinds of investments:

 ____

 ____

6. People with my investment philosophy with $10,000 might expert to have an annual gain of

 ____

 ____

WORKSHEET 47—MY PREFERRED LONG-TERM INVESTMENT STRATEGIES

Most people are long-term investors who seek genuine growth in the value of their investments that exceeds the rate of inflation, usually for 10 or 15 years or longer. Successful investors exercise discipline and follow one or more long-term investment strategies. For each of the strategies below, identify one characteristic you like about it, and note which strategies you might follow during your own investing life. (Use with *Personal Finance*, Ninth Edition, pages 367-376.)

Long-Term Investment Strategies Worksheet

Long-term investment strategies	**One characteristic I like about the strategy**	**Checkmark each of the strategies I will follow myself**
Buy and hold		
Portfolio diversification		
Asset allocation		
Dollar-cost averaging		

WORKSHEET 48—MY INVESTMENT GOALS AND TIME HORIZONS

Some typical investment goals are paying off credit card debts, saving and investing to pay for future college tuition bills, accumulating a down payment to purchase a home, buying a new vehicle, paying for an expensive vacation, and creating a substantial retirement savings nest egg. List below some of your investment goals (one or two for each time period, if appropriate) according to the time horizons when you will need to have accumulated sufficient funds to pay for them. Also identify some possible investments you might consider to achieve those goals. (Use with *Personal Finance*, Ninth Edition, pages 362-363 and 376-377.)

Investment Goals and Time Horizons Worksheet

Time horizon	My investment goals	Investments I might consider
Less than 2 years	1. 2.	
2 to 5 years	1. 2.	
6 to 10 years	1. 2.	
More than 10 years	1. 2.	

WORKSHEET 49—COMPARING TAXABLE AND TAX-FREE INCOME

Use a taxable investment's after-tax yield when making comparisons with tax-free alternatives. Compare only after-tax yields when two taxable investments are subject to different marginal tax rates. To find out whether a taxable investment pays a higher after-tax yield than a tax-exempt alternative, determine the after-tax yield of the taxable alternative. In the appropriate spaces below, insert the taxable yield on one investment and your marginal tax bracket. The result is the equivalent after-tax yield on the taxable investment. An interactive calculator that performs this same procedure can be found on the *Garman/Forgue* website. (The formula can be reversed to solve for the equivalent taxable yield when you know the tax-exempt yield.) (Use with *Personal Finance*, Ninth Edition, page 122.)

After-tax Return on an Investment Worksheet

(A) Steps	(B) Instructions	(C) Example	(D) Your figures
Step 1	Record the taxable return on the investment.	8%	
Step 2	Record the investor's marginal tax rate.	25%	
Step 3	Subtract the investor's marginal tax rate from 1 (1 – MTR).	0.75	
Step 4	Multiply Step 1 by Step 3 to obtain the investment's after-tax rate of return.	6%	
Step 5	Record the rate of return on the tax-exempt alternative.	6.5%	
Step 6	Select the best alternative from Step 4 and Step 5.	6.5%, the tax-exempt alternative	

WORKSHEET 50—MY PREFERENCES AMONG STOCKS

There are different classifications of stocks, and these designations can be used to match an investor's preferences. The three basic classifications of stocks are income, growth, and speculative. A number of other terms are used to meaningfully characterize stocks. For each of the types of stocks below that are of interest to you, identify one characteristic you do or do not like about it, and note those in which you might invest in during your own investing life. (Use with *Personal Finance*, Ninth Edition, pages 390-393.)

Preferences Among Stocks Worksheet

Stock classifications	**One characteristic I do *or* do not like about this type of stock (*Only* comment if the stock is of interest to you.)**	**Checkmark in this column each stock that I might invest in.**
Income stock		
Growth stock		
Speculative stock		
Blue-chip stock		
Value stock		
Cyclical stock		
Countercyclical stock		

WORKSHEET 51—COMPARING STOCKS AS INVESTMENTS

When you invest in the stock market, you buy shares in companies and become one of their owners. To make good choices, you need to understand some important numbers that are key measures of stock performance. Go on-line and search out details on key measures of stock performance for two or three companies that are of interest to you as possible investments. Perhaps use Yahoo Finance (biz.yahoo.com/r/) or CNNMoney (money.cnn.com/). Record the information you find on the worksheet below. Then respond to the question that follows: "Which company appears to be the most suitable investment for you, and why?" (Use with *Personal Finance*, Ninth Edition, pages 394-400.)

Comparing Stocks Worksheet

Key performance measures	Company 1	Company 2	Company 3
Current market price			
Cash dividends			
Dividend payout ratio			
Dividends per share			
Dividend yield			
Book value			
Book value per share			
Price-to-book ratio			
Earnings per share			
Price-to-earnings ratio			
Price-to-sales ratio			
Beta			
Other measure			
Other measure			
Other measure			
Other measure			

Which company appears to be the most suitable investment for you, and why?

____

____

____

WORKSHEET 52—MY PREFERENCES AMONG BONDS

People invest in bonds to increase their current income. For each of the types of bonds below that are of interest to you, identify one characteristic you do or do not like about it, and note those in which you might invest in during your own investing life. (Use with *Personal Finance*, Ninth Edition, pages 417-426.)

Stocks and Bonds Preference Worksheet

Types of stocks and bonds	**One characteristic I do *or* do not like about this type of investment (*Only* comment if the investment is of interest to you.)**	**Checkmark in this column each investment that I might invest in.**
Common stock		
Preferred stock		
Corporate bond (high quality)		
Corporate bond (junk bond)		
Treasury bond (long term)		
Treasury note		
I bond		
TIPS bond		
Treasury bill		
Federal agency debt issues		
Municipal bonds		

WORKSHEET 53–THE CURRENT YIELD ON MY BOND INVESTMENT

The current yield on a bond equals the bond's fixed annual interest payment divided by its current market price. It is a measure of the current annual income expressed as a percentage when divided by the bond's current market price. In the appropriate spaces below, insert the current annual income on a bond and the current market price of the bond. The result of the division is the current yield. An interactive calculator that performs this same procedure can be found on the *Garman/Forgue* website. (Use Equation 14.5 in *Personal Finance*, Ninth Edition, page 423.)

The current yield can be used to compare two or more bonds with differing market values, coupon rates, and annual interest payments. In the example, a bond that has a coupon rate of 5.5 percent would pay $55 (5.5% x $1,000) and might have a market price of $940. Its current yield would be 5.85 percent.

Current Yield on a Bond Worksheet

(A) Steps	(B) Instructions	(C) Example	(D) Your figures: Bond 1	(E) Your figures: Bond 2
Step 1	Annual interest payment on the bond	$55		
Step 2	Current market price of the bond	$940		
Step 3	Current yield on the bond (Step 1 divided by Step 2)	5.85%		

WORKSHEET 54—THE CURRENT MARKET PRICE OF MY BOND INVESTMENT

The current market price of a bond depends on the bond's fixed annual interest payment given current interest rates in the market for bonds with similar levels of risk. In the appropriate spaces below, insert the current annual income on a bond and the current market price of the bond. The result of the division is the current yield. An interactive calculator that performs this same procedure can be found on the *Garman/Forgue* website. (Use with Equation 14.4 in *Personal Finance*, Ninth Edition, page 423.)

In the example, a bond that has a coupon rate of 8 percent would pay $80 (8% x $1,000). If current interest rates for bonds with similar levels of risk were 10.0 percent, the bond would have a market price of only $800.

Current Yield on a Bond Worksheet

(A) Steps	(B) Instructions	(C) Example	(D) Your bond
Step 1	Annual interest payment on the bond	$80	
Step 2	Current market interest rates (as a decimal)	10.0%	
Step 3	Current market price of the bond the bond (Step 1 divided by Step 2)	$800	

WORKSHEET 55—THE REAL RETURN ON MY INVESTMENTS

To identify the real return on your investments, you first need to subtract the negative effects of your marginal tax bracket on the rate of return to obtain the after-tax return. Then you subtract the effects of inflation from the after-tax return. In the appropriate spaces below, insert the rate of return on your investment, your marginal tax bracket, and your estimate of annual inflation. The result is the real return on your investments after taxes and inflation. An interactive calculator that performs this same procedure can be found on the *Garman/Forgue* website. (Use with *Personal Finance*, Ninth Edition, page 368.)

In the example provided, an investor has an investment opportunity that will pay an 8 percent rate of return. After subtracting the effects of taxes, the investment has an after-tax rate of return of 6 percent (Step 4). Further calculations address the effect of inflation on the rate of return. As a result, the real rate of return on this investment is 3.5 percent (Step 6).

Real Return on Investment Worksheet

(A) Steps	(B) Instructions	(C) Example	(D) Your figures
Step 1	Record the taxable return on the investment.	8%	
Step 2	Record the investor's marginal tax rate.	25%	
Step 3	Subtract the investor's marginal tax rate from 1 (1 – MTR).	0.75	
Step 4	Multiply Step 1 by Step 3 to obtain the investment's after-tax rate of return.	6%	
Step 5	Record the current annual inflation rate.	2.5%	
Step 6	Subtract Step 5 from Step 4 to determine the real return on the investment.	3.5%	

WORKSHEET 56—THE YIELD TO MATURITY OF MY BOND

The yield to maturity (YTM) is the total annual effective rate of return earned by a bondholder on a bond when it is held to maturity. It reflects both the current income and any difference if the bond was purchased at a price other than its face value spread over the life of the bond. The YTM can be estimated using a math formula (such as Equation 14.6 on page 425 of *Personal Finance*, Ninth Edition) or using a worksheet such as the one below.

Use the worksheet to calculate the yield to maturity (YTM) on your bond investments. Use column D in the worksheet to record the figures for your bond (bond 1), and use column E if needed. An interactive calculator that performs this same procedure can be found on the *Garman/Forgue* website. (Use with *Personal Finance*, Ninth Edition, pages 424-426.)

Yield to Maturity (YTM) Worksheet

(A) Steps	(B) Instructions	(D) Your figures: Bond 1	(E) Your figures: Bond 2
Step 1	Record the bond's current market value or price.		
Step 2	Record the bond's face value.		
Step 3	Record the number of years until the bond matures.		
Step 4	Record the amount of annual interest the bond is supposed to pay.		
Step 5	Subtract the amount in Step 1 from the amount in Step 2.		
Step 6	Divide the amount in Step 5 by the amount in Step 3.		
Step 7	Add the amounts in Steps 4 and 6; this figure is the average dollar return per year.		
Step 8	Add the amounts in Steps 1 and 2.		
Step 9	Divide the amount in Step 8 by the amount in Step 2.		
Step 10	Divide the amount in Step 7 by the amount in Step 9; this figure is an estimate of the annual yield to maturity.		

WORKSHEET 57—MY MUTUAL FUND PREFERENCES

Each of the thousands of mutual funds has one of four major objectives: income, balanced, growth, or growth and income. Since people usually have a number of different investment objectives with different time horizons, many investors own all four types of funds. Funds do differ, however, on how they achieve their objectives, and this is where investors have to think carefully and make decisions that appropriately fit their investment philosophy. For each of the types of mutual funds below that are of interest to you, identify one characteristic you like about it, and note those in which you might invest in during your own investing life. (Use with *Personal Finance*, Ninth Edition, pages 440-444.)

Mutual Fund Preference Worksheet

Mutual fund objectives and fund types	**One characteristic I like about this type of mutual fund. (*Only* comment if the fund is of interest to you.)**	**Checkmark each fund that I might invest in**
Income objective— Bond fund		
Income objective— Municipal bond fund		
Balanced objective— Balanced fund		
Growth objective— Growth fund		
Growth objective— Value fund		
Growth objective— Aggressive growth fund		
Growth objective— Small-cap fund		
Growth objective— Sector fund		
Growth objective— Precious metals and gold fund		
Growth objective— Global fund		
Growth objective— International fund		
Growth and income objective— Growth and income fund		
Growth and income objective— Life-cycle fund		
Growth and income objective— Socially conscious fund		
Growth and income objective— Mutual fund		

WORKSHEET 58—COMPARING MUTUAL FUNDS AS INVESTMENTS

When you invest in mutual funds, you buy shares in the investment companies and become one of their owners. To make good choices, you need to understand some important numbers that are key measures of fund performance. Go on-line and search out details on key measures of mutual fund performance for two or three companies that are of interest to you as possible investments. Perhaps use CNNMoney (money.cnn.com/funds/) or Kiplinger Personal Finance (kiplinger.com/tools/fundfinder/). Record the information you find on the worksheet below. Then respond to the question that follows: "Which mutual fund appears to be the most suitable investment for you, and why?" (Use with *Personal Finance*, Ninth Edition, pages 444-456.)

Comparing Mutual Funds Worksheet

Key performance measures	Fund 1	Fund 2	Fund 3
Current net asset value (NAV)			
One-year return			
Three-year return			
Five-year return			
Universe			
Category			
Style			
Decile rank within style Last year Two years ago Three years ago			
Down market			
Volatility rank			
Turnover			
Assets (millions)			
Manager since			
Minimum investment			
Maximum load			
Expense ratio			
Other measure			
Other measure			

Which mutual fund appears to be the most suitable investment for you, and why?

____

____

WORKSHEET 59—CALCULATING THE RETURN ON MUTUAL FUND INVESTMENTS

The total return earned by an investor in mutual funds is made up of income from mutual fund dividends (cash distributions) and capital gains from price appreciation [increases in net asset value (NAV)]. Use the worksheet below to calculate your total return on mutual fund investments.

Use column D in the worksheet to record the figures for your mutual fund (fund 1), and use column E if needed. (Use with *Personal Finance*, Ninth Edition, pages 455-456.)

Calculating the Return on Mutual Fund Investments Worksheet

(A) Steps	(B) Instructions	(C) Example	(D) Your figures: Fund 1	(E) Your figures: Fund 2
Step 1	Record the net asset value (NAV) at the beginning of the time period.	$24.00		
Step 2	Record the amount of cash distributions received during the time period.	$1.10		
Step 3	Record the NAV at the end of the time period.	$25.70		
Step 4	Subtract the amount in Step 1 from the amount in Step 3; this figure is the change in NAV.	$1.70		
Step 5	Add the amounts in Steps 2 and 4; this is the total return in dollars.	$2.80		
Step 6	Divide the amount in Step 5 by the amount in Step 1; this is the total return during the time period as a percent.	11.67%		

WORKSHEET 60—EVALUATING THE PERFORMANCE (GAIN OR LOSS) OF MY INVESTMENTS

You should evaluate the performance of your investments at least once a year. To do so, use a form like the one below. List the names of your investments, such as stocks, bonds, and mutual funds, in column 1, the number of shares of securities owned in column 2, and the purchase prices in column 3. Multiply the figures in columns 2 and 3 to obtain the total. Record any purchasing commissions paid in column 4, and add the figures in columns 3 and 4 to obtain the total amount you have invested in each investment. Record the current closing prices as of a certain date for each investment in column 6. Multiply the figures in columns 1 and 6 to obtain the total closing market value of each investment and record those amounts in column 7. Subtract the figures in column 5 from column 7 to determine the gain or loss, and record those amounts in column 8. Record any dividends or interest in column 9. In column 10, record the total gain or loss for each investment by adding the figures in columns 8 and 9. Finally, adding all the figures in each column vertically provides totals for all your investments for the reporting period. (Use with *Personal Finance*, Ninth Edition, Chapter 14.)

Investment Performance (Gain or Loss) Worksheet

Your name: ____________________________

Reporting Period (inclusive dates): ____________________________

Investment	(1) Number of shares	(2) Purchase price per share	(3) Total (1 + 2)	(4) Commission	(5) Total amount invested (3 + 4)	(6) Closing market value	(7) Total closing market value (6 x 1)	(8) Gain or loss (7 – 5)	(9) Dividends, interest, rent	(10) Total gain or loss (8 + 9)
Running Paws (example)	100	$74	$7,400	$148	$7,548	$79	$7,900	$352	$166	$518
Totals										

Gain or loss this reporting period

Dollar return (total of column 10) (Example $518): ____________________________

Rate of return [dollar return (from line above) divided by total of column 5]

(Example $518/$7,548 = 6.86%): ____________________________

SECTION FIVE

Retirement and Estate Planning

This section of your workbook focuses on mechanisms you will use to create a retirement nest egg and then to pass on your estate to your heirs. Each worksheet will allow you to think through a decision or perform calculations related to a specific area of personal financial management in a way that has direct benefit to you.

Worksheet 61 My Estimated Retirement Savings Goal in Today's Dollars

Worksheet 62 Questions to Ask About Your Employer's Retirement Plan

Worksheet 63 My Will, Letter of Last Instructions, and Advance Directive Documents

Worksheet 64 My Assets to be Transferred by Beneficiary Designations

WORKSHEET 61—MY ESTIMATED RETIREMENT SAVINGS GOAL IN TODAY'S DOLLARS

This worksheet will help you calculate the annual amount you need to set aside in today's dollars so that you will have adequate funds for your retirement. The example illustration assumes that a single person is now 35 years old, will retire at age 62, has a current income of $50,000, currently saves and invests about $2,000 per year, contributes zero to an employer-sponsored retirement plan, anticipates needing a retirement income of $35,000 per year assuming a spending lifestyle at 70 percent of current income ($50,000 x 0.70), and will live an additional 20 years beyond retirement. Investment returns are assumed to be 3 percent after inflation. An interactive calculator that performs this same procedure can be found on the *Garman/Forgue* website. (Use with *Personal Finance*, Ninth Edition, pages 494-497.)

Retirement Savings Goal Worksheet

Steps	Instructions	Example	Your Numbers
1	Annual income needed at retirement in today's dollars (Use carefully estimated numbers or a certain percentage, such as 70% or 80%.)	$35,000	________
2	Estimated Social Security retirement benefit in today's dollars	$13,200	________
3	Estimated employer pension benefit in today's dollars (Ask your retirement benefit adviser to make an estimate of your future pension, assuming that you remain in the same job at the same salary, or make your own conservative estimate.)	$5,800	________
4	Total estimated retirement income from Social Security and employer pension in today's dollars (Step 2 + Step 3)	$19,000	________
5	Additional income needed at retirement in today's dollars (Step 1 – Step 4)	$16,000	________
6	Amount you must have at retirement in today's dollars to receive additional annual income in retirement (step 5) for 20 years (from Table A.4, assuming a 3% return over 20 years, or 14.8775 x $16,000)	$238,040	________
7	Amount already available as savings and investments in today's dollars (add Steps 7A through 7D, and record total in Step 7E)		
	A. Employer savings plans, such as a 401(k), SEP-IRA, or profit-sharing plan	0	________
	B. IRAs and Keoghs	$24,000	________
	C. Other investments, such as mutual funds, stocks, bonds, real estate, and other assets available for retirement	$13,000	________
	D. If you wish to include a portion of the equity in your home as savings, enter its present value minus the cost of another home in retirement	0	________
	E. Total retirement savings (add Steps 7A through 7D)	$37,000	________
8	Future value of current savings/investments at time of retirement (Using Table A.1 and a growth rate of 3% over 27 years, the factor is 2.2213: thus, 2.2213 x $37,000.)	$82,188	________
9	Additional retirement savings and investments needed at time of retirement (Step 6 – Step 8)	$155,852	________
10	Annual savings needed (to reach amount in Step 9) before retirement (Using Table A.3 and a growth rate of 3% over 27 years, the factor is 40.7096; thus, $155,852 ÷ 40.7096.)	$3,828	________
11	Current annual contribution to savings and investment plans	$2,000	________
12	Additional amount of annual savings that you need to set aside in today's dollars to achieve retirement goal (in Step 1) (Step 10 – Step 11)	$1,828	________

WORKSHEET 62—QUESTIONS TO ASK ABOUT YOUR EMPLOYER'S RETIREMENT PLAN

As you think about your employer's retirement plan, find out as much as you can. First, identify which type of plan is available. Second, meet with a representative in your employer's human resources department and ask that person the questions indicated by an X for that plan; record the answers. (Use with *Personal Finance*, Ninth Edition, pages 500-506.)

Employer's Retirement Plan Questions Worksheet

Questions to ask	Defined-contribution plan	Defined-benefit plan	Cash balance plan
1. When is an employee eligible to participate in the plan?	X	X	X
2. How much money can the employer or employee contribute?	X		X
3. Is the plan optional or required?	X	X	X
4. How are benefits calculated?		X	X
5. Is the plan insured by the Pension Benefit Guaranty Corporation?		X	
6. When does vesting begin?	X	X	X
7. Can the plan be discontinued or changed by the employer, and if so, how?	X	X	X
8. What is the maximum amount that an employee can contribute?	X		X
9. How much of a matching contribution does the employer contribute?	X		X
10. What investment options are available, and under what rules may the employee switch among investment options?	X		X
11. Are the employer's contributions in the form of company stock?	X		X
12. Are participants required to purchase stock in the company with their retirement savings?	X		X

13. What is the formula used to define the full retirement benefit?		X	X
14. What is the normal retirement age?		X	X
15. What is the amount of the retirement benefit?		X	X
16. What is the amount of survivor's benefits, if any?		X	X
17. What is the earliest retirement age?	X	X	X
18. Is the retirement benefit integrated with Social Security, and if so, how?		X	
19. What is the reduction in benefits for early retirement?		X	X
20. Are the retirement benefits guaranteed for life once a person retires?		X	X
21. What are the disability benefits?		X	X
22. At separation from employment or retirement, does the employee have the right to the vested lump-sum amount in the account rather than take a monthly pension?	X	X	X
23. Are the retirement benefits portable, meaning upon termination of employment, an employee can transfer retirement funds from one employer's account to another without penalty?	X	X	X
24. What are the procedures for applying for benefits?	X	X	X
25. Are financial planning services provided to assist employees when making retirement and other financial decisions?	X	X	X

WORKSHEET 63—MY WILL, LETTER OF LAST INSTRUCTIONS, AND ADVANCE DIRECTIVE DOCUMENTS

You may use an advance directive to establish who will make financial, medical, or other decisions for you should you become mentally incompetent or unable to communicate your wishes. (Use with *Personal Finance*, Ninth Edition, pages 522-530.)

Will, Letter of Last Instructions, and Advance Directives Worksheet

Document	Date prepared	Document location	Person who knows document location or has copy
Will			
Letter of last instructions			
Living will			
Medical power of attorney			
Durable power of attorney			
Limited power of attorney			
Other			